Jesus after Two Thousand Years

For James M. Robinson

Jesus after Two Thousand Years
What he really said and did

Gerd Lüdemann

With contributions by
Frank Schleritt and Martina Janssen

Prometheus Books
59 John Glenn Drive
Amherst, New York 14228-2197

Published 2001 by Prometheus Books

Jesus after 2000 Years: What He Really Said and Did. Copyright © 2001 by Gerd Lüdemann. All rights reserved. No part of this publication may be reproduced, stored in a retrieval system, or transmitted in any form or by any means, digital, electronic, mechanical, photocopying, recording, or otherwise, or conveyed via the Internet or a Web site without prior written permission of the publisher, except in the case of brief quotations embodied in critical articles and reviews.

Inquiries should be addressed to
Prometheus Books
59 John Glenn Drive
Amherst, New York 14228–2197
VOICE: 716–691–0133, ext. 207
FAX: 716–564–2711
WWW.PROMETHEUSBOOKS.COM

05 04 03 02 01   5 4 3 2 1

Library of Congress Cataloging-in-Publication Data

Lüdemann, Gerd.
    [Jesus nach 2000 Jahren. English]
    Jesus after two thousand years : what he really said and did / Gerd Lüdemann ; with contributions by Frank Schleritt and Martina Janssen.
        p. cm.
    Includes bibliographical references and index.
    ISBN 1–57392–890–9 (alk. paper)
    1. Jesus Christ—Historicity. 2. Jesus Christ—Words. 3. Bible. N.T. Gospels—Criticism, interpretation, etc. 4. Jesus Christ—Words—Extracanonical parallels. I. Schleritt, Frank. II. Janssen, Martina. III. Title.

BT303.2 .L84513 2001
232.9'08—dc21   00–068426

Printed in Canada on acid-free paper

Contents

Preface

This book sets out to fill a gap in theological literature. This gap is particularly evident to those who are concerned with the church and Christianity: clergy, teachers of religion and above all the increasing number of people who are interested in Jesus. All of them are being unsettled by an abundance of conflicting books about Jesus in modern times, and also by the conflicting pictures of Jesus in the New Testament itself. Between us and the New Testament lie twenty centuries in which people have understood Jesus in quite different ways. The historical-critical research into Jesus which has been developed for around 250 years may have become the standard for scholars, but it has hardly been able to command a general consensus. Moreover the last decade, particularly in the English-speaking world, has experienced a flood of scholarly and popular literature about Jesus. Its source seems to be inexhaustible and it flows in the most varied directions.

Consequently uninitiated readers get the impression that research is unplanned, full of contradictions, and is going nowhere. This leads them either to sink into resignation or to hold even more firmly to a faith which is above historical questions. Yet neither resignation nor uninformed faith make sense – certainly not in an age which has encouraged the display of an unimagined wealth of knowledge and which at the same time almost daily reminds us of the more modest position of human beings in the cosmos. So it seems to me that a historical stocktaking of critical concern with the central person of Christianity, Jesus of Nazareth, which has been the business of scholars for two hundred and fifty years, is long overdue.

I shall not present this either thematically or in a comprehensive account of the results of the research of other scholars, as did Albert Schweitzer in his *Quest of the Historical Jesus* (of which the first complete translation into English is being published only at the same time as this volume) and later Walter P. Weaver (*The Historical Jesus in the Twentieth Century 1900–1950*, 1999) for the first half of the twentieth century. I must also emphasize that this is not a life of Jesus but only an analysis of the most important words and actions of Jesus as a presupposition of a life of Jesus which is not yet possible (but see the attempt in Chapter VII). My plan is to offer a new translation of the most important extant traditions about Jesus in the first two centuries and then to investigate their historical credibility, in such a way that educated lay people, too, can follow the argument.

The Jesus Seminar founded by Robert W. Funk and the volumes *The Five Gospels* (1993) and *The Acts of Jesus* (1998) have been an important stimulus to such an undertaking. In these volumes the degree of historicity of the words and actions of Jesus are indicated by different colours. But although for several years I have been a fellow of the Jesus Seminar, and concur with its goal of determining the words and actions of the historical Jesus, I prefer to dispense with coloured markings of any kind. Instead I have indicated by *italics* those passages which beyond doubt derive from the particular evangelists. Recognizing their redactional work is a necessary step towards reconstructing the traditions the evangelists received; the third and final step is to identify the sayings and actions of Jesus which are presumably authentic.

This method, in which sometimes the first two stages are completed in the same section, shows its value particularly in the case of those writings the final authors of which we do not know by name (the titles of the four New Testament Gospels date only from the second century), though they can be identified as authors of the writings which are associated with them on the basis of clear characteristics of language and content. By comparison, this mode of procedure is not advisable in the case of the Gospel of Thomas and the sayings and actions of Jesus which have been handed down in isolation, since here the conditions of transmission are different (for the details see the introductions to the writings in question).

The criteria for this investigation are the methods developed in the critical study of the Bible over the last 250 years, and are valid until new and better methods take their place.

Because of the abundance of texts to be discussed and the consequent need for brevity, in this account I have dispensed with explicit discussion of secondary literature and have only occasionally mentioned in brackets the names of scholars from whom particular interpretations derive. Here it seemed to me that titles of books did not need to be mentioned. They say nothing to lay people and specialists know them anyway. Occasional underlinings will make it easier to get into the text.

Some comments on the structure of this book:

The Introduction indicates its presuppositions and develops the modes of procedure and the method.

Chapter I contains a translation and analysis of the earliest Gospel, that of Mark.

This is followed in Chapters II and III by a translation and analysis of the Gospels of Matthew and Luke, which build on the Gospel of Mark independently of each other.

Chapter IV, the translation and analysis of the Gospel of John, has been written by Frank Schleritt.

Chapter V contains the translation and analysis of the Gospel of Thomas.

In Chapter VI, Martina Janssen translates and comments on the rest of the Jesus tradition which has been preserved from the first two centuries.

Chapter VII offers a short life of Jesus. Here I attempt, starting from the historically assured material, to depict the life and fate of Jesus of Nazareth. Reading this final chapter may be recommended as a way into the book as a whole.

The book ends with an index of all the authentic sayings and actions of Jesus.

I am grateful to all those, near and far, who over the last few years have encouraged me to continue research into Christian origins, directly, unerringly and without compromise, and thus to make a contribution to the quest for the truth. I am grateful to Silke Röthke, my secretary of many years, for her repeated typing and correction of the manuscript. Frank Schleritt has also seen to the technical organization of such a large work, and over the last few years has always stood by me as a reliable collaborator. With this volume, my friend Dr John Bowden has already translated my ninth book into English. I will always be in his debt, all the more since thanks to him SCM Press is the only publishing house which has always been loyal to me. I am also grateful to my friend and Nashville neighbour Eugene TeSelle for reading through the English translation and making useful comments. Jim Robinson has allowed me to dedicate this book to him. Hardly anyone else has made a more lasting contribution to the quest of the historical Jesus than he has, and no one else has done more to mediate the best of German theological scholarship to the English-speaking world. This book is a small token of gratitude. It will be published in the United States by Prometheus Books and is an improved second edition of the German original.

Göttingen, 17 April 2000

Introduction: Presuppositions, Method and Interests

The present book subjects *all* the Jesus traditions from the first two centuries to an analysis and investigates their authenticity. It has been written in the conviction that Christians must enter into a credible relationship to Jesus, but that all other men and women in the cultural area stamped by the Christian West should also be enabled to assure themselves of the historical roots of Christianity in the person of Jesus of Nazareth. For both groups, this question of coping with one's own history and shaping the future is vitally important.

Today it is generally recognized that numerous words and actions were attributed to Jesus only after his death. Here to begin with are just two examples:

(a) The 'I am' sayings in the Gospel of John, which make Jesus say of himself in the first person that he is the resurrection, he is the light of the world, he is the vine, etc., certainly do not go back to Jesus but were put on his lips only at a later stage, in order to express the faith of a later generation of Christians.

(b) The same is true of most of the miracle stories. Today no one seriously accepts that Jesus in fact walked on the sea, stilled a storm, multiplied bread, turned water into wine and raised the dead. Rather, these actions were invented for Jesus only after his death or his supposed resurrection in order to heighten his importance.

These better insights, which were first worked out by historical criticism, do not alter the fact that the early Christians regarded all this as authentic within the framework of the canonization of the books of the Bible. Consequently, from then on inauthentic sayings and actions of Jesus have been part of the core of holy scripture. Therefore once again we must rigorously seek clarity about all the traditions of Jesus in early Christianity which possess a claim to authenticity, and clarify what Jesus really said and did, what really happened then and what was clearly added later.

Such a procedure has its foundations in the intellectual history of Western culture and should not be denigrated as European ethnocentricity. For quite apart from the fact that the critical method has become established in all areas of the natural sciences as an experimental mode of procedure and can point to amazing successes, its sister in the disciplines of the humanities, the philological historical method, has led to a completely new view of the past. The question of what was real and what was only asserted has irrevocably become an element in our own lives that we take for granted. Thus one may even speak of a morality of thought which not only works out what is right and wrong, truth and falsehood, but which makes differentiating between the two a public task.

Now occasionally the charge is made against such an undertaking in research into Jesus that:

(a) it overestimates its own possibilities of distinguishing between authentic and inauthentic; (b) it comes to grief on the fact that scholarly verdicts on what is authentic and what is inauthentic sometimes diverge widely; (c) it does not take sufficient account of the fact that the spirit of Jesus could be contained in inauthentic Jesus traditions; (d) it leaves aside reception history, which shows an influence of the biblical traditions about Jesus independently of the question of authenticity, in that millions of people in the past and the present have been nourished by them; and (e) it forgets that the question of whether words or actions are authentic or inauthentic is irrelevant to faith, since one and the same Lord is speaking in the historical Jesus and in the risen Christ.

On (a): I do not understand this objection, especially since it cannot be denied that inauthentic sayings of Jesus are certainly contained in the Bible. But in that case the attempt can, indeed must, be made to work out authentic sayings and actions of Jesus.

On (b): The different reconstructions of the sayings and actions of the historical Jesus which do indeed exist are no argument against such an undertaking: a multiplicity of opinions does not relieve us of the obligation to approach historical reality with the goal of the greatest possible objectivity.

On (c): This cannot be disputed, but in order to identify the spirit of Jesus it is first necessary to make it quite clear where recognizably authentic Jesus traditions are contained.

On (d): Does the influence of texts suffice to make good their claim? In my view this is not how one gets to the bottom of things. If, for example, Jesus did not rise historically, then one cannot rescue the primitive Christian statements which claim this by reflections on the reception history, no matter how powerful the effect of this proclamation may have been and to how many people it has given comfort.

On (e): One can combat any historical work with this theological argument. A historical approach will see the reference to the risen Christ as the speaker of words simply as lying outside its competence. How it is possible to demonstrate with arguments which can be followed that the 'Risen One' said this or that, or even did particular things? In other words, in this sphere nothing at all can be gained directly for historical criticism. But it may be asked whether this or that word of the Risen One goes back to the historical Jesus. And conversely we can check whether words of the Risen One have not been made into words of the historical Jesus. Should the latter be the case, then automatically we would have to judge that they are historically inauthentic. Anyone who unifies the Jesus of history and the Christ of faith is in fact attempting to overturn the historical consciousness of modernity, but that consciousness is vitally necessary, and since the great confessions and religions have failed, it is the only approach which is capable of building up peace between human beings and their ideologies and religions. In any case the historical consciousness forms a firm ingredient of our present-day world. Without this achievement of human culture no reasonable dialogue would be possible either in politics, in business or in the private sphere. How could we possibly abandon it as soon as we enter the sphere of religion? The result is well known: an inner split or a divergence between science and religion, which is a burden on both.

Here are the underlying presuppositions of my work:

On the question of the relationship between the three earliest New Testament Gospels, the analyses are based on a modified two-source theory. This means that the Gospel of Mark is the earliest extant Gospel and dates from around 70. Around twenty years later and independently of each other, Matthew and Luke used both the Gospel of Mark and a Sayings Source (= Q) which might have been as old as Mark or even older. In addition, both used their own special traditions. There is no need for an introduction to the individual Synoptic Gospels, as their theological ideas and their historical origin can be inferred from the original texts. Anyone wanting to have an advance look at the view of the Synoptics and Q gained from the texts is referred to Luke 1.1–4 and the analysis of it.

The Gospel of John comes from the beginning of the second century and pre-supposes the Synoptic Gospels (cf. the introduction to Chapter IV).

The Gospel of Thomas among the discovery near Nag Hammadi in Upper Egypt in December 1945 is beyond question one of the written sources to be investigated here, since, as is becoming increasingly clear, it partly reflects a tradition which is independent of the New Testament (cf. the introduction to Chapter V). Finally, an analysis of the so-called agrapha must be included here, especially as they have been used in a great variety of ways in the history of research for reconstructing the authentic sayings and actions of Jesus and since in recent decades new sources have been uncovered which have laid claim to an unprejudiced examination (see the introduction to Chapter VI).

Before the analysis of the traditions I want to mentioned the following *criteria* for verdicts on the (a) inauthenticity and (b) authenticity of sayings and actions of Jesus which – and this should be emphasized here – have automatically arisen only *after* the analysis of all the texts. Reflection on methods always follows a method which works organically. However, I have not stated explicitly in the case of each individual pericope what criterion has guided me. Readers may discover that for themselves in each case.

(a) Criteria of inauthenticity

First of all, words and actions are inauthentic in which the risen Lord speaks and acts or is presupposed as the one who speaks and acts, for after his death Jesus no longer spoke and acted himself. But as we cannot exclude the possibility that sayings or actions were attributed to the 'Risen One' – the historical Jesus and the Christ of faith were identical for the early Christians – in each case we must check whether perhaps a saying of the earthly Jesus might not underlie particular sayings of the risen Christ.

Secondly, those actions are unhistorical which presuppose that the laws of nature are broken. Here it makes no difference that people at the time of Jesus did not know these laws or did not think in scientific categories.

Thirdly, in the case of all the sayings of Jesus there is a suspicion of inauthenticity if they give answers to community situations at a later time.

Fourthly – closely connected with the last-mentioned criterion – those sayings and actions of Jesus are under serious suspicion of being inauthentic which are indebted to the redactional, i.e. written work of the final author of the source in question.

Fifthly, those words and actions are inauthentic which presuppose a pagan (and not a Jewish) audience. For it is certain that Jesus was active exclusively in the Jewish sphere.

(b) Criteria of authenticity

First, many sayings and actions of Jesus may be demonstrated to be authentic on the basis of the criterion of offensiveness.

Among the actions of Jesus, for example his decision to have himself baptized by John belongs here. Jesus' baptism was offensive to Christians from the very earliest period, and from the beginning it was bent in various ways, passed over completely in silence or rejected by 'Jesus' himself.

Examples of offensive sayings of Jesus are the immoral heroes who appear in the parables of Jesus with striking frequency: the man who finds a treasure in a field and buys the field without mentioning his discovery (Matt. 13.44), or the unjust steward who when called to account by his lord deceives him, in order to find a refuge with his lord's debtors (Luke 16.1b–7). Finally, Jesus himself often acts as an immoral hero and cultivates social dealings with prostitutes and toll collectors. This too is changed or 'interpreted' in the later tradition.

Secondly, the criterion of difference is a plausible way of discovering authentic Jesus material. Its use relates to the question of whether sayings and actions of Jesus can be derived from the post-Easter communities. If the answer to this is negative, when there is a difference between the communities and Jesus, the latter may be taken to have spoken the words or performed the action in question. One example is Jesus' rejection of fasting, which differs from the community's later practice of fasting (cf. Mark 2.18–22).

Thirdly, the criterion of growth offers a good opportunity to identify authentic Jesus material. The final form of a text can be compared with an onion from which one layer after another can be peeled. The older a unit of text is, the more densely it is covered with later tradition. There are examples of this in the ethical radicalisms of the Sermon on the Mount. Thus Jesus' absolute prohibition of swearing oaths (Matt. 5.34a) is supplemented with several instructions by 'Jesus' (Matt. 5.34b–37) which in fact result in the abolition of this prohibition.

Fourthly, mention should be made of the criterion of rarity, which relates to those actions and sayings of Jesus that have few parallels in the Jewish sphere. Jesus' absolute prohibition against judging (Matt. 7.1) is a candidate for this.

Fifthly, the criterion of wide attestation offers some assurance that sayings and actions of Jesus which are attested by sources independently of one another may be authentic.

Sixthly, the criterion of coherence can be used to bring out authentic sayings of Jesus: in each instance this asks whether there is a seamless link between a particular statement or action and assured Jesus material.

The *criterion of plausibility* which recently has sometimes been brought into play is not in my view a suitable method for reconstructing authentic sayings and actions of Jesus. Were that so, then for example the stories of Karl May would also have to be regarded as historically accurate, and so – to give a New Testament example – would be Luke's certainly fictitious account of the revolt of the silversmiths in Ephesus (Acts 19). When all is said and done, for some people one thing is plausible, and for others something else. In other words, the criterion of plausibility is too woolly, and leaves more questions than answers.

From all this it becomes clear that anyone who wants to get through to Jesus – not to Jesus as the early Christians have depicted him but to the man of Nazareth as he really was – must rigorously strip off everything that has come to lie round the words of Jesus, layer by layer – in the hope of thus reaching the bedrock of the authentic sayings of Jesus.

By using the term 'hope' I grant that such a reconstruction, like *any* scientific work, is always open to improvement. The image of bedrock at the same time makes it clear even in the most favourable instance only a high degree of approximation and not the absolutely final form can be achieved. The bedrock that we uncover is at best a close paraphrase of Jesus' words, never the words themselves. That would in any case be out of the question, because Jesus spoke Aramaic and his words are preserved only in Greek translation.

The same goes for the actions of Jesus: here, too, if it is said that something is historically the case, it can only mean that we are very close to what really happened at that time. For narrating always involves a change of tradition.

A further limitation to the present investigation arises from the insight that Jesus' words and actions are rooted in a specific milieu and can really be understood only in the light of that milieu. I regularly take account of this and offer reconstructions of this world of Jesus. But beyond doubt there remains a considerable remnant, the discussion of which belongs to the discipline of the 'environment of early Christianity'. Still we must begin with the analysis of the Jesus traditions and not with the reconstruction of the environment of Jesus, and despite the limitations of this method mentioned above, a high degree of probability can be expected

Clearly a decision on historicity is not *identical* with what Jesus really said or did. But we may say that a decision can correctly identify something that Jesus cannot have said or that certainly did not happen. But these limitations do not alter the value of the judgments made. Anyone who expected more here would get less.

Anything more than what has been said requires the assertion of religious certainty, which is not the business of this book. It is also clear to me that people cannot live only on the bread of the historical facts. But my view is that the analyses and reconstructions of the historical facts carried out in this work are important postulates for religious questions about Jesus.

One more brief comment. Just as Christian faith would collapse if Jesus had never lived, so Christian faith can continue to exist only if it succeeds in gaining support from Jesus on at least some important points. Should this prove impossible, then while Christian faith will not automatically collapse – no faith is ever refuted by arguments – for reasons of honesty it would have to dispense with the adjective 'Christian' and look for another foundation.

I

The Gospel of Mark

Mark 1.1–8: The activity of John the Baptist

1 *Beginning of the Gospel of Jesus Christ, the Son of God.* 2 As it is written in Isaiah, the prophet: ' "Look, I am sending my angel before your face, who will prepare your way", 3 the voice of one crying in the wilderness, "Prepare the way of the Lord, make his path straight," ' 4 so John the Baptizer appeared in the wilderness and preached the baptism of repentance for the forgiveness of sins. 5 *And the whole Judaean land and all the people of Jerusalem went to him and were baptized by him in the river Jordan and confessed their sins.* 6 And John was clothed with camel's hair and a leather girdle around his loins and ate locusts and wild honey. 7 And he *preached* and said: 'The stronger one is coming after me, the thongs of whose sandals I am not worthy to stoop down and untie. 8 I baptized you with water, but he himself will baptize you *with holy spirit.*'

Redaction and tradition

With the term 'gospel' Mark is not yet designating a genre, even if v. 1 has favoured the later formation of a book title ('Gospel according to Mark'). Rather, he has taken the expression from early Christian instruction (cf. I Cor. 15.1 with the pre-Pauline formula which is attached in vv. 3–5) and expressed the connection with that instruction by each time giving 'gospel' a christological reference (1.1, 14f.; 8.35; 10.29; 13.10; 14,9). All the instances cited have been introduced by Mark.

[1] This sums up the whole Gospel of Mark, which sets out to be the gospel of Jesus Christ. The expression 'gospel of Jesus Christ' (v. 1) has a connection with 'gospel of God' in v. 14, the preacher of which is Jesus himself. Mark's concern is the unity of the gospel about Jesus Christ (v. 1) with the gospel of God preached by Jesus (v. 14). This ensures that in his account at the same time he is also addressing his readers.

[2–4] The appearance of the Baptist is designated the beginning of the gospel, because the Baptist is part of it and according to Mark – in contrast to Luke – is its first preacher (!). (For the term 'preach' cf. 1.14, 38f.; 3.14; 6.12, etc.) John's appearance is already predicted by the Old Testament, and he behaves accordingly. John's preparation of the way consists in the fact that he is the forerunner; therefore the emphasis lies on v. 2 although here there is no quotation from Isaiah – as announced – but a quotation from Ex. 23.20a and Mal. 3.1. Only in v. 3 does the quotation from Isa. 40.3 follow. In v. 4 the statement about John's baptism 'for the forgiveness of sins' is in no way a Christianization, but like the report of his appearance in the wilderness goes back to tradition.

[5] This verse is a redactional exaggeration which is inferred from the quotation in v. 3. Of course the first preacher of the gospel *must* attract followers.

[6] These statements are too specific not to reflect tradition.

[7–8] Apart from the baptism with holy spirit, this passage is a tradition incorporated by Mark; v. 8 has a parallel in Q (Matt. 3.11/Luke 3.16). The Sayings Source used by Matthew and Luke shows that John was mainly a preacher of judgment (for a summary see on Matt. 3.1–12). Mark probably knew this, but suppressed it in v. 8 because of his Christianization of John.

Historical

John the Baptist practised baptism for repentance by the Jordan; by it the sins of those being baptized will be forgiven on the day of judgment, which is imminent (though we can infer this only from Q). His claim may have included a criticism of the temple, for sins were forgiven there, not by immersion in the Jordan. He appeared in the wilderness as an ascetic and as one living in the wilderness wore a camel hair garment with a leather girdle. In so doing he sought to recall the prophet Elijah (II Kings 1.8; cf. Zech. 13.4). His appearance in the wilderness may have been a prophetic symbolic action to remind the Israel of his day of Israel in the wilderness. In his own estimation John was in no way a precursor of Jesus. Even after his death he had his own disciples (cf. Mark 6.29; Acts 19.1–7).

Mark 1.9–11: The baptism of Jesus

9 And it happened in those days that Jesus came from Nazareth *in Galilee* and was baptized in the Jordan by John. 10 *And immediately, when* he came out of the water, he saw heaven opened and the spirit descend on him like a dove. 11 And a voice rang out from the heavens: 'You are my beloved son, in you I am well pleased.'

Redaction and tradition

[9–11] The pericope puts the previous announcement of vv. 7–8 into action. The special quality of the person of Jesus, i.e. the further designation of the 'stronger one' of v. 7, follows in God's address to Jesus, 'You are my beloved son.' For the redactional context note in addition the parallels 9.7 and 15.39, where each time there is a proclamation of Jesus as the son of God. Within the pericope Mark has added 'in Galilee'. In so doing he emphasizes that Jesus comes from a different neighbourhood from the crowds coming to the Baptist in v. 5. Galilee was very important to him (cf. 16.7).

In form criticism the pericope is often classified at the level of tradition as a legend of faith, which narrates Jesus' consecration as messiah. At the moment Jesus hears the voice from heaven (v. 11; cf. Ps. 2.7), he is appointed son of God.

As for the significance of John's baptism, in narrating the baptism of Jesus Mark passes over its special content, namely that it took place for the forgiveness of sins. The reason for this is clear: as the son of God Jesus really should not have been baptized for the forgiveness of sins. Here Mark effects the first visible shift in the perception of Jesus' baptism. Similarly, Mark sidesteps the presumption that if Jesus had himself baptized by John, he would have assented to the Baptist's preaching of judgment. (But he had already suppressed this aspect of judgment in v. 8.)

Historical

[9a] Historically, this casts light on the place where Jesus lived, Nazareth (cf. further on Matt. 9.1).

[9b] The baptism of Jesus by John the Baptist is historical. However, Jesus did not regard his baptism as appointment to be the son of God. The underlying concept derives from the community, which believed in Jesus as the son of God (cf. Gal. 2.16; 4.4) and located his appointment as son of God within his lifetime. That was not always the case. In the earliest period, for example, the appointment of Jesus as son of God came only after his resurrection from the dead (cf. Rom. 1.4).

That the baptism of Jesus by John is a historical fact follows no less from the difficulties that the Christian community had with it. Thus Mark had already toned it down, as did Matthew and Luke, according to whom John cannot even have been the one who baptized Jesus. The Gospel of John even thinks that the baptism did not take place; that is also the case in the Gospel of the Nazaraeans, which was not accepted into the NT canon. This says: 'Look, the mother of the Lord and his brothers said to him: "John the Baptist baptizes for the forgiveness of sins; let us go and be baptized by him." But he said to them: "What sin have I committed, that I should go and have myself baptized by him?" ' (Jerome, *Adv. Pelag.* III, 2).

Mark 1.12–13: The temptation of Jesus

12 *And immediately* the spirit drives him into the wilderness. 13 And he was in the wilderness *forty days, tempted by the Satan*, and he was with the wild beasts, and the angels served him.

Redaction and tradition

[12–13] 'The spirit' (v. 12) takes up the same word from v. 10; 'the wilderness' (vv. 12f.) corresponds to the place where John the Baptist appeared (v. 4). The location of the story in the Gospel of Mark – after the baptism and after Jesus' proclamation as son of God – may be attributed to the fact that usually the successful withstanding of temptation occurs at the beginning of the activity of holy men. This feature definitely derives from Mark, if he has added 'tempted by the Satan'. (Mark also uses 'Satan' elsewhere: 3.23, 26; 8.33). Perhaps 'forty days' is also redactional: Israel was forty years in the wilderness, Moses forty days on Sinai, Elijah travelled through the wilderness to Mount Horeb for forty days and nights without food and drink (cf. I Kings 19.8).

The tradition is present only in rudimentary form (cf. by contrast the tradition in Q: Matt. 4.1–11/Luke 4.1–13) and the details can no longer be reconstructed. Perhaps it seeks to depict Jesus as a righteous man, as a new Adam (cf. Rom. 5.12–21; I Cor. 15.45–49), who embodies the righteous son of God.

Historical

The tradition is unhistorical. Cf. the comments on the Q version (Matt. 4.1–11; Luke 4.1–13).

Mark 1.14–15: The preaching of Jesus

14 And after John had been delivered up Jesus came to Galilee and preached the gospel of God, 15 saying: 'The time is fulfilled and the kingdom of God is near, repent and believe in the gospel!'

Redaction and tradition

Mark gives a summary didactic depiction of Jesus' preaching of repentance under the influence of Christian mission terminology (for 'believe in the gospel' cf. I Cor. 15.1–3; Phil. 1.27).

[14] This refers back to v. 1. Jesus *himself* is the preacher of the gospel about himself. Jesus can appear only *after* the end of John the Baptist's preaching, since in Mark's view John is his predecessor. 'Galilee' is certainly redactional (see on v. 9). Jesus' activity, like that of the Baptist and that of Jesus' disciples (6.12), is described as 'preaching'.

[15] For Mark, the nearness of the rule of God is the basis for repentance and belief in the gospel of the son of God (v. 1). He himself lives in expectation of the imminent end (see on Mark 13) and for example believes that the end will come in his generation.

Historical

That Jesus' activity began in Galilee is correct, but not that he began his preaching only *after* the delivering up, i.e. the imprisonment, of John the Baptist. This is improbable simply because after John's death there were disciples of John among whom Jesus no longer belonged, and because Jesus had his own message distinct from that of John. For John and Jesus cf. further on Matt. 11.2–11/Luke 7.18–28.

Mark 1.16–20: Jesus' calling of the first disciples

16 *And as he was going along the Sea of Galilee, he saw* Simon and Andrew, Simon's brother, casting their nets into the sea; for they were fishermen. 17 *And Jesus said to them, 'Here, after me. And* I will make you fishers of men.' 18 *And immediately they left their nets and followed him.*

19 *And when he went a little further he saw* James, the (son) of Zebedee, *and* John, his brother, *also in the boat, mending nets. 20 And immediately he called them. And they left their father Zebedee in the boat with the day labourers and went away after him.*

Redaction and tradition

[16] 'Galilee' takes up the same location from v. 14. The names and the professions of Simon and Andrew come from the tradition.

[17] Verse 17a is the Markan introduction to v. 17b. The saying about fishers of men is rooted in the Easter situation (as is Luke's version of the saying about fishers of men, Luke 5.10).

[18] The motif of discipleship adapts the Easter saying about fishers of men secondarily to the circumstances of Jesus' life.

[19–20] Apart from the names, these verses have been composed redactionally on the basis of vv. 16–18. 'The invitation strikes like lightning. All at once the four fishermen are torn from their trade by an unknown figure who appears by the sea. In truth things probably happened rather differently' (Wellhausen).

Historical

It is impossible to doubt that the two pairs of brothers actually were followers of Jesus and that they were fishermen by profession. However, Jesus did not appoint any missionaries during his lifetime. If he did, they were not fishers of men in the Easter sense, but messengers of the kingdom of God, who spread out into the towns of Galilee.

Mark 1.21–39: Jesus in Capernaum

21 *And they come to Capernaum. And immediately he went into the synagogue on the sabbath and* <u>*taught*</u>. 22 *And they were beside themselves at his* <u>*teaching*</u>. *For he taught them with authority and not as the scribes.* 23 *And immediately in their synagogue* there was a man of <u>unclean spirit</u>, and he cried out, 24 saying, 'What (is there between) us and you, Jesus, Nazarene? Have you come to destroy us? I know who you are, the Holy One of God!' 25 And Jesus threatened him saying, 'Be silent and go out of him!' 26 And the <u>unclean spirit</u> shook him, and uttering a loud cry, he went out of him. 27 And everyone was terrified, so that they *discussed with one another and said,* 'What is this? *A new* <u>*teaching*</u> *in authority?* He commands even the <u>unclean spirits</u> and they obey him!' 28 *And the news of him immediately spread all over the surrounding region of Galilee.*

29 *And immediately, when they went out of the synagogue,* they came into the house of Simon *and Andrew with James and John.* 30 But Simon's mother-in-law was lying down with a fever *and immediately* they speak with him about her. 31 And he went and raised her up, after he had grasped her by the hand. And the fever left her. And she served them.

32 *And when it was evening, when the sun had set, they brought him all sick and possessed.* 33 *And the whole city was gathered before the door.* 34 *And he healed many suffering from various diseases. And he drove out many demons and he did not allow the demons to speak, because they knew him.*

35 *And very early, while it was still night, he arose and went to a lonely place and prayed there.* 36 *And Simon followed him and those who were with him,* 37 *and they found him and say to him, 'All are seeking you.'* 38 *And he says to them, 'Let us go elsewhere into the neighbouring villages, so that I may also preach there. For that is what I have come out for.* 39 *And he went and preached in their synagogues in all Galilee and drove out the demons.*

Redaction

In all likelihood, Mark has probably deliberately formed the present 'pericopes' together with 2.1–12 and 3.1–6 as a unity, for the purpose of depicting the first phase of Jesus' mission (each time it is stressed that the authority of the teaching and the miraculous works of Jesus go together). The present passage gives an example of Jesus' activity.

[21–28] Verses 21–23a and v. 28 are Markan framework. Part of v. 27 intensifies the motif of the authoritative teaching of Jesus.

[29a] This is a Markan link.

[29b] The names of three disciples, whose presence is not at all necessary, come from 1.16–20 and derive from Mark, who has been prompted by the name 'Simon'.

[32–34] The redactional summary depicts Jesus' healing activity at length, as do 3.7–12 and 6.53–56.

[35–39] The verses are a redactional construction and depict an ongoing activity of Jesus. The motif of the disciples' failure to understand appears for the first time in this scene (vv. 36f.); from now on it will govern their description. The activity of preaching in v. 38 links back to 1.14. In v. 39 note the redactional remark about Galilee (previously 1.9, 14).

Tradition

[23–27] Freed from its redactional additions, the story 'displays the typical features of a miracle story, especially the conjuration of a demon: 1. the demon senses the presence of the exorcist and struggles; 2. threat and command by the exorcist; 3. the demon departs with a demonstration; 4. the impression on the onlookers' (Bultmann). Verse 24 contains a formula of the demon to ward off the miracle worker. It recalls I Kings 17.18, where the widow of Zarephath similarly speaks to Elijah, and Elijah goes on to heal her son.

[29–31] The story is a healing miracle simply told, in which the gesture of healing (v. 31: 'he had grasped her by the hand') and the demonstration of the healing which has taken place (v. 31: 'she served them') are typical features. The narrative has been included largely out of a biographical interest in Simon Peter.

Historical

[23–27] The tradition is not the precise description of a miracle in the synagogue of Capernaum at the beginning of Jesus' public appearance. But it does contain a general, accurate recollection of Jesus' work as an exorcist in Capernaum. The activity of Jesus in driving out demons is one of the most certain historical facts about his life.

[29–31] The report about healing Peter's mother-in-law in Capernaum may be accurate, for it is hard to make out a need for constructing such a narrative (criterion of difference). The healing of fever may be the driving out of a demon, since in the ancient world fever was attributed to the activity of demons. The existence of a mother-in-law of Peter corresponds to a note in the letters of Paul that Peter was married (cf. I Cor. 9.5).

Mark 1.40–45: The leper

40 And a leper comes to him, beseeches him, falls at his feet and says to him, 'If you will, you can cleanse me.' 41 And having mercy on him he stretched out his hand, touched (him) and says to him, 'I will, be clean.' 42 *And immediately* the leprous disease left him and he became clean. 43 *And he reproached him, and immediately sent him away* 44 and says to him: '*See that you say nothing to anyone, but* go, show yourself to the priest, and offer a sacrifice for your cleansing, which Moses has commanded as a testimony to them.' 45 *But he went out and began to preach much and to spread the word, so that he could no longer go publicly into a city, but he was outside in solitary places. And they came to him from all around.*

Redaction

[43–44a] This passage is a Markan addition: v. 43 interrupts the connection between v. 42 and v. 44b, and verse 44a corresponds to the messianic secret theory.

[45] This verse is a redactional addition to the narrative which is concluded with v. 44b. Cf. also 1.28 on Mark's interest that the miracles of Jesus are narrated everywhere.

Tradition

[40–44*] The tradition was strongly influenced by the story of the healing of the leper in II Kings 5.1–9 and sought to point out that Jesus is the man of God who surpasses the healing of Naaman by Elisha. The command in v. 44b for the healed leper to show himself to the priest and offer a sacrifice corresponds to the law about the cleansing of lepers in Lev. 14.2–32. Thus the healing is to be confirmed – as a testimony to the people.

Historical

The tradition has no historical value, as its origin and purpose have been made clear.

Mark 2.1–12: The healing of the paralysed man

1 *And when he came to Capernaum again, all day long it was spread around that he was in the house.* 2 *And many people gathered together, so that there was not even enough room for them in front of the door; and he spoke the word to them.* 3 And they come and carry to him a paralysed man, who is borne by four. 4 And as they cannot carry the man to him *because of the people, they uncovered the roof where he was* and dug it up and let down the pallet on which the paralysed man was lying.

5 When Jesus saw their faith,

he says to the paralysed man, 'Child, your <u>sins</u> are <u>forgiven</u> you.' 6 Now some of the scribes were sitting there and thought in their hearts, 7 'Why does this man speak thus? He blasphemes! Who can <u>forgive sins</u> but God alone?' 8 *And immediately* Jesus recognized in his spirit that they were thinking like this and says to them, 'Why are you thinking this in your hearts? 9 What is easier, to say to the paralysed man, "Your <u>sins</u> are <u>forgiven</u> you," or to say, "Arise, take up your pallet and walk?" 10 But so that you know that the son of man has the authority to <u>forgive sins</u> on earth' –

he says to the paralysed man, 11 'I say to you, arise, take up your pallet and go to your house!' 12 And he arose and immediately took up the pallet and went away before them all, so that all were beside themselves and praised God, saying, 'We have never seen anything like this before!'

Redaction and tradition

The pericope has two points: (a) the miracle, (b) the saying about the forgiveness of sins. The latter has been inserted into the miracle story at a secondary stage together with the scene to which it belongs, since the faith of the paralysed man and those who are carrying him, which is spelt out at length in vv. 3–4, and is noted by Jesus in v. 5a, has disappeared in vv. 5b–10. Here vv. 11–12 are the appropriate conclusion to a miracle story.

[1–2] With the mention of the place in v. 1a, Mark picks up 1.21. (Previously Jesus had appeared 'in all Galilee' [1.39].) The transition to the miracle story which now follows derives entirely from Mark, including the end of v. 2: 'He spoke the word to them' (cf. 4.33; 8.32).

[3–5a] The original tradition begins in v. 3. Verses 3f. demonstrate the faith of those carrying the paralysed man. However, 'uncover' and 'dig up' in v. 4 do not match. Probably Mark introduced the uncovering of the roof, because he is thinking of a house covered with tiles, whereas the digging up is possibly only with Palestinian houses which are built of clay (cf. further on Luke 5.19).

[5b–10a] As was already remarked at the beginning, two pieces stand side by side within the pericope: a miracle story (vv. 3–5a, 10b–12) and a dispute over the right of the Son of man to forgive sins (vv. 5b–10a). (a) Verses 3–5a, 10b–12: the faith of those who carry the paralysed man, which overcomes great outward difficulties, sheds even greater radiance on the miracle worker who is worthy of this faith. (b) Verses 5b–10a: with the formation of this passage the community derives its right to forgive sins from Jesus (cf. Matt. 16.19; 18.18).

Since Mark had earlier indicated the clash in principle between scribes and Jesus (cf. 1.22), one can attribute to him the insertion of the forgiveness controversy into the miracle story. At that time the person who narrated healings of the sick by Jesus had to face the objection that sickness was derived from sin. In this pericope Mark disputes this inner connection.

[10b–12] At the level of redaction the miracle is the basis of the authority to forgive sins.

Historical

[3–5a, 10b–12] The healing of the paralysed man cannot be called historical. It belongs to the phase of primitive Christian propaganda in which the figure of Jesus drew every possible miracle to him like a magnet.

[5b–10a] Although the form in which the dispute is presented certainly derives only from the primitive Christian community, the core of Jesus' claim to be able to forgive sins without having formal authority to do so must be historical (cf. also Luke 7.36–50). Any Jewish healer also knew about the traditional connection between sickness and sin (cf. John 5.14; 9.3; I Cor. 11.30, etc.). A capacity for healing could therefore lead directly to the claim to forgive sins, if Jesus had at least latently an attitude which was opposed to the cult. Note, however, that John the Baptist forgave sins, but evidently did not do any miracles.

Mark 2.13–17: The call of Levi and the meal with toll collectors

13 *And he went out again along by the sea. And the whole people came to him, and he taught them.*
14 *And as he was going along, he saw* Levi, the son of Alphaeus, sitting at the toll and says to him, 'Follow me!' And he arose and followed him.
15 And it happens that he is reclining in his house and many toll collectors and sinners were reclining with Jesus *and his disciples. For there were many and they followed him.* 16 And the *scribes* of the Pharisees, when they saw that he eats with the sinners and toll collectors, said to his disciples, 'Is he eating with the toll collectors and sinners?' 17 And when Jesus heard (that), he says to them: 'The strong have no need of the physician, but the sick. I have not come to call righteous, but sinners.'

Redaction

[13] Like 1.22; 1.39f., this is a circumstantial Markan description. As in 1.14f., 21f. Jesus' teaching is put before his actions.

[14] The verse refers back to 1.16 and in part corresponds word for word with this passage.

[15–16] The unexpected mention of the disciples who appear here as a separate entity for the first time in Mark derives from the redactor. He thus prepares for the calling of the twelve (3.13–19), especially as previously he has spoken only of five who are called to discipleship. The mention of the scribes of the Pharisees links the present pericope with the next section (2.18–3.16), in which the Pharisees stand up against Jesus either alone (2.24) or with other adversaries (2.18; 3.6).

[17] In the context of the Gospel of Mark, the statement about the physician, which occurs frequently within the Greek tradition as a proverb, impresses on the readers that Jesus indeed heals the sick (cf. 1.32, 34); that Jesus has come refers back to 1.14. The connection between sin and sickness was the theme in the preceding narrative (2.1–12).

Yield: the pericope consistently continues the tendency which became clear in the Markan insertion of 2.5b–10: Jesus is the one who calls sinners and forgives them their sins.

Tradition

The pericope contains two pieces of tradition: (a) v. 14, the call of Levi the toll collector; (b) vv. 15–17, a controversy which originated in the logion handed down in v. 17c ('I have not come to call righteous, but sinners'). Here v. 17b ('The strong have no need of the physician, but the sick') is a wisdom-type generalization of v. 17c. The scene in v. 15, the colouring of which intrinsically comes from the tradition (Jesus as the guest of a toll collector) has been created subsequently. Verse 16, the question to the disciples, with Jesus' answer in v. 17, shows that the tradition in vv. 15–17 is a community formation.

Historical

[14] That Levi the toll collector was a disciple of Jesus is historical (but the same reservations must be made about the manner of his call as in Mark 1.16–20).

[16] Similarly, that Jesus ate with sinners and toll collectors is historical. Jesus was evidently often a guest in houses whose owners no longer had any real relationship with the Torah and therefore were regarded by the orthodox as godless.

[17b–c] These sayings fit the post-Easter situation well and are therefore unhistorical.

Mark 2.18–22: The question of fasting

18 *And the disciples of John and the Pharisees were fasting.* And they come and say to him: 'Why are the disciples of John *and the disciples of the Pharisees* fasting, but your disciples are not fasting?'

19 And Jesus said to them: 'Can the wedding guests fast while the bridegroom is with them? As long as they have the bridegroom with them, they cannot fast. 20 But days will come when the bridegroom is taken from them, and then on that day they will fast.

21 No one sews a piece of new cloth on an old piece. Otherwise the patch tears from it, *the new from the old,* and there is (only) a worse tear. 22 And no one pours new wine into old skins. Otherwise the wine bursts the skins and the wine is ruined, and the skins. *But new wine in new skins!'*

Redaction and tradition

[18a] 'Disciples' picks up the same expression in v. 15, 'Pharisees' the same word in v. 16.

[18b–20] Mark reproduces word for word a tradition which distinguishes between the time of Jesus and the time after his death. The original tradition consisted of vv. 18b*-19a, which with their argumentative character of the form of a question clearly show their origin in a debate. Verse 19b as a connection between the lifetime of Jesus and the time after his death and v. 20 as a prophecy put on the lips of Jesus are further developments after Jesus' farewell.

[21–22] The redactional insertions (in italics) show Mark's understanding: just as the teaching of Jesus is new, so as new wine the gospel belongs in a new form which is directed against the scribes and Pharisees. The twofold saying – with the Markan additions removed – has its origin in wisdom literature and can be comprehended by anyone who observes reality.

Historical

[18b*-19a] The tradition presupposes that Jesus and his disciples did *not* fast. This presupposition is historically correct (criterion of difference), for fasting as a practice soon developed in the community (see on vv. 19b–20). The present tradition certainly goes back to Jesus and designates the time that Jesus then spent with his disciples as a wedding. Here we will not go wrong in assuming that Jesus celebrated the meals that he had with his disciples, at first occasionally, as an anticipation of the heavenly banquet.

[19b–20] These words are inauthentic and were put on Jesus' lips only after his death in order to provide a basis for the community's practice of fasting. Cf. the rule of piety relating to fasting in Matt. 6.16–18. Jesus and his disciples did not fast (cf. the piece of tradition vv. 18b*-19a discussed above).

[21–22*] These verses can go back to Jesus, but the situation to which they belong is missing. In addition there is the general difficulty in the historical assessment of wisdom material. The verdict remains open.

Mark 2.23–28: Plucking ears of grain on the sabbath

23 And it happened when he was going through the grain fields on the sabbath that his disciples began to pluck ears of grain on the way. 24 And *the Pharisees* said to him, 'Look, why are they doing on the sabbath what is not allowed?'

25 And he says to them, 'Have you never read what David did, when he was in need and was hungry and those with him, 26 how he entered the house of God in the time of the high priest Abiathar and ate the showbread which only the priests are allowed to eat, and also gave (it) to those who were with him?' 27 *And he said to them,* 'The sabbath was made for man and not man for the sabbath. 28 Therefore the Son of man is lord even of the sabbath.'

Redaction

At this point Mark has handed on almost unchanged various pieces of tradition that he had received. Nevertheless the section is firmly rooted in the context of the Gospel of Mark.

The following pericope (3.1–6) is also about Jesus' attitude towards the sabbath. In this section once again we have the conflict of Jesus with the Jewish authorities and their law, over which Jesus stands as Son of man, cf. v. 28: this verse is part of the tradition, but Mark has deliberately put it at the end of the pericope.

[23] 'His disciples' takes up the same expression from v. 15.

[24] 'Pharisees' as opponents of Jesus appear previously in vv. 16 and 18 (twice) and later in 3.6.

[25–26] Cf. I Sam. 21.2–7. However, Abiathar was not high priest but his father Abimelech. Abiathar, Abimelech's successor, is mentioned later in I Sam. 22.20 (correcting Mark, Matthew and Luke therefore omit 'Abiathar').

[27] The beginning ('and he said to them') is a typically Markan transition formula.

Tradition

In the secondary literature the pericope is analysed in two ways: (a) vv. 23f., 27 belong together and vv. 25f., 28 are later additions; (b) vv. 23–26 are an original unit and vv. 27–28 were added, together or individually. However, against (a) there is the fact that in the controversy, Jesus' counter-question (v. 25f.) is typical. Moreover the scriptural proof in vv. 25f. may have played a role in the debates of the primitive community, even without the scenic framework.

Accordingly the following strata in the pericope may be established: vv. 23b–26, controversy; v. 27, individual saying; v. 28, christological conclusion.

Historical

[23b–26] This saying derives from the community, for Jesus is defending an action by his disciples.

[27] This verse is a key saying of Jesus. Behind it may stand the notion that the sabbath is a divine ordinance of creation, but precisely for that reason may in extreme situations be subordinated to human beings as the image of God. For the Jewish background to v. 27 cf. also II Macc. 5.19: 'The Lord (= God) did not choose the people for the sake of the place (= the temple), but the place for the sake of the people.' Apart from that, generally speaking Jesus interprets the Torah in terms of love, i.e. from the perspective of whether it serves men and women. One day he expressed this in the polemical formula of 2.27. No wonder that both Matthew and Luke omit this sentence.

[28] This is a post-Easter interpretation (like 2.10). In place of it, given the train of thought one would really have expected the conclusion, 'Thus the human being is lord over the sabbath'. Such a formula is sometimes also regarded as original on the

assumption of a mistranslation of the Aramaic. In Jesus' Aramaic mother tongue 'son of man' simply means human being. But 'Son of man' remains an honorific title for Jesus, as also emerges from other passages than v. 28 (cf. 2.10).

Mark 3.1–6: The healing on the sabbath

1 *And again he went into a synagogue.* And a man was there with a withered hand. 2 And they watched him, whether he would heal on the sabbath, *so that they could accuse him.* 3 And he says to the man with the withered hand, 'Stand in the middle!' 4 And he says to them, 'Is it allowed to do good on the sabbath or to do evil, to save a life or to kill?' But they were silent. 5 And he looked at them with anger. Sad at the hardness of their hearts, he says to the man, 'Stretch out your hand!' And he stretched it out, and his hand was restored. 6 *And the Pharisees immediately went out with the Herodians and took a decision against him, to destroy him.*

Redaction

In the Markan context the story further heightens the hostility between the Jewish authorities and Jesus. After the healing the authorities take the decision to kill Jesus, and succeed in doing so in Mark 14.15.

[1] 'Again' links the pericope with the context, as in 2.1 and 2.13.

[2] The sabbath theme picks up the previous pericope (2.23–28). Those watching Jesus are the Pharisees from 2.24.

[3] The fact that the sick man goes into the middle indicates that the issue is a human one (not one of the law) – as in 2.27.

[6] This verse is a redactional anticipation of the passion (cf. later Mark 8.31; 9.31; 10.33; 12.12; 14–15).

Tradition

The origin of the tradition is a miracle story. It has many parallels in terminology with the (punitive) miracle story told in I Kings 13.4–6, which depicts the withering and the healing of the ungodly hand of King Jeroboam. This miracle story was later developed into a controversy on the theme of the sabbath.

In the present version of the text the controversy has a coherent construction. 'But they were silent' (v. 4) and the healing (v. 5) formed the organic conclusion to the controversy, into which Mark probably introduced the Jewish leaders and their hostility to Jesus. The logion in v. 4 ('Is it allowed to do good on the sabbath, to save a [human] life or to kill?') never stood in isolation, for the form as a question corresponds to the charge implicitly contained in v. 2 as the typical form of counter-argument.

Historical

The controversy over whether it is allowed to heal on the sabbath never took place. For it is clearly shaped by the needs of the community. Nevertheless, underlying this story is the awareness that Jesus sometimes deliberately transgressed the sabbath commandment (cf. the principle in Mark 2.27).

Because of the parallelism with I Kings 13.4–6, the miracle story about the spontaneous healing of the withered hand is similarly secondary, quite apart from the fact that it would break the laws of nature.

Mark 3.7–12: Drawing great crowds of people and healings

7 *And Jesus went with his disciples to the sea, and a great crowd from Galilee followed (him) and from Judaea* 8 *and from Jerusalem and from Idumaea and from beyond the Jordan and from (the region) around Tyre and Sidon a great crowd. When they heard what he did they came to him.* 9 *And he told his disciples that because of the people he needed a boat so that they should not crush him.* 10 *For he healed many, so that they pressed in on him to touch him, (all) who were tormented by sickness.*

11 *Also the unclean spirits fell down before him when they looked on him, and cried, 'You are the Son of God.'* 12 *And he threatened them many times not to make him known.*

Redaction

Like 1.32–39; 6.53–56 the section is a redactional summary construction (and therefore cannot be counted as a historical source). By comparison with 1.32–34 people's interest in Jesus has intensified (see especially vv. 7f.). Only here do the demons pronounce the confession that Jesus is the Son of God (v. 11). Cf. previously the address to Jesus as the 'Holy One of God' (1.24) by a sick man with an unclean (= demonic) spirit. The narrative focus in this section is more on reactions to Jesus' miraculous deeds than on the healings (v. 10a) themselves.

Mark 3.13–19: The calling of the twelve apostles

13 *And he goes up the mountain and calls those whom he wanted and they went to him.* 14 And he appointed twelve, *to be with him and for him to send out to preach* 15 *and to have the authority to drive out the demons.*

16 And <u>he conferred</u> on Simon <u>the name</u> Peter, 17 and James, the son of Zebedee, and John, the brother of James, and <u>he conferred</u> on them <u>the name</u> Boanerges, *which means sons of thunder.*

18 And Andrew and Philip and Bartholomew and Matthew and Thomas and James the son of Alphaeus and Thaddaeus and Simon, the Canaanean, 19 and Judas Iscariot, *who also delivered him up.*

Redaction and tradition

[13] This is a Markan introduction. As always in Mark, the mountain has a symbolic significance and designates the place of an epiphany (cf. 9.2).

[14b–15] This is a Markan insertion with which Mark provides a motive at the narrative level for the way in which Jesus is constantly accompanied by the twelve disciples and the fact that they are sent out. The disciples receive the same authority to cast out demons that Jesus has demonstrated. As Jesus, so the disciples.

[19b] This verse anticipates 14.10–11. Mark has inserted narrative references by way of incidental remarks into the list of the names of apostles which has been handed down to him and provided it with a narrative framework. At the same time he inserts the notions of mission and authority into the list of names.

As *tradition* we can extract a list of twelve disciples of Jesus which can be reduced to a list of three. This trio consists of Simon, James and John, the three of whom are marked out by special names given to them by Jesus. Here it is striking that the nicknames of John and Andrew are given in Aramaic, and only Simon is given a Greek nickname, Peter, which presupposes his having been given the Aramaic name Cephas. The other known lists of twelve (Matt. 10.2–4; Luke 6.14–16; Acts 1.12–14) are to be compared with this list of twelve, but no great divergences arise; for a summary see on Matt. 10.2–4.

Simon the Canaanean (v. 18 end) means Simon the Zealot (W. Bauer).

Historical

[14] It is very probable that Jesus called a group of twelve during his lifetime. Were we to regard this group as a post-Easter creation, it would be difficult to explain why it disappeared again immediately after its institution. (I Cor. 15.5 mentions the group of twelve, but probably it was no longer in existence at the time of Paul's activity.) Moreover, the existence of Judas as one of the twelve suggests the historicity of the group of twelve in Jesus' lifetime. For who would have invented the existence of Judas who delivered up Jesus as a member of the group of the twelve had this person not been historical?

[16–17a] The conferring of the name Peter (= Aramaic Cephas) is no more historical than the appointment of a college of three, Simon, James and John (cf. on 9.2–8 and Gal. 2.9). Both came about in the primitive community (cf. on Matt. 16.18–19).

[17b] Perhaps Luke 9.54 makes the nickname of the sons of Zebedee, Boanerges, historically plausible. 'Luke does not mention the Aramaic name Boanerges for the sons of Zebedee, but he knows it and explains it here. They themselves want to bring down fire, so they trust that they can do what the Old Testament thunderer could do' (Wellhausen). According to another explanation, their name does not refer

to their character but to their task of prophetic-apocalyptic preaching (cf. John 12.29; Rev. 6.1; 10.3f.; 14.2; 19.6).

Mark 3.20–35: The repudiation of Jesus by his own kin and by scribes

20 *And he (Jesus) comes into a house. And the people again come together so that they could not even eat bread.* 21 And when those close to him heard it, they set about seizing him; for they said, 'He is out of his senses.'

22 *And the scribes who came from Jerusalem said, 'He has Beelzebul,' and,* 'Through the leader of the demons he drives out the demons.' 23 And he called them and spoke to them in parables, 'How can Satan drive out Satan? 24 <u>And if</u> a kingdom <u>is divided</u> in itself, no kingdom can stand. 25 <u>And if</u> a house <u>is divided</u> in itself, that house will <u>not</u> be able to <u>stand</u>. 26 <u>And if</u> Satan arises against himself and <u>is divided</u>, he ca<u>nnot stand</u>, but it has an end. 27 But no one can force his way into the house of the stronger one and plunder his possessions unless first he binds the strong man. Then he will plunder his house. 28 Amen, I say to you, Everything will be forgiven the children of men, the sins and the blasphemies, however much they blaspheme. 29 But whoever blasphemes against the Holy Spirit will have no forgiveness in eternity, but is guilty of the eternal sin.' 30 *For they said, 'He has an unclean spirit.'*

31 And his mother and his brothers come and, standing outside, sent to him and had him called. 32 *And around him sat the people.* And they say to him, 'Look, your mother and your brothers and your sisters *outside* are seeking you.' 33 And he answers them and says, 'Who is my mother and my brothers and sisters?' 34 And he looks around at those sitting round him in a circle and says, 'Look, that is my mother and those are my brothers and sisters. 35 For whoever does God's will, he is my brother and my sister and my mother.'

Redaction

This passage shows the sandwich technique which is typical of Mark. Cf. the large number of examples – the narrative which is sandwiched is each time put in brackets: 5.21–43 (vv. 25–34); 6.7–30 (vv. 14–29); 11.12–25 (vv. 15–19); 14.1–11 (vv. 3–9); 14.54–72 (vv. 55–65). The other New Testament Gospels which make use of the Gospel of Mark often reverse the sandwiching, one more reason for regarding this as one of Mark's stylistic means. He often tears apart a consecutive tradition and works a further narrative into it in order to achieve greater dramatic effect.

[20] For reasons of language and content this verse derives entirely from Mark.

[21] This is the beginning of the piece of tradition which Mark has torn apart.

[22–30] Now follows the sandwiching of a story about 'Jesus and the evil spirits', in which scribes from Jerusalem charge Jesus with having Beelzebul, i.e. of being possessed (v. 22). These attacks intensify the charge of the kinsfolk from v. 21 that Jesus is out of his mind, and Mark puts it in the mouths of the scribes. For Mark,

Jerusalem is the hostile city in which Jesus will be killed and which is therefore doomed to destruction. Thus for Mark scribes from Jerusalem are the worst opponents imaginable.

Next (3.31–35) the narrative which was begun in vv. 20–21 continues:

[31–32] Mark subsequently characterizes 'those close to him' from v. 20 as the physical family of Jesus. On being asked by the people (v. 32), Jesus redefines his family in what follows.

[33–35] Only those can be brother, sister or mother of Jesus who do the will of God. Here the absence of Jesus' father is striking. Mark 10.29–30 provides the key to understanding this:

Jesus said, 'Amen I say to you, There is no one who leaves house or brothers or sisters or father or children or fields for my sake and the gospel's who will not receive them one hundredfold: now in this time houses and brothers and sisters and mothers and children and fields with persecutions – and in the future world eternal life.'

Both passages reflect a fellowship in following Jesus which knows no father of a Jewish patriarchal kind. That need not contradict the theological reason that according to Jesus all have the same heavenly Father and therefore need no earthly fathers, who lay claim to power (cf. Matt. 23.9, 'You shall call no one on earth your Father!').

Tradition

[21, 31–35] Mark found a tradition which formed the basis of vv. 21, 31–35. It can be designated an ideal scene in which Jesus speaks about his true family.

[22–30] The smallest units are vv. 22b–26, v. 27 and vv. 28f. The simile in vv. 23b–25 could have existed by itself, but probably vv. 22b–26 is the basis: the division into attack and response as a two-member simile (divided kingdom and house at odds) corresponds to the typical form of Jewish debates. Verse 27 is a two-membered metaphor, vv. 28–29 a word of law or a community rule. In the present context it hangs somewhat in the air, because the spirit had not been mentioned previously. For blasphemy against the Spirit in v. 29 cf. Luke 12.10 (Q).

Historical

[21, 31–35). Two nuclei of tradition which suggest historical bedrock are contained in the ideal scene: (a) Jesus' family thought that he was 'out of his mind' (v. 21) and wanted to seize him (for further reasons see on Luke 2.7 under 'Historical'). Such a report would have been too offensive for it to have been invented. Moreover, in their use of Mark, Matthew and Luke omit this note without any replacement (cf. Matt. 12.46–50; Luke 8.19–21). Thus they *delete* it. (b) Verse 35 reflects the social structure of communities of followers of Jesus after 'Easter' (cf. above on the redaction). The verse reflects the situation of settled converts who had been thrown out by their families (cf. Luke 14.26/Matt. 10.37) and promises them a substitute social family. But this statement is not historical, since it is to be derived from the community. Moreover Jesus had no substitute family in view, but the kingdom of God, in which he will rule with the twelve after having first judged Israel.

[24–27] Verse 27 was probably spoken by Jesus in an exalted eschatological mood and similarly vv. 24–26, as the interpretation in terms of Satan is probable. Jesus evidently regarded his miracles as signs of the breaking in of the rule of God (Luke 11.20; Mark 3.27; Matt. 11.5). So verse 27 is authentic.

[28–29] These words are not authentic, since they derive from the community. It is interesting that they impose a two-stage sanction: (a) Sins and blasphemies are forgiven (cf. on Matt. 18.15–18); (b) Blasphemies against the holy Spirit cannot be forgiven and will be punished with eternal damnation. Probably this is about malefactors who do not perceive their offence (cf. Matt. 18.17) and have therefore been expelled from the community.

Mark 4.1–20 The parable of the sower and its interpretation

1 *And again he began to teach by the sea. And a very great crowd of people comes to him, so that he gets into the boat and sits on the sea. And the whole people was by the sea on the land. 2 And he taught them many (things) in parables and said to them in his teaching:*

3 'Listen! Look, a sower went out to sow. 4 And it happened that while he was sowing some fell on the way, and the birds came and devoured it. 5 And other fell on rocky ground, where it did not have much earth, and it immediately sprang up, because it had no deep earth. 6 And when the sun rose, it was scorched and, because it had no root, it withered. 7 And other fell among the thorns, and the thorns grew up and choked it, and it bore no fruit. 8 And other fell on the good earth and bore fruit, because it sprang up and grew, and bore thirty- and sixty- and one hundredfold. 9 *And he said, 'He who has ears to hear, let him hear.'*

10 And when he was alone, those around him asked him *with the twelve about the parables.* 11 *And he said to them, 'To you is given the mystery of the rule of God. But to those outside every-thing happens in parables, 12 that seeing they may see and yet not see and hearing they may hear and yet not understand, lest they convert and are forgiven.'*

13 And he says to them: 'You do not understand this parable, *and how will you understand all the parables? 14 The sower sows the word. 15 <u>These are</u> the ones on the way. Where the word is sown and if they hear, immediately Satan comes and takes away the word that was sown in them. 16 And <u>these are</u> those who are sown on the rock who, when they hear the word, immediately receive it with joy, 17 and have no roots in themselves, but are people of the moment. If tribulation or persecution for the word's sake arises, they take offence. 18 And others are those sown in the thorns. <u>These are</u> those who hear the word, 19 and the cares of the world and the deceit of riches and the desire for other things enter them and

choke the word and it becomes barren. 20 And those are the ones sown on the good earth, who hear and receive the word and bear fruit, thirty- and sixty- and one hundredfold.

Redaction

Since 1.14–15 it has often been said that Jesus taught (1.21–22; 2.13), preached (1.38; cf. 1.45), spoke the word (2.2), without mention of any specific content. Rather, 1.14–15 have always been in the background where it is said : Jesus preached the gospel of God, saying: 'The time is fulfilled and the kingdom of God is near, repent and believe in the gospel!"' Only in 4.11, 26, 30 does the key word 'kingdom of God' from 1.15 reappear in the framework of Jesus' discourse in parables. Since in v. 2 Jesus' teaching in parables is introduced as an exemplary extract from Jesus' preaching, 4.1–34 indicates what the nearness of the rule of God, repentance and gospel mean.

[1–2] These verses derive from Mark in their entirety: e.g. the boat from v. 1 which now becomes important as a pulpit on the sea picks up 3.9.

[3–8] The redactional interventions are slight. The summons to hear at the beginning (v. 3) does not refer to the parable but to its interpretation (see further below).

[9] While the awakening call comes from the tradition, it probably did not originally belong to the parable, since it could be attached to a great deal of varied material (cf. only Mark 4.23) and similarly by Mark also here

[10] The disciples' question about the interpretation of the parables in general is surprising, since Jesus has presented only *one* parable. The verse leads to the next redactional passage.

[11–12] These verses have been inserted into the tradition by Mark, quoting Isa. 6.9 in v. 12. Here he has also introduced the twelve into the context. The linking formula 'he said to them' also comes from him.

The statement in vv. 11–12 must be seen in the Markan context in connection with those passages which refer to Israel's unbelief. Cf. the decision of the Pharisees and Herodians to kill Jesus in Mark 3.6; the demand by the Pharisees for signs (8.11); the question of authority raised by the chief priests and the scribes (11.27–33); and the emphasis on the fact that because of the killing of the son the vineyard will be taken away from Israel (Mark 12: namely by the destruction of Jerusalem in the year 70). On the other hand, it is hardly possible to interpret 'those outside' in terms of the kinsfolk of Jesus (cf. 3.31: 'they are standing *outside*'), attractive though that might be in terms of the immediate context. For the kinsfolk are *not* present for the discourse on parables and the later activity of Jesus. Thus the fact remains that 'those outside' designates the Jews who reject Jesus' message.

The logion vv. 11–12 is the positive counterpart to Peter's messianic confession (Mark 8.29) and the confession of the centurion under the cross (Mark 15.39).

[13–20] These verses – apart from v. 13b – have been handed on by Mark practically unchanged. In connection with the chapter on parables, Mark 4, Mark emphasizes the paraenetic aspect by adding the interpretation of the parable in vv. 13–20 – the hearers in vv. 13–20 are to examine their own role as believers – and develops it yet further (cf. vv. 24–25).

Tradition

[3–8, 13a, 14–20] Here we have the tradition of a parable (vv. 3–8) which had already been equipped with an interpretation (vv. 14–20) at the pre-Markan stage. This interpretation is secondary not because it contains allegorical features, but *first* because of the Christian terminology (cf. e.g. the absolute use of 'word'). It is in keeping with this that there is a wealth of sayings about the word in the short passage vv. 14–20 which are alien to the rest of Jesus' preaching but are current in the vocabulary of early Christianity:

The preacher spreads the word (Mark 1.45; Acts.8.4; II Tim. 4.2, etc.); the word is received (I Thess. 1.6; 2.13; Acts 17.11, etc.), and indeed with joy (cf. I Thess. 1.6). Persecution arises because of the word (I Thess. 1.6; II Tim. 1.8; 2.9); the word becomes an offence (I Peter 2.8); the word grows (Acts 6.7; 12.24; 19.20; Col. 1.6); the word brings forth fruit (Col. 1.6, 10). Thus the interpretation reflects negative experiences in the early church (cf. similarly Luke 5.39).

A *second* reason why the interpretation in Mark 4.14–20 cannot go back to Jesus consists in the observation that there are words in this text which do not occur elsewhere among the Synoptists, but are familiar to the rest of New Testament literature: 'sow' in the metaphorical sense of preach (I Cor. 9.11, etc.); 'root' in the metaphorial sense of inner steadfastness (Col. 2.7; Eph. 3.17).

Thirdly, in addition to these linguistic observations comes the serious fact that the interpretation of the parable no longer has an eschatological focus. Rather, the accent is shifted from the eschatological to the psychological. In the interpretation, the parable becomes an admonition to the converts, who are to examine the state of their hearts to see whether they are taking their conversion seriously.

Fourthly, the Gospel of Thomas – where the parable appears without an interpretation (see below) – confirms that it originally circulated without one.

Yield: The interpretation of the parable of the sower in Mark 4.14–20 belongs to the primitive church. This saw the parable as an allegory and expounded it accordingly, feature by feature. First of all the seed is interpreted in terms of the word; then the field, which is described in four ways, is interpreted in terms of four groups of people. Two originally quite different notions stood behind this: on the one hand the comparison of the divine word with God's seed, and on the other the comparison of human beings with God's planting.

Verses 3–8 can be extracted as the oldest tradition, a tradition which has a close parallel in Thomas 9. There we read:

Jesus said, 'Look, a sower went out, filled his hand and threw (the seeds). Some fell on the way; the birds came, they pecked it up. Others fell on the rock and did not take root in the earth and did not bring forth ears <u>heavenwards</u>. And others fell on the thorns; they choked the seeds and the worm ate them. And others fell on the good earth and it brought forth good fruit <u>heavenwards</u>. It bore sixty per measure and one hundred and twenty per measure.'

The comparison between the versions of Mark and Thomas indicates that there is a far-reaching agreement, with two exceptions: *first*, the conclusion differs in that Mark speaks of fruit thirtyfold and sixtyfold and one hundredfold, while Thomas speaks of sixty and one hundred and twenty measures. *Secondly*, in mentioning the rocky ground on which the seed fell Mark additionally writes that the rising sun contributed to the withering (Mark 4.6), whereas Thomas is silent about this. On the whole we must regard the version of Thomas as older than that of Mark, because it is simpler.

[10–13a*] The text which Mark *had before him* ran: 'And when he was alone, those who were around him asked him about the parable. And he said to them, Do you not understand this parable?' (thereupon followed the interpretation of the parable in vv. 14–20). The saying in vv. 11–12 reflects the situation of a community which has accepted apocalyptic notions and is borne up by a sense of being the elite. In *no* way is it a saying of Jesus, since it shows an advanced reflection on scripture and is enigmatic, whereas Jesus' words aimed at agreement and understanding. The contradiction between vv. 11–12 and Jesus' purpose could not be greater. Whereas Jesus spoke in parables in order to be understood, the author of vv. 11–12 states quite the opposite: Jesus spoke in parables in order to be misunderstood, in order to mislead 'those outside' (= the hardening theory).

Historical

[3–8*] With the qualifications mentioned above, the parable goes back to Jesus: however – because we do not know what it really refers to – that does not yet tell us anything about its meaning.

'Is the meaning consolation for everyone, even if not all the work bears fruit? Is the parable in this sense a quasi-resigned, quasi-grateful monologue of Jesus? Is it an admonition to those who hear the divine word? The preaching of Jesus? Or in the original parable is there no reflection on the word at all and is the meaning the people sown in the world?' (Bultmann)

At any rate, in its images the parable goes back to the experiences of a farmer in Galilee. Here and elsewhere in Palestine the sowing came before the ploughing. Therefore the parable depicts a normal case in which failures are 'planned' from the start. 'So the sower of the parable is walking over the unploughed field of stubble. Now we can understand why he sows on the way. He deliberately sows on the thorns that are withered on the fallow field, because they too are to be ploughed in. Nor is it any longer a surprise that grains of seed fall on the rocky ground. What seems clumsy to the Westerner proves to be the rule for conditions in Palestine' (Jeremias).

But what is the meaning of the parable? Though its imagery may be very impressive, its interpretation is highly controversial. This is connected on the one hand with the fact that ignorance of the original narrative situation in this case puts us at a particular disadvantage, while on the other hand the parable was understood either in terms of its interpretation or radically separated from it, so that only uncertain points of contact for the interpretation remained. The uncertainty already expresses itself in the naming of the parable: depending on whether one puts the sower, the field or the ground in the foreground, it is called the parable of the undeterred sower, the scattered seed or the varied field.

The possible understanding which I prefer, on the basis of the criterion of coherence, links the parable with the future expectation of Jesus. Here I classify it with the parables about the kingdom of God, and begin from the contrast in the structure. This lies in the fact that the beginning of the parable describes a different point in time from the end. First the sowing is depicted, and in the final verse it is already harvest time. The breaking in of the kingly rule of God is compared with this. It is confronted with manifold failure and resistance in the present. So the message of the parable calls for confidence. Despite all failure and resistance, God produces the glorious end from the hopeless beginnings. As a parable of Jesus, it then expresses Jesus' confidence – a confidence which suffered a defeat because the kingdom of God did not in fact break in.

[9] Inauthentic as a saying of Jesus.

[10–13a*] Unhistorical.

[13–20] Unhistorical.

Mark 4.21–25: Sayings about the lamp and the measure

21 *And he said to them,* 'Does the lamp come to be put under the bushel or under the bed? Is not it rather put on the lampstand? 22 For nothing is hidden except to be made manifest, and nothing is secret except to come to light. 23 *He who has ears to hear let him hear.*'

24 *And he said to them,*: '*See what you hear*! The measure you give will be the measure you get, and it will be added to you. 25 For to him who has will be given, and from him who does not have, even what he has will be taken away.'

Redaction

[21–22] In the Markan context these verses are probably to be referred to the communication of the mystery of the kingdom of God to the disciples (v. 11). The mystery of the kingdom of God given to the community is to be made manifest and instils courage for the mission. The lamp of the message of the kingdom of God must be put on the lampstand.

[23] Mark inserts this awakening call here and thus repeats v. 9, in order to show that the train of thought is a unity.

[24–25] Redactionally, perhaps these two sayings also explain the mystery of the kingdom of God. The disciples are to pay heed to what they have heard, to believe in the future of the rule of God and to make this faith the measure of their commitment.

Tradition

The key word 'bushel' in v. 21 links the section with the parable of the sower, and has led to the addition of the saying about the measure (v. 24a). The clause 'will be added to you' (v. 24b) has attracted the saying about having and getting (v. 25).

[21] This is a somewhat long-drawn-out simple simile; indeed, it is originally a proverb from profane existential wisdom with parallels in Jewish literature.

[22] A logion formulated in terms of content.

[24] A wisdom maxim (cf. similarly Gal. 6.7).

[25] A logion formulated in personal terms; cf. IV Ezra 7.25: 'Empty for the empty, but fullness for the full.'

Historical

[21 and 22] These words might very well go back to Jesus. He clearly thought that the seed had to be scattered everywhere and that the light had to shine everywhere. This stands in strong opposition to the Markan interpretation of 4.11–12. The nearness of the kingdom of God announced by Jesus is to be scattered everywhere, its light will shine everywhere – this is the meaning which Jesus probably attached to the saying.

[24] The Jewish maxim that people reap what they sow cannot be attributed to Jesus with sufficient probability, though it could be possible.

[25] The verdict on this wisdom saying is the same as that on v. 24.

Mark 4.26–29: The parable of the seed growing by itself

26 And he said, 'The kingdom of God is as if a man casts seed on the land 27 and sleeps and arises day and night, and the seed sprouts and grows, he knows not how. 28 Of itself the earth produces fruit, first the blade, then the ear, then the full-grown wheat in the ear. 29 But when the crop permits, at once he puts in the sickle, for the harvest is there.'

Redaction and tradition

Redactional interventions cannot be established. However, Mark must have been aware of the parallel between this parable and that of the sower (vv. 3–9). It is striking that the parable of the seed is not contained either in Matthew or in Luke. But that should not lead us to the erroneous conclusion that it was inserted only later into the Gospel of Mark. (For example, there is good reason for supposing that with Matt. 13.24–30 Matthew is 'reacting' to the parable of the seed growing by itself, which he has omitted.)

The phrase 'and he said' (v. 26) is probably an element in a pre-Markan collection of parables (cf. v. 30).

Sometimes a tension is noted between vv. 26–28 and v. 29: 'The conclusion in 4.29 overshoots. Through the farmer we get a glimpse of the judge of the world, who has nothing to do here' (Wellhausen). Why not?

The parable underlines the contrast between beginning and end. Its point lies in v. 28: the seed succeeds in maturing in all circumstances, and does so as if by itself. The kingdom of God, a technical term of the preaching of Jesus, is soon established, as is shown by the image of the harvest at the end (cf. Joel 4.13a, 'Seize the sickle, for the harvest is ripe!').

Historical

It is likely that the parable goes back to Jesus, since he himself is not its subject (criterion of difference). Furthermore, the parabolic talk about the kingdom of God is typical of the preaching of Jesus (criterion of coherence). In the parable, we can see Jesus' rock-firm trust that in the immediate future God will finally bring in his kingdom, which is already present in the advent of Jesus.

Mark 4.30–34: The parable of the grain of mustard seed. Conclusion of the parable discourse

30 And he said, 'With what can we compare the kingdom of God, or with what parable shall we describe it? 31 With a grain of mustard seed, which, when sown on the earth, is the smallest of all the seeds on the earth, 32 and when it is sown, it grows up and becomes greater

than all plants and puts forth great branches, so that the birds of the air may take up their abode in its shade.'

33 And in many such parables he spoke the word to them, as they could hear it. 34 *He did not say anything to them without a parable, but privately he explained everything to his own disciples.*

Redaction and tradition

[30–32] Either Mark has put these verses at this point in connection with the parable of the seed growing by itself or – more probably – he has found them with this parable in a collection. There are no redactional interventions. It is worth mentioning that according to Mark the active mission to the Gentiles (Mark 13.10) will replace the pilgrimage of the peoples to Zion which is presupposed in the parable, as will be shown below. Nevertheless, at this point he leaves the words of Jesus unchanged.

The introduction to the parable corresponds to the introduction to the previous parable (v. 26). Sometimes it is said that the seed is no longer the word, but virtually the kingdom of God, which develops as the church on earth, from tiny beginnings (Wellhausen). In that case we would have a post-Easter parable. However, the parable of the grain of mustard seed speaks of the sure coming of the kingdom of God, which is now already at work. We need not see the development of the church on earth in v. 32, but can imagine the messianic kingdom. In that case, at the end stands the consummation of the kingdom of God or the temple as the goal of the pilgrimage of the peoples (cf. Matt. 8.11 par and Ezek. 17.23; 31.6; Dan. 4.9, 18).

[33] This concludes the pre-Markan collection of parables.

[34] This verse comes from Mark and corresponds to the theory of the parable discourse expressed in vv. 11–12: parables are explained to the disciples, and to those outside they produce hardening.

Yield: The parable in vv. 30–32 emphasizes the contrast between beginning and end. The one who speaks it is convinced that God will bring in his kingdom from the most pitiful beginnings, and will do so in the immediate future.

Historical

[30–32] The parable, which has been transmitted in parallel in Q (Matt. 13.31–32/ Luke 13.18–19) and Thomas 20, contains the same message as the parable of the seed which grows by itself (4.26–29) and is authentic (criteria of difference and coherence). It should be emphasized once again that the prospect of the future is an original element of Jesus' message.

Mark 4.35–41: The conjuration of the storm

35 *And he says to them on that day, when evening had come, 'Let us go over to the other shore.'*
36 *And they left the multitude of people and took him with them, as he was in the boat. And other boats were with him.* 37 And a great storm arose. And the waves beat into the boat, so that the boat was already filling. 38 And he himself was asleep in the stern on a cushion. And they wake him and say to him, 'Teacher, do you not care that we are perishing?' 39 And awakened, he threatened the wind and said to the sea, 'Quiet, be dumb.' And the wind ceased, and there was a great calm. 40 *And he said to them, 'Why are you so afraid? Why do you have no faith?'* 41 And they felt great fear, and they said to one another, 'Who is this, that even the wind and the sea obey him?'

Redaction and tradition

Here Jesus brings the forces of nature to rest by his *word*. Mark had already emphasized the presence or the nearness of the kingdom of God in the word or the teaching of Jesus in 1.14–15; 4.1–34.

[35–36] These verses make a connection with v. 1 through the information given here.

[37] This verse recalls Jonah 1.4 ('There arose a great storm on the sea').

[38] Like Jonah (1.5), Jesus sleeps; for the disciples' question in v. 38c cf. Jonah 1.6.

[40] This verse is stamped by the Markan motif of the failure of the disciples to understand. Mark also wishes to make the point that although the disciples do not rightly grasp the presence of the kingdom of God in the word of Jesus, the presence of Jesus can be grasped by faith. Therefore he addresses his readership about this faith.

The *tradition* here is the story of a nature miracle which displays the typical elements of threat by the word (v. 39; cf. 1.25; 9.25) and the description of the impact (v. 41). The drama is heightened by the fact that not only is a great danger posed by the storm, but the one who alone could help is asleep and doing nothing.

Probably an originally alien miracle story was transferred to Jesus, and in addition was furnished with references to the Old Testament story of Jonah. But this reference is not original, since unlike the Jonah narrative, the stilling of the storm is performed as an exorcism of demons. Verse 39 presupposes that angels or demons are directing the wind (cf. Jub. 2.2: 'Angels of the spirit of the winds'; I Enoch 69.22: 'spirits of the winds'). The intention of the narrator of this nature miracle is to show Jesus the equal of Greek magicians and shamans and – at a secondary stage – to make him plausibly fulfil Old Testament models.

Historical

The historical yield is nil, as the tradition can be derived from the community and not even magicians can break the laws of nature. However, the historical Jesus' reputation as an exorcist explains why a nature miracle involving a spell on demons could be attributed to him.

Mark 5.1–20: The demon-possessed man of Gerasa

1 *And they came to the other shore of the sea in the country of the Gerasenes.* 2 *And when he got out of the boat immediately* a man with an unclean spirit came to meet him from the cave tombs, 3 who had his abode in the caves, and no one could bind him with a fetter. 4. For he had already often been bound by fetters and chains, and the chains were torn apart by him and the fetters broken in pieces. And no one could subdue him. 5 And constantly, day and night in the cave tombs and on the hills he cried out and smote himself with stones. 6 And when he saw Jesus from afar he ran and threw himself down before him 7 and cried with a loud voice, 'What have I to do with you, Jesus, son of the most high God? I conjure you by God, do not torment me!' 8 *For he had said to him, 'Depart, unclean spirit, from the man!'* 9 And he asked him, 'What is your name?' And he says to him, 'Legion is my name, for we are many.' 10 And he asked him urgently not to send them out of the region. 11 Now on the mountain there was a herd of pigs, which were feeding. 12 And they asked him, 'Send us into the pigs, that we may enter into them.' 13 And he allowed them, and the unclean spirits went out and entered into the pigs, and the herd rushed down the slope into the sea, around two thousand, and they drowned in the sea.

14 And their herdsmen fled and told (of it) in the city and in the country. And they came to see what had happened, 15 and go to Jesus and see the man possessed of a demon sitting there, clothed and in his right mind, the one who had the legion, and they were afraid. 16 And the eye-witnesses told them what had happened to the possessed man and about the pigs. 17 And they began to ask him to go away from their region.

18 And *when he was getting into the boat* the man who had been possessed asked him if he might *be with him.* 19 And he did not let him, but says to him, 'Go into your house to your own and *tell* them what the Lord has done for you and has had mercy on you!' 20 *And he went and began to proclaim loudly in the ten cities what Jesus had done for him and all were amazed.*

Redaction

[1] This verse derives from Mark. The arrival on the other shore carries out the plan of 4.35. The plural 'they came' is similarly redactional, since the disciples play no further role in what follows.

[2a] The motif of the boat goes back to Mark. Cf. previously 4.36 and later v. 18.

[7] For the encounter with the exorcist cf. 1.23–24 and I Kings 17.18 as a common background.

[8] This verse is probably redactional. Mark loves explanatory sentences which provide additional information: 1.38; 2.15; 3.10; 4.22, 25. Cf. also the similar additions in 3.30; 6.17–29; 15.7, 19.

[18b] The motif of discipleship is redactional (cf. 3.14, 'be with him').

[20] Mark shapes the miracle story to suggest that the healing of the possessed man first brought news of Jesus into the ten cities ('Decapolis'). Decapolis is the name of an alliance originally consisting of ten cities with a territory east of the Jordan (without Scythopolis). The boundaries were Damascus in the north and Philadelphia in the south.

Tradition

The underlying miracle story is the most extended such narrative in the New Testament Gospels. It has numerous parallels with the miracle story in Mark 1.21–28 and is similarly to be designated an exorcism.

The story witnesses to a great delight in narration. This is visible in the duplications: we are told twice that the possessed man lived in the tombs (vv. 3, 5), the request to be spared (vv. 10, 12) and that there were the witnesses (vv. 14, 16). At the same time it should be noted that the underlying motif is that of the cheated devil, which is not without its comic side.

'Contrary to their expectation the demons now see themselves, despite the fulfilment of their wish and precisely as a result of it, forced from their dwelling place, and may see for themselves where to stay (Luke 11.24). That is related with pleasure. Similarly the unclean animals are allowed to drown and their pagan owners suffer the loss: 2000 animals! It is amazing how this comic tale could have been transferred to Jesus' (Wellhausen).

Historical

The historical value of the narrative is nil. It was transferred to Jesus only later, and the formation of its tradition reflects a developed stage. At the same time we should note that such a story could be transferred seamlessly to Jesus. That was possible only because he did in fact perform exorcisms (cf. above on Mark 1.21–28, etc.).

Mark 5.21–6.1a: The healing of the woman with a flow of blood and the raising of Jairus' daughter

21 *And when Jesus had crossed again in the boat to the other shore, a great crowd of people gathered around him, and he was on the sea.* 22 And one of the rulers of the synagogue, Jairus by name, comes to him, and when he sees him he falls down at his feet 23 and asks him urgently, 'My

daughter is dying. Come and lay your hands on her that she may be saved and live!' 24 *And he went with him, and a great crowd of people followed him, and they pressed on him.*

25 And there was a woman who suffered a flow of blood twelve years 26 and had suffered much from many doctors and had spent all that she had, but it had been no use, and her condition had grown even worse. 27 When she heard about Jesus, she came into the crowd from behind and touched his garment. 28 *For she said, 'If I even just touch his garments, I shall be saved.'* 29 And *immediately* her flow of blood dried up and she felt throughout her body that she had been healed from the affliction. 30 And *immediately* Jesus recognized in himself the power that had flowed out; he turned round in the crowd and said, 'Who has touched my garments?' 31 *And his disciples said to him, 'You see that the people is pressing on you, and you say, "Who has touched me?"'* 32 And he looked round to see the one who had done this. 33 But the woman was afraid and trembled, knowing what had happened to her, and came and prostrated herself before him and told him the whole truth. 34 And he said to her, 'Daughter, *your faith has saved you. Go in peace and be healed from your affliction!'*

35 *While he is still speaking,* they come from the ruler of the synagogue and say, 'Your daughter is dead; why do you still trouble the teacher?' 36 But when Jesus heard the word that was spoken he says to the ruler of the synagogue, 'Do not fear, only believe!' 37 And he allowed no one to follow him (= accompany him) *but Peter, James and John, the brother of James.* 38 And *they come* into the house of the ruler of the synagogue and he sees a tumult, weeping and loud lamenting. 39 And when he goes in he says to them, 'Why do you make a tumult and weep? The little child is not dead, but sleeping.' 40 And they laughed at him. But he drove them all out and takes the father of the child and the mother and *his people* and goes in where the child was. 41 And taking the child's hand, he says to her, 'Talitha koum!', *which translated means, 'Little girl, I tell you, arise.'* 42 And *immediately* the little girl arose and went around. For she was twelve years old. And they were overcome with great amazement. 43 *And he commanded them strictly that no one should learn of this.* And he told them to give her something to eat. (6.1a) *And he went away from there.*

Redaction

Mark has sandwiched two stories (for this technique see on 3.20–34). Here it is striking that Jesus performs healings on two women. Mark's awareness of this can be seen in his designation of both women as 'daughter' (vv. 34/35).

[21] This verse is stylistically Markan. The crossing of the sea refers to 5.1f., 18; the stay on the sea back to 4.1.

[24] This verse provides a redactional link between the two narratives in order to create a transition.

[28] The 'flashback' possibly derives from Mark.

[31] The incomprehension of the disciples runs through the Gospel of Mark like a scarlet thread (cf. 4.13; 4.40–41; 6.52; 7.18; 8.17–21, etc.). 'According to the Gospel of Mark, throughout the story the disciples show themselves incapable of understanding Jesus' (Wrede).

[34] For the motif of faith cf. v. 36 and 4.40. For the concept of faith in the preaching of Jesus cf. further on Matt. 17.20b.

[35] This verse is a link (for the construction cf. 14.43).

[37] The group of three comes from 3.16f. Mark also prefers this trio elsewhere, cf. 9.2.

[43a] Mark also adds the prohibition against telling anyone at other points (cf. 7.36; 9.9).

[6.1a] This links the two miracle stories with what follows.

Tradition

(a) The Jairus story (vv. 22–24, 35–43). The model is the Elijah–Elisha story (I Kings 17.17–24; II Kings 4.25–37). The construction of the story, which depicts a raising from the dead, is in keeping with the style.

'Other typical features are the removal of the public in v. 40, the gesture and the magic word in v. 41, the suddenness of the miracle in v. 42, and the indication of age which here is added at an effective point, v. 42, with the report of the impression made by the miracle. A final typical feature is the invitation to give the raised girl something to eat, v. 43, which here forms the motif of demonstration' (Bultmann).

(b) The woman with an issue of blood (vv. 25–34). This miracle story brings out the contrast between the vain quest for healing and sudden, miraculous healing by Jesus. It emphasizes the woman's belief in miracle in the presence of Jesus, the magician (cf. esp. v. 30), whose capability is superior to that of the countless doctors (cf. v. 26). The structure is in keeping with the style.

'Typical features are the information about the duration of the sickness in v. 25 and the emphasis on the vain efforts of the doctors in v. 26, which is meant to emphasize the seriousness of the suffering and thus the magnitude of the miracle. Other typical features are the motif of touching, vv. 27–32, which is especially developed here, and also the suddenness of the healing (v. 29)' (Bultmann).

Both narratives derive from an interest in missionary recruitment: Jesus is superior to other healers and therefore deserves people's trust.

Historical

[22–24, 35–43] Even historical reminiscences of a similar miraculous act by Jesus are improbable, since there are fundamental objections to the historicity of the raising of a dead person both in terms of the tradition and medically.

[25–34] The story has no historical value in terms of the question whether Jesus healed the woman with a flow of blood. For the theme 'Jesus and the women' cf. the summary on Mark 1.29–31; Luke 7.36–50; 8.1–3.

Mark 6.1b–6: The repudiation of Jesus, the son of Mary, in his ancestral town

1b And he comes to his ancestral town, *and his disciples follow him.* 2 And when the sabbath came *he began to teach in the synagogue*, and the many who heard him were amazed and said, 'Where did this man get this? And what kind of wisdom is given him and *such miracles which are performed by his hands?'* 3 Is this not *the craftsman*, the son of Mary *and brother of James and Joses and Jude and Simon? And are not his sisters here with us?'* And they took offence at him.

4 And Jesus said to them: 'A prophet is nowhere without honour except in his ancestral town *and among his kinsfolk and in his house.'*

5 *And he could perform no miracle there, except that he laid hands on a few weak people and healed them.* 6 *And he was amazed at their unbelief. And he went around into the villages and taught.*

Redaction

[1b] The mention of the disciples, who play no role in what follows, derives from Mark.

[2a] This verse contains the motif of Jesus' teaching which is typical of Mark, and thus recalls Jesus' appearance in Capernaum (1.21–28; cf. esp. vv. 21–22).

[2b] Because of the frequent occurrence of the motif of miracle (cf. v. 5), and because of the miraculous actions in the context (ch. 5 alone contains three massive miracles), the question about Jesus' miracles must similarly be redactional.

[3] The question asked by Jesus' hearers emphasizes that there is nothing extraordinary about him: after all he is the craftsman whom they all know. And similarly his brothers and sisters are known. *Therefore* people take offence at Jesus' particular claim. For the unusual phrase 'son of Mary' instead of 'son of Joseph' cf. below under Tradition.

[4] The second half of the verse derives from the redactional link between the wisdom saying and v. 3.

[5] The motif of miracle is redactional (see above on v. 2).

[6] With the closing remark in v. 6a the word-group belief/unbelief occurs for the fourth time within the larger section 4.31–6.6a and is therefore its bracket.

Because of their faith people expect miracles of Jesus; indeed, like the woman with a flow of blood they can cause Jesus to perform a miracle involuntarily. So in this section Mark is encouraging his readership to believe that Jesus performs miracles. The scene and the conduct of the people in Nazareth form the negative counterpart to that.

The teaching of Jesus mentioned in v. 6b runs like a scarlet thread through the Gospel of Mark (cf. 1.21f.; 2.13; 4.1) and picks up v. 2. The content of the teaching of Jesus, which is usually not mentioned at all, is well known: the kingdom of God is near.

Tradition

There are two possible ways of describing the origin of the scene which has been handed down: (a) Mark 6.1–6 contains a prime example of the way in which a narrative has been formed from a general wisdom statement (v. 4a). The key word linking the composition of the story would be 'ancestral town' (vv. 1, 4). (b) Verse 4a , the general wisdom statement, has been inserted by Mark into a story of the unsuccessful appearance of Jesus in his home town (Nazareth). Mark would have been prompted by the word 'ancestral town' to add the wisdom statement.

The latter possibility is more probable, since the information about Jesus' appearance in his ancestral town is too concrete. However, the form of a narrative of the unsuccessful appearance of Jesus in his home town in the tradition cannot be defined. It is worth assuming that Mark has drawn on general knowledge, from whatever source and/or narrative, and worked it into the composition of this scene. I shall designate this piece tradition 1. At the same time the sentence v. 4a, which was handed down separately, might be an attempt to assimilate Jesus' lack of success, a fact which was difficult for the Christian community to understand and offensive to its members. I shall designate this tradition 2.

Within tradition 1, the observation that he is the *son of Mary* stands out as an argument against Jesus. Mark manifestly takes the edge off this argument by a neutral family catalogue, which because of the names given there must go back to tradition. But the phrase 'son of Mary' remains all the more unusual, as a Jewish man was normally associated with the name of his father, even when the father had already died.

The phrase 'son of Mary' probably comes from a tradition which was current in the very earliest time, soon shaped by the controversy over Jesus' authority. The two parallels, Matthew and Luke, provide an important reason for the assumption that 'son of Mary' is meant *polemically;* for each of them changes ' son of Mary' into 'son of Joseph'. Moreover reference should be made to the textual tradition of the Gospel of Mark: a third-century papyrus of the Gospel (unfortunately slightly damaged at this point) makes the following correction to the text of Mark 6.3 with a probability that borders on certainty: 'Is this not the son of the craftsman and of Mary?' (Papyrus 45 from the third century).

The three most important reasons for assuming that the expression 'son of Mary' is about the lack of legitimation for Jesus are:

1. The phrase is uttered in Jesus' home town (Nazareth or Capernaum).

2. It appears on the lips of those who have not completely understood Jesus or are hostile towards him.

3. Mark does not repeat the statement from Mark 6.3. He does not answer the charge by rejecting it, but by declaring the relatives of Jesus unimportant in v. 4b.

In conclusion it should be indicated how tradition 1 and tradition 2 may have grown together. There is a possibility that the charge of being born without honour in tradition 2 (Mark 6.4) is directly connected with the taunt 'son of Mary' from tradition 1. Cf. Wisdom 3.16ff.: 16 'But children of adulterers will not come to maturity, and the offspring of an unlawful union will perish. 17 Even if they live long they will be held of no account, and finally their old age will be without honour . . .' That would then mean that Jesus has no honour because he is illegitimate.

Historical

Tradition 2: the saying underlying Mark 6.4 perhaps goes back to Jesus. But it could also have been put into the mouth of Jesus later.

Tradition 1: Jesus' success in his home town was slight. We may infer as a historical fact that the designation of Jesus as 'son of Mary' was already used against him in his home town. The phrase is then to be designated a taunt which puts a finger on a sore spot in Jesus' descent. For the people of Jesus' home town to call their fellow-townsman Jesus 'son of Mary' is an offensive slur. The key to understanding it is that Jesus is contemptuously named after his mother and not his father, as was usual. So the charge runs: this fellow who wants to preach to us has no proper father; he is a bastard.

In conclusion, we need to look at the following two views of the text, the rejection of which can further reinforce the above analysis.

(a) Mark removed the name of Joseph from the tradition behind Mark 6.3 because Joseph had a place of honour in the church of Jerusalem. At the same time this is a manifesto against the legal and doctrinal hegemony of the Jerusalem church. Hence the strong lack of interest in Joseph. This is a second-degree hypothesis.

(b) The statement that Jesus is the son of Mary is an indirect reference to the virgin birth. Otherwise we should expect Jesus to have been called son of Joseph. But that cannot be derived from the text, all the less so as Mark shows no interest in the virgin birth at any point.

Once again: the father of Jesus is not mentioned at this point because there is doubt about who his real father is. Had Jesus been a physical son of Joseph, the expression 'son of Mary' would never have found its way into an early Christian text. The phrase 'son of Mary' is so shocking that only Mark has the courage to repeat it.

Mark 6.7–13: The sending out of the twelve

7 And he calls the twelve together and began to send them out two by two and gave them authority over the unclean spirits. 8 And he charged them to take nothing with them on the way but a staff, no bread, no bag, no money in their belts, 9 but sandals on their feet and not to wear two undergarments. 10 And he said to them, 'Wherever you enter a house, remain there until you leave again. 11 And whatever place does not receive you and they do not listen to you, go away from there and shake off the dust which is under your feet as a testimony to them.' *12 And they went out and preached that they were to repent 13 and they drove out many demons and anointed with oil many sick and healed (them).*

Redaction and tradition

Mark here parallels Q (Matt. 10.5–16/Luke 10.2–12), though that does not mean that I want to presuppose a *use* of the Q source. Note that the tradition in Mark is drawn quite unapocalyptically, whereas the earlier tradition (Luke 10.2–12) knows the expectation of an imminent end.

[7] This verse is the Markan introduction to the mission discourse. Cf. the almost word-for-word agreement with 3.14.

[8–9] Staff and sandals were conceded at a secondary stage (cf. Q, which differs). The prohibition against putting on two undergarments, one on top of the other, which was the usual custom on journeys, is a watering down of Q (Matt. 10.10/ Luke 9.3). There 'Jesus' even prohibits owning more than one, although even the poorest person attempted to have a second clean garment. The undergarment was worn directly on the body.

[10–11] Cf. on Luke 9.4–5; 10.7–11.

[12–13] These verses describe the result of the mission discourse (cf. 3.15).

Historical

The requirement to go out without any equipment fits Jesus' radical notion of discipleship well.

The historical question is whether Jesus sent out disciples during his lifetime. It is probably to be answered in the affirmative. The commission to preach (the nearness of the rule of God) and to heal are to be regarded as authentic. The missionary instructions of the Synoptics are based on a core of sayings which go back to Jesus (Gnilka).

Mark 6.14–29: King Herod and the beheading of John the Baptist

14 And King Herod heard, for his (Jesus') name became known *and they said, 'John the Baptizer has been raised from the dead and therefore the powers are at work in him.'* 15 *But others said, 'He is Elijah,' and yet others said, 'A prophet like one of the prophets.'* 16 *But when Herod heard this, he said, 'The one whom I beheaded, John, he has been raised.'*

17 For Herod (once) sent and had John arrested and put into prison in fetters because of Herodias, the wife of his brother Philip, because he had married her. 18 For John had told Herod, 'It is not lawful for you to have your brother's wife.' 19 And Herodias bore a grudge against him for this and wanted to kill him and could not. 20 For Herod feared John, knowing that he is a righteous and holy man, and he had him guarded, and when he heard him, he was greatly perplexed, *and heard him gladly.*

21 But on an opportune day, when Herod was giving a meal on his birthday for his courtiers and the officers and the leading men of Galilee, 22 and when his daughter Herodias entered and danced, she pleased Herod and those dining with him and the king said to the girl, 'Ask me for whatever you want and I will give it to you.' 23 And he swore to her: 'Whatever you want to ask me, I will give you, to half of my kingdom.' 24 And she went out and said to her mother, 'What shall I ask for?,' and she said, 'For the head of John *the Baptizer.'* 25 And she immediately went with haste to the king and asked him, saying, 'I want you immediately to give me the head of John the Baptist on a platter.' 26 And the king was very disturbed and did not want to refuse her because of the oath and the guests at table. 27 And the king immediately sent the executioner and commanded him to bring his head. And he went away and beheaded him in the prison. 28 And he brought his head on the platter and gave it to the girl and the girl gave it to her mother.

29 And when his disciples heard of this they came and took his body and put it in a tomb.

Redaction

[14–16] Herod means Herod Antipas, the local ruler of Jesus, who reigned from 4 BC to AD 39 and ruled over Galilee and Peraea. The passage is an introduction to the tradition of the death of John the Baptist, which Mark hands on from v. 17 onwards, but also has an importance in the framework of the Gospel of Mark as a whole. Verses 14a and 16 lead into the story (vv. 17–28), whereas vv. 14b–15 are later taken up in 8.28. In v. 16 resurrection is thought of as a kind of resuscitation.

[17–28] These verses are a parenthesis (cf. most recently 5.8). However, in this unusually extended addition Mark is clumsy in that 6.30, strictly speaking, attaches to the killing of John the Baptist, whereas in the narrative context we are already at a point long after that.

[29] The burial of the body of John the Baptist produces a parallel with the fate of Jesus (15.42–27). For Mark, according to whom the Baptist appeared before the time of Jesus, his fate has a reference to Christ. The fate of the Baptist prepares the way for the Messiah.

Tradition

The form of the tradition employed by Mark in vv. 17–29 is defined in various ways: some speak of a popular narrative which has been handed down in isolation; others of a legend with no Christian character from Hellenistic Jewish traditions or an anecdote about Herod. Yet others prefer the expression martyrdom report. In any case, we can rule out the possibility that the story was told by disciples of the Baptist who buried John (Mark 6.29). For if it were, we would have expected a characteristic of the Baptist's preaching, like the announcement of judgment or the call to repentance, to appear in the tradition.

Historical

According to Josephus, a younger contemporary of the apostle Paul, Herod Antipas had the Baptist executed in order to avoid a possible messianic movement. Josephus relates the killing of John the Baptist in his historical work *Jewish Antiquities* XVIII, 116–119. Granted, this story, too, has a bias, in that e.g. the eschatological character of the Baptist's preaching is suppressed. But it certainly deserves historical priority over the Markan tradition, the implausibility of which is only further intensified by Josephus:

'What Mark narrates here does *not* correspond to the information in Josephus. According to Josephus John was executed at Machaerus beyond the Jordan. By contrast Mark presupposes that the execution took place at the royal court in Galilee . . . According to Josephus the motive for the action was Antipas' fear that the Baptist posed a political danger, according to Mark merely Herodias' hatred of him. The deciding factor in Mark is a scene which certainly brings out vividly the opposition of the ascetic to the frivolous activities at the royal court, but is only a scene and suffers from intrinsic improbability' (Wellhausen).

Mark 6.30–34: The return of the disciples. Jesus has pity on the people

30 *And the apostles again gather round Jesus and told him all that they had done and what they had taught.* 31 *And he says to them, 'Come by yourselves to a lonely place and rest a while!' For there were many people coming and going and they did not even have time to eat.* 32 *And they went away in a boat to a solitary place alone.* 33 *And they saw them depart, and many recognized them. And they came together there on foot from all the towns and reached there first.* 34 *And when he got out, he saw a great crowd of people and he had pity on them, for they were like sheep without a shepherd, and he began to teach them many things.*

Redaction

[30–34] In this section, a summary, Mark shows himself especially concerned with the narrative context, since here he refers back to the sending out of the disciples narrated in 6.7–13. The need of the disciples to rest serves as a motive for seeking out the lonely place (v. 33). The crowd of people which is needed for the feeding of the 5000 that is narrated next is put in place (v. 34). In other passages (1.32–39; 1.45; 3.7–10), at the redactional level Jesus similarly retreats, while at the same time masses of people advance. Like 6.6 previously, v. 34b redactionally describes Jesus as teaching.

Mark 6.35–44: The feeding of the five thousand

35 And when the hour was already advanced, his disciples came to him and said, 'The place is lonely and the hour is already advanced. 36 Send them away, so that they can go into the neighbouring places and villages and buy them something to eat!' 37 *But he answered and said to them, 'You give them something to eat!' And they say to him, 'Shall we go off and buy bread for 200 denarii and give them something to eat?'* 38 But he said to them, 'How much bread do you have? Go, see!' And they looked and say, 'Five loaves and two fishes.' 39 And he commanded them all to settle down by companies on the green grass. 40 And they settled down, the groups like beds in a garden, by hundreds and by fifties. 41 And he took the loaves and the two fishes and looked up to heaven, gave thanks, and broke the loaves and gave them to his disciples, to give to them, and he shared out the two fishes for all. 42 And all ate and were filled, 43 and they took the fragments, twelve baskets full, also of the fishes. 44 And there were five thousand men who ate.

Redaction

[37] The command that the disciples are to give the people something to eat and the reaction of the disciples to it is an expression of their incomprehension (cf. on 5.31) and has probably been inserted by Mark.

[41] Mark himself hardly understood the narrative of the feeding in terms of the eucharist; otherwise he would have assimilated 6.41 and 8.6f. more strongly to 14.22. So for him this is a miracle, which he later interprets further to depict the disciples' failure to understand (6.52; 8.14–21).

Tradition

[35–36, 38–44] The miracle in the story from the tradition is to be described as a gift miracle. *First* it depicts the need (here the lack of food, vv. 35–38); *secondly* the removal of the need by Jesus, who miraculously satisfies so many with the little that there is (vv. 39–42). *Thirdly* follows the confirmation of the miracle by the reference to the remnants (v. 43). With this is contrasted once again the enormous number of those who are fed (v. 44).

The narrative is indebted to II Kings 4.42–44 (Elisha feeds one hundred men with only twenty loaves) for important elements; however, Jesus far surpasses Elisha in his miraculous act. The green grass in vv. 39–40 is enigmatic and may be a reminiscence of Ps. 23.2. For the dividing into groups cf. Ex. 18.25.

Historical

The formation of this story derives from the needs of the community. Its historical value is nil. Anyone is free to accept the table fellowship of Jesus with his followers as a starting point for the rise of this story. But that is rather different from the feeding of the 5000.

Mark 6.45–56: Jesus walks on the sea and heals many sick people

45 *And immediately he urged his disciples to get into the boat* and go before him to the other shore to Bethsaida, *while he himself dismissed the people. 46 And he took his leave of them and went up the mountain to pray.* 47 And when evening had come, the boat was in the midst of the sea and he was alone on land. 48 And he saw them toiling away at the oars, *for the wind was against them,* and in the fourth watch of the night he comes to them walking on the sea. And he wanted to pass by them. 49 But when they saw him walking on the sea, they thought that it was a ghost and they cried out. 50 For all saw him and were perplexed. But he immediately spoke with them and said to them, 'Take courage, it is I, do not fear!' 51 And he went to them into the boat and the wind died down *and they were utterly astounded. 52 For they had not understood about the loaves, but their heart was hardened. 53 And they crossed over to the land and came to Gennesaret and moored.*

54 *And when they were getting out of the boat, immediately they recognized him 55 and ran about in the whole neighbourhood and began to bring the sick on pallets wherever they heard that he was. 56 And where he entered villages or towns or country, they laid the sick in the open places and asked him that they might only touch the hem of his garment. And all who touched him were healed.*

Redaction

[45–46] The motifs of the boat, the people and prayer are redactional.

[48b] 'For the wind was against them' is a Markan addition (cf. on 5.8).

[51–52] Here the Markan motif of the incomprehension of the disciples is particularly evident; v. 52 deliberately refers to the story of the feeding and represents its interpretation. Cf. later 8.14–21.

[54–56] Like 1.32–39; 3.7–12 this passage along with v. 53 is a redactional construction, a summary which depicts Jesus' healing activity at length and takes up the crowd scene of 6.30–34 in the Markan context. Contrary to the two other summaries, Mark does not report any exorcism, probably because there are no such stories in the context. The passivity of Jesus is also striking: he does not heal actively, but is the one who bears power from when the crowds gain the healing force.

Tradition

[45–52] In terms of form this passage is an epiphany story as distinct from the saving miracle in 4.35–41. However, occasionally it is asked whether the two narratives are not variants of one and the same archetype. In that case the stilling of the storm (cf. vv. 48, 51) must have been the original motif, which has been forced into the background by the walking on the sea. But the abrupt statement v. 48 ('He wanted to pass by them') shows that in terms of the tradition the walking on the sea stands at the beginning.

Such a narrative about Jesus' walking on the sea is meant to show his superiority to other sons of god from the environment of earliest Christianity, who could similarly walk on the sea. For in antiquity the capacity to walk on water was regarded as divine power. However, in addition Old Testament parallels are to be noted here, according to which God can walk on the water or on the waves of the sea (cf. Job 9.8; Ps. 77).

Possibly the story of Jesus walking on the sea derives from an Easter story (cf. John 21). Verses 49f. would also fit that: Jesus' presence is emphasized and the disciples' fear that they have seen a ghost is rejected (cf. Luke 24.36–43 in the framework of an Easter story). At a second stage this Easter narrative would have then been expanded into a miracle of rescue from distress at sea.

Historical

Against the historicity of the narrative of Jesus' walking on the sea are (a) the numerous analogies from the contemporary environment and in the Old Testament; (b) the character and the form of the narrative; and (c) its possible derivation from the Easter situation.

Mark 7.1–23: The dispute about clean and unclean

1 *And the Pharisees gather to him and some of the scribes who had come from Jerusalem. 2 And when they saw some of the disciples, that they eat bread with unclean hands, that means unwashed,*
3 for the Pharisees and all the Jews do not eat if they have not washed their hands with a fist and

so they observe the <u>tradition of the elders</u>, 4 *and when they (come) from the market, they eat only when they have sprinkled (= cleansed) themselves. And there is much else that they have adopted, to maintain: the washing of cups and pots and vessels of bronze.*

5 And the Pharisees and the scribes ask him, 'Why do your disciples not walk by the <u>tradition of the elders</u>, but eat bread with unclean hands?'

6 And he answered them, 'Well did Isaiah prophesy of you hypocrites, as it is written: "This people honours me with lips, but their heart is far removed from me. 7 In vain they honour me, teaching as doctrines the commands of men." 8 By dropping the commandment of God, you hold fast the tradition of men.'

9 *And he said to them*, 'You have a fine way of rejecting the commandment of God, in order to observe your tradition. 10 For Moses said, "Honour your father and your mother," and, "Whoever speaks evil of father or mother shall die the death." 11 But you say, "If a man says to his father or mother 'Corban'" – which means "What I owe you is a consecrated gift" – 12 then you do not allow him to do anything more for father or mother. 13 Thus you make void the word of God by your tradition which you have handed on. And you do many more such things.'

14 *And again he called the people and said to them*, 'Hear me all of you and understand! 15 There is nothing that goes into a person from outside which can make him unclean: but those things that come forth from a man, they are what make people unclean.' (Verse 16 is not part of the original text.)

17 *And when he had gone from the crowd of people and entered a house, his disciples asked him about the parable.* 18 *And he says to them, 'Are you so without understanding? Do you not under-*stand that all that enters a person from outside cannot make him unclean, 19 because it does not go into his heart but into his belly and goes into the cesspit?' *Thus he declared all food clean.* 20 *And he said, 'What comes out of a person, that defiles the person.* 21 *For from within, from the human heart, come evil thoughts: fornications, thefts, murders,* 22 *adulteries, covetous-nesses, wickednesses, deceits, licentiousnesses, the evil eye, blasphemy, arrogance, failure to under-*stand. 23 *All this evil comes from within and makes people unclean.'*

Redaction

In the context of the Gospel of Mark, ch. 7 seems like a crude lump because there are very few connections with the context. 'The controversy with Pharisees and scribes is loosely connected backwards by the motif "eat bread" in v. 2 and equally loosely forwards with the same motif in v. 28; the connection in the content is perhaps rather stronger, in so far as the following story tells of the faith of a Gentile woman as opposed to the controversy with the Jews (v. 3). All in all, vv. 1–23 have the function of recalling the opponents of Jesus in Galilee, the Pharisees, to whom are also added here the scribes from Jerusalem' (Lührmann).

Mark must have been aware of the parallelism of the present section with 2.23–28: cf. the parallels (a) the problem (2.23–24/7.1–2, 5); (b) proof from scripture (2.25–26/7.6b–7a); (c) sayings of Jesus (2.27–28/7.9–23).

[1–2] These verses are probably completely redactional. Mark probably composed this introduction on the basis of the tradition in v. 5.

[3–4] '*All* the Jews' is a Markan generalization. Luke too sometimes writes in this way (cf. Acts 18.2, etc.). The passage is a parenthesis deriving from Mark in which he explains to his Gentile Christian readers the Jewish practice of purity by means of select examples. 'With a fist' is almost incomprehensible. Either one omits the expression or reads it with the help of a slight textual emendation, 'often'.

Moreover, as the sequel shows, Mark himself is not well informed on the distinction between laws relating to cleanness and food laws. Thus the main difficulty of the connection between v. 1–13 and v. 15 consists in the fact that v. 15 relates to food laws, whereas vv. 1–13 relate to laws of cleanness, which have to be differentiated from one another. (Therefore historically v. 15 cannot be the answer to what has gone before.) Moreover it is incorrect to say that the Pharisees sprinkle their hands or even what they have bought. Rather, after their return from the market they immerse themselves. This is also said by readings on Mark 7.4, but they are a correction of the more difficult version 'sprinkle themselves', the content of which is wrong.

[17–18a] These verses contain the typically Markan motif of the incomprehension of the disciples.

[19c–23] Verse 19c is the Markan conclusion. Verse 20 is a repetition of v. 15b and vv. 21f. probably derive from Mark himself (cf. similarly vv. 3–4). Mark interprets the dispute about what is clean and unclean from the perspective of behaviour (cf. similarly the insertion of vv. 6–8 and vv. 9–13). Verses 21b–22, in terms of form a catalogue of vices, come from Mark's community or from Mark himself. The individual sins are artistically enumerated in twice three in the plural and in the singular and show antithetically the ideal of the Christian way of life.

Yield: Mark wants to explain to his Gentile Christian readers the law which is binding on Pharisees and all Jews and dissociates from that the law which is binding on Christians, which is presumed to be evident to any reasonable person.

Tradition

[5–8] The polemic against the Pharisees and scribes by means of a quotation from Isaiah and a conclusion (v. 8) is the basis of the tradition. But it has to be noted that the Isaiah quotation is not relevant to the controversy about the practice of eating with unclean hands (v. 5).

[9–13] These verses are a piece of traditional community polemic with the usual Markan connecting formula 'and he said to them'. The passage gives an example of *how* the dropping of God's commandment mentioned in v. 8 becomes concrete. Cf. 'reject' (v. 9) with 'drop' (v. 8), 'make void' (v. 13).

Mark attaches a further element of tradition (the oldest) with v. 15. Here he introduces the distinction between instructing the people and instructing the disciples which is typical of him. Verses 18b–19b derive from the tradition.

Historical

[5–8] This piece of tradition responds to a form of behaviour by the disciples and is therefore not historical.

[9–13] The tradition makes vv. 5–8 concrete and is therefore as unhistorical as the passage vv. 5–8 itself.

[15] The logion is enigmatic, since in the context of the Gospel of Mark it explains why the disciples may eat bread with unclean hands (Mark 7.5). That is surprising, since the saying itself criticizes food laws and not laws of cleanness. In modern terms rules of cleanness have to do with hygiene and relate e.g. to menstruating women, lepers, and issues from the male sexual organs (cf. Lev. 12–15). Food laws relate to nourishment and regulate the consumption of clean and unclean animals (Lev. 11). The saying in Mark 7.15 was therefore originally handed down in isolation and only later inserted by Mark into this piece of text. He was probably led to do this by the consideration that the consumption of unclean animals similarly makes a person unclean, so that the logion in the broad sense can also be taken as a critique of the laws of cleanness. The radical nature of this saying is closely related to that of Mark 2.27, in that it undertakes a grandiose reduction (this time of the food law). The authenticity of the saying is supported first by the criterion of difference, since, as numerous examples show (Gal. 2.11–15; Acts 10; Acts 15.20, etc.), the food laws held without qualification in primitive Christianity. Secondly, the criterion of rarity is to be advanced in support of the authenticity of the saying. As other sayings of Jesus also stand out for their radical quality, the criterion of coherence further suggests the real voice of Jesus here.

[18b–19b] This tradition draws the conclusion from the authentic saying of Jesus in v. 15 and perhaps even goes back to him.

Mark 7.24–30: The Syro-Phoenician woman

24 And he set off from there and went into the region of Tyre. And he came into a house and wanted no one to know (it), and he could not remain hidden.

25 But immediately a woman heard of him, whose little daughter had an unclean spirit. She came and threw herself at his feet. 26 Now the woman was a Greek, a Syro-Phoenician by origin. And she asked him to drive the demon out of her daughter. 27 And he said to her, '*First* let the children be fed. For it is not good to take bread from the children and throw it to the little dogs.' 28 But she replied and says to him, 'Lord, even the little dogs under the table eat the children's crumbs.' 29 And he said to her, 'For this saying, go! The demon has gone

out of your daughter.' 30 And she went away into her house and found the child lying on the bed and the demon gone out.

Redaction

Preliminary comment: together with Matt. 8.5–13 par. and Luke 17.11–19 this section belongs among the reports of the healings of Gentiles at a distance. Perhaps the report of the healing at a distance arose because Jesus never healed Gentiles directly. The genre of the healing at a distance would thus indicate that Jesus first cured Gentiles only as the exalted Lord. The form of the remote healing would then be the attempt to adjust the purely Jewish miracle-working of Jesus in the direction of the miracle-working of the exalted Lord, which embraces all men and women.

[24] The link with the context and indeed the whole journey to Tyre is redactional (cf. v. 31). The content of v. 24 may have been inferred by Mark from v. 26. The statement that Jesus entered a house to remain unknown but could not remain hidden (cf. 1.45; 5.43; 9.30) is typically Markan.

[27] The Markan 'first' weakens the logic of Jesus' argument. For this allows an exception. And in the overall conception of the Gospel of Mark the movement of the preaching of the Gospel to the Gentiles is indicated.

Yield: By this story Mark shows that the miraculous power of Jesus also holds for Gentile communities, indeed – both for the tradition and for Mark himself (cf. 13.10) – it takes on paradigmatic character for the move of the community of Jesus to the Gentiles. The point of the narrative, that Jesus is overcome by the woman's faith, probably derives from Mark. Certainly her faith is not mentioned explicitly as such, but as a phenomenon it is present in the story (cf. 4.40; 5.34, etc).

Tradition

Verses 25–30 contain the unitary composition of a controversy combined with a miracle. 'The miracle here is not told for its own sake; the main thing is the conduct of Jesus which develops in the conversation. And indeed this is a kind of controversy in which this time Jesus is the one who is defeated – though without this casting any shadow on him' (Bultmann). But the typical characteristics of a miracle story can be noted: the description of the need and the request for help (vv. 25f.), the healing by Jesus (v. 29) and the noting of the miracle performed (v. 30). The controversy (between Jesus and the woman) and the miracle originally belong together. The dialogue arises out of the special character of this story.

Debates in the primitive community about the entry of Gentiles into the community must underlie the tradition and explain its origin. The sharp repudiation in Jesus' answer is explained by the harshness of the debate. But the success of the mission to the Gentiles within early Christianity did in the end also lead to a conciliatory conclusion within the narrative.

Historical

The historical yield is nil, as the narrative must be derived from debates in the early Christian community. The attempt sometimes made to rescue a historical remnant or a historical nucleus of the tradition usually consists in the assumption that Jesus sometimes also healed Gentiles (cf. 5.1–20) and thus ultimately documented that the movement which he founded was open to Gentiles as well. But where a core is presupposed it must also be detectable. However, that is nowhere the case in the present story.

Mark 7.31–37: The deaf mute

31 *And again he went away from the region of Tyre and came through Sidon to the Sea of Galilee in the midst of the region of the Decapolis.* 32 And they bring him a deaf mute and ask him to lay hands on him. 33 And he took him aside from the crowd of people and put his fingers in his ears, spat and touched his tongue. 34 And looking up to heaven, he sighed and says to him, 'Ephphatha,' *which means, be opened.* 35 And his ears were opened and immediately the fetter on his tongue was loosed and he spoke properly. 36 *And he commanded them to tell no one. But the more he commanded them, the more they proclaimed it.* 37 *And they were astonished beyond measure and said, 'He has done all things well, he makes even the deaf hear and the dumb speak.'*

Redaction

[31] This verse belongs closely with the redactional v. 24 of the previous story.

[34] Probably the Greek translation of the magic word derives from Mark, as in other passages (cf. 5.41; 15.22, 34).

[36] This verse contains the Markan motif of secrecy (cf. 1.44f.; 5.43a), which is given only to be transgressed.

[37] The joyful exclamation of the crowd could be redactional. It makes the single case an event which is constantly repeated. At the same time, the question of the identity of Jesus is also echoed here (cf. 4.41 and 5.7; 6.3, 14b, 15, 50).

Tradition

[32–35] The present story contains a rich store of healing techniques. Jesus makes use of pharmacological manipulative practices which have a magical impact. The typical features of a miracle story are *first* the manipulation, putting a finger in the ears, *secondly* touching the tongue with spittle, *thirdly* the magic word (Ephphatha), which is needed because the tongue is bound by a demon of sickness, and *fourthly* the segregation of the sick person. It is possible that there is a traditional choral conclusion (cf. Gen. 1.31; Isa. 29.18) also behind v. 37, which has been described above as probably redactional.

Because of the detailed description the story reads almost like instructions for Christian miracle workers (cf. 6.7, etc.).

A variant of the narrative appears later in 8.22–26 (without a magical word).

Historical

First of all something similar is to be said on the question of the healing of a deaf mute to what has been said on the healings of Jesus which relate to possessed people and the like. Individual healings took place, but probably not with the frequency that the New Testament Gospels presupposes. However, because of the specific details the present narrative may have a high claim to authenticity.

Mark 8.1–9: The feeding of the 4000

1 *In those days, when again a great crowd of people was present and they had nothing to eat, he called the disciples and says to them,* 2 'I have compassion on the people, because they have persisted with me now for three days and have nothing to eat. 3 And if I sent them away hungry, they will faint on the way. And some of them have come from afar.' 4 *And his disciples answered him, 'How can anyone feed these people with loaves here in the wilderness?'* 5 And he asked them, 'How many loaves do you have?', and they answered, 'Seven.' 6 And he commands the crowd to recline on the ground. And he took the seven loaves, gave thanks and broke and gave them to his disciples, to set them before them, and they gave (them) to the people. 7 And they had a few small fishes. And he spoke the thanksgiving over them and told them also to set these before them. 8 And they ate and were satisfied; and they took up the fragments which remained, seven baskets. 9 Now there were about four thousand. *And he sent them away.*

Redaction

Mark tells only the story of the feeding twice. The first version, which is narrated in 6.34–44, takes place on Jewish soil and the one here takes place on Gentile soil. His interest in it emerges unequivocally from this, however much in both cases he formulates the story on the basis of tradition. The most important differences between the present story of the feeding and the previous one are as follows: (a) Its style is terser. (b) Jesus – not the disciples – becomes aware of the need of the crowds. (c) The disciples have seven (and not five) loaves. (d) 4000 (and not 5000) are fed and seven baskets (not twelve) remain. (e) Jesus helps exclusively out of bodily need – the people have had nothing to eat for three days and *therefore* Jesus has compassion on them. In the previous story, by contrast, the spiritual need was also indicated because of Jesus' compassion on the flock, which has no shepherd. (f) The role of the disciples has become paler.

In 8.17–21 Mark then explains how he wants the two feeding stories to be understood.

Tradition

The tradition is a second account of the same event and not a narrative about a second event similar to the first. By comparison with the tradition behind 6.35–44 the present tradition may be *more original* in two respects: *first*, there is no substantial redactional expansion at the beginning; *secondly*, in v. 3 there is no reflection on the surrounding fields and villages.

Nevertheless, 8.1–10 is secondary to 6.35–44, for here the action begins with the initiative of Jesus (vv. 1f.); the description 'He had compassion' (6.34) has become the direct speech 'I have compassion' (8.2) and the request of the disciples (6.36) has become a reflection by Jesus (8.3).

Historical

See the observations on 6.35–44. The historical yield of this miracle too is also nil.

Mark 8.10–21: Against the request of the Pharisees for a sign. The incomprehension of the disciples

10 *And immediately he got into a boat with his disciples and came* into the region of Dalmanutha. 11 *And the Pharisees came out and began to dispute with him*, asking him for a sign from heaven *and tempting him.* 12 And he sighed in his spirit and says, 'Why does this generation require a sign? Truly, I say to you, in no way will a sign be given to this generation.' 13 *And he left them, got in again and went away to the other shore.*

14 *And they forget to take bread with them, and had only a single loaf with them in the boat.* 15 *And he admonished them and said, 'Look, take heed of the leaven of the Pharisees and the leaven of Herod.'* 16 *And they discussed among themselves that they had no bread.* 17 *And he is aware of this and says to them, 'Why are you discussing among yourselves that you have no bread? Do you not comprehend and <u>understand</u>? You have a hardened heart.* 18 *Although you have eyes, you do not see, and although you have ears you do not hear. And do you not remember,* 19 *when I broke the five loaves for the 5000, how many baskets full of fragments you gathered up?'* They say to him, 'Twelve'. 20 'When (I broke) the seven for the 4000 how many baskets full of fragments did you take up? And they say, 'Seven.'* 21 *And he said to them, 'Do you still not <u>understand</u>?'*

Redaction

[10a] This is a transition created by Mark, apart from the place name Dalmanutha. Note that the evangelist again introduces the motif of the boat (cf. 4.1, 36 etc.)

[11,13] The introduction and ending have been shaped by Mark. For Mark prefers the Pharisees as opponents of Jesus. Moreover, with them Mark narrows down those to whom his answer is addressed, 'this generation'.

[14–21] These verses are full of Markan motifs and – with the possible exception of v. 15, the meaning of which is obscure – are entirely redactional. The bread motif which comes from the feeding story permeates the whole section (vv. 14, 16, 17, 19). Verse 14 takes up v. 4. Verse 15: 'the Pharisees' refers back to v. 11. Verses 16f.: the motif of incomprehension permeates the Gospel of Mark. Verse 19 takes up 6.41–44, v. 20 refers back to 8.6, 9. Verse 21 heightens the motif of incomprehension.

At the level of the Markan redaction, Jesus' question to the disciples is at the same time addressed to the readership which has read or heard the Gospel from the beginning. Thus Mark wants to indicate indirectly that despite this incomprehension, God nevertheless gives understanding, faith and release from blindness. This will be demonstrated in the next pericope about the blind man in Bethsaida, 8.22–26.

Tradition

[11–12] These verses have a parallel in Q (Matt. 12.38–42/Luke 11.29–32). Whether the form in Q in which this generation is referred to the sign of Jonah is a secondary expansion by comparison with Mark can hardly be decided.

Historical

Verse 12 probably goes back to Jesus, since the saying breathes a characteristic individual spirit. Jesus refuses any authentication for his appearance. Obviously for Jesus himself his power to work miracles was an evident fact. But he refused proof of that to others who ask for authentication. Cf. further on Matt. 12.38–42/Luke 11.29–32.

Mark 8.22–26: The blind man

22 *And they come to Bethsaida.* And they bring him a blind man and ask him to touch him. 23 And he took the hand of the blind man and led him out of the village and spat on his eyes, laid hands on him and asked him, 'Do you see anything?' 24 And looking up he said, 'I see

people, for I see them like trees walking around.' 25 Thereupon he again laid hands on his eyes and he saw sharply and was restored and saw everything clearly. 26 And he sent him into his house *and said, 'Do not go into the village!'*

Redaction

The redactional meaning follows above all from the position of the pericope in the overall framework of the Gospel of Mark. It points forward *on the one hand* to the understanding of the disciple Peter in 8.29. *On the other hand* it takes up the blindness and deafness attributed to the disciples in 8.18. Like the earlier healing of the deaf mute in 7.32–37 the opening of the eyes of the blind man similarly has symbolic meaning.

[26] This verse contains Mark's secrecy theory; one would have expected a continuation similar to 5.16.

Tradition

Mark has handed on at this point a narrative of the same type as the story of the deaf mute in Mark 7.32–37. It displays almost precisely the same features: (a) they bring Jesus a sick man with a request for healing; (b) he takes him aside from the onlookers; (c) he heals him with spittle and the laying on of hands; (d) he forbids the act of healing to be made known. Therefore the story is to be judged a variant of 7.32–37. By comparison with 7.32–37 the only peculiar element in the story is that no magic word is spoken and that the healing takes place in stages.

Historical

The account of the miracle in Mark 8.22–26 may go back to a historical event. The use of spittle as a means of healing eyes was already customary in Judaism at the time of Jesus. Such an abstruse story as this can hardly be derived from the community.

Mark 8.27–33: The messianic confession and Peter's failure

27 And Jesus went away and his disciples into the villages of Caesarea Philippi. And on the way he asked his disciples and said to them, 'Who do people say that I am?' 28 And they told him and said, ' "John the Baptist". And others, "Elijah", and others "one of the prophets".' 29 And he asked them, 'And you, who do you say that I am?' And Peter answered and says to him, 'You are the Christ.' 30 *And he <u>threatened</u> them, to tell no one about him. 31 And he began to teach them, 'The Son of man must suffer much and be rejected by the elders and the chief priests and the scribes and be killed and after three days rise.' 32 And he spoke the word plainly. And Peter took him aside and began to <u>threaten</u> him.* 33 But he turned round, saw his disciples and <u>threatened</u> Peter and says, 'Get behind me, Satan, for you have not God's cause in mind but man's cause.'

Redaction

A new part of the Gospel of Mark begins with 8.27. Jesus discloses to the disciples who he really is, but immediately corrects Peter's misunderstanding.

[27] The first part of this verse is entirely Mark's creation; cf. especially the motif of the way (in what follows 9.33f.; 10.17; 10.32; 10.52).

[28] The form of the questions strongly recalls 6.14f. The question, however, is which passage is dependent on which.

[30] This verse contains the Markan motif of the messianic secret.

[31] This is the first announcement of the passion and resurrection, which like the second (9.31) and third (10.32b–34) has been inserted by Mark. This follows conclusively from the character of its language, which is mostly Markan, and from the fact that they structure Mark 8–10.

[32] 'Boldness' appears only in this passage in the Synoptic Gospels, but is frequent in the Fourth Gospel in connection with 'speaking boldly': 7.13, 26; 10.24, etc. Cf. also Acts 2.29; 4.13, 26 etc. Nevertheless, general considerations suggest that the sentence here must be redactional, all the more so since, like other Markan passages, it shows Jesus' clear foresight about his fate.

[32b] Peter opposes the notion that the Son of man Jesus must suffer. But he cannot understand the statement about the resurrection either. Note that for Mark 'Christ' and 'Son of man' are identical (cf. on Mark 14.61–62).

Tradition

The starting point of the analysis of the tradition is that the addressing of Peter as Satan must go back to a tradition which is to be called reliable. For this 'diabolizing' of the respected disciple cannot be derived from the community.

If we take away the redactional vv. 30–32 it proves that v. 33 is connected to v. 29. The train of thought in the reconstructed tradition then runs as follows: Jesus rejects as a satanic temptation the expectation, attached to him by Peter, that he is the Messiah.

Historical

The reasons which suggest the historical probability that Jesus addressed Peter as Satan have already been mentioned in the previous section. And the occasion for this form of address, Peter's messianic expectation, is likely to be historical. Of course it is another question whether the point in time of the dispute between Jesus and his first disciple which is reflected in the tradition is accurate. I do not want to be definite here. At all events a controversy took place over whether Jesus was the (political) Messiah (who would drive the Romans from the land and restore the kingdom of David, cf. PsSol. 17). Jesus resolutely rejects this expectation of Peter and demonizes his first disciple. Satan, whose fall Jesus has already seen (cf. Luke 10.18), gets in his way precisely in the expectation of his closest confidant. He banishes him and addresses Peter as Satan.

Mark 8.34–38: On being a disciple of Jesus

34 *And he called the crowd of people together with his disciples and said to them,* 'If anyone will come after me, let him deny himself and take his cross upon himself and follow me. 35 Whoever would save his life will lose it; but whoever loses his life for my sake *and the gospel's* will save it. 36 For what use is it for a person to gain the whole world and forfeit his life? 37 For what will a person give in exchange for his life? 38 Whoever is ashamed of me and my words in this adulterous and sinful generation, of him will the Son of man also be ashamed, when he comes in the glory of the Father with the holy angels.'

Redaction

The position of the discourse on discipleship directly after Jesus' rejection of Peter's words allows us to deduce Mark's narrative intention. He is instructing his community on what discipleship can look like in the present. Cf. similar instructions in connection with the second and third prophecies of the passion, each after a failure of the disciples to understand (9.33–37; 10.35–45).

[34a] The introduction is redactional (cf. 7.14; 8.1, etc.).
[35] To reinforce the reference to Jesus, as in 10.29 Mark adds 'and the gospel's (sake)'. For the gospel makes present the word of Jesus (cf. 1.14f.).

Tradition

Various logia of Jesus have been brought together in this section:
[34b] This is a saying of a post-Easter prophet, for the cross can be thought of only as the cross of Jesus; like him, the disciples must be willing to endure martyrdom. This metaphorical use of the crucifixion of Jesus which has not yet taken place sounds very strange indeed on his own lips, as it would inevitably been completely incomprehensible to his hearers. Here the cross already appears as a symbol of Christianity. Cf. also on Matt. 10.38/Luke 14.27.
[35] The Q version of this saying (Luke 17.33/Matt. 10.39) is older, as in its

original form (Luke) it does not yet contain the reference to Jesus. Cf. further on Luke 17.33.

[36–37] Here are two questions with a wisdom-like stamp, both of which are to be answered in the negative. It is useless to gain the whole world. Cf. Ps. 49.8–10; Eccles.1.3; Luke 12.16–20.

[38] This is a saying of Jesus which brings the future Son of man into play and displays a clearly apocalyptic perspective. Cf. the Q parallel Luke 12.8f./Matt. 10.32 and the explanations given on Luke 12.8f.

Historical

[34b] In its Markan form, but also in the Q version, this saying is inauthentic, as it derives from 'the Exalted One'.

[35] The authenticity of this profane proverb is extremely uncertain even without the Markan additions and without reference to Jesus.

[36–37] These verses have a wisdom stamp and have only a slight chance of being authentic.

[38] Cf. on Q (Luke 12.8f.).

Mark 9.1–13: The transfiguration of Jesus and the conversation on the way down the mountain

1 *And he said to them*, 'Amen, I say to you, there are some standing here who will not taste death until they experience the coming of the kingdom of God in power.'
2 And after six days Jesus took Peter and James and John and led them alone *apart* up to a high mountain. And he was transformed before them. 3 And his clothes became quite shining white, as no fuller on earth can whiten them. 4 And Elijah appeared to them with Moses and they carried on a conversation with Jesus. 5 And Peter answered and said to Jesus, 'Rabbi, it is good for us to be here. And we want to build three huts, one for you and one for Moses and one for Elijah.' 6 *For he did not know what to answer, since they were seized with fear.*
7 And a cloud formed which overshadowed them. And a voice came from the cloud, 'This is my beloved son, listen to him!' And suddenly, when they looked around, they saw no one but Jesus alone with them.

9 *And when they were coming down from the mountain he commanded them to tell no one what they had seen, except when the Son of man had risen from the dead. 10 And they did not understand the saying and disputed among themselves what rising from the dead was. 11 And they asked him and said, 'The scribes say that Elijah must come first.' 12 But he said to them, 'Does Elijah come first to restore all things? How then is it written of the Son of man that he will suffer much and be despised? 13 But I say to you, Elijah has come and they did to him what they would, as it is written about him.'*

Redaction

[1] Mark could take over the sentence from the tradition here, since he himself had an expectation of an imminent end, as is shown by 13.30.

The story which is attached nevertheless interprets v. 1, which comes from the tradition. In showing Jesus' glory, it stands in contrast to 8.27–38, where the suffering of Jesus and the disciples is discussed. At the same time the pericope is the divine confirmation of Peter's confession if this is understood rightly: Jesus is the Christ and Son of man, but must suffer first.

The narrative is firmly anchored in the context. The following motifs in the story are known from what has gone before:

[2] Mountain motif (cf. 3.13; 6.46); the three disciples Peter, James and John (cf. 1.16–20; 3.16f.; 5.37; 13.3; 14.33).

[4] Elijah (cf. 8.28 and 9.11).

[5] Peter as spokesman of the disciples (cf. immediately beforehand 8.29).

[6] For the disciples' failure to understand cf. 4.13; 8.14–21 and in the immediate context Mark 9.10. For the flight of the disciples cf. later 14.40b.

[7] The proclamation of Jesus as son of God recalls 1.11 and points forward to 15.39. (Cf. further 3.11; 5.7.)

[9–13] This section consists of two scenes:

(a) vv. 9–10: here the 'Son of man' (4.8, 31) appears who did not occur in the story of the transfiguration. Verse 9 contains a command to the disciples to be silent, which they greet with incomprehension (v. 10). This command to be silent is singular because of the explicit limitation of time associated with it. It means that a proclamation of who Jesus really is will be possible only after Easter. This hermeneutic guideline similarly applies to all the other commands to be silent, for it also becomes clear in all three predictions of the passion and resurrection (8.31; 9.31; 10.32–34) that the mystery of Jesus will be revealed only after his resurrection. But Mark does not leave it at this historicizing view, for at the same time he calls on his readers to be disciples (8.34–35; 9.36–37; 10.42–44) and evidently inculcates the lasting juxtaposition of revelation and concealment.

(b) Verses 11–13 contain a scriptural clarification of the relationship between Elijah (the external occasion is v. 4) and the Son of man. The reference to the suffering of the Son of man (v. 12) refers back to 8.31. Mark sees John the Baptist as Elijah redivivus, who has already been killed (6.14–29).

Tradition

[1] The verse refers to the expectation of the end of the world, the positive counterpart of which is the dawn of the kingdom of God. The saying came into

being in the time after the death and the 'resurrection' of Jesus, when the expectation of the coming of Jesus from heaven was still alive, but some of his disciples had unexpectedly died. The saying of Jesus offers as consolation to these disciples who are still alive the promise that at least a small remnant of the first generation will still experience the dawn of the kingdom of God. You can rely on that.

An insight into the 'delay of the parousia' which is the issue here is provided by the letters of an eyewitness of the first generation of primitive Christianity, Paul. In I Cor. 15.51 he reports a 'mystery' which has been granted him, i.e. a saying of the Lord imparted to him as a prophet which is meant to solve the problems in the community. He writes:

We shall not all sleep,
but we shall all be changed.

Then follows a description of the end, which emphasizes its sudden arrival, stresses the trumpet of judgment and confirms the resurrection of the dead (I Cor. 15.52).

This saying moves within the horizon of the primitive Christian expectation that the end of the world and thus the advent of the Lord Jesus from heaven were imminent. The saying changes this expectation: most would die, but some could reckon on surviving to the end (thus also Mark 9.1).

We find a preliminary stage of this changed expectation of the future in the earliest letter of Paul, that to the Thessalonians (I Thess. 4.15–17), where the word of the 'Lord' vouchsafed to the prophet Paul runs like this:

15 'For this we declare to you with a word of the Lord, that we who are alive and are left until the coming of the Lord will not precede those who have fallen asleep. 16 For he himself, the Lord, when the order sounds out, when the voice of the archangel and the trumpet of God ring out, will descend from heaven, and first the dead who have died in Christ will rise. 17 Afterwards we who live and are left will be transported immediately with them on the clouds into the air to meet the Lord; and so we shall always be with the Lord.'

At the time of the composition of I Thessalonians, Paul evidently presupposes that the majority of Christians, including himself, can reckon on surviving until the advent of Jesus from heaven, while a minority will die.

It follows from this reconstruction that *before* composing I Thessalonians Paul had assumed that *all* Christians would survive until the coming of Jesus from heaven, and in this expectation he must have represented the average Christian view of the first years after the death and 'resurrection' of Jesus.

[2–8] Once the Markan elements have been removed, the tradition is relatively unitary. It should, however, be noted that at the beginning Jesus is the subject, and at the end the disciples. The tradition is rooted in the Jewish milieu. It has some parallels with Ex. 24: Moses ascends the mountain, accompanied by three men (v. 9). A cloud covers the mountain (v. 15) for six days and finally God speaks with

Moses from it (v. 16b). Generally speaking the tradition asserts Jesus' legitimacy by transporting him into the heavenly sphere itself.

The tradition which Mark received as a literary unit can be divided into three parts:

1. Transfiguration of Jesus on the mountain and the appearance of Elijah and Moses;
2. Peter's proposal to build three huts;
3. Cloud and voice from the cloud ('enthronement formula') as the point.

Because of the inventory, namely the motif of light and the mountain, the tradition can with good reason be designated an Easter story. Thus Paul sees the heavenly Christ in a transfigured body of light (I Cor. 15.42–49) and the Risen Christ appears to his disciples on the mountain: Matt. 28.18–20. The inclusion of the transfiguration story in II Peter 1.16–18 manifestly anchors it in an Easter context.

Finally, Mark himself also interprets the tradition as an Easter story through v. 9. The existing tradition may have legitimated the trio 'Peter, James and John', known from Gal. 2.9, in their office as pillars.

Historical

[1] The reconstruction of the origin of the saying proves its inauthenticity. At the same time, together with the instances quoted from the letters of the apostle Paul, it makes clear the burning expectation of an imminent end among the first Christian generation, which can best be understood if Jesus himself reckoned with the coming of the kingdom of God in the very near future.

[2–8] Since the tradition is an original Easter story, its historicity is *a priori* ruled out.

Mark 9.14–29: The epileptic boy

14 *And when they came to the disciples, he saw a great crowd of people around them and scribes who were disputing with them.* 15 *And immediately* the whole people saw him and were alarmed and ran up to greet him. 16 *And he asked them, 'What are you disputing with them?'*

17 And one of the people answered him, 'Teacher, I brought my son to you, who has a dumb spirit. 18 And when it seizes him, it throws him on the ground; and he foams and gnashes his teeth and becomes rigid. And I told your disciples to drive it out and they could not.' 19 *And he answered them and says, 'O unbelieving generation, how long shall I still be with you? How long shall I still endure you? Bring him to me!'* 20 And they brought him to him. And when the spirit saw him, it immediately convulsed him and he fell to the ground and rolled about foaming at the mouth. 21 And he asked his father, 'How long has this been happening to him?' And he said, 'From childhood. 22 And often it also threw him into the fire or into

the water to destroy him. But if you can, help us and have mercy on us.' 23 *And Jesus said to him, 'As for that, I tell you, everything is possible to the one who believes.' 24 Immediately the father of the boy cried out and said, 'I believe, help my unbelief.'* 25 And when Jesus saw that the crowd was gathering, he threatened the unclean spirit and said to it, 'You dumb and deaf spirit, I command you, depart from him and do not return into him again.' 26 And it cried out, convulsed him violently, and went out. And he was as if dead, so that many (literally, the many) said, 'He is dead.' 27 But Jesus took his hand and raised him up and he stood up.

28 *And when he entered the house his disciples asked him privately, 'Why could we not cast it out?' 29 And he said to them, 'This kind can only come out through prayer.'*

Redaction

[14–16] Except for v. 15, these verses are redactional. The return of Jesus to the disciples (v. 14) joins on to vv. 2–3. 'Scribes' (v. 14) picks up the same group from v. 11. Whenever they have been mentioned previously, the issue has always been the authority of Jesus (cf. 1.22, etc.). Here they are discussing with the disciples.

[19] This verse stands within the Gospel of Mark in a long series of passages which strikingly attest the inability of the disciples to understand (cf. previously 8.16–21).

[23–24] These verses explicitly introduce the Markan motif of faith into the story. The faith of the father which is depicted as exemplary stands in marked contrast to the helpless attitude of the disciples, who in v. 19 are described as an unbelieving generation. The readers are thus asked about their own faith and the consequences of faith are specified as performing miracles and praying (v. 29).

[28–29a] These verses are similarly Markan: through v. 28b Mark perhaps attempts to overcome the problem of his community that it has become uncertain of its own capacity to perform exorcisms.

Tradition

After the redaction has been removed, vv. 15, 17–18, 20–22, 25–27 yield a core of tradition. Jesus is the great miracle worker. The disciples could not help the epileptic boy. Now 'Jesus comes at precisely the right moment, the people are amazed and run to him and greet him. The amazement is an expression of the veneration that the crowd offers to the great man and which can also turn into the cultic veneration of a hero. Astonishment belongs with both the miracle and the miracle-worker' (M. Dibelius).

Historical

Sometimes the historical recollection of a failure of the disciples is discovered in the tradition. But we can hardly infer historical reminiscences simply because the failure of the disciples is not a theme in other miracle stories. Moreover the failure of the disciples may have been introduced from the post-Easter situation, since it is also attested for the time after Easter in other places (4.13–20; Luke 22.31f.).

For the historical question of Jesus' activity in exorcisms see also the remarks on Luke 11.20.

For the question whether the motif of faith which was introduced into the story only by Mark was significant for Jesus, cf. the remarks on the faith that moves mountains (11.23).

Mark 9.30–41: Second prediction of the passion. Dispute over rank among the disciples. The strange exorcist

30 And *they went out from there and went through Galilee. And he did not want anyone to know it.* 31 *For he was teaching his disciples and said to them, 'The Son of man will be delivered into the hands of men and they will kill him and, when he is killed, after three days he will rise.'* 32 *But they did not understand the saying, and they were afraid to ask him.*

33 *And they came to Capernaum, and when he was in the house, he asked them, 'What have you been disputing about on the way?'* 34 *But they were silent. For on the way they had been discussing among themselves who was the greatest.* 35 *And he sat down and called the twelve and says to them,* 'If anyone will be first he should be last of all and the servant of all.' 36 *And he took a child and put it in their midst, embraced it and said to them,* 37 'Whoever accepts one of these children in my <u>name</u> accepts me. And whoever accepts me does not accept me but the one who has sent me.'

38 John said to him, 'Teacher, we saw someone driving out demons in your <u>name</u> and we prevented him, because he was not following us.' 39 But Jesus said, 'Do not prevent him. For no one who does a miracle in my <u>name</u> can thereafter speak evil of me. 40 Whoever is not against us is for us. 41 Whoever gives you a cup of water to drink because you belong to Christ, amen, I say to you he will not forfeit his reward.'

Redaction

[30–32] The prediction of suffering and resurrection corresponds to 8.31. Similarly, there is a repetition of the incomprehension of the disciples (v. 32), which was expressed in 8.32 by Peter's reaction. The formulation of secrecy in v. 30 recalls 5.43. In v. 32 there is a redactional mention of the typically uncomprehending attitude of the disciples towards the idea of suffering; cf. similarly 10.32.

[33–34] These verses are the Markan introduction to the following scene.

[35] The mention of the twelve attests that the evangelist has also shaped v. 35a. Cf. 4.10; 6.7 as examples of the way in which the evangelist brings the twelve into the text.

[36–37] Verse 36 is an extremely clumsy introduction to v. 37 and has been created by the evangelist under the influence of 10.16. Verse 37 'gives a rule for the time when Jesus himself will no longer dwell on earth but can receive proofs of love only representatively, as his name lives on among his followers' (Wellhausen).

[38–40] This is a piece of tradition which Mark added here to emphasize further the notion of the uncomprehending disciples. The linkage created by a key word – 'in your name' (v. 38) echoes 'in my name' (v. 37) – may also have played a role. John's appearance in v. 38 might be explained by the joint appearance of the two brothers in 10.35–45, where John similarly approaches Jesus with a concern.

Tradition

[35b, 37] Mark already found both sayings in their secondary version addressed to the community (for v. 37 cf. Luke 10.16/Matt. 10.40; John 13.20). As the following sayings are also addressed quite specifically to community problems, the question already arises at this point whether a short community catechism has been worked into 9.33–50.

[38–40] The disciples appear as a separate group. Verse 38 contains a unique reference to someone who does not follow the disciples. So this is a community problem. There is a secular parallel to v. 40 in Cicero, *Speeches* 41: 'For us, all are opponents except for those who are with us; for Caesar, all are his own in so far as they are not against him.'

[41] This verse (cf. Matt. 10.42) picks up v. 37 and perhaps formed a unit with it in the tradition.

Historical

[35b, 37a] In both sayings, the spirit of Jesus is sometimes rediscovered: 'Whereas the first shows the spirit which is to prevail among the disciples, the second merely indicates the attitude of Jesus to children, who are in a weak social position' (Gnilka). But such an analysis must remain unsatisfactory.

[38–40] The episode is unhistorical, as it is based on a situation in the community. Moreover the possibility that already during the lifetime of Jesus people other than his disciples could have called on his miraculous name seems unlikely. Furthermore, v. 40 is a saying which has been subsequently Christianized. Cf. as an analogy the saying 'To give is more blessed than to receive' (Acts 20.35), put on the lips of Jesus, which appears as a Persian principle in Thucydides II 97, 4.

[41] Belonging to Christ points to the community and not to the life of Jesus. Therefore the saying is inauthentic.

Mark 9.42–43, 45, 47–50: On the temptation to sin. Sayings about salt

42 'Whoever <u>gives offence</u> to one of these little ones who believe, it would be better for him if a millstone were hung around his neck and he were thrown into the sea.

43 And if your hand <u>gives offence</u> to you, cut it off! It would be better for you to enter life maimed than to have two hands and go <u>into Gehenna</u>, into the unquenchable fire.

45 And if your foot <u>gives offence</u> to you, cut it off! It would be better for you to enter life lame than to be thrown with two feet <u>into Gehenna</u>.

47 And if your eye <u>gives offence</u> to you, tear it out! It would be better for you to enter the kingdom of God with one eye than to be thrown with two eyes <u>into Gehenna</u>, 48 where their worm does not die and the fire is not quenched.

49 *For everyone will be salted with fire.* 50 *Salt is good;* but if the salt has lost its saltness, how will you season it? *Have salt in yourselves, and be at peace with one another.'*

Text-critical note: v. 44 and v. 46 are not part of the original text.

Redaction

[42–48] With this series of sayings drawn from the tradition Mark continues the instruction of the disciples. Verse 42: 'little ones' takes up 'children' in vv. 36–37. Verse 48 concludes the unit with a quotation from Isa. 66.24.

[49] This is a Markan transition to the next verse.

[50] With the invitation to have peace Mark harks back to the starting point of the dispute between the disciples in vv. 33–34 and draws the moral from the piece of tradition which has been inserted, namely to keep peace with one another.

Tradition

'The series of isolated and paradoxical sayings of Jesus which stand out like undigested lumps is highly characteristic and without any doubt the primary literary element. How could Mark have come to tear these out of context and thus make them incomprehensible?' (Wellhausen). There are parallels to v. 43 and v. 47 in Matt. 5.30 and 5.29, independently of Mark.

[42–48] These verses are probably parts of the pre-Markan community catechism which has left its mark on 9.33–48. Verse 42 (together with v. 41) refers back to v. 37. The key word 'give offence' (v. 42), which here always means the temptation to fall away from Christianity, is followed in vv. 43, 45, 47f. by three sentences with parallel structures. It is striking that each time in the apodosis there is a contrast between entering into life (vv. 43, 45) or into the kingdom of God (v. 47) and being thrown into Gehenna. (Gehenna is a deep valley south of Jerusalem where, according to Jewish popular belief, the final judgment is to take place.) Previously Jesus states in a radical way the call to destroy part of the body if this causes offence.

Open questions: (a) What is the relationship between 'life' and the 'kingdom of God'? (b) How is the imagery to be explained? I presuppose that the destruction of the limbs which cause offence is not to be taken literally. Does that come from the Markan community, in which other metaphorical interpretations can be noted? For the imagery cf. also on Matt. 5.29–30.

Verse 42, which in technical terminology speaks of the little ones who believe, indicates that generally a situation in the community is the basis of the tradition behind vv. 42–48.

[50] Cf. Matt. 5.13/Luke 14.34. The Q version of the saying about salt which appears there is older.

Historical

[42–50] Even the basic elements of these sayings do not go back to Jesus, as a situation in the community is to be presupposed for all of them. For v. 43 and v. 47 cf. on Matt. 5.29–30. For v. 50 cf. the verdict on Matt. 5.13/Luke 14.34–35, which is an earlier part of the tradition.

Mark 10.1–12: On divorce

1 *And he sets out from there and comes into the region of Judaea and beyond the Jordan, and again crowds of people gather round him and as usual he taught them again.*
2 And Pharisees came to him and asked him whether the husband was allowed to put away his wife, *in order to tempt him.* 3 But he answered and said to them, 'What has Moses commanded you?' 4 And they said, 'Moses said it was lawful to write a document of divorce and to put away.' 5 And Jesus said to them, 'Moses wrote this law for you because of your hardness of heart. 6 But from the beginning of creation he created them as man and woman. 7 Therefore a man will leave his father and his mother. 8 And the two will become one flesh. Therefore they are no longer two, but one flesh. 9 So what God has joined together, let no one separate.'
10 *And in the house the disciples asked him about this again.* 11 And he says to them, 'Whoever puts away his wife and marries another commits adultery against her. 12 And if she marries another after she has put away her husband, she commits adultery.'

Redaction

[1] This is a short Markan summary report with which the journey to Jerusalem for the fatal Passover begins. Both Luke (9.51) and Matthew (19.1) emphasize this turning point more strongly than Mark. However, Mark has announced it through the two predictions of the passion in 8.31 and 9.31, and has spoken of it again later in 10.32.

[4] Cf. Deut. 24.1, 3.

[6–8] Cf. Gen. 1.27; 2.24.

[10] As typically Markan instruction of the disciples in the house (cf. previously 9.33), this is a redactional transition to the originally isolated logion vv. 11f., which has a parallel in Q (Matt. 5.32/Luke 16.18). Cf. the logion I Cor. 7.10f., which is explicitly introduced by Paul as a word of the Lord.

Tradition

In general it can be said that the heart of the pericope, vv. 2–9, has been taken over by Mark without any intervention worth mentioning; similarly vv. 11–12.

Verses 2–9 are a controversy in which Jesus first of all replies to his opponent's question with a counter-question and only later really gives an answer, in v. 9. His opponents' reaction to this is not mentioned because the community is to be instructed and not disturbed.

In the passage vv. 11–12, which originally existed in isolation, the content of Jesus' concluding statement in v. 9 is made more precise in that evidently women also get the possibility of divorce. This possibility, which is inconceivable in the Jewish-Christian sphere, must have existed within the Markan community and corresponds to Roman legislation, which in particular cases presupposes that the woman can separate from her husband. The rare examples of this practice in the Jewish sphere come from regions outside Palestine and from the eccentric family of King Herod.

Historical

[2–9] In the controversy, the earliest stratum is v. 9. Only in v. 9 do the central verbs 'join together' and 'separate' occur, whereas in vv. 2–8 'separate' is never used for the act of divorce, but 'put away'. Moreover the radical repudiation of divorce by Jesus is attested both in the Q tradition (Matt. 5.32/Luke 16.18) and by Paul in I Cor. 7.10–11. It follows that according to all the earliest material Jesus emphasizes the indissolubility of marriage. In 10.9 (= Matt. 19.6b) we are given the real theological basis of this view from the will of God in creation, as already indicated in v. 6 ('beginning of creation'). Perhaps there is a bridge from here to the sabbath commandment in 2.27.

Mark 10.13–16: The children and the kingdom of God

13 And they brought to him children, for him to touch them, *but the disciples threatened them.*
14 *And when Jesus saw that, he became indignant,* and said to them, 'Allow the children to

come to me, do not prevent them, for to such belongs <u>the kingdom of God</u>. 15 Amen, I say to you, whoever does not receive <u>the kingdom of God</u> like a child will not enter into it.' 16 And he embraced them and blessed (them), laying hands on them.

Redaction

Within the framework of the Gospel of Mark the theme of the children follows meaningfully from the theme of marriage (10.1–12). The pericope corresponds to 9.36f. The present pericope contains the original, which at the same time points forward to the problem within the community which is to be discussed in vv. 29f.

[13] The negative portrayal of the disciples in v. 13b derives from Mark.

[14] Only at this point is there mention of Jesus' indignation – elsewhere only of that of the disciples (10.41; 14.4). Matthew 19.14 and Luke 18.16 have omitted these disturbed feelings on the part of Jesus independently of each other.

[15] Mark inserted the saying here (Matt. 19.14–15 reverses that) and thus no longer understood children sociologically, but symbolically (similarly Thomas 22.2). Likewise at this point the expression 'kingdom of God' denotes a present entity. One is to receive it 'like a child'.

Tradition

The starting point of the analysis is the observation that there is a difference of viewpoint in vv. 14 and 15. Verse 15 was originally a detached saying of the Lord which was inserted into the scene vv. 13–16 – not vice versa, since even without v. 15 vv. 13–16 are 'a closed apophthegm which has its point in v. 14' (Bultmann). Verses 13–14, 16 depict an ideal scene which has an occasion in the Jewish custom of blessing; cf. also II Kings 4.27. The truth of v. 15 finds a symbolic depiction in the scene.

The community is to be assumed as the author of this piece. The occasion for its composition may have been a discussion on whether children were to be admitted to baptism. The memory of Jesus' behaviour towards children generally could have been the basis for it.

Historical

[13–14, 16] For traditio-historical reasons this piece is a community formation and therefore inauthentic.

[15] The authenticity of this saying is supported by the possibility of attaching it seamlessly to other logia of Jesus (criterion of coherence). In Matt. 6.25–32 Jesus rejects concern for the wherewithal to live because God as Father will care for his people. Jesus' prayer is also addressed to the 'Father' (Matt. 6.9).

Mark 10.17–31: The rich man's question. The reward for discipleship

17 *And when he went out on the way,* someone ran up, bent the knee and asked him, 'Good teacher, what should I do to inherit <u>eternal life</u>?' 18 And Jesus said to him, 'Why do you call me good? No one is good but God alone. 19 You know the commandments, "You shall not kill, you shall not commit adultery, you shall not steal, you shall not bear false witness, you shall not defraud, honour your father and your mother."' 20 And he said to him, 'Teacher. I have observed all this from my youth.' 21 And Jesus looked on him and loved him and said to him, 'You are lacking one thing. Go, sell what you have and give it to the poor and you will have a treasure in heaven, and come, follow me!' 22 But he was troubled over this saying and went away sorrowfully. For he had many possessions.

23 *And Jesus looked around him and says to his disciples,* 'How hard it will be for those with possessions to <u>enter the kingdom of God</u>.' 24 *And the disciples were dismayed at his words. And Jesus answered again and says to them, 'Children, how difficult it is to <u>enter the kingdom of God</u>. 25 It is easier for a camel to go through the eye of a needle than for a rich man to <u>enter the kingdom of God</u>.' 26 And they were dismayed and said to one another, 'Who then will be saved?' 27 Jesus looked at them and says, 'With men it is impossible but not with God. For everything is possible with God.'*

28 *And Peter began to speak to him, 'Look, we have left everything and followed you.'* 29 Jesus said, 'Amen, I say to you, there is no one who has left house or brothers or sisters or mother or father or children or fields for my sake *and the gospel's* 30 who will not receive one hundredfold – now in this time houses and brothers and sisters and mothers and children and fields – *with persecutions* – and in the age to come <u>eternal life</u>.

31 But many first will be last and last first.'

Redaction

[17–22] Only v. 17a contains typically Markan motifs.

[23–27] These verses are a first Markan appendix on the danger of riches.

[28–30] These verses are a second appendix on the reward of discipleship. The redactional v. 28 picks up v. 21. The unexpressed conclusion runs, 'So have *we* earned entry into the kingdom?' Mark has added vv. 29–30 as an illustration of discipleship.

[31] This verse, an isolated saying, also appears in Matt. 20.16 and Luke 13.30 and was attached here by Mark (cf. above 9.35). It rounds off the section by emphasizing the reversal of earthly criteria before God, partly picking up v. 27.

Tradition

[17b–22] This is a story with a unitary structure (= apophthegm) in which Jesus' words make sense only with reference to the questions. The narrative is not interested in the individual, but only in the subject. For example, we are not told either the name of the rich man or the motive that drove him to Jesus. In v. 19 Mark groups the commandments according to the order in Deut. 5.17–20.

[23–27] This passage is an elaboration of an individual logion of Jesus about riches: 'It is easier for a camel to go through the eye of a needle than for a rich man to enter the kingdom of God' (v. 25). The greatest animal in Palestine is of course too big for the smallest hole known to the culture of that time. This is popular hyperbole which indicates an original speaker. But he does deliberately avoid threats against the rich (unlike I Enoch 94–96).

[29–30] This saying has a lengthy prehistory. Two things come together in it. The *first* point is that individuals – like Jesus himself once – have broken with their own family. *Secondly*, some Christians have ascetically detached themselves from all earthly ties. The question then arises what they are to live on. Answer: the community will support them. The saying may originally have gone only as far as 'hundredfold'. 'What follows is a distinction between a reward in this world and a reward in the world to come; here the former (probably entirely at a secondary stage) is made even more specific. Originally the hundredfold recompense was doubtless one in the other world, i.e. it means reward in the messianic kingdom' (Bultmann).

For the further tradition history of the passage see on Luke 14.26. The absence of an invitation to leave or to hate one's wife in Mark is perhaps explained by the example of Peter, who was (and remained) married.

[31] Cf. Matt. 20.16; Luke 13.30.

Historical

[17b–22] Probably the historical Jesus spoke of God as good and rejected this divine predicate for himself (v. 18). Verse 21 fits the radical nature of Jesus' call to discipleship and the beatitude on the poor (cf. Luke 6.20).

[23–27] The saying in v. 25 is likely to go back to Jesus because of its original hyperbole (cf. 11.23).

[28–30] For traditio-historical reasons most of this section comes from the community. Historically, only Jesus remains as the model of the one who has broken with his physical family. But that does not make all the logia in this section authentic.

[31] The saying can be attached to a great variety of stories and is not suitable as the object for verdicts of authenticity.

Mark 10.32–34: The third announcement of the passion and resurrection

32 *And they were on the way and were going up to Jerusalem. And Jesus was walking ahead of them, and they were terrified. And those who followed were afraid. And again he took the twelve*

*and began to speak to them about what would happen to him. 33 'Look, we are going to Jerusalem
and the Son of man will be handed over to the chief priests and scribes. And they will <u>condemn</u> him
to death and hand him over to the Gentiles 34 and they will <u>mock</u> him and <u>spit on</u> him and <u>scourge</u>
him and kill him, and after three days he will rise.'*

Redaction and tradition

[32–34] Verse 32 has a redactional stamp: cf. the dismay of the disciples, the special
attitude of Jesus to the twelve (cf. 3.14 etc.) and the motif of the way. In vv. 33–34,
some details of the prophecy of the passion which have been underlined in the translation fit in closely with the Markan account of the passion: 'condemn', 14.64;
'spit on', 14.65; 15.19; 'mock', 15.20, 31; for 'scourge' cf. 15.15. Mark himself has
formulated this most detailed announcement of the passion. He attached great
importance to it as the last and longest, and there is a special emphasis on its anti-
Judaistic purpose.

Historical

No discussion of this question is needed.

Mark 10.35–45: The question from the sons of Zebedee

35 And James and John come to him, the sons of Zebedee, and say to him, 'Teacher, we want
you to do for us whatever we ask you.' 36 And he said to them, 'What do you want me to do?'
37 And they said to him, 'Grant that we may sit in your glory, one at your right hand and one
at your left.' 38 *And Jesus said to them, 'You do not know what you ask. Can you drink the cup
that I drink of, or be baptized with the baptism with which I shall be baptized?' 39 And they said to
him, 'We can.' And Jesus said to them, 'The cup that I drink you will drink, and with the baptism
with which I shall be baptized, you will be baptized,* 40 to sit at my right hand and at my left is
not for me to bestow, but is for the one for whom it is prepared.'

41 *And when the ten heard that, they began to be indignant at James and John. 42 Then Jesus
summoned them and says to them,* 'You know that those who are regarded as rulers of the
people subjugate them and their mighty men exercise their power on them. 43 But it is not so
among you, but whoever will be great among you, let him be your servant, 44 and whoever
among you will be first, let him be servant of all. 45 For the Son of man too has not come to
be served but to serve and to give his life as a ransom for many.'

Redaction

Hardly has Jesus ended his third announcement of the passion and resurrection when there
is again a misunderstanding in the circle of disciples. The two brothers, the sons of Zebedee,

act as though they had not heard the words of Jesus immediately beforehand in vv. 34–35. Jesus clarifies this misunderstanding. He shows the appropriate way for a disciple (vv. 43–44), which corresponds to the fate of the Son of man (v. 45). He had already done precisely the same thing after the first and second announcements of the passion and resurrection (cf. on 8.34–35; 9.35–37).

[38–39] These verses have been inserted here by Mark on the theme of disciple-ship. As Mark knows, using the information about the violent death of the two brothers (cf. Acts 12 on the death of James), they will go the same way as Jesus.

[40] This is perhaps a veiled foreshadowing of 15.27.

[41–42a] These verses are a Markan transition to Jesus' teaching from the tradition in vv. 42b–45.

Tradition

[35–37, 40] Jesus is refusing the two brothers what in the Q tradition (Matt. 19.28) he has promised the disciples generally. The apostle Paul offers an illustra-tion, I Cor. 6.2–3, 'Do you not know that the saints will judge the world? . . . Do you not know that we shall judge angels?' Therefore the obvious thing is to understand the unit vv. 35–37, 40 as criticism of such expectations.

[38–39] See under redaction.

[42–45] Seen as a whole, the passage is a community rule in which the risen or exalted Jesus speaks to his community. (For vv. 43–44 cf. 9.35 above.) Their behaviour has to be orientated on that of Jesus the Son of man. However, there is another special feature about v. 45:

Redemption 'through the death of Jesus towers into the Gospel only at this point; immediately beforehand he has not died *for* the others and in their place, but has died *before* them so that they die after him. The step from serving to giving life as a ransom . . . is perhaps to be explained from the diaconia of the eucharist, where Jesus gives his flesh and blood with bread and wine' (Wellhausen).

Historical

[38–39] Underlying this is the historical fact that the two sons of Zebedee suffered martyrdom. For the martyrdom of James cf. Acts 12.2. As John the son of Zebedee was still alive at the time of the Apostolic Council around AD 48 (Paul mentions him in Gal. 2.9 as one of the three pillars), he did not suffer martyrdom with his brother, as is sometimes asserted.

[35, 37, 40] The inauthenticity follows from the analysis of the tradition.

[42–45] The inauthenticity follows from the fact that the 'risen Christ' is speak-ing. Besides, all the details are to be derived from the later community.

Mark 10.46–52: Blind Bartimaeus

46 And they come to Jericho. *And when he was going out of Jericho and his disciples and a large crowd of people,* the son of Timaeus, Bartimaeus, a blind beggar, was sitting *by the wayside.* 47 And when he heard that it was Jesus the Nazarene he began to cry out and to call, '*Son of David,* have mercy on me.' 48 And many threatened him, to be silent. But he cried even more, 'Son of David, have mercy on me!' 49 And Jesus stopped and said, 'Call him!', and they call the blind man and say to him, 'Take heart, arise, he is calling you!' 50 And he threw off his cloak, sprang up, and came to Jesus. 51 And Jesus answered him and said, 'What do you want me to do for you?', and the blind man said to him, 'Rabbuni, let me see again.' 52 And Jesus said to him, 'Go, your faith has saved you.' And immediately he saw and followed him *on the way.*

Redaction

The story of the healing of the blind man recalls 8.22–26, where the blind man who had gained his sight was a counterpart to the blind disciples (8.18). Perhaps in 10.46–52 the blind man stands for all those who have recognized the identity of Jesus and with it the meaning of discipleship and are therefore immediately asked about their faith (cf. v. 52a). At all events the motif of faith is once again a central element of a miracle story (for v. 52 cf. 5.34; 9.23f.).

[46] The duplication in the detail about the location, which has Jesus going to Jericho and leaving it again immediately, is striking. The explanation is that Mark wants to change Jesus' way to Jericho into a way to Jerusalem. This corresponds to the redactional motif of the way that designates Jesus' journey to the passion in Jerusalem on which the disciples are accompanying him (cf. v. 52). Moreover there is also a duplication in the name of the blind man, namely son of Timaeus as a Greek translation of Bar Timaeus.

[47–48] The twofold address as son of David prepares for the story of Jesus' entry into Jerusalem which is told next. It clashes with the address as 'Rabbuni' in v. 51 (thus elsewhere in the New Testament only at John 20.16). 'Rabbuni' means the same thing as 'Rabbi', which occurs in the Gospel of John with reference to Jesus more frequently than in the other Gospels. In John 1.38 'rabbi' is appropriately translated 'teacher', like 'rabbuni' in John 20.16.

[52] See on v. 46.

Tradition

The narrative about Bartimaeus may have been located in Jericho. However, it lacks most of the characteristics of a miracle story. In striking distinction, say, to 8.23, where Jesus applies spittle as a means of working a miracle, Jesus heals the blind man simply by his word (v. 52a). This presupposes later reflection, for the word that works a miracle is the word of the Son of God who is present in worship. Nor is the reaction of the people customary in miracle stories narrated, although it is present (vv. 48f.). Verse 52 almost twists the tradition into a personal legend. Perhaps because the present narrative focusses on the person of Bartimaeus, nothing is said about healing practices, in contrast to Mark 8.22–26; John 9.1.6f. Note that the name Bartimaeus is the only name in a Synoptic miracle story outside 5.22.

Historical

The historical judgment on the tradition is almost zero. The place name Jericho and the name of the blind man given twice are too small a basis for a historical nucleus.

Mark 11.1–11: Jesus' entry into Jerusalem

1 *And when they come near to Jerusalem, to* Bethphage *and Bethany at the Mount of Olives*, he sends out two of his disciples 2 and says to them, 'Go into the village before you *and immediately*, when you enter it, you will find a foal tied, on which no one has yet sat. Loose it and bring (it here)! 3 And if anyone says to you, "Why are you doing this?" answer, "The Lord has need of it," *and immediately* he will send it here.' 4 And they went away and found a foal tied in front of the door outside on the street. And they loose it. 5 And some of those standing there said to them, 'Why are you doing (this) and loosing the foal?' 6 And they told them what Jesus had said to them and they allowed them. 7 And they bring the foal to Jesus and put their clothes on it. And he sat on it. 8 And many spread their clothes on the way, and others branches which they had cut from the fields. 9 And those going before and those going after cried, 'Hosanna! Praised be he who comes in the name of the Lord! 10 Praised be the coming rule of our father David, hosanna in the heights!' 11 And he came to Jerusalem *into the temple*, and looked around at everything. *And since the evening hour was already beginning, he went out with the twelve to Bethany.*

Redaction

The link between this scene and those that follow, and also the scheme of three days (11.11b, 12, 19, 20), derive from Mark. The same goes for the deliberations of Jesus' enemies, which are constantly interspersed (11.18; 12.12; 14.1).

[1] The detail 'to Jerusalem' picks up 10.32. The frequent note about Bethany at the Mount of Olives probably derives from Mark (see vv. 11f.). Note also that the Hebrew Bethphage means 'house of figs'; but Mark does not tell the readers this, although the scene of the cursing of the fig tree (vv. 12–14) follows.
   [2] Jesus' command corresponds to his capacity for clairvoyance. Cf. Jesus' three-fold prediction of his suffering and death (cf. 8.31; 9.31; 10.33f.), the announcement

of Peter's denial (14.26–31) and the prediction of his being delivered up by Judas (14.17–21). Earlier the prophet Samuel made predictions to Saul (I Sam 10.2, 3, 5) which took place immediately (see below on 14.13–16).

[3] The expression 'the Lord' is meant to sound mysterious; elsewhere in Mark Jesus does not designate himself in this way, nor is he given this title by his disciples or the narrator. Probably, however, a christological dimension is decisive – as it is with the title Lord for Jesus in Luke (5.8; 10.1f.).

[4–7] The two disciples do as Jesus has commanded them and find everything as Jesus had predicted. Even the owners of the animal have no objections.

[8] 'The spreading out of the clothes is part of the stylization of a royal ritual. The story finds a continuation in the crucifixion of Jesus as the king of the Jews' (Gnilka).

[9–10] The masses greet Jesus in v. 9 with the cry 'Hosanna' (= 'Help us'), a petition which had become a liturgical formula and was well-known to everyone; it comes from Ps. 117.25f. Verse 10a is evidently a commentary on this word from the psalms. However, 'the kingdom of our father David' had never been the content of the preaching of Jesus, but rather the kingdom of God (1.15). Still, in the previous story Bartimaeus had addressed Jesus as son of David (10.48), though in 12.35–37 Jesus himself refutes the view that the Christ is the son of David. Thus Mark reduces messianic features in the tradition which he used. Jesus has indeed been sent by God and brings in the kingdom of God, but he is not the son of David nor the king of Israel.

Tradition

The tradition used by Mark is a messianic legend which came into being in earliest Christianity. The obtaining of the foal is as much a fairy-tale motif as the finding of the room in 14.12–16. 'Here it is presupposed that this mount has special significance. Therefore it can be found only by divine guidance and also in other respects has characteristics of something special. It has never been ridden before and also stands outside in the street tied up, as though it had been prepared for the disciples. The story of the entry is the direct continuation of the legend of the finding' (M. Dibelius). In the legend the entry of the Messiah into Jerusalem is narrated under the influence of Zech 9.9.

Historical

The tradition is strongly legendary. Nor can Jesus' entry into Jerusalem have been as spectacular as the text describes it. Otherwise the Romans would immediately have made short shrift of him. However, the following historical nucleus is plausible: Jesus went to Jerusalem with a host of festival pilgrims and disciples full of jubilation and in expectation that the kingdom of God would soon come. Under the influence of Zech. 9.9, at a second stage this was made into a messianic legend used by Mark, which accordingly is inauthentic.

Mark 11.12–14, 20: The cursing of the fig tree

12 *And when they went away from Bethany on the next day he became hungry.* 13 And when he saw in the distance a fig tree which had leaves, he went (to see) whether he would find any-thing on it. And he approached, but found nothing but leaves. [For it was not the time of figs.] 14 And he answered and said to it, 'May no one ever eat fruit from you again.' *And his disciples heard it.* 15 . . . 20 And as they passed by in the morning, they saw the fig tree, withered from the roots up.

Redaction

Mark has torn apart a tradition about the cursing of a fig tree and its success (v. 20) and used it in the sandwich technique which is typical of him.

[12] The departure from Bethany is a redactional link.

[13] The 'omniscient' observation at the end of the verse, put in square brackets, is an addition from the time *after* the composition of Mark and seeks to explain why Jesus could find no figs. These appear at the earliest in June, but the time is still March. Like the tradition he has used (see below), Mark understands the symbolism of the fig tree and its fruits in the light of the Old Testament. In Hos. 9.10 the patriarchs are an early fruit on the fig tree. In Jer. 8.13, Israel under judgment is compared to a fig tree without fruits. According to Mark, Israel has opposed Jesus and in so doing can be compared only with the Israel of the Old Testament.

[14c] This introduces the disciples redactionally, since they will be needed in 11.20–25 as the audience for the instruction on faith.

Tradition

[13–14, 20] The underlying tradition is a punitive miracle. Its purpose at the stage of tradition corresponds to that at the level of redaction: Jesus punishes the Jewish people for having missed its time. As a parallel cf. 12.1–12 and the old tradition I Thess. 2.15–16. The narrative is the only instance of a punitive miracle in the Jesus tradition in the New Testament.

Historical

The pericope does not betray any historical knowledge. (a) Jesus was not a clair-voyant but was made one only by the community. (b) The radical anti-Judaism behind the tradition of the cursing of the fig tree is rooted in the early church and not in the preaching of Jesus.

Mark 11.15–19: The cleansing of the temple

15 And they come to Jerusalem. And when he entered the temple he began to drive out those who sold and those who bought in the temple, and he overturned the tables of the money-changers and the seats of those who sold doves. 16 And he did not allow anyone to bear a vessel through the temple. 17 *And he taught and said to them, 'Is it not written, "My house will be called a house of prayer for all peoples?" But you have made it a cave of robbers.'* 18 *And the chief priests and scribes heard of this and reflected on how they could destroy him. They were afraid of him, for the whole people was overcome by his teaching.*

19 *And when evening came, they went out of the city.*

Redaction

[17–18] As teaching accompanying the action narrated in vv. 15–16, in v. 17 Mark couples two Old Testament passages, Isa. 56.7 and Jer. 7.1. The intervention of the chief priests and scribes seems also to be redactional. Their fear of Jesus heightens the drama. For the people is still on the side of Jesus, which would make an immediate intervention difficult.

[19] The Markan scheme of a day is present here (see above on 11.1–11).

Yield: Mark dovetails the pericope with the preceding story of the cursing of the fig tree. At the same time the reflection on scripture in v. 17 has an important task for him. From now on the temple, Jerusalem and Israel no longer play a role in salvation history. Something new will replace the temple. This new thing is indicated with the prospect of all the peoples. The gospel is preached to these peoples (13.10).

Tradition

The tradition, the form of which can no longer be classified, comprised vv. 15–16. It was probably an element in a historical account, possibly even a preparatory part of the passion story.

Historical

In all probability, Jesus' attitude to the temple was the reason for the Jewish authorities to hand him over to the Romans. In Mark, too, Jesus' appearance in the temple is directly connected with his later execution. However, it is not immediately clear what Jesus intended to achieve by the action – presupposing its historicity. (a) Was it intended as a *cleansing of the temple*? But who could have understood the driving out of the merchants and sellers and the overturning of the tables of the money-changers and those who sold doves in this way? (b) Was it to be interpreted as a *reform of the temple*? But the fact that it did not take place in the whole temple but only in a small area does not fit with that. (c) Jesus' action in the temple must have been a *symbolic* action pointing to something else.

Cf. the sign actions of the Old Testament prophets. Thus the prophet Ahijah of Shiloh tears his new cloak into twelve pieces (I Kings 11.29–39), the prophet Isaiah inscribes a tablet with the name of his unborn son, 'Speed-Prey Hasten-Booty' (Isa. 8.1–4), and the prophet Hosea marries the prostitute Gomer and fathers her children (Hos. 1.2–9).

Jesus attempted to abolish the temple symbolically. But this abolition did not take place in order to reform the temple cult or to stop its further profanation, but in order to make room for a completely new temple, eschatological and thus expected from God. There are two presuppositions for this understanding: (a) Jesus understood the saying about the destruction (11.15) literally; (b) he connected with it the hope for a new temple which appears in Judaism in various manifestations (Micah 4.1–2a; Hag. 2.6–9, etc.).

There is a further reflection of Jesus' criticism of the temple in the account of his trial. Cf. 14.58, 'We have heard that he has said, "I will destroy this temple which is made with hands and in three days build another which is not made with hands."' It is very probable that this logion about the temple comes from Jesus, all the more so as 14.57 explicitly depicts it as false witness and Luke transfers it to Acts 6.14 – probably to tone it down. (However, in the logion, under the influence of christology [cf. also the three days which refer to Jesus' resurrection], Jesus – and not God – has become the one who builds the new temple.) In other words, both Mark and Luke blunt the radical character of Jesus' preaching at this point. Jesus' expectation of the heavenly temple is plausible for yet another reason: the primitive community of Jerusalem identified itself with the temple. Its members constantly frequented the temple (Acts 2.46; 3.1–5; Acts 21.26) and here, in accord with Jesus, expected the end of the ages.

Mark 11.20–25: Prayer and faith

20 And as they passed by in the morning they saw the fig tree, withered from the roots up. 21 *And Peter remembers and says to him, 'Rabbi, see, the fig tree which you cursed is withered.'*

22 *And Jesus answered and says to them,* 'Have faith in God! 23 Amen, I say to you, "Whoever says to this mountain, 'Lift yourself up and cast yourself into the sea!' and does not doubt in his heart, but believes that what he says will come true, to him it will be granted." 24 Therefore I say to you: "Whatever you pray and ask for, believe that you have

received (it), and it will be granted to you. [25 And whenever you stand to pray, forgive, if you have anything against anyone, so that your Father in the heavens also forgives you your transgressions.]" ' [26]

Preliminary text-critical comment: While v. 25 is unexceptionally attested in the manuscripts, the language is Matthaean (parallels: Matt. 5.23f. and 6.14; 'your Father in the heavens' appears only here in Mark). Therefore dependence on Matthew is probable and v. 25 is probably a gloss. There is no doubt that v. 26 derives from a secondary addition, as this verse is lacking in the earliest manuscripts.

Redaction

[20–22] Verse 20 redactionally makes a new beginning with the beginning of the next day (cf. above, v. 12). Mark uses the traditional conclusion of the narrative of the cursing of the fig tree to attach instruction to the disciples. It is introduced by Peter's reference to the fig tree. Verse 22a redactionally introduces the answers of Jesus given in the tradition. Here v. 22b is the heading for the following passage and specifies the faith discussed there as faith in God.

[23–24] Mark seeks to show what faith can do (cf. 9.14–29) and what a close relationship it has to prayer.

Tradition

[23–24] These verses contain sayings which were originally handed down in isolation. For v. 23 see the Q parallel (Matt. 17.20/Luke 17.6) and Thomas 48; 106 along with I Cor. 13.2. For v. 24 see Matt. 7.7/Luke 11.9; John 14.13f.; 16.23. Mark may also have found the saying v. 22b, which introduces the two sayings of Jesus, in the tradition. Either Mark himself put the individual sayings together or – more probably – already found them as a piece of tradition.

Verses 23 and 24 have an identical structure in the second half (cf. the underlinings). Verse 24 may have been formulated on the basis of v. 23.

Historical

[23] This saying is based on a hyperbolic metaphor (cf. Matt. 17.20; Luke 17.6) of the kind that Jesus also loved elsewhere (cf. 10.25). It emphasizes the power of a characteristic faith and is probably authentic. Cf. Matt. 7.7–11/Luke 11.9–13.

[24] This verse is very much secondary both in form and in tradition history. Accordingly the saying is inauthentic.

Mark 11.27–33: The question of authority

27 And they come again to Jerusalem. And when he is going round in the sanctuary the chief priests and scribes and the elders come to him 28 and said to him, 'With what <u>authority</u> are you doing this? Or who has given you this <u>authority</u> that you do this?' 29 But Jesus said to them, 'I will ask you a single thing, and answer me, then I will say to you with what <u>authority</u> I do this: 30 The baptism of John, was it from heaven or from men? Answer me!' 31 And they reflected among themselves and said, 'If we say "from heaven" he will say, "Then why did you not believe him?" 32 But if we say "from men"' – they feared the people. For all thought that John really was a prophet. 33 And they answered Jesus and say, 'We do not know.' And Jesus says to them, 'Then I will not tell you either with what <u>authority</u> I do it.'

Redaction and tradition

[27] Here the body which will condemn Jesus to death appears (14.64; cf. 8.31) and is contrasted with the people who have been depicted immediately beforehand, who have faith (11.20–24).

[28] Since the beginning of the Gospel the authority of Jesus has been an issue in the disputes with the scribes (cf. 1.22; 2.1–12; 3.22–30).

[29–30] The readers already know the answer to Jesus' question: the baptism of John must come from heaven and be ordained by God, for it fulfils scripture (1.2–3). Moreover as Elijah, John is the one who puts everything into the state corresponding to the will of God (9.12f.).

[31–33] Jesus' opponents do not answer his question because of their untruthfulness. Therefore Jesus need not answer the question about his authority which was put at the beginning.

Historical

The historical value of the pericope as a whole is nil. The section in its entirety goes back to Mark.

Mark 12.1–12: The wicked tenants

1 And he began to speak to them in parables, 'A man planted a vineyard, and set a hedge around it, and dug a pit for the wine press, and built a tower, and let it out to tenants, and travelled away. 2 And he <u>sent</u> to the tenants at the appointed time a servant, so that he might receive from the tenants part of the fruits of the vineyard. 3 And they seized him, beat him and sent him away (with) empty (hands). 4 And again he <u>sent</u> to them another servant: him too they beat on the head and treated shamefully. 5 And he <u>sent</u> another. They even <u>killed</u> that one, and many others, some they beat and others they <u>killed</u>. 6 He still had one, the *beloved* son. He <u>sent</u> him to them last, saying, "They will respect my son." 7 Those tenants said to one another, "This is the heir. Up, let us <u>kill</u> him and the inheritance will belong to us." 8 And they took him and <u>killed</u> him and threw him from the vineyard. 9 What will the Lord of the vineyard do? He will come and destroy the tenants and give the vineyard to others.

10 Do you not know this scripture, "The stone which the builders have rejected, this has become the corner stone. 11 That has been done by the Lord and it is wonderful in our eyes"?' 12 *And they sought to seize him and feared the people, for they knew that he had told the parable about them. And they left him and went away.*

Redaction

[1a] This verse comes from Mark. 'In parables' means 'in a parabolic way' (4.11). There follows only this one parable.

[1b–11] This section has been adopted by Mark almost unchanged as a block of tradition, including the connecting formula v. 10a, which was also present in the tradition in 2.25 and 12.26. But note that despite the insertion of the extensive passage Mark spans the great arch to 9.7 with the expression 'beloved son' (v. 6) and thus clarifies the legitimation of Jesus.

[12] This verse emphasizes those who are being addressed in vv. 1–11: the chief priest, scribes and elders from 11.27f., against whom Jesus had told this story. The three groups of officials and not the (Jewish) people who prevent immediate action against Jesus, and who are portrayed positively (cf. 11.32), represent the Jews of Mark's time who do not believe in Christ. In further support of this, reference might be made to the corresponding accusation in I Thess. 2.15, where there is similarly mention of the killing of the prophets and the killing of Jesus by the Jews, and above all to the passion account in Mark, in which the Jewish authorities lead the people astray, making them call for the death of Jesus (cf. 15.11–14).

Tradition

The tradition has a parallel in Thomas 65–66.

The text is an allegory which is based on the song of the vineyard in Isa. 5.1–7. In an allegory the true understanding of the story as a whole is achieved only by transferring all its essential elements to another frame of reference. This can be demonstrated completely in the present text, where each of the main terms stands for something else:

The vineyard (v. 1) represents Israel, the tenants (v. 1) are its leaders, the owner of the land (v. 1) is God, the servants (vv. 2–5) are the prophets, the only beloved son (v. 6) is Christ, the killing of the son (v. 8) refers to the murder of Jesus, the punishment of the tenants (v. 9) stands for the rejection of Israel, 'the others' points to the church of the Gentiles.

The yield of the allegory is as follows: because the Jewish leaders have murdered Jesus, they themselves will be killed and Israel will be given to the Gentiles. In order to confirm that by scriptural proof, a quotation (= Ps. 118.22f.) is added in vv. 10–11. The image used here, that of the *rejected* stone which God has made the corner stone, is a popular proof text in the early church for the resurrection of Christ who was *rejected* by the Jews (cf. Acts 4.11).

Historical

As the tradition can be derived from the community, its degree of authenticity is nil. But it is often argued in favour of the historical authenticity of the passage that the imagery (e.g. the rebellious mood of tenants against the owner) is well attested for the world of Jesus. However, this plausibility must not seduce us into historical conclusions. Similarly, two historical reasons which are sometimes advanced in favour of the historical value are useless.

(a) In the text the tenants kill the son, whereas from a historical perspective the Romans killed Jesus. The *counter-argument* is that according to primitive Christian polemic the Jews or their leaders killed Jesus (cf. Mark 8.31; I Thess. 2.15).

(b) Historically speaking, Jesus was killed outside Jerusalem, whereas in the present narrative the tenants kill the son within the vineyard and only then cast him out. The *counter-argument* is that in terms of the narrative strategy, the vineyard commends itself as the place of the killing, since this puts the crown on the wickedness. So the murder takes place at the very place of possession.

Finally one must reject attempts to discover in the actions of the tenants cunning behaviour, corresponding to that of the immoral heroes e.g. in Luke 16.1–7. The *counter-argument* is that in contrast to the case of the unjust steward the fortunes of the tenants do not change by their continued, similar forms of violence.

Mark 12.13–17: The question of the tax for the emperor

13 And they send to him some of the Pharisees and the Herodians to trap him in something. 14 And they came and said to him, 'Teacher, we know that you are truthful and care for no one: *for you do not regard the reputation of people, but in truth you teach the way of God.* Is it right to pay taxes to Caesar or not? Should we pay (them) or not pay?' 15 But he observed their hypocrisy and said to them, 'Why do you tempt me? Bring me a denarius that I may see (it).' 16 And they brought one. And he says to them, 'Whose image is that and whose inscription?' And they say to him, 'Caesar's.' 17 And Jesus said to them, 'Give to Caesar what is Caesar's and to God what is God's!' *And they marvelled at him.*

Redaction

[13] This verse recalls 3.6. The drama of the malicious attacks on Jesus begins. The undefined subject of 'they send' refers to the chief priests, scribes and elders from 11.27.

[14] This verse seems overloaded: the reason given, 'for you do not regard . . . God', is superfluous and probably derives from Mark.

[17] Verse 17b links back to v. 13 and states the amazement of the opponents of Jesus.

Tradition

Question, counter-question and demonstration show that this is a didactic conversation, the decisive word in which stands at the end, as a climax, in v. 17a. Since it is about the question of taxation, Palestine is a likely milieu.

Historical

[17] The saying of Jesus around which the conversation has been conceived seems to be genuine. It is stamped by an accentuation of the first commandment. The answer to the question whether taxes are to be paid to the emperor does not call for a radical decision between the emperor and God in all spheres, as the Zealots, the resistance fighters of the time, had inscribed on their banners. Rather, one owes to the earthly ruler earthly things like taxes, and to the heavenly ruler, God, heavenly things, i.e. obedience, service and love of him and love of neighbour. Whatever bears someone's image is his property and is to be given back to him: money to the emperor and the whole person to God, for human beings were created as his image (Gen. 1.27; cf. Gen. 9.6). The saying is authentic because it reflects the tendency in the proclamation of Jesus to accentuate the law (criterion of coherence). At the same time the criterion of difference applies, because in this saying there is none of the teaching about Christ which characterized the time after the 'resurrection'. Cf. also how another authentic saying of Jesus, Matt. 6.24/Luke 16.13, similarly calls for a decision between worship of God and service of mammon.

Mark 12.18–27: The question of the resurrection

18 And Sadducees come to him, *who say that there is no resurrection*. And they asked him, saying, 19 'Teacher, Moses has written for us, "If someone's brother dies and leaves a wife and has no children, that his brother is to take her as wife and father descendants for his brother." 20 There were seven brothers. The first took a wife; he died and left behind no seed. 21 And the second took her and died without leaving behind seed, and the third likewise. 22 And the

seven left behind no seed. Last of all the wife died. 23 In the resurrection, when they rise, to which of them will the wife belong? *For the seven had her as wife.*' 24 Jesus said to them, 'Is this not why you are wrong, as you know neither the scripture nor the power of God? 25 For when they rise from the dead, they will neither marry nor be given in marriage, but they will be like the angels in the heavens.

26 But as for the dead, that they will be raised, have you not read in the book of Moses how at the burning bush God spoke to him, saying, "I am the God of Abraham and the God of Isaac and the God of Jacob?" 27 He is not a God of the dead but of the living. You are quite wrong.'

Redaction

[18–27] No redactional interventions can be identified apart from the explanation in v. 18 (cf. the analogous explanation of Jewish legal practice in 7.3–4) and the reason given in v. 23b. Mark has attached the piece of tradition at this point for reasons of content. *First*, the Sadducees are to be repudiated, since in the previous pericope the Pharisees vainly turned against Jesus. *Secondly*, the pericope may serve as preparation for the message of the resurrection which the young man in the tomb will proclaim to the women (16.5–7).

Tradition

The underlying tradition is a controversy. Two passages can be differentiated: (a) vv. 18–25 as the original controversy; (b) vv. 26–27 as a later addition. The elaboration of the controversy was necessary because the general resurrection was to be argued for as an outcome of Jesus' resurrection. This happened purposefully in the 'dialogue' with the Sadducees, who completely disputed the resurrection. This is sheer scribal learning, since at the time of Jesus the institution of levirate marriage presupposed in the pericope no longer existed.

The addition vv. 26–27 advances an additional argument in favour of the resurrection. The view of the Old Testament is aptly described by the principle that God is not a God of the dead but of the living. But from that the devout of the Old Testament conclude that in death they are *excluded* from any relationship with God. Cf. Ps. 6.6: 'For in death no one remembers you; who will thank you among the dead?' So vv. 26–27 are an interpretation which, like vv. 19–25, is understandable on the basis of faith in the resurrection of Jesus. In both cases we have a pure community formation.

Historical

The historical yield is nil.

Mark 12.28–34: A question from an individual scribe

28 And a scribe came up, *who had heard them disputing. As he knew that Jesus had answered them well,* he asked him, 'Which commandment is the first of all?' 29 Jesus replied, 'The first is, "Hear, Israel, the Lord, our God, is the Lord alone, 30 and you shall love the Lord, your God, with all your heart with all your life, with all your thought and with all your strength." 31 The second is this: "You shall love your neighbour as yourself." No other commandment is greater than this.'

32 And the scribe said to him, 'Good, teacher, you have spoken in truth. He is only one and there is no other beside him, 33 and to love him with all one's heart, with all one's being, with all one's strength and to love one's neighbour as oneself, (that) is more than all burnt offerings and sacrificial gifts.' 34 And Jesus, when he saw that that he had answered wisely, said to him, 'You are not far from the kingdom of God.' *And no one dared to ask him any more.*

Redaction

Mark hands on the tradition unchanged. He has intervened only at the beginning and the end, to link the section to the context. Mark can identify completely with the content of the pericope. The sayings critical of the cult which Jesus utters on the temple plain, the place of sacrifice, gain in sharpness in the text of the Gospel as a whole. It is no coincidence that the next pericope about the widow's mite takes the same line. There is no further need of sacrifices and burnt offerings. Love of God and of neighbour is the quintessence of the message of Jesus.

[28a] This verse refers back to the 'dispute' in 12.18–27.

[34c] The remark in v. 34c, which is unexpected in view of the positive course taken by the conversation with the scribe, leads to the next section 12.35–44, in which no questions are addressed by outsiders to Jesus.

Tradition

The tradition is a didactic conversation introduced with a question. It emphasizes Jesus' agreement with a scribe over the interpretation of the law, namely the command to love God and neighbour. (For the first commandment cf. Deut. 6.5; for the second commandment Lev. 19.18b.) Note the partial repetition or paraphrase of the issue for catechetical purposes (vv. 30–31/vv. 32–33). The tradition inserted by Mark emphasizes the monotheistic confession of faith (12.29 = Deut. 6.4) and the intellectual dimension of the love of God (vv. 30 and 33). Thus it belongs within Greek-speaking Jewish Christianity.

Historical

The historical yield of the tradition is nil, since it is firmly rooted in the community and is to be derived from its needs. This community has detached itself from the temple cult and justifies this with reference to 'Jesus'. Moreover at another point Jesus gives a completely new definition of the term neighbour (see on Luke 10.30–37).

Mark 12.35–44: The question about the Davidic sonship of the Messiah. Warning against the scribes. The widow's sacrifice

35 And Jesus answered and said, *when he was teaching in the temple*, 'How can the <u>scribes</u> say that the Christ is the son of David? 36 David himself said in the holy Spirit', "The Lord said to my Lord, 'Sit at my right hand until I put your enemies under your feet.'" 37 David himself calls him his Lord. So how can he be his son?' *And all the people heard him gladly.*

38 And *in his teaching* he said, 'Beware of the <u>scribes</u> who go about in long garments and want to have greetings in the market place 39 and seats of honour in the synagogues and places of honour at banquets. 40 Those who devour the houses of <u>widows</u> and pray for a long time for show; these will receive all the more sharp a judgment.'

41 And Jesus sat *opposite the chest for offerings* and saw how people were throwing money into the chest. And many rich people threw much in. 42 And there came a poor <u>widow</u> and threw in two lepta, *that is a quadrans*. 43 *And he summoned his disciples* and said to them, 'Amen, I say to you, this poor <u>widow</u> has thrown more into the chest than all who have thrown something in. 44 For all have thrown in something of their superfluity, but she out of her poverty has thrown in all that she had, (namely) her whole livelihood.'

Redaction

[35] Verse 35a shows itself to be redactional through Mark's favourite word 'teach' and through the mention of the temple (cf. 11.27).

[37] Verse 37c leads to the next scene. The people are still on Jesus' side, so there is reason for his opponents' fear (cf. 11.18, 32; 12.12).

[38–40] After 8.31; 10.33; 11.27, Mark indicates once again the unbridgable opposition between Jesus and the scribes. Verse 38 links up with vv. 35–37 by the motif of 'teaching'.

[41–44] Mark has attached this piece by means of the key word 'widow'. Jesus' knowledge that the widow has given away all her possessions (v. 43) fits the Markan view of Jesus' omniscience.

Tradition

[35–37] The piece has been formed by the community, which in a learned scribal way wanted to demonstrate that Jesus is more than son of David, namely son of God.

Cf. Barn.12.10: 'See, again Jesus, not Son of man but Son of God, who appeared as a model in the flesh. Now as it is to be expected that they say that Christ is a son of David, David himself prophesies . . .: "The Lord said to my Lord, 'Sit at my right hand until I have made your enemies the footstool under your feet.' " '

That need not contradict the differentiation according to which a two-stage christology underlies this passage in Mark 12, as becomes clear in Rom. 1.3–4: during his lifetime Jesus is the Messiah, i.e. of the seed of David. After the resurrection as Son of God he is exalted to be David's Lord.

[38–40] The tradition seems like an extract from the speech against the Pharisees which can be recognized behind Luke 11.37–52/Matt. 23.1–36 as a Q text. The main difference between the Markan version and the Q version lies in those addressed. In Q it is the Pharisees, in Mark the scribes.

[41–44] The story depicts an ideal scene which illustrates the principle that the tiny sacrifice of the poor pleases the deity better than the extravagant gift of the rich. This principle has numerous parallels in antiquity.

Historical

[35–37] The historical value of the pericope is nil, as it can be explained exclusively from discussions in the community.

[38–40] The historical yield is nil. Cf. further on Matt. 23.6–7 (Q).

[41–44] The historical yield is nil. The story shows how a noble principle which was widespread at that time could be put in the mouth of Jesus. This is not to dispute that the content of the principle of the story has affinities with the preaching of Jesus (cf. 10.25; Luke 12.15).

Mark 13: Jesus' discourse on the end time

The basic material in Mark 13 derives from a Jewish original which was composed when the Roman emperor Caligula wanted to erect his statue in the temple of Jerusalem in AD 40 and was prevented from doing so only by his sudden death. This source comprised, say, vv. 7–8, 12, 14–20, 24–27. In view of the threat posed by Caligula's plan, to which reference is made in v. 14, it contained an explicit reference to the approaching end, to the arrival of the Messiah-Son of man, as he was expected in connection with the tradition in the book of Daniel as saviour of the Jewish people.

This source was overlaid by a second stratum of Christian origin. This includes vv. 5b–6, 9, 11, 21–22, 28–32, 34–36. This intermediate Christian stratum comprised not only the description of the tribulations of the end time and the coming of the Son of man but also warnings against heresies and announcements of persecutions. The evangelist Mark has taken over and used this tradition. Verses 10, 13, 23, 33 and 37 are to be regarded as Markan.

The placing of the discourse about the end time near the conclusion of the Gospel is grounded in Christian instruction. The teaching about the end time always comes at the end of this, cf. I Thess. 4.13–5.11; Did.16; Barn. 21.1. The passage is the longest connected discourse of Jesus in the Gospel of Mark; it is not broken up, for example, by transitional formulae like 'and he said to them' or intermediate questions by the disciples (but cf. Mark 13. 4).

Mark 13.1–4: The prophecy of the destruction of the temple

1 *And when he goes out of the temple, one of his disciples says to him, 'Teacher, look at these stones and these buildings!'* 2 And Jesus said to him, 'Do you see these great buildings? Not a stone will be left on another; all will be demolished.'

3 *And when he was sitting on the Mount of Olives opposite the temple, Peter and James and John and Andrew asked him privately,* 4 *'Tell us, when will this happen? And what will the sign be when all this is accomplished?'*

Redaction and tradition

[1–4] Verse 1 is a redactional introduction to v. 2. In this verse Mark uses from the tradition a saying of Jesus about the destruction of the temple which in 14.58 is presented as false witness. In addition he composes a symbolic scene from it and makes a connection between the fate of the temple and the end of the world. Here in vv. 3–4 there is a typical narrowing of focus from the crowd to the closer circle of the four disciples first chosen (1.16–20). The issue is the interpretation of Jesus' saying about the temple in v. 2. The scene is over against the temple on the Mount of Olives, where Jesus will later be once again together with three of the confidants present here, namely in the garden of Gethsemane (14.26).

The first part of the disciples' twofold question ('When will this happen?') is replied to in vv. 5–23, the second part ('What will be the sign?') in vv. 24–27.

Historical

[2] Cf. on 14.58. Jesus never uttered the saying in v. 2 within the framework of a discourse about the end.

Mark 13.5–8: Theme

5 *Jesus began to say to them: 'See that no one leads you astray!* 6 *Many will come in my name and say,* "I am he", *and they will lead many astray.* 7 And when you hear of wars and the tumult of war, do not be afraid. It must happen thus. *But the end is not yet.* 8 For one people will rise up against another and one kingdom against another. There will be earthquakes here and there, there will be famines. *That is the beginning of the birth-pangs.*

Redaction and tradition

[5–8] These verses contain a summary survey in which v. 6, redactionally, antici-pates vv. 21–23. It remains to be noted that in v. 6 Mark begins with the 'christo-logy'. Many will falsely claim to be the Jesus who has returned, but the events described in vv. 7 and 8 are only the beginning.

Historical

The historical yield is nil. For the sayings of Jesus must be derived from the situa-tion of the community, in which numerous adversaries have appeared.

Mark 13.9–13: The present situation

9 *'But look out!* They will hand you over to the courts, and in the synagogues you will be scourged, and you will be led before governors and kings for my sake, as a testimony to them. 10 *And first the gospel must be preached among all people.* 11 And when they lead you away and hand you over, do not be anxious in advance about what you should say; but say whatever is given you in that hour. For it is not you who speak, but the holy Spirit. 12 And brother will hand over (his) brother to death and the father (his) child, and children will rage against parents and will kill them. 13 *And you will be hated by all for my name's sake. But whoever persists to the end, he will be saved.'*

Redaction and tradition

[9–13] The imperative 'Look' corresponds to that in v. 5 (cf. v. 23). The section reflects the experiences of the Markan community and describes its present situa-tion with the point in v. 10. The mission to the Gentiles is in full swing and the delay in the return of Jesus is part of God's plan.

Historical

The historical yield is nil, as the sayings of Jesus derive from problems in the com-munity and have been put on his lips.

Mark 13.14–23: The last segment of history

14 'But when you see the abomination of desolation standing where it should not – let the reader note – then those in Judaea should flee to the mountains. 15 The one who (is) on the roof should not descend and go in to get something from his house. 16 And the one who (is) in the field should not turn back to get his coat. 17 And woe to the pregnant and those who are breast-feeding in those days. 18 Pray that it does not happen in winter. 19 For those days will be a tribulation, such as has never been since the beginning of creation which God has created, until now, nor will there be again. 20 And had the Lord not <u>shortened</u> these days, no one would be saved, but for the sake of the <u>elect</u> whom he has chosen, he has <u>shortened</u> the days.

21 If then anyone says to you, "Look, here is the Christ! Look, there he is!", do not believe! 22 For false Christs and false prophets will be raised up and they will do signs and wonders, in order, if it were possible, to lead astray the <u>elect</u>. 23 *But look out! I have told you all this in advance!*'

Redaction and tradition

[14–20] These verses depict the transition from the present to the future. Verse 14 represents a key to the understanding not only of this discourse but also to the Gospel of Mark generally. Both v. 14a and v. 19 are stamped with clear references to the book of Daniel. For v. 14a cf. Dan. 12.11. For v. 19 cf. Dan. 12.1. 'Jesus' invites the readers to understand the forthcoming events against the background of the pattern of experience and thought of the prophet Daniel, i.e. to understand the decreed erection of the statue of the emperor in the Jerusalem temple specifically in terms of the 'abomination of desolation' in the book of Daniel. In this way the tribulation of the end time is brought in. (For the question of the historical reference in v. 14 cf. the introduction to Mark 13.)

[21–22] The section does not fit well at this point and corresponds to a similar saying in Q (Matt. 24.26–28/Luke 17.23f.).

[23] This verse – after v. 9 – ends with a renewed appeal ('Look out!') and with reference to Jesus, who has predicted everything and whose words therefore cannot be overtaken by current events. As Jesus knew everything in advance and handed on his knowledge to the community (cf. on 11.2), the community need not be worried.

Historical

The sayings of Jesus are inauthentic, because they can be derived completely from a community situation.

Mark 13.24–27: The turning point of salvation with the coming of the Son of man

24 'But in those days, after that tribulation, the sun will be darkened and the moon will not give its light, 25 and the stars will fall from heaven, and the power in the heavens will be shaken. 26 And then they will see the Son of man coming in the clouds with much power and glory. 27 And then he will send the angels, and he will bring together his elect from the four winds, from the end of the earth to the end of heaven.'

Redaction and tradition

The paragraph belongs with v. 8: now, after the earth, even the ordering of heaven gets out of joint. The sun grows dark, the moon loses its light, the stars fall from heaven.

[24–25] These verses disclose the signs which beyond question indicate the end of time, with the saving arrival of the Son of man. The verses depict typical phenomena which accompany the event of an epiphany. Cf. the Old Testament descriptions of the day of Yahweh:

Isa 13.10: 'For the stars in heaven and its Orion (constellation) will not shine brightly, the sun will rise in darkness and the moon give no light'; 34.4: 'And the whole host of heaven will vanish, and heaven will be rolled up like a scroll . . .'

[26–27] Verse 26 is a quotation from Dan. 7.13 (cf. 13.14a, 19; 14.32). Verse 27 depicts the gathering of the elect (cf. 13.20, 22).

Historical

The historical yield is nil, since this is a speculation by the community. Jesus never spoke these words.

Mark 13.28–37: The parable of the fig tree and an admonition to wakefulness

28 'From the fig tree learn the parable: when its branch is already juicy and leaves grow out, you know that the summer is near. 29 So too you, when you see that this is happening, know that he is near, at the door. 30 Amen, I say to you: this generation will <u>not pass away</u>, until all this happens. 31 Heaven and earth will <u>pass away</u>, but my words will <u>not pass away</u>. 32 But about that day and the hour no one knows, not even the angels in heaven, not even the Son, but the Father.

33 *Look out, <u>watch</u>. FOR YOU DO NOT KNOW when the time will come.* 34 It is like a

man who went on a journey and left his house and gave his servants authority, to each one his work, and commanded the doorkeeper to <u>watch</u>; 35 *so watch now*, FOR YOU DO NOT KNOW when the Lord of the house is coming, whether in the evening or at midnight or at cock crow or in the morning, 36 so that when he suddenly comes he does not find you sleeping.

37 *But what I say to you I say to all: <u>Watch</u>!'*

Redaction and tradition

[28–29] Mark here inserts the parable of the fig tree, to admonish his community to wakefulness in the face of the imminent end. No particular tree is meant, for the definite article is part of the style of a parable. The piece has no relation to the person of Jesus.

[30] The saying is closely related to the saying in 9.1, and on this basis could have been adapted by Mark himself for Jesus' discourse on the last things (13.5–37), or inserted here independently as a closing saying. According to the saying the date of the beginning of the end is the dying out of the first generation; here the first deaths probably led the community to modify the expectation of an imminent end: although a number of Christians will not experience the end, nevertheless the first generation will be witnesses to the coming of the Son of man. The most plausible explanation of the phenomenon we have here, the promise that at least some of the first generation will not have to die, is that originally there was an expectation that the first generation as a whole would experience the end of time.

[31] This verse emphasizes the certainty of Jesus' prophecy. 'For Mark's community Jesus' saying already had that eternal validity which the law had for the Jewish community' (Haenchen). The saying is a Christian formation which does not fit well with v. 32 which follows.

[32] This verse is perhaps originally a Jewish saying, apart from the Christian conclusion ('not even the Son, but the Father').

[33] This is a Markan framework saying which is repeated in v. 37 for catechetical reasons.

[34–36] The parable of the doorkeeper with the attached application in vv. 35f. contains a clear allegorization of the situation of the community, whose Lord is temporarily absent. Probably it was never in circulation without the application vv. 35–36. Here the key words about watching and not knowing combine the parable and application with the context.

[37] This verse takes up the admonition of v. 33a and is addressed to the readership of the Gospel of Mark generally.

Historical

[28–29] The parable is authentic. It contains no reference to the person of Jesus, fits his expectation of an imminent end and can hardly be derived from the community.

[30] The saying reflects a delay over the events of the end. By contrast, Jesus expected the final arrival of the kingdom of God in the immediate future. So the saying is certainly inauthentic.

[31] The saying comes from the community and is inauthentic.

[32] The saying is inauthentic as it presupposes the divine sonship of Jesus.

[34–36] The inauthenticity of the passage was already argued for in the section on redaction and tradition.

Mark 14–15: The passion narrative

Mark 14.1–11: Conspiracy. Anointing in Bethany. Contract

1 *Now it was the Passover and the Unleavened (Bread) after two days. And the <u>chief priests</u> and scribes sought how they could seize him by guile and kill him. 2 For they said, 'Not on the festival, so that there is not an uproar in the people.'*

3 And when he was in Bethany in the house of Simon the Leper and was reclining at table, a woman came who had an alabaster jar with genuine, valuable nard, and she broke the alabaster jar and poured it (the oil) on his head. 4 Then some became indignant and said to one another, 'Why this waste of oil? 5 This oil could have been sold for more than three hundred silver coins and the money given to the poor.' And they reproached her. 6 But Jesus said, 'Leave her alone. Why do you cause her trouble? She has done me a good deed. 7 For you always have the poor with you, and if you want, you can do good to them; but you do not always have me. 8 *What she could, she has done; she has anointed my body in advance for my burial. 9 Amen, I say to you: wherever the gospel is preached in all the world, what she has done will be told in memory of her.'*

10 *And Judas Iscariot, one of the twelve, went to the <u>chief priests</u>, in order to deliver him up to them. 11 And when they heard, they were glad, and promised to give him money. And he sought a good opportunity to deliver him up.*

Redaction and tradition

Verses 1–11 are the prelude to the passion story with all the persons involved in it and a mysterious reference forward to the burial of Jesus and the preaching of the gospel. The tradition used by Mark underlies vv. 3–9. As it is focussed on the portrait of a particular woman and comes to a point (vv. 6–7), it may be described as a biographical apophthegm.

[1] The intention of the Jewish opponents to kill Jesus corresponds to 3.6; 11.8 and

12.12, where they do not carry out their plan simply for fear of the people. As well as the chief priests and scribes who are already known, later, in accordance with the prediction in 8.31, the elders are also added (14.43, 53; 15.1). Jesus' Galilean opponents, the Pharisees, do not appear in the passion narrative.

[2] The intention of the enemies of Jesus to act with guile follows for reasons similar to those in 12.12 (concern about the people).

[3–5] The angry questions about waste are put in such a way as to give Jesus the opportunity to explain the meaning of the woman's action.

[6–7] Redactionally, Jesus' answer characterizes the woman's good work as service for his burial. At the level of the tradition, which has nothing to do with the suffering and burial of Jesus, the point comes in vv. 6–7. The intention of performing loving service for Jesus is more important than the giving of alms.

[8] This is a prediction of the burial of Jesus, which will be narrated in 15.42–47.

[9] This verse links the story redactionally with the preaching of the gospel. The expression 'preach the gospel' (cf. 1.14; 13.10) is redactional, as is 'in all the world'. Verse 9 is closely akin in its theme to 13.10. For Mark the woman's service in the burial is evidently an element of the preaching of the gospel.

[10–11] These verses develop vv. 1–2 redactionally. They report how the enemies of Jesus find an ally to liquidate Jesus. The report of the delivering up of Jesus by Judas, i.e. how Jesus is betrayed by one of his disciples, is part of the Judas tradition, which is widely attested in various elaborations (cf. on Matt. 27.3–10).

Historical

[3–7] The historical yield of the tradition is nil. But it does reflect the closeness of Jesus to a probably notorious woman in Galilee (cf. on Luke 7.36–50).

[10–11] Cf. on Matt. 27.3–10.

Mark 14.12–25: Preparation of the Passover Meal. Prophecy of the delivering up. The supper

12 *And on the first day of the Unleavened Bread, when they slaughtered the Passover lamb,* his disciples say to him, 'Where do you want us to go and make preparations, so that you can eat the Passover (lamb)?' 13 And he sends two of his disciples and says to them, 'Go into the city, and a man will meet you carrying a jar with water: follow him, 14 and where he enters, say to the householder, "The teacher says, 'Where is my room in which I can eat the Passover (lamb) with my disciples?' " 15 And he will show you a large upper room which is furnished (with cushions) and prepared. Prepare it for us there!' 16 And the disciples went and came into the city and found (it) as he had told them and prepared the Passover (lamb).

17 And in the evening he comes with the twelve. 18 And when they were reclining at table and eating, Jesus said, 'Amen, I say to you: one of you will deliver me up, who is eating with

me.' 19 And they began to become sorrowful and to say to him, one after the other, 'Is it I?' 20 And he said to them, 'One of the twelve who is dipping with me in the dish. 21 The Son of man goes as it is written of him, but woe to that man through whom the Son of man is delivered up. It would be better for him if he, that man, had not been born!'

22 And while they were eating he took the bread, gave thanks and broke it and gave it to them and said, 'Take, that is my body.' 23 And he took a cup, gave thanks and gave (it) to them; and they all drank of it. 24 And he said to them, 'That is my blood of the covenant which will be shed for many. 25 Amen, I say to you, I will no more drink of the fruit of the vine until that day when I drink it new in the kingdom of God.'

Redaction and tradition

[12] This verse attaches to the dating in v. 1. But it is strange that the disciples are to prepare the Passover meal on the day of the Passover, which began only around six o'clock in the evening. Mark is probably mixing up the day of rest, on which the preparations for the meal were made and the following day of the Passover. As a Gentile Christian he was probably not very familiar with the Passover regulations. Moreover by his dating he wrongly regards the meal narrated in vv. 22–25 as a Passover meal. In view of what is reported there, that is quite out of the question.

[13–16] These verses are a variant of 11.2–6, and considerable agreement in structure and vocabulary can be noted between the two sections. The prediction in vv. 13f. recalls I Sam. 10.2: before Samuel's promise in I Sam. 10.1b that Saul would become the ruler of Israel an anointing similar to Mark 14.3–9 is narrated: 'And Samuel took the flask of oil and poured it over his head' (I Sam. 10.1a).

[17–21] The passage is related to 14.43–45 (Judas betrays Jesus with a kiss) in the same way as the next section 14.26–31 is related to 14.66–72 (Peter denies Jesus).

[22–24] Mark gives the words of institution in parallel, 'That is my body' (v. 22), 'That is my blood' (v. 24), unlike Paul (I Cor. 11.24b–25), who formulates them asymmetrically. On this point Paul's words of institution are older. They run as follows:

24b That is my body for you. Do that in memory of me. 25 . . . This cup is the new covenant in my blood. Do this as often as you drink it in memory of me.

They therefore represent a more difficult version (in them body and covenant correspond) and thus reflect a more original stage of the tradition.

Both the text of Mark and also that of Paul contain an element which must have been added to the original tradition only at a later date: Mark 14.25 is an eschatological prospect on the part of Jesus, which has nothing to do with his gift of bread and wine. With I Cor. 11.26 the community is looking to the coming (again) of Jesus from heaven.

At another point, namely in the twofold command for repetition ('Do this in memory of me') in vv. 24, 25, the text of Paul seems to be later than that found in Mark. For in it liturgical influences are visible which must have been added only at a secondary stage. However, all in all the difference between the words of institution in Mark and Paul is not all that great. I shall therefore ask both as a basis and for the purpose of clarifying the content of Jesus' last meal with his disciples the question, 'How did the first readers understand the texts I Cor. 11.23–25 and Mark 14.22–25?' The answer is clear: they found in them an account of the institution of the Lord's Supper which they celebrated every Sunday and at which they received the body and blood of the Lord Jesus. This 'eating' was interpreted in many ways and in extreme cases understood literally in the sense of consuming real flesh. Cf. the interpretation of the Lord's supper in John 6.51c–58, especially vv. 54–56, where Jesus says:

54 Whoever consumes my flesh and drinks my blood has eternal life, and I will raise him up on the last day. 55 For my flesh is true food and my blood is true drink. 56 Whoever consumes my flesh and drinks my blood remains in me and I in him.

Others, like Paul, interpret the 'eating' as a proclamation of the death of Jesus until his coming from heaven (see above on I Cor. 11.26). In any case it is certain that the meaning of the eucharist was bound up with the situation *after* the death and 'resurrection' of Jesus, in which both were regarded as saving events.

[25] This saying was attached to the report of the institution of the Lord's Supper at a secondary stage. In it Jesus expresses the expectation that he will drink wine again only in the kingdom of God, the image of which as a festal meal also underlies this. Thus at the same time the saying is a kind of prophecy of his death, which does not say anything about Jesus' future relationship to his disciples.

Historical

[17–21] Jesus never spoke the words about the betrayal of Judas. Rather, from the fact that Jesus was betrayed, early Christians concluded that Jesus must have known this in advance and therefore prophesied it.

[22–24] If it is certain that according to the accounts of Paul and Mark (the same is probably true of the accounts of Matthew and Luke) Jesus celebrated the first Lord's Supper with his disciples, at which he distributed to them his body and blood and at which they ate his body and drank his blood symbolically, really or in whatever way, then it is equally certain that the institution of the supper thus described is not historical. The disciples cannot possibly have eaten Jesus' body and drunk his blood, for at the point in time when the Lord's supper was instituted Jesus was not yet dead, and he had said nothing about a saving effect of his death or even his resurrection. Apart from that, Jews were strictly forbidden to consume blood.

However, as has been demonstrated, the eucharistic texts gain meaning if they are read in the light of the liturgical practice of the earliest community.

At this point two other approaches need to be criticized: (a) of course it is open to anyone to assume a last meal of Jesus with his twelve disciples. That is even probable historically, because Jesus and his disciples went to Jerusalem and certainly ate together there. However, such a meal has no genetic relationship to the Lord's Supper which was later understood in cultic terms. (b) It is sometimes assumed that the meal described in vv. 22–24 is a Passover meal, which as a pious Jew of his time Jesus celebrated with his disciples. However, the lack of any Passover symbolism in vv. 22–24 itself and the observation that only Mark has depicted the meal as a Passover meal through the context, tell against that. And that is not enough to discover a Passover meal historically in vv. 22–24.

[25] This saying is probably authentic. It hardly came into being in the early community, for in it Jesus does not exercise any special function for believers at the festal meal in heaven which is imminent. Only Jesus' expectation of the future kingdom of God stands at the centre, not Jesus as saviour, judge or intercessor.

Mark 14.26–31: The announcement of Peter's denial

26 And after they had sung the hymn of praise, they went out to the Mount of Olives. 27 And Jesus says to them, 'You will all take offence, for it is written, "I will smite the shepherd and the sheep will be scattered." 28 But after my resurrection I will go before you into Galilee.' 29 And Peter said to him, 'Though all take offence, I shall not!' 30 And Jesus says to him, 'Amen, I say to you, today, in this night, before the cock crows twice, you will deny me three times.' 31 But he said vehemently, 'Even if I had to die with you, I will not deny you!' And all also spoke likewise.

Redaction and tradition

[26–31] This scene has been formulated by Mark himself in retrospect, using the tradition which will later be developed broadly in his Gospel, that Jesus was denied by Peter before his arrest (14.66–72) and rose after his death (16.1–8: v. 7 explicitly refers back to 14.28, from which the redactional character of both verse emerges). Of course Jesus as the Son of God must also have known of these two future events in advance (cf. the three announcements of the passion and resurrection and the prophecy of the betrayal of Judas). The same goes for the prediction of Jesus that all the disciples will take offence at him. It presupposes the flight of all the disciples which was reported later by Mark (14.50). Significantly it is supported by a scriptural quotation (Zech. 13.7) in v. 27.

Historical

The scene has been composed by Mark and is therefore certainly unhistorical.

Mark 14.32–42: Jesus in Gethsemane

32 And they come to a garden the name of which (is) Gethsemane. And he says to his disciples, 'Sit here until I have prayed.' 33 *And he takes Peter and James and John with him* and began to *tremble* and to quake 34 and says to them, 'My soul is troubled to death, remain here and watch.'

35 And he went a little further, threw himself on the ground and prayed that if it was possible, the hour might pass by him, 36 and he said, 'Abba, Father, all is possible to you: take this cup from me; but not what I will, but what you (will).'

37 And he comes and finds them sleeping and says to Peter, 'Simon, are you asleep? Could you not watch one hour? 38 Watch and pray, that you do not fall into temptation. The spirit is willing, but the flesh is weak.' 39 And he went away again and prayed and said the same words. 40 And again he came and found them sleeping: *for their eyes were very heavy, and they did not know what to answer him.*

41 And he comes a third time and says to them, 'Sleep on and rest!. Enough, the hour has come. See, the Son of man is delivered up into the hands of sinners. 42 Arise, let us go. Look, the one who is delivering me up is here.'

Redaction and tradition

In order to understand the text rightly we must rid ourselves of the prejudice that a conscientious historian is the narrator here. Such an assumption is impossible simply because no one was present at Jesus' prayerful struggle in Gethsemane. Rather, the *edifying* purpose of the whole needs to be evaluated correctly. The story emphasizes the obedience of the son of God as opposed to the dullness of the disciples, for this Son of God is the Lord who is present in the cult of the community on which people mean to rely.

At the same time a parallel tradition to the Gethsemane scene shows the horizon of thought that underlies it. In Heb. 5.7 it is said of Jesus Christ the Son of God, 'And in the days of his earthly life he offered prayers and weeping with loud cries and with tears to the one who could save him from death; and he was heard, because he held God in honour.' This didactic statement derives from the reading of Old Testament psalms, which were also an important source for the shaping of the Gethsemane scene and the passion story. Cf. Ps. 22.25: God 'has not despised nor scorned the misery of the poor and has not hidden his face from him; and when he cried to him he heard it'; Ps. 31.23: 'I said in my alarm: I am driven from your sight. But you heard the voice of my weeping when I cried to you'; Ps. 69.4: 'I have cried myself weary, my throat is parched. My eyes have become dim because I have to wait so long for my God.'

The scene in Gethsemane is not intended to disillusion, but to help to understand revelation; like the whole of the Markan passion its orientation is not towards psychology, but towards salvation history. Mark has developed this material into a process, on the basis of the saying of Jesus handed down in 14.38. Thus the material inferred from the Old Testament about the obedient Son of God arose in opposition to the cowardly and dull disciples.

That Jesus goes to pray three times in the pericope (vv. 35, 39, 41) has its basis in the round number 'three'. Similarly, Jesus endured threefold temptation by the devil (Matt. 4/Luke 4).

[33] For the preferential treatment of the three disciples cf. 5.40; 9.2.

[34] This verse contains prayer language based on Ps. 42.6, 12; 43.5 (LXX Ps. 42.50).

[36] This verse corresponds to the third petition of the Our Father (Matt. 6.10b).

[38] This verse is the traditio-historical starting point of the scene in Gethsemane.

[40b] The second part of this verse is formulated like 9.6a. Mark likes explanations and redactionally emphasizes the failure of the disciples, the fact that they fall asleep three times.

[41] What is the relationship between 'sinner' and the theme that Jesus has come to call sinners? Is sinner here an image for Gentiles? Cf. Gal. 2.15.

Historical

The historical value is nil. The argument occasionally advanced in favour of historicity, that the pericope is too offensive christologically to have been freely invented, quickly comes to grief on the clearly edifying purpose of the pericope, as was noted at the outset.

Mark 14.43–52: Jesus is arrested

43 *And immediately*, while he was still speaking, Judas comes up, one of the twelve, and with him a crowd of people <u>with swords and with staves</u> from the chief priests and scribes and the elders. 44 And the one who was to deliver him up had given them a sign and said, 'The one whom I shall kiss, it is he; <u>seize</u> him and take him away securely.' 45 And when he came, he immediately went up to him and says, 'Rabbi', and kissed him. 46 And they laid hands on him and <u>seized</u> him. 47 And one of them standing there took his sword and struck the servant of the high priest and cut off his ear. 48 Jesus answered and said to them, 'You have come out against me as against a robber <u>with swords and with staves</u>, to catch me. 49 I was daily with you *teaching in the temple*, but you did not <u>seize</u> me. But in this way the scriptures will be fulfilled. 50 Then they left him and *all* fled. 51 Now a young man *followed him* (= accompanied him), who was clothed with a linen garment on his NAKED (skin); and they grabbed at him. 52 But he let his garment go and fled away NAKED.

Redaction and tradition

The report is strongly legendary and in part enigmatic. There seems no prospect of clearly distinguishing the redaction from the tradition. Mark is working with individual elements of tradition available to him – not an account – and from these composes the narrative of the arrest of Jesus as the prerequisite for the hearings before the Supreme Council and Pilate which follow. He has introduced himself quite unobtrusively (vv. 51f.).

[43–46] In the broader context these verses put vv. 10–11 into action. In the immediate context v. 43 takes up v. 42.

[47] The designation 'servant of the high priest' is not attested elsewhere and is probably formed in analogy with 'servant of the king' (I Kings 21.3). Cutting off the ear is a symbolic act of humiliation, not a historical reminiscence.

[48–49] Verse 48 links back to v. 43. Verse 49 contains a reference to the scripture to be fulfilled without indicating the specific (cf. I Cor. 15.3–5). The sayings in these verses resemble apologetics and dogmatics of the Christian community.

[50] This verse depicts the fulfilment of v. 27.

[51–52] These verses are in tension with the previous verse, which reports the flight of all. There has been much puzzling over the young man. He follows or accompanies Jesus. In 5.37 the verb, which literally translated means 'follow along with' relates to the closest circle of disciples. Probably the author of the Gospel of Mark is introducing himself as a follower of Jesus and making the claim that he was with Jesus longer than those followers who fled. The figure of the young man resembles one in the tomb in Jerusalem in 16.5. In each case the young man appears quite suddenly and anonymously, so that his appearance is felt to be not only abrupt but also mysterious and enigmatic. Moreover, special emphasis is put on the form of dress of both these disciples.

Historical

[50] The historicity of the 'flight of the disciples' is certain, even if the verse is in harmony with Zech. 13.7 (14.27), and the Markan account emphasizes the motif of 'all' (14.27, 31, 50; cf. v. 53). It follows on historical grounds that the disciples of Jesus must have forsaken him – otherwise they themselves would have been crucified.

Mark 14.53–65: Jesus before the Supreme Council

53 And they led Jesus away to the high priest; and all the chief priests and the elders and the scribes assemble. 54 And Peter followed him from afar, to the courtyard of the high priest, and sat there among the servants and warmed himself by the fire.

55 But the chief priests and the whole Supreme Council sought testimony against Jesus to kill him, and found nothing, 56 for many gave false testimony against him; and their testimonies did not agree. 57 And some stood up and gave false testimony against him and said, 58 'We have heard that he said, "I will destroy this temple which is made with hands

and in three days build another which is not made with hands."' 59 And even so <u>their testimony did not agree</u>.

60 And the high priest stood up in the midst and asked Jesus and said, 'Have you no answer to what these say against you?' 61 But he kept silent and answered nothing. Again the high priest asked him and said to him, 'Are you the Christ, the son of the Most Blessed?' 62 And Jesus said, 'I am, and you will see the Son of man sitting on the right hand of Power and coming with the clouds of heaven.' 63 And the high priest tore his garments and said, 'What further need do we have of witnesses? 64 You have heard the blasphemy. What is your opinion?' And they all condemned him as deserving death.

65 Then some began to spit on him and to cover his face and to strike him with fists and to say to him, 'Prophesy.' And the servants inflicted blows on him with the scourge.

Redaction and tradition

The Markan account of the trial and condemnation of Jesus before the Supreme Council (14.53–65) is in any case secondary and composed either by Mark himself or by a predecessor. At all events it corresponds item by item to the hearing before Pilate (15.1–5, 15b–20a). Cf. the parallels:

Jesus before the Supreme Council	Jesus before Pilate
14.53a	15.1
14.55	15.3
14.60	15.4
14.61a	15.5
14.61b	15.2
14.62	15.2
14.64	15.15
14.65	15.16–20

It follows from this that the hearing before the Supreme Council has been composed on the basis of the narrative in the tradition about the hearing before Pilate and therefore cannot be regarded as a historical account. (The saying about the temple in v. 58 is an exception here.)

[61–62] These verses are a compendium of the Markan view of Jesus as the Christ, the Son of God *and* the Son of man. Since 1.1 it has been a matter of course that Jesus is the Christ. In 9.41 those who follow Jesus are described as those belonging to Christ. In 8.29 Peter, who is now in the immediate vicinity of the place of the trial, has confessed Jesus as Christ. Jesus is called the son of the Most Blessed, i.e. God, not only at the baptism (1.11) but also at the transfiguration (9.7) and by the demons (3.11; 5.7).

[63–64] The high priest understands Jesus' claim as Mark wants him to: Jesus is not simply the Jewish Messiah – this would have been an indifferent matter in Judaism – he is rather the supernatural son of God and in fact like God.

Historical

It follows from the observations on the history of the tradition that the historical value of the pericope is nil, apart from v. 58 (cf. on 11.15–19; see also on John 2.19). The question what provoked the decisive action of the Jewish authorities against Jesus is a different matter. This must have been Jesus' attitude to the temple (see above on 11.15–19). But there is no mention of that in the present passage.

Mark 14. (54,) 66–72: Peter's denial

54 And Peter followed him from afar, to the <u>courtyard</u> of the high priest, and sat there among the servants and warmed himself by the fire.

66 And when Peter was below in the <u>courtyard</u>, one of the maids of the high priest comes. 67 And when she saw Peter warming himself, she looked at him and said, 'You too were with the Nazarene, Jesus.' 68 But he <u>denied</u> and said, 'I neither know nor understand what you are saying.' And he went out into the forecourt. 69 And the maid saw him and again began to say to the bystanders, 'This man is one of them.' 70 And he again <u>denied</u>. And after a little while the bystanders again said to Peter, 'Truly you are (one) of them; for you also are a Galilean.' 71 And he began to curse and to swear, 'I do not know the man of whom you are speaking.' 72 *And immediately the cock crowed the second time. Then Peter remembered the saying that Jesus had spoken to him, 'Before the cock crows twice you will <u>deny</u> me three times.' And he cast himself down and wept.*

Redaction and tradition

Verses 54, 66–72 refer back to the announcement of the denial (vv. 26–31) and constitute the fulfilment of the second part of Jesus' prediction there. Verse 54, the beginning of the pericope of Peter's denial, was moved forward by Mark in order to link it with the narrative about the proceedings before the Supreme Council (vv. 53, 55–65). Verse 66a ('when Peter was below in the courtyard') takes up the story line which was interrupted after v. 54. This sandwich produces an impressive contrast between Jesus' confession and Peter's denial. The intention of the link between the denial and the proceedings before the Supreme Council in Mark is to contrast the confession of Jesus (14.62) and the threefold, i.e. total, denial by Peter. This contrast admonishes Christians to follow the example of Jesus in open confession.

[66–68a] These verses depict the *first* denial. Peter is in the courtyard, is recognized by a maid of the high priest and asked directly whether he too was with the Nazarene Jesus (v. 67b). Thereupon Peter says, 'I neither know nor understand what you are saying' (v. 68a). Strictly speaking this is a denial of Peter's discipleship (cf. v. 67b) and not yet a denial of Jesus. But since Peter's answer in v. 68a at the same time rejects any knowledge of Jesus, the concrete denial of Jesus in v. 71 is prepared for.

[68b–70a] The section depicts the *second* denial, which takes place in the fore-court. Again the maid sees Peter and now tells the bystanders that Jesus is one of the followers of Jesus ('this man is one of them' [v. 69b]). In contrast to the first denial, this one is not elaborated, but only stated. That fits the fact that the maid is merely 'informing' the bystanders about Peter (and is no longer addressing him, as the first time).

[70b–71] This passage contains the account of the *third* denial. Its location is apparently the same as that of the second (the forecourt), but that is not explicitly mentioned. This time the 'bystanders' to whom the maid had reported Peter's identity in the second denial, take the initiative. The assertion by the bystanders is based on the fact that Peter (like Jesus) is a Galilean. Previously they endorse what the maid has just told them (v. 69b), and this time address Peter expressly: 'You really are with him.' The content of this third denial by Peter is expressed the most strongly by cursing and swearing. Only now is there a concrete denial of Jesus. The announcement of the denial from 14.30 is really fulfilled only here.

[72] The denial in 14.54f., 66–71 and its announcement in 14.27–31 are closely connected redactionally by this verse. Just as Mark's Jesus can see the coming denial of Peter, so he has already known in advance of the betrayal of Judas (14.18–21) and of his own death and resurrection (8.31; 9.31; 10.32–34).

The question of whether the tradition available to Mark had three, two or one denials can hardly be decided. All that is certain is *that* he did have a tradition – although the demarcation of this is not certain – and that the tradition of the denial once circulated in isolation and independently of the passion story, for the link between the two is redaction.

The tradition of the denial, the precise extent of which can no longer be dis-covered, had originally been handed down in isolation from the passion story. It has a rival in the tradition of Luke 22.31f., which speaks of the disciples falling away and of a persistence of Peter in the face of Jesus' passion. Possibly the tradition in Luke 22.31f. sought to *correct* an existing tradition of the denial.

Probably Peter himself told of his denial; not, however, in connection with the passion story but in connection with his Easter experience. As a parallel we may point to the way in which there is a report of Paul's past and his present preaching of the gospel. Galatians 1.23 says, 'The one who once persecuted us now proclaims the faith which he sought to destroy.' This verse is to be designated an oral personal tra-dition which circulated in the Syrian communities persecuted by Paul and which must similarly have been known in the churches which he founded. Indeed in the context of Galatians Paul refers explicitly to the fact that the Galatians have heard of his way of life in Judaism (Gal. 1.16). In a similar way Peter's denial and his Easter experience are now reported in the 'once-now' scheme. In both cases we evidently have personal traditions with considerable historical plausibility.

Historical

In order to save his life, Peter distanced himself from his master in Jerusalem after Jesus' arrest. In this he was like his fellow disciples who had already taken flight (14.50).

Another disciple, Judas, had even collaborated in the arrest of Jesus. Presumably there were considerable tensions within the circle of disciples on the decisive journey to Jerusalem. There may have been real unrest. The saying about Satan (8.33), which is too sharp not to be authentic, indicates ambivalences in the relationship between Jesus and his 'first' disciples. The result was catastrophe, and their togetherness was abruptly ended with the execution of Jesus.

Mark 15.1–20a: Jesus before Pilate. Jesus is condemned and mocked

1 *And immediately* in the morning the chief priests with the elders and scribes, namely the whole Supreme Council, took a decision and bound Jesus, led him away and delivered him up to Pilate.

2 And Pilate asked him, 'Are you the king of the Jews?' And he answered and says to him, 'You say it.' 3 And the chief priests accused him of many things. 4 And Pilate asked him again, 'Do you answer nothing? See how many things they accuse you of!' 5 But Jesus gave no answer, so that Pilate was amazed.

6 Now at the feast he was accustomed to release to them a prisoner for whom they asked. 7 And there was one, named Barabbas, imprisoned with the rebels, who had committed a murder in the rebellion. 8 And the people came up and began to ask him to do as he was accustomed. 9 And Pilate answered them and said, 'Do you want me to release to you the king of the Jews?' 10 For he knew that the chief priests had handed him over out of envy. 11 But the chief priests stirred up the people to have him release to them Barabbas instead. 12 And Pilate answered again and said to them, 'What am I to do with the one whom you call king of the Jews?' 13 And they cried out again, 'Crucify him!' 14 But Pilate said to them, 'What evil then has he done?' But they cried out all the more, 'Crucify him!' 15 But Pilate wanted to satisfy the people and released Barabbas to them. And he had Jesus flogged and handed him over to be crucified.

16 And the soldiers led him away within the courtyard, which is the praetorium, and call together the whole division. 17 And they put a purple cloak on him and set a woven crown of thorns on him 18 and began to greet him, 'Hail, king of the Jews!' 19 *And they smote his head with a reed and spat* on him and fell on their knees and paid homage to him. 20a And when they had mocked him, they stripped him of the purple cloak and put his clothes on him.

Redaction and tradition

[1] The delivering up fulfils Jesus' prophecy from 9.31.

[2] Pilate's question is focussed by the Roman mind-set on the issue of Jesus' royal messiahship and – redactionally – presupposes the messianic confession of Jesus before the Supreme Council (14.62). *But* why does Pilate not immediately condemn Jesus to death?

[4–5] Jesus gave no answer, thus he did not recognize the forum before which he had been led as competent; but the main thing is that in this way he showed himself to be that lamb which is led to the slaughter and does not open its mouth, as the sheep which before its shearers is dumb, i.e. as the servant of God.

Cf. Isa. 53.7: 'When he was tortured, he suffered willingly and did not open his mouth, like a lamb which is led to the slaughter; and like a sheep which before its shearers is dumb, he did not open his mouth.'

[6–15] The Barabbas story is meant to increase the guilt of the Jews, who prefer a murderer to the redeemer. Here v. 10 emphasizes the cunning of the judge with a subsidiary apologetic intent. The Jewish authorities are also successful in turning the people, which previously has been on Jesus' side (cf. 11.32; 12.12) against him. The people now even demand (v. 11) Jesus' crucifixion, a request which is certainly unhistorical. Now all Israel stands against Jesus, who according to 11.10 is the one who fulfils its hopes of salvation. The behaviour announced by 'Jesus' in 12.7 is thus realized.

[15] For 'flog' cf. the prediction of Jesus in 10.34.

[16–20a] In this scene Jesus' prophecy of his own fate is fulfilled. Cf. how vv. 19 and 20a correspond to Jesus' third prediction of his passion and resurrection in 10.33–34. The passage is the basis of the composition of the 'trial' before the Supreme Council (cf. 14.65) and is orientated towards the servant of God in Isa. 50.6: 'I offered my back to those who struck me, and my cheeks to those who plucked out my hair. I did not hide my face from shame and spittle.' The motif of maltreatment in v. 19a interrupts in a nonsensical way the context, which depicts the mockery of Jesus and probably derives from Mark. Thus the scene can be transferred to Christians ('as Christ, so the Christians'), who will suffer something similar to Jesus (cf. 13.9, 11, 13). Verse 19–20a: for 'spitting on' and 'mocking' cf. the predictions of Jesus in 10.34.

Historical

[6–15] The custom of pardoning an individual by a Roman prefect is otherwise unknown and therefore can be ruled out as historical nucleus at this point. Other scholars sometimes decide for the historicity of the Lukan version (Luke 23.18), which knows no amnesty. Against this it should be noted that Luke presupposes the Markan text and has no further information.

[16–20a] The scene is unhistorical and an example of how history has been inferred from prophecy.

Mark 15.20b–41: The crucifixion and death of Jesus

20b And they lead him out to <u>crucify</u> him. 21 And they compel a passer-by, Simon of Cyrene, coming from the fields, the father of Alexander and Rufus, to bear his cross. 22 And they bring him to the place Golgotha, *which being translated means 'Place of the Skull'*. 23 And they gave him wine mixed with myrrh, but he did not take (it). 24 And they <u>crucify</u> him. And they share out his garments, by casting lots for them, who should get what. 25 *And it was the third hour, and they <u>crucified</u> him.* 26 And the inscription of his guilt was written up, 'The king of the Jews'. 27 And with him they <u>crucify</u> two robbers, one on his right hand and one on his left. [28] 29 And the passers-by reviled him and shook their heads and said, 'Ha, you who destroy the temple and build it in three days, 30 save yourself, by coming down from the <u>cross</u>!' 31 So also the high priests mocked him together with the scribes and said, 'He saved others and cannot save himself. 32 Let the Christ, the king of Israel, now come down from the <u>cross</u> that we may see and believe.' And those who were <u>crucified</u> with him also reviled him.

33 And *at the sixth hour* a darkness came over the whole land *until the ninth hour*. 34 And *at the ninth hour* Jesus cried aloud, 'Eloi, Eloi, lama sabachtani?' *Translated that means, 'My God, my God, why have you forsaken me?'* 35 And some of the bystanders, when they heard that, said, 'Look, he is calling on Elijah.' 36 And someone ran (up), filled a sponge with vinegar, stuck it on a reed, gave him to drink and said, 'Wait, let us see whether Elijah will come to take him down!' 37 And Jesus uttered a loud cry and passed away.

38 *And the curtain in the temple was torn into two pieces from top to bottom.* 39 And when the centurion standing there – in front of him – saw that he thus *passed away, he said, 'Truly this man was son of God.'*

40 *And there were also women there, looking on from afar, among them also Mary the woman from Magdala and Mary the mother of the younger James and Joses, and Salome,* 41 *who had followed him when he was in Galilee and served him, and many other (women) who had gone up with him to Jerusalem.*

Preliminary text-critical note: v. 28 runs, 'Then was the scripture fulfilled, he was reckoned among the transgressors.' This verse was certainly added only later, since it is absent from the earliest manuscripts.

Redaction and tradition

[20b–24a] These verses have been interwoven here by Mark as part of a tradition. In particular the personal names Simon of Cyrene, Alexander and Rufus and the place name Golgotha indicate tradition. In v. 23 Jesus rejects the tranquillizing drink and becomes a model in his voluntary obedience and his suffering.

[24b] This is the translation of Ps. 22.18 ('They divide my garments among themselves and cast lots for my raiment') into history.

[25] This corresponds to the Markan scheme of hours.

[26] The tablet indicating guilt points to tradition. However, it should be noted that in Mark (as opposed to Matthew, Luke and John) it is in no way attached to the cross.

[29–32] For v. 29 see 13.2 and later 15.38. The mockery scene derives from the Old Testament.

Cf. Ps. 22.7–8: 'All those who see me mock me, open their mouth and shake their head: "Let him complain to the Lord, let him help him and save him, if he has pleasure in him." '

[34] Jesus' last word corresponds to Ps. 22.2

[38] The rending of the curtain of the temple has an anti-Jewish nuance. The report about it refers back to 13.2 and 14.58. The event is conceived of as a miraculous effect of the death of Jesus, the metaphorical meaning of which must immediately have been clear to the reader of the Gospel. Hebrews 9.8 and 10.19 correspondingly presuppose that the access to the holy of holies closed to the Israelites has now been opened up by the death of Christ.

[39] The confession by the Gentile centurion at the cross that Jesus is Son of God (cf. 1.11) is the climax of the Gospel of Mark. On the cross Jesus is recognized as Son of God.

[40–41] After the disciples have abandoned Jesus (14.50), the women provide the continuity. They have gone with him on the way from Galilee to Jerusalem and are later to deliver the message of the young man in the empty tomb. The list of women in v. 40 with the explanation in v. 41 looks like an addition. As Mark certainly formulated v. 41, probably v. 40 is derived from him. The mention of the three women by name in Mark 15.40 agrees with 16.1 and 15.47: Mary Magdalene, Mary and Salome. On the other hand the surnames of Mary differ in 15.47 and 16.1; this might indicate independent traditions. But each time they agree with a surname of Mary from 15.40.

Historical

[20–24a] Simon of Cyrene did not carry Jesus' cross. Who would have had a correct recollection of that? In any case the whole passage looks like community dogmatics. However, the mention of Simon of Cyrene and his sons Alexander and Rufus by name may be interpreted to mean that these were disciples of Jesus who took up the cross of Jesus into their own lives.

[26] There was a titulus as a historical nucleus, which the other New Testament Gospels have made into the titulus *on the cross*. In the original tradition Jesus probably had a tablet round his neck, or someone else carried a tablet before him which indicated his guilt. There are examples of this from antiquity. Cf. especially Eusebius, *Church History* V, 1, 44: in the second century in Lyons the Christian Attalus was 'led around the amphitheatre; and a placard was carried before him on which was written in Latin, "This is Attalus, the Christian".' Cf. similarly in Suetonius, *Lives of the Emperors*, *Caligula* 32.2; *Domitian* 10.1. This titulus then denotes the alien perception of the Roman state authority about Jesus' aim. They must have regarded him as an emergent political messiah. So the titulus is formulated from a Roman perspective. By contrast, the mocking Jews do not speak of the king of the Jews (15.26), but of the Christ, the king of Israel (15.32). The titulus with the inscription in v. 26 is thus authentic, as it cannot be derived from the community (criterion of difference). The church would have found itself in serious political difficulties had it invented it (criterion of difference).

[34b] Jesus' cry on the cross is a product of the community and is therefore inauthentic. This follows conclusively from the contradiction between the different cries of Jesus on the cross and the lack of an appropriate eye-witness or tradent. Cf. the remarks on the corresponding passages Matt. 27.46; Luke 23.34, 43, 46; John 19.26f., 28, 30.

Mark 15.42–47: The burial of Jesus

42 *And when it was already evening*, and because it was the day of preparation, that is, the day before the sabbath, 43 Joseph of Arimathea, a *respected* member of the council, *who was also awaiting the kingdom of God*, came, *dared (it) and* went in to Pilate and asked him for the body of Jesus. 44 *And Pilate was amazed that he was already dead, and called the centurion and asked him whether he had already died. 45 And when he had learned that from the centurion, he gave Joseph the corpse.* 46 And he bought a linen cloth, took him down and wrapped him in the linen cloth. And he put him in a tomb that had been hewn out of a rock, and rolled a stone before the door of the tomb.

47 But Mary, the woman from Magdala, and Mary the mother of Joses, saw where he was laid.

Redaction and tradition

The present pericope links the narrative of the crucifixion (15.20b–41) with that of the empty tomb (16.1–8). The note of time, 'in the evening' (v. 42) picks up 'the third hour' (15.25) at which Jesus was crucified and the 'sixth . . . until the ninth hour' (15.33), the time at which a darkness set in. I.e. Jesus died at three o'clock in the afternoon (= ninth hour); by the time of the burial it is now already evening. There are two references to the crucifixion scene in v. 44: Pilate's amazement at the rapid death of Jesus makes sense above all in the context of the Markan passion story, since according to that Jesus' time of suffering was unusually short. (That is why Pilate is amazed.)

The scene is linked with what goes before through the questioning of the centurion responsible (v. 44; cf. v. 39, the centurion under the cross). There are further links with the context in the fact that 15.46b and 16.3b correspond almost word for word and the women both look on the cross from afar and also observe the burial and go to the empty tomb (15.40, 47; 16.1).

[42] The note of time 'when it was already evening' is redactional, like 4.35; 6.47; 14.17. Probably tradition underlies the mention of the day of preparation. Mark explains it for his readers as the day before the sabbath (cf. the similar explanation of Jewish customs in 7.3f.).

[43] The characterization of Joseph as a 'respected member of the council' occurs in Mark only here. However, we cannot immediately infer from it that the whole phrase derives from the tradition. The strange note could also be understood as redaction: in this way Joseph is designated a member of the Sanhedrin which condemned Jesus to death (14.55; 15.1). But Mark seems to give the note positive connotations: after all, the 'who was also awaiting the kingdom of God' shows that others than Joseph were doing so. In addition to the disciples (4.11), these included the scribe of whom Jesus says that he is 'not far from the kingdom of God' (12.34). In other words, while Mark does not designate Joseph a Christian, by the characterization mentioned and in view of the completely positive meaning that 'kingdom of God' has in Mark (see 1.15), he excludes him from the opponents of Jesus in the Sanhedrin.

Certainly Mark would have preferred to tell of a burial of Jesus by his followers (cf. 6.29: the burial of John the Baptist by his disciples). But as he had no tradition about this and on the other hand a report of the burial of Jesus by Joseph of Arimathea, a member of the council, was circulating, he made use of this tradition and undertook the improvements to Joseph's character mentioned above. But in that case there is something to be said for the assumption that Joseph's membership of the Supreme Council is part of the tradition, while his characterization as 'respected' is redactional. Matthew and Luke omit the designation of Joseph's action as daring. But precisely by this means Mark makes Joseph, who risks much, more sympathetic to the readership and further tones down his membership of the Supreme Council which is hostile to Jesus.

[44–45] These verses, which appear neither in Matthew nor in Luke, are certainly redactional and unite the scene with the context. They provide official authentication of the death and with a subsidiary apologetic purpose emphasize the reality of the death of Jesus.

[46] The statement about the burial of Jesus by Joseph is part of the tradition. The

information about the rock tomb with a stone rolled in front of it prepares for 16.3 redactionally. It is striking that Joseph *buys* linen. That implies that it is new. If we said that the burial of Jesus derives from tradition, the *new* linen may derive from redaction, which shows itself interested in keeping dishonour away from the burial of Jesus. The wrapping in (used) linen may be part of the tradition. It is customary in all the forms of burial in Judaism (cf. the Jewish abhorrence of nakedness with Acts 5.6). On the other hand there are indications which deviate from the circumstances of a normal burial. Thus we must keep in mind that Jesus was in no way buried in his family tomb in Nazareth, which would have been an essential part of an honourable burial. Furthermore Mark had reported the anointing of Jesus *before* his death in ch. 14 and had understood it as an anointing for death. But this does not amount to an anointing of the *corpse* of Jesus as this is known from Jewish burial ritual. Is there not a suspicion that Mark wanted to reinterpret the tradition of a dishonourable burial?

Yield: the tradition underlying Mark 15.42–47 reports a burial of Jesus by the Joseph of Arimathea, a member of the Supreme Council. In the historical question which is to be put next, John 19.31–37 (cf. Acts 13.29) is to be noted; this text mentions a burial by (hostile) Jews.

Historical

Roman legal practice normally provided for leaving those who had died on the cross where they were, to decay or to be devoured by vultures, jackals or other animals. This was as a warning to the living and as a way of shaming the dead.

This possibility is probably ruled out for Jesus, as the traditions relating to it agree in reporting that he was taken down from the cross (I Cor. 15.4 also presupposes that). Therefore the 'burial of Jesus' may be one of those cases in which the Roman authorities released the corpse.

Cf. Philo, *Flacc.* 83: 'I have heard of those who have been crucified who, because . . . feast days were imminent, were taken down from the cross and given to the relatives, so that they received a dignified burial in accordance with custom. For the dead too should benefit from the birthday of the sole ruler, and at the same time the holiness of the festival should be preserved.'

However, a possibility which is very well worth considering remains, that both in the earliest Markan account and also in I Cor. 15.4 the burial of Jesus was only postulated – in I Cor. 15.4 because in this way the death would be confirmed, and in Mark 15.42–47 in order to avert the rumour of a dishonourable burial which perhaps included the devouring of the corpse by vultures and jackals. In addition, a passage from the prophet Isaiah (53.9) could be a possible catalyst for the formation of the tradition: 'And he was given his tomb with the godless and the transgressors (or 'with the rich') when he had died, although he had done no injustice to anyone and no deceit was in his mouth.'

Presumably Jews took Jesus down from the cross because a crucified man who was dead might not hang on the cross over night (Deut. 21.23) and because a feast day (the Passover) was imminent. Moreover the release and deposition of Jesus from the cross also suited Pilate, because in this way he could prevent in advance any unrest in view of the large numbers of visitors to the feast.

Only conjectures are possible about the precise place of Jesus' burial. The assumption that Jesus was buried in a cemetery for those who had been executed, the location of which can no longer be ascertained by archaeological information, is almost impossible, as Jesus was not executed by the Jewish authorities. The hypothesis of a burial of Jesus in the family tomb of Joseph of Arimathea comes to grief on the tendency of early Christian accounts which betray or fear knowledge of a dishonourable burial of Jesus. The reference to the anointed bones of a crucified Jew by the name of Jejohanan re(!)buried in an ossuary in a rock tomb in the north-east of present-day Jerusalem (Giv'at ha-Mivtar) is not much help, since in that case there is an ossuary while here there is the burial of a corpse (with flesh on). As neither the disciples nor the closest members of the family troubled about Jesus' corpse, it is hardly conceivable that they could have been informed of where it was in order later at least to bury his bones. And I also regard the view sometimes put forward that Jesus was buried by the women disciples (a man by women) as being ruled out as a historical possibility in the Judaism of the time, quite apart from the lack of any attestation in the sources.

The two strands of tradition reconstructed above – Mark 15.42–47 on the one hand and John 19.31–37 and Acts 13.29 on the other – perhaps agree in knowing of Joseph of Arimathea. In that case, from a historical perspective he would have been the one commissioned to see to the burial of Jesus. It is improbable that he was a disciple or a friend of Jesus. The opposite conclusion, that he was one of the enemies of Jesus, would be just as unlikely, since – from a historical perspective – there are serious doubts about the condemnation of Jesus by the Supreme Council. We can no longer say where he (or Jews unknown to us) laid the body.

Mark 16.1–8: The proclamation of the Risen One in the empty tomb

1 And when the sabbath was past, Mary the woman from Magdala and Mary the mother of James and Salome *bought fragrant oils so that they might go and anoint him.* 2 *And very early on the first day of the week they came to the tomb as the sun was rising.* 3 *And they said to one another, 'Who will roll away the stone from the door of the tomb for us?'* 4 *And when they look up, they see that the stone has been rolled away; for it was very great.* 5 *And when they entered the tomb they saw a young man sitting on the right hand, clothed with a long white garment, and they were terrified.* 6 *And he says to them, 'Do not be terrified. You seek* Jesus of Nazareth, the crucified one. He has been raised, *he is not here. See there the place where they laid him.* 7 *But go and tell his disciples and Peter, "He is going before you to Galilee; there you will see him as he has told you."'* 8 *And they went out and fled from the tomb, for trembling and numbness seized them. And they said nothing to anyone, for they were afraid.*

Redaction and tradition

The present pericope is remarkable in a number of ways: the *first* offence that it causes relates to its position at the end of the Gospel. That raises the question: how can a Gospel have ended with the statement 'for they were afraid' (v. 8)? Now attempts have long been made to reconstruct the original ending to the Gospel of Mark. It is pointed out that various conclusions were added to it from the second century on (see on 16.9–20 and the short conclusion to Mark) and that the parallels Matthew and Luke supplemented the Mark that they had before them, which extended as far as 16.8. In view of that it is presupposed that the original conclusion to Mark was broken off at a very early stage (through the loss of a page or by a deliberate excision). That would certainly remove the problem discussed here. However, for reasons of method we must first attempt to understand the Gospel of Mark in its present form.

The *second* offence caused here lies in the content of what Mark reports. If the women did not obey the command of the young man, as v. 8 says, how did the message of the resurrection then reach the disciples and Peter? On the other hand it is certain that the Gospel of Mark was read by Christians. From that we may conclude that even if there is something wrong with this passage historically, nevertheless the message as intended by the author may be clear to the readers of the Gospel. In other words, the purpose of the implicit historical contradiction in v. 8 must be ascertained from the context of the text as a whole.

[1] The date 'third day' presupposed here is certainly part of the tradition. Here we cannot exclude the possibility that the date was meant to justify the church's festival of Easter (cf. Acts 20.7; Rev. 1.10; I Cor. 16.2 [?]). Underlying the planned anointing, the motive of which is redactional, in the tradition there could be the notion of a funeral lament by the women, cf. Luke 23.27. As in 15.42 a note of time introduces the story. The names of the women in the tradition take up those from 15.40 and 15.47. In all three cases Mary of Magdala appears at their head. Mark evidently thought that this was the same group around Mary Magdalene. As so far there had been no mention of these women disciples of Jesus in the Gospel, he adds in v. 41 that they had already followed him in Galilee and served him (cf. 1.31). Furthermore, he points out that additional women went with Jesus to Jerusalem. From this follows a kind of hope for the reader that their faithfulness to Jesus will be stronger than that of the disciples. The intended anointing recalls 14.3–9 (anointing of Jesus by the [anonymous] woman in Bethany). There it is performed 'for burial' (14.8). Because Mark here again introduces the motif of anointing from 14.3–9 in connection with women, he frames the account of the passion with narratives which have similar motifs. Other examples of such Markan frameworks are: 1.21–28 to 6.1–6 (miracle); 6.30–44 to 8.1–9 (feeding story); 8.22–26 to 10.46–52 (healing of a blind man); 15.40–41 to 15.47 (list of women).

[2] The notes of time 'very early' and 'as the sun was rising' are not in tension with one another as is sometimes said. Cf. the passages with double indications of time in Mark: 1.32, 35; 4.35; 10.30; 13.24; 14.21, 30, 43; 15.42. That one could not buy

unguents in the morning before sunrise does not disturb the narrator. The all-important thing is for the women to get to the tomb.

[3] 'Stone' and 'door of the tomb' pick up the same words from 15.46. The women's question who can roll away the stone for them is answered by the following verse.

[4] The explanation that the stone was very great enhances the miraculous deed. It was performed by someone who will be introduced in the next verse.

[5] It is a young man in white who is sitting in the tomb. He recalls the fleeing young man in 14.51–52, who probably represents the author of the Gospel. If this is one and the same person we have to reckon with symbolism. The nakedness has been clothed with a white garment, which symbolizes baptism. Mark speaks here as a preacher of the cross and resurrection of Jesus.

For the figure of the young man cf. II Macc. 3.26, 33 (two young men in splendid garments who take action against Heliodorus, the plunderer of the temple) and Gospel of Peter 9.36 (two young men descend from heaven in great radiance of light); for 'white' cf. Mark 9.3f.; Rev. 7.13. Matthew (28.2) explicitly identifies the young man as an angel, because he no longer understood the original reference to Mark.

The young man in the white garment may denote a heavenly figure. (Thus in Tobit 5.14 the angel Raphael is called a 'young man'.) The whole scene is a kind of epiphany. The 'sitting on the right' gives the message of the young man emphasis and confirms it, as 'right' indicates the correct, happy side (cf. John 21.6, etc.) and 'sit' evidently expresses the authority with which the young man speaks (cf. Dan. 7.9; Rev. 21.5). But all that does not exclude the possibility that the young man is the same figure as that in 14.51, where it is the author of the Gospel of Mark himself. For as a preacher Mark is a heavenly messenger.

The reaction of the women, their terror, has Markan colouring (the word 'be terrified' occurs in the New Testament only in Mark 9.15; 14.33; 16.5, 6; cf. further 1.27; 10.24, 32).

[6] 'Terrified' takes up the same word from v. 5. 'Jesus of Nazareth, the crucified one' refers back to the passion narrative (14–15) and to the predictions of the passion (8.31; 9.31; 10.34). The fact that Jesus is called 'of Nazareth' (cf. 1.24; 10.47; 14.67) makes the identification with the earthly Jesus certain. The message of the young man is that Jesus has been raised. It corresponds to Jesus' own prediction in 8.31; 9.31; 10.34. The reference to the empty tomb ('he is not here') underlines the reality of the resurrection of Jesus. But here the sequence must be noted: first comes the statement 'Jesus has been raised'; only then does the empty tomb appear. So it does not say, 'Because the tomb is empty Jesus was raised,' but, 'Jesus is not here, for he has been raised, so the tomb is empty.'

[7] This verse contains the charge to the women to tell the disciples and Peter that Jesus will go before them into Galilee. The phrase 'the disciples and Peter' recalls

I Cor. 15.5 and may be regarded as an offshoot of that primal tradition of an appearance to Cephas and the twelve. The young man continues, 'There you will see him, as he has told you.' This is an explicit reference back to Mark 14.28 ('But after my resurrection, I will go before you into Galilee'); the redactional character of the two verses emerges from this. Granted, 14.28 does not explicit mention any seeing of Jesus, but that is presupposed, because 16.7 ('go before and see') is emphatically a parallel to 14.28 ('go before'). Here Jesus' going before is related, as in 10.32, to the Christian way which has to be followed in the discipleship of Jesus; Mark stands in the primitive Christian tradition in which the 'way' has become a technical term for the Christian way (cf. Acts 9.2).

[8] The flight of the women recalls the flight of the disciples in 14.50. Their fear is described twice in the present verse (cf. the similar duplication in Mark 10.32). It leads to their telling no one anything, which represents disobedience to the express command of the young man. This is matched by the failure of the disciples through-out the Gospel of Mark, so that 16.1–8 is the last report of a failure of those who were with Jesus – this time it is the women.

Yield: at the end of his Gospel Mark has composed a unit in which he has concen-trated all the points which were important for him: (a) Jesus' death and resurrection; (b) the failure of the disciples, men and women, to understand; (c) the ongoing preaching of the gospel; (d) the important role of Galilee as the location and starting point of the gospel. In addition he has further endorsed his own authority as an eye-witness.

It is doubtful whether a complete story about the tomb existed before Mark, as the text is overlaid with Markan redaction. But the names of the women, the mention of the third day and the figures of Peter and the disciples as those to whom the risen Christ will appear are certainly part of the tradition (cf. I Cor. 15.5: 'Christ appeared to Cephas, then to the twelve'). By saying that the women did not hand on the mes-sage of the resurrection any further, Mark implicitly identifies himself as the first one to tell the story of the empty tomb.

Historical

It follows from the analysis of the tradition that the historical yield is nil: (a) in the story we merely find the claim that the crucified Jesus has been raised and therefore that the tomb is said to have been empty; (b) Mary Magdalene's visit (with the other two women) to the tomb of Jesus on the day after the sabbath is hardly to be termed historical.

Mark 16.9–20: A secondary conclusion to the Gospel of Mark

9 Now when Jesus had risen early on the first day of the week, he appeared first to Mary of Magdala, from whom he had driven out seven evil spirits. 10 She went and proclaimed it to those who had been with him and were (now) mourning and weeping. 11 And when they heard that he was alive and was seen by her, <u>they did not believe it</u>. 12 After that he revealed himself in another form to two of them on the way when they were going through the country. 13 And they went back and proclaimed it to the rest. But they <u>did not believe</u> them.

14 Lastly, when the eleven were reclining at table, he revealed himself to them and rebuked their <u>unbelief</u> and the hardness of their heart, that they <u>had not believed</u> those who had seen him as risen. 15 And he said to them, 'Go into all the world and preach the gospel to the whole creation. 16 Whoever <u>believes</u> and is baptized will be saved; but whoever <u>does not believe</u> will be condemned. 17 And the signs which will follow those who <u>believe</u> are these: in my name they will cast out evil spirits, speak in new tongues, 18 hold up snakes, and if they drink anything deadly it will not harm them; they will lay their hands on sick people and they will recover.'

19 After the Lord Jesus had spoken with them, he was raised to heaven and sat at the right hand of God, 20 and they went out and preached everywhere. And the Lord worked with them and confirmed the word with the signs which followed.

Redaction and tradition

The text shows some peculiarities. It presupposes the first appearance to Mary Magdalene and in so doing probably suppresses the first appearance to Cephas. But at the same time the significance of the appearance to Mary Magdalene is toned down: certainly it appears at the head of a chain of witnesses, but all the weight lies on the later appearance to eleven disciples, to whom indeed Jesus' instructions, related in detail, are given (vv. 15–18).

The motif of unbelief runs through the section (vv. 11, 13 and 14). At the same time there is a call for *right* belief (vv. 16 and 17). Thus the text is to be regarded as a defence of belief in the resurrection with a simultaneous reference to the power of the church (v. 18).

The passage was certainly not first composed specially as a conclusion for the Gospel of Mark, but already existed previously at the beginning of the second century, probably as a kind of Easter catechism in community instruction. It is a kind of collection of the Easter accounts known to the author. It is impossible, however, to demonstrate a knowledge of the Gospels of Mark and Matthew, though there is knowledge of the Gospels of Luke and John and of Acts.

Here the parallel passages are put in brackets after the corresponding verses of the conclusion to Mark: vv. 9f. (Luke 8.2; John 20.1, 11–18); v. 11 (Luke 24.11); vv. 12f. (Luke 24.13–35); v. 14 (Luke 24.36–43; Acts 1.4); vv. 15f. (Luke 24.47); vv. 17f.

(Acts 16.16–18; 2.1–11; 28.3–6; 3.1–10; 9.31–35; 14.8–10; 28.8f.); v. 19 (Acts 1.9; Luke 24,51); v. 20 (Acts generally).

Historical

The historical yield is nil.

Appendix: The short ending to Mark

But everything that was commanded them (= the women) they preached briefly to those around Peter. After that Jesus himself also issued through them from East to West the holy and imperishable preaching of eternal salvation.

Explanation

The text was written in Egypt in the fourth century and is intended to furnish the Gospel of Mark with a conclusion which corresponds to the young man's instruction to the women (16.7) and the church's Easter legend. It was combined later with the long conclusion (= Mark 16.9–20), but its author certainly did not know the latter. Historically it is even more worthless than the long conclusion, but it shows that the early Christians, like Matthew and Luke before them, could not cope with the authentic conclusion to the Gospel of Mark.

II

The Gospel of Matthew

Matthew 1.1–7: The Genealogy of Jesus

1   *Credentials of the origin of Jesus Christ, the son of David, the son of Abraham.*
2   [1]Abraham fathered Isaac.
    [2]Isaac fathered Jacob
    [3]Jacob fathered Judah *and his brothers.*
3   [4]Judah fathered Perez and Zerah *with Tamar.*
    [5]Perez fathered Hezron.
    [6]Hezron fathered Ram.
4   [7]Ram fathered Amminadab.
    [8]Amminadab fathered Nahshon.
    [9]Nahshon fathered Salmon.
5   [10]Salmon fathered Boaz *with Rahab.*
    [11]Boaz fathered Obed with Ruth.
    [12]Obed fathered Jesse.
6   [13]Jesse fathered king David.
    [1/14]David fathered Solomon *with the (wife) of Uriah.*
7   [2]Solomon fathered Rehoboam.
    [3]Rehoboam fathered Abijah.
    [4]Abijah fathered Asa.
8   [5]Asa fathered Jehoshaphat.
    [6]Jehoshaphat fathered Joram.
    [7]Joram fathered Uzziah.
9   [8]Uzziah fathered Jotham.
    [9]Jotham fathered Ahaz.
    [10]Ahaz fathered Hezeiah.
10 [11]Hezekiah fathered Manasseh.
    [12]Manasseh fathered Amon.
    [13]Amon fathered Josiah.
11 [14]Josiah fathered Jechoniah *and his brothers*
    at the time of the Babylonian captivity.
12 *After the Babylonian captivity:*
    [1]Jechoniah fathered Shealtiel.
    [2]Shealtiel fathered Zerubbabel.

13   ³Zerubbabel fathered Abiud.
       ⁴Abiud fathered Eliakim.
       ⁵Eliakim fathered Azor.
14   ⁶Azor fathered Zadok.
       ⁷Zadok fathered Achim.
       ⁸Achim fathered Eliud.
15   ⁹Eliud fathered Eleazar.
       ¹⁰Elieazar fathered Matthan.
       ¹¹Matthan fathered Jacob.
16   ¹²Jacob fathered ¹³Joseph, *the husband of Mary, from whom was fathered Jesus, who is called* ¹⁴*Christ.*

17 *Now all the generations from Abraham to David are fourteen generations. From David to the Babylonian captivity are fourteen generations. From the Babylonian captivity to Christ are fourteen generations.*

Redaction

[1] With 'origin' the introductory sentence points forward to 1.18. The beginnings and conclusions of the works of ancient authors are of great importance for them and they are often the key to our understanding their works. Verse 1 refers to the genealogy in 1.2–16 or the introductory chapters of the Gospel. As Son of David, Jesus is king of Israel; the Abrahamic sonship refers to the underlying theme of the Matthaean prehistory and the Gospel of Matthew generally: the inclusion of the Gentiles in an expanded, new Israel. For in Judaism Abraham is the type of the proselytes.

[2–16a] The genealogy consists of a series of monotonous, short sentences. Additional redactional observations have been inserted into them: women (vv. 3, 5ab, 6b, cf. v. 16), brothers (vv. 2c,11), David as king (v. 6a), and twice the exile (vv. 11f.). All four women are non-Jewish and serve as an indication that the messiah of Israel also brings salvation to the Gentiles (cf. 28.19f.). This produces two further points that the four women have in common by comparison with the fifth woman, Mary.

First, their actions could have offended Jewish sensibilities: *Tamar's* children were born incestuously (Gen. 38); *Rahab* was a prostitute (Josh.2.1); Ruth got her second husband only by sexual incitement (Ruth 3.4, 7–9, 12–13) and *Bathsheba's* relationship to David began with adultery (II Sam. 11). The fact that Matthew does not speak of Bathsheba, but of 'the (wife) of Uriah'; probably indicates that he is not thinking of David's later wife, but of the act of adultery.

Secondly, the text sees all four as heroines, and through their male partners Judah, Salmon, Boaz and David they have become forbears of the Messiah.

Joseph, the husband of the fifth woman, Mary, is initially open to the same misunderstanding that could have been caused to unsuspecting readers of the narratives about the other four women. However, he is led to the right understanding by the revelation of an angel (1.20). This interpretation of the text fits in well with the evidence that Jews related the illegitimate birth of Jesus through Mary (cf. on Mark 6.3). Matthew explains this stain on Mary by referring to the four women in the genealogy mentioned above, who only seemingly had a stain.

[16b] Jesus Christ is the destination of the genealogy. The expression 'Jesus who is called Christ' appears word for word on Pilate's lips in the passion story (27.17); Pilate wants to release Jesus despite bitter Jewish opposition because he is convinced of his innocence. By interrupting the scheme of the genealogy, which laconically introduces one father after another, and by using the same verb in the passive in speaking of Jesus being fathered from Mary, he includes Joseph as Jesus' father. In so doing he prepares the readers for the following narrative about the fathering of Jesus from the spirit of God and his birth from the virgin Mary. Nonetheless the text indicates that Matthew knows the suspicion of illegitimacy which attaches to Jesus.

[17] This verse deciphers the redactional division: the genealogy consists of three times fourteen generations. If the genealogy extends only to Joseph, for this scheme to work David and the Babylonian exile have to be counted twice. But as Christ is explicitly mentioned in v. 17, he is probably the fourteenth member of the series; in that case the Babylonian exile counts only once.

The division into three times fourteen must go back to Matthew. Seven ($14 = 2 \times 7$) is a symbolic number which often appears in the Gospel of Matthew: seven demons (12.45); seven loaves (15.34); seven baskets (15.37); forgiving seven times (18.21f.); seven brothers (22.25); seven woes (23.13–32).

Of the passages mentioned here 12.45 and 23.13–32 occur only in the First Gospel. 15.34, 37 and 22.25 have been taken over from Mark, while 18.21f. goes back to the sayings source Q.

Jesus as Son of David and Abraham: the evangelist gives different directions to the genealogy which he has taken over. Two of them appear only in the superscription, in v. 1, which names Jesus both son of David and son of Abraham. As son of David Jesus is king of Israel. Therefore in v. 6 the author probably emphasized David as king. In the very next chapter (2.1–12), Jesus is the counterpart of king Herod, and in 21.1–11 he enters Jerusalem as the other, gentle king (cf. 21.5).

Tradition

The genealogy, which presumably derives from tradition – or (less likely) goes back to Matthew – belongs to the type of the so-called straight-line genealogies (without branches) which in antiquity very often served the purpose of legitimation (examples of genealogies with branches can be found, for example, in I Chron. 1.1–5, 17; 7; 8). It focusses on Joseph as the father of Jesus and means to show that Jesus is descended from the patriarch Abraham through the royal dynasty of Israel. He is not only a true Jew but a son of David. For an example of another genealogy of Jesus see Luke 3.23–38.

Historical

For a clarification of the historicity of the genealogy cf. the observations on Luke 3.23–38.

Matthew 1.18–25: The announcement of the birth of Jesus

18 *Now the origin of Jesus Christ was as follows* (and not otherwise): When his mother Mary had been betrothed to Joseph, before they had come together, it proved that she was pregnant by Holy Spirit (and not by another man). 19 But Joseph, her husband, who *was righteous and* did not want to expose himself to shame, resolved to put her away secretly. 20 But after he had considered this, look, an angel of the Lord appeared to him in a dream and said, 'Joseph, son of David, do not fear to take Mary, your wife, to you, for that which is fathered in her is of Holy Spirit. 21 And she will bear a son and you shall give him the name Jesus, for he will save his people from their sins.' 22 *Now all this happened to fulfil what the Lord has spoken through the prophet, who says,* 23 'Look, the virgin will become pregnant and bear a son, and she will give him the name Immanuel,' *which being translated means, 'God is with us.'* 24 And Joseph, when he awoke from sleep, did as the angel of the Lord had commanded him and took his wife to him. 25 *And he did not know her until she had borne a son, and he gave him the name Jesus.*

Redaction

[18a] The title clause ('origin') refers back to vv. 1 and 16 and comes from Matthew. He began his work with v. 1: 'Credentials of the *origin* of Jesus Christ, the son of David, the son of Abraham.' After depicting the genealogy from Abraham to Joseph (vv. 2–16a), in v. 16b he goes over to the birth story which now follows. This is done somewhat clumsily, because the story in 1.18–25 will show that the Holy Spirit fathers Jesus, whereas the genealogy leads us to expect Joseph as the father. Matthew resolves this difficulty by stating that Jesus is fathered from Mary (and not through Joseph, see above on 1.16b). Nevertheless Joseph takes his pregnant fiancée into his house and makes her son legitimate by himself naming him (1.20f.,24f.). Thus Jesus has been adopted into the family of the sons of David. In this way there is no longer a contradiction between the genealogy and the birth narrative.

[18b] The observation that Mary is pregnant 'of holy Spirit' anticipates the

instruction which Joseph will be given only later by the angel (v. 20) and really dissolves the narrative tension too early. The reference forward to the fathering by the Holy Spirit presupposes that the reader has some information. By reinforcing v. 18a it is to reject *once again* in advance the Jewish charge that Jesus had been born out of wedlock. Thus the reader already knows what Joseph learns only in v. 20: Jesus has been fathered by the Holy Spirit.

It is striking that the conception of Jesus is not narrated directly, but only its consequences. This is a further point of contact for the suspicion that Matthew is responding to attacks which allude to the questionable origin of Jesus as a child fathered before marriage (and/or in fornication).

[19] With this verse Joseph, who is betrothed to Mary and thus legally married, becomes the centre of the action. At that time the period between betrothal and marriage, during which the engaged couple could not yet have sexual intercourse, usually lasted from six to twelve months. For this period the young fiancée, who was between twelve and fourteen years old, still lived in her parents' house, but was already regarded as the wife of her husband and could theoretically also become a widow. Joseph must suspect Mary of adultery because of her pregnancy and therefore wants to put her away, i.e. divorce her.

He chose a mild kind of separation. Matthew describes Joseph as 'righteous'. That indicates his friendly disposition (cf. 25.37; 10.41; 13.43) and explains his intention not to shame his wife. At the same time doing the will of God, which for example in no way allowed the acceptance of illegitimate children into the family, becomes consonant with being righteous.

[20] As verse 18a already indicated, Matthew's concern is to explain the implantation of the son of a virgin into the tribe of David. The form of address to Joseph, 'son of David', takes up the superscription in 1.1, where Jesus is designated son of David. Only at this point in the New Testament is someone other than Jesus called son of David – an indication of how important the figure of Joseph is for Matthew.

[21] The explanation of the name Jesus indicates the future task of the Messiah: 'He will save his people from their sins.' The forgiveness of sins takes place in Matthew's community (cf. 26.28). 2.6 makes the term 'people' more specific: as 'my people Israel'. But in Matthew 'people' predominantly has negative connotations (cf. 13.15; 15.8; 27.25) or shows a distant relation to Jesus, e.g. in the formula used by the chief priests and elders of the people: 26.47; 27.1; cf. 21.23; 2.4. Thus in 1.21 Matthew is thinking of the *new* people of God.

[22–23] The fulfilment quotation according to which the new-born child is to be called 'Immanuel' interprets 'all this' as the fulfilment of prophetic prediction, indeed as a word which the Lord himself has spoken through the prophet (Isa. 7.14). The Greek translation of the Old Testament (= Septuagint), which wrongly renders the Hebrew word for 'young woman' with 'virgin', underlies this passage. The translation of Immanuel as 'God with us' anticipates the promise of the Risen One that he will be with the community (28.20).

[24] This verse narrates the carrying out of the instructions given in v. 20: Joseph takes his wife to himself. So he does not put her away, as according to v. 19 he had initially planned.

[25] That Joseph has no sexual intercourse with Mary before the birth of the child makes it clear that truly no man has been involved here. This verse does not yet have in prospect the later church view that Joseph did not sleep with Mary after the birth either.

Yield: An important purpose of the story is to make a theological statement: Jesus is the Immanuel. Thus right from the beginning Matthew refers to the living reality of the community in which Jesus is present every day until the end of the world (28.20). Therefore if in 28.16–20 it is true that the Risen One is none other than the Earthly One and that being a Christian means keeping the commandments of the earthly Jesus, 1.18–25 make it clear that the Earthly One is none other than the Exalted One who is with his community. At the same time, the beginning of the Gospel of Matthew – and that is significant in the Gospel of the law and the commandments – contains a clear reference to the grace that has come about through Jesus Christ.

Furthermore the narrative has an *ethical* aspect, which relates to the figure of the righteous Joseph and his obedience.

It is also important because in it an Old Testament prophecy becomes reality. To this extent and only to this extent the virgin birth is also important: it is a fulfilment of Isa. 7. Here – in contrast to later church tradition – it is not regarded as cleanness from impure sexuality, but is a further explanation of the implanting of Jesus in the family of David which was left open in 1.16. To exaggerate somewhat, Jesus is a son of David *despite* the virgin birth which is known to the community.

But this episode is also rooted to controversy. It is related by Matthew in order to ward off hostile Jewish rumours of a scandal surrounding the birth of Jesus and at the same time to explain the true situation.

Tradition

It is almost impossible to reconstruct a precise outline or even a form of the tradition, as Matthew has reworked the story comprehensively. However, the following elements of tradition can be identified: (a) the pregnancy of Mary without the involvement of Joseph; (b) the fathering of Jesus through the Holy Spirit and – connected with this – (c) the birth of Jesus from the virgin Mary on the basis of a wrong translation (see on vv. 22–23).

Historical

The fathering of Jesus from the Holy Spirit and his birth from the virgin Mary are unhistorical:

(a) There are numerous parallels in the history of religion which similarly speak of sons of God who have been fathered and born in a miraculous way. Thus – in legend – Alexander the Great and the emperor Augustus, to mention only these, were fathered by God.

(b) The fathering of Jesus by the Spirit and the virgin birth of Jesus are attested only rarely in the New Testament and moreover exclusively in late strata of the tradition.

(c) If we wanted to regard the virgin birth as historical we would have to assume that Mary gave an account of her intimate experiences only after a long silence. However, what the earliest Synoptic tradition reports about the family of Jesus tells against that (cf. on Mark 3.21).

(d) The historicity of the birth of Jesus from a virgin is also excluded on scientific grounds.

What we can extract as a historical fact behind 1.18–25 is a hostile rumour about the illegitimacy of Jesus which was disseminated by non-Christian Jews. That is the real core of Matthew's story. But in that case it is also clear that the fathering of Jesus by an unknown man must be regarded as a further historical element. This fathering of Jesus by an unknown man might also be concluded from the fact that in the earliest tradition Jesus is called 'son of Mary' (Mark 6.3, see there).

How did the 'virgin' have Jesus as a child if Joseph is not the father? Here Jewish polemic speaks clearly and at the latest in the second century relates that Mary had an affair with the Roman soldier Panthera. If we exclude some elements, this seems to be on the right lines. However, we must rule out a sexual transgression on the part of Mary, which is presupposed there, since in that case Joseph would hardly have taken his fiancée Mary to himself. Moreover we should note that the Jewish patriarchal structure of Mary's family and her presumed age at the time of the betrothal (between twelve and fourteen) make a sexual adventure highly improbable. Therefore – shocking though this may seem to begin with – we are driven to assume the rape of Mary as a likely explanation of this dark stain on her history and that of her son Jesus.

The general objection may be made that in that case Mary would no longer have been acceptable as the Jewish mother of a large family. Mark 6.3 and I Cor. 9.5 indeed presuppose the existence of brothers and sisters of Jesus. But sexual blemishes on women, which included rape, were important in the Judaism of that time only in the case of marriage with a priest (and Joseph was not a priest). For example, a former prisoner of war could not become the wife of a priest, because here the possibility of rape could not be ruled out. Josephus writes this about it in his *Jewish Antiquities* at the beginning of the second century:

'From the priests Moses exacted a double degree of purity. He forbade them to wed a harlot, he forbids them to wed a slave or a prisoner of war or such women as earn their living by hawking or innkeeping or who have for whatsoever reason been cast off by their former husbands' (III, 276)

These regulations are connected with the exegesis of Lev. 21.13f.: 'And he (viz. the high priest) shall take a wife in her virginity. A widow, or one divorced, or a woman who has been defiled, or a harlot, these he shall not marry; but he shall take to wife a virgin of his own people.' Cf. also the fact narrated by Josephus, *Antt.* XIII, 291f., that John Hyrcanus (died 104 BCE) was told by the Pharisee Eleazar that he had to resign from the high priesthood because his mother had been a prisoner of war in the reign of Antiochus Epiphanes (175–164 BCE) (and therefore possibly had been raped).

Now against the reconstruction proposed here it could be pointed out that had Mary been raped, according to Jewish law she remained innocent and therefore the expression 'son of Mary' was unjustified. For if a rape is not a blemish, Jesus could not have been denigrated by the designation 'son of Mary'. Theoretically that is correct. But the modern distinction between law and morality in fact already existed at that time. Arguments were resorted to in the controversy which may not have been legitimate but which were all the more effective – and these always have to do with sexuality.

Matthew 2.1–23: The magicians from the East and Herod's infanticide

1 *Now when Jesus was born in Bethlehem in Judaea in the days of Herod the king, look, magicians from the East came to Jerusalem, saying,* 2 *'Where is the (new)born king of the Jews? For we have seen his* <u>star</u> *in the East, and have come to worship him.'*

3 *When Herod the king heard this, he was troubled, and all Jerusalem with him.* 4 *And he assembled all the chief priests and scribes of the people, and enquired of them where the Christ was to be born.* 5 *And they told him,* 'In Bethlehem of Judaea; for so it is written by the prophet, 6 "And you, O Bethlehem, in the land of Judah, are by no means least among the rulers of Judah; for from you shall come a ruler who will govern my people Israel." '

7 *Then Herod summoned the magicians secretly and ascertained from them precisely when the star had appeared;* 8 *and he sent them to Bethlehem, saying, 'Go and search diligently for the child, and when you have found him bring me word, that I too may come and worship him.'*

9 *And they listened to the king and went away. And look, the* <u>star</u> *which they had seen in the East went before them, till it came to rest over (the place) where the child was.* 10 *When they saw the* <u>star</u>, *they rejoiced exceedingly.* 11 *And they went into the house and saw the child with Mary his mother, and they fell down and worshipped him and opened their treasures and offered him their gifts, gold and frankincense and myrrh.*

12 *And they received a prophecy in a dream not to return to Herod, and departed to their own country by another way.*

13 *Now when they had gone back, look, an angel of the Lord appeared to Joseph in a dream and said, 'Rise, take the child and his mother, and flee to Egypt, and remain there till I tell you; for Herod is about to search for the child, to destroy him.' 14 And he rose and took the child and his mother by night, and departed to Egypt, 15 and remained there until the death of Herod. This was to fulfil what the Lord had spoken by the prophet, 'Out of Egypt have I called my son.'*

16 *Then Herod, because he saw that he had been tricked by the magicians, became very angry, and he sent and had all the male children in Bethlehem and in all that region who were two years old or under killed, according to the time which he had ascertained from the magicians. 17 Then was fulfilled what was spoken by the prophet Jeremiah:* 18 'A voice was heard in Ramah, wailing and loud lamentation, Rachel weeping for her children; she refused to be consoled, because they were no more.'

19 *But when Herod had died, behold, an angel of the Lord appeared in a dream to Joseph in Egypt, 20 and said, 'Arise, take the child and his mother, and go to the land of Israel, for those who sought the child's life are dead.' 21 And he arose and took the child and his mother, and went to the land of Israel. 22 But when he heard that Archelaus reigned over Judaea in place of his father Herod, he was afraid to go there, and being warned in a dream he withdrew to the district of Galilee. 23 And he went and dwelt in a city called Nazareth, that what was spoken by the prophets might be fulfilled,* 'He shall be called a Nazorene.'

Redaction

The present text is independent of the section 1.18–25 and does not presuppose it. Moreover it is not itself a unity, since the combination of the story of the magicians and that of the infanticide is certainly secondary and derives from an unhistorical link which is rooted in dogmatics. The author depicts a sacred past which is governed by the notion of the fulfilment of Old Testament prophecies. The birth in Bethlehem, the stay in Egypt, the journey to Nazareth – all this is backed up with quotations from the Old Testament (vv. 6, 15, 18, 23) which today are rarely construed as predictions of future events (cf. the remarks about this in the next section).

Moreover, even where the author needs the vengeance of Herod to emphasize the deliverance of the child Jesus, he does not hesitate to look in the Old Testament for a basis for this treacherous action. It should be emphasized in advance that all this is sheer invention, which is made even worse by the elaboration of a horrific infanticide.

Division

A.   The magicians (vv. 1–12)
   a.   Arrival of the magicians in Jerusalem (vv. 1f.)
   b.   Privy council in Jerusalem (vv. 3–6)

     c. Interrogation of the magicians (vv. 7f.)
     d. The magicians travel to Bethlehem (vv. 9f.)
     e. Adoration by the magicians (v. 11)
     f. Return of the magicians (v. 12)
B.   Flight of Joseph's family to Egypt (vv. 13–15)
C.   Herod's infanticide (vv. 16–18)
D.   Return of the family from Egypt (vv. 19–23)

The scene of the first three subdivisions of the story of the magicians is Jerusalem; the last two take place in Jerusalem. The individual parts are held together *first* by the twofold journey and arrival of the magicians (vv. 1,9), *secondly* by the motif of the star (vv. 2,9f.), *thirdly* by the contrast between King Herod and the King of the Jews (vv. 1f.), and *fourthly* by the contrast between Herod and the magicians, whose intention to worship the new king (v. 2) Herod hypocritically takes up (v. 8).

[1] This indicates the situation and links the present narrative with 1.18–25. The birth of Jesus in Bethlehem to which 1.25 looks forward and on which 2.1 looks back is not really narrated. The readers know that the magicians (this term is used in a positive sense here, in contrast to the negative usage otherwise customary in early Christianity, as for example in Acts 13.6–8) are Gentiles. That emerges from the next verse.

[2] The magicians paraphrase the messianic expectation known to them and enquire about the birthplace, not of the king of Israel, but of the king of the Jews.

[3] The magicians are met by Herod the Great (37–4 BC) and 'all Jerusalem with him', who react in shock, since they have understood the message. From now on – contrary to the historical facts (Herod the Great was unpopular with the people) – Herod and all the people of Jerusalem form the Jewish front which rejects the new royal child. Their behaviour seems all the more abhorrent since they themselves know the real significance of the star. In this way Matthew gives a foretaste of what will take place in the passion narrative and after the 'resurrection'. There at the end of the Gospel the Jewish people will say, 'His blood be on us and on our children' (27.25), and the Jewish leaders, though they know better, will suppress the news of the 'resurrection' by bribing the Roman soldiers (cf. 28.11–15).

[4] This verse endorses what has been said: Herod gathers all the chief priests and scribes, who are pointedly termed scribes of the (Jewish) people. The combination of Jesus' opponents into groups of two is typical of Matthew. The chief priests, who later appear as the key initiators of the execution of Jesus, and the scribes as stubborn opponents of Jesus in his activity, also appear together in 20.18 and 21.15.

[5–6] Herod asks them about the birthplace of the Messiah. The scribes answer the king's question with the prophet Micah 5.1: Bethlehem in Judaea is the birthplace. Matthew agrees with that, but here avoids using his fulfilment formula (cf.

vv. 15, 17, 23), since the hostile scribes are speaking. Although the Jewish scribes recognize that this is the expected messianic shepherd of the people of God, they go off to Herod. Here we have an anti-Jewish point made by Matthew, the final redactor.

[7] The secret interrogation of the magicians by the king points forward to v. 16, which is couched in similar terms.

[8] This verse serves to show Herod up as a hypocrite. He does not at all want to worship the child, but to murder it.

[9–10] As in related accounts, here too the readers are to detect God's guidance, which is at work in the whole event.

[11] This forms the climax of the story: the magicians find the child and his mother in the house, worship him and bring him precious gifts.

[12] This rounds off the story. The child Jesus remains safe. In a dream the magicians are instructed not to return to Jerusalem.

[13–15] These verses report the flight into Egypt. The narrative is very terse and inculcates two notions: God's guidance alone, God's plan which is expressed in the fulfilment quotation (cf. Hos. 11.1), rescues the small child.

[16] The description of the cruel infanticide in Bethlehem forms a dark foil to this and emphatically expresses the actual threat to Jesus.

[17–18] The fulfilment quotation from Jer. 31.15 indicates that the cruel event, too, corresponds with the divine plan. Originally the 'prophecy' was supposed to have been fulfilled by the deportation of the people of Judah to Babylon: there was no thought of an event lying in a distant future.

[19–21] These verses, which are very similar in language to v. 13f. and thus show themselves to be a redactional link, narrate the rounding off of the divine plan and bring Jesus, the son of David and Abraham, back into the land of the people to whom he is sent.

(22f.) These verses have been entirely composed by Matthew, as is shown by the parallel to them in Matt. 4.12–13. As Matthew needed an Old Testament quotation for Jesus' home town, he filled this gap himself forcibly and understood Nazorene, contrary to its meaning, as an inhabitant of Nazareth.

Tradition

Since the exegesis has shown that the text has been shaped throughout by Matthew, it is difficult to extract a clearly defined text on which this was based. Therefore the task of an analysis of the tradition is to work out motifs and models on the basis of which Matthew may have composed the story.

A Roman historian active in the time of the emperor Augustus (27 BC to AD 14) reports a miraculous star at the birth and accession of Mithridates VI the Great (c.132–63 BC):

'His future greatness was even proclaimed in advance by miraculous heavenly signs. In the year in which he was born and also in the year in which he first began to reign, during the twofold period a comet shone for seventy days, so brightly that it seemed to make the whole heaven glow. For not only did it occupy the fourth part of the heavens with its magnitude, but the gleam which flashed forth from it even surpassed the splendour of the sun; and it occupied the period of four hours each time it rose and set' (Justinus, *Epitome from Pompeius Trogus* 37,2).

There are similarly many parallels to the story of Herod wanting to kill the new-born king. The motif appears both in the Old Testament saga of Moses (Ex. 2) and in many Greek and Roman authors, and is often associated with that of an infanticide. Cf. also the imperial biographer Suetonius (born around AD 70), *Augustus* 94:

'According to Julius Marathus, a few months before he (viz. Augustus) was born a portent was generally observed at Rome, which gave warning that nature was pregnant with a king for the Roman people; thereupon the senate in consternation decreed that no male child born that year should be reared; but those whose wives were with child saw to it that the decree was not filed in the treasury (i.e. did not assume the force of law).'

History

In view of the thorough redactional shaping of the text, the observations at the beginning of the redactional analysis, and the parallel motifs mentioned, the historical yield for Matt. 2 is nil.

Similarly, the fact that Luke as well as Matthew has a birth narrative does not contribute anything to the historical credibility of Matthew's narrative. On the contrary, because the two accounts are incompatible their historical value is even less.

(a) Matthew and Luke do not agree in dating the birth of Jesus. In Matthew the birth of Jesus is said to have taken place while Herod the Great was still alive (he died in 4 BC); by contrast, in Luke Jesus was born shortly after a tax assessment ordered by the emperor Augustus at the time when Quirinius was governor of Syria (from AD 6). However, we know nothing from non-Christian sources of a census under Augustus which extended throughout the empire. The first census in Judaea (not in the whole of the Roman empire) was only taken in AD 6/7.

(b) In Matthew, Jesus' parents live in Bethlehem and move to Nazareth only after the return from Egypt. By contrast, Luke has the parents go to Bethlehem from their abode in Nazareth before the birth of Jesus.

(c) Luke reports nothing about magicians from the East, a miraculous star, a flight to Egypt and an infanticide by Herod; conversely, Matthew knows nothing of a proclamation of Jesus' birth to the shepherds.

A last attempt, as desperate as it is misplaced, to harmonize the two narratives would be to assume that both sought to depict the same thing in different ways or that what was reported by Matthew presupposed the already Lukan account existing (or vice versa). Rather, we have two equally unhistorical narratives.

Matthew 3.1–12: John the Baptist

1 In those days John the Baptist comes and preaches in the wilderness of Judaea 2 and says, 'Repent, for the kingdom of heaven has come near! 3 For this is he who was named by Isaiah the prophet when he says, "It is a voice of a preacher in the wilderness, 'Prepare the way for the Lord and make his paths level.'" 4 Now he, John, had a garment of camel hair and a leather girdle around his loins; and his food was locusts and wild honey. 5 Then the city of Jerusalem and all Judaea and all the region around the Jordan went out to him 6 and had themselves baptized by him in the Jordan and confessed their sins.

7 *But when he saw many Pharisees and Sadducees coming to his baptism,* he said *to them,* 'You brood of vipers, who assured you that you would escape the future wrath? 8 See that you bear fruit worthy of repentance. 9 Do not simply think that you can say among yourselves, "We have Abraham as our father." For I say to you, God can raise up children to Abraham from these stones. 10 Already the axe is laid to the roots of the trees. Now every tree that does not bear good fruit will be cut down and cast into the fire.

11 I baptize you with water for repentance; but he who comes after me is stronger than I. I am not worthy to carry his shoes; he himself will baptize you with holy Spirit and fire.

12 The winnowing fork is in his hand, and he will sweep his threshing floor and gather his wheat into the barns; but the chaff he will burn with unquenchable fire.'

Redaction

[1–6] To some degree these verses correspond to the Mark 1.2–6 which Matthew had before him. But Matthew omits the purpose of the baptism of John, namely forgiveness of sins. Moreover Matthew differs from Mark in describing the exterior appearance of the Baptist (v. 4) before the note of the success of his activity (vv. 5f.). In this way it forms a better transition to vv. 7–10.

[7a] This verse introduces Pharisees and Sadducees as those addressed in John's preaching of judgment (cf. later ch. 23). Here Matthew explicitly distinguishes them from the people who are willing to repent in vv. 5f., but like Mark (!) he does away with these differentiations in the passion story (27.25).

[7b–10] Cf. Luke 3.7–9 (= Q).

[11] This verse corresponds to Mark 1.8: by the combination of the Markan and Q originals (cf. Luke 3.16) in v. 11d the baptism with the spirit is added to the baptism with fire.

[12] Cf. Luke 3.17 (Q). Note that in the concluding preaching of the Son of man Jesus (Matt. 25.41) 'fire' remains a key word.

Tradition

The Q version which Matthew had before him appears in vv. 7b–10 and 11–12. Sometimes this is seen as a Christian formation:

'That these words are put in the mouth of John the Baptist in Q does not of course mean that he spoke them. We can hardly go wrong in assuming that the words were circulating in the Christian tradition and were put on the lips of the Baptist because there was a concern to report something of his penitential preaching. The verses Luke 6.24; 11.31f.; 13.28f. have been attributed to him (= John the Baptist). It must be judged sheer chance that Jesus does not utter these threats (of Matt. 3.7–9)' (Bultmann).

The first important point is not only that the Q source contains the outline of the Baptist's preaching but that this preaching even forms its beginning.

Now Mark and Q agree that John is a preacher of repentance, who calls on all Israel to repent. He finds a great echo among the people, not least among groups which are regarded as particularly 'sinful' (toll collectors, prostitutes, soldiers), but also faces resistance.

The Baptist's real preaching of judgment, which displays many points of contact with Old Testament and apocalyptic prophecy of judgment, has been handed down only in Q (Matt. 3.7–10,12/Luke 3.7–9,17) and (contrary to Bultmann) seems hardly to have undergone a Christian revision. The imminent judgment of wrath on all Israel, from which the children of Abraham cannot escape, is announced under the image of the axe which has already been laid to the roots of the tree. Only baptism for the forgiveness of sins and 'fruit worthy of repentance' will preserve those addressed being cast into the fire as barren trees. But beyond the judgment a Stronger One appears (v. 11a), who will bring salvation (v. 12a). It is impossible to say any longer who this is. Christian interpreters have seen it as a reference to Jesus, who as Son of man will hold judgment and usher in salvation. This is certainly wrong.

Historical

Cf. on Mark 1.1–8.

Matthew 3.13–17: The baptism of Jesus

13 *Then* Jesus comes from Galilee to the Jordan to have himself baptized by him. 14 *But John sought to prevent him and said, 'I need to be baptized by you, and do you come to me?'* 15 *But Jesus answered and said to him, 'Let it be so now, for thus it is fitting for us to fulfil all righteousness.' And he let him.*

16 And when Jesus had been baptized, he immediately got out of the water. And behold, the heavens opened, and he saw the spirit *of God* descend like a dove and come upon him. 17 And look, a voice said from the heavens, '*This is* my beloved son, in whom I am well pleased.'

Redaction and tradition

Matthew is using Mark 1.9–11.

[13] This verse uses Mark 1.9 and picks up 3.1. The present narrative fulfils the prediction made in the previous pericope. At the same time in designating Jesus as the Son of God Matthew arrives at his real theme.

[14–15] As John knows that Jesus has a superior status and dignity to him, he does not want to baptize him. Moreover the baptism of John served to forgive sins, and Matthew had already *omitted* this statement in revising Mark 1.4. Jesus' answer, v. 15, is the first word of Jesus in the Gospel of Matthew. It serves as a signal and points forward to 5.17.

[16–17] These verses correspond to Mark (1.10f.) with slight differences.

Historical

Cf. on Mark 1.9–11.

Matthew 4.1–11: The temptation of Jesus

1. *Then* Jesus was led by the Spirit into the wilderness, to be tempted by the devil. 2 And after he *had fasted* forty days and forty nights he was hungry.

3 And the tempter came to him and said, 'If you are God's Son, tell these stones to become bread.' 4 But he answered and said, 'It is written, "Man will not live by bread alone, but by every word that proceeds from the mouth of God."'

5 Then the devil takes him to the holy city and sets him on the pinnacle of the temple 6 and says to him, 'If you are God's Son, throw yourself down; for it is written, "He will give his angels orders about you; and they will bear you in their hands, so that you do not strike your foot against a stone."' 7 Jesus said to him, '<u>Again</u> it is written, "You shall not tempt the Lord, your God."'

8 <u>Again</u> the devil takes him to a very high mountain and showed him all the kingdoms of the world and their glory 9 and said to him, 'All this I will give you, if you fall down and worship me.' 10 *Then* Jesus says to him, 'Away, Satan! For it is written, "You shall worship your God as Lord, and serve him alone."'

11 *Then* the devil leaves him. And look, angels came and ministered to him.

Redaction

[1–2] These verses use Mark 1.12–13; 'Spirit' takes up 'spirit of God' from 3.16. The result of the proclamation of Jesus as son of God from 3.17 finds corroboration in the first two temptations.

[3] Only here is the devil called 'the tempter'. Jesus' hunger is the starting point for the first temptation. Allegedly other 'sons of god' like Simon Magus had the ability to make bread from stones (cf. the early Simon Magus tradition especially in the Pseudo-Clementines and in the Acts of Peter, of which Acts 8.9–24 is only one extract).

[4] Jesus counters with a verse from the Septuagint, Deut. 8.3.

[5–7] The devil challenges Jesus with Ps. 91.11f. and Jesus replies with a reference to Deut. 6.16. Is it a coincidence that 'tempt' (v. 7 end) and 'the tempter' (v. 3) correspond? If it is thought that Jesus is to fly down from the pinnacle of the temple we may again think of the flying of the son of God Simon Magus (cf. on v. 3).

[8–10] For the high mountain cf. 17.1 and 28.16. The point of the third temptation is that Jesus could have ruled the whole world, but he is obedient to God and not to the devil. That is shown by the quotation from Deut. 6.13 (LXX).

[11] This verse corresponds to Mark 1.13b.

Tradition

The basis of this passage is Q tradition; here Matthew has preserved the original sequence of the temptation, in contrast with Luke. This is indicated *first* by the appearance of 'Son of God' in the first and second temptations, *secondly* by the position of the third temptation at the end, since it represents a heightening which cannot be further surpassed, and *thirdly* by the following observation; only in the third temptation does the devil show what he really requires – idolatry – whereas in the second temptation he had still sanctimoniously quoted the word of God.

The tradition that Jesus successfully withstood temptation stems from the belief that he was already the Son of God during his lifetime and had already given a proof of this at the beginning of his activity. That is certainly a stylistic element, especially as it is also reported of Buddha that he successfully withstood temptation at the beginning of his public activity.

Historical

From a historical perspective the temptation stories are offshoots of the encounter of Jesus with Satan. He saw him fall like lightning from heaven (cf. Luke 10.18).

Matthew 4.12–17: The beginning of Jesus' activity in Galilee

12 Now when he *heard* that John had been delivered up, *he withdrew* to Galilee. 13 *And he left Nazareth, came and dwelt in Capernaum, which is by the sea in the neighbourhood of Zebulun and Naphthali,* 14 *that what was spoken by the prophet Isaiah might be fulfilled, who says,* 15 'The land of Zebulun and the land of Naphthali, way of the sea beyond the Jordan, the Galilee of the Gentiles, 16 the people which sits in darkness has seen a great light; and on them who sat in the place and in the shadow of death, a light has dawned.' 17 *After that* Jesus began to preach, 'Repent, for the kingdom *of heaven* has come near.'

Redaction and tradition

The section uses the Markan summary Mark 1.14–15.

[12] This verse mentions the reason why Jesus withdraws to Galilee: the imprisonment of John the Baptist.

[13] Matthew reads out of Mark 1.21 that Jesus really resettled in Capernaum; cf. 9.1; 11.23; John 2.12–8.20 differs. This Matthaean conclusion may be based on tradition.

[14] This is a typical Matthaean fulfilment formula (cf. 1.22; 3.14, etc.), which designates Jesus' move to Capernaum as part of the divine plan of salvation.

[15–16] Matthew puts the reflective quotation from Isa. 8.23; 9.1 after the geographical information. 'Galilee of the Gentiles' is most important for Matthew (cf. 28.16–20).

[17] Matthew describes the content of the preaching of Jesus *in precisely the same way* as he describes the preaching of John the Baptist earlier (3.2) and that of the disciples later in 10.7 (without a call to repentance).

Historical

The tradition perhaps aptly reflects Capernaum as the (birthplace and) home town of Jesus. But cf. also on 9.1.

Matthew 4.18–22: The calling of the first disciples

18 Now when Jesus was going along by the Sea of Galilee he saw two brothers, Simon, *who is called Peter*, and Andrew, his brother; they were casting their nets into the sea, for they were fishermen. 19 And he said to them, 'Follow me; I will make you fishers of men.' 20 And immediately they left their nets and followed him.

21 And when he went on from there he saw *two other brothers*, James the son of Zebedee and John his brother, in the boat with Zebedee, their father, casting *their* nets. And he called them. 22 And immediately they left the boat and their father and followed him.

Redaction and tradition

[18–22] Apart from a few deviations (e.g. he omits the 'day labourers' in Mark 1.20), Matthew completely follows Mark (1.16–20), which he has before him. However, the callings as individual events do not fit in well here, since before them and after them Matthew describes general happenings. Their appearance here is therefore to be explained exclusively from Matthew's use of Mark. Matthew emphasizes the calling of Simon with the addition 'who is called Peter'. The person of Peter has special importance for the Matthaean community of Syria and for the Gospel of Matthew.

Historical

Cf. on Mark 1.16–20.

Matthew 4.23–25: Healings of the sick in Galilee

23 *And he went around throughout Galilee, teaching in their synagogues and preaching the gospel of the kingdom and healing every disease and every infirmity among the people. 24 And the news of him resounded throughout Syria. And they brought to him all the sick with various sufferings and afflictions, the possessed, the epileptic and the paralysed; and he healed them. 25 And great crowds of people followed him from Galilee and the Decapolis, from Jerusalem and from Judaea and from beyond the Jordan.*

Redaction and tradition

[23–25] By using and shaping Mark 1.39 Matthew paints an overall picture of the activity of Jesus. Only in later chapters does he produce the details which sometimes word for word refer back to the present summary account. Matthew repeats v. 23 almost word for word in 9.35 and in so doing creates a kind of framework for chs. 5–9. But cf. also 8.1,16; 12.15f.; 14.35; 19.2 as references to the present summary.

Historical

Cf. on Mark 1.39.

Preliminary comment on Matthew 5–7
('The Sermon on the Mount')

The Sermon on the Mount is the first great discourse composition of the First Evangelist. Its concluding formula 7.28 corresponds to the conclusion of other Matthaean discourse compositions. 'And it happened when Jesus had ended these words' appears word for word at 13.53; 19.1; 26.1 (cf. already 11.1). Matthew has composed the Sermon on the Mount on the basis of Q (cf. Luke 6). In analysing it we must always investigate the relationship to the Lukan account, as Matthew's intention and the history of the tradition of the various material are to be defined in the light of this.

Matthew 5.1–12: The Beatitudes

1 *Now when he saw the multitudes, he went up the mountain, and when he sat down his disciples came to him.* 2 *And he opened his mouth, taught them and said,*
3 'Blessed are the poor *in spirit*;
for theirs is the kingdom *of heaven*.
4 Blessed are *the sorrowful*,
For they shall be comforted.
5 Blessed are *the meek*,
for they shall inherit the earth.
6 Blessed are they who hunger and thirst *for righteousness*,
for they shall be filled.
7 Blessed are the merciful,
for they shall obtain mercy.
8 Blessed are the pure in heart,
for they shall see God.
9 Blessed are the peacemakers,
for they shall be called the sons of God.
10 *Blessed are they who are persecuted for righteousness' sake*,
for theirs is the kingdom of heaven.
11 Blessed are you when men revile you and persecute you and utter all kinds of evil against you falsely for my sake.
12 Rejoice and be jubilant; for your *reward* will be great in heaven. For so did they persecute the prophets before you.'

Redaction and tradition

[1–2] Unlike Luke, Matthew locates Jesus' discourse on the mountain. In so doing he is not setting it parallel to Sinai as the mountain of the old covenant and the law of Moses, for according to Old Testament notions Sinai is the seat of Yahweh, not the seat of Moses. But by means of the motif of the mountain Matthew is indicating that in Jesus' discourse a divine revelation is taking place (cf. 28.16). Matthew addresses the Sermon on the Mount to the people and the disciples. By contrast, Luke addresses his statements initially only to the disciples, but at the end in 7.1 also has the people addressed. Moreover the content of the Sermon on the Plain indicates that others too, e.g. the rich, have been addressed (6.24–26), who may be members of the Lukan community.

[3] Matthew supplements the first beatitude with the addition 'in spirit'. With this addition he hardly wanted merely to emphasize the ideal significance of earthly poverty. Matthew has in view people who regard themselves as lowly, who are humble. The concept of poverty that appears in the Lukan parallel (6.20) and Thomas 54, and originally was understood literally, is interpreted in a spiritualizing – and here that means an ethicizing – way.

[4] 'The sorrowful' may be redactional because of 9.15, where it certainly comes from the pen of Matthew.

[5] Cf. Ps. 37.11. For 'meek' cf. 11.29; 21.5. Matthew is thereby issuing an indirect summons to action. Perhaps this beatitude even derives from Matthew in its entirety.

[6] Matthew adds 'righteousness'. The beatitude is then to be read to mean that the kingdom of God is promised to those who long for righteousness. The term righteousness already appears in 3.15 in Matthaean redactional material and is also redactional in what follows: 5.10, 20; 6.1, 33; 21.32. Here too Matthew spiritualizes his original (cf. Luke 6.21a) and understands 'hunger' and 'thirst' in a metaphorical sense.

[7–9] These three beatitudes were added before the redactional stage.

Verse 7: Matthew later speaks of mercy having priority over sacrifice (cf. 9.13; 12.7). Verse 8 has a model in Ps. 24.3–6. Verse 9 contains the seventh member in the table of the beatitudes. Matthew does not reward any peacemakers with divine sonship (cf. James 3.18; on this see Rom. 8.23; Gal. 4.5).

[10–11] Verse 10 was formulated by Matthew. In content v. 10a is an excerpt from v. 11. Here 'for righteousness' sake', which designates a right attitude, corresponds to 'for my sake' in v. 11. Verse 10b repeats verse 3b word for word and thus holds together the preceding beatitudes as a unity in form and content. From v. 11 on, the discourse is given as an address (cf. Luke 6.22 and Thomas 68.1).

[12a] This verse interprets the beatitudes. Because of the reversal of relationships which the future will bring there is reason for joy, for in the last judgment the reward will be great. Verse 12b is an explanatory additional comment (cf. 23.31) which takes up v. 10a. The persecuted community is being addressed.

Historical

Cf. on Luke 6.20–23.

Matthew 5.13–16: Discipleship

13 '*You are the salt of the earth*. If the salt has lost its flavour, how will people salt things? It is no longer good for anything but to be thrown away and trampled on by people. 14 *You are the light of the world*. A city which lies on a hill cannot be hidden. 15 Nor does one kindle a light and put it under a bushel, but on a lampstand, and it lights all those who are in the house. 16 *So let your light shine before people that they see your good works and praise your Father in heaven.*'

Redaction and tradition

[13] As the introductory address shows, Matthew refers the parable, which comes from Q (cf. Luke 14.34–35), exclusively to the disciples. The tradition is similar in Mark 9.50.

[14] The address to the disciples in v. 14a is formulated by analogy with v. 13a. For the image cf. Isa. 49.6. What Matthew says of the disciples the Johannine Jesus asserts of himself (John 8.12; 12.35). Verse 14b is an appended profane proverb, which has an offshoot in Thomas 32.

[15] Cf. Luke 11.33 (= Q). A variant tradition also appears in Mark 4.21. Matthew refers the imagery to the disciples.

[16] This verse is an exegesis and application of vv. 13–15. This confirms that the whole opening of the Sermon on the Mount has a paraenetic focus. In terms of content, the call for good works prepares for the fundamental statement from v. 20.

Historical

It is hardly possible to make any certain assertions about the three aphorisms in vv. 13, 14, 15. But they seem to be to be authentic – without the redactional interpretation in each case – since they say impressively what is important in life. To this degree I am inclined to regard them all as authentic on the basis of the criterion of coherence. Insights of Jesus presented in a similarly aphoristic way appear e.g. in Mark 2.27; 7.15; Thomas 98.

Matthew 5.17–20: The new righteousness

17 '*Do not think that I have come to abolish the law or the prophets; I have not come to abolish but to fulfil. 18 For amen, I say to you,* till heaven and earth pass away, not the smallest stroke nor a dot in the law will pass away, *until all is fulfilled.* 19 Whoever now relaxes one of the least of these commandments and teaches people so will be called the least in the kingdom of heaven; but whoever does and teaches (it) will be called great in the kingdom of heaven. 20 *For I say to you: unless your righteousness far exceeds that of the scribes and Pharisees, you will not enter the kingdom of heaven.*

Redaction and tradition

[17] The verse derives from Matthew in its entirety. The beginning corresponds to the introduction in 10.32 which is similarly redactional. 'Fulfil' is a favourite word of the First Evangelist. The phrase 'law and prophets' is also attested as Matthaean in 7.12 and 22.40. In principle, 'fulfil' has a positive significance, as emerges from the contrast with 'abolish'. In this verse Matthew is possibly correcting a reputed saying of Jesus which he regards as false, 'I have come to abolish law and prophets.' Cf. 13.41, where the Matthaean interpretation of the parable of the weeds among the wheat mentions those who do lawlessness. Such a 'false' saying of Jesus could derive from them.

[18] The introduction and conclusion give the verse a Matthaean character, whereas probably Q is the basis for the central part (cf. Luke 16.17; see further the tradition there). In accord with 24.34, v. 18d refers to the end of the world.

[19] 'The least of these commandments' probably refers to the teaching presented by Jesus from 5.21 on. Matthew found the whole saying in existence as an isolated saying and gave it a place here. Perhaps 'least' is an allusion to the apostle Paul, who designates himself with this predicate (I Cor. 15.9). But it remains worth noting that according to v. 19 even this 'least' comes into the kingdom of heaven – but in a subordinate position.

[20] This verse makes a statement of principle. Matthew rounds off the preceding words with the explanatory 'for' and at the same time prepares for the following section. The attitude of righteousness called for by 'Jesus' measures itself antitypically by the caricature of the scribes and Pharisees and is orientated on good works or fruits (cf. 4.16).

Historical

[18] (Without Matthaean redaction) Jesus never uttered this saying; for the reasons cf. on Luke 16.17.

[19] The saying is inauthentic, since its roots are in the situation of the community and its was spoken by the 'Exalted One'.

Matthew 5.21–26: The first antithesis: On killing

21 'You have heard that it was said to those of old, "You shall not kill; and whoever kills <u>will be liable to</u> judgment." 22 But I say to you, Whoever is angry with his brother <u>will be liable to</u> judgment; and whoever says to his brother "Raka" (stupid) <u>will be</u> <u>liable to</u> the Supreme Council; and whoever says, "Fool" <u>will be liable to</u> the Gehenna of fire.

23 So if you are offering your gift on the altar and there remember that your brother has

something against you, 24 leave your gift there before the altar and first go and be reconciled with your brother and *then* come and offer your gift.

25 Agree quickly with your enemy while you are still with him on the way, lest your enemy hand you over to the judge and the judge to the guard, and you are put in prison. 26 Amen, I *say* to you, You will not get out of there until you have paid the last penny.'

Redaction and tradition

[21–22a] Verse 21 is a combination of Ex. 20.13 and 21.12. Verse 22a is an accentuation of v. 21 and was evidently already handed down in the tradition as an antithesis to v. 21. The tradition vv. 21–22a as an accentuation of the fifth commandment corresponds to the accentuation of the sixth commandment which follows in the context in vv. 27–28.

[22b–c] This passage is an old addition to the original antithesis in the casuistic style which has become attached by the key word 'be liable to'.

[23–24] To the theme of murder Matthew adds the admonition to be reconciled, which in terms of form may be regarded as a rule of piety. Other sections in the immediate context of the present pericope have a similar structure: cf. the relationship of vv. 29–30 to vv. 27–28 and of 6.9–13 to 6.5–8.

[25–26] Here Matthew adds a parable from Q (cf. Luke 12.58–59), because it inculcates the threatening approach of judgment on the last day as a foil to the preaching of Jesus.

Historical

[21–22a] Like the second antithesis (vv. 27–28), the first is historical. In both cases we have an accentuation of the law to which the criterion of offensiveness applies. At the same time the criterion of growth is to be applied, for both antitheses are provided with further interpretations. Jesus does not abolish the Torah but calls for its fulfilment even in the realm of the emotions or the unconscious. Jesus is concerned to affirm the divine demand which includes the whole person.

[22b–c] The passage is unhistorical, since it has been attached secondarily to a saying of Jesus.

[23–24] For reasons of form the rule of piety is unhistorical, since on the whole it was the community that first collected such rules (cf. Matt. 6.1–6, 16–18). But it presupposes the existence of the temple and therefore comes from the time before AD 70.

[25–26] Cf. on Luke 12.58–59, where reasons are given for the authenticity of the Q parable.

Matthew 5.27–30: The second antithesis: On adultery

27 'You have heard that it was said, "You shall not commit adultery." 28 But I say to you, Whoever looks on a woman coveting her has already committed adultery with her *in his heart*.

29 If your right eye offends you, tear it out and throw it from you. For it is better for you that one of your members should perish and your whole body not be thrown into Gehenna. 30 And if your *right* hand offends you, cut it off and throw it from you. For it is better for your that one of your members should perish and your whole body not go into Gehenna.'

Redaction and tradition

[27–28] Verse 27 is based on Ex. 20.13 (cf. Deut. 5.17). The second antithesis has a shorter introduction than the first; those of old are not mentioned nor is the punishment for transgressing the Old Testament commandment. The passage is a unit of tradition which in the form of an antithesis – like vv. 21f. before it – accentuates a commandment of the Decalogue. The content of v. 28 picks up the ninth commandment, 'You shall not covet your neighbour's wife' (Deut. 5.21). For the Matthaean addition 'in his heart' cf. 12.40; 5.8.

[29–30] The passage has been added to the second antithesis by an association with the key word 'eye', and as a consequence which arises from the strict view taken of adultery. Originally it has nothing to do with vv. 27f. and appears a second time in Matthew outside the present passage (18.8–9), in connection with Mark 9.42–48. The structure of the two sentences is parallel. Their perspective is orientated on the last judgment. However, the statements are meant to be understood metaphorically. It is important for Matthew that in both antitheses there is mention of condemnation to Gehenna (= a valley south of Jerusalem, where according to Jewish popular belief the last judgment is to take place).

Historical

[27–28] The second antithesis goes back to Jesus. For the reasons see what is said on the first antithesis, 5.21–22a.

[29–30] The observation that this passage has been attached to the authentic antithesis only at a secondary stage tells against its originating with Jesus. Furthermore the saying fits ascetic Christian itinerant prophets better. The decisive argument in favour of inauthenticity is that Jesus nowhere threatened people so undisguisedly with Gehenna (= hell).

Matthew 5.31–32: The third antithesis: Divorce

31 'It is also said, "Whoever divorces his wife is to give her a letter of separation." 32 But I say to you, Whoever divorces his wife, *except for fornication,* makes her an adulteress, and whoever marries a divorced woman commits adultery.'

Redaction and tradition

[31–32] The antithesis derives from Matthew. It does not quote a prohibition, as in the first and second antitheses, but a commandment which does not appear in this form in the Old Testament (cf. the remote parallel Deut. 24.3). But v. 31 aptly reproduces the Jewish marriage law according to which divorce is largely up to the husband. For the redactional revision of v. 32 cf. 19.9 ('except for fornication'), where it has been added by Matthew to Mark, which he had before him. The saying of Jesus in v. 32 appears in Luke 16.18 (Q) and Mark 10.11f., but not as an antithesis. The non-antithetical form is beyond doubt the more original version.

Historical

Cf. on Mark 10.1–12.

Matthew 5.33–37: The fourth antithesis: On swearing

33 'Again you have heard that it was said to those of old, "You shall not swear falsely and shall keep your oath to the Lord." 34 But I say to you, Do not swear at all, either by heaven, for it is God's throne; 35 or by the earth, for it is his footstool, or by Jerusalem, for it is the city of the great king. 36 Nor should you swear by your head, for you cannot make a single hair white or black. 37 *But let your speech be yes, 'Yes; No, no''. Anything more than this is of the evil one.'*

Redaction and tradition

[33–36] In v. 33b a statement is presented as tradition which, freely basing itself on the Old Testament, forbids perjury (Lev. 19.12) and calls for the fulfilling of vows (cf. Num. 30.3; Deut. 23.21; Ps. 49.14), without itself speaking directly of swearing. By comparison, the new antithesis, which for the first time is formulated as a prohibition, does not relate to observing oaths and vows but to swearing generally. Here is an accentuation of the law. Verses 33–36 are of pre-redactional origin, but once again there are different strata in them. The original tradition comprised either v. 34a alone or already the antithesis vv. 33–34a. As the parallel James 5.12 shows, vv. 34b–37a* have been added to this before Matthew, probably in stages: first vv. 34b–35, then v. 36, then v. 37.

[37] This verse introduces a new main clause with the form of address – like v. 34 – in the second person plural. Verse 37b is to be assigned to Matthew because of its language. But v. 37a also goes back to him in its present form. Here Jesus' prohibition against oaths becomes a substitute for oaths. The verse recommends a form of affirmation which is used without being guaranteed by an oath. Cf. similarly James 5.12, 'Above all, my brothers, do not swear, either by heaven or by earth or with any other oath, but let the yes be yes and the no be no, that you may not fall under condemnation.' However, in v. 37, by comparison with James 5.12 there is no article. That allows us to conclude that v. 37 is a formula which was current in the Matthaean community. Cf. II Enoch 49.1: 'If there is no truth in human beings, then let them make an oath by means of the words "Yes, Yes!," or, if it should be the other way round, "No, No!"'

Historical

The uncompromising absolute prohibition of oaths goes back to Jesus. This thesis can be justified by various criteria: (a) the criterion of growth, since the prohibition expressed above is embedded in traditions which know an oath or a similar phenomenon: v. 36 ('Nor should you swear by your head, for you cannot make a single hair white or black') and the formula of asseveration in v. 37 ('But let your speech be "Yes, yes," "No, no" '), presuppose an oath or come close to one. (b) For the same reason the criterion of difference applies, all the more so since in primitive Christianity the absolute prohibition of oaths was by no means observed. Paul often employs oaths. Cf. Rom. 9.1, 'I tell the truth in Christ and do not lie!'; Gal. 1.20, 'What I write, see, I do not lie!' (c) The absolute prohibition against oaths almost never occurred in Jewish tradition. To this degree the criterion of rarity applies.

Matthew 5.38–42: The fifth antithesis: On non-violence

38 *'You have heard that it was said, "An eye for an eye, a tooth for a tooth." 39 But I say to you, Do not resist evil, but,*

If anyone strikes you on the *right* cheek, turn to him the other cheek also. 40 And if anyone would sue you and take your undergarment, give him your cloak also. 41 And if anyone presses you to accompany him a mile, go two with him. 42 Give to him who begs from you, and do not refuse him who would borrow from you.'

Redaction and tradition

The substance of the fifth antithesis derives from Q (cf. Luke 6.29–30), but it is not formulated antithetically there.

[38–39a] These verses are a Matthaean construction analogous to the antitheses which precede it. Matthew has formed them, like the third (and the sixth) for the purpose of instruction. The quotation in v. 38 from Ex. 21.24; Lev. 24.20; Deut. 19.21 corresponds to the LXX text. In form, v. 39a takes up v. 34 ('not' plus the infinitive). This part of the verse is a kind of superscription over what follows and is a call not to recompense evil with evil.

[39b–42] Here Matthew is handing on Q material (cf. Luke 6.29–30) with the possible exception of v. 41, which has no parallel in Luke. But Luke may have omitted the verse for apologetic reasons, as the right contained in it to compel a person to accompany a soldier on the way would have had negative connotations among his Roman readership.

These verses are not words of the law but aphorisms which, taken literally, would have had a comic effect. Cf. the possible result if after following the advice in v. 40 the person concerned were to stand naked before the other. Or what would the soldier say if someone voluntary doubled the distance he was compelled to accompany him? The aphorisms need no explanation to make their point. Either they are convincing or they are not. It would be wrong to expect them to be grounded in a reference to the kingdom of God. Nor do they have anything to do with the commandment to love one's enemy. It is Q which first makes the connection by framing the present logia with the command to love one's enemy. – For v. 42b cf. also Thomas 95.1–2.

Historical

[39b–42] The five aphorisms are original, offensive, and at the same time comic, so that Jesus must have uttered them.

Matthew 5.43–48: The sixth antithesis: On love of enemy

43 '*You have heard that it was said, "You shall love your neighbour and hate your enemy."* 44 But I say to you, Love your enemies *and pray for those who persecute you,*

45 *that* you may become sons of your *Father in heaven.* For he makes the sun rise on *the evil and the good* and makes it rain on the just and the unjust. 46 For if you love those who love you, what reward do you have? <u>Do not</u> the toll collectors <u>also do the same?</u> 47 And if you greet only your brothers, what *more* are you doing? <u>Do not</u> the Gentiles <u>also do the same?</u> 48 So become *perfect*, as your *heavenly Father* is *perfect*.'

Redaction and tradition

The substance of the sixth antithesis derives from Q (cf. Luke 6.27–28, 32–36), but is not formulated as an antithesis there.

[43] Matthew quotes the Old Testament commandment to love one's neighbour (Lev. 19.18) from the LXX and adds the second part as a rhetorical counter-formulation. In so doing he wants to express Judaism's restricted understanding of the commandment to love.

[44] The commandment to love one's neighbour is an isolated tradition, as is shown by a look at the Q tradition (Luke 6.27). Matthew formulates the second part of the verse with a view to the persecution of his own community (cf. already 5.10–12, etc.).

[45] The motivation to love one's enemy is not completely clear. What has the image of the universal goodness of God to do with loving one's enemy? The basic material goes back to Q (cf. Luke 6.35c,d).

[46–47] Cf. Luke 6.32–34 (= Q). Already in Q the commandment to love one's enemy was further substantiated by negative examples. In v. 47 Matthew inserts 'more' into his original. In view of the parallel in 5.20 we may interpret this to mean that quantitatively more righteousness is to be shown by his disciples than by the Jewish representatives.

[48] Matthew replaces the demand for mercy in Q, which he has before him (cf. Luke 6.36) with the demand for perfection (cf. 19.21). The perfection to be striven for is a share of God's perfection. It is made concrete in doing righteousness (cf. 3.15; 5.20 etc.).

Historical

[44a] The saying is certainly authentic: (a) It was evaded in primitive Christianity (criterion of difference). The apostle Paul virtually hates his enemies (II Cor. 11.13–15), as does the author of II Peter (2.12–22). At the same time it should be noted that Matthew hands down Jesus' command to love one's enemy and not only passes on the hate-filled accusations of Matt. 23 but even accentuates them. (b) The commandment to love one's enemy is rare within Judaism (criterion of rarity). (c) Moreover the criterion of coherence comes to bear in it, since it again attests the radical ethic of Jesus. If we ask what particular enemy Jesus had in mind when he formulated the present commandment we might best think of the Samaritans. They were hated by the Jews. But Jesus must have been concerned with them, as the authentic parable of the good Samaritan (Luke 10.25–37) shows.

[45–48] As far as they go back to tradition, these verses are secondary reflections on the command to love one's enemy which breathe the spirit of the community.

Matthew 6.1–18: Rules for piety

1 *'Beware of practising your piety before people in order to be seen by them; for then you will have no reward from your Father who is in heaven.*

2 Now when you give alms, you are not to sound a trumpet before you, as the hypocrites do in the synagogues and in the streets, that they may be praised by men. <u>Amen, I say to you: they already have their reward</u>. 3 But when you give alms, do not let your left hand know what your right hand is doing, 4 so that your alms may be in secret. <u>And your Father who sees in secret will recompense you</u>.

5 And when you pray, you are not to be like the hypocrites, for they love to stand and pray in the synagogues and on the street corners, so that they PUT themselves ON SHOW to people. <u>Amen, I say to you, they already have their reward</u>. 6 But when you pray, go into your room and shut the door and pray to your Father who is in secret; <u>and your Father who sees in secret will recompense you</u>.

7 And when you pray, you are not to babble like the Gentiles, for they think that they will be heard for their many words. 8 Therefore you are not to be like them. For your Father knows what you need before you ask him. 9 So now you are to pray:

Our Father *in heaven,*
hallowed be your name.
10 Your kingdom come,
Your will be done, as in heaven so on earth.
11 Our daily bread give us today.
12 And forgive us our debts, as we too forgive our debtors.
13 And lead us not into temptation,
but deliver us from evil.

14 *For if you forgive people their transgressions, your heavenly Father will also forgive you.* 15 *But if you do not forgive people, neither will your Father forgive your transgressions.*

16 And when you fast, do not look dismal, like the hypocrites; for they disfigure their face in order to PUT themselves ON SHOW to people as fasting. 17. But when you fast, anoint your head and wash your face, 18 that your fasting may not be seen by men but by your Father who is in secret. <u>And your Father who sees in secret will recompense you</u>.'

Redaction and tradition

Three rules of piety form the core of this section. Each introduced by a 'when' clause (vv. 2, 5, 16), they are constructed in the same way: they deal with almsgiving (vv. 2–4), prayer (vv. 5–6) and fasting (vv. 16–18). Matthew has inserted the Our Father into the context in the tradition (vv. 7–13) as an example of a proper, short prayer and provided it with an interpretation (vv. 14–15).

The rules of piety in vv. 2–6 have a wisdom-type structure. They concentrate on a private piety. The public cult in the temple is not mentioned; the individual stands at the centre. Radical asceticism is commended in this religious self-portrait.

[1] Matthew has put the introductory verse at the head as a superscription for the whole section. Observations on its language suggest that it is redactional: thus the designation of God as the 'Father in heaven' and the term 'righteousness' are typically Matthaean. That means that the First Evangelist has deliberately given the key word 'righteousness' to the three rules of piety in vv. 2–6, which he found as a catechism in the tradition.

[2–6(,16–18)] Cf. the underlinings for the repetitions in the rules of piety. For v. 3b see Thomas 62.2.

[7–13] 'Our' Father (v. 9) takes up 'your' Father (v. 8; cf. v. 14). Matthew inserts the Our Father in contrast to the hypocritical prayer of the Pharisees and scribes (v. 5) and the babbling prayer of the Gentiles (vv. 7–8) as an example of devout prayer to God. The Our Father comes from Q (cf. Luke 11.2–4). Logia from Mark also correspond to it (14.36,38). Didache 8.2f. is closely related to the Matthaean version, but will not be commented on here. The Lukan version consists of five petitions, the Matthaean version of six (v. 10b is thus surplus). The addition to v. 13 ('for yours is the kingdom and the power and the glory for ever'), which is offered by less important textual witnesses, is along this line (cf. I Chron. 29.11–12). In terms of the history of tradition the Lukan version is probably more original, as the third petition in Matthew might be understood as an attempt to have two times three petitions and thus achieve a greater symmetry between the petitions in the second person addressed to God (vv. 9–10) and the petitions in the first person plural (vv. 11–13).

[14–15] Linking up with v. 12, these verses provide an interpretation of the Our Father from Matthew's perspective. According to him human readiness to forgive is a precondition for the divine action in forgiving. This corresponds very precisely to the Jewish wisdom writing Sirach 28.2–5:

2 'Forgive your neighbour the wrong he has done, and then your sins will be pardoned when you pray. 3 Does a man harbour anger against another, and yet seek for healing from the Lord? 4 Does he have no mercy towards a man like himself, and yet pray for his own sins? 5 If he himself, being flesh, maintains wrath, who will make expiation for his sins?'

[16–18] Cf. on vv. 2–6.

Historical

[1–6,16–18] In no way did Jesus speak these words. *First*, they have nothing to do with Jesus' call to repentance grounded in the nearness of the kingdom of God and his radical ethical demands. *Secondly*, the rules about fasting stand in direct opposition to the authentic saying of Jesus in Mark 2.19, according to which the presence of the bridegroom Jesus makes the observing of the commandments to fast superfluous. By comparison Mark 2.20 comes from the time after the death and 'resurrection' of Jesus. This says: 'But days will come when the bridegroom is taken from them; and then on that day they will fast.' This is the situation in which rules about fasting like those in Matt. 6.16–18 could be developed. But if these are inauthentic, then because of the similar form the same is to be said of the first and second rules.

[9–13] With the exception of v. 10b, in all probability the Our Father goes back to Jesus. That is certain for the original address 'Father', which has been preserved in the Lukan version and which goes back to the Aramaic Abba (cf. Mark 14.36). In the time of Jesus very few Jews spoke to God in such a trusting, indeed intimate way; probably, it was never forgotten that this was originally children's language (Abba = Papa, J. Jeremias). (Thus in the family children small and adult addressed their father as Papa.) Had it been usual to put prayers in the mouth of Jesus, we would have had more Jesus prayers than just this one, which indeed is not specifically a Christian prayer. Here the first of the 'we' petitions may be focussed on the specifically daily necessities in the life of Jesus and his disciples, namely having food. For they did not engage in any regular activity. Furthermore, the second petition of the Our Father, focussed on the imminent coming of the kingdom of God and, included in that, the end of the world which was soon to take place, is certainly an authentic saying of Jesus. In accord with the basic structure of the preaching of Jesus it is focussed on a future kingdom (criterion of coherence). The petition is in a tense (aorist) which emphasizes the unique, future coming of the kingdom of God. The phrase about the coming of the kingdom is relatively new with Jesus (criterion of rarity). It takes the place of talk of the coming of God which can be found, for example, in the Old Testament (cf. e.g. Isa. 35.4: 'Say to those who are of a fearful heart, "Be strong, fear not! Behold, your God will come with vengeance, with the recompense of God. He will come and save you"'). By contrast, the primitive Christian expectation was directed towards the coming of the Lord (cf. I Cor. 11.26; 16.22), so that the second petition of the Our Father cannot be derived from the earliest communities (criterion of difference). It seems generally to be the key to the overall understanding of the Our Father against the background of the imminent dawn of the rule of God.

Matthew 6.19–24: Against the accumulation of earthly treasures

19 'Do not gather treasures for yourself on earth where moth and rust consume and where thieves break in and steal. 20 But gather treasures in heaven, where neither moth nor rust consume and where thieves do not break in nor steal. 21 For where your treasure is, there your heart will be also.

22 The light of the body is the eye. Now if your eye is sound, your whole body will be bright. 23 But if your eye is evil, your whole body will be dark. Now if the light that is in you is darkness, how great then will the darkness be!

24 No one can serve two masters: either he will hate the one and love the other, or he will be devoted to the one and despise the other. You cannot serve God and mammon.'

Redaction and tradition

In this section Matthew uses sayings of Jesus from Q which vary in content.

[19–21] Matthew takes over Q, which he has before him (cf. Luke 12.33–34), because it fits in with his intentions (see also Thomas 76.3). Cf. the purely wisdom-type criticism of riches in Prov. 23.4f.: 'Do not toil to acquire wealth; be wise enough to desist. When your eyes light upon it, it is gone; for suddenly it takes to itself wings, flying like an eagle toward heaven.' But here and in Q the criticism is intertwined with an implicit reference to the last judgment (even more strongly in I Enoch 94.7–10).

[22–23] Matthew formulates these verses on the basis of Q (cf. Luke 11.34–36) to make 'Jesus' utter a saying about possessions: greed corrupts the whole person and makes it dark.

[24] Matthew's formulation is again based on Q (Luke 16.13), Matthew formulates this verse. The logion also appears in Thomas 47.2. In bringing 'God' into play at this point, he makes a link back to the Our Father and gives the present section a climax: he makes Jesus say that the question of true humanity has nothing to do with money and other things, but is based on the question of the right worship of God.

Historical

[19–21] We have no means of tracing this wisdom saying back to Jesus.
[22–23] Cf. on Luke 11.33–36.
[24] The saying is authentic (cf. on Mark 12.17).

Matthew 6.25–34: On anxiety

25 'Therefore I say to you: Do not be <u>anxious</u> about your life, what you shall eat or what you shall drink, nor about your body, what you shall put on. Is not life more than food and the body more than clothing?

26 Look at the birds of the air; they neither sow nor reap nor gather into barns, and yet your heavenly Father feeds them. Are you not worth more than they? 27 Who among you can add one cubit to his life span by <u>anxiety</u>? 28 And why are you anxious about <u>clothing</u>? Consider the lilies of the field, how they grow; they do not work, nor do they spin. 29 But I tell you, even Solomon in all his glory was not <u>clothed</u> like one of these.

30 Now if God so clothes the grass of the field, which today is alive and tomorrow is cast into the oven, will he not much rather <u>clothe</u> you, O you of little faith? 31 *So* you are not to be

anxious and say, "What shall we eat?", or "What shall we drink?", or "With what shall we be clothed?" 32 All these things the Gentiles seek. For your heavenly Father knows that you need all this. 33 Seek *first* the kingdom of God *and his (= God's) righteousness*, and all these things shall be added to you.

34 So do not be anxious about tomorrow, for tomorrow will be anxious about itself. It is enough that every day has its own troubles.'

Redaction and tradition

[25–33] Matthew uses Q (cf. Luke 12.22–31) and largely corresponds to his original. The key word of the text handed down by Matthew is the commandment not to be anxious (v. 25), which stands like a superscription over what follows. The text is a unity and inculcates the same ideas through different approaches. The end of the Q section comes in v. 33, as the parallel in Luke (12.31) attests. Matthew has made a small insertion in v. 33. Precisely because Matthew elsewhere follows the Q text, this addition of 'first' and 'and his righteousness' is all the more striking. All the instances of righteousness in Matthew are redactional in origin (3.15; 5.6, 10, 20; 6.1; 21.32) and mostly denote an action. But at this point righteousness is the righteousness of God. It is for the disciples to realize and thus become perfect like God (cf. 5.48).

[34] This verse is an addition which sounds more pessimistic and in fact takes back what has been said previously. It reflects the reality of the community and its failures.

Historical

[25–33*] The sayings are authentic because they cannot be derived from the community (but cf. v. 34). They fit a situation when Jesus sent out his disciples or went with them himself – with a notable lack of anxiety – from village to village in Galilee in the service of the kingdom of God, which was in the process of dawning.

For the relationship between wisdom and eschatology cf. the remarks on Luke 12.22–34. At any rate the predominantly wisdom-type content of Matt. 6.25–33 is no reason for regarding the passages as inauthentic, even when one thinks that Jesus expected the kingdom of God in the very near future.

Matthew 7.1–6: Against judging

1 'Judge not, that you be not judged. 2 For with the judgment that you pronounce you will be judged, and the measure you give will be the measure you get.

3 Why do you see the speck in your brother's eye, but do not notice the log that is in your eye? 4 Or how can you say to your brother, "Let me take the splinter out of your eye," and

look, a log is in your eye. 5 Hypocrite, first take the log out of your eye; then you may see to take the splinter out of your brother's eye.

6 Do not give what is holy to the dogs, and do not cast your pearls before swine, lest they trample them with their feet and turn and rend you.'

Redaction and tradition

Matthew uses Q (cf. Luke 6.37–38, 41–42; see also Thomas 26) and supplements the Q section with an enigmatic saying (v. 6). The whole pericope illustrates for Matthew the demand for perfection (5.48).

[1] The prohibition against judging (cf. Luke 6.37a) stands as a threatening notice at the beginning of the section. The prospect of judgment (v. 1b) also fits well with Matthew.

[2] This verse is a secondary substantiation of v. 1, but was already in Q as well (cf. Luke 6.38). That God recompenses people according to their actions is not only the conviction of the Q group and Matthew but is good Old Testament thought (cf. Prov. 24.12; Ps. 62.13).

[3–4] Two rhetorical questions with the character of examples make specific the demand not to judge in the interpersonal sphere. The word 'brother' identifies the context of the admonitions as the Christian community.

[5] This verse draws conclusions from vv. 3–4 and calls for the removal of the discrepancy. For the charge of hypocrisy cf. 6.2, 5; 23.13–15.

[6] This saying, which stands in isolation, has an artificial chiastic construction ('dogs' and 'tear' belong together) and appears in the New Testament only in Matthew. Cf. however, Thomas 93.1–2. The connection with what goes before is a riddle. In Didache 9.5 the logion is interpreted in quite secondary fashion in terms of the eucharist, i.e. already in the first century people no longer understood the saying. The saying is an example of countless proverbs the original reference of which has become enigmatic. Cf. only Matt. 24.28/Luke 17.37.

Historical

[1] The absolute prohibition against judging goes back to Jesus, for various criteria of authenticity apply to this prohibition: ethical radicality, offensiveness, rarity in Jewish tradition (but cf. Rom. 2.1; James 4.11 – each time without reference to Jesus) and finally the criterion of growth (vv. 2–6 are various rings around v. 1, which comprises one argument against their authenticity).

[2] This verse is inauthentic and secondary by comparison with v. 1.

[3–5] These verses have their context in the community and therefore do not go back to Jesus.

[6] This verse is obscure and also because of that can hardly be linked with Jesus.

Matthew 7.7–11: On the hearing of prayer

7 'Ask, and it will be given to you; seek and you will find; knock, and it will be opened to you. 8 For everyone who asks, receives; and the one who seeks finds; and to the one who knocks it will be opened.

9 Or what man among you, if his son asks for bread will give him a stone? 10 Or if he asks for a fish will he give him a serpent?

11 Now if you who are evil know how to give your children good gifts, how much more will your Father in the heavens give good things to those who ask him!'

Redaction and tradition

Matthew formulates this passage in close connection with Q (cf. Luke 11.9–13) and understands the passage as a piece of teaching on the hearing of prayer, which can refer to the fact that the exalted Lord Jesus is with his community to the end of the world (28.20).

[7–8] The section, with which not only Q but Thomas 92.1 and 94 are to be compared, has a marked symmetry: the threefold invitation corresponds to a threefold substantiation.

[9–10] The double parable inculcates the notion of the unconditional hearing of prayer which is given in vv. 7–8.

[11] This verse is a conclusion which once again is the basis for the whole. The indication that human beings are evil is a contrast to the goodness of God.

Yield: the pericope is a unit and shaped by the single same notion of God's hearing of prayer.

Historical

[7–11] The sayings are authentic and correspond to Jesus' unconditional trust in his heavenly Father. They stand very close to Jesus' words about the faith which moves mountains (Mark 11.23). Cf. Matt. 17.20/Luke 17.6.

Matthew 7.12: The Golden Rule

12 'Now *everything* that you want people to do to you, do so to them. *That is the law and the prophets.*'

Redaction and tradition

Matthew formulates this on the basis of Q (cf. Luke 6.31); here I presuppose that the traditional saying must in some way have been regarded – albeit not in the same way as in Matthew – as the yield of Old Testament law.

The Golden Rule sums up the experiential wisdom of people of Greek, Roman and Jewish cultures in antiquity, and is attested from the fifth century BC on. The fact that this rule is often formulated in the negative makes no difference to its content. Cf. from the Jewish tradition II Enoch 61.1: 'What a man asks for himself from the Lord he is also to do to every living being;' Tobit 4.15: 'And what you hate, do to no one!' The earliest evidence for the content of the Golden Rule is to be found in Herodotus III 142, 3: 'I will not do that for which I censure my neighbours.' Verse 12b links back to 5.17–20. Evidently Matthew is summing up all the individual instructions he has given so far with the Golden Rule.

Historical

In view of the widespread attestation of the Golden Rule in antiquity and its generality it cannot be attributed to Jesus. Had the Rule run, 'Treat people as they want to be treated,' a positive verdict on the historicity would have been more possible.

Matthew 7.13–23: Eschatological warnings

13 'Enter by the narrow gate. For the gate is wide and the way is broad which leads to damnation, and those who enter by it are many. 14 For narrow is the gate and the way is hard which leads to life, and few are those who find it!

15 *Beware of false prophets, who come to you in sheep's clothing, but inwardly they are ravening wolves.* 16 <u>*By their fruits you shall know them.*</u> Do people gather grapes from thorns or figs from thistles? 17 Thus every good tree brings forth good fruit, but the bad tree brings forth evil fruit. 18 A good tree cannot bring forth evil fruit, nor can a bad tree bring forth good fruit. 19 *Every tree which does not bring forth good fruit will be cut down and thrown into the fire.* 20 So <u>*by their fruits you shall know them.*</u>

21 Not everyone who says to me "Lord, Lord", *will enter the kingdom of heaven, but the one who does the will of my Father in the heavens.* 22 On that day many will say to me, "Lord, Lord, did we not prophesy <u>in your name</u>? Did we not drive out evil spirits <u>in your name</u>? Did we not do many miracles <u>in your name</u>?" 23 *Then* I will declare to them, "I never knew you; depart from me, you doers of *lawlessness*!" '

Redaction and tradition

[13–14] The way through the narrow gate that leads to life is the way of righteousness which is marked out in the instructions of the Sermon on the Mount. (Cf. Luke 13.24 as a reworking of the Q text, which is better preserved in Matthew.)

[15] This is a Matthaean formation which is a prelude to what follows.

[16a] This is a redactional transition which is repeated in v. 20 to round off the unit vv. 16–20.

[16b–18] The passage (cf. Thomas 45.1–2) partly corresponds to the Q parable (cf. Luke 6.43–45) of the tree with the fruits and its application to a person's speech. Matthew presents it more completely in 12.33–35.

[19] Matthew repeats part of the preaching of John the Baptist (Matt. 3.10). John and Jesus also say the same thing at another point (cf. Matt. 3.2 = 4.17).

[20] This is a summary conclusion, a Matthaean application which takes up v. 16a and thus frames the passage.

[21] Matthew reformulates the principle on the basis of Q (= Luke 6.46). Verse 21 summarizes vv. 22–23 by way of anticipation.

[22–23] Matthew is directing these verses against false prophets in his own community (cf. Luke 13.26–27 on the Q version). There is much to be said for the hypothesis that the 'false' prophets stand behind 5.17 and are missionaries similar to the apostle Paul (H. D. Betz).

Historical

With the possible exception of vv. 17–18 (original version) these passages are inauthentic and have been formulated by the community or by Matthew himself. Cf. also the remarks on the Q parallels.

[17–18] These verses go back to an authentic simile of Jesus (cf. on Luke 6.43–45).

Matthew 7.24–29: A double parable as an epilogue

24 Now everyone who hears these my words and does them is like a wise man who built his house on the rock. 25 And torrential rain fell and the waters came and the winds blew and beat upon that house, and it did not fall, because it had been founded upon the rock.

26 And everyone who hears these my words and does not do them is like a foolish man who built his house on the sand. 27 And torrential rain fell and the waters came and the winds blew and beat upon that house, and it fell, and its fall was great.'

28 *And it happened that when Jesus had completed these discourses, the multitudes were amazed at his teaching;* 29 *for he taught them like one who had authority, and not like their scribes.*

Redaction and tradition

[24–27] The parable is connected in two ways to the preceding pericope: (a) the requirement of action from v. 21 is inculcated once more; (b) the prospect of the end is again emphasized. At the same time, at the end of Jesus' discourse (cf. similarly 'Moses' in Deut. 30.15–20) Matthew again presents his hearers with the great alternative. The passage derives from Q (cf. Luke 6.47–49), where it already stood at the end of a discourse. Matthew has preserved it better because unlike Luke he has kept the symmetrical structure of vv. 24–25 and vv. 26–27, which are constructed as antitheses and have the same wording even in detail. Only the concluding members of vv. 25 and 27 are not parallel. They contain the decisive sentences about building on a rock on the one hand and the terrible fall on the other.

[28–29] These verses mark the end of the Sermon on the Mount and the return to the Markan framework with a concluding phrase which is typical of Matthew (however, Mark 1.22 is also used).

Historical

The historical yield is nil, as these sayings of Jesus are tied to the post-Easter notion of Jesus as the judge of the world.

Matthew 8.1–9.35: The miraculous power of Jesus

In what follows Matthew brings together ten miracles, in part contrary to the outline of his original, Mark (e.g. in Mark the healing of Peter's mother-in-law comes *before* the healing of a leper, and in Matthew the latter stands at the beginning of the miracle cycle). It is not by chance that these miracles *follow* the discourse complex of the Sermon on the Mount.

Matthew 8.1–4: The healing of a leper

1 *Now when he came down the mountain, great crowds of people followed him.* 2 And look, a leper approached and *fell down before him* and said, 'Lord, if you will, you can make me <u>clean</u>.' 3 And he stretched out his hand, touched him and said, 'I will, be <u>clean</u>!' And at the same time he was <u>cleansed</u> of his leprosy. 4 And Jesus said to him, 'See that you say nothing to any one, but go, show yourself to the priest, and make the offering that Moses commanded as a testimony to them.'

Redaction and tradition

Matthew is using Mark 1.40–45.

[1] This verse is the transition from the Sermon on the Mount to healing stories.

[2–3] The leper prostrates himself before Jesus like a disciple (cf. 28.17) and addresses him as Lord. Otherwise Matthew's report is close to Mark 1.40–42, but (as in Luke 8.13) he leaves out Mark 1.43, evidently because the threatening gesture of Jesus reported there did not fit the healing.

[4] The command to be silent, taken over from Mark 1.44a, really no longer fits because of the multitude which has been inserted redactionally in v. 1.

Historical

Cf. on Mark 1.40–45.

Matthew 8.5–13: The centurion of Capernaum

5 As Jesus was entering Capernaum, a centurion came to him, asked him 6 and says, 'Lord, my servant is lying at home paralysed and in terrible torment.' 7 He says to him, 'Shall I come and heal him?' (or 'I shall come and heal him.') 8 The centurion answered and said, 'Lord, I am not worthy to have you come under my roof; but only say the word, and my servant will be healed. 9 For I too am a man under authority, with soldiers under me; and I say to one, "Go," and he goes, and to another, "Come," and he comes; and to my servant, '"Do this," and he does it.' 10 When Jesus heard that he wondered and said to those who followed him, 'Truly I say to you, *in no one* in Israel have I found such faith!'

11 But I say to you, 'Many will come from east and west and recline at table with Abraham and Isaac and Jacob in the kingdom *of heaven*. 12 But the *sons of the kingdom* will be cast out into *deep darkness*; there will be wailing and gnashing of teeth.'

13 *And Jesus said to the centurion, 'Go, be it for you as you have believed.' And his servant was healed in that hour.*

Redaction and tradition

[5–10(,13)] Matthew again follows Q closely in the wording of the story, which may be a variant in the tradition of Mark 7.24–30. In both cases people are successful in causing Jesus to act through a skilful request, and in both cases we have a healing at a distance. 'In no one' (v. 10) is a change to the Q original, which is preserved in Luke: 'not even in Israel . . .' (Luke 7.9). The redactional intervention anticipates the Matthaean interpretation which follows (see on vv. 11–12).

[11–12] Matthew here inserts an originally independent Q saying (cf. Luke 13.28–30) and makes the exceptional case of the faith of a Gentile the rule (cf. 1.1; 2.1–12; 28.19). The other side of this is that the real 'sons of the kingdom', the Jews, will be cast out.

[13] This verse has been reformulated by Matthew as a consequence of the insertion of vv. 11–12 (cf. 15.28).

Historical

[5–10,13] Most details are certainly unhistorical and derive from a community construction. Sometimes it is assumed that the historical nucleus is the recollection of the healing of a pagan person in Capernaum. But where there is talk of a nucleus, it must also be possible to identify it (W.Wrede). That does not seem to be the case here.

[11–12] The sayings are inauthentic, as they presuppose anti-Judaism which only arose after 'Easter'.

Matthew 8.14–17: The healing of Peter's mother-in-law. Healings of the sick

14 And *Jesus* came into Peter's house and saw his mother-in-law lying (in bed) with a fever. 15 And he touched her hand, and the fever left her. And she arose and served *him*.

16 And in the evening they brought many possessed by demons to him; and he drove out the spirits *through (the) word* and healed all the sick, 17 in order to fulfil what is spoken by the prophet Isaiah, who says, 'He took our weakness upon him and bore our illnesses.'

Redaction and tradition

Matthew uses Mark 1.29–34. He makes the piece into a Jesus story by tightening up and deleting the parts relating to the disciples.

[14–15] Matthew omits both the names of the three disciples (Mark 1.29a) and the question to Jesus (Mark 1.30b). Peter's mother-in-law serves only Jesus after she is healed.

[16] Matthew abbreviates the abundant information about time and persons in Mark 1.32–33. Jesus drives out the (evil) spirits by the power of his word. Matthew passes over the command to the demons to be silent from Mark 1.34c.

[17] This is a fulfilment quotation from Isa. 53.4, which has had no influence on the text. In other words, Matthew is the first to combine it with the revised Markan original. Here it is striking that this quotation is a basis for *healing miracles* and not, say, for the atoning death of Jesus (cf. I Cor. 15.3).

Historical

Cf. on Mark 1.29–34.

Matthew 8.18–22: On discipleship

18 *Now when Jesus saw great crowds around him, he gave orders to go over to the other shore.* 19 And a scribe came up and said to him, 'Teacher, I will follow you wherever you go.' 20 And Jesus says to him, 'The foxes have holes, and the birds of heaven have nests; but the Son of man has nowhere to lay his head.' 21 And another of the disciples said to him, '*Lord,* let me first go and bury my father.' 22 But *Jesus* says to him, 'Follow me, and let the dead bury their dead!'

Redaction and tradition

The passage derives from a revision of Q (cf. on Luke 9.57–60).

[18] Jesus wants to depart, but only in v. 23 is he said to enter the boat. Did the two men wanting to become disciples delay his departure? It is no coincidence that vv. 23–27 will say what discipleship is – to be in the ship of the church.

[19–21] Note how consistently Matthew makes distinctions in the way in which Jesus is addressed: the scribe says 'Teacher' (v. 19). Whereas in what Matthew has before him Jesus is addressed by his followers as 'Teacher', this is deleted (cf. Mark 9.38; 10.35; 13.1) or replaced by 'Lord' (Matt. 8.25; 17.15). In v. 21 the form of address 'Lord' is reserved for the disciples or those seeking healing (8.2, 6, 8, 21, 25; 9.28; 14.28, 30, etc.).

[22] Note that in contrast to the Q version (Luke 9.59) Jesus' instruction is addressed to a disciple. As 'Lord' Jesus can also call someone to a discipleship which severs family ties in Matthew's community.

Historical

Cf. on Luke 9.57–60.

Matthew 8.23–27: The stilling of the storm

23 And when he got into the boat, his disciples followed him. 24 And look, a great upheaval happened on the sea, so that the boat was covered by waves. But he was asleep. 25 And they came up, woke him and said, '*Lord, save*, we perish.' 26 And he says to them, 'Why are you so fearful, *O you of little faith*?' *Then he stood up* and threatened the winds and the sea. And a great calm arose. 27 And *the people* wondered and said, 'What sort of a man is this that even the winds and the sea obey him?'

Redaction and tradition

Matthew uses Mark 4.36–41 and by prefacing it with the saying about discipleship in 8.18–22 makes this passage an allegory about preservation in discipleship. The narrative of the stilling of the storm now depicts the ship of the church, threatened by wind and waves, which despite all the dangers does not sink.

[23] This verse takes up v. 18.

[24] Matthew writes 'upheaval' instead of 'storm' in order to remind his Christian readers of their experiences (cf. 5.11f.; 10.16–19; 23.34–37).

[25] For 'Lord' cf. the address in v. 21.

[26–27] These verses derive from a reversal of the Mark original. Mark makes Jesus reproach the disciples for their lack of faith (Mark 4.40) after the miracle (4.39) and then depicts the positive reaction of the disciples to the miracle (4.41). Matthew changes the order. First comes the rebuke to the disciples, then the stilling of the storm and afterwards the effect of the miracle; here it is no longer the disciples (thus Mark 4.41) but 'the people' who are made to wonder. This is an indication of the universal claim of the Christian message in the time of Matthew. The way in which the disciples are addressed as being 'of little faith' recalls the situation of Matthew's community. It is referred to the presence of the Lord until the end of the world (28.20), which it is to experience in faith. Here we have a Christianizing of the Markan original similar to that noted in Luke 8.25.

Historical

Cf. on Mark 4.35–41.

Matthew 8.28–34: The healing of two men possessed by demons

28 And when he came to the other shore into the region of the Gadarenes, *two men possessed by demons* came to meet him. They came from the cave tombs and were *very fierce, so that no one could pass that way.* 29 And *look*, they cried out and said, 'What have we to do with you? *Have you come to torment us before the time?*' 30 And *a long way from them* there was a herd of many pigs, who were feeding. 31 And the demons asked him, 'If you want to drive us out, send us into the herd of pigs.' 32 And he said to them, 'Go!' And they came out and went into the pigs. And *look*, the whole herd rushed down the slope into the sea, and they perished in the water. 33 And the herdsmen fled and went into the town and told everything, also about those possessed by demons. 34 And *look, the whole town went out to meet Jesus.* And when they saw him, they asked him to *depart* from their region.

Redaction and tradition

Matthew considerably abbreviates what he has before him (Mark 5.1–20), replacing e.g. the broad description in Mark 5.3–6 by the brief sentence v. 28b. He turns the one man possessed into two. For that reason he also omits the legion episode (Mark 5.9–10). 'A legion of demons can be housed in one man, but not in two' (Haenchen).

[28] The popular motif of duality has probably influenced the fact that there are two possessed men (instead of one in the Markan original). Matthew also makes the one blind man in Mark (10.46–52) into two blind men in 20.29–34 (to say nothing of turning one ass into two in 21.2–7). Instead of the one possessed person, v. 28b depicts two dangerous bandits and thus abbreviates Mark 5.3–6 while at the same time clarifying it.

[29–30] Matthew passes over Mark 5.8–10 and by doing so achieves a tighter account. Unlike Mark he puts the herd of pigs far away, probably because pigs are unclean and are to be kept away from Jesus.

[31–34] Cf. Mark 5.12–17. Matthew passes over the scene which follows in Mark (vv. 18–20) in order to confirm that Jesus' activity among the Gentiles has no consequences (cf. 15.24).

Historical

Cf. on Mark 5.1–20.

Matthew 9.1–8: The healing of a paralysed man

1 Then he got into a boat and crossed over and came to his *own* town.

2 *And look*, they brought to him a paralysed man, *who was lying on a bed*. Now when Jesus saw their faith, he said to the paralysed man, 'Take heart, my son, your sins are forgiven.' 3 *And look*, some of the scribes *said among themselves*, 'This man blasphemes God.' 4 But when Jesus *saw* their thoughts he said, 'Why do you think *evil* in your hearts? 5 What is easier, to say "Your sins are forgiven," or to say, "Rise and walk"? 6 But that you may know that the Son of man has authority to forgive sins on earth' – *then* he says to the paralysed man, 'Arise, take up your *bed* and go into your house.' 7 And he arose and went into his house.

8 And when the multitudes saw (it), they were afraid and praised God *who has given such authority to people*.

Redaction and tradition

Matthew uses Mark 2.1–12. In Matthew the hostility of the scribes towards Jesus first becomes clear in this story (v. 3). Here it is only a sample and will continue as the Gospel of Matthew goes on (12.38; 15.1; 16.21; 26.57; 27.41).

[1] Matthew was thinking of a particular house in Capernaum (cf. 4.13) and emphasizes a geographical detail in Jesus' life. Apart from 8.23–34, Matthew deliberately concentrates the miracles on the place where Jesus lives.

[2] Here Matthew tightens up Mark 2.3–5.

[3–4] Cf. Mark 2.6–8.

[5–6] Matthew means the authority of the Son of man for the forgiveness of sins in the sense indicated by 28.18. The forgiveness of sins is an important Matthaean theme (cf. 16.19; 18.18; 26.28).

[8] 'Authority' refers to the same word in v. 6. For 'people' cf. the comments on 8.27. Matthew not only passes over the unique situation in the life of Jesus but also

that of his community and makes the message of Christ 'universal', at least in its claim (cf. the end of the Gospel of Matthew).

Historical

[1] From the striking concentration of the miracles in Matt. 8–9 on Capernaum some scholars conclude that this was Jesus' home. But what we have is Matthaean redaction. And it is a considerable step from here to historical reality, especially as Nazareth is attested by Mark 1.9 as Jesus' native town. I leave the question open, but incline towards Nazareth.

[2–8] Cf. on Mark 2.1–12.

Matthew 9.9–13: The call of Matthew and the meal with the toll collectors

9 And when *Jesus* went away from there he saw a man sitting at the toll, *who was called Matthew*; and he said to him, 'Follow me!', and he arose and followed him.

10 And it *happened* that when he was reclining at table in the house, *look*, many toll collectors and sinners came and reclined at table with Jesus and his disciples. 11 When the Pharisees saw that, they said to his disciples, 'Why does your *teacher* eat with the toll collectors and sinners?' 12 And when Jesus heard that, he said, 'The strong have no need of the physician, but the sick. 13 *But go and learn what this means, "I desire mercy and not sacrifice." For* I have not come to call the righteous, but sinners.'

Redaction and tradition

Matthew is using Mark 2.13–17. Whereas Mark narrates the call of Levi (similarly Luke 5.27), Matthew makes it a call of Matthew, who was a member of the group of twelve (cf. 10.3). However, we can rule out the possibility that Matthew's community venerated the 'Matthew' of 9.9. as an apostolic authority or even that the apostle Matthew composed the Gospel of Matthew. The latter already comes to grief on the fact that Mark 2.14 was used as a source.

[9] Matthew passes over Mark 2.13 with the information that Jesus taught the people.

[10] Matthew makes the house of Matthew alias Levi the house of Jesus (!). Matthew thinks that Jesus lives in Capernaum (see on 9.1).

[11] This verse simplifies the difficult expression 'the scribes of the Pharisees' to 'the Pharisees'.

[12] Perhaps 'your teacher' has been influenced by Mark 2.13 (Matthew had passed over this verse).

[13] Jesus quotes Hos. 6.6 and breaks up the context, which is not about sacrifice. Matthew will introduce this prophetic saying once again in 12.7 as an expansion of Mark 2.26. So he is interested in this Hosea quotation, which in the present context explains Jesus' dealings with sinners and toll collectors. At the same time the quotation is a commentary on 5.17 and 5.20. It gives the centre from which the Matthaean Jesus expounds the law.

Historical

Cf. on Mark 2.13–17.

Matthew 9.14–17: The question of fasting

14 *Then* the disciples of John come to him and say, 'Why do we and the Pharisees fast, but your disciples do not fast?'

15 And Jesus said to them, 'Can the wedding guests *mourn* as long as the bridegroom is with them? But days will come when the bridegroom is taken away from them; then they will fast.

16 And no one puts a piece from a cloth which comes fresh from the loom on an old garment; for its patch tears away from the garment and a worse rent is made. 17 *Nor* does one put new wine in old skins; otherwise the skins burst and the wine is spilled, and the skins are destroyed. But one puts new wine in new skins, and both are preserved.'

Redaction and tradition

Matthew is using Mark 2.18–22. With the tightening up of the Markan original the circumstantial introduction in Mark 2.18a and the dispensable intermediate sentence in Mark 2.19c drop out.

[14] Matthew makes the disciples of John come to Jesus of their own accord and ask him, as he connects 'come' from Mark 2.18 with 'the disciples of John' as subject.

[15] Matthew replaces 'fast' from Mark, which he has before him (2.19), with 'mourn' (cf. 5.4 in connection with the beatitudes). However, this hardly designates the time between the death of Jesus and his coming again as a time of mourning. Cf. 25.1–30: the time of Jesus' absence is a time of wakefulness. I therefore understand 'mourn' exclusively as part of the image: where a wedding is being celebrated one cannot be sad.

[16–17] The double saying is hardly changed from Mark (2.21–22). In the context (9.2–17) of the Gospel of Matthew this double saying emphasizes the incompatibility of Jesus and the Jewish leaders.

Historical

Cf. on Mark 2.18–22.

Matthew 9.18–26: The healing of the woman with a flow of blood and the raising of Jairus' daughter

18 While he was thus speaking with them, *look*, a ruler (of the synagogue) *fell down before him* and said, 'My daughter has *just died*, but come and lay your hand on her, and she will live.' 19 And Jesus arose and followed him with his disciples.

20 *And look*, a woman who had a flow of blood for twelve years, approached him from behind and touched *the hem* of his garment. 21 For she said to herself, 'If I could only touch his garment, I will be saved.' 22 Then Jesus turned round, saw her and said, 'Take heart, daughter, your faith has saved you.' And the woman was saved at that hour.

23 And when he came into the ruler's house and saw *the flute players* and the people making a tumult, 24 he said, '*Get out*! For the girl is not dead but sleeping.' And they laughed at him. 25 But when *the people* had been driven out he went in and seized her by the hand and the girl got up. 26 *And news of this resounded throughout that land.*

Redaction and tradition

Matthew uses Mark 5.21–43 and abbreviates the Markan original more strongly than anywhere else: from twenty-three verses to nine.

[18–19] In contrast to the Markan version (5.23) the girl has just died. This intensifies the magnitude of the faith which the father has. In keeping with this he falls down before Jesus (cf. 28.17).

[20] Matthew makes the woman touch only the hem of Jesus' garment and not the garment itself (thus Mark 5.27). For touching the hem cf. Mark 6.56.

[21–22] The healing takes place only through the word of Jesus, not through the touch. Matthew deletes possible traits of Jesus' ignorance about the person touching him (Mark 5.29–33) for dogmatic reasons.

[23–25] Matthew reduces the Markan original to essentials. He supplements it with the flute players who are part of a funeral cortege. 'Go in' (v. 25) is remarkable, since Jesus had already gone into the house (v. 23) and had sent the people out (v. 24). The explanation of this remarkable detail is Matthew's use of the Markan original, in which there was a distinction between the house and the room in which the girl died (Mark 5.40).

[26] Here too (cf. on Mark 1. 34c) Matthew omits the Markan command to be silent (Mark 5.43) and replaces it with a closing note which emphasizes the activity of Jesus.

Historical

Cf. on Mark 5.21–43.

Matthew 9.27–35: The healing of two blind men and a dumb man with a summary concluding note

27 *And when Jesus went away from there, two blind men followed him, crying out, 'Have mercy upon us, Son of David!' 28 And when he entered the house the blind men came to him and Jesus says to them, 'Do you believe that I can do this?' They say to him, 'Yes, Lord.' 29 Then he touched their eyes and said, 'According to your faith be it done to you.' 30 And their eyes were opened. And Jesus threatened them and said, 'See that no one learns (of this).' 31 But they went out and made him known throughout that land.*

32 *Now when they had gone out, look, they brought to him a man who was dumb and possessed. 33 But when the demon had been driven out, the dumb man spoke. And the multitudes wondered and said, 'Never has such a thing been seen in Israel.' 34 But the Pharisees said, 'By the ruler of the demons he casts out the demons.' 35 And Jesus went around in all the towns and villages, taught in their synagogues and proclaimed the gospel of the kingdom and healed every sickness and ailment.*

Redaction and tradition

'The two stories are not told with love and for their own sakes. They stand as instances of Matt. 11.5 and have been put together from Mark 7.31–37 and Mark 8.13–21, narratives which Matthew passes over in their place' (Wellhausen). These are secondary constructions on the basis of 12.22–24 and 20.29–34.

[27] The petition for mercy recalls 9.13. The address to Jesus as Son of David echoes the first verse of the Gospel of Matthew, 1.1. In the healing of a blind man which is related later (20.29–34), the address as son of David recurs on the basis of Mark 10.46–52. This suggests that Matthew understands 'blindness' also metaphorically as the hardening of Israel, which Jesus as messiah of Israel has come to heal.

[28] In contrast to 20.32 (= Mark 10.49) Jesus does not react to the address by the blind man at all.

[30] The command to be silent sounds Markan.

[31] This verse takes up v. 26, in part word for word.

[32–34] The story illustrates the divided reaction to Jesus (cf. 12.22–24; 21.14–16).

[35] This verse repeats 4.23 with only a slight difference.

Historical

The historical yield is nil.

Matthew 9.36–38: The people's distress

36 *And when he saw the multitudes he had compassion on them; for they were harassed and down-cast like sheep which have no shepherd.*

37 *Then* he says to his disciples, 'The harvest is great but the labourers are few. 38 Therefore ask the Lord of the harvest to send labourers into his harvest.'

Redaction and tradition

[36] Verse 36a attaches directly to the preceding summary. In v. 36b Matthew inserts a note from the Markan story of the feeding (Mark 6.34) which he will pass over in 14.14. The readers have long been aware that God's mercy with Israel has become reality in Jesus.

[37–38] These verses correspond word for word with Luke 10.2 and derive from Q (cf. also Thomas 73). The transition from the image of the shepherd to that of the harvest is somewhat harsh and is to be explained by the presence of different literary strata. The saying is focussed on the Christian mission; the last judgment is also implied here in the image of the 'harvest' (cf. Mark 4.29). Perhaps the logion has an earlier history and form. But neither of these can be ascertained any longer.

Historical

[37–38] The saying is inauthentic as it comes from the community.

Matthew 10.1–5a: The calling of the twelve apostles

1 And when he called *his* twelve *disciples* to him, he gave them authority over the unclean spirits, *to drive them out* and to heal every disease and every infirmity. 2 And *the* names *of the twelve apostles* are these:

　first Simon, named Peter,
　and Andrew, his brother;
　James the son of Zebedee,
　and John, his brother;
3 Philip
　and Bartholomew;
　Thomas
　and Matthew *the toll collector*;

James the son of Alphaeus,
and Thaddaeus [or Lebbaeus];
4 Simon the Canaanean
and Judas Iscariot who delivered him up.
5a These twelve Jesus sent out and commanded them as follows . . .

Redaction and tradition

Matthew is using Mark 3.13–19.

[1] Matthew brings the two notes in Mark 3.15 and 6.7 together.

[2] This verse corresponds to Mark 3.16. By connecting Andrew with Peter, vv. 2b–e become a recollection of the call of the disciples in 4.18–22. Matthew attaches the complete list of names to this in a 'didactic aside' (Luz).

[5a] This half-verse picks up vv. 1–4. There we are shown that Jesus gave authority to the disciples mentioned by name. With v. 5a Matthew reports their sending and at the same time introduces the discourse which now follows.

Historical

Cf. on Mark 3.13–19.

Matthew 10.5b–15: The charge to the disciples

5b *'Do not take the way to the Gentiles and do not go into a <u>town</u> of the Samaritans! 6 Go rather to the lost sheep of the house of Israel! 7 And when you go, preach and say, 'The kingdom of heaven is at hand.' 8 Heal the sick, raise the dead, cleanse lepers, drive out demons. Freely you have received, freely give!* 9 Take no gold nor silver nor copper in your belts, 10 no bag for your journey, nor two undergarments, no shoes and no staff. For a worker is <u>worthy of</u> his food.

11 And if you enter a <u>town</u> or a village, find out who in it is <u>worthy</u> (of it) in it; and remain with him until you depart. 12 And if you come into a house, greet it; 13 and if the house is <u>worthy</u> (of it), let your peace come upon it. But if it is not <u>worthy</u>, your peace is to return to you. 14 And whoever does not receive you and will not hear your words – depart from this house or this town and shake the dust from your feet. 15 Amen, I say to you, it will be more tolerable for the land of Sodom and Gomorrah on the day of judgment than this <u>town</u>.'

Redaction and tradition

In vv. 9–15 Matthew uses Mark 6.8–11 and Q (cf. Luke 10.4–12). Verses 5–8 have been formulated by Matthew.

[5b–6] According to Matthew the preaching of Jesus (cf. 15.24) is addressed both to the disciples and to the people of Israel. The expression 'the lost sheep of the house of Israel' has been formulated with a clear allusion to I Kings 22.17, as in Matt. 15.24. This parallelization extends also to actions (cf. 7–8). For linguistic reasons ('go', 'sheep', lost') v. 6 is redactional, but has a basis in the tradition in that, like Jesus, the disciples originally worked only among the Jews. That Matthew puts this saying about concentrating on Israel at the beginning is striking and calls for an explanation. In contrast to this, at the end of the Gospel of Matthew, exclusively Gentiles are the target of the mission command, which deliberately refers back to 10.5f. This is suggested first by the consideration that because of the reference from 28.19 back to 10.5f. the Greek *ethne* (= 'peoples' in 28.19 = Gentiles in 10.5b) must mean the same (i.e. Gentiles) in both passages. For in 10.5, because of the contrast with Israel, the people are clearly understood as Gentiles. Secondly, Matthew could hardly have included the Jews under the term Gentiles. He still lived and thought too much in a Jewish framework in which the term 'peoples' exclusively designated Gentiles and not Jews.

[7–8] Matthew consistently sets the disciples in parallel with Jesus. Like his actions, theirs point to the imminence of the kingdom of God (cf. 4.17); as in his case, their preaching is accompanied by mighty acts: raisings of the dead (cf. 9.18ff.; 11.5); healings of lepers (cf. 8.2ff.11.5) and of the possessed (cf. 4.24; 8.16; 8.28ff.; 9.32). Possibly the instances in v. 8 have been deliberately chosen in order to emphasize the relationship to the miracles in Matt. 8–9.

[9] The rules about equipment go back to Q (cf. Luke 10.5–7). Matthew also inserts them because for him poverty is of fundamental importance (cf. 6.19–34). For the Q group it is a matter of demonstrating a shocking poverty and need, which can be related to the beatitude on the poor (6.20), defencelessness (Q = Luke 6.29), the love of enemy (Q = Luke 6.27f.), the break with all earthly kinsfolk (Q = Luke 14.26) and living only for the kingdom of God (Q = Luke 12.31).

[11–15] These verses are a unit and depict the modes of mission. Matthew reproduces the Q text (cf. Luke 10.8–12).

Historical

[6] For the orientation of the activity of Jesus on Israel only see on 15.21–28.

[9–10] The radically ascetic feature of the mission rule cannot be connected with Jesus historically, since he was not incorrectly regarded as a 'glutton and drunkard' (Matt. 11.19). Nor should the authentic Q saying Matt. 8.20/Luke 9.58 be used here as an argument in favour of the historicity of vv. 9–10. But a heightening and development of tendencies to be found with Jesus may become visible in the mission rule. (Cf. the parallel I Cor. 7.1, where Pauline disciples concluded from Paul's appearance as an unmarried man that it was good not to touch a woman.)

[11–14] This mission tradition goes back to the time after 'Easter'. The 'Risen One' is speaking in it (cf. 28.19f.).

Matthew 10.16–26a: The announcement of persecutions to come

16 '*Look*, I am sending you out like sheep among the wolves. *So be as wise as serpents and as innocent as doves;* 17 *Beware of men;* for they will hand you over to courts and they will flog you in their synagogues. 18 And for my sake you will be led before governors and kings, to bear witness to them and the Gentiles.

19 But when they hand you over, do not be anxious how or what you should say; for at that hour it will be given to you what you should say. 20 For it is not you who speak, but the Spirit of your Father is the one who speaks in you.

21 And a brother will deliver (his) brother to death, and the father (the) child, and the children will rise against parents and will kill them. 22 And you will be hated by all for my name's sake. But whoever perseveres to the end will be saved.

23 And if they persecute you in this city, flee to the next! Amen, I say to you, you shall not have gone through the cities of Israel before the Son of man comes.

24 A disciple is not above his teacher nor a servant above his master. 25 It is enough for the disciple to be like his teacher and the servant like his master. If they have called the master of the house Beelzebul, how much more those of his household! 26a *Therefore* do not fear them!'

Redaction

Matthew combines material from Mark and Q (for both cf. the exegesis) to inculcate in his community that preaching necessary provokes conflicts.

[16] Verse 16a = Q (Luke 10.3). Verse 16b is probably redactional, because its wisdom content fits Matthaean theology (cf. immediately 11.25–30).

[17–22] Verse 17a is a Matthaean introduction (cf. 6.1; 7.15; 16.11f.). The section which follows, vv. 17b–22, has been taken over essentially unchanged from Mark 13.9, 11–13. (Mark 13.10 has been saved for Matt. 24.24, because this verse did not fit the theme.)

[23] The saying is relatively isolated in the context – one more reason to regard it as a saying of Jesus which has been handed down in isolation; Matthew got to know it and wove it into his Gospel in order to augment Jesus' discourse to the disciples about their future fate (vv. 17–23).

[24–25] These verses come from Q (= Luke 6.40 with parallels in John 13.16; 15.20). The explanation for the addition of these sentences from the tradition is that from v. 5 Jesus and his disciples have been presupposed to have the same task (cf. on vv. 5–6). But in that case – thus v. 25b – the disciples will be open to the same charge as Jesus, namely of being in league with Beelzebul (cf. 12.26–28).

[26a] Matthew clearly feels that the reference to the slander against Jesus in v. 25 offers consolation. Hence the admonition not to fear the adversaries mentioned in vv. 17–23.

Tradition

All in all there are five individual logia here:

(a) Verse 16a reflects the situation of persecution in the Q community (cf. on v. 23).

(b) Verses 17b–20 (= Mark 13.9, 11; Luke 12.11f.) derive from a promise by the exalted Jesus to the missionaries of Israel.

(c) Verses 21–22 (cf. Mark 13.12f.) derive, like 10.34–36, from an oracle of the exalted Jesus on the basis of Micah 7.6. The occasion of the formation of this saying was rifts in the family which had been produced by the preaching.

(d) Verse 23 reflects an ardent expectation of an imminent end. For the one who uttered it and those whom he addressed it was bound up with the conviction that he would experience the day of the Son of man in his own lifetime. The end of the world is given a date with this saying. With its statement that the disciples will not have to endure persecution long, it contains the clear presupposition that none of them (or only a minority) will die. Otherwise the address to the disciples would have been meaningless. To this degree this text belongs to an even earlier period than Mark 9.1.

(e) For verses 24–25 cf. the remarks under 'redaction'.

Historical

Logia (a), (b) and (c) are inauthentic, because they can be derived from the situation of Matthew's community,

Some hold logion (d) to be authentic since v. 23b is a prediction which remained unfulfilled. This argument is not convincing, as a primitive Christian prophet could also have expressed an unfulfilled prophecy. But the saying can be derived in its entirety from the situation of the community after the death and 'resurrection' of Jesus in which the missionaries were canvassing in Israel for faith in Christ and were exposed to many difficulties. Again Paul provides a parallel; he instructs his communities in advance about the persecution that they are to expect because Jesus' advent is imminent (I Thess. 3.3–4). Another factor which tells against the authenticity of the saying is that an extreme situation of persecution or a flight of the disciples in Jesus' lifetime would be hardly conceivable.

Logion (e) is historical in that in all probability the same charges were made against the disciples as were made against Jesus. However, Jesus did *not* speak this logion.

Matthew 10.26b–33: Invitation to fearless confession

26b 'Nothing is concealed that will not be manifested, and nothing is hidden that will not be known. 27 *What I say to you in the dark, speak in the light! And what you hear whispered, proclaim on the rooftops.* 28 And do not <u>fear</u> those who kill the body, but cannot kill the soul. <u>Fear</u> rather him who can destroy body and soul in hell. 29 Are not two sparrows bought for a penny? And not one of them falls to the ground without your Father. 30 All the hairs of your head are also numbered. 31 *So* do not <u>fear</u>; you are worth more than many sparrows.

32 *Now* everyone who confesses me before men, I will also confess before my Father *in heaven*. 33 But whoever denies me before men, him will I also deny before my Father *in heaven.*'

Redaction and tradition

Matthew's formulation is based on Q (cf. Luke 12.2–9). The whole section is held together by the commandment not to fear (or to fear the right person). Thus the pericope is linked with the preceding passage which Matthew has concluded with the demand not to fear (the adversaries).

[26b] In Mark 4.22; Luke 8.17 the logion relates to the parable discourses; in the present context it is a statement which takes on meaning only in the next verse.

[27] The disciples are already to proclaim now what will emerge at the last judgment (thus Q: cf. Luke 12.3).

[28–31] These verses are a comforting warning from Q (cf. Luke 12.4–7), which emphasizes the main issue in the situation of persecution. Note that the wisdom demonstrations (sparrows, hairs of the head) are an element of the warning against perishing in hell.

[32–33] The double saying about confessing and denying Jesus already stood at this point in Q (cf. Luke 12.8–9 and the remarks on the tradition made there). It also emphasizes at the level of the Matthaean redaction that there is still the possibility of a condemnation even for the disciples (cf. vv. 28, 33). But the main emphasis is on the consolation of v. 32.

Historical

[26b] cf. on Mark 4.22.

[27–33] All the sayings are inauthentic as they derive from a later situation of the community stamped by persecution.

Matthew 10.34–39: Divisions for Jesus' sake

34 *Do not think* that I have come to bring peace on the earth. I have not come to bring peace, but the sword. 35 For I have come to set a man against his <u>father</u> and a daughter against her <u>mother</u> and a daughter-in-law against her mother-in-law. 36 And a man's enemies will be those of his own household.

37 Whoever loves <u>father</u> or <u>mother</u> more than me, <u>is not worthy of me</u>; and whoever loves son or daughter more than me, <u>is not worthy of me</u>. 38 And whoever does not take up his cross and follow me <u>is not worthy of me</u>. 39 He who finds his life will lose it; and he who loses his life for my sake will find it.

Redaction and tradition

Matthew formulates this passage on the basis of Q and Mark. For vv. 34–36 cf. Luke 12.51–53; for vv. 37–39 cf. Luke 14.26–27; 17.33 and Mark 8.34–35.

[34–36] For 'do not think . . .' (v. 34a) cf. 5.17a. The mission of Jesus serves necessarily to bring about divisions within a person's family, as is concluded in Q in connection with Micah 7.6 (cf. on Luke 12.49–53). Here vv. 34–36 are a further accentuation of vv. 26–31, because here the closer members of the family are the person's enemies.

[37–38] The passage derives from Q (Luke 14.26–27); here Luke 14.26* comes closer to the original. There is a parallel in Thomas 55.1–2. The saying in the Gospel of Thomas is probably a mixed quotation from Matthew and Luke.

[39] Cf. Mark 8.35; Luke 17.33 and John 12.25.

Historical

[34–36] Cf. on Luke 12.51–53.
[37] Cf. on Luke 14.26.
[38] Cf. on Luke 14.27.
[39] Cf. on Mark 8.35.

Matthew 10.40–11.1: Acceptance for the sake of Jesus and the conclusion of the discourse to the disciples

40 <u>He who accepts</u> you, accepts me; and <u>he who accepts</u> me accepts the one who has sent me. 41 *<u>He who accepts</u> a prophet because he is a prophet will receive a prophet's <u>reward</u>. <u>He who accepts</u> a righteous man because he is a righteous man will receive a righteous man's <u>reward</u>.* 42 And he who gives one of these little ones even a cup of cold water to drink, because he is a disciple, Amen I say to you, he will not lose his <u>reward</u>.' 11.1 *And it happened, when Jesus had completed the instructions to his twelve disciples, that he went on from there to teach and preach in their towns.*

Redaction and tradition

[40] Cf. on Luke 10.16 (Q). The saying is rooted in mission and authorizes the preacher to speak in the name of the exalted Lord.

[41] This verse probably derives from Matthew, who has created it as a substitute for the narrative of the alien exorcist (Mark 9.38–40). Evidently 'prophet' and 'righteous man' denote different ranks in his community (cf. 23.34: Christian prophets, wise men, scribes).

[42] Cf. Mark 9.42; for the expression 'little ones' cf. 18.6–14. Matthew emphasizes that Christians from the lower 'ranks' have the same worth as 'prophets' and the 'righteous' (cf. 18.1–14; 23.8–12).

[11.1] This verse marks the conclusion of the second complex of discourses in Matthew after 7.27 and before 13.53; 19.1; 26.1. With these stereotyped sentences Matthew emphasizes that preaching is the essential characteristic of the earthly activity of Jesus.

Historical

[40] Cf. on Luke 10.16.
[42] Cf. on Mark 9.42.

Matthew 11.2–19: The Baptist's enquiry and Jesus' testimony about him

2 Now when John heard *in prison the works of Christ*, he sent word by his disciples 3 and said to him, 'Are you he who should come, or shall we expect another?' 4 Jesus answered and said to them, 'Go and proclaim to John what you hear and see: 5 the blind see and the lame walk, lepers are cleansed and the deaf hear, and the dead are raised, and the gospel is preached to the poor. 6 And blessed is he who does not take offence at me.'

7 When they went away, Jesus began to say to the crowds about John, 'What did you go out into the wilderness to look at? A reed shaken by the wind? 8 Or what did you go out to see? A man in soft garments? See, those who wear soft garments are in king's houses. 9 Or what did you go out to see? A prophet? Yes, I tell you, more than a prophet. 10 This it is of whom it is written, "Look, I send my messengers before you, to prepare your way before you."

11 Amen, I say to you: of all those born of women none greater has been raised than John the Baptist. But the least in the kingdom *of heaven* is greater than he. 12 But from the days of John the Baptist until now the kingdom *of heaven* suffers violence, and men of violence take it by force. 13 For all the prophets and the law have prophesied up to John; 14 *and if you will accept (it): he is Elijah who is to come.* 15 *He who has ears let him hear.*

16 With whom shall I compare this generation? It is like children sitting in the market who call to the others and 17 who say, 'We have played for you and you have not danced, we have

sung laments and you have not wept.' 18 John came and did not eat and drink, *and they say,* "He is possessed." 19 The Son of man came, eats and drinks, *and they say,* 'Look, a glutton and a drunkard, a friend of tax collectors and sinners. And wisdom is justified by her *works*.'

Redaction and tradition

Matthew is using Q. For vv. 2–6 cf. Luke 7.18–23. For vv. 7–19 cf. Luke 7.24–35 and 16.16.

[2] The works of Christ refer to what is related in chs. 5–9 of Christ: his words and actions. For 'Christ' in Matthew cf. Matt. 1.1, 16f.; 2.4.

[3] Matthew is thinking of John's saying about the Stronger One in 3.11, i.e. of the Son of man.

[4–5] Jesus answers John's question about his person by referring to the time of salvation which is accessible to those who ask. For the details cf. chs. 8–9. However, no dead person is raised in these chapters devoted to the miraculous power of Jesus (but cf. Q: Luke 7.22).

[6] This beatitude has threatening connotations in so far as now is the time of decision, but the opportunity can be squandered. Accordingly, after the demonstration of the miraculous power of Jesus in Israel the disciples had received the charge to confront its inhabitants with the choice.

[7–9] Cf. on Luke 7.24–26.

[10] A scriptural proof from Mal. 3.1. Cf. on Luke 7.27.

[11] This verse derives from Q (cf. Luke 7.28). There its meaning is that John the Baptist is the turning point in history. Certainly he is the greatest figure in history so far. But the least in the kingdom of God is superior to him.

[12–13] The logion in v. 12 comes from Q (cf. Luke 16.16). In the original version it may have run: 'The law and the prophets (are) up to John. From then on violence is done to the rule of God and violent men seize it.' The saying presupposes the rule of God as a present entity. The 'men of violence' refers to Jesus and his disciples, because that is the only interpretation which makes the note of time 'from the days of John' plausible.

[14–15] In this redactional part inspired by Mark 9.13 Matthew emphasizes that John is the Elijah announced by the prophets (cf. vv. 10,13). For the identification of John the Baptist with Elijah redivivus cf. also 17.13.

[16–19] The passage consists of a parable (vv. 16–17) and an interpretation (vv. 18–19). As the interpretation fits the parable very well, I regard the piece as a unity. The interpretation itself has been enriched in Q with v. 19c (cf. Luke 7.35). Here the Q group as the children of wisdom sets itself against Israel, which has rejected Jesus. Matthew writes 'by her works' (v. 19c) instead of 'by her children' (Luke 7.35). In so doing he relates the works to the acts of the wisdom 'Christ' in vv. 2–5.

Historical

[2–6, 7–10] Cf. on Luke 7.18–27.

[12–13] Because of its offensive language the Q version of v. 12 may go back to Jesus (it recalls Thomas 98). But Jesus' relationship to the prophets and the Torah is also indicated aptly in these verses. Jesus sees his own ethics as a fulfilment of the prophets and the Torah and thinks that the promises given there were fulfilled in his activity.

[16–19] Within the interpretation of the parable the outside testimony about John and Jesus is authentic. It is orientated on the appearance of John and Jesus and can be attested from other sources. John appeared as an ascetic; Jesus (after his detachment from John) lived in the Jewish community of his time in relative openness to the world.

Matthew 11.20–24: Jesus' woes on Galilean cities

20 *Then he began to revile the cities in which most of his deeds had been done, since they had not repented:*

21 'Woe to you Chorazin! Woe to you Bethsaida! For had such deeds been done in Tyre and Sidon which have been done in you, they would long since have repented in sackcloth and ashes. 22 <u>But I say to you, it will be more tolerable for</u> Tyre and Sidon <u>on the day of judgment than for</u> you.

23 And you, Capernaum, will you be exalted to heaven? You will go down to Hades. For if the deeds had been done in Sodom which have been done in you, it would still be standing today. 24 <u>But I say to you: it will be more tolerable for</u> the land of Sodom <u>on the day of judgment than for</u> you.'

Redaction

Here Matthew is incorporating Q material which also occurs in Luke 10.13–15, to a large degree word for word.

[20] This verse is a Matthaean summarizing transition.

[21–22] These verses correspond almost word for word with Luke 10.13–14 (= Q). Matthew can take this passage over because the notion of judgment is important for him, in particular in connection with the unsuccessful mission of his community carried on in these places.

[23–24] Verse 23, a partly inaccurate quotation of Isa. 14.13, 15, corresponds with Luke 10.15 (= Q) almost word for word. Verse 23b corresponds with v. 21 stylistically. Verse 24 corresponds with v. 22: it will be more tolerable for the land of Sodom, as for Tyre and Sidon than for the places in Galilee where Jesus was active.

Tradition

The passage from Q (= vv. 21–23 [24]) consists of two threats in which the Old Testament form of the oracle against the nations is adopted by the Q community, but directed polemically against places in Israel itself. It is striking that this time it is not Jewish opponents like the Pharisees who are the target of polemic, but places in the activity of Jesus himself. The polemic is crude and total.

Historical

The threats are to be derived from the situation of later communities, all the more so as they look back on the completion of Jesus' activity. 'Even Jesus hardly felt that Capernaum had been exalted to the heavens by his activity' (Bultmann, following Wellhausen). The argument in favour of the authenticity of the threats, namely that after 'Easter' there are no references to the two places, is inadequate in view of our sparse knowledge of Galilee after the 'resurrection' of Jesus.

Matthew 11.25–30: Jesus' praise and the Comfortable Words

25 *At that time Jesus answered and said,* 'I praise you, Father, Lord of heaven and earth, because you have hidden this from the wise and understanding and <u>revealed</u> it to babes. 26 Yes, Father, for this was your gracious will.

27 All things have been delivered to me by my Father, and no one knows the Father except the Son and the one to whom the Son chooses to <u>reveal</u> it.

28 Come to me all who labour and are heavy laden, and I will give you rest. 29 Take my yoke upon you and learn from me; for I am gentle and lowly in heart, and you will find rest for your souls. 30 For my yoke is easy and my burden is light.'

Redaction and tradition

[25–27] Verse 25a is Matthaean. Verses 25b–27 come from Q (= Luke 10.21–22), probably as a continuation of Luke 10.13–16 (= Q; cf. Matt. 11.20–24). Jesus' activity as revealer is expressed in the style of the revelation discourse. (Cf. again on Luke 10.21–22.) Verse 27 is clearly formulated as a commentary by the community on vv. 25b–26.

[28–30] These verses are known as the Comfortable Words. There are countless parallels to them in wisdom: Prov. 8.1–21; Sirach 51.23–29 LXX, etc. 'Gentle' and 'lowly' have an ethical significance in Matthew, cf. 5.5, 7; 21.5. In the context of the Gospel of Matthew the 'weary and heavy laden' probably refer to those burdened with Pharisaic precepts: cf. 23.4.

Historical

[25b–27] Cf. on Luke 10.21–22.

[28–30] The sayings are inauthentic. The passage presupposes the identification of Jesus with 'wisdom' and thus a post-Easter situation.

Matthew 12.1–8: Plucking ears of corn on the sabbath

1 *At that time* Jesus went through the grain fields on the sabbath; and his disciples *became hungry* and began to pluck ears of grain *and to eat.* 2 When the Pharisees saw this, they said to him, 'Look, your disciples are doing what is not lawful to do on the sabbath.' 3 But he said to them, 'Have you not read what David did when he was hungry and those who were with him? 4 How he went into the house of God and ate the showbread which *neither he nor those who were with him* might eat, but only the priests? 5 *Or have you not read in the law how the priests in the temple profane the sabbath, and are* guiltless? 6 *But I say to you, something greater than the temple is here.* 7 *And if you knew what this means,* "I have pleasure in mercy and not in sacrifice," *then you would not have condemned the* guiltless. 8 For the Son of man is lord of the sabbath.'

Redaction and tradition

Matthew is using Mark 2.23–28.

[1] Matthew adds 'become hungry' and 'eat' to the Markan original. In Mark (and Luke) the sin of the disciples lies in the eating, whereas in Matthew it consists in the work of plucking ears of corn. In keeping with that, Matthew's community observed the sabbath (24.20) and certainly would not have allowed the plucking of ears of corn.

[2–4] Cf. Mark 2.24–26. In v. 3 Matthew corrects Mark's erroneous reference to Abiathar and like Luke omits his name.

[5] This is a reference to Num. 28.9f., which contains a second argument from scripture for the conduct of the disciples.

[6] This is a sentence constructed like 12.41f. Its meaning follows from v. 7.

[7] This is a quotation from Hos. 6.6 which was previously used redactionally in 9.13. 'Guiltless' takes up the same word from v. 5. Matthew means to say that the Pharisees have wrongly attacked the disciples. These are innocent, as scripture shows.

[8] Matthew (like Luke) omits Mark 2.27 and with Mark 2.28 emphasizes the sovereignty of Jesus the Son of man over the sabbath.

Historical

Cf. on Mark 2.23–28. Matthew has omitted the only historical sentence of the pericope which he has used, Mark 2.27, and removed himself still further from history.

Matthew 12.9–14: The healing on the sabbath

9 *And he went on from there, and entered their synagogue.* 10 And *look,* there was a man who had a withered hand. And they asked him and said, 'Is it lawful to heal on the sabbath?', so that they could accuse him. 11 But he said to them, 'Who among you, if his only sheep falls into a pit on the sabbath, does not seize it and help it out? 12 Of how much more value is a man than a sheep! So it is lawful to do good on the sabbath.' 13 Then he said to the man, 'Stretch out *your* hand!' And he stretched it out, and it was *sound* again *like the other.* 14 But the Pharisees went out and took counsel against him, in order to do away with him.

Redaction and tradition

Matthew uses Mark 3.1–6 and interprets the passage by the parable vv. 11–12.

[9] Matthew introduces the second saying of Jesus about the sabbath *immediately* after the first, by making Jesus go from the scene in vv. 1–8 into a synagogue (Luke would wait until the next sabbath, Luke 6.6).

[10] Matthew makes Mark 3.2 a direct question (for the construction see Acts 1.6; 7.1).

[11–12] The parable inserted here deals with a question often discussed in Judaism: may one rescue an animal which has fallen into a pit on the sabbath? It occurs at another point in Luke (14.5) and here responds to the direct question in v. 10. Thus Matthew turns the story into a controversy. Verse 12 clarifies the issue: doing good, i.e. practising mercy, stands above sacrifice and sabbath.

[13] Matthew elaborates the healing.

[14] The departure of the Pharisees rounds off the whole section 12.1–14.

Historical

[10,13–14] Cf. on Mark 3.1–6.
[11–12] Cf. on Luke 14.5.

Matthew 12.15–21: The servant of God

15 *But when Jesus was aware (of this), he withdrew from there.* And many followed him, and he healed them all. 16 And he threatened them not to make him known. 17 *This was to fulfil what is spoken by the prophet Isaiah, who says:*

18 'Look, this is my servant whom I have chosen, my beloved, in whom my soul is well pleased. I will put my spirit upon him, and he will proclaim justice to the Gentiles. 19 He will not dispute nor cry aloud, nor will anyone hear his voice in the streets. 20 A bruised reed he will not break and a smouldering wick he will not quench, until he brings justice to victory; 21 and in his name the Gentiles will hope.'

Redaction and tradition

[15] This verse is based on Mark 3.7, but in addition to Mark the decision of the Pharisees in v. 14 is mentioned as a motive for Jesus' departure. As in 8.16, Jesus heals *all*.

[16] The echo of the command to keep silent in Mark (3.12) is surprising (but cf. already 9.30). Is that an anticipation of v. 19?

[17] This verse is an introduction to the fufilment quotation (cf. 1.22; 2.15,23; 4.14; etc.)

[18–21] These verses are a quotation from Isa. 42.1–4. Matthew wants to depict the whole of the figure of Jesus with the help of a quotation. With the conclusion of the quotation Matthew is pointing forward to 28.16–20; the meekness of v. 19 recalls 11.29.

Historical

The historical yield is nil.

Matthew 12.22–37: Jesus – not in league with the devil

22 Then a man possessed who was blind and dumb was brought to Jesus; and he healed him so that the dumb man spoke and saw. 23 And all the multitudes were amazed and asked, 'Is this the Son of David?' 24 And when the Pharisees heard it they said, 'This man drives out the evil spirits only through Beelzebul, their prince.'

25 But knowing their thoughts he said to them, 'Every kingdom which is <u>divided</u> against itself is laid waste; and every city or a house which is <u>divided</u> against itself cannot stand. 26 Now if Satan drives out Satan, he is <u>divided</u> against himself; how then will his kingdom stand?

27 And if I cast out the demons through Beelzebul, by whom do your sons cast (them) out? Therefore they shall be your judges. 28 But if I cast out demons by the spirit of God, the kingdom of God has come upon you. 29 Or how can anyone enter the strong man's house

and plunder his possessions if he has not first bound the strong man? Then he will plunder his house.

30 He who is not with me is against me; and he who does not gather with me, scatters.

31 *Therefore* I say to you, every sin and blasphemy will be forgiven people, but the blasphemy against the Spirit will not be forgiven. 32 And whoever says a word against the Son of man will be forgiven ; but whoever says (something) against the Holy Spirit will not be forgiven, *either in this world or in that world.*

33 Either assume that the tree is good, so that its fruit will also be good, or assume that a tree is bad, and so its fruit will also be bad. For the tree is known by its fruit.

34 *You brood of vipers! How can you speak good, when you are evil? For out of the abundance of the heart the mouth speaks.* 35 The good man out of his good treasure brings forth good, and the evil man out of his evil treasure brings forth evil.

36 *But I tell you, on the day of judgment people will render account for every careless word that they utter. 37 For by your words you will be justified, and by your words you will be condemned.'*

Redaction and tradition

[22–24] The exorcism, which Matthew previously reported in 9.32–34 (there following Mark 3.20–22) has a parallel in Luke 11.14–15 and thus derives from Q. In the present context, which is strongly shaped by Matthew, it serves as an exposition of the following controversy. The supposition of the crowds that Jesus must be the Messiah – this is doubtless what is meant by 'son of David' – is immediately replaced by the supposition of the Pharisees that he is in league with Beelzebul.

[25–30] Matthew combines two blocks of text in the controversy, Mark 3.24–27 and Q (cf. Luke 11.17–23).

[31–32] The saying about blasphemy against the Spirit appears in Q in the context of logia about persecution (cf. Luke 12.2–12, especially v. 10) and in Mark (3.28–29) in the context of the Beelzebul conversation. Matthew takes up this Markan sequence.

[33–35] Verses 33 and 35 'elsewhere come at the conclusion of the Sermon on the Mount, and in Luke 6.43–45 are more similar in wording than in Matt. 7.17–18' (Wellhausen). With v. 34 Matthew makes a connection with the Beelzebul section and has Jesus say, 'You cannot but blaspheme because an evil tree necessarily brings forth evil fruit.' But that should be no excuse, as the concluding passage will show.

[36–37] The passage concludes Jesus' discourse shaped in controversy with the Pharisees. Jesus continues to speak with them, but in v. 36 he addresses all and inculcates the notion of judgment. Because of the sudden shift to the second person and because of its sententious character, v. 37 is perhaps a quotation.

Historical

[22–24] Cf. on Luke 11.14–15.
[25–30] Cf. on Mark 3.24–27 and Luke 11.17–23.
[31–32] Cf. on Mark 3.28–29.
[33,35] Cf. on Luke 6.43–45.

Matthew 12.38–45: The Pharisees' demand for signs. The return of the evil spirit

38 Then some of the scribes and Pharisees answered him and said, 'Teacher, we want to see a sign from you.' 39 But he answered and said to them, 'An evil and adulterous <u>generation</u> requires a sign, and no sign will be given to it except the sign of Jonah the prophet. 40 *For as Jonah was in the belly of the sea monster three days and three nights, so the Son of man will be in the heart of the earth three days and three nights.* 41 The people of Nineveh will rise up at the judgment with this <u>generation</u> and condemn it; for they repented at the preaching of Jonah. <u>And look, more than</u> Jonah <u>is here.</u> 42 The queen of the south will be raised up at the judgment with this <u>generation</u> and will condemn it; for she came from the ends of the earth to hear Solomon's wisdom. <u>And look, more than</u> Solomon <u>is here.</u>

43 Now when the unclean spirit goes out of a person, he passes through waterless places seeking rest, and does not find it. 44 Then he says, 'I will return to my house from which I came.' And when he comes, he finds it empty, swept and put in order. 45 Then he goes and brings with him seven other spirits, more evil than himself, and they enter and dwell there; and the last state of this man is worse than the first. *So too it will be with this evil <u>generation</u>.*'

Redaction and tradition

Matthew uses Q: for vv. 38–42 cf. Luke 11.29–32, where the Q text is better preserved. For vv. 43–45 cf. Luke 11.24–26.

[38] Cf. Mark 8.11 and Matt. 16.1.
[40] This verse is taken up later in Matt. 27.63 and probably comes from Matthew.
[41–42] Matthew reverses the order of the Q original. In so doing he brings together the statements about Jonah.
[43–45b] Cf. the remarks on Luke 11.24–26 (= Q).
[45c] 'With the closing sentence which is absent from Luke Matthew wants to justify the wrong position which he has assigned to the passage. This point is utterly contrived' (Wellhausen), for Matthew makes this parable (cf. on Luke 11.24–26) a prediction of disaster for this generation.

Historical

[38–42] Cf. on Luke 11.29–32 and Mark 8.11–12.
[43–45] Cf. on Luke 11.24–26.

Matthew 12.46–50: The true kinsfolk of Jesus

46 *And while he was still speaking to the crowds, look*, his mother and his brothers were stand-ing outside, who <u>wanted to speak with him</u>. 47 Then *someone* said to him, 'Look, your mother and your brothers are standing outside and <u>want *to speak with you*</u>.' 48 But he answered and said *to the one who told him*, 'Who is my mother, and who are my brothers?' 49 And he *stretched out his hand over his disciples* and said, 'Look, my mother and my brothers! 50 For whoever does the will *of my Father in heaven*, he is my brother and sister and mother.'

Redaction and tradition

Matthew uses Mark 3.21, 31–35. In relation to the harsh rejection of the family depicted in Mark the Matthew text (like Luke 8.19–21) is somewhat more friendly. It is toned down in two ways: *first*, Matthew (like Luke 8.19–21) simply omits Mark 3.21 – the assumption of the kinsfolk that Jesus is out of his mind; *secondly*, he abbreviates the report of the arrival of the kinsfolk: these are now no longer separated from Jesus by the assembled multitude (Mark 3.32a).

[46] Verse 46a is a Matthaean transition.

[47–48] It is not the crowd but an unnamed person who reports the arrival of the kinsfolk. Verse 47b picks up v. 46b. Verse 48 presupposes v. 47 and for this reason, contrary to ancient textual witnesses, is an ingredient of the text of Matthew.

[49] Jesus' gesture emphasizes his concern for the disciples. Indeed in the meta-phorical sense these are to be identified with his mother and his brothers.

[50] In contrast to Mark 3.35 ('God') this verse speaks in a way typical of the First Evangelist of 'my Father in heaven'.

Historical

Cf. on Mark 3.21, 31–35.

Matthew 13.1–9: The parable of the sower

1 On the same day Jesus went out of the house and sat beside the sea. 2 And great multitudes gathered around him, so that he got into a boat and sat there, and the whole people stood on the shore. 3 And he *told* them many things in parables and *said*,

'Look, a sower went out to sow. 4 And as he sowed some fell on the path; and the birds came and devoured it. 5 And other seeds fell on rocky ground, where it did not have much earth, and immediately it sprang up, since it did not have any deep earth. 6 But when the sun rose, it was scorched, and because it had no roots it withered away. 7 And other seeds fell among the thorns, and the thorns grew up and choked it. 8 And other seeds fell on the good earth and produced fruit, some one hundred fold, some sixtyfold and some thirtyfold. 9 He who has ears let him hear!'

Redaction and tradition

Matthew uses Mark 4.1–9 and reproduces what he has before him word for word with few exceptions.

[1–3a] Matthew (like Luke) twice deletes the motif of the teaching of Jesus (Mark 4.1, 3). Cf. previously 9.9 (Mark 2.13).

[3b–9] In v. 8 Matthew introduces a descending series of numbers, contrary to Mark 4.8 (cf. similarly 25.20–24/Luke 19.16–20).

Historical

Cf. on Mark 4.1–9.

Matthew 13.10–17: The meaning of the parable discourse

10 *And the disciples came to him and said,* 'Why do you speak to them in parables?' 11 And he answered and said, 'To you is given to know the mysteries of the kingdom of heaven, but to them it is not given. 12 For to him who has will be given, and he will have abundance; but from him who does not have, even what he has will be taken away. 13 This is why I speak to them in parables. For seeing they do not see and hearing they do not hear, nor do they understand. 14 *And with them is fulfilled the prophecy of Isaiah, which says,*

"You shall indeed hear and not understand; and you shall indeed see but not perceive. 15 For this people's heart has been hardened. And their ears are heavy of hearing and they have closed their eyes, so that they do not perceive with their eyes and hear with their ears and understand with their hearts and convert, and I will heal them."

16 But blessed are your eyes, *that* they see, *and your ears, that they hear.* 17 *Amen,* I say to you, many prophets *and righteous men* desired to see what you see and did not see (it), and to hear what you hear and did not hear (it).'

Redaction and tradition

[10–13] The passage is based on Mark 4.10–12; here Matthew has inserted v. 12 from Mark 4.25.

[14–15] Matthew had recognized that there is an allusion to Isa. 6 in v. 13 and in a learned way adds the complete quotation from Isa. 6.9–10, with an introductory formula, here.

[16–17] Cf. Luke 10.23–24 (= Q). Because of the context in the parable chapter Matthew adds the part about hearing. He replaces 'kings' with 'righteous men' because the term is important to him (cf. 1.19; 5.45, etc.). For 'prophet and righteous man' cf. 10.41.

Historical

[10–15] Cf. on Mark 4.10–12,25.
[16–17] Cf. on Luke 10.23–24.

Matthew 13.18–23: The interpretation of the parable of the sower

18 'Now hear the parable of the sower,

19 When anyone hears the word of the kingdom and *does not understand, the evil one* comes and snatches away what is sown *in his heart*; this is he who was sown along the path. 20 As for who was sown on rocky ground, this is he who hears the word and immediately receives it with joy. 21 Yet he has no root in himself, but endures for a while; when tribulation or persecution arises on account of the word, he takes offence. 22 As for who was sown among the thorns, this is he who hears the word, and the cares of the world and the deception of riches choke the word, so that it becomes unfruitful. 23 As for who was sown on good soil, this is he who hears the word *and understands* and then also bears fruit and does (it); one a hundredfold, another sixtyfold, the third thirtyfold.'

Redaction and tradition

Matthew is using Mark 4.13–20.

[18] Matthew passes over the rebuke to the disciples.

[19–23] Matthew skilfully improves the disconnected text he has before him and replaces the plural of the interpretations with the singular 'this is' formula plus interpretation. In terms of content Matthew has changed the Markan text by adding 'understand' in vv. 19 and 23. The type of person mentioned first in v. 19 hears and does not understand (cf. vv. 13f.), whereas the type of person mentioned last in v. 23 hears and understands. Cf. 15.10; 16.12; 17.13 for the significance of 'understand' in Matthew.

Historical

Cf. on Mark 4.13–20.

Matthew 13.24–30: The weeds among the wheat

24 He put another parable before them and said,
'The kingdom *of heaven* is like a man who sowed good seed in his field. 25 But while the people were sleeping, his enemy came and sowed weeds among the wheat and went away. 26 And when the plants grew and bore fruit the weeds also *appeared.* 27 And the servants of the householder came and said to him, "Lord, did you not sow good seed on your field? How then does it now have weeds?" 28 And he said to them, "An enemy has done this." And the servants said to him, "Then do you want us to go and gather them?" 29 But he said, "No, lest in gathering the weeds at the same time you tear up the roots of the wheat. 30 Let both grow together until harvest; and at harvest time I will say to the reapers, "First gather the wheat and bind it in bundles to burn it; but gather the wheat into my barns." '

Redaction and tradition

[24a] The introduction links the present parable with the previous one and prepares for following two (cf. vv. 31a, 33a).

[24b–30] The parable, which has an offshoot in Thomas 57, stands in place of the parable of the seed growing by itself (Mark 4.26–30), which Matthew has omitted, probably deliberately. The present parable has in common with this parable the feature that one is not to intervene in the process of growth between sowing and harvest. But it differs from the Markan parable in that this is not an everyday occurrence but an unusual individual action which seeks to inculcate the fact that despite the 'sowing' of the kingdom of God, evil remains present. At the same time this indicates that the parable is using experiences of the young community with 'the evil one' and calls for patience. The figure of the enemy (v. 28) is an image for the devil (cf. Mark 4.15). So the parable has an allegorical feature at a decisive point.

[30] Cf. 3.12.

Historical

The parable is inauthentic, as it reflects a community situation. Moreover Jesus himself saw the devil fall (Luke 10.18), so that he can no longer have an effect as in the present parable.

Matthew 13.31–32: The parable of the mustard seed

31 *He put another parable before them and said*, 'The kingdom *of heaven* is like a grain of mustard seed which a man took and sowed in his field. 32 It is the smallest of all seeds, but when it has grown it is the greatest of all shrubs and becomes a tree, so that the birds of heaven come and make nests in its branches.'

Redaction and tradition

[31–32] The parable uses Mark 4.30–32 and Q (cf. Luke 13.18–19), Mark more in the middle part (v. 32a–c) and Q more at the beginning and end. In Q the passage is a parable of growth, in Mark a parable of contrast, in Matthew a mixture of both. See further Thomas 20.

Historical

Cf. on Mark 4.30–32 and Thomas 20.

Matthew 13.33: On leaven

33 *He spoke another parable to them*, 'The kingdom *of heaven* is like leaven which a woman took and hid in three measures of meal, until it was all leavened.'

Redaction and tradition

The parable corresponds to Luke 13.20–21 (= Q). Cf. Thomas 96.1–2. Matthew adds this to the parable of the mustard seed taken over from Mark and Q. Although the word 'hide' comes from Q (cf. Luke 13.21), it nevertheless recurs in the Matthaean context (cf. vv. 35,44). Consequently for Matthew the parable may illustrate the hiddenness of salvation, which has always to be discovered (cf. 13.44; 10.26f.).

Historical

Cf. on Luke 13.20–21.

Matthew 13.34–35: The method of speaking to the people in parables

34 All this Jesus said to the crowds in parables, and he said nothing to them without a parable. 35 *This was to fulfil what was spoken by the prophet, who says*, 'I will open my mouth in parables and will utter what has been hidden since the beginning of the world.'

Redaction and tradition

[34] With this verse, which abbreviates Mark 4.33–34, Matthew is referring back to vv. 2–3 and 10–13.

[35] The fulfilment quotation (cf. most recently 12.17–21) comes from Ps. 78.2, the author of which Matthew understands as a prophet. It brings together all the parables that Jesus has so far told the people. The hardening theory of the Markan original (4.33–34) is not taken over directly here, but it is presupposed in the overall context (cf. 13.10–17).

Historical

The historical yield is nil.

Matthew 13.36–43: The interpretation of the parable of the weeds

36 *Then Jesus let the people go and came home. And his disciples came to him and said,* 'Interpret to us the parable of the weeds in the field!' 37 He answered and said, 'The one who sows the good seed is the Son of man; 38 and the field is the *world*; the good seed means *the sons of the kingdom*; the weeds are the sons of the evil one; 39 the enemy who sowed it is *the devil*; the harvest is the end of the world; and the reapers are the angels. 40 *Just as the weeds are collected and burned with fire, so it will be at the end of the world.* 41 *The Son of man will send his angels, and they will gather out of his kingdom all who give offence and do lawlessness,* 42 *and throw them into the fiery oven; there will be wailing and gnashing of teeth.* 43 *Then the righteous will shine like the sun in their father's kingdom. He who has ears, let him hear!'*

Redaction and tradition

This interpretation of the parable of the weeds (vv. 24–30) hardly goes back to its narrator. The reasons are: *first,* the interpretation nowhere touches on the key point of the parable, the admonition to patience. *Secondly,* the interpretation is selective, since there is no interpretation of the people sleeping (v. 25) or the servants and their conversation with the master (vv. 27–29) or the barns (v. 30).*Thirdly,* Matt. 13.36–43 shows a great accumulation of the linguistic peculiarities of Matthew (the most important are printed in italics in the translation). It follows from these observations that the interpretation derives from another narrator than the 'Jesus' of the parables and may come from Matthew himself, who has put his own view into the mouth of Jesus. Here Matthew is instructing the members of his community that they still face judgment and are therefore summoned to act righteously in order to bear fruit.

[36a] Cf. on v. 35.

[37–39] The passage contains what Luz calls a 'lexicographical interpretative catalogue' for many individual terms in the parable to be expounded.

[40–43] The theme of judgment occurs often in Matthew (cf. esp. 25.31–46). The emphasis that the righteous will enter the Father's kingdom (v. 43) is as Jewish as it is Matthaean (for the two cf. chs. 5–7). For the shining of the righteous cf. 17.2; Dan. 12.3; I Enoch 39.7; 104.2.

Historical

The historical yield is nil.

Matthew 13.44–46: The treasure in the field. The precious pearl

44 'The kingdom *of heaven* is like a treasure hidden in a field, which a man found and hid; and in his joy he goes and sells all that he has and buys that field.

45 Again the kingdom of heaven is like a merchant in search of fine pearls, 46 and when he found a precious pearl he went and sold all that he had and bought it.'

Redaction and tradition

This pair of parables, which appear in the New Testament only in Matthew (but for v. 44 cf. the offshoot in Thomas 109.1–2 and for vv. 45–46 that in Thomas 76.1–2), do not depict the coming of the kingdom but its value, which puts everything in the shade. Everything must be sacrificed for it: cf. Mark 10.29; Matt. 19.12.

[44] The field contains a treasure and not the seed as in the two parables told previously.

[45–46] 'The individual can and should buy the kingdom of God, sacrificing all else' (Wellhausen), similarly in v. 44.

Historical

[44] This verse is authentic. It describes an immoral hero (cf. Luke 16.1–7 and Thomas 98), for the man should have reported his discovery.

[45–46] These verses are authentic: the merchant is an example of all those who – like Jesus himself – give up everything in the face of the discovery of the kingdom of God in order to surrender to it completely (cf. on Luke 9.57–62).

Matthew 13.47–52: The parable of the net and its interpretation

47 'Again the kingdom *of heaven* is like a net which was thrown into the sea and gathered (fish) of all kinds. 48 When it became full, they draw it to shore, sit down and put the good into vessels but threw away the bad.

49 *So also it will be at the end of the world: the angels will come out and separate the evil from the righteous* 50 *and they will throw them into the fiery oven; there will be weeping and gnashing of teeth.*

51 *Have you understood all this?' They answer, 'Yes.'*

52 *Then he said to them, 'Therefore every scribe who has been (made) a disciple of the kingdom of heaven is like a householder who brings out of his treasure things new and old.'*

Redaction and tradition

[47–48] The parable recalls that of the weeds among the wheat (13.24–30). Instead of the image of sowing, which probably derives from preaching, there is the image of the fishing, which suggests mission. The parable (like that of the weeds) is about the last judgment. For another version of the parable of Thomas 8.

[49–50] These verses contain the interpretation. The hearers are prepared for it by vv. 40–43. In terms of content the being thrown into the fiery oven has nothing to do with the throwing out of the bad (v. 48).

[51] This verse refers back to v. 34.

[52] Like 23.34 this verse presupposes the existence of Christian scribes in Matthew's community. 'The scribe who is trained for the kingdom of God is Christian as distinct from Jewish (5.19). He creates new things and hands on old ones' (Wellhausen).

Historical

[47–48] The parable is authentic. It show no signs of having been shaped by the community. For example, the church does not appear in it at all.

[49–52] These verses are unhistorical, as Matthew's community is speaking in them.

Matthew 13.53–58: The repudiation of Jesus in his ancestral town

53 *And it happened when Jesus had ended these parables, that he went away from there.* 54 And he came into his ancestral town and taught them in *their* synagogue, so that they were amazed and asked, 'Where did this man get this wisdom and these mighty works? 55 Is not this the *craftsman's son? Is not his mother called Mary?* And his brothers James and *Joseph* and Simon and Jude? 56 And are not all his sisters with us? Where then did he get all this?' 57 And they took offence at him. But Jesus said to them, 'Nowhere is a prophet without honour except in his ancestral town and in his home.' 58 And he did not do many mighty acts there because of their unbelief.

Redaction and tradition

Matthew is using Mark 6.1–6.

[53a] This is a stereotyped phrase, which concludes the parable discourse (cf. on 7.28).

[53b] This is a transition.

[54] The verse displays three changes as compared with Mark 6.1f.: *first*, the disciples are not mentioned; *secondly*, Jesus teaches in 'their' synagogue; *thirdly*, the miracles are not defined further (Mark 6.2: 'which are performed by his hands').

[55–56] By contrast with Mark 6.3 Jesus is not described as a 'craftsman' and 'son of Mary' but as 'the craftsman's son'. In other words, Matthew suppresses (cf. 1.18ff.) the contemporary Jewish tradition which was derogatory about Jesus on the grounds of his illegitimate birth. As in the original, the extended listing of the members of the family, slightly changed from Mark 6.3, illustrates the position of the neighbours: Jesus cannot be powerful and wise because his family is well known locally.

[57] Matthew deletes the relatives from the series of three in Mark 6.4.

[58] Matthew tightens up the conclusion in Mark 6.5f. by omitting both the statement 'he could perform no miracles there', which might have caused offence to the Christian reader, and the observation that Jesus was amazed. In so doing Matthew emphasizes the superiority of Jesus as the ruler of this world (cf. 18.16–20).

The focal point of the Matthaean revision lies in the emphasis on the unbelief of the people in Nazareth. This anticipates the unbelief of the whole Jewish nation towards Jesus.

Historical

Cf. on Mark 6.1–6.

Matthew 14.1–12: The end of John the Baptist

1 At that time Herod the tetrarch heard the news about Jesus. 2 And he said to his servants, 'That is John the Baptist; he has risen from the dead; that is why these powers are at work in him.'

3 For Herod had John seized, bound and thrown into prison because of Herodias, his brother's wife. 4 For John had said to him, 'It is not lawful for you to have her.' 5 *And he would have liked to kill him, but he feared for the people, for they regarded him as a prophet.* 6 And when Herod celebrated his birthday, the daughter of Herodias danced in the midst and pleased Herod. 7 Therefore he promised with an oath to give her whatever she wanted. 8 Prompted by her mother, she (said), 'Give me the head of John the Baptist on a platter.' 9 And sorrowfully, the king commanded that (it) should be given to her because of the oaths

and those who were reclining with him at table, 10 and he sent and had John beheaded in prison. 11 And his head was brought in on a platter and given to the girl; and she brought it to her mother. 12 And his disciples came and took his corpse and buried him; and *they came and told Jesus.*

Redaction and tradition

Matthew uses Mark 6.14–19 and tightens up his original.

[2–3] In contrast to Mark 6.14 Herod is rightly given the title 'tetrarch'. This is Antipas, the local ruler of the area where Jesus lived; from AD 4 to 39 he was ruler of Galilee. (Later in v. 9 Matthew, on the basis of the Markan original [6.26], speaks of 'king'.) Matthew omits Mark 6.15, which spoke of belief in John as Elijah or one of the prophets, without providing any substitute.

[3–4] Cf. Mark 6.17–18.

[5] By comparison with the Markan original Matthew shifts Herod into the background and depicts him as John's opponent, not his protector. For the role of John as a prophet cf. 21.26 and Mark 6.15. As in 21.46, the fear of the people prevents the high priests and Pharisees from killing Jesus.

[6–11] These verses markedly abbreviate Mark 6.21–28.

[12] Matthew alters the typically Markan parenthesis and attaches the narrative of the death of John the Baptist directly to the overall context with v. 12b.

Historical

Cf. on Mark 6.14–29.

Matthew 14.13–21: The feeding of the five thousand

13 Now when Jesus heard (it), he went away from there in a boat to a lonely place apart. And when the crowds of people heard that, they followed him on foot from the towns. 14 And when he got out he saw a great crowd, and he had compassion on them and he healed their sick. 15 And in the evening his disciples came to him and said, 'This is a lonely place and the hour is now past; send the crowds of people away, so that they may go into the villages and buy food for themselves.' 16 But Jesus said to them, *'They need not go away;* give them something to eat.' 17 And they say to him, 'We have nothing here but five loaves and two fishes.' 18 And he said, 'Bring them here to me.' 19 And he ordered the crowds of people to recline on the grass, and took the five loaves and the two fishes, looked up to heaven, gave thanks and broke (them) and gave the loaves to the disciples, *and the disciples (gave them) to the people.* 20 And they all ate and were full and gathered up the fragments that were left over, twelve baskets full. 21 And those who had eaten were around five thousand men, *not counting women and children.*

Redaction and tradition

Matthew is using Mark 6.30–44.

[13] In contrast to Mark, this verse links up with the report of the death of John the Baptist. In v. 13b Matthew tightens up the Markan report (Mark 6.33b) of the people gathering.

[16] The addition 'they need not go away' shows that Jesus intended the miracle from the start (cf. John 6.6).

[17] The disciples' question in Mark (6.37), which betrays incomprehension, is omitted.

[19] This verse involves the disciples more closely in the distribution of the bread.

[21] The statement that the number applies only to the men *not counting women and children* accentuates the miracle by comparison with the Markan original, since now the number of women and children, which is not given, has to be added.

Historical

Cf. on Mark 6.35–44.

Matthew 14.22–36: Jesus and the sinking Peter on the sea. Healings

22 And immediately Jesus made the disciples get into the boat and go before him to the other side, while he dismissed the multitudes. 23 And he dismissed the crowds of people and went up the mountain *by himself*, to pray. And when evening came, *he was there alone*.

24 And the boat was already many stadia from land and was in trouble from the waves, for the wind was against it. 25 But in the fourth watch of the night Jesus came to them and walked on the sea. 26 And when the disciples saw him walking on the sea, they were terrified and cried, 'It is a ghost.' And they cried out for fear. 27 But immediately Jesus spoke with them *and said*, 'Take heart, it is I; do not be afraid.'

28 *And* Peter *answered* him and said, '*Lord*, if it is you, *command* me to come to you *over the waters*.' 29 And he said, 'Come here!' And Peter got out of the boat and walked on the water and came to Jesus. 30 But when he saw the strong wind he *took fright* and began to sink and cried, 'Lord, save me!' 31 Immediately Jesus stretched out his hand and caught him and says to him, '*O man of little faith, why did you doubt?*' 32 And when they had got *into the boat the wind ceased*. 33 And those who were in the boat fell down before him and said, 'Truly you are the Son of God.'

34 And they crossed over and came to land, to Gennesaret. 35 And when the men at this place recognized him, they sent them into the whole region and brought all the sick to him. 36 And they asked that they might only touch the fringe of his garment. And all those who touched (him) were healed.

Redaction and tradition

Verses 22–27 and 34–36 presuppose Mark 6.45–56 as an original, whereas vv. 28–31 are Matthaean special material.

[22] Matthew deletes the detail 'Bethsaida' (Mark 6.45) because this place had already been rebuked in 11.21 (= Luke 10.13).

[23–24] These verses largely correspond to Mark 6.46–47. But Matthew prefaces them (v. 23b) with the statement that Jesus was alone (Mark 6.47b).

[25] Matthew omits the difficult sentence Mark 6.48b ('And he wanted to pass by them').

[26] Matthew passes over the sentence Mark 6.50a ('all saw him') in order to excuse the disciples.

[27] This verse largely corresponds to Mark 6.50b–c.

[28–31] The passage has numerous Matthaean linguistic elements. For Peter's walking on the sea cf. the analogies from the history of religion cited at Mark 6.45–52. In the Matthaean context vv. 28–31 prepare for Peter's confession in 16.16. At the same time, for Matthew the figure of Peter may be a symbol of the believers generally, who although they possess little faith can overcome this situation. At any rate even some of the twelve have doubts on their encounter with the 'Risen One' (Matt. 28.17; cf. 18.16).

[32] This verse is a link from the inserted episode about Peter back to the story about the disciples (vv. 22–27).

[33] Instead of being beside themselves because of their hardened hearts (Mark 6.51b–52) the disciples fall down and confess that Jesus is Son of God, anticipating Peter's confession (16.16).

[34–36] Part of this corresponds to the Markan original, Mark 6.53–56, which Matthew has abbreviated. Verse 34 is a transition. Verses 35f. are the summary of healings (cf. 4.24; 8.16; 9.35; 12.15; 14.14; 15.29–31; 21.14).

Historical

[22–27, 34–36] Cf. on Mark 6.45–56.
[28–31] Peter did not walk on the sea.

Matthew 15.1–20: On cleanness and uncleanness

1 *Then* Pharisees and scribes come to Jesus from Jerusalem and said, 2 'Why do your disciples transgress the tradition of the elders? For they do not wash their hands when they eat bread.'

3 But he answered and said to them, 'Why then do you transgress the commandment of

God for the sake of your precepts?' 4 For God said, "Honour your father and mother", and "Whoever speaks evil of father and mother shall die the death." 5 But you say, "Whoever says to father and mother, 'What I owe you is a consecrated gift', 6 need not honour his father." And you have annulled God's commandment for your precepts.

7 You hypocrites, well has Isaiah prophesied of you, saying, "This people honours me with their lips, but their heart is far from me; 9 in vain do they worship me, teaching as doctrines the precepts of men.""

10 And he called the people and said to them, 'Listen and understand:

11 It is not what goes into the mouth that makes a person unclean, but what comes out of the mouth makes a person unclean.'

12 *Then his disciples came up and say to him, 'Do you know that the Pharisees were offended when they heard the saying?' 13 And he answered and said, 'Every plant which my heavenly Father has planted will be rooted up. 14 Let them alone: they are blind guides! And if a blind man leads a blind man, they both fall into the pit.'*

15 *Then Peter answered and said to him,* 'Interpret the parable for us.' 16 And he said, 'Are you still without understanding? Do you not comprehend that all that goes *into the mouth* goes into the belly and after that is emptied into the cesspit? 18 But what comes *out of the mouth* comes from the heart, and that makes people unclean. 19 For out of the heart come *wicked* thoughts, murders, adulteries, fornications, thefts, false witnesses, blasphemies. 20 These are the things which make people unclean. *But eating with unwashed hands does not make people unclean.'*

Redaction and tradition

Matthew uses Mark 7.1–23. He simplifies what he has in front of him and adds the announcement of judgment on the Pharisees in vv. 12–14.

[1] Matthew passes over Mark 7.2–4. He does not need to remind his community, which is rooted in Judaism, about the custom of washing hands before meals, as Mark had needed to do for his Gentile-Christian readership.

[2] Cf. Mark 7.5.

[3–9] Matthew transposes Mark 7.6-8 and Mark 7.9–13. In so doing he skilfully creates a textual unit which censures the misuse of the Decalogue by the tradition of the elders and makes the prophet Isaiah pass the final verdict on such hypocrisy. For vv. 3–6 cf. Mark 7.9–13. Note the counter-question in v. 3, which rejects the charge of transgression with a charge of transgression. For vv. 7–9 cf. Mark 7.6–8.

[10–11] For v. 10 cf. Mark 7.14. Verse 11 simplifies Mark 7.15.

[12–14] This passage accentuates the anti-Jewish criticism. Verse 14b goes back to Q (cf. on Luke 6.39b).

[15] Peter (and not the disciples, Mark 7.17) asks Jesus about the meaning of the parable.

[17] This verse deletes the rationalistic freeing of foods by Mark 7.19d ('With this he declared all foods clean').

[19] This verse abbreviates the Markan catalogue of vices (Mark 7.21–22) by some misdeeds: covetousnesses, wickednesses, deceist, licentiousness, the evil eye, arrogance, failure to understand. The vices omitted stand somewhat apart from the Decalogue, which is the issue in vv. 3–6. Matthew has kept the misdeeds corresponding to the commandments of the Decalogue.

[20b] This is a concluding observation with which Matthew refers back to the problem of washing hands and rounds off the section.

Historical

[1–11, 15–20] Cf. on Mark 7.1–23.
[14b] Cf. on Luke 6.39b.

Matthew 15.21–28: The Canaanite woman

21 *And* Jesus *went away from there and withdrew* into the region of Tyre and Sidon. 22 *And look, a Canaanite woman came from this region and cried, saying, 'Have mercy on me,* <u>Lord</u>, *son of David! My daughter is severely plagued by a demon.' 23 But he did not answer her a word. Then his disciples came to him, asked him and said, 'Send her away, for she is crying after us.' 24 And he answered and said, 'I was sent only to the lost sheep of the house of Israel.' 25 And she came and prostrated herself before him and said, '*<u>Lord</u>, *help me!'* 26 And he answered and said, 'It is not right to take the children's bread and throw it to the dogs.' 27 But she said, 'Yes, <u>Lord</u>, but after all, the little dogs eat the crumbs *which fall from their lords'* table.' 28 *Then Jesus answered and said to her, 'Woman, your faith is great. Be it done to you as you will!'* and her *daughter was healed in the same hour.*

Redaction and tradition

Matthew is using Mark 7.24–30; here vv. 22–25 go beyond the Markan original and have been reformulated by Matthew. The Matthaean revision recalls Mark 10.46–52, for there too the sick person twice makes his request for healing (vv. 47, 51). In the present story this happens in vv. 22, 25.

[21] As elsewhere (cf. 13.26 with Mark 5.43), Matthew omits the secrecy motif from Mark 7.24.

[22] The address 'son of David' emphasizes that Jesus is the messiah of Israel (cf. 9.27).

[23] For the reactions of the disciples cf. 14.15 and 19.13.

[24] This verse is a Matthaean formulation on the basis of the logion from the tradition in 10.5–6.

[25] This verse reinforces the petition to Jesus with the renewed form of address as Lord (cf. previously v. 22).

[26] Here the second rejection by Jesus takes place, following the first (v. 24). By comparison with the Markan original (7.27), Matthew puts the emphasis elsewhere: now Jews and Gentiles are not even to get the same bread any more.

[27] This verse contains the most verbal agreements with Mark (7.28).

[28] This verse recalls 8.10,13. Like the Gentile centurion, so too this time a Gentile woman has her wish granted. In this story the Matthaean community, which indeed has already begun on its mission to the Gentiles (28.16–20), is once again (cf. above, the prehistory, Matt. 1–2) given a signal that the gospel will go beyond the frontiers of Israel. But this is possible only because Jesus had been sent to the lost sheep of the house of Israel.

Historical

Cf. on Mark 7.24–30. Otherwise this pericope raises clear historical reservations about the assumption that Jesus was active among the Gentiles. This is because for Matthew's community the mission among Gentiles began only after 'Easter' and from this perspective, at any rate in Matthew, there was a cautious reference to the relationship of Jesus to individual Gentiles. Time and again we must be clear that the mission among the Gentiles was raised as a theme for the earliest community only by the Hellenists around Stephen (cf. Acts 6–8) and especially by the apostle Paul, who did not know Jesus. Had Jesus shown the openness *in principle* that we find here, the mission to the Gentiles would not have been so difficult to establish (cf. Gal. 2/Acts 15).

Matthew 15.29–31: Further healings

29 *And when Jesus had gone away from there, he came to the sea of Galilee. And when he had climbed a mountain, he sat down there.* 30 *And great multitudes came to him who had with them the lame, the maimed, the blind, the dumb and many other sick people. And they put them at the feet of Jesus, and he healed them,* 31 *so that the multitudes wondered when they saw that the dumb spoke, the maimed were made whole, the lame walked and the blind saw. And they praised the God of Israel.*

Redaction and tradition

The passage is a quite colourless summary of healing which has been fashioned by Matthew himself. In his Gospel it takes the place of the healing of the deaf mute (Mark 7.31–37) which Matthew could not accept. For the expression 'God of Israel' in v. 31, which reflects the language of the Psalms, cf. Luke 1.68.

With this summary of healings (for this phenomenon see most recently 14.35–36), which presupposes a great crowd of people, Matthew prepares for the feeding of the four thousand which is narrated next.

Historical

The pericope has no historical value at this time and in this place, however much individual exorcisms of Jesus may have been the occasion for its composition.

Matthew 15.32–39: The feeding of the four thousand

32 And Jesus called his disciples to him and said, 'I have compassion on the people; for they have already persisted three days with me and have nothing to eat, and I do not want to let them go hungry lest they faint on the way.' 33 And his disciples say to him, 'Where shall we (get) so much bread in the wilderness to feed so many people?' 34 And Jesus said to them, 'How many loaves have you?' And they said, 'Seven and a couple of little fishes.' 35 And making the people recline on the earth, 36 he took the seven loaves and the fishes, gave thanks, broke (them) and gave to the disciples, and the disciples to the people. 37 And they all ate and were filled. And they took up the fragments which remained, seven baskets full. 38 And those who had eaten were four thousand men, *not counting women and children.*

39 And when he had sent the people away, he got into the boat and went into the region of Magadan.

Redaction and tradition

Matthew uses Mark 8.1–9 and in particular in vv. 35–39 emphasizes the parallels to the story of the first feeding (14.13–21). Note, however, that in Mark the second feeding takes place on Gentile soil, but not in Matthew. In Mark we are in the Decapolis (Mark 7.3), in Matthew by Lake Gennesaret (Matt. 15.29).

[32] Matthew abbreviates Mark 8.1–3 at the beginning (v. 1a) and at the end (v. 3b).

[33–36] The passage corresponds to Mark 8.4–7, where Matthew has included the distribution of the fish in the giving of the bread. Mark 8.7 can therefore be passed over.

[37–38] Cf. Mark 8.8–9.

[39] In both Matthew and in Mark there is a note about a crossing in the boat in connection with the story of the feeding, each with a different note of place, Magadan or Dalmanutha (Mark 8.10). Both places are unknown.

Historical

Cf. on Mark 6.34–44.

Matthew 16.1–12: The Pharisees and Sadducees ask for a sign. Warning against their teaching

1 And the Pharisees an*d Sadducees* came. And to tempt him they called on him to show them a sign from heaven.

2 But he answered and said to them, '[In the evening you say, "Good weather, for the sky is red." 3 And in the morning, "Tomorrow a storm is coming, for the sky is red and threatening." Can you interpret the appearance of the sky; but not the signs of the time?] 4 An evil and apostate generation calls for a sign, and no sign will be given it but the sign of Jonah.' And he left them and went away.

5 And when the disciples had come to the other shore, they had forgotten to bring bread with them. 6 And Jesus said to them, 'Look out and beware of the leaven of the Pharisees *and Sadducees!*' 7 And they discussed it among themselves and said, 'We did not bring bread.' 8 When Jesus saw (this), he said, 'Why are you discussing among yourselves, *O you of little faith,* that you have no bread? 9 Do you still not <u>understand</u>? Do you not remember the five loaves for the five thousand and how many baskets you gathered up? 10 Or the seven loaves for the four thousand and how many baskets you collected? 11 How is it that you do not <u>understand</u> that I was not talking to you about bread? *Beware rather of the leaven of the Pharisees and Sadducees!'* 12 *Then they understood that he had not told them to beware of the leaven of bread, but of the teaching of the Pharisees and Sadducees.*

Preliminary text-critical note: vv. 2b–3 are missing in important manuscripts. Nevertheless some commentators (cf. e.g. Gnilka) hold that they belong to the original text. Cf. however, Luz: 'Matthew 16.2f. presumably came into being as a gloss without the direct influence of Luke 12.54–56.'

Redaction and tradition

Matthew is using Mark 8.10–21. Yet Matthew had already reported a request for a sign from the Pharisees and scribes in 12.38–40; the reader is reminded of this and its details might have an influence here.

[1] Matthew adds 'and Sadducees' to prepare for 16.6.

[2–3] For the textual criticism see above.

[4] Cf. 12.39; Mark 8.13. A heightening can be noted by comparison with the first request for a sign (12.38–40). 'Jesus' does not explain what the sign of Jonah is and therefore leaves his conversation partners abruptly. They will encounter him again only in Jerusalem, when the sign of Jonah will be given in real earnest: Jesus' death and his resurrection after three days.

[5] Cf. on v. 7.

[6] Verse 6b is explained by Matthew in vv. 11–12.

[7] This verse takes up again the disciples' problem mentioned in v. 5.

[8–10] These verses discuss the anxieties of the disciples from the perspective of Jesus.

[11–12] The disciples come to understand as a result of the interpretation, which takes up v. 6 again (cf. similarly 13.11–23, 36–50; 15.15–20). However, it remains unclear what could be meant by the *teaching* of the Pharisees *and* Sadducees, by which Matthew interprets Mark (8.15) and his talk of the leaven of the Pharisees and that of Herod.

The healing of the blind man which is related next in Mark (8.22–26) and symbolically depicts the opening of the disciples' eyes is omitted in Matthew. For him the disciples already see.

Historical

[1–3, 5–12] Cf. on Mark 8.10–11, 13–21.

[4] Cf. on Mark 8.12, where we have the authentic saying of Jesus in a more original form.

Matthew 16.13–20: Peter's confession and the promise to him

13 Then Jesus came into the region of Caesarea Philippi and asked his disciples and said, 'Who do people say that *the Son of man* is?' 14 They said, 'Some (say that you are) John the Baptist, others (that you are) Elijah, *yet others (that you are) Jeremiah* or one of the prophets.' 15 And he said to them, 'But who do you say that I am?' 16 Simon Peter answered and said, 'You are Christ, *the son of the living God.*'

17 *And Jesus answered and said to him, 'Blessed are you, Simon bar Jonah; for flesh and blood have not revealed (that) to you, but my Father in heaven.* 18 And I also say to you, You are rock (Peter) and on this stone I will build my community, and the gates of hell shall not prevail against it. 19 *I will give you the keys of the kingdom of heaven*: and what you bind on earth shall also be bound in heaven, and what you loose on earth shall also be loosed in heaven.'

20 Then he *commanded* the disciples to say to no one that he was the Christ.

Redaction

The source for vv. 13–16 and v. 20 is Mark 8.27–30. Matthew has inserted special material in vv. 17–19.

[13] Matthew brings forward the title Son of man for Jesus here from Mark 8.31.

[14] Matthew inserts the popular expectation that Jeremiah will come again (cf. II Macc. 15.14–16: the appearance of Jeremiah, the heavenly intercessor, to Onias), and has people making the identification of Jeremiah with Jesus.

[16] For talk of the 'living God' cf. 26.63; I Thess. 1.9; Ps. 42.3; 84.3.

[17] Because of the overlappings with 11.25–27, this verse is redactional and is to be understood as a Matthaean transition to vv. 18–19.

[18–19] In the context of the Gospel of Matthew the piece of tradition has the task of providing a basis for the authority of the community and its leader (cf. 18.15–18). The name 'Peter' is *not* attested before Christianity, but from the beginning was a Greek counterpart to the Aramaic Cephas (= rock), which was Simon's surname. Because of its agreement with 23.13, and as a counter formulation to it, v. 19a perhaps derives from Matthew.

[20] This verse links back to v. 16.

Tradition

[18,19b] Here the 'Risen One' is speaking; he transfers to the first witness Simon/Cephas/Peter (cf. I Cor. 15.5) the leadership of the church including the authority to forgive sins. For the disciplinary authority cf. also 18.18; John 20.23. 'The community, whose authority Peter is, will be saved in the end time, when the powers of the underworld overwhelm people. Here is an expression of the eschatological consciousness of the Palestinian community that it is the community of the righteous of the end time' (Bultmann). The community is presumed to be a building. Simon is the firm foundation.

Historical

[13–16, 20] Cf. on Mark 8.27–30.

[18,19b] Jesus cannot have spoken these words as he did not found a church. Rather, these are words of the 'Risen One', which are based on the fact that after the death of Jesus Simon Cephas was in fact the first to have seen the 'Risen One' (cf. I Cor. 15.5). The passage was then put in the mouth of Jesus by Peter himself or his followers and subsequently predated by Matthew into the life of Jesus. It is inauthentic.

Matthew 16.21–23: The first announcement of Jesus' passion and resurrection. Peter's objection

21 From that time Jesus began *to show* his disciples that he had to go to Jerusalem and suffer much from the elders and chief priests and scribes and be killed and *on the third day* be raised.

22 And Peter took him aside and began to threaten him and said, '*God forbid, Lord! Do not let this happen to you.*' 23 But he turned round and said to Peter, 'Get behind me, Satan. You are an *offence* to me; for you are not on God's side but on that of men.'

Redaction and tradition

Matthew is using Mark 8.31–33.

[21] This verse links to the prohibition in v. 20 and discloses new knowledge about the fate of Jesus to the disciples. Matthew passes over the statements about Jesus being rejected (Mark 8.31) and his plainness of speech (Mark 8.32a).

[22–23] Matthew deletes any reference to the disciples and concentrates the passage on Peter, by having him address and even remonstrate with Jesus in direct speech.

Historical

Cf. on Mark 8.31–33.

Matthew 16.24–28: On discipleship of Jesus

24 *Then* Jesus said to his disciples, 'If anyone will come after me, let him deny himself and take up his cross and follow me. 25 Whoever shall save his life shall lose it; but whoever shall lose his life for my sake shall *find* it. 26 What does it benefit a man if he gains the whole world but forfeits his life? Or what will a man give in exchange for his life? 27 For the Son of man will come in the glory of his father with his angels, and *then he will recompense everyone for what he has done.* 28 Amen, I say to you: there are some standing here who will not taste death until they see the Son of man coming in his kingdom.'

Redaction and tradition

Matthew is using Mark 8.34–9.1.

[24–26] This passage largely corresponds to the Markan original (8.34–37). Here, however, Jesus addresses the instructions *only* to the disciples, whereas Mark 8.34 also includes the people as audience. So Matthew deletes the people as those who receive Jesus' instructions.

[27] Matthew tightens up Mark 8.38 because he has already partly incorporated this verse into 10.33. However, the hand of Matthew is particularly evident in v. 27b, where there is emphasis on judgment according to works (cf. 25.31–46).

[28] The kingdom of God in Mark (9.1) becomes the Son of man. In this way Matthew makes a smoother connection with v. 27.

Historical

Cf. on Mark 8.34–9.1.

Matthew 17.1–13: The transfiguration of Jesus and the conversation on the descent from the mountain

1 And after six days Jesus took with him Peter and James and John, *his brother*, and led them apart up a high mountain. 2 And he was transfigured before them, a*nd his face shone like the sun*. 3 And *look,* Moses and Elijah appeared to them; they spoke with him. 4 And Peter began and spoke to Jesus, 'Lord, it is good to be here. *If you will,* I shall make three booths here, one for you and one for Moses and one for Elijah.' 5 *While he was still speaking,* look, a bright cloud overshadowed them. And *look*, a voice from the cloud said, 'This is my beloved son, in whom I am well pleased; listen to him.' 6 *When the disciples heard that, they fell on their faces and were greatly afraid.* 7 *But Jesus came to them, touched them and said, 'Arise and have no fear.'* 8 But when they opened their eyes they saw no one but Jesus alone.

9 And when they were going down from the mountain, Jesus commanded them and said, 'Tell no man this vision until the Son of man has risen from the dead!' 10 And his disciples asked him and said, 'Why do the scribes say that Elijah must first come?' 11 Jesus answered and said, 'Elijah is indeed coming and will restore all things. 12 But I say to you, Elijah has already come, and they did not know him, but did to him whatever they wanted. *So also the Son of man will have to suffer at their hands.'* 13 *Then the disciples understood that he had spoken to them of John the Baptist.*

Redaction and tradition

Matthew is using Mark 9.2–13.

[1] For the three named disciples as companions of Jesus cf. later 26.37 (= Mark 14.33).

[2] Matthew relates the transfiguration to a transformation of the face of Jesus (cf. Rev. 1.16); similarly Luke 9.29: the appearance of his face was 'altered'.

[3] The sequence 'Moses and Elijah' is chronologically correct (Mark 9.4, 'Elijah with Moses').

[4] There is no longer any mention of Peter's incomprehension (Mark 9.5–6).

[5] This verse corresponds to Mark 9.7.

[6–7] The depiction of the disciples' reaction to the voice from the cloud (cf. 28.16) and their raising up by Jesus derive from Matthew. Thus the disciples are portrayed in a more positive way than in Mark, and on the redactional level the episode is brought close to being an Easter story.

[8] This verse corresponds to Mark 9.8.

[9] This verse corresponds to Mark 9.9; here Matthew deletes the failure of the

disciples to understand, which follows in Mark (9.9), in accord with his own positive picture of the disciples in vv. 6–7.

[10] This verse corresponds almost word for word with Mark 9.11.

[11–12] These verses use Mark 9.12–13. The references to the fulfilment of scripture in Mark 9.12b and 9.13c are omitted as superfluous.

[13] As in 16.12, this verse adds that the disciples gained an insight – here into the point that John the Baptist is Elijah redivivus, as is presupposed in the Markan original (9.13).

Historical

Cf. on Mark 9.1–13.

Matthew 17.14–20: The epileptic boy

14 And when they came to the people, a man came up to him, fell at his feet 15 and said, 'Lord, have mercy on my son! For he is an epileptic and suffers terribly; often he falls into the fire, and *often* into the water; 16 and I brought him to your disciples, and they could not heal him.' 17 And Jesus answered and said, 'O unbelieving and perverse generation, how long shall I be with you? How long shall I endure you? Bring him here to me.' 18 And Jesus threatened him and the demon went out of him and the boy was healed from that hour. 19 Then his disciples came to him when they were alone and asked, 'Why could we not drive it out?' 20 And he said to them, 'Because of your *little faith*. Amen, I say to you, if you have faith like a mustard seed, you can say to this mountain "Move to there", and it will move, and nothing will be impossible for you.' [21]

Preliminary text-critical note: v. 21 ('But this kind only comes out with prayer and fasting') is absent from the most important manuscripts. It was inserted at a secondary stage on the basis of Mark 9.29.

Redaction and tradition

The text of Mark 9.14–29 was striking for its almost intolerable length. Matthew has abbreviated it to about a third of its original extent (cf. the similarly drastic abbreviation of Mark 5.1–20 in 8.28–34). At the same time, the assumption that the existing Matthaean version represents a working over of the Markan narrative mentioned comes up against difficulties. For Luke 9.37–42 has numerous agreements with Matthew against Mark, so that the thesis is also possible that Matthew and Luke used another basis than Mark 9.14–29. However, I shall leave that aside here and presuppose exclusively the use of Mark.

[15] Matthew immediately inserts the (second) description of the illness from Mark 9.22 here.

[16] Cf. Mark 9.18.

[17] Cf. Mark 9.19.

[18] Matthew suppresses the fact that the young man was possessed to the point that it is almost unrecognizable, but he has to mention it here, since v. 19 which follows contains a question from the disciples.

[19–20] Cf. Mark 9.28. It follows from 7.22 that in the Matthaean community miracles took place, though in a dubious way. Possibly the disciples' question reflects the absence of healing and Jesus explains how true miracles are to be done (cf. similarly the original Mark 9.28f. and James 5.13–16). The saying about a faith which moves mountains derives from Q (cf. Luke 17.6). Cf. also Mark 11.23; Thomas 48; 106.2. Paul seems to be reacting to this in I Cor. 13.2.

Historical

[14–20a] Cf. on Mark 9.14–29.

[20b] The saying about faith moving mountains is probably authentic, since it is widely attested for Jesus and fits his notion of God. Cf. on Mark 11.23.

Matthew 17.22–23: The second prediction of the passion and resurrection

22 As they *were gathering* in Galilee, Jesus said to them, 'The Son of man will be delivered into the hands of men, 23 and they will kill him and on the third day he *will be raised.' And they became very sorrowful.*

Redaction and tradition

[22–23] The source of this section is Mark 9.30–32. Matthew has abbreviated what he had before him and replaced the typical Markan motif of incomprehension (Mark 9.32) with the disciples' sorrow.

Historical

Cf. on Mark 9.30–32.

Matthew 17.24–27: Paying the temple tax

24 When they came to Capernaum, the collectors of the didrachm came to Peter and said, 'Does not your teacher pay the didrachm?' 25 He says, 'Of course.' And when he went home, Jesus spoke to him first and said, 'What do you think, Simon? From whom do the kings of

the earth take toll or taxes, from their sons or from strangers?' 26 When he answered, 'From strangers,' Jesus said to him, 'So the sons are free.

27 But so that we do not cause them offence, go to the sea and cast a hook, and take the first fish that comes up; and when you open its mouth, you will find a stater (didrachma); take that and give it to them for me and you.'

Redaction and tradition

[24–27] The passage derives from the community, for the question is put to Peter, the leader of the earliest community. The topic is whether Christians are to pay the temple tax (cf. Ex. 30.11–16; Neh. 10.32f.). The pericope consists of a didactic conversation (vv. 24–26) and a kind of miracle story (v. 27). However, strictly speaking v. 27 does not report a miracle but an order for a miracle. Moreover v. 27 makes sense only in connection with vv. 24–26 and never existed on its own. The passage comes from the time before the destruction of the temple, i.e. before AD 70.

Historical

The historical yield is nil.

Matthew 18.1–5: The greatest in the kingdom of heaven

1 At that hour the disciples came to Jesus and said, 'Who is the greatest *in the kingdom of heaven*?' 2 Jesus called a child to him and put it in their midst 3 and said, 'Amen, I say to you, Unless you repent and become like children, you will not enter the kingdom *of heaven*. 4 Whoever humbles himself *like this child, he is the greatest in the kingdom of heaven*. 5 And whoever receives such a child in my name receives me.'

Redaction and tradition

With this section Matthew begins the fourth great discourse of Jesus, the end of which is indicated in 19.1 with the typical concluding formula. The discourse deals mainly with the life of the disciples in the community and the norms which apply there. Mark 9.33–37 is used in the opening section.

[1] This is an abbreviation of Mark 9.33–35. In Mark the disciples had been disputing, and Jesus learns this only by enquiring: in Matthew they themselves approach Jesus. The addition 'in the kingdom of heaven' effects a transition from the earthly to the heavenly sphere.

[2] Cf. Mark 9.36.

[3] Cf. Mark 10.15. (Matthew later omits this verse when he uses Mark 10.13–16 in 19.13–15.)

[4] For v. 4a cf. Q (= Matt. 23.12/Luke 14.11); v. 4b takes up vv. 2–3; v. 4c links back to the end of v. 1.

[5] Cf. Mark 9.37.

Historical

Cf. on Mark 9.33–37.

Matthew 18.6–9: A warning against being led astray

6 'But whoever causes offence to one of these little ones who believe *in me*, it would be better for a millstone to be hung about his neck and for him to be drowned in the *deepest* sea. 7 *Woe to the world for offences. Indeed offences must come, but woe to the one by whom the offence comes.* 8 And if your hand or your foot causes you offence, cut it off and throw it from you. IT WOULD BE BETTER FOR YOU TO ENTER INTO LIFE lame or maimed than with two hands or two feet to be thrown into eternal fire. 9 And if your eye causes you offence, pluck it out and throw it from you. IT WOULD BE BETTER FOR YOU TO ENTER LIFE with one eye than with two eyes to be thrown into hell fire.'

Redaction and tradition

Matthew is using Mark 9.42–28 and for v. 7 perhaps Q (Luke 17.1b).

[6] Matthew found the phrase 'one of the little ones who believe' in Mark 9.42 and understands it christologically by the addition of 'in me'. He repeats the designation 'these little ones' often (10.42; 18.10,14; cf. 25.40, 45). This indicates their importance for Matthew. The expression states Matthew's concern: to become lowly because it is precisely there that the promise of greatness in the kingdom of heaven lies. Cf. the beatitudes (5.3–12).

[7] Matthew is probably thinking of the false prophets against whose coming he has already warned the community. For the possible Q original cf. on Luke 17.1b.

[8–9] These verses correspond almost word for word with Mark 9.43, 45, 47; here Matthew combines 'hand' and 'foot' in one sentence. He had already reported a similar saying of Jesus in 5.29–30.

Historical

Cf. on Mark 9.42–48.

Matthew 18.10–14: The lost sheep

10 *'See that you do not despise one of these little ones; for I tell you that in heaven their angels always behold the face of my Father in heaven.* [11] 12 *What do you think?* If a man had a hundred sheep and one of them <u>went astray</u>, would he not leave the ninety-nine on the hills and go in search of the one that <u>went astray</u>? 13 And if it happens that he finds it, amen, I say to you, he rejoices over it more than over the ninety-nine which did not <u>go astray</u>. 14 *So too it is not the will of your Father in heaven that even one of these little ones should perish.'*

Preliminary text-critical note: v. 11 ('For the Son of man came to save the lost') is not an original element of the text.

Redaction and tradition

Matthew is using a Q parable (cf. Luke 15.4–6). Verses 10 and 14 form the framework. Cf. also the link words 'little one' and 'Father in heaven' in the context: vv. 6, 19, 35. Matthew emphasizes the exemplary nature of the search and suggests this to community leaders in dealing with those who have gone astray.

[10–14] For the redaction see the preliminary notes. For the tradition cf. the remarks on Luke 15.4–6. In contrast to the Lukan version the present text does not offer a narrative but an argument, a conversation with readers to convince them.

Historical

Cf. on Luke 15.4–6.

Matthew 18.15–20: Reproof and prayer in the community

15 'And if your brother sins against you, go to him and tell him, the two of you alone. If he listens to you, you have gained your brother. 16 But if he does not listen, take one or two others along with you, that every word may be confirmed by the evidence of two or three witnesses. 17 And if he refuses to listen to them, tell (it) to the community. And if he does not listen to the community, let him be to you as a Gentile and a toll collector. 18 Amen, I say to you, whatever you bind <u>on earth</u> will also be bound <u>in heaven</u>, and whatever you loose <u>on earth</u> will also be loosed <u>in heaven</u>.

19 *Again* I say to you, if two of you agree <u>on earth</u> about anything they ask, it will be done by my Father <u>in heaven</u>. 20 For where two or three are gathered in my name, there I am in their midst.'

Redaction and tradition

The section consist of two parts: vv. 15–18 and vv. 19–20. Verses 15–18 were perhaps already a piece of tradition which has developed on the basis of a Q tradition (on v. 15a cf. Luke 17.3). Matthew has added the unit vv. 19–20 to the 'community order' (vv. 15–18).

[15–17] These verses contain a community order in the form of sayings of Jesus and regulate procedure in the case of conflict, if a member of the community has committed a sin. If no reconciliation proves possible, the brother is to be treated as a Gentile or a toll collector. It is illuminating that here the community still lives completely apart from the Gentiles (cf. similarly 6.7).

[18] Looked at from the outside, the saying of Jesus has been added to vv. 15–18 at a secondary stage, as it discusses another topic and has nothing to do with community discipline. At the same time it gives the procedure in vv. 15–17 the necessary endorsement. According to Jesus, God will confirm the community's verdict on the sinner who is not ready to repent. Cf. 16.19.

[19–20] Contrary to appearances these verses have a close connection with vv. 15–17 (cf. the links which are brought out by underlinings). Matthew makes the link with v. 18 by 'again' (beginning of v. 19). The passage is meant generally to bring out the power of the community's prayer, as it is grounded in coming together in the name of Jesus (v. 20).

Historical

[15–17] These verses are completely rooted in a particular community situation after the death of Jesus, and for that reason alone cannot go back to Jesus.

The same is true of v. 18, which – as a saying of Jesus – gives the community heavenly sanctions for its effective jurisdiction.

[19–20] The passage is rooted in the Easter situation (cf. 28.20). The Saviour is speaking. These verses are inauthentic.

Matthew 18.21–35: On forgiveness

21 Then Peter came up and said to him, 'Lord, how often may my brother sin against me and I must forgive him? As many as seven times? 22 Jesus says to him, 'I do not say to you seven times but seventy-seven times.

23 *Therefore* the kingdom of *heaven* is like a king who wished to settle accounts with his servants. 24 And when he began the reckoning, one was brought to him who owed him ten thousand talents. 25 And as he could not pay, the lord commanded that he and his wife and his children and all that he had should be sold and (thus) payment be made. 26 Then the servant fell at his feet and said, "Have patience with me and I will pay you all." 27 Then the

lord of that servant had compassion and released him, and forgave him the debt. 28 But that servant went out and met one of his fellow servants, who owed him a hundred denarii; and he seized him by the throat and said, 'Pay me what you owe me.' 29 Then his fellow servant fell down and asked him and said, "Have patience with me and I will pay you." 30 But he would not, but went and threw him into prison until he had paid back the debt. 31 But when his fellow servants saw that *they became very troubled* and told their lord all that had happened. 32 Then his lord summoned him and says to him, 'You wicked servant! I forgave you all that debt because you asked me; 33 should you not also have had compassion on your fellow servant, as I had compassion on you?'

34 *And his lord became angry and handed him over to the torturers, until he had paid back the whole debt. 35 So also my heavenly Father will do to every one of you if you do not forgive your brother from the heart.'*

Redaction and tradition

Matthew understands the parable in vv. 23–33 as an illustration of the admonition that forgiveness is to be repeated without limit (vv. 21f.). At the same time he makes Jesus threaten judgment in the present case (vv. 34f.).

[21–22] Verse 21 takes up v. 15: Peter in fact proposes forgiving up to seven times; Jesus' answer intensifies the demand for forgiveness. It knows no limits. For the Q basis to this passage cf. on Luke 17.3–4.

[23–33] Matthew is reproducing a parable which was handed down to him by oral tradition (cf. on Luke 7.41–43). The admonition to unlimited forgiveness is not central to it, as it is in the Matthaean redaction, for there is no mention of any repetition of forgiveness. The thought of the parable is forceful. The first servant receives complete remission of his debts from his lord. But this does not motivate him to act in the same way towards his fellow servant, who owes him much less than he had owed his master. The closing question (v. 33) provides the moral: those who live by grace received should themselves be gracious. Otherwise their own behaviour, which is to be rejected, already bears within it its own punishment.

[34] This verse shifts the focal point of the parable from goodness to judgment; the shift in accent may derive from Matthew.

[35] This verse, following on from v. 34 and taking up 6.14f., formulates the meaning. The parable speaks of God and the forgiveness of sins in the sphere of the community, but at the same time also of judgment; cf. 7.26f.; 13.49f.; 24.37–25.46. The community also consists of good and evil people (cf. 13.37–43, 49f.; 22.11–14) and therefore stands under judgment. Verse 35 thus enables Matthew, starting from the penal character of v. 34, to emphasize the answer to Peter's question. Whoever does not forgive his brother feels the weight of divine punishment.

Historical

The parable is about interpersonal relationships, not about the relationship to God or God's relationship towards human beings. In any case this fine parable could have been told by any sage in Israel. There are no criteria for attributing it to Jesus.

Matthew 19.1–12: Marriage, divorce and celibacy

1 *Now when Jesus had completed these discourses, he went away from Galilee and entered* the region of Judaea beyond the Jordan; 2 and large multitudes of people *followed him, and he healed them there.*

3 Then Pharisees came up to him and tempted him and said, 'Is it lawful to divorce one's wife *for any reason whatever?*' 4 And he answered and said, 'Have you not read that he who made human beings in the beginning created them as man and woman?' 5 And said, 'Therefore a man will leave father and mother and be joined to his wife, and the two will become one flesh?'. 6 So they are now no longer two but one flesh. What God has joined together let no one separate.'

7 They say to him, 'Why then has Moses commanded that she should be given a bill of divorce and be put away?' 8 He says to them, 'For your hardness of heart Moses allows you to put away your wives; but it was not so from the beginning.

9 But I say to you, Whoever divorces his wife, *except for adultery,* and marries another, commits fornication.'

10 *His disciples say to him, 'If such is the case of a man with his wife, it is not expedient to marry.'*

11 *But he said to them, 'Not all can receive this saying but only those to whom it is given.* 12 For there are eunuchs who have been so from birth, and there are eunuchs who have been castrated by men, and there are eunuchs who have castrated themselves for the kingdom *of heaven.* Let him who can receive it, receive it!'

Redaction and tradition

Matthew is using Mark 10.1–9 and inserts further sayings material from his special material in vv. 11–12.

[1–2] These verses are mostly redactional. For the closing formula in v. 1a cf. 7.28; 11.1; 13.53; 26.1. Jesus' teaching in Mark 10.1 is here replaced by his healing.

[3] Matthew formulates the question of the Pharisee from Mark 10.2 already with a view to the exception of v. 9 and adds 'for any reason whatever'.

[4–6] Cf. Mark 10.6–9. Matthew turns the Markan text round and reserves Mark 10.3–5 for the following two verses.

[7–8] The transposition brings out the point better.

[9] This verse omits Mark 10.10 and formulates the yield on the basis of Mark

10.11; here there is also a reference to the initial question of the Pharisees (v. 3) with the insertion of the clause about adultery (cf. similarly 5.32). Matthew deletes the adjoining verse from what he finds in Mark (Mark 10.12) because here the divorce of the man by the woman is mentioned as a possibility and thus Roman law is presupposed.

[10] This is a transition formulated very clumsily on the model of 19.25. 'As if all the disciples expected to get intolerable wives whom they nevertheless could not send away!' (Haenchen).

[11] Matthew forms a transition to the next verse.

[12] 'Jesus' uses the observation of the disciples, which betrays their perplexity, as 'a welcome occasion to report a saying which hardly corresponds to the intention of what preceded. For marriage here is to be hallowed and not discredited' (Wellhausen). The traditional saying knows three different kinds of eunuchs of which the first two classes mentioned refer to known types and the third class, 'eunuch' related to the kingdom of God, is understood in a metaphorical sense.

Historical

[3–9] Cf. on Mark 10.2–9.

[12] The saying is probably authentic. Jesus himself was unmarried and was criticized for this; perhaps he was taunted as a eunuch. Here he takes the offensive and formulates an offensive saying about his own celibacy and that of some of his own followers.

Matthew 19.13–15: The children and the kingdom of God

13 *Then* children were brought to him, that <u>he might lay his hands on them</u> *and pray*. But the disciples threatened them. 14 But Jesus said, 'Let the children come to me, and do not hinder them, for to such belongs the kingdom *of heaven*.' 15 And <u>he laid hands on them</u> and went away from there.

Redaction and tradition

[13–15] Matthew uses Mark 10.13–16 and tightens it up. He deletes Jesus' strong feelings in Mark 10.14 and passes over Mark 10.15. In other passages, too, Matthew deletes Jesus' strong feelings. For example Jesus avoids anger: 8.13; 12.12 over against Mark 1.53; 3.5.

Historical

Cf. on Mark 10.13–16.

Matthew 19.16–30: The rich young man. The reward for discipleship

16 *And look*, someone came to him and asked, 'Teacher, what *good* shall I do to receive eternal life?' 17 And he said to him, 'Why do you ask me *about the good*? Only one is good. *But if you want to enter into life, keep the commandments*!' 18 He says to him, 'Which?' And Jesus said, '"You shall not kill, you shall not commit adultery, you shall not steal, you shall not bear false witness; 19 honour your father and mother" and "*You shall love your neighbour as yourself.*"' 20 The *young man* says to him, 'I have done all this; *what do I still lack*?' 21 Jesus said to him, 'If you want to be *perfect*, go, sell what you have and give (it) to the poor, and you will have treasure in heaven; and (come) here, follow me!' 22 When the *young man* heard the saying he went away troubled, for he had many possessions.

23 And Jesus said to his disciples, 'Amen, I say to you, it will be hard for a rich man to enter the kingdom of heaven. 24 And I also say to you, it is easier for a camel to go through the eye of a needle than for a rich man to enter the kingdom of God.' 25 When his disciples heard that they were greatly astonished and said, 'Who then can be saved?' 26 But Jesus looked at them and said to them, 'With men it is impossible, but with God all things are possible.'

27 Then Peter answered and said to him, 'Look, we have left everything and followed you, what will be given to us for that?' 28 And Jesus said to them, 'Amen, I say to you, You who have followed me, at the rebirth, *when the Son of man sits on the throne of his glory*, will also sit on twelve thrones and judge the twelve tribes of Israel. 29 And anyone who has left houses or brothers or sisters or father or mother or children or fields for my name's sake will receive one hundredfold and inherit eternal life.

30 But many first will be last and last first.'

Redaction and tradition

Matthew uses Mark 10.17–31 and inserts special material in v. 28.

[16–17] Matthew makes the young man (v. 20) ask about the good (Mark 10.17, 'eternal life').

[18–19] Matthew inserts the commandment to love one's neighbour from Lev. 19.18.

[20] The questioner becomes 'a young man' (similarly v. 22). At the same time Matthew deletes Mark's remark (10.21) that Jesus loved the young person who asked Jesus a question.

[21] This verse contains the Matthaean theme of perfection. It applies in ethical terms (cf. on 5.48), but also and above all has a personal component: discipleship of Jesus, who makes the disciple go the way of righteousness (cf. on 5.6).

[22–23] Cf. Mark 10.22–23.

[24] Matthew deletes Mark 5.24 with its observation how difficult it is to enter the kingdom of God, as he regards this generalization on the basis of Mark 5.22–23 as superfluous.

[25–26] Cf. Mark 10.26–27.

[27] Cf. Mark 10.28. As in 18.1 and 18.21 (Peter is speaking), a question from a disciple introduces a new section.

[28] This saying is an isolated logion which Matthew has inserted into his text following Mark 10.28–30 (= Matt. 19.27, 29), promising a reward to all disciples. He promises the twelve disciples that in the near future they will judge the house of Israel; here the clause printed in italics in the text probably derives from Matthew because it largely agrees with 25.31.

There is a similar saying in Luke 22.28–30, but it is probably not to be attributed to Q with Matt. 19.28, though it similarly comes from oral tradition. It runs: 28 'But you are those who have persevered with me in my temptations. 29 And I assign to you the kingdom, as my Father has assigned it to me, 30 that you may eat and drink at my table in my kingdom, and sit on thrones judging the twelve tribes of Israel.'

[29] This verse abbreviates Mark 10.29–30.

[30] This verse looks ahead to the next section. Cf. 20.16.

Historical

[16–27, 29] Cf. Mark 10.17–31.

[28] At first sight the logion looks like a product of the 'risen Christ'. For it is lofty in its vision of the future, when one thinks that in the time of Jesus only two of the twelve tribes of Israel were left, Judah and Benjamin. According to the view at the time the other ten had been systematically destroyed by the Assyrians 700 years previously.

On the other hand, fantasy in itself is not an adequate criterion for historical judgements. And there is much in support of the authenticity of this saying. *First*, it is closely connected with the conception of the group of twelve. If the founding of this group really goes back to Jesus (see on Mark 3.14), the logion in a unique way indicates the significance that Jesus attached to the group of twelve: to symbolize the twelve tribes of Israel and to predict its restoration in the near future. *Secondly*, this saying helps us to understand the Jewish side of Jesus better (criterion of coherence). In this way Jesus can be better understood as a Jew of his time, who like many others believed in the restoration of the twelve tribes of Israel (cf. Sir. 36.13; PsSol. 17.26–29; Qumran War Scroll 2.2; 7.8; 5.1). *Thirdly*, the authenticity of the saying is endorsed by the criterion of difference, since it cannot be derived from the earliest community. The logion assigns the twelve exclusively to Israel and does not make any reference to the church. It may be added that the authenticity of v. 28 also sheds light on Jesus' expectation of the future. For if the twelve whom he has called exercise the function of judges at the judgment on the twelve tribes of Israel, he himself

of course has the main function. The only question is, which? One might recall
PsSol. 17.26, where the Messiah will judge the twelve tribes of Israel. Do we then
have what Theissen calls a group messianism here?

Matthew 20.1–16: The labourers in the vineyard

1 'For *the kingdom of heaven is like* a householder who went out early in the morning to hire
labourers for his vineyard. 2 And when he <u>agreed</u> with the labourers <u>for a denarius</u> as a day's
pay, he sent them into his vineyard. 3 And when he went out at the third hour, he saw others
standing idle in the market place 4 and said *to those*, "You too go into the vineyard; I will give
you what is right." 5 And they went. Again he went out around the sixth and the ninth hour
and did likewise. 6 And around the eleventh hour he went out and *found* others and says to
them, "Why are you standing there all day?" 7 They say to him, "No one has hired us." He
says to them, "*You too go* into the vineyard." 8 *Now when evening came the lord of the vineyard
says to his steward*, "Call the labourers and give them their *recompense*, beginning from the last
up to the first." 9 And when those hired about the eleventh hour came, they each *received* a
denarius. 10 and when the first came, they thought that they would *receive* more, and they
too each *received* a denarius. 11 And when they *received* (it), they murmured against the
householder 12 and said, "These last have laboured only one hour, but you have made them
equal with us, who have born the burden and heat of the day." 13 *He answered one and said*,
"My friend, I do you no wrong. Did you not <u>agree with me for a denarius</u>? 14 Take what is
yours and go. I will give the same to this last as to you. 15 Is it not lawful for me to do what I
will with what belongs to me? Or is your *eye evil* because I am good?"
    16 *So the last shall be the first and the first the last.*'

Redaction and tradition

[1–15] This piece, which has been handed down only by the First Evangelist, is
stamped with Matthaean language (cf. the selection in the translation printed in
italic). But we can rule out the possibility that the whole pericope is a Matthaean
construction, since v. 16 has been put here by Matthew taking up 19.30, and picks
up only *one* detail of the pericope: the *order of payment* in v. 8b. Here Matthew
understands the parable wrongly, since it in fact stresses the equality of the recompense and the reason for it (v. 15). 'Like the householder in the parable, God gives
the same recompense of the kingdom to all, regardless of whether they can lay claim
to it for their achievement or only receive it through his grace' (Klostermann).

[16] It is often proposed that in the case of the first Matthew is thinking of Jews
and in the case of the last of Gentiles (cf. 21.43). But what tells against that is that the
denarius is by no means taken away from the first. Therefore it is more probable that
with these two groups Matthew has members of the community in view. In that
case, v. 16 is a warning in the spirit of 18.3–4 and 23.12.

Historical

[1–15] The parable inculcates one notion. God is gracious without discrimination to all who are active in his vineyard, Israel. It is free from ideas which could have come from the community, and also corresponds to Jesus' message that God seeks the lost (cf. Luke 15.11–32; 18.9–14). The parable certainly goes back to Jesus.

Matthew 20.17–19: The third announcement of the passion and resurrection

17 And when Jesus was going up to Jerusalem, he took the twelve *disciples aside* and said to them *on the way*, 18 'Look, we are going up to Jerusalem, and the Son of man will be handed over to the chief priests and scribes; and they will condemn him to death 19 and will hand him over to the Gentiles to be mocked, scourged and crucified; and on the third day he *will be raised.*'

Redaction and tradition

[17–19] Matthew is using and abbreviating Mark 10.32–34. In v. 17 he deletes the anxious reaction of his followers (Mark 10.32). Verse 18 corresponds almost word for word with Mark 10.33. In v. 19 the Gentiles (= Romans) appear as mere instruments of the wickedness of the Jewish authorities depicted in v. 18, for unlike Mark 10.34 they do not appear as a grammatical subject.

Historical

Cf. on Mark 10.32–34.

Matthew 20.20–28: The question of the sons of Zebedee

20 *Then the mother of the sons of Zebedee came up to him with her sons, fell before him and wanted to ask him for something.* 21 He said to her, 'What do you want?' She says to him, 'Command that these my two sons sit one at your right hand and the other at your left in your kingdom.' 22 But Jesus answered and said, 'You do not know what you are asking for. Can you drink the cup that I shall drink? They answered, 'Yes, we can.' 23 He says to them, 'You will indeed drink my cup, but to sit at my right hand and at my left is not mine to give but is for those for whom it has been prepared *by my Father.*'

24 And when the ten heard it they were indignant about the two brothers. 25 But Jesus called them to him and said, 'You know that the rulers of the people subjugate them and the powerful exercise power over them. 26 It shall not *be* so among you; but whoever among you will be great, let him be *your* servant; 27 and whoever among you will be first, let him be your

slave, 28 just as the Son of man has come not to be served but to serve, and to give his life as a ransom for many.'

Redaction and tradition

Matthew is using Mark 10.35–45. Matthew gives this section with few changes, but again abbreviates it.

[20–21] The mother of the sons of Zebedee – and not the sons themselves – takes the initiative with her request. Thus the two apostles are excused at the expense of their mother.

[22–23] Faithful to the Markan text which Matthew has before him (10.38), Jesus' answer is given to the two sons of Zebedee – a stylistic harshness, as the mother had after all addressed Jesus. Matthew omits the two references to the baptism of death (Mark 10.38–39).

[24–28] The passage corresponds almost word for word with Mark 10.41–45. Verse 28 with its notion of expiation is an isolated verse in Matthew (cf. also 26.28), as is Mark 10.45 in the Second Gospel.

Historical

See on Mark 10.35–45.

Matthew 20.29–34: The healing of the two blind men before Jericho

29 And when they went out of Jericho a great crowd of people followed him. 30 *And look, two blind men* were sitting by the wayside; and when they heard that Jesus was passing by they cried out, saying, 'Have mercy on us, Lord, Son of David!' 31 But the people threatened them, and told them to keep quiet. But they cried all the more and said, 'Have mercy on us, Lord, son of David!' 32 And Jesus stopped, called them and said, 'What do you want me to do for you?' 33 They say to him, 'Lord, that our eyes may be opened.' 34 *And Jesus had compassion on them and he touched their eyes*; and immediately they saw again and followed him.

Redaction and tradition

The present story already occurred in a freer form in Matt. 9.27–31, there too on the basis of Mark 10.46–52. Matthew introduces it again here, basing it more closely on the Markan passage mentioned above.

[29] The blind man Bartimaeus (Mark 10.36), who is mentioned by name, here becomes two anonymous blind men.

[30–31] This passage corresponds to Mark 10.47–48; here Jesus is twice addressed as 'Lord' over and above Mark.

[32] This verse abbreviates the Markan original (10.49–51a) and brings the two men together with Jesus more quickly.

[33] For the third time, in contrast to Mark, Jesus is addressed as 'Lord'.

[34] Jesus touches the eyes. Matthew adds this individual feature to the Markan original, but omits the motif of faith (but cf. 9.29).

Historical

Cf. on Mark 10.46–52.

Matthew 21.1–11: Jesus' entry into Jerusalem

1 And when they drew near to Jerusalem and came to Bethphage to the Mount of Olives, Jesus sent two disciples, 2 and said to them, 'Go into the village before you and immediately you will find an ass tied and a colt with her; untie them and bring them to me. 3 And if anyone says anything to you, say, "'The Lord needs them." And immediately he will send them.' 4 *That happened to fulfil what was spoken by the prophet, who says*, 5 'Say to the daughter of Zion, See, your king comes to you, meek and riding on an ass and on a colt, the foal of a beast of burden.' 6 The disciples went and did as Jesus had commanded them. 7 They brought the ass *and the colt* and laid their garments on them, and he sat on them. 8 And a very great crowd spread their garments on the way; others cut *branches from the trees and spread them on the way.* 9 And the multitudes which went before him and followed him cried, 'Hosanna to the Son of David! Blessed is he who comes in the name of the Lord! Hosanna in the highest.' 10 And when he entered Jerusalem, the whole city was excited and asked, 'Who is this?' 11 And the multitudes said, 'This is the prophet from Nazareth in Galilee.'

Redaction and tradition

Matthew is using Mark 11.1–11.

[2] Matthew turns one ass (Mark 11.2) into two and presupposes this in what follows.

[4–5] Faithful to his theology and giving it a specifically Matthaean introduction (v. 4a, cf. similarly 1.22 etc.), Matthew adds a prophetic proof from Zech. 9.9, from which he has got the two asses (cf. already v. 2).

[6–7] In accordance with the fulfilled prophecy from Zech. 9.9, Jesus rides on two asses. 'Only "Christian" theology can possibly justify these two asses' (Wernle).

[8] This verse turns the prophecy from v. 5 into history and further specifies the details of the entry.

[9] Matthew replaces the archaic phrase 'the kingdom of our father David' (Mark 11.10) with the term 'son of David', i.e. Messiah, used more frequently among Christians.

[10–11] Matthew composes a dialogue between the multitudes and the whole city of Jerusalem (cf. 2.3) on the significance of Jesus.

Historical

Cf. on Mark 11.1–11. By his expansions, which have a redactional motivation, Matthew has moved yet further from history.

Matthew 21.12–17: The cleansing of the temple

12 And Jesus entered the temple and drove out all who bought and sold in the temple and overturned the tables of the money changers and the seats of those who sold doves, 13 and he says to them, 'It is written, "My house shall be called a house of prayer," but you are making it a den of robbers.'

14 *And the blind and the lame came to him in the temple, and he healed them.* 15 *But when the chief priests and scribes saw the wonderful things that he did, and the children who were crying out in the temple and saying, 'Hosanna to the Son of David!', they were filled with indignation* 16 *and said to him, 'Do you hear what these are saying?' Jesus says to them, 'Yes, have you never read, "Out of the mouths of babes and sucklings you have prepared praise?"'* 17 And he left them and went out of the city to Bethany, and remained there overnight.

Redaction and tradition

Matthew is using Mark 11.15–19.

[12–13] Cf. Mark 11.15.

[14] This is a Matthaean addition. It thus points to 11.5–6; 15.30–32 and especially back to the pericope 20.29–34 which immediately precedes it, thus putting special emphasis on Jesus' healing of the blind and lame.

[15–16] These verses may also have been prompted by Mark 11.18. Matthew once again heightens the opposition of the chief priests and scribes towards Jesus. The saying quoted by Jesus in v. 16 comes from Ps. 8.3. The positive attitude of the children is a contrast to the negative reaction of the leaders in Jerusalem.

[17a] This verse corresponds to 16.4c.

[17b–c] Cf. Mark 11.11b, 19b.

Historical

Cf. on Mark 11.15–19.

Matthew 21.18–22: The cursing of the fig tree. Prayer and faith

18 Now when he returned to the city the next day, he was hungry. 19 And when he saw a fig tree by the wayside he went up to it and found on it nothing but leaves. And he says to it, 'You shall never again bear fruit!' And the fig tree withered on the spot. 20 When *the disciples* saw (this), they marvelled and said, 'How has the fig tree withered so quickly?' 21 And Jesus answered and said to them, 'Amen, I say to you, If you have faith and do not doubt, *you will not only do what has been done to the fig tree* but also, if you say to this mountain, "Lift yourself up and cast yourself into the sea," it will happen. 22 And whatever you ask in prayer you will receive it, if you believe.'

Redaction and tradition

Matthew is using Mark 11.12–14, 20–24. He does away with the sandwich in Mark and omits the 'know it all' observation in Mark 11.13c if this did in fact stand in the original text of Mark.

[18–20] Matthew further intensifies the miracle by comparison with Mark (11.12–14, 20–21). Hardly has Jesus cursed the guilty tree when it withers. In Mark, by contrast, a whole day elapses between the curse and its fulfilment.

[21–22] Cf. Mark 11.22–24. The verses contain the answer to the question why the fig tree withered immediately. The reason is the boldness of faith, which can achieve even more than merely making this fig tree wither. With v. 21 Matthew points back to 17.20.

Historical

[18–20] Cf. Mark 11.12–14, 20–21. As the Markan pericope formed a sandwich and therefore the episode of the cursing of the fig tree had to be divided differently, the historical yield may be repeated once again here. Jesus never cursed a fig tree (in the literal sense). If Matthew's fig tree was seen as a metaphor for Israel on the basis of Mark, then we have to pass a negative historical judgment as well. Jesus never cursed Israel; the condemnation in the Markan original (Mark 11.14) and other corresponding statements in Matthew derive from the view of Christian communities after the death and 'resurrection' of Jesus. In the battle against non-Christian Jews their members took refuge in these wicked condemnations and put them directly into the mouth of Jesus.

[21–22] Cf. on Mark 11.23.

Matthew 21.23–32: The question of Jesus' authority. The unequal sons

23 And when he had come into the temple, the chief priests and elders *of the people* came up to him while he was teaching and asked, 'With what <u>authority</u> are you doing this? And who has given you this <u>authority</u>?' 24 And Jesus answered and said to them, 'I too will ask you a single question; *if* you tell me the answer, I will also tell you with what <u>authority</u> I do this. 25 Whence was the baptism of John? Was it from heaven or from men?' And they reflected among themselves, saying, 'If we say, "From heaven", he will say *to us,* "Then why did you not believe him?" 26 If we say, "From men", we (have to) fear the people. For all regard John as a prophet.' 27 And they answered Jesus and said, 'We do not know.' Then he also said to them, 'Neither will I tell you by what <u>authority</u> I do this.

28 Now what do you think? A man had two children (sons) and went to the first and said, "Child, go and work today in the vineyard," 29 But he answered and said, "No, I will not." <u>Later he repented</u> and went. 30 And the father went to the other son and spoke likewise. And he answered and said, "Yes, lord," and did not go. 31 Which of the two has done the will of the Father?' They answered, 'The first.' Jesus says to them, 'Amen I say to you, the toll collectors and prostitutes will go *before you* into the kingdom of God. 32 *For John came to you on the way of righteousness and you did not believe him, but the toll collectors and prostitutes believed him. But you have seen (it), and did not <u>repent later</u>, and believe him.*'

Redaction and tradition

In v. 23–27 Matthew is using Mark 11.27–33 as a model. To it he has added the parable of the two unequal sons and an interpretation (v. 28–32); these are to be found only in his Gospel.

[23–27] These verses largely correspond to Mark 11.27–33. The small differences are indicated by italics. The only difference worth mentioning is to be found in v. 26, where their own fear of the people and its view of John is part of the reflections of the chief priests and elders, whereas in Mark (11.32) this is an explanation by the Second Evangelist. This is clearly an improvement of Mark which Luke (20.6) has made independently of Matthew.

[28–31b] Matthew adds a parable which, starting with two sons and the task given to them, emphasizes that doing the will of God is the most important thing.

[31c] This verse begins with the application of the parable to Jesus' opponents. The expression 'kingdom of God' (elsewhere in Matthew 'kingdom of heaven') shows that Matthew's formulation is based on tradition. However, the application does not fit the parable, which is orientated on the contrast between hearing and doing. So Matthew might himself have added a saying from the tradition here in order to create a transition to v. 32. That this is tradition is also supported by the observation that prostitutes and toll collectors cannot be compared with the two sons, for they never said no, and then yes, but immediately yes.

[32] This verse describes the yield of vv. 23–31, in that it demonstrates the unreadiness of Jesus' Jewish opponents to believe in John at least after the event, just as the first son did the will of his father (= God), albeit belatedly (cf. the parallels in v. 32 with v. 29).

Historical

[23–27] Cf. on Mark 11.27–33.

[28–31b] The parable is a good Jewish one and clearly inculcates one idea. It is too general in its orientation to be unquestionably attributed to Jesus. Matthew could be the narrator.

[31c] The saying is authentic (without the addition 'before you'), since it is offensive, rare in the world of Jesus, cannot be derived from the community and fits the main thrust of the preaching of Jesus (cf. on 11.18–19a; Luke 7.36–50). In content it corresponds with the authentic beatitudes on the poor, the hungry and those who weep (cf. on Luke 6.20–26).

Matthew 21.33–46: The wicked tenants

33 '*Hear another parable*: there was a householder who planted a vineyard and set a hedge around it and dug a winepress in it and built a tower and let it out to tenants and travelled away. 34 *Now when season of fruit came near*, he sent his servants to the tenants, to get his fruits. 35 Then the tenants seized his servants: the first they beat, *the second they killed, the third they stoned*. 36 Again he sent other servants, *more than the first time*, and they did the same thing to them. 37 Lastly he sent his son to them and said, "They will respect my son." 38 But when the tenants *saw the son*, they said to one another, "This is the heir, come, let us kill him and have his inheritance." 39 And they took him and cast him out of the vineyard and killed him. 40 Now when the Lord of the vineyard comes, what will he do with these tenants?' 41 They say to him, 'He will prepare an evil end for *the evil men* and lease his vineyard to other tenants *who will give him the fruits in their seasons*.'

42 Jesus says to them, 'Have you never read *in the scriptures*, "The stone which the builders have rejected, this has become the corner stone. It is the Lord's doing and it is marvellous in our eyes"? 43 *Therefore I say to you, The kingdom of God will be taken from you and given to a people which brings forth its (the kingdom of God's) fruits*. 44 And whoever falls on this stone will be broken in pieces; and on whomever it falls, it will crush him.'

45 And when the chief priests and the Pharisees heard his parables, they recognized that he was speaking of them. 46 And they sought to seize him; (but) they feared the multitudes, *for they regarded him as a prophet*.

Redaction and tradition

Matthew 21.33–36 virtually turns the Markan passage on which it is based (Mark 12.1–12) into a sketch of salvation history from the covenant on Sinai through the destruction of Jerusalem (21.41; cf. 22.7) and the foundation of the church of the Gentiles (21.43) to the last judgment (21.44).

[33] The introduction is necessary, since unlike Mark, Matthew had told a parable immediately beforehand (of the unequal sons).

[34–36] In Mark 12.2–5a three servants are sent out one after another and as the action steadily heightens are treated increasingly badly, whereas Matthew has a group of three sent out immediately and afterwards (v. 36) even more, all of whom suffer the same fate. This is a climax.

[37–39] Matthew's formulation closely follows Mark, which he has before him (12.6–8), but reverses the sequence of the killing and the throwing out of the vineyard. Thus he takes account of the historical fact that Jesus was crucified outside Jerusalem.

[41] This verse makes a far-reaching change to Mark. In Matthew's version, Mark 12.9, 'The Lord of the vineyard . . . will give the vineyard to others', becomes: 'The Lord of the vineyard . . . will lease the vineyard to other tenants, who will give him the fruits in their season.'

[43] This verse is a Matthaean addition to the text of Mark. That means that God's kingdom will be taken away from Israel and given to a people which brings forth 'fruits of the kingdom of God'. The word 'people' refers to Gentiles and is also used in this sense in other passages in Matthew (cf. 10.5, 'Way of the Gentiles'; 28.19, 'Make disciples of all Gentiles!'). In other words, Matthew takes over all the anti-Jewish statements in Mark; he accentuates them further by emphasizing the explicit transfer of the vineyard to the Gentiles and denies Israel any promise.

[45–46] Cf. Mark 12.12. According to Matthew the parable is no longer addressed to chief priests and elders of the people in v. 23, but to chief priests and Pharisees, as in 27.62.

Historical

Cf. on Mark 12.1–12.

Matthew 22.1–14: The parable of the wedding feast

1 *And Jesus answered and again spoke to them in parables and said*, 2 'The kingdom of heaven is like a king who prepared a wedding feast for his son. 3 And he sent out his servants to invite the guests to the wedding; but they did not want to come. 4 *Again* he sent out other servants

and said, "Tell the guests, 'Look, I have prepared my banquet, my oxen and my fat calves are killed, and all is ready; come to the wedding feast.'" 5 But they scorned (it) and went away, one to his own field, the other to his business. 6 *And the rest seized his servants, treated them shamefully and killed them.* 7 *Then* the king grew angry *and sent out his armies and killed these murderers and burned down their city.* 8 *Then* he says to his servants, "The wedding is ready, but the guests were not worthy. 9 Therefore go out into the thoroughfares and invite to the wedding whoever you find." 10 And the servants went out on to the streets and gathered together whom they found, *bad and good*; and the wedding hall was filled with guests.

11 But when the king entered to look at those reclining at table, he saw a man without a wedding garment. 12 And he says to him, "Friend, how did you get in here without a wedding garment?" But he was silent. 13 *Then* the king said to his servants, "Bind him hand and foot and throw him into the darkness outside. There will be weeping and gnashing of teeth. 14 For many are called but few are chosen."'

Redaction and tradition

The parable of the wedding feast follows that of the wicked tenants (21.33–46) the purpose of which may be recalled here: the church replaces Israel in so far as it observes Jesus' words. Israel is disqualified without exception and completely robbed of its salvation by the destruction of Jerusalem.

Like Luke 14.16–24, vv. 2–10 derive from Q. Matthew has interpreted the existing Q tradition by additions. Verses 11–13 are originally a Jewish parable. It has probably been added by Matthew (like v. 14), but in its present state is only a fragment, the original form of which can no longer be arrived at. It must therefore be regarded as a piece added ad hoc by Matthew.

[1] This links the following section with 21.46.

[2–10] These verses are an allegory of salvation history, through to the period after Easter. The king, i.e. God, arranges a banquet for his son, namely Jesus Christ. Matthew changes the individual servant in the Q parallel (as in Luke 14.16 = Q) into several groups of servants. These can only be understood only as the apostles. 'They invite the Jews to enter the kingdom of God by their preaching of the gospel, but come up against indifference among the upper classes' (Wellhausen). The first group of servants (v. 3) stands for the prophets and the repudiation of their message; the second group (v. 4) denotes the apostles and missionaries sent to Israel (Jerusalem) and the maltreatment and martyrdom (v. 6) that some of them suffered. Sending out into the streets (vv. 9f.) suggests the mission to the Gentiles, and the entry into the wedding hall (v. 10b) baptism. The vivid statement in v. 7 shows a heightening of anti-Judaism: the murderous Jews are killed and their city (= Jerusalem) is set on fire; Matthew can depict this with a retrospect to the destruction of Jerusalem in AD 70. With 'bad and good' in v. 10b Matthew prepares for vv. 11–14 which follow.

[11–13] Like the allegory of the wicked tenants, these verses inculcate the role of good works and are further evidence that Matthew is concerned with conduct. For

v. 9, which relates the indiscriminate invitation of guests, could have given the impression of indifference on ethical matters. For 'weeping and gnashing of teeth' (v. 13) cf. 8.12; 13.42; 13.50; 24.51; 25.13.

[14] Matthew inserts a logion from the tradition in order to comment on a whole passage, here vv. 2–13, as in 20.16. Certainly many are invited from Israel and the Gentiles, but only few are saved. For the contrast between 'many' and 'few' cf. 7.13f. The saying in v. 14 contradicts both vv. 11–13 and vv. 2–10. For in vv. 11–13 only a single guest is not chosen, and in vv. 2–10 not a single individual accepts the invitation.

Historical

[1–10] Cf. on Luke 14.15–24.
[11–14] Cf. the introduction to 'redaction and tradition'.

Matthew 22.15–22: The question of tax for the emperor

15 Then the Pharisees went and *made a decision* to trap him in a saying. 16 And they send their disciples to him along with the supporters of Herod, who said, 'Teacher, we know that you are truthful and teach the way of God in truth and care for none; for you do not regard people's reputation. 17 Therefore tell us what you think: is it right to pay tax to Caesar or not?' 18 And when Jesus observed their malice, he said, 'Why do you tempt me, you hypocrites? 19 Show me the money for the tax!' And they brought him a denarius. 20 And he says to them, 'Whose image is that and whose superscription?' 21 They say, 'Caesar's.' Then he says to them, 'Then give to Caesar what is Caesar's and to God what is God's.' 22 And when they heard that, they marvelled. *And they left him and went away.*

Redaction and tradition

Matthew is using Mark 12.13–17.

[15] This verse corresponds in some respects to Mark 12.13b, but Matthew emphasizes 'the' Pharisees as the chief enemies of Jesus. Redactionally it forms the exposition for the major section vv. 15–46.

[16–21a] These verses largely follow the Markan original (12.14–17).

[21b] This verse corresponds to Mark 12.12. Matthew had previously omitted it (21.46). He inserts it here and thus creates a better transition to the conflict which is narrated next, in which the disciples of the Pharisees from v. 16 are no longer involved.

Historical

Cf. on Mark 12.13–17.

Matthew 22.23–33: The question of the resurrection

23 On that day the Sadducees came up to him and said that there is no resurrection. And they asked him 24, saying, 'Teacher, Moses said, "If a man dies and has no children, his brother must marry his wife as brother-in-law and father descendants for his brother." 25 Now among us there were seven brothers. And the first married and died; and because he had no seed, he left his wife to his brother; 26 similarly the second and the third, up to the seventh. 27 Last of all the woman died. 28 In the resurrection, therefore, whose wife of these seven will she be? For they all had her.' 29 But Jesus answered and said to them, 'You are wrong, because you know neither the scriptures nor the power of God. 30 For in the resurrection they will neither marry nor be given in marriage, but they are like angels in heaven.

31 As for the resurrection of the dead, have you not read what was spoken to you by God, who says, 32 "I am the God of Abraham and the God of Isaac and the God of Jacob"? *God* is not a God of the dead, but of the living.' 33 And when the crowd of people heard that, they were astonished at his teaching.

Redaction and tradition

Matthew is using Mark 12.18–27.

[23–32] Matthew largely takes over Mark, which he has in front of him, and occasionally tightens it up (cf. vv. 25–26 with Mark 12.20–22a). In v. 23 the Sadducees themselves present their view that the dead are not raised, in contrast to Mark (12.18b).

[33] As the immediate Markan original does not contain any reaction on the part of the people, this verse – based on Mark 11.18 – describes the impression that Jesus' answer has made on the crowds of people. Matthew had been able to make a similar report in 7.28 (after the Sermon on the Mount) and in 13.54 (in connection with the preaching in the synagogue in Nazareth).

Historical

Cf. on Mark 12.18–27.

Matthew 22.34–40: The question of the greatest commandment

34 *And when the Pharisees heard that he had silenced the Sadducees, they gathered at the same place.* 35 And one of them, an expert in the law, *asked him, putting him to the test*, 36 *'Teacher,*

which commandment is great in the law?' 37 And he said to him, ' "You shall love the Lord your God with all your heart, with all your life and all your thought." 38 This is the great and first commandment. 39 And the second is like it, "You shall love your neighbour as your-self." 40 *On these two commandments hang all the law and the prophets.'*

Redaction and tradition

Matthew is using Mark 12.28–34, but omits the whole of the second half, vv. 32–34, in which Jesus praises the one who asks the question. The reasons for this is the following discourse condemning the Pharisees and scribes, who here too do not merit any recognition.

[34] The question is not put by a scribe (thus Mark 12.28a), but by a Pharisee.

[35] The questioner appears as a tempter, whereas in Mark he is an honest seeker (Mark 12.28a).

[36–39] Cf. Mark 12.29–31. The passage consists almost entirely of biblical passages (v. 37, Deut. 6.5; v. 39, Lev. 19.18), it is very thin.

[40] All the commandments from the Torah and prophets 'hang' on these two main commandments. For the expression 'the law and the prophets' cf. 5.17 and 7.12.

Historical

Cf. on Mark 12.28–34.

Matthew 22.41–46: The question about the son of David

41 *Now when the Pharisees had assembled, Jesus asked them and said,* 42 'What do you think of the Christ? Whose son is he?' They answered, 'David's.' 43 He says to them, 'How then does David in the spirit call him Lord, when he says, 44 "The Lord said to my Lord, 'Sit at my right hand until I put your enemies under your feet' "? 45 Now if David calls him Lord, how then is he his son?' 46 *And no one could answer him a word, nor from that day on dared anyone ask him any more questions.*

Redaction and tradition

Matthew reproduces Mark 12.35–37 almost word for word.

[41] Again Jesus' main enemies, the Pharisees, are introduced by Matthew (cf. most recently v. 34). Matthew turns the scene into a dialogue. This makes the whole thing more lively than in Mark.

[46] By comparison with Mark this verse is a new concluding sentence.

Historical

Cf. on Mark 12.35–37

Matthew 23.1–39: The discourse against scribes and Pharisees

1 *Then* Jesus *spoke* to the multitudes and his disciples, 2 *and says,* 'The scribes and the Pharisees sit on Moses' seat. 3 Now do and observe all that they tell you, but not according to their works; for they say (it) and do not do (it). 4 They bind heavy burdens, hard to bear, and lay them on men's shoulders; but they themselves will not move them with their fingers. 5 They do all their deeds to be seen by men. They make their phylacteries broad and the fringes on their garments long. 6 They love the top places at feasts and the best seats in the synagogues, 7 and greetings in the market places, and being called "Rabbi" by people. 8 But you are not to be called rabbi, for you have <u>one</u> teacher, and you are all brothers. 9 And do not call (anyone) among you father on earth, for you have <u>one</u> Father, who is in heaven. 10 And do not be called masters, for you have <u>one</u> master, Christ. 11 The greatest among you shall be your servant. 12 Whoever exalts himself will be humbled, and whoever humbles himself will be exalted.

13 <u>*Woe to you*</u>, *scribes and Pharisees, you hypocrites*, for you shut the kingdom of heaven against men. You neither enter yourselves, nor allow those who (want to) go in to enter. [14]

15 <u>*Woe to you*</u>, *scribes and Pharisees, you hypocrites,* who traverse sea and land to make a single proselyte, and when he becomes (one), you make him a child of hell, twice (as bad) as yourselves

16 <u>Woe to you</u>, blind guides, who say, "If any one swears by the temple it is nothing; but if any one swears by the gold of the temple, he is bound by his oath." 17 You fools and blind! Which is greater, the gold or the temple that makes the gold sacred? 18 Or, "If any one swears by the altar it is nothing; but if any one swears by the gift that is on the altar, he is bound by his oath." 19 You blind men! For which is greater, the gift or the altar that makes the gift sacred? 20 So whoever swears by the altar, swears by it and by everything on it. 21 And whoever swears by the temple, swears by it and by him who dwells in it. 22 And whoever swears by heaven, swears by the throne of God and by him who sits upon it.

23 <u>*Woe to you*</u>, *scribes and Pharisees, you hypocrites*, for you tithe mint and dill and cumin, and have neglected the weightier matters of the law, justice and mercy and faith; these you ought to have done, without neglecting the others. 24 You blind guides, straining out a gnat and swallowing a camel!

25 <u>*Woe to you*</u>, *scribes and Pharisees, you hypocrites*, for you cleanse the outside of the cup and of the plate, but inside they are full of extortion and rapacity. 26 You blind Pharisee, first cleanse the inside of the cup and of the plate, that the outside also may be clean.

27 <u>*Woe to you*</u>, *scribes and Pharisees, you hypocrites*, for you are like whitewashed tombs, which outwardly appear beautiful, but within they are full of dead men's bones and all uncleanness. 28 So you also outwardly appear righteous to men, but within you are full of hypocrisy and iniquity.

29 <u>*Woe to you*</u>, *scribes and Pharisees, you hypocrites*, for you build tombs for the prophets

and adorn the graves of the righteous, 30 and say, "If we had lived in the days of our fathers, we would not have taken part with them in shedding the blood of the prophets." 31 Thus you witness against yourselves that you are sons of those who murdered the prophets. 32 Fill up, then, the measure of your fathers. 33 You serpents, you brood of vipers, how are you to escape being sentenced to hell?

34 Therefore, look, I send you prophets and wise men and *scribes;* and (some) of them you will kill and crucify, and (some) you will scourge in your synagogues and persecute from town to town, 35 that upon you may come all the righteous blood shed on earth, from the blood of innocent Abel to the blood of Zechariah the son of Barachiah, whom you murdered between the sanctuary and the altar. 36 Amen, I say to you, all this will come upon this generation.

37 Jerusalem, Jerusalem, who kills the prophets and stones those who are sent to you! How often would I have gathered your children together as a hen gathers her brood under her wings, and you would not! 38 See, your house is forsaken and desolate.

39 For I tell you, you will not see me again until you say, "Blessed is he who comes in the name of the Lord." '

Preliminary text-critical note: v. 14 ('Woe to you, scribes and Pharisees, you hypocrites, who devour widows' houses and for a pretence make long prayers, therefore you will receive the greater condemnation') is not part of the original text. The verse is only weakly attested and is a woe formed on the basis of Mark 12.40.

Redaction and tradition

Deviating from my procedure elsewhere, here I am analysing a lengthy text *en bloc*. I am doing so because this brings out better Matthew's overall statement. Thus the discourse in Matt. 23 is less well known than another great speech in Matthew, the Sermon on the Mount, which is investigated in units.

Matthew uses the Markan warning against the scribes (Mark 12.37c–40 = Matt. 23.1–2a, 6–7) as a place to anchor the discourse in the course of Mark. Moreover he elaborates the discourse using Q (Luke 11.37–52; 13.34f.). In Mark the discourse is addressed to the people (12.37f.), in Matthew also to the disciples (Matt. 23.1.8–12). Mark speaks only of the scribes (Mark 12.38), whereas Matthew puts the scribes and Pharisees together (Matt. 23.2) and Luke artificially distinguishes them (Luke 11.39, 46). Matthew leaves the discourse in the context which he found in Mark 12.38–40; but here the scribe who in Mark was not far from the kingdom of God (12.34) has become a mere tempter (Matt. 22.35) – a gloomy foretaste of the fire, brimstone and pitch that Jesus will pour on the scribes and Pharisees in the view of the First Evangelist.

In the composition of discourses Matthew proves to be a first-class writer. That is true not only of his most famous composition, the Sermon on the Mount, but also of the present discourse against scribes and Pharisees, which for the reasons given at the start will be analysed as a single piece.

[1–3a] The discourse begins with words of recognition for the Jewish leaders. But v. 3a is meant only theoretically. 'So for my sake observe all that the scribes and Pharisees tell you – that is not so bad – the main thing is that you do not follow their actions' (Luz).

[3b–7] Here the tone changes: they do not do what they teach and seek only external recognition. Because of this contradiction in themselves they are not a suitable model. This anticipates the main charge of *hypocrisy*, which follows.

[8–12] These verses form a paraenetic part of the discourse on Christian humility which after the preceding attacks offers a degree of rest. Matthew concludes this unit with v. 12, a widely known saying of Jesus from Q (cf. Luke 14.11; 18.14).

[13–33] But now the storm breaks. Seven woes establish the scribes and Pharisees as hypocrites. The number seven is intended by Matthew to heighten further the force of the charge. He may have inserted the third woe himself. Verses 16–19 have an introduction which is different from that of the other six woes. In addition, the third woe is lengthier than each of the other six woes and corresponds to 15.14 and 5.33–37. Verses 16–19 have a parallel structure and, by giving various examples, make a single point: it is absurd to maintain that to swear by what is lesser is not binding, while to swear by what is greater is binding. The tradition presupposes the existence of the temple and therefore goes back to the time before AD 70. It is certainly to be derived from a Christian tradition and not from Jesus. For Jesus taught not to swear at all (cf. 5.34). The other six woes derive from tradition as well and have a similar style. Hence they stem from the same layer of tradition and were given the same introductory formula by Matthew. The explanation of their harsh polemic may be that these are controversies within an association of synagogues. In v. 13 the scribes and Pharisees are made a negative counterpart of Peter. They close the kingdom of heaven instead of opening it, as was said of Peter in 16.19a. Verse 15 is a reflection of Jewish missionary activity. For vv. 29–32 cf. on Luke 11.47–48.

If the preaching of judgment up to v. 33 was addressed only to the scribes and Pharisees, this is no longer the case in

[34–36] This is a composition on the basis of Q (cf. Luke 11.49–51). The formal address to the Pharisees and scribes is dropped here. The Christian prophets are focussing on the present time of Q; the wise men and scribes refer to the situation of Matthew's community. They will suffer the fate of killing, crucifixion and scourging (cf. 10.17; 22.6) by the Pharisees and scribes whom Jesus chastizes for their hypocrisy. Verses 35–36 show that Matthew is thinking of a judgment on all Israel. Thus the goal of the whole chapter is reached.

[37–39] These verses correspond almost word for word with Luke 13.34–35 and derive from Q (for the reconstruction of the meaning in Q cf. on Luke 13.34–35). The lament on Jerusalem presupposes the punishment of the destruction of Jerusalem (in the Jewish War). There is nothing more to hope for, even in the future. If according to v. 39 Jesus is coming (again) in his parousia as judge of the world, the scribes, Pharisees and hostile Jews will be forced to greet him. But then it will be too late.

The sharpness and polemic of these condemnations by Matthew become even more questionable in that they are not simply handed on as the statement of a prophet, but are put in the mouth of Jesus himself.

Historical

[2–12] The passage is inauthentic, since it must be derived in its entirety from the situation of Matthew's community.

[13–32] As above.

[33–39] As above.

Matthew 24–25: Jesus' discourse on the end time

Matthew 24.1–3: Prophecy of the destruction of the temple

1 And Jesus came out of the temple and went away. And his disciples came to point out the buildings of the temple to him. 2 But he answered and said to them, 'Do you not see all this? *Amen, I say to you*, not one stone will remain here upon another, which will not be turned to ruins.' 3 And when he was sitting on the Mount of Olives, his disciples came to him privately, and said, 'Tell us, when will all this happen, and what will be the sign for your coming and for the consummation of the world?'

Redaction and tradition

Matthew is using Mark 13.1–4.

[1–2] This passage has been taken over from Mark 13.1–2, but in contrast to Mark all the disciples ask the questions and not the four who were first to be called, Peter, James, John and Andrew. Verses 1–2 serve Matthew as a narrative interlude between the discourses of ch. 23 and the discourse about the end time which now follows.

[3] The disciples' two questions are formulated on the basis of Mark 13.3–4. Into the Markan text which he has before him Matthew inserts the coming (again) of Jesus before the consummation of the world. 'Only this is of interest to the

Christians, for whom the catastrophe which befell the temple already lies in the past' (Wernle).

Historical

Cf. on Mark 13.1–4.

Matthew 24.4–14: The beginning of the woes

4 And Jesus answered and said to them, 'See that no one leads you astray. 5 For many will come in my name, saying, "I am the Christ," and they will lead many astray.

6 And you will hear of wars and rumours of wars; see that you are not alarmed. For this must take place. But the end is not yet. 7 For one people will rise up against another, and one kingdom against another, and there will be famine and earthquakes here and there. 8 But all this is the beginning of the woes.

9 *Then* they will deliver you up to tribulation, and will put you to death. And you will be hated by all peoples for my name's sake. 10 *And then many will take offence and betray one another and hate one another.* 11 *And many false prophets will arise and lead many astray.* 12 *And because lawlessness gains the upper hand, the love of many will grow cold.* 13 But whoever endures to the end will be saved. 14 And this gospel of the kingdom *will be* preached *throughout the whole world*, as a testimony to all peoples, and *then* the end will come.'

Redaction and tradition

Matthew is using Mark 13.5–13.

[4–8] Cf. Mark 13.5–8.
[9–14] Matthew has recreated vv. 10–12 (cf. John 15.18–21). Matthew passes over parts of Mark 13 which should have followed in the present passage (13.9, 11–13), because he had already used them in his mission discourse (10.18–22). Verse 14 is a reformulation of Mark 13.10.

Historical

Cf. on Mark 13.5–13.

Matthew 24.15–28: The last period of history

15 'Now when you see the abomination of desolation *spoken of by the prophet Daniel*, standing *in the holy place* – let the reader understand – 16 then those who are in Judaea should flee into the mountains. 17 The one on the roof should not descend to take things from his house. 18 And the one in the field should not turn back to get his cloak. 19 And woe to the pregnant

and those who are breast-feeding in those days! 20 Pray that *your flight* may not be in winter or *on the sabbath.* 21 For then there will be great tribulation, such as has not been from the beginning *of the world* until now, and never will be. 22 And if those days had not been short-ened, no human being would be saved; but for the sake of the elect those days will be short-ened.

23 Then if any one says to you, "Look, here is the Christ!", or "There", do not believe (it). 24 For false Christs and false prophets will arise and do *great* signs and wonders, so as to lead astray, if possible, even the elect. 25 *Look,* I have told you beforehand.

26 So, if they say to you, "Look, he is in the wilderness," do not go out; "Look, he is in the inner rooms," do not believe (it). 27 For as the lightning comes from the east and shines as far as the west, so will be the coming of the Son of man. 28 Where the body is, there the eagles will gather together.'

Redaction and tradition

Matthew's source in vv. 15–25 is the section Mark 13.14–23. For the most part Matthew takes over this section word for word, with the partial exception of v. 14 (cf. Mark 24.15). Q (cf. Luke 17.23–24,37) is the basis of vv. 26–28.

[15] Matthew recognizes the reference to Dan. 12.11 and designates this with a quotation formula which in part recalls his fulfilment quotations (cf. on 1.22). As a result the character of the tradition behind Mark 13 as a pamphlet becomes com-pletely unrecognizable.

[20] Matthew (or his informant) adds 'or on the sabbath'. Here we see that Jesus words about the sabbath (cf. 12.1–14), and Jesus' principle that when there is a danger to life the sabbath commandment may be broken, evidently no longer apply.

[26–28] Matthew adds Q material and thus gives the passage about the last period of history a powerful conclusion. Verse 26 (cf. Luke 17.23) links up with v. 23. Verse 27 (cf. Luke 17.24) describes the cosmic aspect of the parousia. Verse 28 (cf. Luke 17.37b) is a proverb which in the present context is based on the insight that the coming of the Son of man is a certain as the fact that the eagles (here = vultures) will always find the corpse (= the carcass).

Historical

[15–25] Cf. on Mark 13.14–28.

[26–28] None of these Q sayings is authentic, as they are based on a community situation. But v. 27 perhaps contains illustrative material for the final expectation of Jesus.

Cf. Syrian Baruch 53.9–11 (on the end): 9 'That lightning shone much more, so that it lighted the whole earth and healed the regions where the last waters had descended and where it had brought about destruction. 10 And it occupied the whole earth and took command of it. 11 And after this I saw, behold, twelve rivers came from the sea and surrounded the lightning and became subject to it.'

Matthew 24.29–31: The turn towards salvation with the coming of the Son of Man

29 '*And immediately* after the tribulation of that time the sun will be darkened, and the moon will not give its light, and the stars will fall from heaven, and the powers of the heavens will be shaken. 30 And then *will appear the sign of the Son of man in heaven. And then all the generations of the earth will mourn, and* they will see the Son of man coming on the clouds of heaven with power and great glory. 31 And he will send out *his* angels *with a loud trumpet call*, and they will gather his elect from the four winds, from one end of heaven to the other.'

Redaction and tradition

[29–31] Matthew uses Mark 13.24–27. With v. 29 he describes the end which begins with cosmic catastrophes. In v. 30 Matthew has borrowed from Zech. 12.10,12 and combined this prophetic passage with the prophecies given in Dan. 7.13 from Mark (Mark 13.26 = Matt. 24.30b, cf. similarly Rev. 1.7). The sign of the Son of man is probably the Son of man himself. In v. 31 the 'loud trumpet call' added to the Markan original (13.27) is part of the imagery of the end time. Paul already says in his earliest letter that the 'Lord' will descend from heaven and the voice of the archangel and the trumpet of God will ring out (I Thess. 4.16; in v. 17 the motif of the cloud is also attached to that, cf. Matt. 24.30).

Historical

Cf. on Mark 13.24–27.

Matthew 24.32–44: Admonition to watchfulness

32 'From the fig tree learn the parable: when its branch is already juicy and the leaves grow out, you know that summer is near. 33 So too you, when you see all this, know that he is near, at the very door.

34 Amen, I say to you, this generation will not pass away until all this happens. 35 Heaven and earth will pass away, but my words will not pass away.

36 But of that day and hour no one knows, not even the angels of heaven, nor the Son, but the Father *only*.

37 For as (were) the days of Noah, so will be the coming of the Son of man. 38 For as in

those days before the flood they were eating and drinking, marrying and being married until the day when Noah entered the ark, 39 and did not notice until the flood came and swept them all away, so will be the coming of the Son of man. 40 Then two men will be in the field; one will be taken and the other left. 41 Two women will be grinding at the mill; one will be taken and the other left. 42 *Watch, therefore, for you do not know on what day your Lord is coming.*

43 But you should know this, that if the householder had known in what watch of the night the thief was coming, he would have watched and would not have let his house be broken into. 44 Therefore you also must be ready; for the Son of man is coming at an hour you do not expect.'

Redaction and tradition

[32–36] In this passage Matthew takes over Mark 13.28–32 almost word for word.

[37–39] Matthew is using Q (cf. Luke 17.26–28) in order to inculcate the negative side of the coming of the Son of man.

[40–41] These verses derive from Q (cf. Luke 17.34–35) and bring out another negative aspect of the final catastrophe: the inexorable division between individuals.

[42–44] These verses are traditional paraenesis about being watchful. For Matthew, the consequences of not knowing the time when Jesus will come (again) is the admonition to be on guard. Matthew has transposed v. 42 here from Mark 13.35. With this admonition to be watchful he emphasizes what is important for him. Verses 43–44 are a Q parable with an application (cf. Luke 12.39–40).

Historical

[32–36] Cf. on Mark 13.28–32.

[37–39] The sayings are not authentic, for Jesus did not speak of the coming of the Son of man in the imminent future. Kingdom of God and Son of man are never mentioned in parallel in the preaching of Jesus. From this we must conclude that only one way of talking can be 'authentic', either about the future kingdom of God or about the Son of man who will come soon.

[40–41*] The nucleus of these verses is an authentic saying of Jesus since there are no Jewish parallels, nor are there christological references.

[43–44] Cf. on Luke 12.39–40.

Matthew 24.45–51: The faithful and wicked servants

45 'Who then is the faithful and wise servant, whom his master has set over those whom he serves, to give them their food at the proper time? 46 Blessed is that servant whom his master, when he comes, finds so doing. 47 Amen, I say to you, he will set him over all his

possessions. 48 But if that *wicked* servant says to himself, "My master is delayed," 49 and begins to beat his fellow servants (and) eats and drinks with the drunken, 50 the master of that servant will come on a day when he does not expect him and at an hour he does not know, 51 and he will punish him, and put him with the *hypocrites; there will be weeping and gnashing of teeth.'*

Redaction and tradition

Matthew does not use the parable of the gatekeeper from Mark 13.34–36, which he has before him because he has noted the affinity of the present parable about the faithful and wicked servants to it.

[45–51a] The present parable derives from Q (cf. Luke 12.42–46) and its essential wording has been preserved, as is shown by the considerable agreement between the Matthaean and Lukan versions. But already in Q it was related to Christ as judge of the world (cf. especially the conclusion in Matt. 24.51/Luke 12.46 which completely fails to fit the picture), and in view of the delay in the coming of Christ the Son of man seems to invite correct behaviour.

[51b] For Matthew the hypocrites relate to the scribes and Pharisees (23.13–33). They – but also the members of the community who follow the way of the wicked servant – are punished. For the fifth time Matthew makes Jesus threaten with the sentence in vv. 51f. (cf. previously 8.12; 13.42, 50; 22.13; cf. later 25.30).

Historical

The parable is inauthentic, as it is governed by the problem of the delay of the parousia (v. 48b). This was alien to Jesus.

Matthew 25.1–13: The wise and foolish virgins

1 *'Then the kingdom of heaven is to be compared to ten virgins who took their lamps and went <u>to meet</u> the bridegroom. 2 And five of them were foolish, and five were wise.* 3 For when the foolish took their lamps, they took no oil with them. 4 But the wise took oil in their vessels with their lamps. 5 Now when the bridegroom was delayed, they slumbered and slept. 6 But at midnight there was a cry, "Look, the bridegroom is coming! Go out <u>to meet</u> him." 7 Then all those virgins arose and trimmed their lamps. 8 And the foolish said to the wise, "Give us some of your oil, for our lamps are going out." 9 But the wise replied, "No, otherwise there would not be enough for us and for you; go rather to the dealers and buy for yourselves." 10 And while they went to buy, the bridegroom came, and those who were ready went in with him to the marriage feast; and the door was shut. 11 Later the other virgins came and say, "'Lord, lord, open to us.'" 12 But he replied and said, "Amen, I say to you, I do not know you."

13 *Watch therefore, for you know neither the day nor the hour.'*

Redaction and tradition

The narrative of the wise and foolish virgins is a mixture of parable and allegory. A pure parable would have led us to expect a mention of the bride who was being married to the bridegroom. But the place of the bride has already been taken by the believers, the virgins, who are waiting for the Messiah. To this degree it can be said that the present narrative uses the theme of delay.

[1] This is a redactional construction as a superscription and a summary of what follows. 'Then' refers back to the parousia mentioned in 24.44 and 50.

[2–5] These verses contain the exposition of the story and provide all the knowledge necessary. In relation to v. 2, in 7.24–27 a man is similarly characterized as wise or foolish depending on whether he builds his house on the rock or on sand.

[6–9] The middle section comes to a climax in the conversation between the foolish and the wise women.

[10–12] Verse 10 depicts the coming of the bridegroom, the wedding feast and the closing of the door to the wedding feast. Verses 11–12 reproduce a conversation between the bridegroom and the foolish women. Cf. 7.21.

[13] 'Watch' has a metaphorical significance and means 'Be prepared'. It is not a reproach for going to sleep, for even the wise virgins went to sleep.

Historical

The narrative is inauthentic since the semi-allegorical form derives from the needs of the community to find themselves in the parable. Furthermore the parable reflects the delay of the coming of the bridegroom Christ.

Matthew 25.14–30: The parable of the talents

14 'For it will be like a man who went abroad: he called his own servants and entrusted his property to them; 15 to one he gave five talents, to another two, to a third one, to each according to his ability, and he went away. Immediately 16 the one who had received the five talents went and traded with them and made five talents more. 17 Likewise the one who had received two talents made two talents more. 18 But the one who had received one talent went away and dug in the ground and hid his lord's money.

19 After a long time the lord of those servants came and settled accounts with them. 20 And the one who had received five talents came forward, bringing five talents more, and said, "LORD, YOU ENTRUSTED ME WITH FIVE TALENTS; HERE I HAVE MADE FIVE TALENTS MORE." 21 His lord said to him, "Well done, good and faithful servant. You were faithful over a little, I will set you over much. *Enter into the joy (ful feast) of your lord*."

22 The one who had two talents also came forward and said, "LORD, YOU

ENTRUSTED ME WITH TWO TALENTS; HERE I HAVE MADE TWO TALENTS MORE." 23 <u>His lord said to him, "Well done, good and faithful servant. You were faithful over a little, I will set you over much.</u> *Enter into the joy (ful) feast of your lord."*

24 And the one who had received the one talent also came forward and said, "Lord, I knew that you were a hard man: <u>you reap where you have not sowed, and gather where you have not scattered</u>; 25 and as I was afraid, I went and hid your talent in the ground. Here you have what is yours." 26 But his lord answered and said to him, "You wicked and slothful servant! Did you know that <u>I reaped where I had not sowed, and gathered where I had not scattered?</u> 27 Then you ought to have invested my money with the moneychangers, and at my coming I should have received what was my own with interest. 28 So take the talent from him, and give it to him who has ten talents." 29 For to every one who has will be given, and he will have abundance; but from him who has not, even what he has will be taken away. 30 *And cast the worthless servant into the outer darkness; there will be wailing and gnashing of teeth.'*

Redaction and exposition

The text is genetically connected with Luke 19.11–27 and probably derives from Q. However, because of the great differences between the Matthaean and Lukan versions I think it no longer possible to reconstruct the Q version (see also the introduction to the Lukan version). Matthew understands the parable as an admonition to watchfulness because the hour of the parousia is uncertain (25.13). This interpretation leaves its mark on his version of the parable at two points, in vv. 21 and 23 and in v. 30, for in these verses Christ the judge of the world is speaking and not the businessman of v. 14. Verses 21 and 23 have no equivalent in the parallel version of Luke (vv. 17f.). By contrast the allegorical feature of v. 30 has an analogy in Luke 19.27.

[14–18] These verses contain the exposition.

[19–28] These verses display a symmetrical construction (cf. the different under-linings in the translation). The delay of the parousia has left its mark on v. 19. In the reckoning with the servants in vv. 20–32 Matthew is thinking of the last judgment for the members of his community (cf. 18.23–24).

[29] This verse has been added at a secondary stage. Cf. the parallels Luke 19.27; also Mark 4.25 (= Matt. 13.12); Thomas 41.

[30] This verse contains Matthew's commentary, cf. 8.12; 13.42, 50; 22.13. Matthew is again clear in the elaboration of hell.

Historical

There is no hope of getting any answer to historical questions, in view of the numerous elaborations by the community of an original which can no longer be reconstructed.

Matthew 25.31–46: The judgment of the world

31 '*Now when the Son of man comes in his glory, and all the angels with him, then he will sit on the throne of his glory,* 32 *and all the peoples will be gathered before him. And he will separate them one from another as a shepherd separates the sheep from the goats,* 33 *and he will place the sheep at his right hand, but the goats at the left.*

34 *Then the king will say to those at his right hand, "Come, you blessed of my Father, inherit the kingdom prepared for you from the foundation of the world.* 35 <u>*For I was hungry and you gave me food. I was thirsty and you gave me drink, I was a stranger and you welcomed me.*</u> 36 <u>*I was naked and you clothed me. I was sick and you visited me. I was in prison*</u> *and you came to me."*

37 THEN THE RIGHTEOUS WILL ANSWER HIM AND SAY, "LORD, WHEN DID WE SEE YOU HUNGRY AND FEED YOU, OR THIRSTY AND GIVE YOU DRINK? 38 AND WHEN DID WE SEE YOU A STRANGER AND WELCOME YOU, OR NAKED AND CLOTHE YOU? 39 AND WHEN DID WE SEE YOU SICK OR IN PRISON AND VISIT YOU?"

40 *And the king will answer and say to them, "*<u>*Amen, I say to you, what you have done to one of the least of these my brothers, you have done to me.*</u>*"*

41 *Then he will say to those at his left hand, "Depart from me, you cursed, into the eternal fire prepared for the devil and his angels!* 42 <u>*For I was hungry and you gave me no food. I was thirsty and you gave me no drink.*</u> 43 <u>*I was a stranger and you did not welcome me. I was naked and you did not clothe me. I was sick and in prison and you*</u> *did not* <u>*visit me.*</u>*"*

44 THEN THEY ALSO WILL ANSWER HIM AND SAY, "LORD, WHEN DID WE SEE YOU HUNGRY OR THIRSTY OR A STRANGER OR NAKED OR SICK OR IN PRISON, AND DID NOT MINISTER TO YOU?"

45 *Then he will answer them and say, "*<u>*Amen, I say to you, what you have not done to one of the least of these, you have not done to me.*</u>*"*

46 *And these will go away into eternal punishment, but the righteous into eternal life.'*

Redaction and tradition

In this section, which is often wrongly headed 'Parable of the Judgment of the World', the two great dialogues vv. 34–40 and vv. 41–45 with their symmetrical construction strike the eye. The moral of the passage corresponds to Isa. 58.7: 'Break your bread with the hungry and bring the homeless poor into your house. When you see the naked, clothe him.' Cf. further Ezek. 18.7, 16; TestJos.1.

This concluding text of Jesus' eschatological discourse fits Matthaean theology seamlessly. After the paraenesis in 24.32–25.30 the judgment by the Son of man is depicted in a great painting. The judgment is of all human beings, but Matthew has his community in particular in view: cf. 13.37–43, 49–50. In view of this similarity we must seriously consider whether the whole passage should be regarded as a Matthaean construction.

[31–32a] This introduction picks up 13.40–43, 49–50; 16.27; 19.28 and 24.30–31.
[32b–33] The theme of judgment is typically Matthaean.

[34–36] Cf. vv. 41–43. The king is not God but Jesus, the Son of man and judge. He had already taken his place on the throne of glory (v. 31).

[37–39] Cf. v. 44.

[40] This verse completes the identification of the Son of man or God with the least of the brothers. Against the identification of God with the brother is the fact that in early Christianity (including the authentic Jesus tradition), God is not put into close relations with a brother but is the Father. By contrast the identification of Jesus the Son of man with the brother in our text makes sense; cf. Mark 9.37/Matt. 18.5.

[41–43] These verses correspond almost word for word with vv. 34–36, which this time are formulated in the negative. However, in v. 41 Matthew does not make Jesus say 'Accursed of my Father' and also avoids a statement about being pre-destined to the curse. Verse 43 is slightly abbreviated by comparison with v. 36.

[44] This is a short version of the question from vv. 37–39.

Historical

The historical question does not arise, as the text is a Matthaean compendium. Jesus never spoke the words which it contains.

Matthew 26–27: The passion story

Matthew 26.1–16: Conspiracy. Anointing in Bethany. Contract

1 *And it happened, when Jesus had finished all these sayings, he said to his disciples,* 2 'You know that in two days it is Passover, and the Son of man will be delivered up to be crucified.'

3 Then the chief priests and the elders of the people *gathered in the palace of the high priest, who was named Caiaphas,* 4 and took counsel together so that they could arrest Jesus by guile and kill him. 5 But they said, 'Not during the feast, lest there be a tumult among the people.'

6 Now when Jesus was at Bethany in the house of Simon the leper, 7 a woman came up to him with an alabaster flask of very expensive oil, and she poured it on his head, as he reclined at table. 8 But when *the disciples* saw it, they became indignant and said, 'Why this waste? 9 For this oil might have been sold for a large sum, and the money given to the poor.' 10 When Jesus noticed (this), he said to them, 'Why do you trouble the woman? For she has done a good work for me. 11 For you always have the poor with you, but you will not always have me. 12 In pouring this oil on my body she has done (it) to prepare me for burial. 13 Amen, I say to you, wherever this gospel is preached in the whole world, what she has done will be told in memory of her.'

14 Then one of the twelve, *named* Judas Iscariot, went to the chief priests 15 and said, 'What will you give me if I deliver him to you?' And they paid him *thirty* pieces of silver. 16 And *from then on* he sought an opportunity to deliver him up.

Redaction

Matthew is using Mark 14.1–11.

[1] This verse is the last of the five concluding and transitional formulae (previously 7.28; 11.1; 13.53; 19.1) with which Matthew rounds off the discourse sections of his work. 'All' indicates that there will be no further discourses.

[2] The direct speech enlivens the account and adds a further prediction of Jesus' death over and above the passages taken from Mark.

[3–5] These verses are an expansion of Mark 14.1b–2; in them Matthew (cf. further Matt. 26.57), like the Fourth Gospel (cf. John 11.49; 18.13–14, 24, 28), goes beyond Mark in knowing the name of the high priest Caiaphas for the passion story. But this is hardly because both are dependent on a common original. At any rate Caiaphas is also known to Luke (cf. Luke 3.2; Acts 4.6).

[6–13] These verses contain numerous word-for-word agreements with Mark 14.3–9. Strangely in Matthew (v. 8) the disciples express their indignation, whereas Mark (14.4) generalizes and makes only 'some' speak like this. The indignation of the disciples (who fail to understand) would have fitted Mark better; but cf. Mark 14.5c, where the disciples are certainly the subject and reproach the woman.

[14–16] These verses correspond to Mark 14.10–11. 'Named' (v. 14) picks up 'named' in v. 3. The direct speech in v. 15 enlivens the narrative (cf. previously v. 2). At the same time Judas' greed appears as a reason for his action. Matthew has inferred the thirty pieces of silver from the prophet Zechariah (11.12f.; cf. on 27.3–10). 'Alongside the two asses (21.1–9), that is the clearest example of how Matthew has written history' (Wernle).

Historical

Cf. on Mark 14.1–11.

Matthew 26.17–29: Preparation of the Passover meal. Prediction of the delivering up. The supper

17 Now on the first (day) of the Unleavened (Bread) the disciples came to Jesus, saying, 'Where will you have us prepare the Passover lamb for you to eat?' 18 He said, 'Go into the city to a certain one and say to him, "The teacher says, '*My time is near*; I will keep the Passover at your house with my disciples."' 19 And the disciples did as Jesus had commanded them, and prepared the Passover lamb.

20 And in the evening, he reclined at table with the twelve. 21 And as they were eating, he said, 'Amen, I say to you, one of you will deliver me up.' 22 And they became very sorrowful, and began to ask him one after another, 'Is it I, Lord?'23 He answered, 'The one who has

dipped his hand in the dish with me, *this one will deliver me up*. 24 The Son of man indeed goes as it is written of him, but woe to that man by whom the Son of man is delivered up! It would have been better for that man if he had not been born.'

25 *Judas, who delivered him up, answered and said, 'Is it I, rabbi?' He says to him, 'You say so.'*

26 Now as they were eating, Jesus took the bread, gave thanks and broke it and gave it *to the disciples* and said, 'Take, *eat*; this is my body.' 27 And he took the cup and gave thanks, gave it to them and said, '*Drink* of it, all of you; 28 for this is my blood of the covenant, which is poured out for many *for the forgiveness of sins*. 29 I tell you, *from now on* I shall not drink of this fruit of the vine until that day when I drink it anew with you in *my Father's* kingdom.'

Redaction and tradition

[17–19] Matthew has tightened up the Markan original (14.12–16) considerably. He does not have Jesus sending two of his disciples as in Mark (14.13), but all the disciples. The new clause added in v. 18, 'My time is near', sounds almost Johannine (cf. John 7.6,8).

[23] The change from Mark 14.20 is striking (cf. John 13.26). See further on v. 25.

[24] Cf. 18.7.

[25] This verse describes the unmasking of the traitor, linking up with the end of v. 23.

[26–27] The institution of the eucharist largely corresponds to Mark, which Matthew has before him (14.22–23). However, in Matthew, unlike Mark, Jesus issues an explicit invitation to eat and drink. This is governed on the one hand by the liturgical practice in Matthew's community, and on the other indicates that the celebration of the eucharist has been commanded by the 'Lord'. Similarly, the 'Lord' will later ordain baptism (28.19).

[28] Matthew adds 'for the forgiveness of sins'. However, neither in the Matthaean passion story nor in the other New Testament passion narratives is there any elaboration in terms of the obliteration of sins brought about by the death of Jesus.

Historical

Cf. on Mark 14.12–25.

Matthew 26.30–35: The announcement of Peter's denial

30 And when they had sung a hymn, they went out to the Mount of Olives. 31 Then Jesus said to them, 'You will all take offence *at me this night*. For it is written, "I will strike the shepherd, and the sheep *of the flock* will be scattered." 32 But after my resurrection, I will go before you to Galilee.' 33 But Peter answered and said to him, 'Though all take offence *at*

you, I will never *take offence*.' 34 Jesus said to him, 'Truly, I say to you, <u>this night</u>, before the cock crows, you will deny me three times.' 35 Peter says to him, 'Even if I must die with you, I will not deny you.' And *so* said all the *disciples*.

Redaction and tradition

Matthew is using Mark 14.26–31.

[30–35] The changes to Mark are insignificant. In v. 31 the offence taken by the disciples is personalized (a) through an emphatic 'you' which is untranslatable and (b) by the addition 'at me'. The characterization of Peter's assertion (v. 33) as an answer continues the personalization.

Historical

Cf. Mark 14.26–31.

Matthew 26.36–46: Jesus in Gethsemane

36 *Then* Jesus goes with them to a garden, named Gethsemane, and says to the disciples, 'Sit here, while I go over there and pray.' 37 And he took with him Peter and the two sons of Zebedee, and began to be sorrowful and troubled. 38 Then he said to them, 'My soul is troubled, even to death; remain here, and watch *with me.*'

39 And he went a little further, fell on his face and prayed, '<u>My Father, if it is possible</u>, let this cup *pass by* me; nevertheless, not as I will, but as you (will).'

40 And he comes *to his disciples* and finds them sleeping and says to Peter, 'Could you not watch *with me* one hour? 41 Watch and pray that you do not enter into temptation. The spirit is willing, but the flesh is weak.' 42 Again he went away a second time, prayed and said, '<u>My Father, if it is impossible</u> for this (cup) to pass by me, without my drinking it, let your will be done.' 43 And again he came and found them sleeping, for their eyes were very heavy. 44 And he left them and again went away and prayed for the third time, saying the same words.

45 Then he comes *to his disciples* and says to them, 'Sleep on and take your rest! Look, the hour has come and the Son of man is delivered into the hands of sinners. 46 Rise, let us be going. Look, the one who will deliver me up is there.'

Redaction and tradition

Matthew is using Mark 14.32–42.

[36–46] The changes to Mark are slight, but evocative. Matthew intensifies Jesus' submission to God's will by describing Jesus' two prayers in direct speech. The positive conditional clause (v. 39, 'if it is possible') is followed by a negative one (v. 42, 'if it is impossible'). Verse 42 quotes the third petition of the Our Father (6.10b). Jesus' submission is understood as a practising of the prayer that he himself taught the disciples. His attitude is the model for such prayer.

Historical

Cf. on Mark 14.32–42.

Matthew 26.47–56: The arrest of Jesus

47 And while he was still speaking, look, Judas came, one of the twelve, and with him a *great* crowd of people with swords and staves, from the chief priests and the elders of the people. 48 Now the betrayer had given them a sign and said, 'The one whom I shall kiss is the man; seize him.' 49 And immediately he came up to Jesus and said, 'Hail, rabbi!', and kissed him. 50 And Jesus said to him, '*Friend, why are you here?*' *Then they came up* and laid hands on Jesus and seized him. 51 *And look,* one of those who were with Jesus stretched out his hand and drew his sword, and struck the slave of the high priest and cut off his ear. 52 *Then Jesus said to him, 'Put your sword in its place. For all who take the sword will perish by the sword. 53 Or do you think that I cannot ask my Father, and he will at once send me more than twelve legions of angels?*

54 *But how then would the <u>scriptures be fulfilled</u>, that it must happen in this way?*' 55 *At that hour* Jesus said *to the crowds of people*, 'You have come out as against a robber, with swords and clubs to capture me. Day after day I *sat* in the temple teaching, and you did not seize me. 56 But all this has taken place, that <u>the scriptures</u> *of the prophets* might <u>be fulfilled</u>.' *Then* all the *disciples* forsook him and fled.

Redaction and tradition

Matthew is using Mark 14.43–52.

[50] The address with 'friend' has negative connotations (cf. 20.13; 22.13).

[52–54] Matthew emphasizes Jesus' obedience. He is deliberately defenceless (v. 52; cf. 5.39–42) although as Messiah he is ruler of the world and would immediately get superhuman help (v. 53). The Matthaean Son of man–judge has power to command the angels (13.41; 16.27). But it is his will to fulfil scripture.

[55] Sitting emphasizes the dignity of a teacher.

[56] Matthew adds 'the prophets' because the prediction of flight comes from the prophet Zechariah (13.7). He had used it in 26.31, taking up Mark 14.27. In the preceding passage Matthew had introduced 'disciples' several times into Mark that he had in front of him: 26.35, 40, 45. Cf. the overall situation indicated by the italics.

Like Luke, Matthew omits the episode of the young man who flees, which follows in Mark.

Historical

Cf. on Mark 14.43–52.

Matthew 26.57–68: Jesus before the Supreme Council

57 But they seized Jesus and led him to *Caiaphas* the high priest, where the scribes and the elders *had gathered.* 58 And Peter followed him at a distance, as far as the palace of the high priest, and entered and sat with the servants to see the outcome (of the matter). 59 Now the chief priests and the whole Supreme Council sought *false* testimony against Jesus that they might put him to death. 60 And they found none, though many false witnesses came forward. At last *two* came forward 61 and said, 'This man said, "I can destroy the temple of God and build it in three days."'

62 And the high priest stood up and said to him, 'Have you no answer to make to what these men say against you?' 63 But Jesus was silent. And the high priest said to him, '*I adjure you by the living God, tell us* if you are the Christ, the Son *of God.*' 64 Jesus said to him, 'You have said so. *But I tell you, hereafter* you will see the Son of man seated at the right hand of Power and coming on the clouds of heaven.' 65 *Then* the high priest tore his robes, and said, '*He has blasphemed God.* Why do we need further witnesses? *Look, now* you have heard his blasphemy. 66 What do you think?' They answered and said, 'He deserves death.'

67 *Then* they spat in his face and struck him with their fists. And some scourged (him) 68 and said, 'Prophesy *to us, Christ, who is it who struck you?*'

Redaction and tradition

Matthew uses Mark 14.53–65 and reproduces the original with slight differences.

[59] Matthew explains the intention of the Supreme Council to kill Jesus (cf. Mark 14.55) *right at the beginning* of the investigation by observing that an attempt was made to establish this by false testimony.

[63–64] His question, put in connection with Mark (14.61) and Jesus' answer, takes on special significance as a result of the high priest's adjuration.

[67] Members of the Supreme Council – not 'some' (Mark 14.65a) – spit on Jesus. Whereas in Mark (14.65c) the servants of the Supreme Council scourge Jesus, in Matthew this is done by some of the members of the Sanhedrin themselves.

[68] Members of the Supreme Council mock Jesus as Christ. Evidently for Mark the messianic dignity of Jesus was the main cause of offence for the Sanhedrin.

Yield: Matthew has further accentuated the opposition between Jesus and his Jewish enemies.

Historical

Cf. on Mark 14.53–65.

Matthew 26.69–75: Peter's denial

69 Now Peter was sitting *outside* in the courtyard. And a maid came to him, and said, 'You also were with Jesus *the Galilean*.' 70 But he denied it before them all and said, 'I do not know what you are saying.' 71 And when he went out to the porch, another maid saw him, and she said to those who were there, 'This man was with Jesus the Nazorene.' 72 And again he denied it *with an oath*, *'I do not know this man.'* 73 And after a little while the (by)standers came up and said to Peter, 'Certainly you are also one of them, for *your speech betrays you.*' 74 *Then* Peter began to curse and to swear, 'I do not know the man.' And immediately the cock crowed. 75 Then Peter thought of the words that Jesus had spoken, 'Before the cock crows, you will deny me three times.' And he went out and wept *bitterly*.

Redaction and tradition

Matthew is using Mark 14.54, 66–72. The whole passage is an example of Matthew's literary practice: he has abbreviated the original and improved it stylistically, but has essentially maintained the content.

[71] In Mark 14.69 it is the same maid as in 14.66f., in Matthew another one in v. 69–71 and in v. 71.

[72] Peter already swears at the second denial, and not at the third as in Mark (14.71).

[74–75] Because of the change in the Markan prediction by Jesus in Matt. 26.34 (cf. Mark 14.30) the cock may crow only once to fulfil Jesus' prediction precisely.

Historical

Cf. on Mark 14.54, 66–72. The thesis developed there that Peter himself spoke of his denial of Jesus in connection with the Easter experience is the reason why Peter does not fall under the verdict of Matt. 10.33. The Q saying in Matt. 10.33 is focussed on the denial of being a Christian during persecutions; the story of Peter's denial goes back to the decisive prehistory of belief in the Risen One.

Matthew 27.1–31a: Jesus before Pilate. The end of Judas. Condemnation and mockery of Jesus

1 When morning came, all the chief priests and the elders of the people took a decision on Jesus, *to kill him*, 2 and they bound him, led him away and delivered him to Pilate *the governor.*

3 When Judas, who had delivered him up, saw that he was condemned, he repented and brought back the thirty pieces of silver to the chief priests and the elders, 4 and said, 'I have done wrong, in that I have delivered up innocent blood.' But they said, 'What is that to us? See to it yourself.' 5 And he threw down the pieces of silver in the temple, departed, went out and hanged himself. 6 But the chief priests took the pieces of silver and said, 'It is not lawful to put them into the treasury, since they are blood money.' 7 So they took a decision and bought with them the potter's field, to bury strangers in. 8 Therefore that field is called the Field of Blood to the present day. 9 *Then was fulfilled what is spoken by the prophet Jeremiah, who says,* 'And they took the thirty pieces of silver, the price of the him on whom a price had been set by some of the sons of Israel, 10 and they gave them for the potter's field, as the Lord commanded me.'

11 *Now Jesus stood before the governor;* and the governor asked him and said, 'Are you the King of the Jews?' Jesus said, 'You say (it).' 12 And when he was accused by the chief priests and elders, he answered nothing. 13 *Then* Pilate said to him, 'Do you not hear how many things they testify against you?' 14 And he answered him not a single word, so that the governor wondered greatly.

15 Now at the feast the governor had *the custom* of releasing for the people a prisoner whom they wanted. 16 And at that time they had a *notorious prisoner*, called Barabbas. 17 *And when they had gathered*, Pilate said to them, 'Whom do you want me to release for you, Barabbas or Jesus who is called Christ?' 18 For he knew that they had delivered him up out of envy.

19 *And while he was sitting on the judgment seat, his wife sent word to him saying, 'Have nothing to do with that righteous man, for I have suffered much over him today a dream.'*

20 And the chief priests and elders persuaded the people to ask for Barabbas and kill Jesus. 21 Then the governor again answered and said to them, 'Which do you want? Which of the two shall I release to you?' And they said, 'Barabbas!' 22 Pilate says to them, 'What then shall I do with Jesus, the so-called Christ?' They all said, 'Let him be crucified.' 23 And he said, 'Why, what evil has he done?' But they cried out all the more, 'Let him be crucified.' 24 *And when Pilate saw that he was achieving nothing, but rather that a riot was beginning, he took water and washed his hands before the people and said, 'I am innocent of this man's blood; see to it yourselves.'* 25 *Then the whole people answered and said, 'His blood be on us and on our children!'*

26 *Then* he released Barabbas to them, but he had Jesus scourged and delivered him to be crucified.

27 *Then* the soldiers of the governor took Jesus with them into the praetorium and gathered the whole division before him. 28 And they stripped him and put a scarlet robe upon him 29 and plaited a crown of thorns *and put it on his head, and gave him a reed in his right hand and knelt before him and mocked him* and said, 'Hail, king of the Jews!', 30 and they spat at him and took the reed and struck him on the head with it. 31a And when they had mocked him, they stripped him of the robe, and dressed him (again) in his own clothes.

Redaction and tradition

Matthew is using Mark 15.1–20a but subjects this section to more reshaping than elsewhere. Moreover in vv. 3–10, developing 26.14–16 he inserts a further tradition about the suicide of Judas.

[1–2] Matthew clarifies the Markan narrative, which he has in front of him (15.1–2). The decision which the Jewish leaders make is one to *kill* Jesus (cf. similarly in terms of content Mark 14.64).

[3–10] Matthew uses a tradition about the death of Judas and shapes it on the basis of a prophecy which in v. 9 he wrongly attributes to Jeremiah instead of Zechariah (11.13).

The scene has the following further Matthaean purpose. With the suicide of Judas the proceedings against Jesus are from the start presented as reprehensible, and redactionally a devastating judgment is pronounced on the Jews who are hostile to Jesus. If a disciple who has betrayed Jesus cannot make good his action despite repentance and therefore has to die, that is nothing by comparison with the chief priests and elders who do not even repent of their action.

The death of Judas is also described in Acts 1.18–20 and by the bishop Papias of Hierapolis in Asia Minor (beginning of the second century) independently of the present tradition. The Matthaean version differs from the versions of Acts and Papias in that it reports the repentance of Judas and therefore makes him return the money and commit suicide. By contrast, Luke in Acts and Papias depict the fearful manner of the traitor's death. Common to all three accounts is the connection of Judas with a piece of land; here Matthew and Acts have a particularly affinity in that they call the piece of land the Field of Blood. According to Matt. 27.7 the chief priests buy a field with the thirty pieces of silver which Judas returns; according to the Acts version Judas buys a field himself with his reward (Mark 14.11/Luke 22.5 do not know the precise amount – the number thirty in Matt. 26.15 has been taken from Zech. 11.12f.), on which he evidently hastens to his terrible end. Papias relates how Judas dies in a similarly cruel way on his own property and how the stink of his putrefying body spreads everywhere. The versions of Papias and Luke converge on the following two points: 1. Acts reports that Judas bursts as the result of a fall and that his entrails spill out. According to Papias, Judas swells up tremendously and – one might add – as a consequence bursts, so that his entrails spill out. 2. In the Papias story the fearful swelling up of Judas' body seems to be depicted in connection with Ps. 109.18. Much as the result of the above comparison of the Judas traditions establishes the genetic connection between the three narratives, nevertheless one cannot speak of a well-rounded story about the death of Judas as a basis for the three versions. All that have emerged have been elements of tradition: fearful death, a field as the place of death, and an enrichment with passages from the Old Testament.

[11a] This is a transitional phrase which, after the insertion of vv. 3–10, links back to the narrative thread in v. 2. Matthew gives Pilate the title 'governor' more frequently than Mark: vv. 14–15, 21.

[11b–14] These verses emphasize the silence of Jesus rather more strongly than Mark does.

[19] This verse prepares for vv. 24–25. The motif of the dream already appears in 1.20; 2.12, 19, 22. The designation of Jesus as righteous occurs only here, but righteousness is a key term in Matthew. The recognition of Jesus' status by Pilate's wife recalls the scene in 2.1ff., where the Gentiles come from the East and ask about the newborn king of the Jews in order to pay homage to him, while all Jerusalem is terrified instead of rejoicing at the news. Occasionally scholars wonder whether the community before Matthew knew the content of the dream (Dibelius). However, that must be left unresolved.

[24–25] For Pilate's washing of his hands cf. Ps. 26.6, 'I wash my hands in innocence' and Deut. 21.6–7. Pilate endorses his wife's verdict: as a righteous man Jesus is innocent. This further intensifies the guilt of the Jews. The gesture which the pagan Roman performs, the Jewish-biblical rite of expiation, is very striking and demonstrates Matthew's purpose to foist guilt for the death of Jesus on the Jews. This intention is expressed climactically in the curse that the Jewish people bring down upon themselves immediately after the hand-washing, which occurs only in Matthew: 'And all the people answered and said, "His blood be on us and on our children"' (Matt. 27.25). With this verse Matthew is referring back to 23.34–36:

34 'Therefore, look, I send you prophets and wise men and scribes; and some of them you will kill and crucify, and some you will scourge in your synagogues and persecute from town to town, 35 that upon you may come all the righteous blood shed on earth, from the blood of innocent Abel to the blood of Zechariah the son of Barachiah, whom you murdered between the sanctuary and the altar. 36 Amen, I say to you, all this will come upon this generation.'

Granted, Pilate has given orders for the crucifixion, but according to Matthew Israel is to blame for Jesus' death, and in so doing has finally forfeited its special election. The Jews themselves must assent to that, because, convinced of the guilt of Jesus, they have uttered a limited curse upon themselves. But as Jesus is certainly innocent, they will be responsible for the consequences, so that Jesus' blood comes on them and on their children. None of the anti-Judaistic statements in the New Testament has caused so much murder, distress and desperation among Jews as this.

[29] Matthew puts here the reed which in Mark appears somewhat later (15.19) as an instrument for striking and effectively places it in Jesus' right hand for a moment. The soldiers will immediately snatch it away to strike Jesus.

Historical

For vv. 1–2, 11–18, 20–23, 26–31 cf. on Mark 15.1–20a.
    [3–10] The historical value is nil.

[19] The historical value is nil.
[24–25] The historical value is nil.

Matthew 27.31b–56: The crucifixion and death of Jesus

31b And they lead him away to crucify him. 32 And as they were going out, they found a man from Cyrene, Simon by name. This man they compelled to carry his cross. 33 And when they came to a place called Golgotha – which is called the place of the skull – 34 they gave him wine to drink mixed with gall; *but when he tasted it,* he would not drink it. 35 And when they had crucified him, they divided his garments among them and cast lots. 36 And they sat down and kept watch over him there. 37 And over his head they fastened the charge against him (which was) written, 'This is Jesus the King of the Jews.' 38 Then two robbers were crucified with him, one on the right and one on the left. 39 And those who passed by blasphemed, shaking their heads 40 and saying, 'You who would destroy the temple and build it in three days, save yourself, *if you are the Son of God,* and come down from the cross.' 41 So also the chief priests with the scribes *and elders* mocked him, saying, 42 'He saved others; he cannot save himself. He is the king of Israel; let him come down now from the cross, and we will believe *in him.* 43 *He trusted in God; let God deliver him now, if he will; for he said, "I am the Son of God."* 44 And the robbers who were crucified with him also reviled him in the same way.

45 And from the sixth hour darkness came over all the land until the ninth hour. 46 And about the ninth hour Jesus cried with a loud voice, 'Eli, Eli, lama sabachthani?', that is, 'My God, my God, why have you forsaken me?' 47 And some of those standing there, when they heard it, said, 'This man is calling Elijah.' 48 And one of them at once ran (up) and took a sponge, filled it with vinegar, and put it on a reed, and gave it to him to drink. 49 But the others said, 'Wait, let us see whether Elijah will come and save him.' 50 But Jesus cried again with a loud voice and yielded up his spirit.

51 And *look*, the curtain in the temple was torn from top to bottom, *in two pieces.* 52 And the earth shook, and the rocks were split, and the tombs were opened, and many bodies of the saints who had fallen asleep were raised, 53 and came out of the tombs *after his resurrection* and went into the holy city and appeared to many.

54 And the centurion *and those who were guarding Jesus with him were very frightened when they saw the earthquake and what had taken place, and* said, 'Truly this was the Son of God!'

55 And there were *many* women there, looking on from afar; they had followed Jesus from Galilee and had served him. 56 Among them were Mary Magdalene, and Mary the mother of James and Joses, and the mother of the sons of Zebedee.

Redaction and tradition

Matthew is using Mark 15.20b–41 and for the most part reproduces what he has before him word for word. Only in vv. 52–54 does he use a special tradition.

[32] Like Luke (23.26), Matthew passes over the names of Alexander and Rufus (Mark 15.21) because they no longer meant anything to him.

[40] The introduction of the motif of the son of God prepares for v. 43 and v. 53.

[43] Matthew expands the taunts with a borrowing from Ps. 22.9. The opponents of Jesus react to Jesus' claim to be son of God as they do in v. 40.

[46–47] Matthew alters Elohi to Eli, in order to explain why the bystanders could hear this as a cry for help to Elijah.

[52–53] After the removal of the Matthaean phrase 'after his resurrection' we get the tradition of a (general?) resurrection of the dead, which took place at the time of Jesus' death. The earliest Christians thought of the resurrection of Jesus as taking place immediately on his death ('ascension of Jesus from the cross'), which is matched by the statement of the exaltation of Jesus to the right hand of God, which followed immediately after the humiliation (of the death). Cf. Phil. 2.8–9: 8 'He humbled himself and became obedient to death, the death on the cross. 9 Therefore God has exalted him . . .'

The tradition in Matt. 27.52–53 could be combined with the tradition preserved in Paul of Jesus as the firstfruit of those who have fallen asleep (I Cor. 15.20). Accordingly, Jesus' 'resurrection' is the beginning of the general resurrection of the dead. But Matthew fits this tradition to his view that Jesus was raised on the third day and therefore the resurrection of the righteous from their tombs which is mentioned could take place only *after* the resurrection of Jesus and not on the day of Jesus' death.

[56] In the enumeration of the women who witnessed the death, Matthew writes 'the mother of the sons of Zebedee' instead of Salome. That may derive from tradition.

Historical

For Matt. 27.31b–51, 54–55, cf. Mark 15.20b–41.

[52–53] The verses are an imaginative description of the resurrection of the dead saints and their going to Jerusalem. (Their tombs lay outside the city.) These events did not take place.

Matthew 27.57–61: The burial of Jesus

57 Now when it was evening, there came a *rich* man from Arimathea, named Joseph, *who had also himself become a disciple of Jesus.* 58 He went to Pilate and asked for the body of Jesus. Then Pilate *ordered* it to be given (to him). 59 And Joseph took the body, and wrapped it in a *clean* linen cloth, 60 and laid it in *his own new tomb*, which he had hewn in a rock; and rolled a *great* stone before the door of the tomb, and departed.

61 And Mary Magdalene and the other Mary were there; *they sat opposite the tomb.*

Redaction and tradition

Matthew is using Mark 15.42–47. As Luke (23.50–56a), like Matthew, does not reproduce the passage Mark 15.44–45 in his version of Mark 15.42–47, it has been asked whether they read these two verses in their copy of Mark.

[57] Matthew makes Joseph a disciple of Jesus and is silent about the fact that as a counsellor he had been a member of the Supreme Council which had condemned Jesus to death.

[59] Instead of 'bought a linen cloth' Matthew writes 'clean linen cloth'. This confirms that the linen cloth was not only new but also 'clean', which was fitting for the special body of Jesus (a clean cloth for a clean tomb). Of course Matthew knew that according to Jewish belief a dead body is unclean (cf. Num. 5.2; 9.6–7). With Jesus it was different, for he will be raised, and as Christ *is* already the Lord of the world.

[60] There is a special reason for Jesus' tomb. It is Joseph's tomb and it is new, i.e. it has not yet been made unclean by another corpse. In this way Matthew reinforces the idea from v. 59.

Matthew 27.62–28.20: The resurrection narratives

In the resurrection narratives Matthew bases himself on the Markan account of the empty tomb but supplements this with two appearances of the risen Lord (28.9f. to the women at the tomb; 28,16–20 to the eleven in Galilee), because the conclusion of Mark's Gospel was as unsatisfactory for him, as it was for Luke and the later readers of the Gospel of Mark. Moreover he contributes a story about the guards at the tomb which provides a framework for the narrative of the journey of the women to the empty tomb, reported in Mark 16.1–8. Indeed, 27.62–66 and 28.11–15 'belong together like the two halves of a ball, which when put together produce a perfect sphere' (Lohmeyer).

Matthew 27.62–66: The guard on the tomb

62 *On the next day, which follows the day of rest, the chief priests with the Pharisees gathered before Pilate* 63 and said, 'Lord, we have remembered how this <u>deceiver</u> said, when he was still alive, "After three days I will be raised." 64 Therefore *command* the tomb to be <u>made secure</u> until the third day, so that his disciples do not go and steal him away and tell the people, "He was raised from the dead." And the last <u>deceit</u> will be worse than the first.'

65 Pilate said to them, 'You have a guard; go, make (it) as <u>secure</u> as you can." 66 So they went and made the tomb <u>secure</u> with the guard and sealed the stone.

Redaction and tradition

[62] The verse introduces the narrative with Matthaean vocabulary (cf. only 'gathered', 26.3, 57; 27.17,27; 28.12). The note of time 'next day' follows from the 'evening' of v. 57. The 'Pharisees' appear only here in the passion story and reflect the real counterparts of the many Christian communities in the time of Matthew. (The controversy with the official representatives of Judaism has become harsher than it was in the time before the Jewish War, as is clear from a comparison of Matt. 23 and Mark 12, see below on 28.13). Strikingly, the session before Pilate takes place on the sabbath (= Saturday), not for historical reasons but because this is necessary for the narrative. The death of Jesus on Friday, and the resurrection or discovery of the empty tomb two days after his death, the day after the sabbath, were presupposed by the Markan tradition (cf. Mark 16.1).

[63] The chief priests and Pharisees explicitly 'remember' in their speech to Pilate a saying of Jesus, 'This deceiver said when he was still alive, "After three days I will be raised."' This is not a reference to the predictions of the passion, where Matthew (16.21; 17.23; 20.19), contrary to Mark, which he had before him (8.31; 9.31; 10.34), each time alters 'after three days' to 'on the third day' (cf. I Cor. 15.4), but to Matt. 12.40: 'For as Jonah was three days and three nights in the belly of the whale, so will the Son of man be three days and three nights in the heart of the earth.' In keeping with that, Pharisees are present in the scene in Matt. 12.38f., as they are here in v. 62. The divergent formula 'after three days' is evidently meant to recall this passage.

[64] The Jewish authorities ask Pilate to put a guard on the tomb: 'deceit' refers back to 'deceiver' in v. 63. Verse 64c ('and that last deceit will be worse than the first') corresponds to 12.45c, 'And the last state of this man is worse than the first.' If one allows the disciples to preach the resurrection, matters will be worse than they previously were with Jesus.

[65–66] These verses narrate how Pilate accedes to the request of the Jewish authorities.

28.1–10, the pericope about the empty tomb and the appearance of Jesus to two women disciples, follows. After this Matthew continues his account of the bribing of the guard at the tomb (28.11–15).

Historical

Cf. the remarks on the section 28.11–15.

Matthew 28.1–10: The empty tomb and the appearance of Jesus to two women disciples

1 Now after the sabbath was over and the first day of the week dawned, Mary of Magdala and the other Mary went to see the tomb.

2 *And look*, there was a great earthquake. For an angel of the Lord came down from heaven and came and rolled back the stone, and sat upon it. 3 His appearance was like lightning and his garment white as snow. 4 And for fear of him the guards trembled and became like dead men.

5 But the angel answered and said to the women, 'Do not be afraid! I know that you seek Jesus the crucified. 6 He is not here; he has been raised, *as he said*. Come, see the place where he lay. 7 Then go quickly and tell his disciples *that he has been raised from the dead. And look*, he will go before you to Galilee; there you will see him. Look, I have told you (it).' 8 And they departed quickly from the tomb with fear and great joy, and ran to proclaim (it) to his disciples. 9 *And look, Jesus met them and said, 'Hail!' And they came up to him and took hold of his feet and fell down before him.* 10 *Then Jesus said to them, 'Do not be afraid! Go and* proclaim *to my brothers that they are to go to Galilee. There they will see me.'*

Redaction and tradition

[1] This verse can be explained completely on the basis of Mark. The reason why only two women come to the tomb in Matthew (who are identical with those of 27.61) whereas there were still three in Mark, is that here Matthew probably felt a tension between Mark 15.47 and 16.1 and smoothed it out accordingly. The women's intention in the Markan account to anoint the body in the tomb is absent from Matthew. The phrase 'to see the tomb' is to be explained from the influence of Mark 15.47, for after the stay of the women at the tomb in Matt. 27.61 (they 'sat opposite the tomb') a 'seeing of the tomb' is otherwise quite puzzling.

[2–4] There is a tension between vv. 2–4 and 5–8, where again Mark's account is the basis, for the mighty events of vv. 2–4 bear no relation to the communication of the message in vv. 5–8. It hardly needed such powerful events to get rid of these guards and allow the women to see the empty tomb. Verses 2–4 depict the opening of the tomb by an angel from heaven, confronted with whom the guards become helpless. In vv. 5–8 the message of the resurrection is addressed to the women by the same angel; here what was said in vv. 5–10 must have taken place while the soldiers were helpless. (According to the tradition used by Matthew the angel has evidently opened the tomb so that the revived Jesus can come out.) In vv. 5–8, Matthew again follows the Markan account with some deviations.

[5] This verse is parallel to Mark 16.6a.

[6] This corresponds to Mark 16.6b, where the statement of the resurrection is derived from a prediction of Jesus. This is absent from Mark, who a little later

(Mark 16.7) derives the future seeing of Jesus by the disciples from a prediction of Jesus. Matthew is probably referring back to 26.32.

[7] This has a parallel in Mark 16.7. However, the message is said to be directed only to the disciples as a whole; Peter is not specifically mentioned, as in Mark. In Matthew the content of the message is the resurrection of Jesus; in Mark it is that Jesus is going before the disciples into Galilee and they will see him there. In Mark that is connected with the prediction of Jesus; Matthew makes this a saying by the angel, 'Look, I have told you (it).'

[8] In contrast to Mark (16.8: the women are silent for fear), Matthew narrates that in fear (= taking up what is said in Mark) and in great joy the women want to pass on the message of the angel. That is not surprising, since previously (vv. 2–4) they have *indirectly* been made witnesses to the event of the resurrection. This is a good preparation for the next episode (vv. 9–10), in which Jesus will appear *directly* to them.

[9–10] These verses have no parallel in Mark and might derive from Matthew in their entirety. The verses depict an encounter of Jesus with the two women mentioned in v. 1, who take hold of his feet (cf. II Kings 4.27) and fall down before him, i.e. worship him (cf. later v. 17).

Matthew uses the verb 'fall down' (cf. 8.2; 9.18; 14.33; 15.25; 20.20), differing from Mark, which he has before him, and in so doing indicates that the earthly Jesus already has the authority of the Risen One. (Consistently he does not take over the worship in the mockery scene [Mark 15.19].) Jesus orders them not to fear, and to tell his brothers (cf. Matt. 18.15f.; and 23.8, the fellowship of the disciples among themselves) to go to Galilee, where they will see him.

Apart from the greeting, the risen Jesus does not say anything to the women that the angel at the tomb has not already said: 'Do not be afraid! Go and proclaim to my brothers that they are to go to Galilee. There they will see me' (v. 10; cf. v. 7). However, in connection with Matthew's intention it should be noted that we have 'brothers' instead of 'disciples' (vv. 7f.). But despite the mutual brotherhood of the disciples they have a pupil-teacher relationship with Jesus (Matt. 23.8, 10).

Historical

[1, 5–10] Cf. on Mark 16.1–8.

[2–4] The depiction of the descent of an angel from heaven, his opening of the tomb and the emergence of the revived and transformed Jesus belong in the realm of fantasy. The historical value is nil.

Matthew 28.11–15: The bribing of the guards

11 *Now while they were going, look*, some of the guard went into the city and *proclaimed* to the chief priests all that had taken place. 12 And they assembled with the elders, *made a decision* and gave sufficient silver pieces to the soldiers 13 and said, 'Say, "His disciples came by night and stole him away while we were asleep." 14 And if this comes to the governor's ears, we will satisfy (him) and keep you out of trouble.' 15 So they took the silver pieces and did as they were directed. And this story has been spread among the Jews to this day.

Redaction

[11] Verse 11a links the previous scene with the present one. While the women are making their way to Galilee, the guards themselves report to the Jewish leaders all that has happened, i.e. about the resurrection of Jesus. So the chief priests and elders know of this, just as it was clear to them that by his own testimony Jesus would rise after three days (27.63).

[12] The bribery of the guards recalls the bribery of Judas (26.15).

[13] This verse takes up 27.64. Although they know otherwise, the soldiers are to spread the rumour that the disciples stole the body while they themselves were sleeping. But precisely this had previously been the fear which the Jewish authorities had expressed to Pilate (27.64). Now that Jesus has really risen, they bribe the soldiers to spread this false news nevertheless. (The anti-Jewish criticism is here heightened as in Matt. 23.1–36 in relation to Mark 12.37b–40, on which that passage is based.)

[14] This provides the necessary supplement to the soldiers' action. Should the governor hear that the soldiers neglected their duty and slept on watch – the guard had in fact been agreed on with him – the Jewish authorities will intervene with Pilate on their behalf.

[15] This verse concludes the story. The Roman soldiers do what the Jewish authorities ask of them. The second half of the verse looks forward to Matthew's time: 'and this story has been spread among the Jews to the present day'. That means that the story of the theft of Jesus' body by the disciples was evidently quite widespread among the Jews of Matthew's time and previously. Whether the details of the story told by Matthew belong to this is very questionable, since the Jews are depicted in an extremely negative way and even know of the resurrection of Jesus. They could hardly have exposed themselves to such damning testimony.

The apologist Justin in the middle of the second century, in dialogue with the Jew Trypho, similarly knows this Jewish assertion (though he does not mention the guards).

Justin, *Dial.* 108.2: 'After you heard of his resurrection from the dead you did not convert but chose . . . select people and sent them all over the world to proclaim that a godless and wicked sect had been called to life by a certain Galilean Jesus: we crucified him, but his disciples stole him by night from the tomb in which he had been placed after being taken down from the cross, and told people that he had risen from the dead and ascended into heaven.' Cf. Eusebius, *Church History* IV 18, 7.

Therefore we can imagine the following history of the tradition: (a) the earliest Christians concluded from visions of Christ that there had been a bodily resurrection from the dead; (b) Mark (or a predecessor) composed a story about the empty tomb; (c) Jews claimed that the corpse of Jesus had been stolen by the disciples; (d) Matthew reacts to that with the story of the bribery of the guards at the tomb which we read in his Gospel.

Now it is claimed time and again that the Jewish news presupposes the recognition of the empty tomb: the Jewish polemic never disputed that the tomb was empty but attempts to explain it away. But it is hard to explain how the (unbelieving) Jews could have arrived at the view that the tomb was empty otherwise than through this particular Christian tradition.

Historical

Three historical judgments can be given:

(a) The rumour of a theft of the corpse of Jesus is certainly historical, but not the theft itself. For the disciples did not even know where Jesus had been 'buried', and furthermore, because of their utter disappointment, they would not have been in a position to perpetrate such a fraud.

(b) The tradition about the bribing of the guards at the tomb cannot be taken seriously, because it too clearly has partisan features of Matthew or the Matthaean tradition. (By confessing that they had slept at the tomb the guards would have been risking their necks.)

(c) The Jewish authorities did not know anything about an actual resurrection of Jesus. This too is a supposition which is rooted in Matthew's anti-Jewish attitude.

Matthew 28.16–20: The appearance of Jesus and the mission command

16 Now the eleven disciples went to Galilee, to the mountain to which Jesus had directed them (to go). 17 And when they saw him they fell down, but some doubted. 18 And Jesus *came and spoke with them and said,* 'All authority in heaven and on earth has been given to me. 19 *Therefore go and make disciples of* all peoples, baptizing them in the name of the Father and of the Son and of the Holy Spirit, 20 and teaching them to *observe* all that I have *commanded* you. And *look,* I am with you always, to the *end of the world.*'

Redaction and tradition

At this point Matthew narrates an appearance story. Generally speaking, it is striking that the account of Jesus' real appearance is brief. It is expressed only by a terse 'when they saw him'; here the reaction of the eleven disciples is identical to that of the women in v. 9 ('they prostrated themselves'). The emphasis here is not on the appearance itself, but on the subsequent words of Jesus (vv. 18–20).

[16] This describes the carrying out of Jesus' command from v. 10. The 'mountain' here is the place of the epiphany (cf. 5.1; 15.29; 17.1).

[17] 'They prostrated themselves' takes up the same verb from v. 9. 'Doubt' appears in the New Testament elsewhere only in Matt. 14.31 (Jesus to the sinking Peter, 'O man of little faith, why did you doubt?') and may be redactional. For doubt – in substance a motif which occurs frequently in the Easter stories (Luke 24.11, 25, 37f., 41) – cf. esp. John 20.29.

The motif of doubt addresses problems of Christians of the second and third generations, who no longer have any direct access to the original Easter experience. In this way they can recognize their own situation in the text and are more inclined to accept Jesus' answer to this question which is oppressing them.

[18] The verb 'to come' is typically Matthaean language (4.3; 8.19; 9.28, etc.). In v. 18b the notion of the enthronement of the Son of Man as ruler (cf. Dan. 7.14) is transferred to Jesus. The exaltation of Jesus and the power thus bestowed on him (cf. Matt. 11.27; John 3.35; Phil. 2.9–11) is a traditional piece of doctrine. With the partial exception of 9.6 (= Mark 2.10), the phrase 'in heaven as on earth' occurs as a whole or in part only in Matthaean special material (6.10; 16.19; 18.18).

[19] With its mission command, v. 19 deliberately refers back to 10.5–6. Its target is exclusively Gentile, for 'peoples' must be understood in the same way in 10.5–6 and here, namely as Gentiles. Matthew would hardly have counted the Jews among the peoples.

Presumably Matthew has replaced a command standing in the original, 'preach the gospel', with the invitation 'make disciples' (cf. 13.52; 27.57), and this may perhaps have been preserved in the secondary conclusion to Mark (16.15). The baptism 'in the name of the Father and of the Son and of the Holy Spirit' is striking for its triadic formula, since in the early period baptism was simply into Christ (Gal. 3.27) or in the name of Jesus (I Cor. 1.13; Acts 8.16; 19.5; cf. Did.9.5), though the combination of God, Jesus and Spirit has already been prepared for by Paul (II Cor. 1.21f.; II Cor. 13.13; I Cor. 12.4–6). Probably this was a baptismal formula with a liturgical character with a parallel in Didache 7.1, which runs: 'Baptize in the name of the Father and of the Son and of the Holy Spirit.'

[20] This verse is saturated with Matthaean vocabulary: 'observe', 'all',

'command' and 'look' (cf. 28.9); 'end of the world' (13.39f., 49; 24.3). Matthew makes Jesus refer to the exclusive authority of his words in the present. The Matthaean proclamation has become the preaching of the commandments of the Torah rightly understood. The place of the appearance of the risen Christ which has become impossible in Matthew's community has been taken by the word of the exalted Christ who is identical with the earthly Jesus. His teaching is present in the Gospel of Matthew.

Historical

[16–20] The historical yield is extremely meagre. It is true that Jesus 'appeared' (to Peter and) to the twelve (I Cor. 15.5), though Matthew explicitly speaks only of the eleven disciples (28.16), as do some codices on I Cor. 15.5. But that is a rationalization which has removed the figure of Judas from the twelve. Originally the tradition reported an appearance to the twelve (I Cor. 15.5) with Cephas as leader. They saw Jesus and on the basis of this founded a community which preached the resurrection and exaltation of Jesus as the Messiah and/or the Son of Man among their Jewish contemporaries. That is the historical nucleus of the scene reported by Matthew. Whether this vision took place in Galilee, as the text indicates, remains uncertain on the basis of the present passage, since Matthew has inferred 'Galilee' from Mark 16.7. But from general considerations, the location of this first vision in Galilee may be historically correct. In the first panic the disciple fled to their homes in Galilee and thus at the same time to the places where Jesus had been active.

In this closing scene of the Gospel, Matthew and/or his tradition has concentrated later theological conclusions like the 'mission to the Gentiles', which were never formulated in that way by the twelve (cf. on 19.28), though they already had been by Paul and other Jewish-Hellenistic Christians. Cf. Paul's autobiographical retrospect in Gal. 1–2.

III

The Gospel of Luke

Luke 1.1–4: Preface

1 *Since many have undertaken to compose a narrative about the events which have come to fulfilment among us, 2 as they have been handed down to us by those who from the beginning were themselves eyewitnesses and servants of the word, 3 I too have thought it good, since I have investigated everything carefully from the beginning, to write them out in order for you, excellent Theophilus, 4 that you may know the certain basis of the teaching in which you have been instructed.*

A general comment on the aim of Luke's work

The preface to the Gospel of Luke (and that to Acts, see below) is a magnificently stylized Greek sentence without any parallel in the New Testament, which emphasizes the literary claim of Luke's work. It is the only passage in the Synoptic Gospels in which an evangelist gives information about the aim of his work and his sources. This provides us with important insights: *first*, there were other (= 'many') authors of Gospels already before Luke (v. 1). *Secondly*, these were not present at the events – any more than Luke was. This condition is only fulfilled by the group of eyewitnesses and servants of the word who are the source of the tradition (v. 2). *Thirdly*, Luke wants to surpass his predecessors, since he has once again investigated everything carefully from the beginning, so as to write it down in order (v. 3).

The appropriate chronological sequence of events is also important (cf. the position of the Nazareth pericope in Luke 4.16–30). Here Luke infers the correct chronological sequence out of what for him is an evident dogmatic necessity. In this connection the geographical course taken by the events depicted in the Gospel of Luke and Acts is important. Jesus' way begins in Nazareth. The world mission takes its beginning in Jerusalem, finally to reach its goal in Rome, the capital of the world (Acts 28).

Fourthly, according to Luke his work serves as a support for faith; here the relevant story prepares the basis of Christian doctrine (v. 4). In other words, faith is grounded in historical realities which are no delusion.

The preface is important for judging the question of the origin of the Jesus traditions. What emerges from it is this: at the beginning stands the oral tradition of the eye-witnesses and servants of the word (v. 2). None of them set down his knowledge about Jesus in writing. That happened only later, and certainly not only one or two Gospels came into being in this way, but a larger number. However, the individual writings did not yet enjoy significant respect. Luke has continued this line with his own work and has used at least Q and Mark.

There are parallels to Luke's prologue in the prefaces to classical historical works of antiquity (Herodotus, Thucydides, Polybius). But the prologue and its continuation at the beginning of Acts (1.1) also have a striking parallel in the work *Against Apion* by the Jewish historian Josephus, a younger contemporary of Paul, where similarly the continuation of the preface of Book I 1 appears in Book II 1:

In the previous book, esteemed Epaphroditus, I attempted to prove the great age of our people and the truth of my descriptions through the writings of the Phoenicians, Chaldaeans and Egyptians and also by many Greek historians whom I cited as witnesses . . .

On the composition of Luke 1.5–2.52

The narrative of the proclamation to Zechariah and of the birth and naming of the Baptist (Luke 1.5–25, 57–66) was originally an individual narrative handed down in isolation and was first torn apart by the redactional activity of Luke. That emerges from the fact that v. 57 attaches smoothly to v. 25 and the story presupposes neither the announcement of the birth of Jesus (1.26–38) nor the visit of Mary to Elizabeth (1.39–56). Conversely, however, the Jesus stories surpass the John the Baptist narrative (cf. esp. Luke 1.39–45 and the birth from the virgin which is announced only of Jesus).

Moreover the evangelist had in isolation two psalms (1.46–55* and 1.68–79*) and four independent traditions on the birth and childhood of Jesus.

Luke has put the narrative about John in parallel with the corresponding stories about Jesus and linked them by the story of the encounter of the two mothers in Luke 1.39–45, (46–55,) 56.

Original consecutive tradition about the Baptist	*Redactional link*	*Traditions about Jesus originally independent of one another*
1.5–25: Announcement of the birth of John the Baptist		1.26–38: Announcement of the birth of Jesus
	1.39–56: Visit of Mary to Elizabeth	

(vv. **46–55**: Mary's song
of praise)

1.57–80: birth and naming
of the Baptist
(vv. **67–79**: Zechariah's
 song of praise)

2.1–21: Birth of Jesus

2.22–41: Presentation of
Jesus in the temple
2.42–52: The twelve-year-
old Jesus in the temple

Luke 1.5–25: The announcement of the birth of John the Baptist

5 *It happened in the days of Herod, the king of Judah,* that there was a priest by the name of
Zechariah from the class of Abijah, and he had a wife from the daughters of Aaron, and her
name was Elizabeth. 6 They were both righteous before God and walked blamelessly in all
the commandments and precepts of the Lord. 7 And they had no child, because Elizabeth
was barren, and both were already advanced in age.

8 *Now it happened* when he was performing his priestly ministry after the order of his class
9 that the lot fell on him according *to the custom* of the priestly ministry to make the incense
offfering and he went into the temple of the Lord 10 *and the whole crowd of the people was
praying outside at the hour of the incense offering.* 11 And an angel of the Lord appeared to him
standing on the right hand of the altar of *incense. 12 And Zechariah was disturbed when he saw
it and fear fell upon him. 13 But the* angel *said to him*:

'Fear not, Zechariah,
for your prayer has been heard,
and your wife Elizabeth will bear a son
and you will give him the name John.
14 And you will have joy and gladness,
and many will rejoice at his birth.
15 For he will become great before the Lord
and he will not drink wine and intoxicating drink,
and with holy Spirit *he will be filled*
from his mother's womb
16 and many of the children of Israel will he turn
to the Lord their God.
17 *And he himself* will go before him
in the spirit and power of Elijah,
to turn the hearts of the fathers to children
and disobedient to the wisdom of the righteous
to prepare a well-equipped people for the Lord.'

18 And Zechariah said to the angel, 'How shall I know that? For I am old and my wife is of
an advanced age.' 19 The angel answered and said to him, 'I am Gabriel who stands before

God and has been sent to speak to you and to bring you this good news. 20 *And look*, you will become <u>dumb</u> and will not be able to speak until the day on which this happens, because you have not believed my words, which are to be fulfilled in their time.'

21 *And the people was waiting for Zechariah and wondering at his long stay in the temple.* 22 And when he came out he could not speak to them and they perceived that he had seen a vision in the temple; and he nodded to them and remained <u>dumb</u>.

23 *And it happened* when the days of his service were fulfilled that he went back to his home. 24 *After these days* Elizabeth his wife became pregnant *and hid herself five months and said,* 25 'Thus the Lord has done for me in the days when he looked on me to take away my reproach among men.'

Redaction

[5a] The linking of the following narrative to Herod (the Great) corresponds to Luke's concern, which we often meet, to give the dates of salvation history profane roots. Later he will date the birth of Jesus to the time of the emperor Augustus and the governorship of Quirinius (2.1f.) and the appearance of John the Baptist to the fifteenth year of the rule of the emperor Tiberius (3.1). This concern is continued in Acts: the prophecy of a world-wide famine by the prophet Agabus became historical reality under the emperor Claudius (Acts 11.28).

[5b–7] These verses form the exposition: Zechariah and Elizabeth, both of priestly origin and morally blameless, are childless. Elizabeth's barrenness and the great age of the couple heighten the magnitude and the extraordinary and miraculous character of the event which is reported in what follows.

[8–9] These verses introduce the decisive scene: by the casting of lots, one day the task falls to Zechariah to offer the incense offering in the temple.

[10] This verse derives completely from Luke. He adds to the tradition the *motif of prayer* at decisive points in the history of individual people and groups. Two examples are: (a) at the baptism of Jesus by John the son of God prays (Luke 3.21), something that the Markan original (1.9–11) did not contain. (b) In Acts Luke makes the prayer of the community (Acts 4.24–30) follow the scene before the Supreme Council (Acts 4.1–22) and thus creates an impressive scenario. The young community has a strong God on its side, who protects it despite all the opposition of its enemies.

[11–12] Zechariah's fear in the face of the appearance of the angel is the typical human reaction to contact with the divine.

[13–17] The formula 'Do not fear' as an introduction to the speech of the angel is equally typical. The speech is divided into three parts. Verses 13–14 refer to the immediate future: a son is promised to Zechariah whose name is predetermined by God. Verse 15 says that John will already be a prophet from his mother's womb, so that he did not need a special calling. Verses 16–17 mention the future success of his activity: he will go before God or the Lord (here Luke is certainly thinking of the Messiah Jesus) to prepare for him a well-equipped people.

[18] In view of his own great age and that of his wife (cf. v. 7), Zechariah asks for a sign to confirm the promise.

[19–20] The angel replies to the request for a sign with the mention of his name: he is Gabriel, one of the archangels (cf. Dan. 8.16f.; 9.21). Thus it is said that the message comes directly from God and needs no confirmation through a sign. Therefore the sign that Zechariah will nevertheless be given is at the same time a punishment for his unbelief: he is to remain dumb until the birth of his son.

[21] This verse is a redactional edition. That emerges not only from Luke's preferred words ('people', 'wait') but above all from the fact that the phrase 'and the people was waiting' recurs almost word for word in 3.15, and that the focus here, as in v. 10, is directed to the people before the temple.

[22] The 'punitive sign' announced in v. 20 has already been given when Zechariah leaves the temple. Instead of bestowing the expected blessing on the people, he can only nod.

[23–24a] But the promise also begins to be fulfilled immediately: as soon as Zechariah has returned home, Elizabeth's pregnancy begins.

[24b] This verse serves to join the story of John to the story of Jesus and is redactional: 1.26 ('in the sixth month') refers back to the five months.

[25] This verse rounds off the story redactionally. Elizabeth thanks God for removing the shame associated with her barrenness (cf. the Old Testament example of Hannah: I Sam. 1.2, 11).

Yield: Luke has adopted an existing narrative, supplemented by some elements which slow it down (vv. 10 and 21), and has only made deeper interventions in it at the end, in order to produce the link with the story of Jesus.

Tradition and historical

Cf. as a summary the remarks on the section Luke 1.57–66 which at the preredactional level forms a unity with 1.5–25.

Luke 1.26–38: The announcement of the birth of Jesus

26 Now *in the sixth month* the angel Gabriel was sent by God to a town of Galilee called Nazareth, 27 to a virgin *who was betrothed to a man by the name of Joseph* from the house of David, and the name of the virgin was Mary. 28 And after he came to her, he said to her, 'Hail, favoured one, the Lord is with you.' 29 And she was *overwhelmed* at the saying and *considered* what this greeting might mean. 30 And the angel said to her:

'Fear not, Mary,
for you have found favour with God.

31 And look, you will become pregnant
and bear a son,
and you will give him the name Jesus.
32 He will become great
and be called the son of the Most High,
and God the Lord will give him the throne of David, his father,
33 and he will be king over the house of Jacob for ever,
and his kingdom will have no end.'

34 And Mary said to the angel, 'How will this happen, as I know no man?' 35 And the angel answered and said to her,

'Holy Spirit *will come upon you*, and power of the Most High will overshadow you, therefore the holy thing to be born will be called Son of God. 36 *And look, Elizabeth, your kinswoman, she too has become pregnant with a son in her old age, and this is the sixth month for her who was called barren. 37 For with God nothing is impossible.'* 38 *And* Mary said, 'Behold the handmaid of the Lord, let it be to me as you have said.' And the angel went away from her.

Redaction

[26] The date ('in the sixth month') refers to the note in 1.24 that Elizabeth hid herself for five months, and serves as a redactional link between the two stories. The angel Gabriel is known from 1.5–25. Nazareth in Galilee is a possible historical reminiscence of the birthplace of Jesus. But because according to the Old Testament prophecy in Micah 5.1f. the Messiah 'had to' come from *Bethlehem*, Luke later has the parents of Jesus travel there (2.1ff.).

[27] This verse introduces Mary and Joseph; here Mary is presented very ponderously as Joseph's betrothed.

[28–29] The scene corresponds to 1.11f.: the way in which Zechariah is disturbed corresponds to the way in which Mary is overwhelmed.

[30–33] The two five-line strophes in which the words of the angel are contained are *not*, with one exception, in accord with Luke's style.

[34–35] Mary's question corresponds to Zechariah's question (1.18). It is hardly compatible with v. 27: a bride can hardly be amazed that a child is promised her, even when she has so far had no sexual intercourse with her betrothed. Therefore on occasion it has been assumed that vv. 34–35 are a secondary Lukan addition which introduces the notion of the virgin birth into the original story. However, against this is the fact that in the following narratives which deal with the fulfilment of the promise (with the exception of 2.21) Luke makes no connection with the scene of the promise and in particular never mentions the virginal conception again either in the Gospel or in Acts. It is therefore more likely that not the virgin birth, but in v. 27 *Joseph* has been introduced at a secondary stage into the narrative, especially as he plays no further role in the following story, which is completely orientated on Mary (vv. 28–38).

[36–37] These verses refer back to 1.24, 26 and serve to provide a redactional link between the two narrative strands.

[38] This verse surpasses 1.20: whereas Zechariah doubted (and therefore became dumb for a while), Mary complies with the will of the angel.

Yield: Luke has inserted into the story of John a narrative which he had about the proclamation to Mary, linked it through v. 26 and vv. 36–37 and added 'Joseph' (v. 27). In so doing he did not mind the manifest contradiction between vv. 27 and 34. By making the story parallel to the narrative of the announcement to Zechariah, at the same time he goes beyond this with the motif of the virginal conception and the obedience of Mary.

Tradition

The legend probably derives from Jewish Hellenistic circles, which wanted to keep together the procreation by the Spirit, the true sonship of the Messiah and the virgin birth.

The structural parallels with the story of the announcement of the birth of John are explained from the fact that both narratives follow the pattern of announcements of births in the Old Testament (cf. on 1.57–66).

Historical

The thoroughly legendary character of the story in the tradition shows it to be a community formation and therefore unhistorical.

Luke 1.39–45: Mary's visit to Elizabeth

39 *In those days Mary set off and went in haste into the hill country to a town in Judah* 40 *and entered the house of Zechariah and greeted Elizabeth.* 41 *And it happened that when Elizabeth heard Mary's greeting* <u>*the child leapt in her body*</u>*. And Elizabeth was filled with the holy Spirit* 42 *and cried aloud and said, 'Blessed are you among women, and blessed is the fruit of your body!* 43 *And how do I deserve this, that the mother of my Lord should come to me?* 44 *For look, when I heard the voice of your greeting, the* <u>*child in my body leapt*</u> *for joy.* 45 *And blessed is she who believed that what was said to her by the Lord would be fulfilled.'*

Redaction

[39–40] Mary's journey to Elizabeth is motivated by the reference of the angel in 1.36. 'Hill country' is taken from 1.65.

[41a] The leaping of the child in its mother's womb emphasizes the inferiority of John the Baptist: even before his birth, John exercises his prophetic function as a forerunner. Probably 1.15 had an influence on the formulation of this verse.

[41b] This corresponds word for word with the redactional verse 1.67.

[42] Through the beatitude Elizabeth subordinates herself to Mary and her still unborn child.

[43] An answer to Elizabeth's question is neither given nor expected: rather, 'How do I deserve this?' again emphasizes the superiority of Mary and her child to John the Baptist and his mother.

[44] This verse repeats v. 41 in the first person singular.

[45] This verse refers back to the prophecy of the angel and Mary's reaction in 1.26–38. However, Elizabeth cannot know of that, any more than she can know of Mary's pregnancy (v. 42). Luke probably understands her mention of it in the light of the fact that she is filled with the Holy Spirit.

Yield: the section provides the link between the stories of John the Baptist and Jesus and at the same time emphasizes Jesus' superiority to John. It is redactional throughout and its content is unhistorical.

Luke 1.46–56: Mary's song of praise ('Magnificat')

46 *And Mary said,*
'My soul exalts the Lord,
47 and my spirit rejoices in God my saviour;
48 for he saw the lowliness of his handmaid.
For look, from now on all generations will call me blessed.
49 For the Mighty One did great things by me,
and holy (is) his name,
50 And his <u>mercy</u> (lasts) from generation to generation
among those who fear him.
51 He showed power with his arm
and scattered the proud in the imagination of their heart.
52 He cast down the mighty from the throne
and exalted the lowly.
53 The hungry he filled with good things
and sent the rich empty away.
54 He accepted Israel, his servant
in remembrance of his <u>mercy</u>,
55 as he spoke to our fathers,
Abraham and his children for ever.'
56 *And Mary stayed with her three months; after that she returned home.*

Redaction

[46a] The name Elizabeth appears instead of 'Mary' in several Latin manuscripts. According to *Luke*, however, it is beyond doubt Mary who speaks the hymn. Nevertheless – independently of textual criticism – the question arises whether at the pre-redactional level the song was handed down as a hymn of Elizabeth (see below).

[46b–55] The hymn, which is usually called 'Magnificat' ('Exalts'), after the first word of the Latin translation of v. 46b, has been inserted into the story of Mary's visit to Elizabeth (cf. a similar literary technique in Ex. 15.1–18; Deut. 32; Judg.5, etc.) and cannot be recognized with certainty as a redactional intervention in either language or content. The only exception is v. 48b., which makes a reference to the situation and moreover indicates a change of subject from God to the children's children (on v. 48a see below).

[56] This verse is the redactional conclusion to the narrative of Mary's visit to Elizabeth. Together with 1.26, the 'three months' produce nine months in all and lead on to the following story of the birth of the Baptist.

Yield: Luke has taken up an existing psalm and in the framework of the encounter of the two expectant mothers which he has created (1.39–45, 56) put it in the mouth of Mary to subordinate Elizabeth even more clearly to her and to legitimate the high esteem for Mary (v. 48b). The thesis that Luke himself composed the psalm in the style of the Greek translation of the Old Testament (= Septuagint) is contradicted not only by v. 48b but also by the fact that on this presupposition clearer references to the context might have been expected (there is no mention at all of a pregnancy or birth).

Tradition

The *first* part of the hymn in the tradition has features of an individual thanksgiving (vv. 46b–49); the *second* (vv. 50–53) describes the general action of God with human beings (here vv. 52ab/53ab have a chiastic formulation [A-B-B-A]; the third describes God's special care for Israel (vv. 54f.).

Numerous Old Testament parallel phrases can be adduced for each individual verse, but the song has been most strongly influenced by the song of the formerly barren Hannah after the birth of Samuel (I Sam. 2.1–10), which the author doubtless knows. The similarity of Luke 1.46–55 to this song is a strong argument for the assumption that the Magnificat was originally handed down as a hymn of Elizabeth. For *first* she – as opposed to Mary – had been barren for a long time, like Hannah, and *secondly*, the vow of the still childless Hannah in I Sam. 1.11 ('Lord Sabaoth, if you will look upon the affliction of your handmaid . . . and give your handmaid a son, I will give him to the Lord all his life long . . .') is similar to v. 48a (the Lord 'saw the lowliness of his handmaid').

If, however, we begin by assuming that the traditional psalm was originally independent of Elizabeth, we must probably also attribute v. 48a to Luke, who will then have taken Mary's designation of herself as 'handmaid' from Luke 1.38 and by 'lowliness' have understood not the shame of barrenness but a humble attitude.

Historical

The Magnificat may or may not have been originally handed down as a psalm of Elizabeth, but neither she nor Mary ever spoke the psalm. That is already evident from the fact that the scenic framework in which it is spoken is sheer fiction.

Luke 1.57–66: The birth of John the Baptist

57 For Elizabeth the time came for her to be delivered, and she gave birth to a son. 58 And her neighbours and kinsfolk heard that the Lord had shown rich mercy on her and rejoiced with her.

59 And *it happened* on the eighth day that they came to circumcise the child and wanted to name it after his father Zechariah. 60 And his mother answered and said, 'No, it is to be called John.' 61 And they said to her, 'There is no one of your family who is named by this name.' 62 And they nodded to his father *to see what he wanted it to be named.* 63 And he asked for a writing tablet and wrote, 'John is his name.' And they were all amazed. 64 And *immediately* his mouth was opened and his tongue, and he spoke and *praised* God.

65 And *fear came on all* who lived in their neighbourhood, and throughout the hill country of Judaea all these events were discussed, 66 and *all who heard it kept it in their hearts and* said, *'What will become of this little child?' And the hand of the Lord was with him.*

Redaction

After the interruption by 1.26–38 and 1.39–56, this section takes up once again the narrative thread of 1.5–25:

[57–58] These verses report first of all the fulfilment of the message which had been given to Zechariah by the angel (1.13d).

[59–63] These verses then depict the naming of the child as commanded by the angel (1.13e).

[64] This verse refers back to 1.20: as the day has arrived up until when Zechariah is to be dumb, he now gets his voice back.

[65–66] These verses round off the story; in v. 66 the motif of the heart corresponds to 2.19, 51b and the concluding remark in v. 66 to 2.40.

Tradition

Luke may have had before him a prophecy of the birth of John the Baptist and its fulfilment; here redaction and tradition cannot always be separated clearly. It is to be called a personal legend of the birth of a hero.

The original purpose of this legend was to depict John as a 'great man' who, chosen by God and deriving from a priestly family, has the task of converting the people of Israel and preparing for the advent of God himself.

John as forerunner and his inferiority to Jesus, which it is indispensable for Christians to emphasize – that is what makes the story of the Baptist worth telling for Christians in the first place – play no role whatsoever here. For this reason the legend can hardly be of Christian origin. Rather, this is a tradition from the followers of John the Baptist. The motifs in the legend are Old Testament throughout (cf. e.g. Gen. 17.17–19; Judg. 13.2–5).

Historical

The legendary and edificatory character, and the parallel motifs from the Old Testament which appear throughout, show the tradition underlying 1.5–25, 57–66 to be unhistorical. Only the proper names and the priestly origin of John take us back to historical ground.

Luke 1.67–80: Zechariah's song of praise ('Benedictus')

67 *And Zechariah, his father, was filled with holy spirit and prophesied and said:*
68 'Blessed be the Lord, the God of Israel!
For he has visited (his people) and brought redemption to his people,
69 and he has raised up a horn of salvation for us,
in the house of David, his servant,
70 *as he has spoken through the mouth of his holy prophets from of old,*
71 salvation from our enemies and from the hand of all who hate us,
72 to perform mercy with our fathers
and to remember his holy covenant,
73 the oath which he swore to Abraham our father,
and to grant us 74 without fear, freed from the hand of enemies,
to serve him 75 in piety and righteousness
before him all our days.
76 *And you, little child, will be called prophet of the Most High,*
for you will walk before the Lord to prepare his ways
77 *and to give knowledge of salvation to his people*
in forgiveness of their sins,
78 through the compassionate mercy of our God,

with which the dawn from on high will visit us,
79 to appear to those who sit in darkness and the shadow of death,
to guide our feet on the way of peace.'
80 *And the child grew and became strong in the spirit and was in the wilderness until the day of his manifestation to Israel.*

Redaction

Zechariah's song of praise, which has come to be known as the 'Benedictus' after the first word of the Latin translation, follows when the story of the birth of the Baptist has already been concluded. This position makes it clear that it was not part of the original personal legend, in which it would have had an appropriate place after v. 64. Rather, it was added only later, probably by Luke, at the end of the previous narrative.

Within the section 1.67–80 the following elements are to be attributed to Luke's redaction:

[67] This verse is Lukan in language and a redactional transitional verse.

[70] This verse corresponds almost word for word with Acts 3.21b, and for that reason must derive from Luke.

[71] 'Salvation' takes up the same word from v. 69 and marks a new beginning of the piece of tradition which was interrupted by v. 70.

[76–77] Verse 76a forms a counterpart to 1.32 with a redactional motivation. Verses 76b–77 are a Lukan insertion. This emphasizes the role of John as forerunner – a motif which will later be developed further: 3.2–6 (with the use of Mark 1.2) and 7.26f. John's message, 'to give knowledge of salvation to his people in forgiveness of their sins', anticipates 3.3. 'Salvation' does not appear in Mark and Matthew; it appears once in John (4.22), three times in the Lukan prehistory (1.69, 71, 77) and six times in Acts (4.12; 7.25; 13.26, 47; 16.17; 27.34).

[78] Was Luke aware that this verse only expects something that according to v. 68 has already happened (cf. the key word 'visit')?

[80] This verse bridges the time to the public appearance of John in ch. 3 and corresponds to 2.40, 52. Luke gives a stereotyped description of the healthy growth of a child. In Acts he will later describe in a similar way the successful dissemination of the word of God and the constant growth of the church (Acts 1.15: approximately 120 believers; 2.41: 3000).

Yield: Luke has taken a psalm known to him and expanded it to emphasize the role of John as forerunner.

Tradition

The psalm is of Jewish origin. As with Mary's hymn (1.46–55), there are numerous Old Testament parallel phrases to every verse, cf. especially the Old Testament psalms. Here is a selection: v. 68, Ps. 40.14; 71.18; 110.9; v. 71, Ps. 105.10; v. 72, Ps. 105.45; v. 79, Ps. 106.10.

Cf. further Psalms of Solomon (first century BC) 17.30–31: 'And he (= the Messiah) will have Gentile nations serving him under his yoke, and he will glorify the Lord (= God) manifestly before the whole world, and will make Jerusalem clean and holy as it was at the beginning, so that peoples come from the end of the earth to see his glory, bringing as gifts her exhausted sons, and to see the glory of the Lord with which God has glorified her.'

Historical

Zechariah never spoke the psalm attributed to him.

Luke 2.1–21: The birth of Jesus

1 *Now it happened in those days that a command went out from Emperor Augustus that the whole earth should be enrolled. 2 This census was the first; at that time Quirinius was governor of Syria. 3 And all went to be enrolled, each to his city. 4 And Joseph also set out from Galilee, from the town of Nazareth, to Judaea to the city of David which is called Bethlehem, because he was of the house and family of David, 5 to have himself enrolled with Mary his betrothed, who was pregnant.*

6 Now it happened *when they were there*, the days were fulfilled for her to be delivered. 7 And she bore her firstborn son and <u>wrapped him in swaddling cloths and</u> <u>laid him in a</u> <u>manger</u>, because there was no room for them in the inn.

8 And shepherds were camping in the same area and keeping watch over their flocks by night. 9 *And the angel of the Lord came to them, and the glory of the Lord shone around them;* and they were very afraid.

10 And the angel said to them, 'Do not fear! For look, I *proclaim* to you a great joy which shall be for all the people; 11 for to you today the saviour is born *who is Christ the Lord*, in the city of David. 12 And (let this be) the sign to you: you will find the child <u>wrapped in</u> <u>swaddling cloths and lying in a manger</u>.'

13 And suddenly there was with the angel the multitude of the heavenly hosts, praising God and saying, 14 'Glory to God in the highest and on earth peace among the men with whom he is well pleased.'

15 *And it happened* when the angel had gone away from them into heaven, that the shepherds said to one another, 'Let us now go to Bethlehem and see the thing which has happened which the Lord has made known to us.' 16 And they came *in haste* and found both Mary and Joseph and the child lying in the manger. 17 *And when they had seen it* they spread the word that had been said to them about this child. 18 And *all who heard it* were amazed at what the shepherds had said to them. 19 *And Mary kept all these words and pondered them in her heart.* 20 And the shepherds *returned, praised and glorified God for all that they had seen and heard, as it had been told them.*

21 *And when eight days had been fulfilled and they had to circumcise the child, they gave him the name Jesus, as he had been named by the angel before he was conceived in his mother's womb.*

Redaction

[1–5] With the mention of the census Luke puts the birth story in the context of world history (cf. on 1.5). Moreover, Joseph's journey to his home town required by the census makes it possible for Luke to include in his narrative the salvation-historical requirement for the Messiah to be born in Bethlehem (cf. Micah 5.1).

By describing Mary as Joseph's betrothed in v. 5, Luke links the story with 1.26–38 (see below). But given the context, Mary must already be Joseph's wife. For as a fiancée she would still count with the house of her own father and neither could nor might travel with Joseph.

[6–7a] The information 'when they were there' refers to Bethlehem (v. 4) and accordingly derives from Luke. The prophecy is fulfilled in the birth, which is briefly reported, without explicit reference being made to it.

[7b] The sentence 'and laid him . . . was no room for them' follows abruptly. No inn had been mentioned previously.

[8] This verse brings a change of scene and introduces a self-contained narrative about the proclamation of the birth to the shepherds.

[9] In a typical way there is a report of the appearance of an angel with radiant light and of the reaction of the shepherds.

[10–12] Similarly typical is the formula 'Do not fear' with which the angel introduces his speech (cf. also 1.11–13). The focus in v. 11 differs from that in the message of the angel in 1.32f.: whereas there the royal function of the child is delineated, here the emphasis is on the task of Jesus as a saviour – an indication that the traditions underlying the two passages are independent (see below). The manger as a sign points back to v. 7.

[13–14] The news given by the angels is supplemented with a song of praise from the heavenly host.

[15–18] These verses report the reaction of the shepherds to the message of the angel. As announced in v. 12, they find the child in the manger.

[19] This corresponds to 2.51b and is redactional. Doubtless Luke's view is that Mary was the source of his narratives, at least the story of the proclamation. However, it cannot be assumed that in v. 19 (and 2.51b) he wants to make an explicit reference to Mary as a guarantor of his tradition, for elsewhere too he does not name his sources. Rather, here his special interest in the person of Mary herself is evident. In v. 19 she proves to be almost a believing Christian, as emerges later from an application of the parable of the sower: 'And that on the good soil are those who with a noble and good heart hear the word and hold it fast and bring forth fruit with patience' (8.15).

[20] This verse rounds off the narrative with a choral conclusion.

[21] This verse is independent. It refers back to the story of the annunciation and is a redactional formation in parallel to the narrative about John (cf. 1.59).

Yield: Luke has taken a narrative about the proclamation of the birth to the shepherds and provided it with a new introduction (vv. 1–5). It is clear that at the pre-redactional level this narrative cannot have been the continuation of 1.26–38 ('The announcement of the birth of Jesus'). For it betrays nothing of a miraculous conception, and Mary evidently first learns from the visit of the shepherd what kind of a child she has (v. 19). The difficulty in combining the two stories from the tradition lay in the fact that whereas Joseph did not appear in the narrative of the birth of Jesus, the story of the shepherds was about an ordinary married couple. Luke solved the problem by adding Joseph to the first story and making his wife Mary into a fiancée in the second.

Tradition

The basis of vv. (6–7,) 8–20 is an originally independent narrative about how the birth of the Messiah is revealed to the shepherds. It is a narrative about a proclamation the beginning of which has been overlaid with the redactional insertion of the census motif and can no longer be reconstructed. Probably only fragments of the original beginning have been retained in vv. 6–7.

The sudden appearance of a great host of angels who join an angel who is already present raises the question whether vv. 13–15a were not added to the story in the course of the tradition.

The terms 'proclaim' (v. 10) and 'saviour' (v. 11) suggest that the legend came into being in Hellenistic Christianity. The motif of the proclamation of the birth to the shepherds also points in this direction. For in Judaism shepherds were in no way regarded as being particularly pious; rather, their profession was despised. They were suspect of not taking personal possessions too seriously. Therefore they were also excluded from those who could give evidence to a court.

By contrast, in oriental and above all in Greek sagas shepherds had an exalted status. Here the shepherd is following a calling which is well-pleasing to God and recalls the primal age when the gods still had dealings with human beings. In his contemplative existence he is regarded as particularly capable of hearing divine voices.

The expectation that the Messiah will come from Bethlehem, the home town of David (I Sam. 17.12–15; 20.6), is widespread in Judaism.

Historical

The historical yield of the Lukan infancy narrative in respect of the birth of Jesus is virtually nil (cf. on Matt. 2.1–23). However, the note (v. 7) that Jesus was Mary's first child may be correct. Only in this way can we understand the note in Mark 3.21, which is beyond suspicion, that the family of Jesus wanted to seize him because he was out of his mind. As the eldest he had the duty to feed his family after the death of his father.

Luke 2.22–40: The presentation of Jesus in the temple: Simeon and Anna

22 *And when the days of her purification according to the law of Moses were fulfilled, they brought him to Jerusalem, to present him to the Lord,* 23 *as it is written in the law of the Lord,* 'Every male who first breaks through his mother's womb is to be called holy to the Lord,' 24 *and to offer the sacrifice as it is said in the law of the Lord,* 'a few turtle doves or two young doves'.

25 And see, a man was in Jerusalem by the name of Simeon, and this man was pious and godfearing and waited for the consolation of Israel, and the holy Spirit was with him. 26 And a word had been given to him by the holy Spirit that he should not see death before he had seen the Lord's Christ. 27 And on the prompting of the Spirit he came to the temple. And when the parents had brought the child Jesus into the temple to do with him according to the custom of the law, 28 he took it in his arms and praised God and said,

29 'Lord, now let your servant go in peace, as you have said;
30 for my eyes have seen your salvation,
31 which you have prepared before all people,
32 a light for the revelation for the Gentiles
and for the glorification of your people Israel.'

33 And his father and his mother marvelled at what was said of him. 34 And Simeon blessed them and said to Mary, his mother, 'Look, this child is appointed for the fall and the rising for many in Israel and as a sign which will be contradicted – 35 *and a sword shall pierce your soul also* – that the thoughts of many hearts may become open.'

36 And (there) was a prophetess, Anna, a daughter of Phanuel, from the tribe of Asher; she was very old, since she had lived with her husband (only) seven years from her virginity with her husband, 37 and now she was a widow of eighty-four years. She did not depart from the temple and served (God) with fasting and prayer day and night. 38 And at the same hour she went up and praised God and spoke of him (= the child) to all who were waiting for the redemption of Israel.

39 *And when they had accomplished everything according to the law of the Lord, they returned to Galilee, to their town of Nazareth.* 40 *And the child grew and became strong, full of wisdom, and God's grace was with him.*

Redaction

[22–24] These verses introduce the two following scenes and serve to give a reason for Jesus' presence in the temple. The ignorance of Jewish legal prescriptions shows this introduction to be redactional: the author thinks that mother *and* child (or father?) must be cleansed. In fact all that was necessary was the cleansing of the mother thirty-three days after the circumcision (Lev. 12.2–8). Contrary to the assertion, there was no legal prescription that the firstborn should be presented in the temple.

Elsewhere Luke is not very familiar with the Jewish law, as is shown by the two following examples: (a) Acts 16.3 presupposes that the status of Timothy is determined by his Greek father – and not, as was customary in Judaism in the case of mixed marriages, by his Jewish mother; (b) Luke assumes that a Nazirite vow lasts seven days (Acts 21.27); in reality it extended over at least thirty days.

[25–28] These verses introduce Simeon. Living in expectation of the consolation of Israel (cf. Isa. 40.1f.; 49.3), he enters the temple at the precise moment that Joseph and Mary bring in the child.

[29–32] With a prophetic song of praise (the so-called 'Nunc dimittis') he praises God for the fulfilment of a revelation which concerns him personally (v. 26) and for the universal salvation realized in Jesus, one which also embraces the Gentiles.

[33] Father and mother marvel at Simeon's words, a reaction which is more than amazing after 1.26–38 and 2.8–21.

[34–35] Simeon once again takes the initiative. He blesses the parents and addresses Mary directly. In speaking of the decision with which Jesus will confront the people Israel, he to some degree narrows down the universal perspective of vv. 31f. The saying about the sword (v. 35a) is a somewhat clumsy intervention, probably by Luke: in the context of vv. 34, 35b it suggests a conflict between the mother and the son, but is meant to prophesy the mother's pain at the passion of Jesus.

[36–38] The second scene is a mere report about the prophetess Anna: much is said about her, but she herself has nothing to say.

[39] This verse, which rounds off the story, is similar to 2.51a and refers back to v. 22.

[40] This verse is a summary concluding formula which has a parallel in 1.80 (of John the Baptist) and moreover in 2.52.

Yield: the Lukan redaction is visible only in the framework of the narrative and in the introduction of the motif of the mother's pain in v. 35a.

Tradition

The story which Luke had before him might have already contained the juxtaposition of Simeon's different prophecies in vv. 29–32 and vv. 34–35 and also the scene with Anna which was added at a secondary stage. Had Luke himself created or inserted one of the two Simeon sayings it would be difficult to imagine why he did not put the other in the mouth of the 'speechless' prophetess.

It is certain that the Simeon legend was originally an independent individual story which presupposed neither the story of the announcement nor that of the shepherds. For the prophecy of Simeon makes sense and is impressive only if it is the first, and the amazement of the parents (v. 33) can be explained only if previously they had had no idea that their child was destined to be the saviour.

Historical

The story projects post-Easter faith in Jesus on to his childhood. Therefore its historical value is nil.

Luke 2.41–52: The twelve-year-old Jesus in the temple

41 And his parents *travelled* each year to Jerusalem to the feast of the Passover. 42 And when he was twelve years old, they went up according to the custom of the feast. 43 And when the days were past and they *were returning home* again, the boy Jesus *remained behind* in Jerusalem, and his parents did not know it. 44 But they thought that he was among the travellers, and they went a day's journey and looked for him among their kinsfolk and acquaintances. 45 And as they did not find him, they returned to Jerusalem and sought him.

46 *And it happened* after three days they found him sitting in the temple in the midst of the teachers, listening to them and asking them questions. 47 *But all who heard him were amazed at his understanding and answers.* 48 And when they saw him they were astonished. And his mother said to him, 'Child, why have you done this to us? See, your father and I have been looking for you *with grief.*' 49 And he said to them, 'Why were you looking for me? Do you not know that I must be in what is my Father's?' 50 And they did not understand the saying that he spoke to them. 51 *And he went down with them and came to Nazareth and was obedient to them. And his mother kept all these sayings in her heart.*

52 *And Jesus increased in wisdom, age and grace with God and man.*

Redaction

[41–45] These verses contain the information about the situation: after the end of a pilgrimage, the twelve-year-old Jesus, unnoticed by his parents, remains behind in Jerusalem. When the parents note his absence, they return to look for him.

[46] This verse reports the success of the search: Joseph and Mary find Jesus among the teachers in the temple.

[47] Whereas in v. 46 Jesus was the one who listened and asked questions, here it is presupposed that he also gives answers. That does not yet support the assumption that this is a redactional addition; however, that is confirmed by the fact that – quite apart from the Lukan vocabulary (cf. Acts 9.21) – in v. 48 the subject changes abruptly from the audience to the parents. With Jesus' answer in v. 49 – the first

words spoken by Jesus in the Gospel of Luke – the point of the story follows the mother's question: as son of God Jesus belongs in his Father's house.

[50] The parents react to their child's answer with incomprehension (cf. 2.33), as human beings react to a divine message. The redactional v. 51b conflicts with this.

[51a] The information about the return to Nazareth derives wholly from Luke (cf. 2.39).

[51b] This verse echoes 2.19 and is redactional (for the opposition to v. 50, see above).

[52] The maturing of the child corresponds to 1.80 and 2.40 and to some degree bridges the period up to the baptism and the public appearance of the adult Jesus (3.21, 23).

Yield: Luke has taken up a well-rounded individual story and put it into his own words. With the additional v. 47 he has given the unusual wisdom of the child as much weight as the point in v. 49b.

Tradition

The original individual story about the wisest child in Israel, who knows the law, does not presuppose either the miracle of the annunciation or that of the birth or a knowledge on the part of the parents that their child is the Messiah.

The narrative contains the theme widespread in antiquity that a great personality already stands out in childhood for his towering capacities. Cf. only what is said by Philo of Alexandria, a contemporary of the apostle Paul, about the young Moses:

Soon teachers came from every region, some of their own accord from the adjacent lands and parts of the land of Egypt, others brought from Greece at great expense. But soon he surpassed them by far in ability – for through his natural gifts he advanced beyond their teachings, so that it seemed to be a recollecting and not a learning – and in addition he himself devised difficult questions (*Life of Moses* I 21).

We cannot claim a valuable old source for this story. However, v. 51b seeks to give the contrary impression. Like Mark 16.8 it explains why the story became known only relatively late. Certainly both the women who discovered the empty tomb, and Mary, who heard the words of the twelve-year-old, were silent for a long time. But in the light of the Easter event or the fulfilling of the promises they finally break their silence.

Historical

This episode is unhistorical for the reasons just mentioned, nor does it have a historical nucleus.

Luke 3.1–20: John the Baptist

1 *In the fifteenth year of the reign of Tiberius Caesar, when Pontius Pilate was governor of Judaea and Herod tetrarch of Galilee, his brother Philip tetrarch of Ituraea and Trachonitis and Lysanias tetrarch of Abilene, 2 in the high priesthood of Annas and Caiaphas – the word of God came to John, the son of Zechariah, in the wilderness; 3 and he went into all the region around the Jordan,* preaching the baptism of repentance for the forgiveness of sins, 4 as it is written *in the book of the words* of the prophet Isaiah, 'A voice calls in the wilderness: prepare the way of the Lord, make his paths straight. 5 Every ravine shall be filled and every mountain and hill shall be levelled; and what is crooked shall become straight; and what is rough shall become a smooth way. 6 And all flesh will see the salvation of God.'

7 *Now he said to the multitudes* which went out to be baptized, 'You brood of vipers, who has assured you that you will escape the future wrath? 8 See that you bear righteous *fruits* of repentance, and do not begin to say to yourselves, "We have Abraham as our Father." For I say to you, God can raise up children to Abraham from these stones. 9 Already the axe is laid to the roots of the trees: every tree that does not bear good fruit will be cut down and thrown into the fire.'

10 *And the multitudes asked him and said, 'What then shall we do?'* 11 *He answered and said to them, 'Let him who has two undergarments give (one) to him who has none; and let him who has food do likewise.'* 12 *And the toll collectors also came to be baptized, and said to him, 'Teacher, what then shall we do?'* 13 *And he said to them, 'Collect no more than is prescribed for you.'* 14 *Then soldiers also asked him and said, 'What then shall we do?' And he said to them, 'Do violence or injustice to no one, and be content with your wages.'*

15 *And when the people was full of expectation and all wondered in their hearts whether he was perhaps the Christ,* 16 *John answered and said to all,* 'I baptize you with water; but one is coming who is stronger than I, the thongs of whose sandals I am not worthy to loose. He himself will baptize you with holy Spirit and fire. 17 The winnowing fork is in his hand, to sweep his threshing floor and to gather the wheat into his barns; but the chaff he will burn with unquenchable fire.'

18 *And with many other admonitions he preached the message to the people.* 19 But Herod the ruler, who had been reproved by John over Herodias, his brother's wife, and over all the evil that he had done, 20 added this to everything: he shut up John in prison.

Redaction

[1–2] The note of time – as already in Luke 2.1 and 3.1 – corresponds to Luke's concern to anchor the story of Jesus (and the church) in the framework of world history. Luke has added the name of John the Baptist's father, Zechariah, to Mark, which he has before him.

[3–6] Luke has worked over the Markan text stylistically.

It was not the whole land of Judaea which went out to John (thus Mark 1.5), but John came into the whole region around the Jordan. Luke omits the description of John the Baptist's dress and food (from Mark 1.6); he corrects the quotation from 'Isaiah' in Mark and expands it. Instead of 'in the prophet Isaiah' Luke writes more clearly 'in the book of the words of the prophet Isaiah' and (like Matthew) omits the first part of the quotation in Mark 1.2, because it does not come from Isaiah (but from Mal. 1.3). Instead, in connection with the Markan original (Mark 1.3) he quotes not only Isa. 40.3 but Isa. 40.4–5, with the conclusion, 'And all flesh will see the salvation of God'. The words 'all flesh' (= all human beings) already refers to the universal character of this coming salvation. Here 'salvation of God' recalls Luke 2.30; Acts 28.28.

[7–9] Luke takes over John the Baptist's penitential preaching from Q (cf. Matt. 3.7–10) but significantly adds the 'multitudes' to the audience.

[10–14] John the Baptist's teaching consists of three questions and three answers. Purely in terms of form this already suggests Lukan authorship, and this is confirmed on grounds of content. Verses 10f. conclude vv. 7–9 ('multitudes' had already been inserted in v. 7 by Luke) and introduce the Lukan notion of giving away half (cf. 19.8: Zacchaeus). The second and third group of questioners (toll collectors and soldiers) accord with Luke's interest; for the toll collectors cf. Levi (5.27); Zacchaeus (19.8). Loyalty to the Roman state is included in the moral advice to the soldiers (v. 14), who had not shown themselves at all interested in John's baptism. (Here at the latest, Luke is addressing his readership.)

[15–16a] This is a redactional introduction to the account of the preaching of the Baptist in vv. 16b–17.

[16b–17] In v. 16b 'with holy Spirit' comes from Mark and 'with fire' from Q (v. 17 = Matt. 3.12).

[18] The language of this verse is purely Lukan and the conclusion of the report on the preaching of John the Baptist. We get the impression that Luke regards the preaching of John the Baptist as preaching of salvation and not just as a transitional preaching. But this can also be an imprecise formulation by Luke, especially since in the present passage (later 16.16) Luke sets the appearance of John the Baptist apart from that of Jesus, giving the impression that these are two different eras. For in

[19–20] Luke puts the account of the imprisonment of John the Baptist in connection with the account of his preaching before the baptism of Jesus (v. 21f.).

That is an improvement on Mark 6.17–29, where a retrospect is inserted somewhat ponderously (but cf. already Mark 1.14). Luke passes over the end of John the Baptist reported there – perhaps because he knew the divergent report of Josephus (*Jewish Antiquities* 18, 116–19; cf. on Mark 6.14–29) or even for the same reason that he passed over the death of Paul at the end of Acts, namely that it was too cruel and disrupted the salvation history (cf. his minimizing or omission of conflicts in Acts). At all events, Luke thus avoids John being unduly brought to the fore as a martyr (as in Mark). John the Baptist appears again only in 7.18f., where he sends from prison to ask whether Jesus is the Coming One. Luke already works in Mark 6.17f. here and reinforces the Baptist's accusation against

Herod – whom he correctly specifies as Herod Antipas – because of all the evil that he did (v. 19). He sees the crime against John as the pinnacle of his wickedness and further corrects his original by omitting 'Philip'. This example shows that Luke did not work without criticism and research, for Philip married Salome, Herodias's daughter (Josephus, *Jewish Antiquities* VIII, 137). So she was the mother-in-law and not, as Mark 6.17 states, the wife of Philip.

Tradition

In verses 7–9,16–17 there is an account of the preaching of John the Baptist following Q, which corresponds almost word for word with Matt. 3.7b–12. As Matthew has handed on the Q text rather more faithfully, for an analysis of the Q tradition see the remarks on Matt. 3.1–12.

Historical

Luke has bent the historically valuable tradition about John the Baptist which he has taken over from Q to make it seem as if John had referred to Jesus (v. 16). Furthermore he has falsified it for the purpose of edification and made John a moral preacher (vv. 10–14). Thus the historical value of Luke's account is considerably diminished.

Luke 3.21–22: The baptism of Jesus

21 *And it happened, when all the people had themselves baptized*, and Jesus had also been baptized *and was praying, the* heaven was opened, 22 and the *holy* Spirit descended upon in him bodily form, as a dove, and a voice came from *the* heaven, 'You are my dear son; in you I am well pleased.'

Redaction and tradition

The basis is the Markan account (Mark 1.9–11). Luke's authorial intent can be seen in his deviations from it.

[21] This verse plays down the individual baptism of Jesus, because this already caused confusion for Luke and the early Christians, and combines it with the baptism of the whole people. In fact Luke describes the baptism of Jesus and of the people without the main person, John the Baptist, since previously he had already been put in prison. By a change in sentence construction the baptism of Jesus is stated in a subordinate clause and supplemented with the mention of Jesus praying, an act which here causes heaven to open, and which in Luke is generally the occasion

for miraculous events (cf. 5.16; 6.12; 9.13, 28f.; 11.1). Doubtless we have here a record of the Lukan experience of the connection between prayer and miracle.

[22] 'Holy Spirit' appears far more frequently in Luke (13 times) than in Mark (4 times) and Matthew (5 times) and gains even more importance in Acts (42 times).

Historical

In this narrative the baptism of Jesus is seriously distorted and, because of the lack of the Baptist, far removed from the historical event. The pericope may therefore be classed as virtually unhistorical.

Luke 3.23–38: The genealogy of Jesus

23 *And Jesus himself was, when he appeared, around* thirty years old, and was, *as was supposed*, a son of Joseph
    the son of Eli,
24 the son of Matthat,
    the son of Levi,
    the son of Melchi,
    the son of Jannai,
    the son of Joseph,
25 the son of Mattathias,
    the son of Amos,
    the son of Nahum,
    the son of Hesli,
    the son of Naggai,
26 the son of Maath,
    the son of Mattathias,
    the son of Shimi,
    the son of Josech,
    the son of Joda,
27 the son of Johanan,
    the son of Rhesa,
    the son of Zerubbabel,
    the son of Shealtiel,
    the son of Neri,
28 the son of Melchi,
    the son of Addi,
    the son of Cosam,

    the son of Elmadam,
    the son of Er,
29 the son of Joshua,
    the son of Eliezer,
    the son of Jormi,
    the son of Mattatha,
    the son of Levi,
30 the son of Simeon,
    the son of Judah,
    the son of Joseph,
    the son of Jonam,
    the son of Eliakim,
31 the son of Melea,
    the son of Menna,
    the son of Mattatha,
    the son of David,
32 the son of Jesse,
    the son of Obed,
    the son of Boaz,
    the son of Sala,
    the son of Nahshon,
33 the son of Amminadab,
    the son of Admin,
    the son of Arni,
    the son of Hezron,
    the son of Perez,
    the son of Judah,

34	the son of Jacob,		the son of Shem,
	the son of Isaac,		the son of Noah,
	the son of Abraham,		the son of Lamech
	the son of Terah	37	the son of Methuselah,
	the son of Nahor,		the son of Enoch,
35	the son of Serug,		the son of Jared,
	the son of Reu,		the son of Mahalalel,
	the son of Peleg,		the son of Cainan,
	the son of Eber,	38	the son of Enos,
	the son of Shelah,		the son of Seth,
36	the son of Cainan,		the son of Adam,
	the son of Arphaxad,		the son of God.

Redaction

[23a] This verse derives from Luke; similarly, 'as was supposed' is an incidental remark by the redactor, who now wants to produce a genealogy built on physical descent but without dropping the virgin birth which was reported previously (there is similar redactional work in Matt. 1.16f.).

Tradition

As is shown by the tracing back of the genealogy to God himself (v. 38d), it probably derives from circles which were concerned – like the author of the Matthaean genealogy (Matt. 1.2–6) – not only to demonstrate that Jesus was a son of David and a son of Abraham, but above all to depict Jesus as the goal of salvation history and the one who completes it.

Since Joseph is regarded as the father of Jesus without any qualification, at the time of the composition of the genealogy the virgin birth still evidently lay outside the field of view.

There are Old Testament parallels e.g. in Gen. 5.3–32 (genealogy from Adam to Noah) and 11.10–26 (genealogy from Shem to Abram).

Historical

The lack of connection between the genealogies in Matthew and Luke and their large degree of incompatibility tell against their historical reliability:

(a) Matthew takes the genealogy from David through Solomon, Luke through Nathan; (b) Shealtiel and his son Zerubbabel indeed appear in both genealogies (Matt. 1.12; Luke 3.27), but whereas Luke gives nineteen names in all between

Zerubbabel and Jesus, in Matthew there are only ten; (c) the name of Jesus' grandfather is already uncertain (Matt. 1.15f., Jacob; Luke 3.23, Eli).

The Lukan and Matthaean genealogies correspond to some degree only in the generations from Abraham to David, because both follow the Old Testament; cf. Ruth 4.18–22; I Chron 2.1–14.

So neither the Matthaean nor the Lukan genealogies is based on historically reliable accounts. References to the authenticity of other contemporary genealogies and the high civil and religious value attached to preserving traditions about the legitimacy of descent generally cannot alter this verdict. For in the present case this evidence only explains the interest which led to the composition of the genealogy of Jesus.

Luke 4.1–13: The temptation of Jesus

1 *And Jesus, full of holy Spirit, returned from the Jordan* and was led by the Spirit into the wilderness 2 and tempted forty days by the devil. And he ate nothing in these days, and when they were at an end, he was hungry.

3 And the devil said to him, '<u>If you are God's Son</u>, tell this stone to become bread.' 4 And Jesus answered him, 'It is written, "Man does not live by bread alone."' 5 And he *led* him *up* and showed him all the kingdoms *of the earth in a moment*, 6 and the devil said to him, 'To you I will give all this power *and glory, for it has been delivered to me, and I give it to whom I will.* 7 If you now fall down before me, *all (that) shall be yours.*' 8 Jesus answered him and said, 'It is written, "You shall worship the Lord your God and serve him alone."' 9 And he led him to Jerusalem and puts him on the pinnacle of the temple and said to him, '<u>If you are God's Son</u>, cast yourself down here; 10 for it is written, "He will command your angels for your sake, to preserve you", 11 also, "They will bear you in their hands, so that you do not strike your foot against a stone."'

12 Jesus answered and said to him, 'It is said, "You shall not tempt the Lord your God."'

13 *And when the devil had ended every temptation, he departed from him until the (appointed) time.*

Redaction

Luke (like Matthew and Mark) puts the temptation story at the beginning of the public activity of Jesus. Like the proclamation of Jesus as Son of God at the baptism narrated previously (Luke 3.21–22, similarly by Mark and Matthew), it is the effective prelude to the story of the Son of God which is now to be told. To some degree the quality of Jesus' divine sonship is guaranteed by his rejection of Satan.

[1a] This verse links the temptation story closely with the pericope about the baptism; here the Holy Spirit, which after 3.22 is already being mentioned for the

second time, is a person which can no longer be distinguished from Jesus as in Mark 1.22

[1b–2] These verses follow Mark, which Luke has before him; Luke omits the sentence 'and he was with the wild beasts' which occurs there, because it no longer fits.

[3–12] These verses narrate three temptations – on the basis of Q. Luke has put the third version (in Q) in second place. Possible reasons are:

Verse 12 is a weighty closing quotation, *after* which no temptation will be possible any longer.

This necessitates only *one* change of scene, from the wilderness to Jerusalem (cf. Matthew: from the wilderness to Jerusalem and back to a high mountain) – thus it is a simplification.

The *drama is heightened* by the devil, who has twice been repudiated through scripture, the third time himself referring to scripture (however, he is again repudiated by a scriptural quotation).

In addition, by transposing the second and third temptations Luke makes Jesus' way begin at the place – Jerusalem – where it will also end (cf. 9.31). The preaching of the gospel will then start from Jerusalem (cf. Acts 1.8).

[5] The mountain is deleted by Luke to simplify things; however, in the verb 'lead up' the Q original shines through. Thus for the author 'the mountain' remains the place of prayer and the esoteric epiphany, the place of communication with the world above, and does not become the place of temptation.

[6] Satan's position of power which is presupposed here is later transcended in the experience of Jesus (10.18: 'I saw Satan fall like lightning from heaven').

[13] This verse marks the beginning of the 'Satan-free time' (Conzelmann) which comes to an end in 22.3, when Satan enters into Judas, the one who betrays Jesus.

Tradition

Matthew has preserved the original sequence of Q, as can be seen in the twofold 'Are you God's Son?' (Matt. 4.3, 6/ Luke 4.3, 9) in the first two temptations, and generally gives a more original version of Q.

Historical

Cf. on Matt. 4.1–11.

Luke 4.14–30: The preaching of Jesus in Nazareth

14 *And Jesus returned in the power of the Spirit to Galilee. And the news of him resounded through all the surrounding places.* 15 *And he taught in their synagogues and was praised by all.*

16 *And he came to Nazareth, where he had been brought up,* and went *according to his custom* on the sabbath day into the synagogue *and stood up to read.* 17 *And the scroll of the prophet Isaiah was given to him, and when he unrolled the scroll, he found the place where it is written:*

18 'The spirit of the Lord is upon me,
because he has anointed me.
To preach the good news to the poor
he has sent me,
to proclaim freedom to the prisoners
and sight to the blind,
to set at liberty those who are oppressed,
19 to proclaim a <u>welcome</u> year of the Lord.'

20 *And he rolled up the scroll, gave (it) back to the servant and sat down. And all eyes in the synagogue were fixed on him.* 21 *And he began to speak to them, 'Today is this scripture fulfilled in your ears.'* 22 *And all gave testimony about him and marvelled at the words of grace which came from his mouth and said, 'Is this not the son of Joseph?'* 23 And he said to them, 'Doubtless you will quote me this proverb, "Physician, heal yourself!' *What we have heard has happened in Capernaum, do also here in your ancestral city."* 24 But he said, 'Amen, I say to you, no prophet is <u>welcome</u> in his ancestral city. 25 But in truth I say to you, there were many widows in Israel in the days of Elijah, when the heaven was shut up for three years and six months, when a great famine came over all the land, 26 and Elijah was not sent to any of them except to Zarephath in Sidon, to a woman who was a widow. 27 And there were many lepers in Israel in the time of the prophet Elisha, and none of them was healed but Naaman the Syrian.'

28 *And all in the synagogue were filled with rage when they heard this,* 29 *arose and cast him out of the city and took him to the slope of the hill on which their city was built, in order to cast him down.* 30 *But he passed through their midst and went away.*

Redaction and tradition

This section, using Mark 6, puts Jesus' inaugural sermon in his home town of Nazareth programmatically at the beginning of his activity, using Mark 6. It is the only speech in Luke which he addresses to a regular assembly (cf. the corresponding speeches Paul makes in his defence in Acts: 22.1–21; 24.10–21; 26.2–23). That keynote address stands within Luke where Mark relates the calling of the first disciples (Mark 1.16–20). At the same time Luke is putting a typical event at the head. For the rejection of Jesus in Nazareth foreshadows his later fate.

Here Luke expands Mark, *first* with a prophetic testimony which is put on the lips of Jesus in vv. 18f., *secondly* by the prediction in vv. 25–27 that salvation will pass to another people, and *thirdly* by a redactional rounding off of the event which anticipates the future fate of Jesus (vv. 28–30).

[14–15] These verses are a Lukan superscription to what follows; 14b echoes Mark 1.28. Luke replaces the information about the content of Jesus' preaching in Mark (1.14f.) with the summary description of the whole Galilean period of Jesus' activity.

[16] The basis of the verse is Mark 6.1f. Luke identifies Jesus' 'ancestral city' as Nazareth.

[17] Unrolling the scroll, Jesus finds unsought and miraculously a passage from the book of Isaiah which is fulfilled in him. (The motif of the fulfilment of scripture in Jesus pervades the whole of Luke-Acts, cf. later especially 24.26.)

[18–19] The words found by Jesus are a combination of Isa. 61.1f. and 58.6d (both LXX). Luke indicates different passages of scripture which had been combined in a Greek-speaking Christian community as a unitary prophetic text read aloud by Jesus.

[20–21] The combination of history and scripture is redactionally important. Whereas in Mark the 'time' was still fulfilled (Mark 1.15) and the rule of God was imminent (ibid.), in Luke there is a shift. *At that time* – at the time of Jesus – the 'scripture' was fulfilled (cf. 5.26). Similarly the enmity of his fellow citizens (v. 29) points in a historicizing way to the passion of Jesus.

[22] Mark's son of Mary (Mark 6.3) becomes the son of Joseph in Luke. He omits the brothers and sisters of Jesus.

[23] This verse can be understood only from Luke's incorporation of Mark 6 (vv. 2c and 5b). But the composition is not a complete success, since the (miraculous) deeds in Capernaum will be narrated only in the next chapter. Luke probably imagines the episode in Capernaum from Mark 1.21–28 (= Luke 4.31–37), but chronologically he had put it after his inaugural sermon.

[24] The sentence 'but he said' is surprising, since Jesus is already speaking. From the series of three in Mark 6.4 Luke deletes not only the kinsfolk – like Matthew – but also the house. If the prophet is thought to be 'without honour' in Mark, here he is 'not welcome' ('welcome' takes up v. 19). Luke makes Jesus speak in a hostile way to a crowd which is well disposed towards him, and thus initiate the conflict himself, because in obedience to God, he does not want to perform any miracles. At the same time v. 24 leads on to anti-Jewish polemic in the following verses.

[25–27] These verses give two probably redactional examples from scripture (vv. 25f., I Kings 17; v. 27, II Kings 5) of the way in which Jesus' activity benefits another people, because God has not destined his 'son' for Israel.

[28–30] These verses show how Luke wants vv. 25–27 to be understood. Jesus' Jewish contemporaries are lost irredeemably, as is shown by their anger against Jesus. Salvation *must* go to another people, which in the context of Luke-Acts suggests the Gentiles (cf. the conclusion to Acts).

Historical

[18–19] Jesus cannot have spoken the relevant verses from Isaiah, simply because they have already been manipulated dogmatically and moreover are quoted in the LXX version.

The rest of the story told on the basis of Mark is a crude distortion of Jesus' view of himself, as it already includes the Gentile mission among his tasks and – as the other side of this – has a strongly anti-Jewish stamp.

Luke 4.31–44: Jesus in Capernaum

31 And he went down to Capernaum, a city in Galilee. And he taught them on the Sabbath. 32 And they were astonished at his teaching, for *his speech* was with authority.

33 And in the synagogue was a man who had the spirit of an unclean *demon*, and who cried aloud, 34 'Stop, what do you want of us, Jesus of Nazareth? You have come to destroy us. I know who you are, the Holy One of God.' 35 And Jesus threatened him and said, 'Be dumb and go out of him!' And the *demon* cast him in the midst (of them) and went out of him and did him no harm.

36 And *a fear came over them all*, and they spoke with one another and said, '*What kind of speech is this?* He commands the unclean spirits with authority and *power* and they go out.'

37 And the news of him resounded in all the places in the surrounding region.

38 And he arose from the synagogue and came to Simon's house. And Simon's mother-in-law had a high fever, and they asked him (to do something) for her. 39 And he went to her and commanded the fever, and it left her. And immediately she stood up and served them.

40 *And when the sun had set they all brought their sick with many kinds of suffering to him. And he laid hands on each and made them healthy.* 41 *The evil spirits also went out of many and cried, 'You are the son of God!' And he threatened them and would not let them speak; for they knew that he was the Christ.*

42 *And when it was day* he went out to a lonely place, *and the multitudes sought him, and they came to him and wanted to keep him, so that he did not depart from them.* 43 But he said to them, '*I must also preach the kingdom of God to the other cities, for that is why I was sent.*' 44 And he preached in the synagogues *of Judaea.*

Redaction and tradition

The whole section has been completely constructed on the basis of Mark 1.21–39. The following observations arise from a comparison.

[31] The move from Nazareth to Capernaum is prepared for by the pericope 4.16–30, which is set earlier than in the Markan outline. Capernaum is described as a 'city of Galilee' – an aid for the readers.

[32] Luke emphasizes the authority of Jesus' *speech* (similarly v. 36); there is no comparison with the scribes.

[33–37] In v. 36, 'speech' and 'power' go beyond Mark in denoting the miracle-worker. 'Demon' has been added in vv. 33, 35. Verse 37 picks up v. 14 and describes the carrying out of the prospect given there.

[38–39] Luke deletes Andrew, James and John, whose call Mark had reported in

1.16–20, a narrative which Luke similarly omits. All this happens in order to go on to relate the call of Simon Peter, whose figure Luke kept in the present pericope. The gesture with which Jesus threatens the fever (like a demon) takes up vv. 33 and 35, where Luke had similarly inserted the motif into Mark.

[40–41] These verses are a prime example of stylistic improvement of Mark. The confession of the evil spirits that Jesus is the Son of God takes up the confession of the demon in v. 34 and is absent from Mark.

[42–43] The 'multitudes' (cf. above Luke 3.7,10) replace the 'disciples'. The phrase 'preach the kingdom of God' is the Lucan form of the preaching of the kingdom, which has been detached from the framework of the expectation of an imminent end (cf. Mark 1.15) and from now on will stamp the Gospel of Luke: 9.2, 11, 60; 16.16; 18.29; 21.31. Cf. further below on 10.9. The 'must' denotes the necessity in the history of salvation.

[44] This indicates positively the territory of the other cities in which the proclamation of the kingdom of God takes place.

Historical

[33–36] Cf. on Mark 1.23–27.
[38–39] Cf. on Mark 1.29–31.
[40–42] The information is certainly unhistorical, since it exaggerates excessively either for the purpose of propaganda or as a generalization (vv. 41, 42).
[43] The self-attestation attributes a later view to Jesus and is certainly not historically accurate.

Luke 5.1–11: Peter's fishing trip

1 Now *it happened that when the crowd was pressing on him and hearing the word of God, he stood by Lake Gennesaret* 2 *and saw two boats lying on the shore; but the fishermen had got out of them and were washing their nets.* 3 *Then he got into one of the boats, which belonged to Simon, and asked him to go out a little way from the land. And he sat down and taught the multitude from the boat.*

4 *And when he had finished speaking, he said to Simon,* 'Put out into the deep, and cast your nets for a catch.' 5 And Simon answered and said, '*Master*, we have worked all night and caught nothing; but at your word I will let down the nets.' 6 And when they did that, they caught *a great mass* of fish, and their nets began to break. 7 And they *beckoned* to their comrades in the other boat to come and pull with them. And they came and filled both boats, so that they were (almost) sinking. 8 When Simon Peter *saw* that, he fell at Jesus' feet and said, 'Lord, depart from me! I am a sinful man!' 9 For *terror had come over him* and all those who were with him, about this catch which they had made together, 10 likewise also James

and John the sons of Zebedee, Simon's companions. And Jesus said to Simon, 'Do not be afraid, from now on you will catch men.'

11 And they brought the boats to land and left all and followed him.

Redaction

This call story is to be seen in connection with the Nazareth story (4.16) – over and above the account of Capernaum. It offers the positive supplement to it. The critical attitude in Jesus' home country forms the background for the description of the appropriate relationship to Jesus which comes about through a calling.

[1–3] These verses are an exposition formed on the basis of Mark 1.16–20 and Mark 4.1. Verse 1 contains the Lukan designation for the *Sea* of Gennesaret, namely *Lake* Genessaret. Again the crowd of people appears – in good redactional style – and presses in on Jesus. 'Word of God' (v. 1) recalls the twofold occurrence of the word (= speech) of Jesus (4.32, 36) in the previous pericope. Here 'word of God' is used for the first time, although Luke already referred to 'the word' in the preface (Luke 1.2). Luke knows the expression 'the word of God' from the Christian tradition (cf. esp. Mark 4.13–20) and above all from the language of the (Pauline) mission (cf. I Thess. 1.6–8). The mention of the two boats in v. 2 prepares for v. 7. 'Simon's boat' (v. 3) takes up 4.38 (Simon's house).

[4] First the main character, Simon, is addressed, and then the whole group (cf. v. 9).

[5] The description of the fruitless effort prepares for the great miracle. For the 'word' cf. above on v. 1. Peter's obedience had been prepared for by 4.38f.

[6–7] These verses depict the miracle of the giant catch of fish, which is grounded in the power of the word of Jesus.

[8] This verse is in tension with what has gone before. Peter cannot fall at the feet of Jesus in a boat which is on the verge of sinking, nor ask him to go away in this situation. Moreover the confession of being a sinful man does not fit the miracle. The picture of the repentant sinner is generally Lukan (7.36–50; 15.1–10; 18.9–14; 19.1–10).

[9–10a] These verses link the miracle back to vv. 6–7. Verse 10a is an addition. On the basis of Mark 1.19 Luke inserts the sons of Zebedee among those who are amazed at the miracle.

[10b] This is in tension with the context and refers to the missionary activity of Peter after Easter. We must conjecture a connection between vv. 8 and 10b on the level of tradition (see below).

[11] This verse stands in tension with v. 10b, where there is no invitation to discipleship. By means of v. 11 Luke makes the whole pericope the narrative of a call in the lifetime of Jesus.

Tradition

The present story can be understood initially only on the basis of its use of Mark 1.16–20. But in vv. 8, 10b a further tradition is visible which belongs to the time after Easter. This can be further substantiated, as there is a related narrative in John 21.

The two pericopes belong together genetically. Thus the following motifs agree in them:
1. The fruitless fishing trip;
2. Allusions to the denial of Peter (cf. Jesus' threefold question in John 21.15–17 and the confession of sins in Luke 5.8b);
3. The abundant catch (John 21.6/Luke 5.6);
4. John 21.11 is parallel to Luke 5.10c (motif of the catch both times in connection with Peter);
5. The call to discipleship in John 21.19 corresponds to Luke 5.11;
6. The evaluation of Peter is given by a saying of the Lord (John 21.17d/Luke 5.10c).
7. Peter is the main character in the narrative (alongside Jesus).

Over against this comparison it can be pointed out that the second and the fifth points do not come from the pericope John 21.1–15, but only from the context. Further, John 21.15–17 can hardly be regarded as early tradition, for the precise way in which it follows the story of the denial betrays later reflection. And the Lukan parallel to John 21.19 in the fifth point, Luke 5.11, does not belong to the same stratum of tradition as Luke 5.10 (see above). Still, on the basis of the other parallels cited above it remains very probable that by means of John 21 the pericope Luke 5.1–11 can be designated a former Easter story, all the more so since in its focus on Peter Luke 5.10b conclusively presupposes the Easter situation. For Peter, his mission coincides with his vision of the Risen Christ.

Whereas Mark 1.17 merely relates a promise of the future appointment to be fishers of men, Luke 5.10b ('from now on') describes the appointment itself, which follows immediately upon this word being said to Peter. Moreover Mark 1.18 contains a call to discipleship which has been applied at a *secondary* stage to the circumstances of the life of Jesus, whereas Luke 5.10 contains the invitation, 'Do not be afraid!' The latter has hardly developed from Mark 1.18, but is original in this appearance story, which fits the situation of the disciples after the death of Jesus. Of course not every scene in which Jesus reveals himself is to be rooted in the Easter situation. But a further point of contact lies in the fact that Luke 5.8b narrates a confession of guilt on the part of Peter for which there is no occasion in the situation presupposed in Luke 5.

Historical

[4–10] The historical nucleus of the tradition lies in the fact that after Easter (and not during his lifetime, as Luke writes) Peter saw Jesus as a figure of light. Thus the historical recollection is somewhat distorted.

The miracle with the fish is certainly unhistorical.

Luke 5.12–16: The healing of a leper

12 And it happened when he was in one of the cities, and look, there was a man, full of leprosy. And when he saw Jesus, he fell down on his face and *besought* him and said, '*Lord*, if you will, you can make me clean.' 13 And he stretched out his hand and touched him and said, 'I will; be clean!' And immediately the leprosy departed from him. 14 *And he himself commanded* him to say nothing to anyone, but, 'Go away, show yourself to the priest and bring for your cleansing what Moses has ordained, as a testimony to them.' 15 The word about him spread still more, and a great multitude came together to hear and to be healed of their sickness. 16 *But he himself withdrew into the wilderness and prayed.*

Redaction and tradition

This section is based on Mark 1.40–45 (for the strata see there).

[12] This verse refers back to 4.43f. Matthew 8.2 also includes 'Look' and the appellation 'Lord', both absent from Mark.

[13] This verse corresponds to Mark 1.41f., but Luke (like Matt. 8.3) omits both Mark 1.42b ('and he became clean') and Mark 1.43, evidently because the hostile reaction of Jesus reported there does not fit the healing.

[14–15] In Mark the man who is healed is ordered to tell nothing, yet he disobeys the order (Mark 1.45). Luke passes over this and reports that the word about Jesus spreads (and not – as in Mark – that the man who has been healed passes on the word about his own healing).

[16] This verse contains the Lukan motif of prayer (see on 3.21).

Historical

See on Mark 1.40–45.

Luke 5.17–26: The healing of a paralysed man

17 And it happened that on one of those days he himself was teaching, and Pharisees and teachers of the law were sitting there who had come from every village of Galilee and Judaea and from Jerusalem. And it was a power of the Lord that he healed. 18 *And look, men* carried on a pallet a man who was paralysed, *and they tried to bring him in and lay him before him.* 19 And as they were not able to bring him in, because of the crowd, *they climbed on to the roof* and let him down with his pallet *through the tiles into the midst before Jesus.* 20 And when he saw their faith he said, 'Man, your sins are forgiven you.' 21 And the scribes *and the Pharisees began* to discuss, 'Who is this who speaks blasphemies? Who can forgive sins but God only?' 22 But when Jesus perceived their thoughts, he answered and said to them, 'What do you think in your hearts? 23 Which is easier, to say, "Your sins are forgiven you," or to say, "Rise and walk"? 24 But that you may know that the Son of man has authority on earth to forgive sins,' he said to the man who was paralysed, 'I say to you, rise, take up your pallet and go home.' 25 And immediately he got up before them, took up that on which he lay, went home *and praised God.* 26 And amazement seized them all, and they glorified God *and were filled with fear,* saying 'We have seen *unexpected things today.'*

Redaction and tradition

This section is based on Mark 2.1–12.

[17] From Mark (2.1) Luke deletes the place name Capernaum and describes the region of Jesus' influence: Galilee, Judaea, Jerusalem (cf. the programme of 4.43–44). He introduces the Pharisees as arch-enemies.

[19] Luke replaces the sentence 'they uncovered the roof . . . and dug it up' (Mark 2.4) with 'they climbed on to the roof'. He probably thinks that the men took off the tiles in order to be able to let the sick man down. Mark is thinking of a clay roof, Luke of a tile roof, a kind that did not exist in Palestine.

[20] Jesus addresses the sick man in Luke as 'man', not 'my son', as in Mark 2.5.

[21] Luke introduces the Pharisees, who after the preliminary reference in v. 17 appear for the first time in a story in his Gospel, into the Markan text and thus associates them with the scribes. He knows the partial identity of the two groups from Mark 2.16.

[26] 'Today' picks up 'today' from 4.21 (cf. earlier 2.21).

Historical

Cf. on Mark 2.1–12.

Luke 5.27–32: The call of Levi

27 And *afterwards* he went out, and saw a tax collector *named* Levi sitting at the toll office; and he said to him, 'Follow me.' 28 And *he left everything,* rose, and followed him. 29 And Levi *made him a great feast* in his house, and there was a large crowd of toll collectors and others reclining at table with them. 30 And the Pharisees and their scribes murmured against his disciples, saying, 'Why *do you eat and drink* with tax collectors and sinners?' 31 And Jesus *answered and said* to them, 'The *healthy* do not need the physician, but those who are sick. 32 I have not come to call the righteous, but sinners *to repentance.'*

Redaction and tradition

This section is based on Mark 2.13–17 (for the strata see there).

[27] Luke removes the shore scenery from Mark 2.13 and deletes the name of the father (Alphaeus) from Mark 2.14, because a James, son of Alphaeus, appears in Luke 6.15 and he wants to avoid confusion between the two.

[28] As in 5.11, this verse adds the leaving of all possessions.

[29] Luke changes the sitting together in Mark 2.15 into a great banquet given by Levi.

[30] The disciples are asked why they themselves are eating with sinners and toll collectors, and not, as in Mark (2.16), why Jesus is doing so. For 'Pharisees and scribes' cf. v. 21.

[31] The 'healthy' appear in the Gospels only in Luke (cf. also 7.10; 15.27).

[32] 'To repentance' is a commentary on 'call'. In contrast to Mark, Luke has Jesus eat with *converted* sinners (cf. 15.7, 10 with Matt. 18.12–14). Accordingly, in the Lukan church the forgiveness of sins which follows baptism can be granted only on the condition of a change of conduct (= repentance, cf. 3.3; 24.47; Acts 5.31). Whereas in Mark 'repentance' designates the whole process of conversion, Luke splits this up. He supplements as follows: Acts 5.31 ('and forgiveness of sins'); Luke 24.47; Luke 3.3 ('for the forgiveness of sins').

Historical

Cf. on Mark 2.13–17. The same provisos apply to the present narrative as apply to Mark, on which it is based; here the addition of the situation of the meal in v. 29 and the question to the disciples (instead of to Jesus) in v. 30 represent a further removal from history.

Luke 5.33–39: On fasting

33 *And they* said to him, 'The disciples of John fast *often and offer prayers*, like those of the Pharisees, but yours *eat and drink.*' 34 And Jesus said to them, '*Can you* make wedding guests fast while the bridegroom is with them? 35 But days will come, and when the bridegroom is taken away from them, then they will fast in those days.' 36 *And he told them a parable*, 'No one tears a piece *from a new garment* and puts it on an old garment. If he does, he will tear the new, and the piece *from the new* will not match the old. 37 And no one puts new wine into old wineskins; if he does, the *new* wine will burst the skins and *it will flow out*, and the skins will be destroyed. 38 But new wine *should be put* into fresh wineskins. 39 *And no one who has drunk old (wine) will want new, for he thinks, "The old tastes better."*

Redaction and tradition

This section is based on Mark 2.18–22 (for the strata see there).

[33] The questioners are identical with the speakers of v. 30, although 'like those of the Pharisees' is in tension with that. Thus the present story is closely linked with the previous one. 'Eat and drink', a key phrase which links back to v. 30, anticipates 7.34, where the same charge is addressed to Jesus.

[36] This verse contains a new formula completely in the Lukan style: 'And he spoke a parable to them' (cf. 6.39; 15.3); it clarifies the next saying in Mark 2.21, which is difficult to understand. Luke intensifies the folly of the procedure by having the patches cut out of a new skin. In that way both this skin and the old one are damaged.

[39] This verse has been added by Luke (perhaps he has in view the repudiation of Jesus by the scribes and Pharisees in vv. 21, 30, 33). The verse explains to the Lukan readership why so many contemporaries of Jesus rejected his message.

Historical

Cf. on Mark 2.18–32. The historical nucleus underlies vv. 33–34 (= Mark 2.18–19*). Luke has developed further away from history (cf. esp. v. 39) the Markan scene, which clusters round the historical nucleus in Luke 5.34 (= Mark 2.19a).

Luke 6.1–5: Plucking ears of grain on the sabbath

1 And it happened that he was going through grain fields on a sabbath; and his disciples plucked ears of grain and <u>ate</u> *them, rubbing them in their hands.* 2 But *some* of the Pharisees said, 'Why are you doing what is not lawful to do on the sabbath?' 3 *And Jesus answered them* and said, 'Have you not read what David did when he was hungry, and those who were with him? 4 How he entered the house of God, and *took* and ate the showbread which it is not lawful for any but priests to <u>eat</u>, and also gave it to those with him?' 5 And he said to them, 'The Son of man is lord of the sabbath.'

Redaction and tradition

Luke is using Mark 2.23–28.

[1] The 'they ate' which has been added to Mark takes up 5.33; 'rubbed' makes it more precise. In Luke (and Matthew) the sin of the disciples lies in the eating, whereas in Mark it consists in the work of plucking the ears.

[5] This verse passes over the offensive saying of Jesus, 'The sabbath is made for man and not man for the sabbath' (Mark 2.27). Here Luke has him justifying the action of the disciples solely from the rule of the exalted Son of man (Jesus).

Historical

Cf. on Mark 2.23–28. Luke deletes the only element of the Markan text which can be said to be historical, v. 27, and in so doing robs the whole pericope of any historical value.

Luke 6.6–11: The healing of the withered hand on the sabbath

6 *Now it happened on another sabbath that* he entered *the* synagogue and taught. And a man was there, and his *right* hand was withered. 7 And *the scribes and the Pharisees* watched him, to see whether he would heal on the sabbath so that they might find an accusation against him. 8 *But he knew their thoughts,* and he said to the man with the withered hand, 'Stand up *and come* into the midst.' *And he stood up and came.* 9 *And Jesus* said to them, '*I ask you*, is it lawful on the sabbath to do good (rather) than evil, to save a soul or to destroy it?' 10 And he looked round at them all, and said to him, 'Stretch out your hand.' And he did so, and his hand was restored. 11 *And they were filled with blind rage and discussed with one another what they could do to Jesus.*

Redaction and tradition

This section is based on Mark 3.1–6 (for the stratification and the construction of this controversy see there).

[6] Luke *deliberately* introduces this story as another sabbath narrative. For the right hand cf. the right ear (22.50) and the right eye (Matt. 5.29).

[7] Luke replaces the Pharisees and Herodians who appear at the end in Mark, which he has before him (Mark 3.6), with the scribes and the Pharisees, here right at the beginning, so as to achieve a greater dramatic effect.

[8] Jesus knows the thoughts of his opponents in advance. In this way Luke emphasizes the miraculous power of Jesus.

[9] Luke omits the silence of the opponents (Mark 3.4 end) to Jesus' question.

[10] Luke deliberately passes over Jesus' strong feelings (anger and sorrow) in Mark (3.5b).

[11] This verse represents a further heightening of the hostility of Jesus' enemies towards him. This is probably true even by comparison with the intention of Jesus' opponents to kill him which is narrated in Mark. Luke's readership indeed knows the consequences of blind fury, which will be depicted in the Lukan passion story even more vividly than in Mark.

Historical

Cf. on Mark 3.1–6

Luke 6.12–19: The call of the twelve apostles. Healings

12 *And it happened in these days that* he went up a mountain to pray; *and he spent the night in prayer to God.* 13 *And when it was day*, he called his disciples and chose from them twelve, *whom he also named apostles*: 14 Simon, *whom he also named* Peter, and Andrew his brother, and James and John and Philip and Bartholomew, 15 and Matthew and Thomas and James the son of Alphaeus, and Simon the *so-called* Zealot, 16 and Judas the son of James, and Judas Iscariot who became (his) betrayer.

17 *And he went down with them and stood on a level place*, and (with him was) a crowd of his disciples and a great multitude of people from *all* Judaea and Jerusalem and the coastal region of Tyre and Sidon, 18 *who came to hear him and to be healed of their diseases. And those who were troubled with unclean spirits were healed,* 19 *and the whole people sought to touch him, for a power came forth from him and healed them all.*

Redaction and tradition

This section is based on Mark 3.7–19. Luke exchanges Mark 3.7–12 with Mark 3.13–19. First of all his formulation follows Mark 3.13–19 and then Mark 3.7–12 (for the strata see there).

[12] Here Luke introduces the motif of prayer once again. Jesus prepares himself for the choice of the apostles, which is made the next day, by a prayer to God which lasts all night.

[13] This verse explicitly calls the twelve also apostles. In this way the apostolate of the twelve is formed, which according to Luke is to be of great significance for the post-Easter church (cf. Acts 1). In contrast to Mark (and Matthew), the twelve are chosen from the wider group of disciples. In contrast to Mark there is as yet no mention of sending them out.

[14–16] Like Matthew, Luke puts the disciples in pairs; cf. especially the two persons named Judas at the end. As in Matthew, the first pair are the brothers Peter and Andrew (against Mark 3.16 and Acts 1.13, where – governed by their joint appearance in Acts 3–5 – Peter and John appear as a pair), the second pair James and John (with Mark and Matthew against Acts 1.13); here Luke omits their designation as 'sons of thunder' from Mark 3.17b. For Simon the Zealot cf. Acts 1.13.

[17–19] These verses are based in general on Mark 3.7–12 and are put in the style of a summary report. The section functions as a transition to the Sermon on the Plain which immediately follows (cf. a similar transition to the Sermon on the

Mount in Matt. 4.23–25). Verse 17 replaces the sea with a 'level place' and omits Galilee. Verses 18–19 emphasize more strongly than Mark the miraculous power which once again went forth from Jesus (cf. previously 5.17), but pass over the confession of the demons and the command to silence in Mark, which he has in front of him (Mark 3.11b–12).

Historical

Cf. on Mark 3.7–19. In addition the following needs to be said:

The names of the twelve disciples are predominantly those of followers of Jesus in his lifetime. But Jesus did not call these either as apostles or even as twelve apostles.

[18–19] The miracles narrated over and above those in Mark, on which the passage is based, rest on generalizations and exaggerations. Their historical value is therefore nil.

Preliminary observation on Luke 6.20–49 ('Discourse on the Plain')

By comparison with Mark, Luke has introduced extra material in two insertions, *first* the so-called Sermon on the Plain in Luke 6.20–49 and *secondly* the so-called travel account, Luke 9.51–18.14. Here he is more conservative than Matthew, who composes several discourses and has inserted into them material which goes beyond Mark. In terms of content, Matthew's first discourse composition (chs. 5–7, 'Sermon on the Mount') corresponds to the present 'Discourse on the Plain'; both derive from Q material. However, here Luke is not simply reproducing traditions. The introduction (6.20) and the retrospect (7.1) indicate that Luke regarded this discourse as a unit and attached a specific meaning to it.

Luke 6.20–26: Beatitudes and woes

20 *And he lifted up his eyes on his disciples, and said,*
'Blessed are you poor, for yours the kingdom of God.
21 Blessed are you that hunger *now*, for *you* shall be satisfied.
Blessed are you that weep *now*, for *you* shall laugh.
22 Blessed are you when men hate you, and when they exclude you (from the community) and revile you, and bring your name into disrepute because of the Son of man! 23 Rejoice in that day, and dance for joy, for look, your reward is great in heaven; for so their fathers did to the prophets.
24 *But woe to you rich, for you have received your consolation. 25 Woe to you that are full now, for you shall hunger. Woe to you that laugh now, for you shall mourn and weep. 26 Woe to you, when all men speak well of you, for so their fathers did to the false prophets.'*

Redaction

[20a] What follows is addressed to the disciples, who were mentioned in v. 13.

[20b–23] These verses as a whole go back to Q, which Luke uses along with Matthew. The twofold 'now' (v. 21) probably comes from Luke, who in this way historicizes the address: accordingly it applies to those addressed by Jesus at the time, as was the 'today' of 4.21 to the people of Nazareth. For the same reason Luke each time alters the third person to the second person in the apodosis.

[24–26] These verses are either an antithesis to the beatitudes formed in the tradition or – more probably – Luke's updating of the blessings. Several observations support this.

(a) Only in v. 27 does the address return to the hearers, whereas with 'but', v. 24 turns to outsiders;

(b) Luke knows the genre of the woes (10.13; 11.42–52; 17.1; 21.23; 22.22);

(c) The contrast between rich and poor is typical of Luke – cf. the parable of the rich man and poor Lazarus (16.19–31);

(d) Linguistically, the passage contains favourite words of Luke: e.g. 'but', 'all men' and 'speak good';

(e) The second person of the woes corresponds to the second person of the Lukan beatitudes.

Tradition

Within the Q tradition taken over by Luke, vv. 20b–21 and vv. 22–23 can be distinguished from each other on grounds of form, since they display a different sentence construction. (But both passages can be assigned to Q because of the Matthaean parallel Matt. 5.3–12.)

Chronologically vv. 20b–21 stand at the beginning of the beatitudes (for v. 20b cf. Thomas 54) and do not contain any reference to Jesus. Verses 22–23 presuppose talk of (Jesus as) the Son of man (v. 22). They are specific in view of a particular situation (v. 22) and connect the persecution with the previous persecutions of the prophets. Cf. a similar view in I Thess. 2.14–16 and Mark 12.1–12. Verses 22–23 reflect experiences of early Christian communities.

For the original beatitudes (vv. 20b–21), poverty, hunger and suffering are not positive characteristics. But God soon turns the fate of the poor, the hungry and those who weep to good fortune in accordance with the royal ideal expressed in Ps. 72:

4 The king will judge the people with righteousness and the poor with justice and crush the oppressor . . .

12 He will deliver the poor who cries for help, and the wretched who has no helper. 13 He will be gracious to the little ones and the poor, and the poor he will help.

The coming kingdom, the announcement of which makes sense only if the distress will be transformed in the near future, is bound up with expectation of a heavenly banquet.

Historical

[20b–21] The earliest stratum of the beatitudes goes back to Jesus. This judgment is based on two observations: (a) the beatitudes form a much longer series in Matthew and there consist of ten individual blessings (Matt. 5.3–12); here we can already note processes of growth within the tradition (cf. Matt. 5.7–9 as an element of the Q original of Matthew). (b) Luke 6.22/Matt. 5.11–12 (cf. Thomas 68.1) are focussed on the situation of the post-Easter community and are clearly of later origin.

The spiritualization of the beatitudes in Matthew is also part of the community situation, in that he makes the poor the poor *in spirit* and interprets the hungry as those who hunger and thirst *for righteousness* (cf. Matt. 5.3,6). It emerges from this that in the earliest community the concrete material promises of Jesus were interpreted in a metaphorical sense. The reason for this lies in their radical and offensive nature. Moreover Christians increasingly recognized that the coming of the kingdom of God, which was finally to bring about the promised changes, was delayed.

Around the historical nucleus we have two rings of expansions in Q (vv. 22–23) and the expansion by Luke himself (vv. 24–26), neither of which, like the introduction (v. 20), has any claim to historicity. By contrast, the criteria of growth, offensiveness and difference support the historicity of vv. 20b–21.

Luke 6.27–38: On love of enemy and on judging

27 '*But I say to you that hear*, <u>Love your enemies</u>, do good to those who hate you, 28 bless those who curse you, pray for those who abuse you. 29 To him who strikes you on the cheek, offer the other also; and from him who takes away your coat do not withhold even your undergarment. 30 Give *to every one* who asks you; and if someone takes your goods, do not ask for them back. 31 *And as you wish people to do to you, do so to them.*

32 <u>If you</u> love those who love you, *what thanks do you get for that*? For even sinners love those who love them.

33 And <u>if you</u> do good to those who do good to you, *what thanks do you get for that*? For even sinners do the same.

34 *And <u>if you</u> lend to those from whom you hope to receive, what thanks do you get for that? Even sinners lend to sinners, to receive the same again.*

35 No, <u>*love your enemies*</u> and do good and lend without hoping for anything, and your reward will be great, and you will be sons of the Most High; for he is gracious to the ungrateful and the wicked. 36 Be merciful, as your Father is merciful.

37 And do not judge, *and* you will not be judged (in turn). Do not condemn, and you will not be condemned (in turn). Forgive (debts), and you will be forgiven (as a debtor). 38 Give, and it will given to you. *A good measure, pressed down, shaken together, running over will be put into your lap.* For the measure you give will be the measure you get back.'

Redaction

Luke composes quite independently, on the basis of Q (cf. the Matthew parallels under 'Tradition'), a brief treatise on the relationship between love of enemy and problems with money. By enemy Luke does not think, as Matthew does, of 'national enemy' but of the debtor as a possible enemy. At other points in his two-volume work, like Acts 6.1–6 or Acts 19.23–40, he also shows a sensitivity to tensions which have arisen for financial reasons, not to mention the rich persons in his Gospel: the rich farmer (12.16–20), Zacchaeus (19.1–10).

[27a] This verse is a Lukan transition which links back to the hearers present (v. 20), since in vv. 24–26 the rich who were not present and the other groups of people depicted in negative terms had been addressed.

[27b] The invitation to love one's enemy is introduced in connection with Q (cf. Matt. 5.44).

[27c–30] These verses contain several concrete examples of love of enemy based on Q. For the undergarment see on Mark 6.8–9.

[31] The so-called Golden Rule here sums up the command to love one's enemy and the specific details in vv. 28–30. Unlike the Matthaean parallel (Matt. 7.12), it contains no reference to the Old Testament and in this generally valid form was deliberately put at this point by Luke. He wants to make clear to his readers that the harsh commandment to love one's enemy does have universalistic features.

[32–34] These verses contain three sentences with a parallel structure, each of which has an identical question ('What thanks do you get for that?'), and an additional reason, that sinners also do the same thing. The passage is first about love for those who also love (v. 32), secondly about doing good to those who do the same thing (v. 33) and thirdly about lending to those from whom one hopes to receive again (v. 34).

[35a] This verse links back to the command to love one's enemy in v. 27b (but omits blessing and praying for enemies) and develops vv. 33f. with the commandment to do and lend without expecting any good thing back. So the verse depicts the Lukan yield of the remarks so far: love of enemy is made concrete in doing good and in lending – without the principle of mutuality.

[35b] This verse rounds off the admonition with the prospect of heavenly reward from God who is gracious to good and bad alike.

[36] The merciful behaviour of those addressed, which does not rest on the principle of reciprocity as this has been developed previously, has its foundation in the mercy of God himself. ('Merciful' appears only here in Luke.)

[37–38] In contrast to the Matthaean parallel (Matt. 7.1 = Q), where there is an absolute prohibition against judging in view of the last judgment, four imperatives follow here as the last instruction. Two prohibitions (vv. 37a–b) and two command-ments (vv. 37c–38a) are put side by side. To these Luke adds two sayings about measuring. With the tremendous accumulation of just four attributes in v. 38 he emphasizes the measure that one is to receive if, as 'Jesus' instructs in v. 37f., one loves the (private) enemy with whom one has money problems. Cf. Sir. 29.1–17 for the connection between mercy, treasure (in heaven), debtors, and enemy.

Tradition

The section is based on Q passages, as the comparison with the Matthaean parallel (Matt. 5.39–42, 44–48; 7.1, 12) shows. Cf. the parallels: v. 27/Matt. 5.44a; v. 28/ Matt. 5.44b; v. 29/ Matt. 5.39–40; v. 30/Matt. 5.42; v. 31/Matt. 7.12; v. 32/Matt. 5.46–47; v. 35b/Matt. 5.45; v. 36/Matt. 5.48; vv. 37–38/Matt. 7.1–2.

As Matthew has preserved the Q basis better, it is investigated in the section on Matthew (see on Matt. 5.38–42, 43–48; 7.1–6, 12).

Historical

Cf. on Matt. 5.39–42, 44–48; 7.1, 12. The parts of v. 28 which are not attested by Matthew are a community construction and therefore not historical.

Luke 6.39–49: Parable discourse

39 *He also told them a parable,* 'Can a blind man lead a blind man? Will they not both fall into the pit? 40 A disciple is not above his teacher; *if he is fully trained, he will be like his teacher.*

41 Why do you see the speck in your brother's eye but do not notice the log in your *own* eye? 42 How can you say to your brother, "Brother, let me take out the speck that is in your eye," when you yourself do not see the log in your own eye? You hypocrite, first take the log out of your own eye and then you will see clearly to take out the speck that is in your brother's eye.

43 For no good tree bears bad fruit, nor conversely does a bad tree bear good fruit; 44 for each tree is known by its own fruit. For figs are not gathered from thorns, nor are grapes picked from a bramble bush. 45 A good man out of the good treasure of his heart produces good, and an evil man out of evil produces evil. *For of the abundance of his heart his mouth speaks.*

46 Why do you call me 'Lord, Lord,' and not do what I say? 47 Every one *who comes to me* and hears my words and does them – *I will show you what he is like.* 48 He is like a man who wanted to build a house, *who dug deep*, and laid the foundation upon rock; *and when a flood came*, the wave broke against that house, and could not shake it. 49 But whoever hears and

does not do, he is like a man who built a house on the ground without a foundation; when the flood wave broke against it, immediately it fell, and the ruin of that house was great.'

Redaction

The section vv. 39–49 concludes the Discourse on the Plain with a collection of parables which essentially consists of Q material (see on tradition).

[39a–40] Verse 39a is a Lukan introductory formula (cf. 5.36). Luke probably wants v. 39b to be understood in parallel to vv. 37f.: how can you set yourself up as a judge if you yourself are blind? Alongside it Luke puts the saying about the pupil and the master (v. 40), deleting half of the parallelism which does not fit the context, namely 'nor a servant above his master' (cf. Matt. 10.24b). That would seem to make a clear statement that there is only one judicial authority, namely Jesus. But in that case the extra redactional v. 40b would still remain unclear. Therefore it seems more likely that at the redactional level vv. 39–40 are addressed to disciples who exalt themselves to be community leaders. Luke accuses them of blindness. It is true of the community leader, too, that he has (only) to be like the teacher. Luke uses this insight in Acts for his depiction of Peter, Stephen and Paul, all of whom he partly portrays like Jesus: cf. simply the parallel between Jesus (23.46) and Stephen (Acts 7.59) in the cries they utter at their deaths.

[41–42] These verses, formulated in connection with Q (cf. Matt. 7.3–5), are focussed on Christians of Luke's time, who with a claim to moral superiority criticize other members of the community (cf. their claim to teaching qualities greater than those of Jesus, a claim which has just been rejected in vv. 39f.).

[43–45] These verses develop the criticism of false teachers which so far has been presented only indirectly. To rebuke fellow Christians, one must be better than they are, and evidently the false teachers addressed were not. Taking up a simile from Q (cf. Matt. 7.16–18), vv. 43–44 give criteria for false teachers. Over and above the Q original, v. 45 explicitly applies the image to people and focusses it further in the second part of the verse: speech reveals the heart from which it flows. While this part of the verse corresponds to Matt. 12.34b (Q), it has been deliberately inserted at this point by Luke and corresponds with his picture of human nature. In the context it refers to the false teachers, from whose mouth only evil can come.

[46] This verse is a transition to the closing parable in vv. 47–49, which is a forceful admonition to do what one has heard.

[47] With 'who comes to me', this verse picks up the summary report of the miracles of Jesus (cf. 6.18). On v. 47c cf. 12.5.

[48] This verse narrates the activities of a builder building a house more vividly than the Q version in Matthew (7.24), and redactionally includes working on the foundation. At the same time it tones down the environmental catastrophe and

speaks of 'inundation' rather than the downpour of the Q version (= Matt. 7.25), which is like a torrent.

[49] This verse develops the negative side of the image of the house-building which is depicted positively in v. 48. Within the Gospel of Luke this contrast corresponds to that between the beatitudes (6.20–23) and the woes (6.24–26).

Tradition

[39b] This saying about the blind leading the blind probably derives from Q, as is attested by Matt. 15.14. Whereas in Matthew it has an explicit anti-Pharisaic reference, this is lacking in Q. As the saying has been handed down in isolation without a recognizable context, its original intent can no longer be recognized. The parallel in Thomas 34 also attests this. Moreover the logion was a proverb in antiquity and therefore could also have been attached to the Jesus tradition as an independent saying only at a later stage.

[41–42] These verses correspond to Q (cf. Matt. 7.3–5) and have a parallel in Thomas 26.

[43–45] These verses derive from a parable in Q (cf. Matt. 7.16–20) which in vv. 43–44 contains three images and in v. 45 the application.

[46] This is an individual logion from Q handed down in isolation (cf. Matt. 7.21). It presupposes faith in Jesus, the Lord, and is thus post-Easter.

[47–49] These verses correspond to Q (cf. Matt. 7.24–27). The passage is a double parable and in the Q source already stood at the end of a discourse (cf. the analogous position in Matthew at the end of the Sermon on the Mount). It is better preserved in Matthew than in Luke, who has considerably altered the symmetrical construction.

Historical

[39b] There are no criteria for attributing this to Jesus because the original meaning has become obscure. For example, an anti-Pharisaic orientation (J. Jeremias) is only a remote possibility.

[41–42*] Cf. on Matt. 7.3–5.

[43–45] There are probably no direct parallels for this simile (but cf. Sirach 27.7). It matches the authentic saying of Jesus in Mark 7.15 well.

[46] Jesus could certainly have meant the address 'Lord, Lord' ironically. However, a post-Easter context is likely, since addressing Jesus as Lord is rooted there.

[47–49] Cf. on Matt. 7.24–27, where reasons are given why it is improbable that the saying originates with Jesus. However, since Luke has changed the parable further the historical verdict here must be completely negative.

Luke 7.1–10: The centurion of Capernaum

1 *After he had finished all his sayings in the hearing of the people* he entered Capernaum. 2 Now the *slave* of a centurion was sick and on the point of death, *who was valuable to him.* 3 And when he heard of Jesus, he sent to him *elders of the Jews* to ask him to come and heal his slave. 4 *And they came to Jesus, besought him earnestly and said, 'He is worthy to have you do this for him,* 5 *for he loves our people, and he has built us our synagogue.'* 6 *Then Jesus went with them. However, when he was not far from the house, the centurion sent friends to him, saying to him,* 'Lord, do not trouble yourself. I am not worthy to have you come under my roof. 7 *Therefore I did not think myself worthy to come to you.* But say a word, and my servant will be made healthy again. 8 For I too am a man set under authority, and have soldiers under me; and I say to this one, "Go," and he goes; and to another, "Come," and he comes; and to my servant, "Do this," and he does it.' 9 When Jesus heard this, he marvelled at him, and turned and said to the crowd that followed him 'I tell you, not even in Israel have I found such faith.' 10 *And when they returned to the house*, those who had been sent found *the slave* healthy.

Redaction and tradition

The basis is Q, whose version Matthew has preserved most faithfully (cf. further on Matt. 8.5–13). Whereas Matt. 8.5 depicts the centurion simply as a Gentile who turns humbly and in trust to Jesus and is heard by him, in 7.3–5 Luke inserts the elders of the Jews: they intercede for the centurion with Jesus and in addition emphasize his love for the Jewish people; for example, he has had the synagogue built for them. This redactional description corresponds to the description of Cornelius in Acts 10 who is similarly a Gentile, but is God-fearing and has given the Jewish people much alms. Moreover Luke 7 and Acts 10 are similar in that Jesus is asked into the centurion's house as Peter is asked into Cornelius's house by delegates (cf. Luke 7.3/Acts 10.7f.). However, Luke 7 and Acts 10 are fundamentally different in that the content of one story is a miracle (the centurion's servant is healed) and of the other a conversion (of Cornelius). However, the agreements between the present story and Acts 10 must be regarded as redactional.

[1] Verse 1a is a Lukan transition. Like Matthew, Luke attaches the narrative of the centurion of Capernaum to a great discourse. In both instances the order is based on Q.

[2] Luke changes the expression 'servant' in Q, which he has before him (cf. Matt. 8.6), into 'slave' (cf. v. 10), but leaves 'servant' in v. 7 (out of carelessness?).

[3–5] These verses give the story a stronger Jewish colouring (cf. the introductory remarks). The commendation of the Gentile centurion by the Jewish presbyters is an apologetic feature. In this way Luke is expressing the correctness of the mission to the Gentiles.

[6] This verse with its redactional construction of the second delegation drama-

tizes the narrative. The word 'friends' suggests that the centurion has a harmonious, hospitable home.

[7] This verse reinforces the centurion's sense of unworthiness, which has already been expressed in v. 6.

[10] This verse rounds off the story as a narrative. The delegation can convince themselves of the healing of the servant on their return. By his redactional work Luke has created the paradox that the main figure, the centurion of Capernaum, has never appeared on stage in person. In contrast to the Q version, he remains at home.

Historical

Cf. on Matt. 8.5–13.

Luke 7.11–17: The young man at Nain

11 And *it happened afterwards* that he went into a city called Nain, and his disciples went with him and a great crowd. 12 And as he came to the gate of the city, *look*, they were carrying out a dead man who was the *only son* of his mother, and she was a widow; and *a great crowd from the city* went with her. 13 And when *the Lord* saw her, he had compassion on her and said to her, 'Do not weep.' 14 And he came up and touched the bier, and the bearers stood still. And he said, 'Young man, I say to you, arise.' 15 And the dead man got up and began to speak, and Jesus *gave him to his mother*. 16 *And fear seized them all*, and they praised God and said, 'A great prophet has been raised up among us!', and 'God has visited his people (graciously).' 17 *And this report concerning him spread through the whole of Judaea and all the surrounding country*.

Redaction and tradition

The narrative has been inserted at this point by Luke (in the Q context of 7.1–10, 18–35) in order to give an anticipatory illustration of the later statement in 7.22 ('dead are raised'). At the same time it represents a heightening by comparison with the healing of the dying slave of the centurion of Capernaum which has just been narrated.

[11] At the beginning this verse contains a Lukan connecting formula.

[12–16] Apart from a few details, these verses reproduce what Luke has before him. The story corresponds to the Hellenistic type of resurrection miracle. Here the miracle-worker similarly meets the bier or the coffin and does the miracle before a crowd of people on his own initiative. Such a story, transferred to Jesus, has taken on features from the Elijah tradition at a second stage (cf. I Kings 17.10, 17–24), which explains the confession that Jesus is a great prophet (v. 16). Luke himself extends this line in v. 15 by a literal quotation of I Kings 17.23 (LXX). Cf. also Luke 9.42 (Mark 9.27/Matt. 17.18 differ).

[17] This verse is a redactional conclusion (cf. similarly 4.37; 5.15), as v. 16 had already rounded off the narrative with a choral conclusion. 'This news' refers either to the praise in v. 16b or to the whole miracle story or to both.

Historical

Jesus never raised the young man of Nain.

Luke 7.18–35: The Baptist's enquiry and Jesus' testimony about him

18 *And the disciples of John told him of all this.* And John called *two of his* disciples to him 19 and sent them *to the Lord* to ask him, '<u>Are you he who is to come, or shall</u> <u>we wait for</u> <u>another?</u>' 20 *And when the men came to him, they said, 'John the Baptist has sent us to you to ask,* "<u>*Are you he who is to come, or shall we wait for another?*</u>" 21 *In that hour Jesus cured many of diseases and plagues and evil spirits, and to many who were blind he gave sight.* 22 And he answered and said to them, 'Go and proclaim to John what you have seen and heard: the blind see, the lame walk, lepers are cleansed, the deaf hear, dead are raised, the gospel is preached to the poor; 23 and blessed is he who takes no offence at me.'

24 *Now when the messengers of John had gone,* Jesus began to speak to the crowds of people concerning John: '<u>What did you go out</u> into the wilderness to see? A reed shaken by the wind? 25 Or <u>what did you go out</u> to see? A man clothed in soft clothing? Look, those who wear gorgeous clothes and live in luxury are *in royal palaces.* 26 Or <u>what</u> then <u>did you go out</u> to see? A prophet? Yes, I tell you, more than a prophet. 27 This is he of whom it is written, "Look, I send my messenger before you, who shall prepare your way before you." 28 I tell you, among those born of a woman none is greater than John; but the least in the kingdom of God is greater than he.'

29 *And all the people that heard him and the toll collectors justified God and had themselves baptized with the baptism of John. 30 But the Pharisees and the scribes rejected the counsel of God for themselves and were not baptized by him.*

31 'To what shall I compare *the men* of this generation, and what are they like? 32 They are like the children who sit in the market place and call *to one another,* "We played for you, and you did not dance; we sang lamentations, and you did not weep." 33 For John *the Baptist* has come, eats no *bread* and drinks no *wine;* and *you* say, "He has a demon." 34The Son of man has come, eats and drinks, and *you* say, "Look, this man is a glutton and drunkard, a friend of toll collectors and sinners." 35 And wisdom has been justified by all her children.'

Redaction

[18–19] Verse 18 is a redactional transition; in v. 18b, for 'two disciples' cf. 10.2; 19.29; v. 19, for 'Lord' cf. 6.46.

[20–21] These verses repeat the charge given in v. 19 and emphasize the healings of Jesus, which he carries out in the presence of the messengers. Verse 21 has developed from 'what you have seen and heard' (v. 22) and the language is word for word Lukan. The healing of the blind is mentioned because Luke has not yet narrated any healing of the blind in his Gospel.

[22–23] The preaching to the poor stands emphatically at the end of the list in v. 22 and takes up 6.20b. In other words, miracles are an expression of Jesus' concern for the poor. The beginning of the time of salvation can be recognized from Jesus' preaching and his miraculous deeds. The beatitude refers back to the Baptist's question in v. 19.

[24–26] These verses contain three rhetorical questions to convince the readers. John is neither a reed shaken by the wind nor a man in fine garments but more than a prophet. Verse 25b contains an explanation for Luke's readership (cf. Matt. 7.8).

[27] This verse develops the significance of John for salvation history with a quotation from Mal. 3.1. Cf. 1.17, 76 and similarly Mark 1.2, from where Luke has transposed it here following Q (?).

[28] This verse is taken over by Luke unchanged from Q and appears similarly in Thomas 46.

[29–30] These verses contain a narrative which is nevertheless part of Jesus' discourse. The passage probably derives from Luke. The verses are meant to clarify to readers the enigmatic saying v. 35. Wisdom probably means God, her children the people and toll collectors, as opposed to the Pharisees, and 'justify' the praise of God through the fulfilment of his will, baptism. Here vv. 29–30 have the function of a transition. They lead from one section in which the people has a positive attitude to John (vv. 24–28) to another in which a negative form of behaviour emerges (vv. 31–34).

[31] Luke adds 'men'.

[33] 'Bread' and 'wine' are added by Luke to the Q text.

[35] This verse takes up v. 29 (key word 'justify'). According to the context the people, the toll collectors and the sinners are regarded as children of wisdom, which because of v. 29 is to be identified with God (vv. 29, 34). For they heard John and Jesus as messengers of God.

Tradition

[18–28] This passage has been composed on the basis of Q, as is evident from a comparison with Matt. 11.2–11. The Q text centres on the question whether Jesus really is the one to come in the end time as announced by the Baptist himself, and answers it positively. But at the same time the beatitude in v. 23 sounds like a threat against the Baptist's disciples, who do not recognize the claim of the followers of

Jesus. The miracles enumerated in v. 22 take place in the time of salvation which has dawned with Jesus.

[24–28] John remains only the forerunner of the kingdom of God and is the messenger announced in Mal. 3.1.

[31–35] These verses come from Q (cf. on Matt. 11.16–19). Within the Q parable there are two testimonies by others about John and Jesus (vv. 33–34) which must still be analysed individually.

Historical

[18–28] These verses are generally formulated from a post-Easter perspective and are therefore inauthentic – including v. 28. John could not have put the question attributed to him to a historical person, for he expected the coming judgment and the Stronger One, who at all events is a heavenly figure. But vv. 22–23 may give an accurate historical account of Jesus' understanding of himself without reference to John.

[31–35] Cf. on Matt. 11.16–19.

Luke 7.36–50: The anointing of Jesus by the woman who was a sinner

36 One of the Pharisees invited him to eat with him. And he went into the Pharisee's house, and reclined at table. 37 And look, a woman was in the city, who was a sinner. When she learned that he was reclining at table in the Pharisee's house, she brought a glass with oil for anointing, 38 and came from behind *to his feet*, wept, and began to wet his feet with tears and to dry them with the hair of her head, and kissed his feet and anointed them with the oil. 39 Now when the Pharisee who had invited him saw (it), he said to himself, 'If this man were *a prophet*, he would have known who and what sort of woman this is who is touching him, for she is a sinner.' 40 Jesus answered and said to him, 'Simon, I have something to say to you.' And he said, 'Teacher, speak!'

41 'A creditor had two debtors. One owed five hundred silver coins, and the other fifty. 42 And when they could not pay, he forgave them both. Now which of them will love him more?' 43 Simon answered and said, 'I think the one to whom he forgave more.' And he said to him, 'You have judged rightly.'

44 And he turned towards the woman and said to Simon, 'Do you see this woman? I entered your house; you gave me no water for my feet, but she has wet my feet with her tears and wiped them with her hair.

45 You gave me no kiss, but from the time I came in this woman has not ceased to kiss my feet.

46 You did not anoint my head with oil, but she has anointed my feet with oil of anointing.

47 Therefore I say to you, her many sins have been forgiven, for she showed much love; but he who is forgiven little, loves little.'

48 And he said to her, 'Your sins have been forgiven.'

49 *Then those who were reclining at table with him began to say among themselves, 'Who is this who even forgives sins?' 50 And he said to the woman, 'Your faith has saved you; go in peace.'*

Redaction

The basis of the analysis is the observation that Luke has read the anointing at Bethany in Mark 14.3–9 and deliberately omitted it, although in the passion story he follows Mark relatively closely. In other words *he deliberately brings this story forward* and provides it with additional detail.

Luke adds this story because of the situation of the meal, Jesus' dealings with sinners and the criticism of the Pharisees (cf. vv. 30,34). Is the narrative meant e.g. to defend eating with 'sinners' in the community?

[36] Cf. v. 49; 11.37; 14.1.

[37] 'Sinner' – to be specific historically, 'prostitute' – links to '(friend of toll collectors and) sinners' in v. 34 and foreshadows v. 39 end. Judging from the context, 'the town' might be Nain (cf. v. 11).

[38] This verse depicts a grateful gesture on the part of the woman; here the loosing of the hair has erotic connotations. Luke tells a gripping story.

[39] 'Prophet' takes up the same expression from v. 16. The hospitable Pharisee is indignant that Jesus lets himself be touched by an unclean prostitute, and thus provides Luke with the background for the following remarks.

[40] This verse leads on to vv. 41–43.

[41–43] For the parable of the two debtors see under Tradition.

[44–46] In Lukan style, these verses contain three contrasts between the woman who is a sinner and the Pharisee.

[47] The first part of the verse gives the impression that the woman is promised forgiveness in gratitude for her demonstration of love, whereas in the second part of the verse the relationship between forgiveness and love is almost reversed.

[48–49] These verses derive from Luke. With them he manages to make Jesus forgive more clearly than in vv. 41–43 and in v. 47 itself.

[50] Luke emphasizes that the faith of the woman who is a sinner has brought about forgiveness and salvation. Cf. elsewhere 8.48 and 18.42 – each time in connection with Mark (5.34; 10.52) – on the statement that faith has saved the woman who is a sinner. In both the passages mentioned and in the Lukan special material (17.19), Jesus' statement each time follows a healing of the sick.

Tradition

The narrative of the anointing of Jesus by the woman who is a sinner is a development of Mark 14.3–9 or a combination of this pericope with a tradition about Jesus' encounter with a prostitute. At the same time there was a fusion with a parable which was not an intrinsic part of the story, vv. (40,) 41–43 (,47). But the different directions of statements in the passages have not completely been smoothed out: whereas in the parable the remission of debts comes first and is then the criterion for the debtor's love of the creditor, in the narrative the love of the prostitute seems to bring forgiveness.

All in all, the tradition has become a story of love for Jesus. The result is that the sins of anyone who loves Jesus in this way must be forgiven. Cf. a corresponding example from the Arab world:

'On a journey a prostitute went past a dog which was lying panting and perishing at the side of a well – then she took off her shoe, tied it to her head scarf and drew water for the dog with it. Therefore her sins are forgiven' (Wellhausen).

Historical

If the story of the woman who was a sinner must be regarded as a mere development of Mark 14.3–9 it is unhistorical. But as the encounter of Jesus with a prostitute comes from the Lukan special tradition, this may be historical. For the contact of Jesus with shady people is a fact. The historicity of the encounter of Jesus with a prostitute is supported by the criterion of offensiveness. 'We would be indignant about the invasion by a prostitute of a party, even if it consisted only of men, in quite a different way from the Pharisees' (Wellhausen). However, the details of the encounter are unclear. For example, I do not think that it is possible to decide whether Jesus forgave this woman her sins. But for the historicity of the claim of Jesus to forgive sins cf. on Mark 2.1–12.

The parable of the two debtors in the tradition (vv. 41–43) has a resemblance to Matt. 18.23–33, and for the same reasons as the parable contained there goes back to Jesus.

Luke 8.1–3: The discipleship of women

1 *And it happened in the following time, that he wandered from town to town and from village to village, preaching and proclaiming the kingdom of God. The twelve (were) with him. 2 And some women who had been healed of evil spirits and sicknesses,* Mary, called Magdalene, *from whom seven demons had gone out,* 3 *and* Joanna, the wife of Chuza, Herod's steward, and Susanna, *and many others, who provided for him out of their means.*

Redaction and tradition

The passage gives a summary survey of the next major section 8.4–9.50. Jesus is travelling and addresses the message of the kingdom of God to every place in the land. That he is accompanied by the twelve is highly important to Luke. Apart from the proper names, 8.1–3 is word for word Lukan.

[1] For the travel motif cf. 9.6; 13.22. For the preaching of the kingdom of God see on 4.43.

[2] Luke derives information about the others who accompany Jesus on his travels from Mark 15.41. The reference to the evil spirits and the seven demons who have gone out of Mary Magdalene similarly derive from Luke, who alone inserts the word 'demon' ten times into Mark, which he has in front of him (cf. 4.33, 35; 8.27, 29, 30, 33, 35, 38; 9.1, 42).

[3] For Joanna cf. 24.10. Only the information that she was married to Chuza, a steward of Herod, and the name Susanna reflect tradition. The note about well-to-do women in the company of Jesus derives from later times (cf. Acts 16.14; 17.4, 12). Luke has projected them back into the time of Jesus.

Historical

Apart from the names, the historical yield is nil.

Luke 8.4–15: The parable of the sower and its interpretation

4 *Now when many people came together and (people) from all the towns flocked to him, he said in a parable:*

5 'A sower went out to sow *his seed*. And in *his* sowing, some fell along the path, and *it was trodden under foot* and the birds of the air devoured it. 6 And some fell on the rock and grew up and withered away, because it had no *moisture*. 7 And some fell *in the midst of thorns*; and the thorns grew with it and choked it. 8 And some fell into good soil and *grew* and yielded a hundredfold.'

As he said this, *he called out*, 'Whoever has ears to hear, let him hear.'

9 *And his disciples* asked him what *this* parable meant. 10 And he said, 'To you it has been given *to know the* mysteries of the kingdom of God, but for the others (they are only) in parables, so that they may see and yet not see, and hear and yet not understand.

11 Now the parable is this: *The seed is the word of God.* 12 Those along the path are those who hear it, then the *devil* comes and takes away the word from their hearts, *that they may not believe and be saved.* 13 And those on the rock (are) they who, when they hear it, receive the word with joy, but they have no root; they *believe* for a while and in time *of temptation fall away.* 14 And that which fell among the thorns is those who hear, but as on the way they are choked by the cares and riches and *the pleasures of life* and *do not come to maturity.* 15 And that

on the good soil is those who *with a noble and good heart* hear the word and *hold it fast* and bring forth fruit *with patience*.

Redaction

This section is based on Mark 4.1–20 as a source.

[4] This is a typical Lukan introduction. Luke has already worked Mark 4.1, which he has before him at this point, into 5.3 and therefore does not use it here.

[5] Luke introduces his interest in the word of God here (cf. later 11b). Furthermore he emphasizes that the seed is trodden on the path. The interpretation (v. 12) does not go into this.

[6] This verse abbreviates Mark 4.5–6. It does not say that the seeds shoot up quickly because of a lack of depth, nor does it speak of the scorching heat of the sun, but merely of a lack of moisture, whereas the interpretation (v. 13) speaks with Mark 5.6 of a lack of roots.

[7] This verse omits the observation about the total failure (cf. Mark 4.7 end).

[8] This does not note the success graded into three groups, but one which is overwhelming, 'a hundredfold'.

[9–10] Luke makes the section about the meaning of the parable discourse, which in Mark 4.10–12 can still clearly be recognized as a secondary insertion, into an introduction to the following interpretation of the parable which brings it up to date. In contrast to Mark, the interpretation relates only to the one concrete parable. The disciples are no longer a special group which receives secret knowledge. As in Matthew (13.11), Jesus emphasizes that it has been given to the disciples to *know* the secrets of the rule of God (the verb is absent from Mark). Luke passes over the harsh talk of hardening in Mark 4.12 (similarly Matthew) and transposes it to the end of Acts (28.27).

[11–15] For the changes to Mark in the interpretation of the parable cf. the italics in the translation. Here are some examples: instead of 'Satan' (Mark 4.15), Luke writes devil (v. 12); Luke in v. 13 splits the unusual expression 'people of the moment' (Mark 4.17) into two ways of believing, premature faith on the one hand and apostasy on the other. Only Luke uses the word 'bring to maturity' (v. 14). Instead of mentioning the success at three levels Luke mentions it in one form in v. 9, this time with the admonition to be patient.

Historical

Cf. on Mark 4.1–20.

Luke 8.16–18: Sayings about hearing rightly

16 'No one lights a lamp and covers it with a vessel or puts it under a bed; rather, he puts it on the lampstand, that those who enter may see the light. 17 For nothing is hid that will not be made manifest and nothing is secret that will not be known and come to light. 18 So take heed *how* you hear! For to him who has will more be given, and from him who has not, even what he thinks that he has will be taken away.'

Redaction and tradition

In this section Luke is using Mark 4.21–25 and Q.

[16] This verse is also contained in Q (Matt. 5.15f./Luke 11.33). The Q version is included in the use of Mark, the beginning of which (Mark 4.21a) has been omitted.

[17] This verse takes over Mark 4.22, but similarly has a parallel in Q (Matt. 10.26/Luke 12.2). Luke means to indicate that the community of disciples keeps nothing secret. Its knowledge must come to light.

[18] The beginning of what Luke has before him in Mark (4.24–25) is omitted (as in v. 16). The commandment to hear rightly relates to the nature of hearing in the parable vv. 11–15.

Historical

Cf. on Mark 4.21–25.

Luke 8.19–21: The true kinsfolk of Jesus

19 And his mother and his brothers came to him, but they could not reach him because of the crowd. 20 And he was told, 'Your mother and your brothers are standing outside and want to see you.' 21 But he answered and said to them, 'My mother and my brothers are these who *hear* the *word* of God *and* do it.'

Redaction and tradition

Luke uses Mark 3.31–35, but like Matthew omits Mark 3.21 (Jesus is said by his family to be crazy) in order to tone it down. He puts the story about Jesus' true kinsfolk after the discourse on parables in which the people of 8.4 is present. It serves to explain v. 15: 'who . . . hear the word and hold it fast.'

[19–21] Luke's point corresponds to that of Mark, which he has in front of him: the true kinsfolk of Jesus are those who hear and do God's word (Mark 3.35: 'those who do the will of God'). Thus Luke makes a connection with the preceding parable of the sower and its interpretation. In agreement with v. 15, v. 21 speaks of hearing and doing the word of God. Of course Luke identifies the preaching of Jesus and the word of God (cf. 5.1; 8.11; Acts 4.31; 6.2, 7; 8.14, etc.). The listening community is the real family of Jesus.

Historical

Cf. on Mark 3.31–35.

Luke 8.22–25: The stilling of the storm on the lake

22 *It happened one day that he got into a boat* with his disciples. And he said to them, 'Let us go across to the other side *of the lake*.' So they set out. 23 And as they were sailing he fell asleep, and a squall came down *on the lake, and their boat was filling with water, and they were in danger.* 24 *And they went to him,* woke him, *and said, 'Master, Master,* we are lost!' But when he awoke he threatened the wind and the waves of water and they ceased, and there was a calm. 25 And he said to them, '*Where is your* faith?' Full of fear, they marvelled and said to one another, 'Who then is this, that *he commands wind and water,* and they obey him?'

Redaction and tradition

Luke is using Mark 4.35–41

[22] The point of time is not defined: Jesus is not already in the ship but gets in, and not on the same day (Mark 4.35), but *one* day (8.22).

[23] Like Matthew, Luke deletes the superfluous mention of the other boat (Mark 4.36). Verse 23b is an abbreviation of Mark 4.37.

[24] The rebuke to Jesus is toned down and is more modest than in Mark, which says, 'Do you not care that we are perishing?' (4.38).

[25] The reproof to the disciples (Mark 4.40, 'Why are you so afraid?') is deleted; the address is a kind of Christianization (Wellhausen), which turn the question 'Why do you have no faith?' (Mark 4.40b) into the question of (Christian) faith. The motif inserted by Luke here, that Jesus commands winds and waters, comes from Mark 1.27.

Historical

Cf. on Mark 4.35–41.

Luke 8.26–39: The healing of the possessed man of Gerasa

26 And they went into the region of the Gerasenes, *which lies opposite Galilee.* 27 And as he stepped out on land, there met him a man *from the city* who had *demons* and for a long time *had worn no clothes*, and he lived not in a house but in the tombs. 28 And when he saw Jesus, he cried out and fell down before him, and cried with a loud voice, 'What have you to do with me, Jesus, Son of the Most High God? I *beseech* you, do not torment me!' 29 *For he had commanded the unclean spirit to come out of the man; for often it had seized him and he had been fettered hand and feet and guarded, but he broke the bonds and was driven by the demon into a lonely region.* 30 And Jesus asked him, 'What is your name?' He said, 'Legion' – because many demons had entered him. 31 And they begged him not to command them *to go to hell.*

32 Now a herd of many pigs was feeding on the pasture on the mountain; and they begged him to let them enter these. So he let them. 33 And when the *demons* went out of the man, they entered the pigs, and the herd rushed down the slope into the lake and were drowned.

34 And when the herdsmen saw what had happened, they fled and told it in the city and in the country. 35 Then they went out to see what had happened, and they came to Jesus, and found the man from whom the demons had gone out, clothed and in his right mind, sitting *at the feet of Jesus*; and they were afraid. 36 And those who had seen (it) told them how the possessed man had been saved. 37 And all the people of the region of the Gerasenes asked him to leave them; *for they were seized with great fear.* And he got into the boat *and returned.* 38 And the man from whom the demons had gone begged to be allowed to remain with him. But he sent him away and said, 39 'Return to your home, and tell what a great thing *God* has done for you!' Then he went away and proclaimed throughout the city what Jesus had done for him.

Redaction and tradition

Luke is using Mark 5.1–20.

[26] This verse identifies the area which is the Lukan counterpart to Peraea and the Decapolis in Mark. The significance of the story in Luke, which because of the note of place in v. 26b is meant to be an excursion into foreign territory, is that it gives an exemplary demonstration of power outside Jewish territory; for that was of fundamental importance for the mission.

[27] Luke has inferred the lack of clothing from Mark 5.15. Initially he passes over Mark 5.3b–5, so that he can go on without delay to relate the encounter of the possessed man with Jesus.

[28] The man asks to be spared and does not conjure Jesus (thus, however, Mark 5.7). Here he fully acknowledges the dignity of Jesus.

[29] Here Luke so to speak puts Mark 5.4f. after Mark 5.8. In doing so he has hardly improved the flow of the text.

[30] The legion consists of many demons.

[31] Instead of 'send out of the region' (Mark 5.10), Luke reads 'drive to hell'. The demons are afraid of going immediately where they will really go only at the last judgment, to hell. This corresponds to the picture of history in the parable of the rich man and poor Lazarus (16.19–13), where the rich man goes to hell immediately after his death and not at the last judgment.

[36] 'And about the pigs' (Mark 5.16) is omitted, and with it an important reason for the request for him to go away.

[37] For the motif of numinous fear cf. 1.12, 65; Acts 5.5, 11.

[39] 'Lord' is here replaced with 'God' in order to exclude possible misunderstandings of the following clause ('what Jesus had done for him').

Historical

Cf. on Mark 5.1–20.

Luke 8.40–56: The raising of Jairus' daughter and the healing of the woman with a flow of blood

40 *Now when Jesus returned*, the people welcomed him. *For they were all waiting for him.* 41 *And look*, a man came named Jairus, and he was *a ruler* of the synagogue. And he fell at Jesus' feet and begged him to come to his house, 42 for he had an *only* daughter, about twelve years old, and she lay dying. But as he went there, the crowds of people pressed in on him.

43 And a woman who had suffered from a flow of blood for twelve years, which no one had been able to cure, 44 came up and touched the fringe of his garment from behind, and immediately the flow of her blood ceased. 45 And Jesus said, 'Who was it who touched me?' *Now when all denied (it), Peter said, 'Master,* the crowds are surrounding you and pressing in on you.' 46 But Jesus said, 'Someone touched me; *for I perceived that power went out from me.'* 47 And when the woman saw that she had not remained hidden she came trembling, and fell down before him and *reported* in the presence of all the people why she had touched him, and how she had been immediately healed. 48 And he said to her, 'My daughter, your faith has saved you. Go in peace.'

49 While he was still speaking, someone from the ruler of the synagogue's people came and said, 'Your daughter is dead; do not trouble the teacher any more.' 50 But when Jesus heard that, he answered him, 'Do not fear; only believe, *and she will be saved.'* 51 And when he came to the house, he permitted no one to enter with him except Peter and John and James, *and the father of the child and the mother.* 52 And all were weeping and bewailing her. But he said, 'Do not weep! She is not dead, but sleeping.' 53 And they laughed at him, *as they knew that she was dead.* 54 But he took her hand and called, 'Child, arise.' 55 *And her spirit returned*, and she got up at once; and he commanded that something should be given to her to eat. 56 And her parents were amazed. But he charged them to tell no one what had happened.

Redaction and tradition

Luke is using Mark 5.21–43.

[40a] This verse is a Lukan link. The people was last mentioned in 8.4 as the audience of the parable.

[41] Luke corrects the information in Mark, which presupposes several rulers in a synagogue.

[42–43] The way in which the information about the age of the girl, who in Luke becomes an only daughter (cf. 7.12), is put in parallel with the duration of the woman's illness is a literary artifice on the part of Luke. Moreover, bringing the note about the girl's age forward is an improvement, since in Mark, which Luke had in front of him, it only appears at the end of the story (5.42). Luke has abbreviated Mark's account of the sickness. The unfavourable verdict on the physicians (Mark 5.26) is lacking in the earliest manuscripts (it has been introduced here from Mark by later texts).

[44] Whereas most scholars assume that Luke is dependent on Mark, the similarity in drift and content between this verse and Matt. 9.20 is remarkable.

[45–46] Peter becomes the disciples' spokesman (Mark 5.31, 'his disciples'). At the same time Luke tones down the disciples' lack of respect in Mark 5.31 and emphasizes the omniscience of Jesus by making v. 46b link back to v. 45a.

[47] This verse almost turns the scene into a public confession.

[50] In the answer to the ruler of the synagogue, who has just heard of the death of his daughter, Jesus appears as the saviour in need, for Luke adds to the Markan text, 'she will be saved'.

[51] The placing of John before James is characteristic of Luke (9.28; Acts 1.13). The presence of the parents at the healing is already mentioned here.

[52] This verse omits the driving out of the wailing women (Mark 5.40).

[53] This verse tightens up and passes over the further notice in Mark (5.40) that Jesus goes to the girl and the parents and takes his disciples with him.

[54–55] The mysterious *talitha koum* from Mark 5.41 is missing from the awakening call: the raising itself is depicted as a return of the spirit, which has heard Jesus' call. The instruction to give the child something to eat (cf. 24.41f.) serves to demonstrate that the miracle has actually happened. It is appropriate at this point and not, as in Mark (5.43c), after the command to go on telling the story.

[56] Luke had already brought forward (v. 42) the note about the age of the girl which Mark somewhat clumsily put here. The subject of the astonishment is the parents, who were already present at the healing (v. 51). All in all, Luke has improved the conclusion of the story stylistically.

Historical

Cf. on Mark 5.21–43.

Luke 9.1–6: The sending out of the twelve

1 And he called the twelve together and gave them *power* and authority *over all demons and (authority)* to heal diseases. 2 *And he sent them out to preach the kingdom of God and to heal.* 3 *And he said to them,* 'Take nothing with you on the way, neither a staff, nor a bag, nor bread, nor money; nor (should you) have two undergarments. 4 And whatever house you enter, stay there, and depart again from there 5 and wherever they do not receive you – go away from *that town* and shake off the dust from your feet as a testimony against them.'

6 And they departed *and wandered from village to village. They preached the good news* and healed *everywhere.*

Redaction and tradition

Luke uses Mark 6.7–13 in this section, but at the same time is influenced by the Q tradition (Luke 10.1–12). Note that in 22.35–38 the Lukan Jesus takes back the mission instructions of vv. 3–5.

[1] In contrast to Mark, Luke narrates the sending of the disciples only after these have been endowed with power and authority. 'Power and authority' refers back to 4.36, where 'all' are amazed at Jesus' capacity for miraculous healing. This capacity is important for Luke. Therefore he already mentions it here and not at the end of the depiction of the activity of the twelve, as Mark (6.13) does.

[2] This is a summary note with two themes which are important for Luke: the proclamation of the kingdom of God (cf. 8.1; Acts 28.31) and the healings by the disciples. Both also correspond to the activity of the early church.

[3] The prohibition of money, which Mark does not mention, is clearly influenced by Q (cf. Matt. 10.9).

[4–5] In these verses instructions are given about staying in lodgings: the missionaries are not to change their place without reason. There is clear influence from Q in the word 'dust' used in the act of repudiation (cf. 9.5 with Matt. 10.14; Luke 10.11; Acts 15.51; 22.23). There is no mention at all of driving out demons or anointing with oil (Mark 6.13).

[6] In contrast to the Markan account, which depicts them as preachers of repentance, the messengers proclaim the good news, the kingdom of God (cf. v. 2); 'everywhere' is a Lukan generalization (cf. Acts 18.2, etc.).

Historical

For the historical question cf. the summary discussion on Matt. 10.5b–15.

Luke 9.7–9: Herod's perplexity

7 Now Herod, *the tetrarch*, heard of all that was done, and he *was perplexed, because it was said by some,* 'John has been raised from the dead', 8 by others, 'Elijah has appeared', and by others, 'One of *the old* prophets has arisen'. 9 And Herod said, 'John I beheaded; *but who is this about whom I hear such things?' And he sought to see him.*

Redaction and tradition

The section has been composed solely on the basis of Mark 6.14–16. In the framework of the Gospel of Luke the scene looks forward to the passion story (23.6–16) and at the same time points forward to 13.31–33. There is a commentary on the present pericope in 9.18–22.

[7] This verse makes it clear that the Herod mentioned by Mark is Herod Antipas, the ruler of the territory in which Jesus is active. Luke also makes Mark, which he has in front of him, more precise at other points, like 3.19f. Luke deliberately passes over the mention of the miracles (Mark 6.14) so that no miracle is attributed to John even indirectly (cf. similarly John 10.41). Herod is introduced as a questioner who is tormented by public opinion.

[8] This verse transforms the expectation of a prophet into that of one of the old prophets. These are not the same thing.

[9] Herod's answer in v. 9a is quite different from that in Mark. He does not share the belief in the risen prophet. The beheading of the Baptist is reported here on the basis of Mark 6.16; his arrest had already been mentioned in 3.19–20. Herod's question in v. 9b finds its fulfilment in 23.8 and a provisional answer in the story of the feeding which follows. His kinsmen had already desired to see Jesus (8.19f.). For Luke this is nothing but mere 'curiosity'. Luke omits the supplement Mark 6.17–29.

Historical

The historical plausibility of the scene shaped by Luke disappears with the improbability of Luke 23.6–12. Herod Antipas did not want to see Jesus.

Luke 9.10–17: The feeding of the five thousand

10 And the apostles *returned and told him what they had done*. And he took them and withdrew apart to a city called Bethsaida. 11 But the crowds of people noticed it and followed him. *And he welcomed them and spoke to them of the kingdom of God, and cured those in need of healing.*

12 *Now the day began to decline. The twelve* came to him and said, 'Send the crowd away, so that they (can) go into the neighbouring villages and farms, to find lodgings and food; for here we are in a lonely place.' 13 But he said to them, 'You give them something to eat.' But they answered, '*We have no more than* five loaves and two fishes, unless we are to go and buy food for all these people.' 14 For there were *about* five thousand men. And he said to his disciples, 'Make them settle down in companies, of about fifty each.' 15 And they did so and made them all settle down. 16 And he took the five loaves and the two fishes, looked up to heaven, blessed and broke them and gave (them) to the disciples to set (them) before the crowd. 17 And they ate and were all filled. And they took up the fragments of bread left over, twelve baskets full.

Redaction and tradition

Luke is using Mark 6.30–44. Herod's question who it is about whom great things are being heard is given a first answer by the present pericope. At the same time it creates the possibility of Peter's confession which follows. That its content cannot be taken for granted is shown by the verdict of the multitudes on Jesus that he is John, Elijah or a prophet. Peter's confession is then followed by the first prediction of the passion. We also find this contrast between miracle and prediction of the passion in 9.43b–45. For Peter the miracle of the feeding is the impetus to confession, and thus a real epiphany; however, the nature of the divinity of Jesus is then defined more closely by the proclamation of the passion. The transfiguration which follows is similarly orientated on the passion (cf. 9.31).

[10–11a] The statement about the return clarifies Mark 6.30 and picks up 9.6, which had spoken of the preaching and healing activity of the twelve. Luke omits the phrase 'what they taught' (6.30) from Mark. Luke replaces 'to a lonely place' with 'to a city called Bethsaida'. Luke simplifies the note of place in Mark 6.33, which is difficult to understand (similarly also Matthew).

[11b] Luke reports Jesus' twofold activity: speaking about the kingdom of God – its nearness is not a theme – and healing those in need of help. By contrast Mark reports Jesus having compassion on the people and his teaching.

[12] Luke alters the clause 'and the hour was already advanced' (Mark 6.35) into 'the day began to decline' (cf. 24.29). As already in v. 10 he speaks of 'the twelve' instead of 'the disciples' (thus Mark 6.35). In Luke the disciples not only suggest getting food but also think of lodgings for the crowd.

[13] The disciples' reaction to Jesus' invitation resembles the Matthaean version (Matt. 14.17). They immediately know how much food they have. Here the com-

parative in the answer 'we have no more than five loaves' is meant to mark the contrast with the later multiplication of the loaves.

[14–15] In contrast to Mark, Luke gives the number of the people *before* the feeding, evidently in order to emphasize the miracle which follows (cf. the contrast motif in v. 13b). He does not mention the green grass and has the crowd settling down only in groups of fifty, as opposed to Mark, where the crowd reclines in fifties and hundreds. Mark 6.40 describes how the crowd obeys the command of the disciples and v. 15 how the disciples obey the command of Jesus.

[16] This verse largely corresponds to Mark (6.41). Luke only makes an accusative dependent on 'bless'. It is worth noting that, like Matthew (14.19), Luke omits the Markan apodosis about the distribution of the fish.

[17] This verse largely corresponds to Mark 6.42–43.

Yield of the comparison with Mark 6.30–44: (a) The story contains marked tendencies to emphasize the miracle. (b) In contrast to Mark (and Matthew), Luke speaks of the twelve. (c) In Luke, too, we can see a reduction of the motif of the fishes in contrast to Mark. After the mention of the fishes in v. 16a we hear no more of them. Although the fishes could be included in 'them' (v. 16b), it is not explicitly said either that they are distributed or that their remnants are collected.

Historical

Cf. on Mark 6.30–44.

Luke 9.18–27: Peter's messianic confession and call to discipleship

18 *And it happened that as he was praying alone* the disciples were with him, and he asked them and said, 'Who do the people say that I am?' 19 And they answered and said, 'John the Baptist; but others say Elijah, others (think) that *one of the old* prophets has risen.' 20 And he said to them, 'But you, who do you say that I am?' And Peter answered and said, 'The Christ *of God.*' 21 But he threatened them and commanded them to say this to no one, 22 saying, 'The Son of man must suffer many things and be rejected by the elders and chief priests and scribes and be killed *and on the third day be raised.*'

23 And he said *to all*, 'If anyone would come after me, let him deny himself and take up his cross *daily* and follow me, 24 for whoever would save his life will lose it; and whoever loses his life for my sake will save it. 25 For what does it profit a man if he gains the whole world and destroys or forfeits himself? 26 For whoever is ashamed of me and of my words, of him will the Son of man be ashamed when he comes in *his* glory and (the glory) of the Father and of the *holy* angels. 27 But I tell you *in truth*, of those standing *there* some will not taste death before they see the kingdom of God.'

Redaction and tradition

Unlike Matthew, Luke passes over the great section Mark 6.45–8.26. He might have known it but deliberately omitted it. *Possible reasons*: (a) Luke saw the second feeding story (Mark 8) as a superfluous repetition of the first and (b) the dispute about clean and unclean (Mark 7) as uninteresting or as too aggressive and antinomian for his readers. Moreover he wanted to put the feeding and Peter's confession directly one after the other, for feeding, confession, proclamation of suffering and transfiguration represent a block to which Luke gives a special function in the construction of his Gospel.

Mark 8.34–9.1 is the sole source for the present section.

[18] As in 3.21; 6.12; 9.28, Jesus' prayer prepares for an important event. The harshness of the style and content of the statement – Jesus' prayer in loneliness on the one hand and the presence of the disciples on the other – suggests a literary seam which is typical of a new beginning. (The first part of v. 18 recalls Mark 6.46.)

[19] Cf. 9.8, where as here the expression in Mark, 'one of the prophets', is changed into 'one of the old prophets'.

[20] 'The Christ of God' (cf. 2.26) replaces 'the Christ' (Mark 8.29).

[21] This' instead of 'about him' (Mark 8.30) is a clarification. In this way the Markan messianic secret is restyled into a misunderstanding of the passion.

[22] 'On the third day' (cf. 13.32; 18.33; 24.21, 46; Acts 10.40) is a correction or clarification of 'after three days'; 'be raised' makes the Markan 'rise' more precise. Luke deletes the conversation between Jesus and Peter which follows in the Markan original (8.32), because in it Jesus had addressed Peter as Satan. To address this man as Satan was too harsh for the author of Acts, who will celebrate Peter's successes. (It is no coincidence that in Luke, as well as the denial of Jesus by Peter which is narrated on the basis of Mark we also have the section Luke 22.31–32, see there.)

[23] Not only the disciples from vv. 18–22 are addressed, but *all*. This is a re-interpretation of Luke which is addressed to the readership. The instruction for *daily* discipleship applies to them.

[24–25] These verses adopt Mark 8.35–36 almost word for word, but 'and for the sake of the gospel' is omitted. The question in v. 25 is meant to make clear to the reader the uselessness of striving for earthly gain. Cf. the Lukan parallel 12.16–21: the Christian is to collect treasures *before God*.

[26] This verse, too, makes bearing the cross concrete.

[27] Luke deletes the words 'come in power' from the Markan original. In this way the event of the future coming becomes the present reality of the kingdom, for this is the object of the preaching. With Jesus the kingdom is present. The old man Simeon can die in peace, as he has seen salvation (2.30).

Historical

Cf. on Mark 8.34–9.1. By his redactional treatment Luke has further reduced the historical value of the scene.

Luke 9.28–36: The transfiguration of Jesus

28 *And it happened about eight days after these words,* that he took Peter and John and James and went up a mountain *to pray.* 29 *And it happened, while he was praying, the appearance of his face was altered,* and his clothing became *dazzling* white. 30 And look, two men talked with him, who were Moses and Elijah. 31 They appeared *in glory and announced his departure, which he was to accomplish in Jerusalem.* 32 *Now Peter and those who were with him were heavy with sleep. And when they awoke they saw his glory and the two men standing with him.* 33 *And it happened that as they were parting from him,* Peter said to Jesus, '*Master,* it is good that we are here, and we want to make three booths, one for you and one for Moses and one for Elijah.' Here he did not know what he was saying. 34 *And as he was speaking like this,* a cloud came and overshadowed them. *And they were afraid as they entered the cloud.* 35 And a voice came from the cloud, which said, 'This is my *chosen* Son, hear him.' 36 *And when the voice had spoken,* Jesus *was found* alone. And they kept silence and proclaimed in those days nothing of what they had seen.

Redaction and tradition

The Lukan peculiarities in the transfiguration story are so numerous that sometimes they are thought to be based on other traditions than Mark 9.2–8. But that is unnecessary, for to some degree Luke is rewriting the Markan version and making it serve his particular view.

[28–29] Why Luke changes the Markan number 'six' into 'about eight' is puzzling. The purpose of going up the mountain is prayer, which may look forward to Jesus' last prayer on the Mount of Olives (22.29). Jesus is again separated from the people (cf. v. 37). Luke here (and at other places, cf. Acts 1.13) alters the Markan order James/John.

[30–31] Moses and Elijah confirm Jesus' departure in Jerusalem which he had himself predicted (v. 22). The suffering is reported to Jesus himself. This is not a legitimation before the disciples but a confirmation for Jesus himself on his way of suffering. This corresponds to the way in which the scene of the baptism is shaped in Luke (3.21–22); it is focussed more strongly than in Mark on Jesus himself, not on the onlookers and John.

[32–33] The disciples' sleep similarly refers to the passion story, cf. 22.39–46.

[34] The disciples' fear is not caused by the appearance of Moses and Elijah (thus Mark) but is based on the fact that they enter the cloud. In this verse, as already in

vv. 32–33, Luke gives a particularly lively description of the situation and the persons involved.

[35] Luke writes 'chosen' instead of 'beloved' son, just as previously he wrote 'Christ of God' instead of 'Christ' (9.20b). In this way he aims at a greater solemnity of expression.

[36] By saying 'Jesus was found alone' Luke sees that the heavenly voice is clearly related to Jesus. Whereas in Mark the disciples say nothing without having to be commanded by the Lord, Luke reports that 'in those days' the disciples were silent, but not that in this they were following an order of Jesus.

Luke has deliberately omitted the conversation which follows in Mark (9.9–13). For Elijah to be forerunner, as he is in Mark 9.9–13, clashes with Luke's notion of the end events. He rejects any assumption of prophets returning from the past (cf. 9.7f.,19) and *contrary* to Mark 9.13a wants to save his readers from seeing John the Baptist as Elijah redivivus.

Historical

Cf. on Mark 9.2–8.

Luke 9.37–43a: The epileptic boy

37 *Now it happened on the next day, when they came down from the mountain, that a great crowd came to them.* 38 *And look*, a man from the crowd cried and said, 'Teacher, I beg you *to look on* my son, *for he is my only child,* 39 *and look, a spirit seizes him, and it suddenly cries out and convulses him till he foams and will hardly leave him and shatters him.* 40 And I begged your disciples to cast it out, but they could not.' 41 And Jesus answered and said, 'You faithless *and perverse* generation, how long am I to be with you and bear with you? Bring *your son* here.' 42 And as he was still on the way the demon tore him and convulsed him. But Jesus rebuked the unclean spirit and healed the boy and gave him back to his father. 43a *And all were astonished at the greatness of God.*

Redaction and tradition

Luke presents the narrative in a very much shorter form than Mark (9.14–29) and in so doing partially agrees with Matthew (17.14–21). But I presuppose that Mark was the only source for Luke.

[37] This verse is a link with the transfiguration story formulated by Luke, using Markan material.

[38] Luke says specifically that the sick child is the *only* son (cf. similarly 7.12).

[39] The sickness is told of in a different way from Mark 9.18a.

[40–41] The failure of the disciples is related in close agreement with Mark

(9.18b–19). But Luke no longer discusses the reason for the disciples' failure (later Mark 9.38f. differs).

[42–43a] Luke considerably abbreviates Mark (9.20–27), and adds a concluding sentence which contains the praise of God by the crowd (cf. 13.17; Acts 19.17).

Historical

Cf. on Mark 9.14–29.

Luke 9.43b–50: The disciples' incomprehension

43b *But while they were all marvelling at everything he did, he said to his disciples,* 44 '*Let these words sink into your ears:* for the Son of man is to be delivered into the hands of men.' 45 But they did not understand this saying, *and it was concealed from them, that they should not perceive it;* and they were afraid to ask him *about this saying.*

46 *And a discussion arose among them as to which of them was the greatest.* 47 *But Jesus knew the thought of their hearts,* took a child, put it in front of him 48 and said to them, 'Whoever receives this child in my name receives me, and whoever receives me receives him who sent me. For he who is the least among you all is the one who is great.'

49 And John answered and said, '*Master,* we saw a man casting out demons in your name, and we attempted to prevent him, because he does not follow *with* us.' 50 But Jesus said to him, 'Do not forbid him; for whoever is not against you is for *you*.'

Redaction and tradition

Luke presupposes Mark 9.30–41.

[43b–44] These verses develop 9.31 further. Verse 43b is a Lukan transitional phrase. In the instruction about his fate which follows, contrary to Mark Jesus says nothing about his resurrection. In this, Jesus' second announcement differs from the first (9.22). Thus the Lukan Jesus emphasizes an interpretation of his death which is important to Luke, namely Jesus' exemplary suffering (cf. 17.25; 18.32f.; 24.46).

[45] This verse reinforces Mark 9.32 ('but they did not understand the saying and were afraid to ask him') and by a general remark refers it to the plan of the saving event.

[46–48] The language of v. 46 is word for word Lukan, but presupposes Mark 9.33f. Luke attaches Mark 9.36–37 here and puts Mark 9.35 afterwards. In vv. 47–48a Jesus then presents a child as a model for the disciples and understands acceptance of it as acceptance of both him and his Father who has sent him. Partly changing Mark, which Luke has in front of him (9.35), and linking up with the dispute of the disciples in v. 46, v. 48b says that whoever has made himself like the child in the smallest things is in reality great.

[49b–50] Luke's formulation follows Mark 9.38–41, but omits vv. 39b and 41 and then passes over Mark 9.42–10.12. Verse 50b supports 'tolerant' behaviour towards another exorcist. Behaviour towards him is based on the fact that now the issue is common discipleship (of Christ) and no longer as in Mark the discipleship of the disciples. Cf. also the form of address' 'Master' (Luke), compared with 'Teacher' in Mark.

Historical

Cf. on Mark 9.30–41.

Luke 9.51–56: Turning towards Jerusalem

51 *Now it happened, when the days for him to be received up (from earth to heaven) were fulfilled, he set his face to travel to Jerusalem.* 52 And he sent messengers ahead of him, and they travelled and entered a village of the Samaritans to find lodgings for him. 53 And the people did not receive him, because his face was going in the direction of Jerusalem. 54 And when the disciples James and John saw it, they said, 'Lord, do you want us to tell fire to come down from heaven and consume them?' 55 But he turned round and threatened them. 56 *And they travelled to another village.*

Redaction and tradition

After Luke's formulation in 8.4–9.50 has followed Mark, here he begins his travel account, which extends from 9.51 to 19.27.

[51] This verse speaks in solemn style of the beginning of the journey which will end in Jerusalem. 'Receive up' comprises both being taken away from the earth as a result of death and being received into heaven through resurrection and ascension.

[52–53] The sending out of the messengers takes place just as it does a little later in 10.1. That the Samaritans do not receive them because they want to travel to Jerusalem is based on the conflict between Samaritans and Jews of which Luke knew. Thus he may have formulated the scene himself.

[54–55] The punitive judgment (on Samaria) suggested by the sons of Zebedee and the repudiation of this enterprise by Jesus has been inserted by Luke in the context on the basis of a tradition. Here v. 54 is too concrete not to derive from tradition. The verse indicates a specific attitude of the sons of Zebedee. They also appear very self-confident at other points, cf. Mark 9.38; 10.35.

[56] This verse is a Lukan framework which takes up v. 51.

Historical

[54] It seems natural to connect the reaction of the sons of Zebedee depicted here at the level of the tradition with the Aramaic name Boanerges ('sons of thunder') which Jesus gave them in Mark 3.17. 'The passionate remark of the sons of Zebedee shows them worthy of the name sons of thunder' (Wellhausen). They themselves wanted to bring fire down, and thus were confident that they could do what the God of the Old Testament, the thunderer, could do. But the verification of the name of the sons of Zebedee by this tradition does not necessarily make this tradition historically credible, if it means that the sons of Zebedee would have spoken the words in v. 54 at this time and on the occasion mentioned.

Luke 9.57–62: On discipleship

57 *And as they were travelling on the way*, someone said to him, 'I want to follow you wherever you go.' 58 And Jesus said to him, 'The foxes have holes and the birds of the air have nests, but the Son of man has nowhere to lay his head.' 59 *And he said to another, 'Follow me.'* But he said, '<u>First allow me</u> to go and bury my father.' 60 But he said to him, 'Let the dead bury their dead. *But as for you, go and proclaim the kingdom of God.*' 61 *And another said, 'I want to follow you, Lord; but first allow me to say farewell to those in my house.'* 62 *And Jesus said*, 'No one who puts his hand to the plough and looks back is fit for the kingdom of God.'

Redaction

This passage, which has been formulated on the basis of Q (cf. Matt. 8.19–22), prepares for the report of the mission of the seventy-two in 10.1–16. It is meant to prevent 9.51–55 (esp. 9.52) and 10.1–16 from clashing with each other. However, here in Luke it has a more appropriate place than in Matthew, because discipleship in the higher sense only takes place after Jesus goes to Jerusalem to take up his cross.

[57–58] The introduction (v. 57a) continues the beginning of the travel report which has just been given. The rest of the passage corresponds closely with Matt. 8.19–20.

[59–60] The beginning and end have been formulated by Luke. In Luke (v. 59a), Jesus takes the initiative, but in Q (cf. Matt. 8.21) it is another disciple. Verse 60b contains the typically Lukan notion that the kingdom of God must be proclaimed (cf. 8.1; 9.2, etc.), and prepares for 10.9, 11.

[61–62] The third follower, who like the first presents himself (cf. v. 54), but like the second makes a condition (v. 59), has probably been added here by Luke on the basis of a saying about discipleship in the tradition. That emerges from his absence in Matthew and from the number of three followers, which is conditioned by the redaction. Note too that he has been attached to the second saying, as is shown by the linking phrase 'first allow me'.

Tradition

The first two sayings about discipleship in vv. 57–60a derive from Q.

[57b–58] The homelessness of the wandering Jesus is described in the logia source *secondarily* as that of the Son of man. It is thus made clear to the community that discipleship of the homeless Jesus nevertheless means discipleship of the one to whom authority over all has been given.

[59–60a] These verses are a radical call to discipleship, which leads to a departure from the burial of parents required by the law.

[62] This is an isolated saying of Jesus, which in the form of a simile expresses the radical nature of the demand for decision. One may hardly use its commonplace nature as an argument against its origin from the tradition. For looking back cf. Gen. 19.26: Lot's wife is turned to a pillar of salt for looking back at Sodom and Gomorrah.

Historical

[57b–58] The first saying about discipleship is an authentic saying of Jesus if the secondary title 'Son of man' is replaced by 'the man' (Jesus). In it Jesus speaks of himself as man and in contrast to the foxes and the birds. This creates a sharp rhetorical point: I myself, Jesus, in contrast to the animals, have no firm abode and no home. Its authenticity is supported by its radical nature and by the ethos of homelessness which generally fits Jesus' activity.

[59–60a] The second saying about discipleship has a high degree of historicity. Jesus' criticism of the living burying dead members of their family is a clear 'transgression' of the law. For in Judaism, burial of the dead, and especially of parents, was a duty. Cf. e.g. the book of Tobit. But at any rate there were also examples from the prophetic tradition of the Old Testament which come near to Jesus' criticism. Thus God forbade Ezekiel to utter lament and to perform the ritual of mourning for his dead wife (Ezek. 24.15–24), or required Jeremiah to abstain from lamenting the dead (Jer. 16.5–7).

Note additionally that Jesus speaks of his contemporaries as dead. With them are to be included all those who find no access to the kingdom of God as Jesus proclaims it. This radical character, too, fits the preaching of Jesus.

[62] The saying in the third remark about discipleship is probably historical. This

is one of those sayings which are driven by the energy of the call to repentance, like v. 60a; Mark 8.35; 10.23b, 25; Matt. 7.13f.; 22.14.

Luke 10.1–20: The sending out of the seventy-two and their return

1 *After this the Lord appointed seventy-two others and sent them on ahead of him in pairs into every town and place where he himself wanted to enter.* 2 And he said to them, 'The harvest is great, but the labourers are few. Therefore pray the Lord of the harvest to send labourers into his harvest. 3 Go, *look*, I send you out as lambs in the midst of wolves. 4 Carry no purse, no bag, no sandals with you and greet no one on the way.

5 Whatever house you enter, first say, "Peace to this house!" 6 And if a son of peace is there, your peace shall rest upon him; but if not, it will return to you. 7 Remain in the house, eat and drink what (is set) before you by them. For the labourer is worthy of his wages. Do not go from one house to another house.

8 And whatever town you enter and they receive you, eat what is set before you. 9 And heal the sick in it and say to them, "The kingdom of God has come near *to you*." 10 But whatever town you enter and they do not receive you, go into its streets and say, 11 "Even the dust of your town that clings to our feet we shake off against you; nevertheless know this, that the kingdom of God has come near." 12 I tell you, it shall be more tolerable on that day for Sodom than for that town.

13 Woe to you, Chorazin, woe to you, Bethsaida; for if the mighty works done in you had been done in Tyre and Sidon, they would long since have repented, sitting in sackcloth and ashes. 14 But it will be more tolerable in the judgment for Tyre and Sidon than for you. 15 And you, Capernaum, will you be exalted to heaven? You will go down to Hades.

16 Whoever hears you hears me, and whoever rejects you rejects me, and whoever rejects me rejects him who has sent me.'

17 *And the seventy-two returned with joy and said,* 'Lord, even the demons are subject to us in your name.' 18 *He said to them,* 'I saw Satan fall like lightning from heaven. 19 *Look,* I have given you *authority* to tread on serpents and scorpions and over all the power of the enemy; and nothing shall hurt you. 20 But do not rejoice in this, that the spirits are subject to you, but rejoice that your names are inscribed in heaven.'

Redaction and tradition

Luke is prompted to such a discourse, which was framed by the sending out and the return of the disciples, by Mark (cf. Luke 9.1f., 10a with Mark 6.7, 30). On the whole Luke preserves the order of the logia from Q, whereas Matthew rearranges the material more. He combines Mark 6.6b–13 with the Q account.

[1] This verse is a Lukan introduction to the Q discourse. In Luke it has the task of preparing for Jesus' coming. But that does not fit Q very well, where those sent out do not prepare at all for Jesus' arrival, but are doing independent missionary work.

[2–3] 'Harvest' in v. 2 is an image for the kingly rule of God. The logion in v. 2 derives from Q (cf. on Matt. 9.37–38). It also occurs in Thomas 73. As Matt. 10.16 shows, v. 3 did not stand at the beginning of the discourse, since it does not fit at all after v. 2. In Matt. 10.16 the emphasis lies on the threat to which the disciples are exposed (cf. the context, Matt. 10.14, 17f.). However, in Luke it is on the protection under which they stand in the midst of danger.

[4] In Luke the money is carried in a purse (12.33; 22.35f.), in Mark (6.8) and Matthew (10.9) in the belt. The lack of equipment translates the admonition not to be anxious from Matt. 6.25–33 (Q) into action. The prohibition against greeting is meant to prevent the power of the messenger as a bearer of the blessing from being diminished by the greeting. Cf. II Kings 4.29: '(Elisha) said to Gehazi, "Gird up your loins and take my staff in your hand, and go. If you meet any one, do not greet him; and if anyone greets you do not reply, and lay my staff upon the face of the boy."'

[5–7] Cf. the Q parallel Matt. 10.11–13.

[8–12] Verse 8: the introduction of the sentence takes up that of v. 5 ('Whatever house/town you enter . . .'). Verse 9: the preaching takes place in Luke only in the town, not in the house. The kingdom of God is not future but already there, and takes root specifically among the inhabitants of that city. That follows from the addition 'to you'. For then the messengers preach the arrival of Jesus, who is bringing the kingdom of God; the important thing is whether he is welcomed. Verse 10 is a negative imitation of v. 8 or an antithesis to the statement made there. In v. 11 we have a statement about the *nearness* of the kingdom, which is rare in Luke. Luke has taken it over from Q (cf. Matt. 10.7), but modified it by the addition 'to you'. Verse 12 is the conclusion of v. 10–11 and a transition to vv. 13–15, where the fate of two cities is dealt with.

[13–15] These verses are a threat from Q (= Matt. 11.21–23; cf. further there on the form). Luke adds it here in order to make the threat of judgment in v. 12 concrete by means of two examples. The passage cannot originally have belonged with the previous section, because in v. 12 'you' refers to the disciples but in vv. 13–15 to quite different people.

[16] This is the closing sentence of the discourse. It sums up succinctly what has been said so far and derives from God the authority promised by Jesus to the preachers. For the saying cf. Mark 9.37 par. and Matt. 10.40 and Matt. 18.5. One's attitude to the community determines one's attitude to Christ and that in turn one's attitude to God. The saying corresponds to the community, but not to the preaching of Jesus and already has a Johannine ring (cf. John 5.23; 15.23).

[17] Verse 17a links up with v. 1. The driving out of the demons by a conjuration formula using the name of Jesus in v. 17b is regarded, as in 11.20 (Matt. 12.28), as a victorious battle against the kingdom of Satan. (Later in v. 20 it is relativized.)

[18] This verse confirms the experience of the disciples. The defeat of the devil

agrees with Jesus' own experience. This experience of Jesus has been recorded in an isolated saying which has preserved the vision at Jesus' call in the first-person form. The saying gives the impression of being a fragment, since miracles by the disciples and a vision of Jesus hardly fit together, but rather Jesus' vision and his miraculous power which follows. At the same time the saying is unique, in that it is the only one in which Jesus appears as a visionary.

In Judaism at the time of Jesus the overcoming of Satan was expected in the *future*. Cf. Ascension of Moses 10.1: 'And then God's rule will appear over his whole creation, and then Satan will be no more and sorrow will be taken away with him.' According to the speaker in Luke 10.18, what was still expected in the Jewish tradition has already taken place in heaven.

[19] This verse makes a new beginning with a promise of Jesus. For the background cf. Ps. 91.13. (Ps. 91.11f. is taken up in the temptation story [Luke 4.10].) See further Mark 16.18. The authority expressed in v. 19 is the 'faith of all primitive Christianity' (J.Weiss).

[20] This verse might originally have existed as an individual saying. It relativizes what was said immediately beforehand in a Lukan way. The saying added by Luke here is meant to warn the community against overestimating miracles.

Historical

[2–3] The words presuppose the situation of the community (cf. on Matt. 9.37–38; 10.16).

[4] The missionaries go through the land as living proof of God's care. I regard this as authentic evidence for the practice and ethos of the Jesus movement and thus possibly also for Jesus. Moreover, it fits Matt. 6.25–33.

[5–12] These verses reflect the situation of the itinerant missionaries after 'Easter' who are already engaging in mission with a purpose.

[13–15] See on Matt. 11.21–23.

[16] Jesus certainly did not utter the saying in its present wording, because the transference of the authority of Jesus to the disciples presupposes the situation of the community (cf. on Matt. 18.5).

[17b] The saying is rooted in the community, for the name of Jesus became a means of doing miracles only after 'Easter'.

[18] The saying is authentic, since it cannot be derived from the primitive community (criterion of difference). There the victory of Jesus himself was attributed to the victory over Satan (cf. John 12.31; Rev. 12.7). At the same time the criterion of coherence comes to bear, since generally speaking Jesus has intimate contact with the devil and with the demons subordinate to him. A legendary echo of this side of Jesus which is often overlooked appears in the temptation stories (Mark 1.12–13; Matt. 4.1–11 = Mark 4.1–13) and in the countless reports of encounters of Jesus

with demons who virtually sense his nearness (cf. only Mark 5.1–20; Luke 13.32). Similarly, the criterion of rarity can be applied, for the idea of Satan's defeat as a past event underlying the saying was very rare in the Judaism of the time (cf. the example from the Ascension of Moses quoted above). The end of the rule of the devil is the key conviction of the religious life of Jesus. Occasionally the vision of the fall of Satan is taken to be the decisive event of the detachment of Jesus from John the Baptist. But that is only a third-degree hypothesis – attractive though it is.

[19] As the bestowing of miraculous power is first rooted in the Easter situation, the saying is inauthentic.

[20] The Exalted One speaks in order to warn the community against over-estimating the earliest faith. The saying is a community construction and does not go back to Jesus himself, who in it 'looked back to the excitements and successes of his initial period with some coolness' (J.Weiss).

Luke 10.21–24: Jesus' cry of jubilation and the beatitude on the disciples

21 *In that hour he was jubilant in the Holy Spirit* and said, 'I praise you, Father, Lord of heaven and earth, because you have hidden these things from the wise and understanding and revealed them to babes. Yes, Father, for that was your gracious will.

22 All things have been delivered to me by my Father, and no one knows who the Son is except the Father, and who the Father is except the Son and any one to whom the Son wills to reveal him.'

23 *He turned to the disciples alone and* said , 'Blessed are the eyes which see what you see; 24 for I say to you that many prophets and kings wanted to see what you see, and did not see it, and to hear what you hear, and did not hear it.'

Redaction and tradition

[21] 'In that hour' comes from Luke and refers to the point of time of the return of the seventy-two. The parallel in Q (Matt. 11.25, 'at that time') connected the cry of jubilation with the point in time when the disciples were sent out. Luke has also formulated other expressions of jubilation at the fulfilment of a prophecy (cf. 1.14, 44, 47; Acts 2.26, 46; 16.34) and of jubilation in the Holy Spirit (cf. Acts 2.46f.). The joy of the disciples in v. 17 and the jubilation of Jesus in v. 21 are rooted in the same situation. At the level of the tradition the speaker in v. 21 is already a divine being who is uttering a prayer of thanksgiving only in the wording. In reality he is speaking about the true recipients of the revelation, namely the babes and not the wise (cf. I Cor. 1.18–31).

[22] The saying gives the impression of being a 'thunderbolt from the Johannine

heaven' (K.Hase). This is indicated by (a) the mutual knowledge and (b) Jesus' designation of himself as 'the Son', used in the absolute.

[23–24] Verse 23a is a Lukan transitional construction in order to attach the saying about the blessedness of the eyewitnesses to the preceding words. This makes the beatitude point quite clearly to the disciples of Jesus. Verses 23b–24 come from Q (cf. on Matt. 13.16–17).

Historical

[21] The saying is inauthentic, as the 'Risen One' is speaking.

[22] This verse is inauthentic. The Johannine terminology is not that of the historical Jesus. Moreover v. 22a attests the Easter situation (cf. Matt. 28.18: 'All authority has been given to me'; v. 22a: 'everything has been given to me by my Father').

[23b–24] The Q saying is probably authentic, since in it Jesus is addressing a beatitude to his disciples and his hearers without a community situation being visible. The beatitude is uttered on the presupposition that with the appearance of Jesus the time of salvation has dawned: cf. similarly Matt. 11.5–6/Luke 7.22–23 (= Q). In Judaism, Psalm of Solomon 17.44 ('Blessed is he who may live in those days and see the salvation of Israel in the union of the [twelve] tribes, as it is brought about by God') and I Enoch 58.2–6 say that those who have a share in the time of salvation are to be praised.

Luke 10.25–37: The parable of the good Samaritan

25 *And look*, an expert in the law stood up to tempt him and said, 'Teacher, *what shall I do to inherit eternal life?*' 26 *And he said to him*, 'What is written in the law? How do you read?' 27 And he answered and said, 'You shall love the Lord your God with all your heart and all your soul and all your strength and all your mind; and your neighbour as yourself.' 28 *And he said to him*, 'You have answered rightly; *do this, and you will live.*'

29 But he wanted *to justify himself* and *said to* Jesus, 'Who is my neighbour?' 30 Jesus took that up and said,

'A man was going down from Jerusalem to Jericho and fell among robbers. They stripped him and beat him and departed, leaving him half dead. 31 Now by chance a priest was going down that road, <u>and when he saw him he passed by</u>. 32 So likewise a Levite came to the place <u>and when he saw him he passed by</u>. 33 But a Samaritan, as he journeyed, came there <u>and when he saw him</u>, he had compassion. 34 And he went up to him and bound up his wounds, pouring on oil and wine, set him on his own beast and brought him to an inn, and took care of him. 35 And the next day he took out two denarii and gave them to the innkeeper and said, "Take care of him, and if you need any more, I will repay you when I come back."

36 Which of these three, *does it seem to you*, proved neighbour to the one who fell among

the robbers?' 37 *And he said*, 'The one who showed mercy on him.' And Jesus said to him, 'Go and *do likewise*.'

Redaction and tradition

The passage can be divided into three strands: (a) introduction, the occasion of the question about the neighbour (vv. 25–28); (b) question about the neighbour and the answer to it (vv. 29, 36–37); (c) the parable or the example narrative itself (vv. 30–35).

[25–28] This is a revision of Mark 12.28–34 which has been inserted here, since the Markan pericope is absent from its original place between 20.39 and 20.40. Luke has transposed the question about eternal life to v. 25 from Mark 10.17 (par. Luke 18.18). Therefore vv. 25–28 have been worked over in connection with the exemplary story and so already differ from Mark 12.28–34.

[29] Luke depicts the Pharisee as in 16.15 as someone who justifies himself, whereas the toll collector justifies God (cf. 7.19).

[30–35] The story has its 'point in the contrast between the loveless Jews and the loving Samaritan' (Bultmann). This narrative has nothing to do with the question about one's neighbour. It begins from the man who has been attacked (v. 30) and relates what happens to him: three times people come and 'see' him and twice they 'pass by' him; the third time someone comes who in vv. 34f. will be shown to be a person who provides comprehensive help. Beyond doubt v. 33 represents the climax. Help comes from the enemy of the people, from whom the victim had not expected it.

[36–37] These verses artificially take up the question of the neighbour in v. 29 and stand it on its head. The question of the neighbour as object of my action is thoroughly changed into the one in the narrative who is the neighbour as the one who acts. In this way Luke makes the Samaritan an example of action who puts the Jews to shame.

Historical

The historical question is meaningful only in connection with the example story, since the framework derives from Luke. For vv. 25–28 cf. the historical evaluation of Mark 12.28–34.

[30–35] The example story certainly goes back to Jesus and illustrates love of enemy (cf. Matt. 5.44a). Jesus shows how a Samaritan who is hated by the Jews performs a loving service towards a Jew whom he really should have hated. The story is so impressive because it is not a Jew who loves his enemy but the Samaritan, regarded as *the* enemy, who loves a Jew.

Luke 10.37–42: Mary and Martha

38 *While they were journeying, he entered a village. And a woman named* Martha *received him into her house.* 39 *And she had a sister called* Mary, *who sat at the Lord's feet and listened to his words.* 40 *But* Martha *was utterly taken up in much serving. She went to him and said, 'Lord, do you not care that my sister has left me to serve alone? Tell her then to help me.'* 41 *But the Lord answered her and said, 'Martha, Martha, you are anxious and troubled about many things,* 42 *but only one thing is needful; Mary has chosen the good portion which shall not be taken away from her.'*

Redaction and tradition

According to John 11 the two sisters Mary and Martha live in Bethany, where Jesus raises Lazarus. There is probably no genetic connection.

[38] This verse recalls the journey which Jesus has been on since 9.51.

[39] The sitting at the feet of the Lord and hearing his word are Lukan constructions. Similarly the fact that a woman is allowed to listen to Jesus fits well into the use of the motif of women, which can also be recognized elsewhere in Luke's work (cf. only 8.2–3; the women in Acts: 16.14; 17. 4, 12).

[40] This verse is a redactional formation antithetical to v. 39.

[41] Jesus criticizes Martha's objection by characterizing her activity as trouble and anxiety.

[42] The saying about the choice of the good part derives from Luke. The emphasis on the important thing, what lasts and remains for people, corresponds to his concern.

Yield: the passage is a unitary composition, an ideal scene which impresses on the reader that it is important to hear Jesus' word.

Historical

The story is a Lukan formation. Apart from the two names, its historical value is nil.

Luke 11.1–13: On prayer

1 *And it happened when he was praying in a certain place, when he had ended (it), one of his disciples said to him, 'Lord, teach us to pray, as John also taught his disciples.* 2 *And he said to them, 'When you pray, say,*
"Father,
hallowed be your name,
your kingdom come,

3 Give us our bread for the coming day *daily*

4 and forgive us our *sins,* for we ourselves *forgive* everyone who *is* indebted to us,
and lead us not into temptation.'

5 *And he said to them,* 'Which of you will have a friend and go to him at midnight and say to him, "Friend, I need three loaves; 6 for a friend of mine has arrived on a journey, and I have nothing to offer him," 7 and the person inside will answer, "Do not bother me; the door is now shut, and my children are with me in bed. I cannot get up and give you anything"? 8 I tell you, even if he will not get up and give him anything because he is his friend, yet because of his importunity he will rise and give him whatever he needs.

9 *And I tell you,* Ask and it will be given to you; seek, and you will find; knock, and it will be opened to you; 10 for everyone who asks receives, and whoever seeks finds, and to him who knocks it will be opened.

11 Or what kind of father among you, if his son asks for a fish, will instead of a fish give him a serpent? 12 Or if he asks for an egg, will give him a scorpion? 13 Now if you, who are evil, know how to give your children good gifts, how much more will the Father from heaven give *Holy Spirit* to those who ask him!'

Redaction and tradition

Three sections follow with statements of Jesus about prayer: vv. 1–4, Our Father; vv. 5–8, the parable of the friend's request; vv. 9–13, sayings about prayer being heard. The whole section is introduced by an initiative on the part of the disciples (v. 1) and rounded off by the promise that the disciples will be given Holy Spirit if they ask for it (v. 13).

[1] This verse is the introduction; it derives wholly from Luke and shows Jesus as the great man of prayer (cf. 6.12). Elsewhere, too, in Luke someone inside or outside the circle of disciples (cf. 9.57; 11.15; 21.5, 7, always against Mark or Matthew; cf. 10.25; 20.27) puts a question directly or through his behaviour and by it evokes Jesus' teaching. For John the Baptist cf. 3.15–20 and 5.33. Luke emphasizes praying after Jesus' example and thus, with a redactional motivation, gives the occasion for the communication of the Our Father.

[2] The first two petitions correspond with those in Matt. 6.9f. and derive from Q. Because of the end of v. 13, the reading 'may your spirit come and cleanse us' which is offered by some manuscripts is not original, but a later liturgical application of the second petition.

[3–4] For 'daily' as a Lukan addition cf. 19.47; Acts 17.11. Through it Luke ensures that it is God's *providence* that is thought of. Faithful to the extension of the time, it shows itself over a lengthy period. Luke replaces the aorist of the fourth and fifth petitions (cf. Matt. 6.11f. = Q) with the present tense. This clearly indicates a change of perspective, which is no longer primarily future-orientated. Like the addition 'daily' to the third petition, the forms in the present give the impression of a long duration.

[5–8] The parable emphasizes redactionally that the Our Father is to be regarded as a petitionary prayer. The new introduction 'and he said to them' (v. 5a) leads from the right *form* of prayer to *perseverance* in prayer. The question in v. 5b invites identification with the one asking. The parable emphasizes that the one making the request may be confident in his expectation.

At the level of tradition the parable about the friend's request may have formed a pair with that of the widow and her judge (18.1–8). 'Both illustrate in a sharply popular way that persistent requests help. It is worth noting that neither the friend nor the judge agrees to grant the request for noble motives, but only to get rid of the burdensome petitioner. That is deliberately emphasized' (J.Weiss).

[9–13] This section occurs almost word for word in Matt. 7.7–11 and thus is clearly Q. At the level of redaction Luke develops the idea that prayer can count on being heard. As in 16.9 (18.6 differs somewhat), v. 9a ('And I tell you') attaches instruction on the hearing of prayer to the parable. But we must completely rule out the possibility that these sayings are the original application of the preceding parable. For example, the invitation 'seek and you will find' is not contained in the parable at all.

Historical

[1–4] Cf. on Matt. 6.9–13.

[5–8] It is very probable that the parable comes from Jesus, since with respect to a case of importunate behaviour it displays what matters (criterion of offensiveness). However, that is not yet a reconstruction of the historical situation in which Jesus spoke the parable. I would suggest with J. Jeremias that Jesus wants to say here, 'God hears those who are in distress. He helps them. He does more than they ask. You can rely on that with the utmost certainty.'

[9–13] Cf. on Matt. 7.7–11.

Luke 11.14–23: A discourse in defence of Jesus

14 And he was driving out a demon, and it was dumb. *And it happened* that when the demon went out, the dumb man spoke, and the crowds of people marvelled. 15 But *some* of them said, 'He drives out demons by Beelzebul, the prince of demons.' 16 And others, to tempt him, requested from him a sign from heaven. 17 But he knew their thoughts and said to them, 'Every kingdom that is divided against itself is laid waste, and one house falls on another. 18 And if Satan also is divided against himself, how will his kingdom stand? For you say that I drive out demons by Beelzebul. 19 But if I drive out demons by Beelzebul, by whom do your sons drive them out? Therefore they shall be your judges. 20 But if I by the finger of God drive out demons, then the kingdom of God has come upon you. 21 When the strong man, fully armed, guards his palace, his *property* is in peace. 22 But when one comes

who is stronger than he and overcomes him, he takes away his armour in which he trusted, and divides his spoil. 23 He who is not with me is against me, and he who does not gather with me scatters.'

Redaction

After the petition for the coming of the kingdom of God (v. 2), Luke makes it clear that this kingdom has already come to men and women in the activity of Jesus (cf. esp. v. 20). Luke passes over the Markan tradition on the same theme (Mark 3.22–30) and follows Q in his formulation (cf. Matt. 12.22–30).

[14] The driving out of demons reported of Jesus takes up the narrative of the return of the disciples and the statement made here (10.17): 'Lord, even the demons are subject to us in your name.'

[15] In Luke it is not the Pharisees (Matt. 12.24) or the scribes (Mark 3.22) who speak, but 'some'.

[16] This verse interrupts the context and brings forward a verse which appears only later in Q (Matt. 12.38) in order to prepare for 11.29–32.

[17–23] These verses answer the charge from v. 15. According to Luke they do not focus on Jesus' constant fight against Satan but at the level of redaction are meant as principles and in the first instance offer comfort to Luke's church, which since the story of Jesus' passion (cf. 22.3) must again grapple with Satan (Conzelmann). In Luke, vv. 19–20 are illuminated in advance by the redactional alteration of the Q original in 10.9 (see there). The kingdom of God is present and the battle goes against the kingdom of Satan. Jesus does works, the significance of which is to be inferred from 4.18–21. 'Thus Luke can immediately use the passage in the sense of his own future expectation. The "to you" in 10.9 and 11.20 further corresponds to the "in you" in 17.21' (Conzelmann). In Luke, as in Q, v. 19 is about Jewish exorcists generally; in Matthew (18.27) about exorcists among the Pharisees. Verse 23 derives from Q. Cf. the verbal correspondence with Matt. 12.30. Luke probably interprets the saying in terms of the gathering of the community (cf. 12.32).

Tradition

At the beginning (Luke 11.14/Matt. 12.22) the Q original contains the driving out of a demon which is told in summary fashion; alongside the story of the centurion of Capernaum it is the only miracle story in Q. Attached to it is the charge that Jesus drives out the demons by Beelzebul, the chief of the demons (Luke 11.15/Matt. 12.24). Jesus defends himself against this accusation with two comparisons, (a) Luke 11.17–18/Matt. 12.25–26; (b) Luke 11.21–22/Matt. 12.29, between which stands the positive statement of Jesus that he drives out the demons (not by

Beelzebul but) by the finger of God (11.20/Matt. 12.28). Already in Q to this scene in defence of Jesus is attached the statement Luke 11.23/Matt/12,30, a call to decision which is not directed to the opponents addressed in the preceding text but to interested hearers.

Historical

Verse 20 comes from Q; 'finger of God' – instead of 'spirit of God' – certainly reflects the original (Q) reading. For on the one hand the Matthaean version has probably been conditioned by the context, in which there is similarly talk of the spirit of God (cf. Matt. 12.18 = Isa. 42.1; Matt. 12.32). And on the other hand, in view of the importance of the Spirit in Luke's two-volume work (the Gospel and Acts) it would have been impossible for him to delete this term. 'Finger of God' alludes to the miracles of Moses at the exodus from Egypt (Ex. 8.15). The Egyptian magicians here recognize the superiority of Moses with the words, 'That is the finger of God.'

The reasons which support the authenticity of the logion 10.18 (criteria of coherence, difference and rarity) also apply to v. 20. The most famous New Testament scholar of this century, Rudolf Bultmann (1884–1976), thought that the present saying could claim the highest degree of originality which may be assumed for a saying of Jesus. He said that it was supported by the eschatological feeling of power which must have governed the behaviour of Jesus. In his activity Jesus presupposes the fall of Satan. His exorcisms make that evident for him. The flight of the demons is a sign that the power of evil has been overcome, even if the final destruction of the evil power will take place only in the imminent final judgment. At the same time the rule of God has already come, for the expulsions of demons are already constantly taking place in the present, irreversibly and visible to all.

Possibly the following can be said about the closer context of the saying: Jesus is defending himself, faithful to the Q context, against the charge of driving out demons and answers: 'If the exorcisms by your sons do not come from Satan, how much more do my exorcisms then show the power of the rule of God' (Theissen).

Luke 11.24–26: The return of the unclean spirit

24 'When the unclean spirit has gone out of a man, he passes through dry places seeking rest. And when he finds none he says, "I will return to my house from which I came." 25 And when he comes and finds it swept and put in order, 26 then he goes and brings seven other spirits more evil than himself. They enter and dwell there. And the end of that man becomes worse than before.'

Redaction and tradition

The present passage corresponds almost word for word with Matt. 12.43–45 and derives from Q. However, as it speaks of unclean spirits and not of demons as the previous section (vv. 14–23), it is already clear from the terminology that the texts did not originally belong together. At the level of the Lukan redaction the text expounds the call to decision in v. 23: in Christ there is only for or against.

[24–26] The text is either an instruction for exorcism, a piece of popular wisdom which draws on the experience of the return of evil spirits, or a parable. In the latter case, which seems to me to be the most probable, the parable is saying that half a beginning is worse than no beginning at all. 'The house may not stand empty when the recalcitrant spirit is driven out. A new master must rule in it. Jesus' instructions must rule in it and the joy of the kingdom of God have an effect on it' (J. Jeremias).

Thus the issue is one of total decision, so that half-heartedness does not result in a lapse.

Historical

The parable is a further example of the radical character of Jesus' call for decision. The probability of its authenticity also follows from the fact that it presupposes an expulsion of unclean spirits. And that is to be presupposed for Jesus, cf. v. 20.

Luke 11.27–28: A beatitude on Jesus' mother and a correction of it

27 Now it happened, when he said this, that a woman in the crowd raised her voice and said to him, 'Blessed is the womb which bore you, and the breasts which you sucked!' 28 But he said, 'Blessed rather are those who hear the word of God and keep it!'

Redaction and tradition

[27–28] The occasion for this beatitude is the expulsion of demons which preceded it in the context of the Gospel of Luke (v. 14). Whereas this provokes a negative reaction in the crowd (vv. 15f.), for a woman it indicates the greatness of Jesus. She calls the body and breasts of the mother of Jesus holy. Verse 27b is probably a saying to glorify Mary, which Luke has woven in here in order to correct it. On the basis of 1.48, Jesus' answer is to be understood more as a correction than as a strict repudiation of the beatitude. In the end, the question whether the mother of Jesus is to be called blessed is not decisive. Rather, it is important for the disciples to hear and do the word of God. To this degree the relationship between vv. 27 and 28 corresponds to the first and second part of the question 6.46: 'Why do you call me "Lord, Lord" and do not do what I say?'

Historical

Verse 27b was not spoken in the lifetime of Jesus, but probably later, to glorify his mother. In any case, the present scene has no claim to historicity.

Luke 11.29–32: The refusal of a sign of authentication

29 *Now when the crowds of people were increasing*, he began to say, 'This generation is an evil generation; it seeks a sign, but no sign shall be given to it except the sign of Jonah. 30 For as Jonah became a sign to the Ninevites, so will the Son of man be (a sign) to this generation. 31 The queen of the South will be raised at the judgment with the men of this generation and condemn them; for she came from the ends of the earth to hear the wisdom of Solomon, and look, here is more than Solomon. 32 The men of Nineveh will arise at the judgment with this generation and condemn it; for they repented at the preaching of Jonah, and look, here is more than Jonah.'

Redaction and tradition

Luke follows the Logia source Q and is closer to its text than Matt. 12.38–42, for he sees in the Son of man the future sign for this generation (v. 30), and in accordance with this, previously in the person of Jonah the sign for the inhabitants of Nineveh (v. 29). The Q text at this point is a variant of Mark 8.11–12.

[29] The real introduction to this section came earlier, in 11.16. Therefore Luke can content himself with the formulation of a looser transition.

[30] For Jesus as sign cf. 2.34: there the old Simeon denotes Jesus as a sign which will be spoken against.

[31–32] These verses were originally a threat against the present generation (= the Jews). Its place in the present context gives it a clear reference to Jesus. Because of the parallelism with the Q section Luke 10.13–15/Matt. 11.21–24, it must be assumed to originate in early Christian polemic.

Historical

The individual formulations in this section are inauthentic, since they can be derived from the community (see under tradition). I assume the polemic against this generation (cf. Mark 8.12) to be the sole historical basis. It is probably Jesus' continuation of John the Baptist's preaching of judgment .

Luke 11.33–36: The similitude of light

33 'No one takes a lamp and puts it in a hidden corner or under a bushel, but on the lamp-stand, so that those who enter may see the shining <u>light</u>. 34 Your eye is the lamp of your body. If your eye is clear, your whole body is also <u>light</u>; but if it is evil, your body is also dark. 35 *So see that* the <u>light</u> in you is not darkness. 36 Now if your whole body is <u>light</u> and has no dark part, it will be all *<u>light</u>*, as when the lamp shines on you with the brightness.'

Redaction and tradition

The passage derives from Q. For v. 33 cf. Matt. 5.15; for vv. 34–35 cf. Matt. 6.22–23. Verse 36 is Lukan special tradition. Luke adds the image of light at this point as a second answer to the demand for a sign in v. 29.

[33] The saying has already appeared earlier (8.16). In the present context it is probably meant to say, 'Now that the light is there it should shine; the coming of Jesus has failed in its purpose if one does not listen to him' (J.Weiss).

[34–36] The redactional context is the discourse on judgment. The right understanding of discipleship of Jesus is explained by the image of the clear eye. The hearers of Jesus are called to this, as the Lukan imperative (v. 35 beginning) emphasizes.

Historical

[33] Cf. on Matt. 5.15.

[34–36] The historical question cannot be decided, as the meaning of the similitude on light cannot be defined.

Luke 11.37–12.1: Woes against Pharisees and scribes

37 *Now while he was speaking like this, a Pharisee asked him to eat with him. So he went in and reclined at table. 38 And when the Pharisee saw that, he was astonished that* he did not first wash before the meal. 39 But *the Lord* said to him, 'Now, you Pharisees, you cleanse the outside of cup and dish, but your inward self (is) full of extortion and wickedness. 40 *You fools!* Did not he who made the outside make the inside also? 41 But give as alms *what is within*; and *look*, all will be clean for you. 42 But <u>woe to you, Pharisees</u>, for you tithe mint and rue and every garden herb, and pass over justice and *the love of God*. These you ought to have done, without neglecting that. 43 <u>Woe to you, Pharisees</u>, for *you love* the best seat in the synagogues and greetings in the market place. 44 Woe to you; for you are like unrecognizable graves, and men walk over them without knowing it'.

45 *But one of the experts in the law answered and says to him, 'Teacher, if you say this you also insult us.'* 46 And he said, '<u>Woe to you, experts in the law</u>, for you load men with burdens

hard to bear, and you yourselves do not touch the burdens with one finger. 47 Woe to you, for you build the tombs of the prophets, but your fathers killed them. 48 So you are witnesses and consent to the works of your fathers; for they killed them, and you build their tombs. 49Therefore the Wisdom of God said, 'I will send them prophets *and apostles*, and (some) of them they will kill and persecute, 50 that the blood of *all the prophets*, shed from the foundation of the world, may be required of this generation, 51 from the blood of Abel to the blood of Zechariah who perished between the altar and the house. Yes, I tell you, it will be required of this generation. 52 <u>Woe to you, experts in the law</u>. For you have *taken away the key of knowledge*. You have not entered yourselves, and you have hindered those who were entering.'

53 *And as he went away from there, the scribes and the Pharisees began to press him hard, and to provoke him to speak of many things.* 54 *They lay in wait for him to catch at something he might say. 12.1 (Now) when tens of thousands of the crowd of people gathered, so that they trod on one another, he began to say to his disciples first, 'Beware of the leaven, of the hypocrisy of the Pharisees.'*

Redaction and tradition

'This discourse corresponds to that of Matt. 23 in content but not in situation. In Luke it is not delivered in Jerusalem or publicly in the temple, but in the house of a Pharisee at a feast (7.36; 14.1) outside Jerusalem at the time of Jesus' journey there. However, that does not fit at all well. Where does the crowd of scribes and Pharisees which is evidently presupposed come from?' (Wellhausen).

[37] For the invitation of Jesus by a Pharisee cf. 7.36; 14.1. It is quite uncouth and in need of explanation that Luke has Jesus addressing the sharp criticism which follows to his host, and describing his fellow guests as fools.

[38] This is redactional exposition, in order to create a link for the following reckoning.

[39] This verse has a remote parallel in Matt. 23.25f. There it is a woe; here it is a redactional conversation at table, reproachful and instructive, about the outside of cup and plate as opposed to what is inside a person. Here Mark 7, which Luke has omitted, has probably had an influence. The connection with the previous section 11.33–36 may consist in the following thought: 'The centre dominates the periphery, the eye must be light so that the body is light; the inside must be clean so that the outside is clean' (Wellhausen).

[40] Luke inserts 'fools' and probably passes over a 'woe' that stands in the Q original (cf. later vv. 43, 44, 46, 47) in order to achieve a smoother connection with vv. 37–39. Cf. further Thomas 89.2.

[41] 'What is inside' means what is present. 'Alms here appears as a universal means which is neither Christian nor Jewish. It will not have occurred to any Jew that unclean foods become clean by almsgiving, or to any Christian that foods are unclean, since Jesus has spoken Matt. 15.11' (Merx).

[42–44] Cf. Matt. 23.23–27 (= Q).

[45] This verse introduces the legal experts who become the target of the criticism as a second group after the Pharisees. However, the redirection of the speech is contrived. For in what follows the experts in the law are addressed only in vv. 46 and 52.

[46] Jesus replies to an objection by the legal experts with a woe the content of which derives from Q (cf. Matt. 23.4). However, it has been recast as a woe by Luke in order to make a better connection with v. 45 (cf. v. 52).

[47–48] The Lukan form of the woe is original (= Q), whereas the parallel Matt. 23.29–32 can be recognized as an extension. Already in Q the saying about the murderers of the prophets led to the insertion of a saying of the divine Wisdom.

[49–51] These verses contain the original wording of Q (Matt. 23.34–35 is slightly different). The Q logion was probably a saying spoken by Wisdom that Jesus commented on – in Q – in v. 51b: 'Yes, I tell you . . .'

[52] Cf. Matt. 23.13 (= Q). But Luke transposed this saying to the conclusion as a transition to the following discourse and changed 'kingdom of God' into 'key of knowledge', although with 'enter' he again presupposes 'kingdom of God', since Q is about entering the kingdom of God (cf. Matt. 23.13).

[53–12.1] This conclusion has been constructed by Luke. Together with similar notes (6.11; 19.47; 20.19f.; 22.2), the verses illustrate the growing hostility of the opponents of Jesus, among whom the scribes are particularly prominent. Here 12.1 is at the same time a transition to what follows. For the figure 'ten thousand' cf. the similar Lukan exaggeration in Acts 21.20.

Historical

For the historical questions cf. on Matt. 23. In addition the following historical clarification is necessary at this point:

[49–51] The wisdom saying in these verses is sometimes regarded as authentic by analogy with Luke 7.35/Matt. 11.19. It is said to be an example of how Jesus' main image of God was wisdom and not the Father (E.Schüssler Fiorenza). But the logion in vv. 49–51 cannot support this far-reaching thesis. The same is true of Luke 7.35/Matt. 11.19e: the passage was inserted into Q at a secondary stage. It is an expansion presupposing Luke 7.31–34 (or Matt. 11.16–19d). It has nothing to do with the generation which repudiates Jesus, but here contrasts the Q community itself as "children of wisdom" with the generation of Israel which rejects Jesus' (Luz).

Luke 12.2–12: Admonition to bold confession

2 'But nothing is covered up that will not be revealed, and nothing is hidden that will not be known. 3 Therefore whatever you have said in the dark shall be heard in the light, and what you have whispered in private rooms shall be proclaimed upon the housetops.

4 *I tell you, my friends*, do not fear those who kill the body, and after that have no more that they can do. 5 *But I will show you whom you are to fear:* fear him who, after he has killed, has power to throw into hell. *Yes, I tell you*, fear him! 6 Are not five sparrows sold for two pennies, and not one of these is forgotten before God? 7 But even the hairs of your head are all numbered. Fear not, you are worth far more than many sparrows.

8 *I tell you*, everyone who acknowledges me before men, the Son of man also will acknowledge before the angels of God. 9 But he who denies me before men will be denied before the angels of God. 10 And every one who speaks a word against the Son of man will be forgiven. But he who blasphemes against the <u>Holy Spirit</u> will not be forgiven.

11 When they bring you before the synagogues and the powers and the authorities, do not be anxious how or what you are to answer or to say in your defence; 12 for the <u>*Holy* Spirit</u> will teach you in that very hour what you ought to say.'

Redaction and tradition

The passage derives from Q, where individual sayings already stood side by side. For vv. 2–9 cf. Matt. 10.26–33; for v. 10 cf. Matt. 12.32 (and Mark 3.28–29); for vv. 11–12 cf. Matt. 10.19–20.

[2–3] These verses are explanations of the warnings to the Pharisees which were given in v. 1 and provide further reasons for them. On v. 2 see Mark 4.22. The train of thought is: beware of hypocrisy which conceals evil under pious forms – for the concealed evil will become manifest – for even what you say in secret will become known publicly. Only then does the real theme of fearless confession follow. Verse 3 has been put into Lukan language: Matthew's version (Matt. 10.27) is more original.

[4] Verse 4a is a redactional transition (cf. 6.27). For the form of address 'friends', cf. John 15.14, but also the general evidence relating to friend: the word does not appear in Matthew and Mark; it appears fifteen times in Luke and six in John.

[5] Verse 5a, like 6.47, is oratorical shaping; 'throw into hell' occurs only here in Luke.

[6–7] By comparison with 'does not fall to earth' (Matt. 10.29), 'is not forgotten by God' may be a toning down by Luke.

[8–9] The content of these words occurs in several traditions: Mark 8.38 is quoted in 9.26. Here, however, a non-Markan tradition appears, in which a positive version precedes Mark's negative version (cf. similarly Matt. 10.32 = Q). Q prefers 'deny' to 'be ashamed of' (Mark 8.38) and with this clarifies the meaning of the saying: anyone who 'denies' or 'is ashamed' in this way is asked whether he belongs to the Jesus community. So this is a prophetic admonition from the post-Easter community. For it ,Jesus and the Son of man were 'identical in the future: Jesus will return in the near future as the Son of man with the clouds of heaven. In his earthly life he was not yet the Son of man, since he will come to judgment only with the clouds of heaven (Dan. 7.13f.) at the end of days' (Haenchen). Therefore other people hardly spoke of Jesus as Son of man during his lifetime.

In Luke, the Son of man confesses before the angels of heaven those who confess him. These angels carry out the divine judgment, in the face of which the Son of man does not give orders as one in charge but only bears testimony. These angels have been removed in Matthew, and God the Father has taken their place (Matt. 10.32). Therefore Luke is probably reproducing the original Q text. Cf. also Matt. 13.49 on the angels as judges who elect the good; that is also the basic notion in Matt. 13.39, but already in v. 41 these angels have become angels of the Son of man, though they were originally angels of God.

[10] This saying seems out of place here and has been inserted from another context (cf. Matt. 12.31–32). It joins up with v. 8 by means of the key word 'Son of man', whereas 'Holy Spirit' leads on to v. 12. 'It is more likely that the word really belongs to v. 12; whoever blasphemes the Holy Spirit which speaks from the disciples will not be forgiven' (J. Weiss).

[11–12] This is a word of consolation (from Q: cf. on Matt. 10.19–20) for the trials which face the disciples.

Historical

[2] Cf. on Mark 4.22.
[10] Cf. on Mark 3.28–29.
The rest of the section derives from the community and is inauthentic.

Luke 12.13–21: The parable of the rich fool

13 *Now one of the multitude said to him, 'Teacher,* tell my brother to divide the inheritance with me.' 14 But he said to him, 'Man, who made me a judge or divider over you?' 15 *And he said to them, 'Take heed and beware of all covetousness; for a man's life does not consist in his abundance and in what belongs to him.'*

16 *And he told them a parable, saying,* 'The land of a rich man brought forth plentifully, 17 and he thought to himself, "What shall I do, for I have nowhere to store my crops?" 18 And he said, "I will do this: I will pull down my barns and build larger ones; and there I will store all my grain and my goods, 19 and I will say to my soul, 'Soul, you have ample goods laid up for many years. Take your ease, eat, drink and rejoice.'" 20 But God said to him, "You fool, this night they require your soul of you; and the things you have put in store, whose will they be?" 21 *So is he who gathers for himself, and is not rich toward God.'*

Redaction and tradition

[13a] this verse is a Lukan transition, since as in 11.45 a hearer interrupts Jesus and allows him to start on a new theme.

[13b–14] These verses contain a didactic conversation on a dispute over an inheritance (cf. Thomas 72.1–2). It is a unitary conversation in which what Jesus says makes sense only in relation to the question.

[15] This verse is a transition constructed by Luke. It anticipates the moral of vv. 16–21.

[16–20] These verses are an example story (for the narrative cf. 10.29–37; 16.19–31; 18.9–14) which is based on tradition. (See the related story Thomas 63.1–3.) In content it corresponds to Sir. 11.17–19:

17 'Some stint and save and thus become rich 18 and think that they have achieved something 19 and say, "Now I will make myself a good life, eat and drink of what I have" – but they do not know that their hour is near and that they must leave everything to others and die.'

Cf. also a Jewish legend in which a king is taken away by the angel of death while at a banquet he is saying to himself, 'O soul, you have accumulated to yourself all the good of this world, and now enjoy it and let these treasures taste good to you in a long life and rich happiness' (cf. Klostermann).

[21] This verse rounds the section off: it contains specifically Lukan individual eschatology (cf. on 23.43) and at the same time leads on to the next series of sayings (cf. esp. v. 33).

Historical

[13b–14] Jesus' repudiation of being a judge or divider is probably historical (cf. the attestation in Thomas 72.1–2 which is independent of Luke). It cannot be derived from any need of the community.

'It is customary in the East to turn to a religious authority even in secular affairs; Jesus rejects that. But the church behaved otherwise, and Luke (12.15) already derives from the saying in 12.14 a moral which it does not contain' (Wellhausen).

[16–20] The authenticity of this passage is sometimes defended by designating it an 'eschatological parable' (J. Jeremias). But it is certainly not that. It is the narrative by a wise man indicating that riches mean nothing in the face of death. As one who knew the traditions of Israel, especially as he had called the poor blessed (6.20), Jesus may have thought that. But each time the context is quite different. If 6.20 is authentic, then 12.16–20 must be inauthentic. Jesus had other concerns than the fate of individual rich men, all the more so as the case mentioned in the parable was not and is not the rule.

Luke 12.22–34: The right orientation of life

22 *And he said to his disciples, 'Therefore I tell you,* Do not be <u>anxious</u> about life, what you eat, or about the body, what you put on. 23 For life is more than food, and the body (more) than clothing. 24 *Look at* the ravens: they do not sow, they do not reap, they have neither store-house nor barn, and God feeds them. Of how much more value are you than the birds! 25 And which of you by being <u>anxious</u> can add a cubit to his span of life?

26 If then you are not able to do the *least* thing, why are you <u>anxious</u> about the rest? 27 *Look at* the lilies, how they grow; they do not toil and do not spin. But I tell you, even Solomon in all his glory was not clothed like one of these.

28 But if God so clothes the grass which stands in the field today and tomorrow is thrown into the oven, how much more (will he clothe) you, O you of little faith! 29 And as for you, do not <u>*seek*</u> what you are to eat and what you are to drink, and do not be anxious; 30 for all the peoples *of the world* seek these things. But your Father knows that you need them. 31 <u>Seek</u> *instead* his kingdom, and these things will be given to you as well. 32 *Fear not, little flock, for it is your Father's good pleasure to give you the kingdom.* 33 *Sell your possessions, and give alms.* Get yourselves purses that do not grow old, with an *imperishable* treasure in the heavens, where no thief *approaches* and no moth *destroys*; 34 for where your treasure is, there your heart will be.'

Redaction and tradition

Luke is using Q (cf. Matt. 6.25–34 and 6.19–21).

[22] This verse refers to the preceding discourse ('eat' takes up 'eat' from v. 19). However, it was addressed to the people, whereas the speech which now begins addresses the disciples (cf. later v. 32). It is to explain to them further the parable of the rich fool (vv. 13–21).

[25–26] Verse 25 clearly stands out as an insertion which brings an interruption: v. 26 is attached to it in order to use the insertion of v. 25 for the context.

[29–30] 'Eat' and 'drink' in v. 29 pick up 'eat' from v. 19 (cf. v. 22). In v. 30, in contrast to the Q original (= Matt. 6.30), which betrays a Jewish standpoint, Luke introduces a Gentile Christian perspective. I have therefore deliberately translated 'peoples of the world' instead of 'Gentiles of the world'.

[31–32] The prophecy of salvation in v. 32 which Luke has woven in here derives from a prophet (similarly 10.20) speaking in the name of the 'Exalted One'. The verse renews the address to the disciples (cf. v. 22) and endorses the promise of v. 31.

[33–34] Cf. Q (Matt. 6.19–21). The call to sell possessions and give alms (v. 33a) comes from Luke, who here has rich Christians in his community in view. The second half of the verse also shows Lukan traces, especially the characterization of the treasure in heaven as an imperishable possession which does not disappear even in death (by comparison cf. the deterrent example in 12.16–20 and 16.9). In conclusion v. 34 explains why earthly cares and troubles hinder the quest for the kingdom of God (v. 31).

As a summary comment on the Q tradition behind these passages cf. the remarks on Matt. 6.25–33 and 6.19–21. In addition, we may consider the problem here whether the 'carefree cheerfulness' (Wellhausen) of vv. 22–34 no longer presupposes the imminent expectation and parousia of the Son of man. Here one can adopt another view and regard wisdom sayings and apocalyptic as quite compatible. In general cf. the apostle Paul (see Chapter VII) and as a further example the author of the first-century writing attributed to Enoch, which threatens with the imminent judgment of God but at the same time says:

'Observe how all the works in the heaven do not change their courses, consider the earth, consider the summer and winter, consider and see, then consider . . . observe . . ., take heed and note all his works, and you will recognize how he who lives for ever has done all this for you. All his works which he has made happen from year to year in always the same way, and all the works which do him service, do not change in their doing, but everything happens as God commands. But you have not persevered and have not fulfilled the law of the Lord, but have fallen away' (I Enoch 2.1–5.4).

Historical

[22–32] Cf. on Matt. 6.25–34.
[33–34] Cf. on Matt. 6.19–21.

Luke 12.35–48: The watchful and the negligent servants

35 'Your loins are to be girded and your lamps lit. 36 And you are to be like men who are waiting for their <u>lord</u> to come home from the marriage feast, so that they may open to him at once when he comes and knocks. 37 <u>Blessed</u> are those servants whom the <u>lord</u> finds awake when he comes. Amen, I say to you, he will gird himself and have them recline at table, and he will come and serve them. 38 And if he comes in the second watch or third watch of the night and finds them so, they are <u>blessed</u>. 39 But know this, that if the householder had known at what hour the thief was coming, he would not have let his house be broken into. 40 You also must be ready; for the Son of man is coming at an unexpected hour.'

41 *Peter said, 'Lord, are you telling this parable to us or to all?'* 42 *And the Lord said,* 'Who then is the faithful and wise *steward* whom the <u>lord</u> will set over his servants, to give them

their portion of food at the proper time? 43 Blessed is that servant whom his lord, when he comes, will find so doing. 44 In truth, I say to you, he will set him over all that he has. 45 But if that servant says to himself, "My <u>lord</u> is delayed in *coming*," and he begins to beat the menservants and the maidservants, and to eat and drink and get drunk, 46 the <u>lord</u> of that servant will come on a day when he does not expect and at an hour he does not know, and will punish him and give him his portion among the unfaithful.

47 And that servant who knows his <u>lord</u>'s will and did not make preparations and did not act according to his will will receive many strokes. 48 But he who does not know (him) and does what deserves strokes will receive only a few strokes. Of everyone to whom much is given, much be required, and of him to whom they have entrusted much they will require all the more.'

Redaction and tradition

[35–38] These verses are an admonition about a householder returning home late, which have a secondary character: it is impossible to tell whether they already stood as a whole or in part in Q and whether Matthew thought to replace them by 25.1–13. Verse 35 is a metaphorical admonition to wakefulness which may have been original and used by Luke as an introduction to what follows. Cf. Didache 16.1: 'Watch over your life. Your lamps must not go out and your loins must not sleep, but be prepared. For you do not know the hour in which our Lord comes.' Verse 36 varies v. 35 in the form of a comparison. Verses 37–38 develop the comparison of v. 36 allegorically (the 'lord' means Jesus).

[39–40] These verses contain the Q parable of the thief (cf. Matt. 24.43–44). The image of the thief already occurs in early Christianity in I Thess. 5.2; cf. also Thomas 21.5; II Peter 3.10a; Rev. 3.3b. The existing Q parable is to be regarded only as a fragment, for the householder does not know when the thief is coming. Thus there is still a notion missing here (see my proposal under 'Historical'). Luke understands the lord in the preceding admonition (v. 37) as the Son of man from v. 40 (cf. v. 46b).

[41–46] The parable of the householder comes from Q (cf. Matt. 24.45–51). The introduction in vv. 41–42a gives it another target from that in Q, where it is asking about the faithful and wise servant. In v. 41 Luke substitutes 'steward' for 'servant' and thus relates it to the leader of the community.

[47–48] Luke combines the similitude of the servant's reward, which occurs only in him, with the parable in vv. 42–46. In Paul, too, sin as ignorance weighs more lightly than sin in the face of better knowledge (cf. I Cor. 10.28–29). According to Luke, the person who knows the will of the Lord (v. 47) is probably the leader of the Christian community in v. 46; the one who does not know (v. 48) is probably the Christian lay person.

Historical

[35–38, 41–46, 47–48] These passages presuppose the delay of the end or the coming of the Son of man. Since Jesus knew of no delay, they are therefore all unhistorical.

[39–40] Verse 39 is probably authentic. Its continuation, which has been broken off, may have been, 'but he did not know and that is why the thief was so successful'. This parable exhibits the theme of the immoral hero in Jesus, which is always an indication of authenticity.

Luke 12.49–53: Jesus' coming as the hour of decision

49 '*I have come to cast fire upon the earth, and how I wish that it had already been kindled!*
50 *I have a baptism to be baptized with, and how I am constrained until it is accomplished!*
51 Do you think that I have come to give peace on earth? No, I tell you, but rather division.
52 For there will be *henceforth in one house five divided, three against two and two against three;*
53 *they will be divided,* father against son and son against father, mother against daughter and daughter against her mother, mother-in-law against her daughter-in-law and daughter-in-law against her mother- in-law.'

Redaction and tradition

The passage concludes the instruction of the disciples which has continued since 12.1 and calls for discipleship with all its consequences, including splits in the family. This is an element of the expectation of the end. Cf. only Micah 7.6: 'The son despises the father, the daughter opposes her mother, the daughter in law is against the mother in law; and a man's enemies are those of his own house.'

[49–50] At the level of redaction both sayings are a further reference to the mission which leads to division (v. 49) and to the death of Jesus (v. 50). Moreover they again attest (cf. 2.34) the basic notion in Luke that Jesus' mission to the people of Israel brings division.

A distinction has to be made between v. 49 and v. 50. Certainly the formulation of the two sayings seems to be parallel. But they do not fit together: v. 49 is evidently about the goal of Jesus' activity, whereas v. 50 speaks of a temporary personal experience of Jesus, namely his death, about which he is anxious (Wellhausen). Verse 50 must therefore be a *vaticinium ex eventu* like Mark 10.38. It was either attached to Jesus' saying in v. 49 after the death of Jesus or Luke has formulated it himself in retrospect. In the latter case v. 49 may also come from Luke. The express identification of Jesus with the one involved in the event of the end time and the cosmic universalization of his eschatological function as one who brings fire fit better with Luke's christology and eschatology. According to Acts 17.31 Jesus is the judge of the ecumene predestined by God. In 21.10–11, 25–26 Luke introduces additional references to the eschatological cosmic catastrophes and emphasizes the world-embracing character of the event. The suspicion of Lukan redaction also holds for the elements expressing feeling in Luke 12.49. Such psychologizing corresponds generally with Luke's mode of description (cf. 2.19, 35; 4.38, 39; 6.11) and also determines the picture which he draws of Jesus: Jesus weeps over Jerusalem (19.41).

At the same time it is worth noting the attempt to understand v. 49 as part of Q. In that case one would have to presuppose that Jesus is the one baptizing with fire who had been announced by John (Luke 3.16).

[51] This is the heading of the next section, and like the saying Matt. 5.17 which arose in the community repudiates doubt about the person and cause of Jesus.

[52–53] Verse 52 has no parallel in Matthew and may be an expansion inserted by Luke. That is shown (a) by the phrase 'henceforth', typical of Luke, which is always followed by a verb form in the future and in Luke describes not the end time but the era of struggle which is now beginning (cf. Luke 22.69); (b) the 'division' with its Lukan language, which appears twice; and (c) the numbers which correspond precisely to the examples cited in v. 53, the next verse: the five persons in a house are father, mother, son, daughter and mother-in-law.

The prediction in v. 53 is the well-known eschatological prediction of the confusions of the end time according to Micah 7.6 (see the preliminary comment) which is also present in Mark 13.12. 'The fulfilment of that prophecy is seen in the experiences of the community and there is an awareness – a comfort in suffering – that Jesus spoke like this and brought it about' (Bultmann).

Historical

[49–50] These verses have been defined as a Lukan construction. If v. 49 derives from Q, the understanding of Jesus as the 'one baptizing with fire' announced by John is in any case inauthentic. It would be too singular.

[51–53] These verses reflect experiences of rifts in the families of early Christians and for this reason are inauthentic.

Luke 12.54–59: Estimating the time rightly and its consequences

54 *And he said to the crowds of people*, 'If you see a cloud rising in the west, you immediately say, "Rain is coming," and so it happens. 55 And if (you see) the south wind blowing, then you say, "It will be hot," and it happens. 56 *Hypocrites*, you know how to interpret the face of earth and heaven, how then can you not interpret the present time?

57 *Why do you not judge for yourselves what is right?* 58 For when you go with your

adversary to the *magistrate, make an effort* to *settle* with him on the way, lest he drag you before the judge, and the judge hand you over to the officer, and the officer throw you in prison. 59 I tell you, you will not get out of there until you have paid the last *penny*.'

Redaction and tradition

[54a] As previously in 12.13–21, the multitudes are being addressed.

[54b–56] These verses are a parable about time which has been handed down only by Luke and has been inserted into Matt. 16.2–3 at a secondary stage. It inculcates the threatening seriousness of the hour of decision, but does not contain any reference to the person of Jesus. 'There is no comparative particle, the parable has the form of a statement, and one in the second person at that. The application follows *e contrario* as a rhetorical question and seems to be quite original' (Bultmann).

[57] The non-disciples are to recognize what is right themselves (cf. Acts 4.19). The verse is a redactional transition to

[58–59] The form of address in the second person singular begins here. Luke has probably interpreted the original parable allegorically: in that case 'adversary' means Satan. The parable about agreeing at the right time, which is attested for Q by Matt. 5.25–26, is a typical example of a parable developed from a similitude. 'Because here there is neither comparative particle nor application, the tradition no longer understood the parable as such but made it into an admonition about being reconciled with earthly opponents in law, whereas the original sense was probably, "Just as you attach great importance in civil life in not coming before the judge, so be careful that you do not need to fear any accuser before the heavenly judge"' (Bultmann).

Historical

[54b–56, 58–59] At the level of the tradition both parables have a high claim to historicity. Each deals with a crisis in the face of which the hearer must make the right decision. As the situation of the later community is not visible and Jesus himself is not part of the parable, he may have spoken them. The subject about which he spoke in metaphor is the rule of God which breaks in unexpectedly, and the judgment associated with it.

Luke 13.1–9: The call to repentance and the parable of the fig tree

1 *Now some came at that very time who told him of the Galileans whose blood Pilate had mingled with their sacrifices.* 2 *And he answered and said to them, '*Do you think *that these Galileans were worse sinners than all the other Galileans, because they suffered this?* 3 No, I tell you,

but unless you repent you will all likewise perish. 4 Or those eighteen upon whom the tower in Siloam fell and killed them, do you think that they were more guilty than all the people who live in Jerusalem? 5 No, I tell you, but unless you repent you will all likewise perish.'

6 *And he told this parable*, 'A man had planted a fig tree in his vineyard; and he came seeking fruit on it and found none. 7 And he said to the vine-dresser, "Look, these three years I have come seeking fruit on this fig tree, and I find none. Cut it down; why should it use up the ground?" 8 But he answered him, "Lord, let it alone this year also, while I dig around it and put on manure, 9 (and see) if it bears fruit in the future; but if not, you can cut it down."'

Redaction and tradition

Verses 1–5 are a two-part composition which invites the hearers to repent with reference to a 'historical' example. Verses 6–9 are a counterpart to what has gone before: those to whom God still leaves an interval for repentance should use this, since it will not last much longer.

[1] This is a Lukan introduction with an apparently precise note of time. But it has long been established that the historian Josephus would not have passed over a massacre of Galileans while they were sacrificing in Jerusalem. More important is the observation that Josephus (*Jewish Antiquities* 18, 85ff.) reports a blood bath on the occasion of Pilate's action against the Samaritans on Mount Gerizim, the sanctuary of the Samaritans. This provoked a great stir and even led to the deposition of Pilate. But it did not take place until AD 35, when Jesus was no longer alive. Accordingly Luke has confused things.

[2–5] Note the symmetrical construction. The notion that guilt may not be inferred from misfortune (John 9) does occur in Luke. Those concerned even deserve their fate, but not more than the others who could have been killed with just as much justification. The question why God makes an example of them in particular is not touched on.

[6a] This is a formula by means of which Luke creates series (cf. 4.23; 5.36; 6.39; 12.16a, 41; 14.7; 15.3; 18.1, 9; 19.11; 20.9; 21.29). Luke combines two different traditions with this.

[6b–9] For Luke the interpretation of the fig tree in terms of the people of Israel seems settled (cf. 21.29). The tradition is a real parable without an application. There is a parallel to it in the fifth-century BC Story of Ahikar:

'My son, you are like a tree which bore no fruit, although it stood by the water, and its lord was compelled to cut it down. And it said to him, "Transplant me, and if even then I bear no fruit, cut me down." But its lord said to it, "If you bore no fruit when you stood by the water, how will you bear fruit in another place"' (J. Jeremias).

Historical

[1–5] For chronological reasons this passage does not go back to Jesus.

[6–9] The parable might be authentic, for (a) Jesus is not part of the parable; (b) it does not yet reflect the replacement of Israel with the church; (c) it corresponds to John the Baptist's preaching of judgment (Matt. 3.10) which Jesus has taken over from his teacher.

Luke 13.10–17: The healing of the woman bent over

10 *Now he was teaching in one of the synagogues on the sabbath.* 11 And *look*, there was a woman who had had a spirit of infirmity for eighteen years; and she was bent over and could not fully straighten herself. 12 When Jesus saw her, he called her and said to her, 'Woman, be freed from your infirmity,' 13 *and he laid his hands upon her, and immediately she stood upright and praised God.* 14 But the ruler of the synagogue, indignant because Jesus had healed on the sabbath, said to the people, 'There are six days on which work ought to be done. You may come on those days and be healed, and not on the sabbath day.' 15 But *the Lord* answered him and said, '*Hypocrites,* does not each of you on the sabbath untie his ox or his ass from the manger, and lead it away to drink? 16 And should not this woman, a daughter of Abraham whom Satan has bound, *look,* for eighteen years, be loosed from this bond on the sabbath day?' 17 *And as he said this, all his adversaries were put to shame; and all the crowd rejoiced at all the glorious things that were done by him.*

Redaction and tradition

Redactionally, Luke wants to show that the actions and words of Jesus give occasion for division between the people and its leaders. At the level of *tradition* there is a miracle story which is connected with the sabbath theme. This composition 'is the clumsiest of the three healings on the sabbath, because here – unlike 14.1–6 and Mark 3.1–6 – it takes place before the debate, so that the conclusion (v. 17) does not seem organic; for the shaming should have followed the miracle' (Bultmann).

[10] Luke presents the following story as a contribution to the sabbath problem.

[11–13] He narrates a self-contained story of illness and healing which in keeping with the style ends with praise from the woman healed. (Verse 16 adds the reason for the healing: the woman bent over is a daughter of Abraham; cf. 19.9.)

[14] The ruler of the synagogue does not turn to Jesus in his indignation but to those present, and introduces the sabbath theme, taking up v. 1.

[15–16] With the form of address 'Hypocrites' (plural), the 'Lord's' answer takes up the same form of address from 12.56 and is directed to his Jewish opponents. Verses 15b and 16 contain two different reasons for the healing; here 'on the sabbath' (v. 16 end) connects the two reasons. Probably here a healing story has later been developed into the narrative of a sabbath conflict (cf. John 5.9b; 9.14).

[17] This depicts the success of the discourse and Jesus' miracle with a conclusion to the narrative in v. 17b which is in keeping with the style (cf. 9.43).

Historical

The observations on the literary strata exclude the possibility that the narrative contains historical elements (authentic words or deeds of Jesus). Nevertheless it is clear for other reasons that Jesus came into conflict with the sabbath commandment (cf. on Mark 3.1–6).

Luke 13.18–21: The parables of the mustard seed and the leaven

18 *He said now*, 'What is the kingdom of God like and to what shall I compare it? 19 It is like a grain of mustard seed which a man took and sowed in *his garden*; and it grew and became a tree and the birds of the air made nests in its branches.'

20 *And again he said*, 'To what shall I compare the kingdom of God? 21 It is like leaven which a woman took and hid in three measures of wheatmeal, until it was all leavened.'

Redaction and tradition

Luke attaches two parables here, following Q (cf. Matt. 13.31–33). At the stage of redaction they relate to the world-wide progress of the proclamation of the kingdom, namely mission.

[18–19] The parable of the mustard seed is introduced by a Lukan linking formula and the traditional comparative formula. Luke doubtless intends the birds of the air to represent the Gentiles. The proclamation of the kingdom of God began with Jesus (16.16) and will reach the ends of the earth (Acts 1.8; 28.31). The parable which has been handed down is a parable of growth, unlike the Markan version (4.30–32), which is orientated on contrast. However, as the expectation of an imminent end also predominated in the Q community (cf. v. 19 end with the comments on Mark 4.30–32), the difference between parable of growth and parable of contrast is relativized. See also Thomas 20, where both features are united in the same parable.

[20–21] The parable uses the image of leaven and its permeating effect to portray the effect of the kingdom of God. Two things are striking. *First*, the formulation 'hid' is anything but normal. One would rather have expected a description of kneading. *Secondly*, the reference of the leaven to the kingdom of God is surprising, all the more so as leaven has negative connotations. According to Ex. 12.15–20, anything leavened must be kept away from the celebration of the Passover. It is even thought deserving of death to eat leavened bread during this period (Ex. 12.15).

Historical

[18–19] The parable is authentic (cf. on Mark 4.30–32).

[20–21] Because of its offensiveness the parable is to be termed authentic. At the same time the verb 'hide' points to the invisible beginning of the kingdom of God, and in this statement corresponds to other authentic parables of Jesus like the parable of the mustard seed which immediately precedes it.

Luke 13.22–30: The narrow door

22 *And he went on his way town by town and village by village, teaching, and journeying toward Jerusalem.* 23 *And someone said to him, 'Lord, will those who are saved be few?' And he said to them,* 24 'Strive to enter by the narrow <u>*door*</u>; for many, I tell you, will seek to enter and will not *be able*.

25 *As soon as the householder has got up and the <u>door</u> is shut and you begin to stand outside and knock at the <u>door</u> and say, "Lord, open to us," he will answer you, "<u>I do not know where you come from</u>."* 26 Then you will *begin to say, "We ate and drank in your presence, and you taught in our streets."* 27 And he will say, "<u>I do not know where you come from</u>; depart from me, all you workers of iniquity!" 28 There will be wailings and gnashing of teeth, when you see Abraham and Isaac and Jacob and all the prophets in the kingdom of God, and you yourselves are cast out. 29 And they will come from east and west, and from north and south, and recline at table in the kingdom of God. 30 *And look*, some are last who will be first, and some are first who will be last.'

Redaction and tradition

[22] The evangelist recalls that Jesus is travelling to Jerusalem. The language is Lukan. Luke does not imagine the journey as a short one but as long, purposeful activity.

[23–24] For the introductory phrase cf. 9.57; 10.25; 11.1, 27, 45; 12.13; 14.15; 18.18. The question of v. 23 is predetermined by 13.3,5 and occasioned by the universal aspect of 13.18–21. Therefore the whole of v. 23 is probably redactional. Verse 24 is a reworking of Q (cf. Matt. 7.13–14).

For the narrow gate in v. 24 cf. IV Ezra 7.6–8: 6 'There is a city built which lies in a plain and is full of all good things; but the entrance to it is narrow and leads to abysses where fire threatens on the right and deep water on the left; 8 and there is only a single path between the two, between fire and water, and this path is so narrow that it can take the footstep only of one man.'

[25] This verse is a redactional transition to v. 26. Still, it begins abruptly.

However, the key word 'door' which Luke has first made possible by changing the Q original 'gate' (Matt. 7.14) into 'door', provides a little hook, as the narrow door in v. 24 has become the closed door in v. 25.

[26–27] These verses derive from Q and have a parallel in Matt. 7.22–23. The prophetic saying looks back to Jesus' activity as concluded and therefore comes from the community. In Luke the logion rejects the unbelieving Jews but in Matthew Christian false teachers, which is probably secondary.

[28–29] These verses have a parallel in Matt. 8.11–12 (= Q). This is a prophetic threat which has no relation to the person of Jesus. It contrasts Gentiles with Jews. The former will recline at table in the kingdom of God and the latter will be shut out. The separation between Jews and Christians is presupposed. The saying derives from the community (cf. also on Matt. 8.11–12).

[30] In this context Luke refers the saying to Jews and Gentiles. The Gentiles as 'last' will finally become 'first'. For the traditional logion in this verse cf. further on Mark 10.31.

Historical

None of the sayings is authentic. For the reasons see above.

Luke 13.31–35: Jesus must die in Jerusalem

31 *At this hour some Pharisees came and said to him, 'Get away from here, for Herod wants to kill you.' 32 And he said to them, 'Go and tell that fox, "Look, I drive out evil spirits and perform cures today and tomorrow, and on the third day I shall be fulfilled. 33 But I must go on my way today and tomorrow and on the day following; for it cannot be that a prophet should perish outside Jerusalem."*

34 Jerusalem, Jerusalem, you who kill the prophets and stone those who are sent to you, how often I have wanted to gather your children as a hen gathers her brood under her wings, and you would not! 35 See, your house is to be forsaken. But I tell you, you will not see me until (the time) comes when you say, "Blessed is he who comes in the name of the Lord!" '

Redaction and tradition

[31–33] The passage takes up two sections from Q (Luke 13.25–30 and Luke 13.34–35) and explains (a) Jesus' further travelling; (b) his miracle-working activity; and (c) the necessity of his death in Jerusalem (and not in Galilee). All these – like the appearance of the Pharisees in v. 31 – are frequently recurring notions in the Gospel of Luke, so that the section as a whole is to be attributed to the redaction. For the redactional Herod motif cf. on 9.9.

[34–35] Luke inserts the threat against Jerusalem, which comes from Q (cf. Matt.

23.37–39) through the key word 'Jerusalem' (at the end of v. 33) at this point, whereas Matthew may have preserved the Q order. The saying about the necessity of Jesus' death in Jerusalem leads to the lament over Jerusalem, the city which has always murdered God's prophets. The threat is purely of Jewish origin and has a Christian addition only in v. 35b (cf. Matt. 23.39b). It fits well the Q polemic against whole cities: Chorazin, Bethsaida, Capernaum (cf. 10.13–16) and now Jerusalem. In this way *all* the Jews of the last generation are accused. As in 11.49 the speaker is Wisdom, with whom Jesus is identified here. Moreover, Wisdom, Jesus and the judge of the world are to be identified (v. 35b: Ps. 118.26 is understood in apocalyptic terms).

Historical

[34–35] These verses are inauthentic as sayings of Jesus, for they presuppose supra-historical Wisdom as the speaker (see under Tradition). For wisdom christology as a construction by the community cf. the summary on 11.49.

Luke 14.1–6: The healing of a man with dropsy

1 *And it happened, when he had entered the house of a ruler of the Pharisees to eat on the sabbath, they were there to spy on him.* 2 *And look, there was a man before him who had dropsy.* 3 *And Jesus answered and spoke to the experts on law and Pharisees and said,* 'Is it lawful to heal on the sabbath, or not?' 4 *But they were silent. And he took him and healed him, and let him go.* 5 *And he said to them,* 'Which of you who has a son or an ox that has fallen into a well, will not immediately pull him out on a sabbath day?' 6 *And they could not reply to this.*

Redaction and tradition

The present text stands in a longer section (14.1–24) which consists of sayings of Jesus to teachers of the law and Pharisees, on the occasion of a meal. On the level of the tradition the passage is a variant of Mark 3.1–6.

[1a] This is a redactional resumption from 7.36.

[3–4] Here, as in 6.9, the opponents are put to silence by a question which is constructed in parallel.

[5] This verse contains a traditional argument in the debates about the sabbath in the primitive community (cf. Matt. 12.11).

[6] This verse emphasizes the superiority of Jesus.

Historical

Only in the case of the logion on the sabbath, v. 5 (cf. Matt. 12.11) does there remain
a possibility – but no more – that from the beginning it served to justify Jesus' healings on the sabbath.

Luke 14.7–14: Hierarchy of guests

7 *And he told a parable to those who were invited, when he observed how they chose the first places
at table, and said to them,* 8 'When you are invited by any one to a marriage feast, do not
recline in the first place, lest a more worthy man than you has been invited by him, 9 and the
one who invited you both will say to you, "Give place to this man," and then you *begin* with
shame to take the lowest place. 10 But when you are invited, go and recline in the lowest
place, so that when the one who has invited you comes, he will say to you, "Friend, go up
higher." Then you will be honoured in the presence of all who recline at table with you.
11 For every one who exalts himself will be humbled, and he who humbles himself will be
exalted.'

12 *He said also to the man who had invited him, 'When you give a breakfast or a dinner, do not
invite your friends or your brothers or your kinsmen or rich neighbours, lest they also invite you in
return, and you be repaid.* 13 *But when you give a feast, invite the poor, the maimed, the lame,
the blind,* 14 *and you will be blessed, because they cannot repay you. You will be repaid* at the
resurrection of the just.'

Redaction and tradition

The two parts of the discourse (v. 7–11 and vv. 12–14) have fundamentally the same structure. First of all the mode of behaviour to be criticized is mentioned and then what is called
for positively is described. In each case there is a promise at the end (vv. 11, 14).

[7] This verse is a Lukan introduction and designates what follows as a parable.

[8–10] The parable is to be understood as an admonition to be modest at a meal to
which one is invited. In fact it is a bit of 'table manners' (M.Dibelius). Cf. Prov.
25.6–7: 'Do not put yourself forward in the king's presence and do not stand in the
place of the great. For it is better to be told, "Come up here," than to be humiliated
before a superior.'

[11] Cf. 18.14. In any case v. 11 has been added to vv. 8–10 only at a later stage.

[12–14] A rule for hosts follows the table manners (vv. 7–11). The list of those
who have not been invited betrays Lukan diction. The passage is addressed to
Christians who can afford to offer breakfast or supper to a large number of guests,
but in so doing, in keeping with the Greek ethic of reciprocity, remain among themselves and exclude socially weak members of the community or even outsiders (cf.
further on v. 21). Verse 14 contains a view of the resurrection which in its limitation

to the righteous is to be judged pre-Lukan. In Acts 24.15 Paul repeats this saying in his own words, evidently as a polemic against limiting the expectation of the resurrection to the righteous.

Historical

The historical yield is nil, as all the words in this section can be derived from the community or attributed to Luke.

Luke 14.15–24: The parable of the great feast

15 *When one of those who were reclining at table with him heard this, he said to him, 'Blessed is he who eats bread in the kingdom of God!'*

16 But he said to him, 'A man once gave a great banquet *and invited many.* 17 And at the time of the banquet he sent his servant to say to those who had been invited, "Come, for all is now ready." 18 And they all alike *began to make excuses. The first said to him. "I have bought a field, and I must go out and see it; I beg you, have me excused."* 19 And another said, "I have bought five yoke of oxen, and I am going to inspect them; *I pray you,* have me excused." 20 *And another said, "I have married a wife, and therefore I cannot come."* 21 And when the servant came to him, he *reported* this to his lord. Then the householder became angry and said to his servant. "Go out quickly to the streets and lanes of the city and bring here *the poor and maimed and blind and lame."* 22 *And the servant said, "Lord, what you commanded has been done, and still there is room."* 23 *And the lord said to the servant, "Go out to the highways and hedges (outside the city), and compel them to come in, that my house may be filled.* 24 *For I tell you, none of those men who were invited shall taste my banquet."'*

Redaction

The parable of the banquet comes from the Q tradition, as the Matthaean parallel (22.1–10) shows (see under 'Tradition').

[15] This verse has a transitional function. One of those present takes up the beatitude from v. 14 and understands the restitution announced there as taking place at the resurrection of the righteous to mean participation in the heavenly feast.

[18–20] The symmetry of the three excuses is matched by the threefold parallelism in 20.10–12 (cf. 8.3–8, 12–15). The parallel texts from Matthew and Mark do not contain this careful symmetry. Because of v. 26 below, v. 20 is probably redactional.

[21] Here the same list appears as in the context 14.13: poor, maimed, lame, blind. In the context of the Gospel of Luke – that is the *first* point – the parable thus serves as an exemplary narrative on the invitation issued in 14.12–14 to invite the poorest.

[22–23] In these verses a *second* point of the parable for Luke becomes clear: the people living outside the city might refer to the Gentiles. In this way, according to Luke Jesus opens up access to the kingdom of God for the Gentiles (cf. Acts 28.28).

[24] Luke's *third* point lies here. Those originally invited to the meal (namely the Jews) are denied access to the meal because they did not accept the invitation. Matthew reinforces what Luke only states and depicts it in a violent way: the (unbelieving) Jews are killed and are excluded from salvation for ever (see on Matt. 22.1–10). In other words, the positive move to the Gentiles is matched negatively by the rejection of the Jews – and this explicitly on the instructions of 'Jesus'.

Tradition

'It is a sorry fate that in the case of this parable too we know what Matthew intended by it and what Luke discovered in it, but only by bold hypotheses can we approach the form in which it came from Jesus' mouth and thus approach its original thought' (Jülicher).

The possibility of getting back to the earliest tradition has been improved by the discovery of the Gospel of Thomas. For here a further version of the parable of the feast occurs as Logion 64. And not only this. Here the parable seems to have been handed on intact.

'According to this a messenger of the lord goes to those invited, all of whom – here there are four – excuse themselves. When he reports this to the lord, he replies, "Go out into the streets; bring those whom you find so that they share in the meal." Then Thomas adds as a conclusion, "Businessmen and merchants will not enter the places of my Father"' (Haenchen).

Apart from (a) the abbreviated introduction, (b) the extension of the invitation from three to four (three is a round number and thus original) and (c) the interpretation of the parable in terms of merchants, the rest may be a version free of allegorical features and therefore original.

Historical

Because of the redactional features, the present parable in the Lukan version has departed from history and is inauthentic. In the original parable, which is represented most clearly by Thomas 64, the focus is the refusal of the invitation. At the same time it is indicated that despite the unexpected rejection of the invitation the feast can nevertheless be held. A historical point of contact for the meal is presented by the meals in which Jesus was involved, which were increasingly frequented by shady people. Jesus resorts to a parable to defend the company he keeps.

Luke 14.25–35: Jesus' discourse on discipleship

25 *Now a great crowd came together, and he turned and said to them,* 26 'If anyone *comes to me* and does not hate his father and mother *and his wife* and children and his brothers and his sisters, yes, *and even his own life,* he <u>cannot be my disciple</u>. 27 Whoever does not bear his cross and come after me, <u>cannot be my disciple</u>.

28 For which of you, who wants to build a tower, does not first sit down and count the cost, whether he is in a position to complete it? 29 Otherwise, when he has laid the foundation and is not able to finish (it), all who see it *will begin* to mock him, 30 saying, "This man *began* to build and was not in a position to complete it." 31 Or what king, who wants to encounter another king in war, will not sit down first and take counsel whether he is able with ten thousand to meet one who comes against him with twenty thousand? 32 And if not, while the other is still distant, he sends a delegation and asks for peace. 33 *So therefore, whoever of you does not renounce all that he has* <u>*cannot be my disciple*</u>.

34 Now salt is good, but if salt has lost its taste, what will be used for seasoning? 35 It is fit neither for the land nor for the dunghill; people throw it away. *He who has ears to hear, let him hear.'*

Redaction and tradition

This is a further discourse composition. Luke had already made Jesus give a discourse on the goods of this world in 12.13–34, in 12.35–39 a discourse on the last things and in 14.7–24 a discourse on hospitality; in 15.1–32 a discourse on the lost will follow.

[25] This is a Lukan construction. 'The appearance of the people shows that again the effect is to be emphasized – but on the journey' (Conzelmann).

[26–27] The passage derives from Q (cf. Matt. 10.37–38). Thomas 55 as a mixed quotation comes between the Lukan and Markan versions. With the verb 'hate' Luke has certainly preserved the original expression. Similarly, the discourse on discipleship in Luke may give the Q text, since it is more concrete than the version '(not) be worthy of Jesus' (Matt. 10.37f.). By contrast, Luke must have added 'and his wife' and 'even his own life' to the Q text. In 18.29, too, Luke also inserts 'wife' into Mark (10.20). 'His own life' has been added here by Luke for the sake of completeness, cf. Luke 9.24 (= Mark 8.35). In v. 27 the negative version of Q seems to be more original than the positive version in Mark (8.34), where 'discipleship is no longer the condition but already has the radiance of a value in itself' (Bultmann).

[28–33] Verses 28–32 support community paraenesis. The community finds itself again in the double parable, insofar as it is summoned to persist on the way it has taken. Verse 33 is a direct application of the parables to the Lukan community; here the phrase 'cannot be my disciple' includes the passage vv. 25–27. Thus for Luke the occasion to emphasize the break with wives probably lies in the specific experiences of his community, all the more so as in 14.20 marriage was the occasion for declining the invitation to the feast.

For the double parable of the building of the tower and waging war which Luke has inserted cf. Prov. 24.3, 'By wisdom a house is built and by understanding it is established'; 24.6a, 'For by wise guidance you can wage war'. The speaker has used such notions, which are widespread in the wisdom literature, in order to call for self-examination.

[34–35] Luke renders the parable according to Q (cf. Matt. 5.13, where in contrast to Luke the explicit reference is to the disciples). But he adjusts the text to that of Mark 9.50a. Luke has taken over the closing sentence word for word from 8.8.

Historical

[26] This verse, without the redactional additions, is an authentic saying of Jesus. Hating parents is a phrase which is deliberately used to denote the actual relationship. 9.59f. offers one of the possible concrete forms of this, namely not being concerned about burying one's dead father. The theological reason for this radical quality is based on the advent of the kingdom of God. The destruction of Jesus' relationship with his own family may have been an additional factor. For according to Mark 3.21, they think that he is out of his mind. The saying cannot be derived from the community, since in the framework of Christian families such a saying would be ruled out.

[27] This verse is probably inauthentic, as here 'cross' is understood in the metaphorical sense (cf. on Mark 8.34).

[28–32] In my view there is more to be said for the authenticity than for the inauthenticity of these verses. Here the speaker is a wise man who, as in Thomas 98, observes the harsh reality and foresees the difficulty of carrying out a challenging plan. Unfortunately the context of these parables is unclear, so it does not become evident what kind of self-examination is called for.

[34–35] Cf. on Matt. 5.13.

Luke 15.1–10: The parables of the lost sheep and the lost drachma

1 *And all the toll collectors and sinners were drawing near to him to hear him. 2 And the Pharisees and scribes murmured, saying, 'This man receives sinners and eats with them.' 3 And he told them the following parable and said,*

4 'What man of you has a hundred sheep and loses one of them, and does not leave the ninety-nine in the wilderness and go after the one which is lost, until he finds it? 5 And when he finds it, he lays it on his shoulders full of joy, 6 and when he comes home he calls together his friends and neighbours, and says to them, "Rejoice with me, for I have found my sheep

which was lost." 7 *I tell you, there will be more joy in heaven over one sinner who repents than over ninety-nine righteous persons who need no repentance.*

8 Or what woman, having who has ten drachmas, if she loses one, does not light a lamp and sweep the house and seek diligently until she finds (it)? 9 And when she finds (it), she calls together her friends and neighbours, saying, "<u>Rejoice with me, for I have found</u> my drachma which I had lost." 10 *So I tell you, there is joy before the angels of God over one sinner who repents.'*

Redaction and tradition

[1–2] These verses are details of a situation which derive from Luke.

[3] The introduction to the first parable similarly derives from Luke (cf. by analogy 5.36).

[4–6] The parable of the lost sheep taken over from Q (cf. Matt. 18.12f.) inculcates the notion that finding brings very great joy. This clause evidently relates to God, who rejoices over all in Israel who allow themselves to be found by him and his messenger, Jesus. The version of the lost sheep in Thomas 107 is secondary in terms of the history of the tradition, since there the lost sheep is said to be the largest.

[7] This verse contains the Lukan application of the first parable which corresponds to the second (cf. v. 10). Also in support of the redactional character of v. 7 is the fact that this application is absent from the parallel in Matthew (18.14).

[8–9] The parable of the lost drachma taken over from the tradition inculcates the same idea as vv. 4–6, except that with the shepherd metaphor God is immediately thought of (cf. Ps. 23). But this second parable might also have been handed down with the parable of the lost sheep because of its structure, which is parallel with vv. 4–6. Perhaps it comes from Q and was omitted by Matthew because it did not fit into the community rule in Matt. 18.

[10] This verse gives the Lukan application of the second parable: it is about the repentance of the sinner, and the resulting joy in heaven.

Historical

[4–6, 8–9] It is highly probable that both the parable of the lost sheep and that of the lost drachma go back to Jesus. Indeed, Jesus exaggerates the behaviour of the shepherd who leaves behind ninety-nine sheep in order to seek the one. With this behaviour he in fact endangers the existence of the ninety-nine, who could fall victim to predatory animals. This kind of exaggeration can often be found in Jesus' sayings and parables and is therefore a sign of the authenticity of the parable. (The same goes for the woman who although she has nine drachmae, turns everything upside down to find the one lost drachma.) According to Jesus, God seeks the lost and these do not first have to resolve to repent.

Luke 15.11–32: The parable of the father's compassion

11 *And he said,* 'A man had two sons. 12 And the younger of them said to his father, "Father, give me the share of property that falls to me." And he divided his living between them. 13 And not *many days* later, the younger son gathered all he had and went from there into a far country. And there he wasted his property senselessly. 14 And when he had spent everything, a *severe famine* arose in that country, and he *began* to suffer want. 15 And he went and joined himself to a citizen of that country, and he sent him into his fields to feed pigs. 16 And he would gladly have filled his belly with the pods that the pigs ate; and no one gave them to him. 17 Then he came to himself and said, 'How many of my father's hired servants have more than enough to eat, but I perish here with hunger! 18 *I will arise and go to my father, and I will say to him, "Father, I have sinned against heaven and before you*; 19 *I am no longer worthy to be called your son. Treat me as one of your hired servants."* 20 And he set off and came to his father. But when he was still a long way off, his father saw him and had compassion on him, and ran *and fell on his neck and kissed him.* 21 *And the son said to him, "Father, I have sinned against heaven and before you; I am no longer worthy to be called your son."* 22 *But* the father *said* to his servants, "Bring quickly the best robe, and put it on him, and put a ring on his hand, and shoes on his feet. 23 And bring the fatted calf and kill it, and let us eat and make merry; 24 for this my son was dead and is alive again; he *was lost*, and is found." And they began to make merry.

25 Now his elder son was in the field; and as he came and drew near to the house, he heard music and dancing 26 and he called one of the lads and *asked what this meant.* 27 And he said to him, "Your brother has come, and your father has killed the fatted calf, because he has received him back safe and sound." 28 But he became furious and refused to go in. But his father came out and spoke to him. 29 And he answered and said to his father, "Look, for many years I have served you like a slave, and never disobeyed your command; yet you never gave me a kid, that I might make merry with my friends. 30 But now when this son of yours comes, who has devoured your living with prostitutes, you have killed the fatted calf!" 31 And he said to him, "Child, you are always with me, and all that is mine is yours. 32 It was fitting to make merry and be glad, for this your brother was dead and came to life again; and was lost, and is found."'

Redaction

The parable stands in the wider context of Jesus' discourses about the lost and is its third part. It serves as an illustration of 15.1–3. 'The example of a father who lovingly receives his son who has returned home laden with guilt, but penitent, and justifies his joy in the face of the wrath of the older son who has always remained faithful is meant to justify Jesus who welcomes toll collectors and sinners, although the Pharisees and scribes murmur about it' (Jülicher).

[18–19] These verses have been added by Luke with the aim of heightening the drama of the narrative.

[21] Cf. on vv. 18–19.

Tradition

The basis is a parable with two points; it is impossible to decide with certainty whether the second part was originally told with the first part or was added only at a later stage of the tradition. The father figure is doubtless a metaphor for God. It is in keeping with this that the compassion (v. 20) is best related to God. The son is probably to be interpreted in individualistic terms, i.e. as the person entangled in sin. The older brother represents a Jewish person who objects to God's compassion. For the interpretation, this means that the parable tells of God's mercy on people which is unconditional and in which God takes the initiative. This concern is shown in the preaching of the approaching rule of God. In this respect the one who tells the parable, Jesus, is indirectly an element of the parable. And he himself illustrates by the figure of the prodigal son that God cares for sinners.

Historical

The parable goes back to Jesus. *First,* no kind of influence of later community theology or even of Luke's theology can be discovered in it. Thus the parable is not a reflection of the Lukan view that the gospel is offered to the Jews and then in their place to the Gentiles (cf. Acts 28.17–28). Rather, at the end of the parable the elder brother is invited to take part in the celebration and the father asks him to understand it. The parable represents the reconciliation of the Jews among themselves, not the replacement of the Jews by Gentiles. The return of the prodigal son means the restoration of the family and that means that it is time to celebrate, if the elder brother can bring himself to take part in the feast. *Secondly,* the parable contains features of Jesus' picture of God, according to which along the lines of Jesus' discourses and actions God seeks out the lost without any preconditions. Jesus' life actualizes the love of God, and the parable is an illustration of this. *Thirdly,* the anthropomorphic character of the parable suggests that it originates with Jesus. 'In a markedly anthropomorphic way the bliss of God's discovery is compared with the happiness of undisturbed possession; this anthropomorphic character is one of the true signs of the authenticity of our parable' (Jülicher).

Luke 16.1–13: The parable of the unjust steward and various applications

1 *And he also said to the disciples,* 'There was a rich man who had a steward, and charges were brought to him that this man was wasting his goods. 2 And he called him and said to him, "What is this that *I hear about you?* Give account of your stewardship, for you can no longer be steward.'" 3 And the steward *said to himself,* "What shall I do? For my <u>lord</u> is taking the stewardship away from me. I cannot dig, and I am ashamed to beg. 4 *I know what I shall do, so*

that when I am put out of the stewardship <u>they will receive</u> me <u>in</u> their houses. 5 And he called his <u>lord</u>'s debtors *one by one*, and said to the first, "How much do you owe my lord?" 6 He said, "One hundred bath of oil." And he said to him, "Take your bill, and sit down and quickly write fifty." 7 Then he said to another, "And you, how much do you owe?" He said, "A hundred cor of wheat." He said to him, "Take your bill, and write eighty."

8 And the <u>lord</u> commended the steward OF UNRIGHTEOUSNESS because he had acted wisely, *because the sons of this world are wiser towards their own generation than the sons of light. 9 And I tell you, make friends with the mammon OF UNRIGHTEOUSNESS, so that when it fails* <u>*they will receive*</u> *you* <u>*in*</u> *the eternal habitations.*

10 *He who is faithful in the least is also faithful in much; and he who is dishonest in the least is also dishonest in much. 11 If then you are not faithful in the unrighteous mammon, who will entrust to you the true riches? 12 And if you are not faithful in that which is another's, who will give you that which is your own? 13 No servant can serve two lords; for either he will hate the one and love the other, or he will hold to the one and despise the other. You cannot serve God and mammon.'*

Redaction and tradition

Luke links the story to the three parables which in ch. 15 had been addressed to the Pharisees by a loose 'and he also said to the disciples' (cf. 18.1; 17.1); v. 14 below explicitly says that the Pharisees are to be thought of as still present. Verses 15–31 again contain a discourse spoken directly to the Pharisees. That Luke designates 16.1–13 a discourse to the disciples despite this framework follows from the section vv. 8–13, which is addressed to the Lukan community. In vv. 1b–7 it is prefaced by the parable of the shrewdness of a cheat around which various rings of tradition have formed. No wonder, since here Jesus is introducing a criminal as a model for his followers to imitate in one way or another.

[1] 'Waste' corresponds to 15.13,

[2] The question is redactional, as a look at Acts 14.15 shows. Moreover the construction 'hear about someone' appears only in Luke: cf. 9.9.

[3] For the steward's reflection about his situation cf. 12.17; 15.17; 18.4.

[8a] According to Luke 'the lord' refers to the lord in the parable (vv. 3 and 5), whereas at the level of the tradition 'the lord' refers to the Lord Jesus. The christological interpretation of the parable after 'Easter' begins with v. 8a and is continued in v. 9. Note the immediate context in 18.6, where the Lord Jesus is similarly speaking in the application of the parable by 'the lord' and at the same time the main character of the parable, the judge, is designated 'judge of unrighteousness' – just as the main character of the parable 16.1–7 in the interpretation is named 'steward of unrighteousness' (v. 8). Probably both parables came down to Luke with an application already appended.

[8b] As a new interpretation this verse develops v. 8a and depicts the steward as a model of shrewdness for believers. But who would doubt that shrewdness is praiseworthy?

[9] This verse provides an additional interpretation and makes Jesus give further advice about being accepted into heaven through money. Cf. the way in which 'receive in houses' (v. 4) and 'receive in habitations' (v. 9) correspond. Any natural dislike for the steward of unrighteousness (v. 8b) is overcome to some degree by the fact that the mammon of unrighteousness (v. 9) is at least used for acceptance into the eternal habitations. The narrative of the rich man and poor Lazarus (16.19–31) will later continue the theme of mammon (= wealth) and make it clear what a rich man has to expect if he does not use mammon in the way called for in v. 9.

[10–13] These verses are an appendix 'made up of various sayings which above all want to avoid the possible misunderstanding that disloyalty is something commendable for a steward' (Klostermann). Cf. v. 10 with 19.17; here there is an antithetical proverb on faithfulness and unfaithfulness in the smallest things. The proverb in vv. 11–12 is 'applied to mammon and eternal goods. This interpretation says that the man is not a model but a deterrent!' (J. Jeremias). Verse 13 is a redactional conclusion from the pericope. The warning against serving two masters similarly occurs at Matt. 6.24; Thomas 47.2. By inserting 'servant' Luke makes specific what Matthew and Thomas formulate as a general principle.

Historical

[1b–7] It is very probable that the parable goes back to Jesus. It is clearly offensive, as the subsequent interpretations in the present pericope show. The criteria of offensiveness and growth apply to it, as at least five rings of tradition have formed round vv. 1b–7: first v. 8a, secondly v. 8b, thirdly v. 9, fourthly vv. 10–12 and fifthly v. 13.

However, I find doubtful the *eschatological interpretation of the parable* according to which it is important to use the time wisely at the last moment. Rather, the parable seems to be about using the present as the time of decision, not in view of a coming catastrophe but in view of a crisis which is apparently impossible to overcome. 'The resolute use of the present as a precondition for an enjoyable future, and an assessment of circumstances which is completely without illusions, are to be inculcated with the story of the steward. But certainly not the right use of riches' (Wellhausen). If one wishes, this is about a strategy for survival, the type of the immoral hero which Jesus himself was in part (7.34), which included many of his hearers like toll collectors and prostitutes, and which similarly appears in other parables (Thomas 98; Matt. 13.44; 24.43–44 and Luke 18.2–5).

[8–13] With the exception of v. 13a (cf. on Matt. 6.24), the sayings are inauthentic. For the reasons see above.

Luke 16.14–18: Jesus' verdict on the Pharisees, the law and divorce

14 *The Pharisees, who were lovers of money, heard all this, and they scoffed at him.* 15 *And he said to them, 'You are those who justify yourselves before men, but God knows your hearts; for what is exalted among men is an abomination before God.*

16 The law and the prophets extend up to John; from then on *the kingdom of God is preached*, and every one enters it violently.

17 It is easier for heaven and earth to pass away, than for one dot to fall from the law.

18 Whoever dismisses his wife (from a marriage) *and marries another* commits adultery; and every one who marries a woman dismissed by her husband (from marriage) commits adultery.'

Redaction and tradition

[14–15] These verses are completely rooted in the situation of Luke's community and have similarities with the admonitions to the rich in I Tim. 6.9–10, 17–19. The warning against ambition is combined with that against arrogance also in this letter attributed to Paul, which comes from the beginning of the second century. Rich Christians from the Lukan communities can recognize themselves in the artificial picture of the Pharisees.

[16–19] Exegetes have been endlessly ingenious in producing a smooth train of thought between these three logia; how successful they have been remains to be seen. But these difficulties have one advantage. They demonstrate that all these sayings are logia of Jesus handed down in isolation, each of which was known in the communities before the composition of the Gospel of Luke. The phrase 'the kingdom of God is preached' in v. 16 clearly derives from Luke (cf. on 8.1). 'From then on' can be understood inclusively or exclusively. In the latter case the preaching of the kingdom of God is begun by Jesus and has been continued by his disciples. Thus according to v. 16 the time of the preaching of the kingdom of God (by Jesus and the church) is contrasted with a time of the law and the prophets (including John). (For the Q basis of this verse cf. Matt. 11.12–13.)

It is remarkable that Luke hands on the rigorous saying of Jesus in v. 17 without changing it, and does so in a far harsher form than Matt. 5.18. But he has relativized it in advance by v. 16, as here the law is replaced by the preaching of the kingdom of God. For the Q tradition cf. on Matt. 5.18. The prohibition of divorce in v. 18 endorses the previous verse about the validity of the law and shows 'that the dissolution of the law by Jesus is in truth fulfilment' (Conzelmann). Luke adds 'and marries another' from Mark 10.11 to the Q logion he has (cf. on Matt. 5.32). (The section Mark 10.1–12 was passed over by him.) In so doing the Lukan Jesus does not declare the man guilty because he dismisses his wife but because he remarries.

Historical

[16] Cf. on Matt. 11.12–13.
[17] Cf. on Matt. 5.18.
[18] Cf. on Matt. 5.32.

Luke 16.19–31: The parable of the rich man and poor Lazarus

19 '*Now a man was rich*, and clothed himself in purple and finest linen and feasted sumptuously every day. 20 And a poor man *named* Lazarus, covered with sores, was laid on his threshold, 21 full of longing to be filled with what fell from the rich man's table; and even the dogs came and licked his sores. 22 *Now it happened* that the poor man died and was carried by the angels to Abraham's breast. The rich man also died and was buried. 23 And in the underworld he lifted up his eyes when he *found himself* in torment, and saw Abraham far off and Lazarus on his breast. 24 And he called out and said, "Father Abraham, have compassion on me, and send Lazarus to dip the end of his finger in water and cool my tongue, for I am *suffering torments* in this flame." 25 *But* Abraham *said*, "Child, remember that you in your lifetime received your good things and Lazarus likewise evil things. But now he is comforted here, and you are suffering torment. 26 *And besides all this, between us and you a great gulf has been fixed, so that those who want to pass from here to you could not, and so that they would not cross from there to us.*"

27 *And he said, "Then I beg you, father, to send him to my father's house, 28 for I have five brothers, so that he may testify to them, lest they also come into this place of pain." 29 But Abraham says, "They have Moses and the prophets, let them hear them." 30 And he said to him, "No, father Abraham, but if someone came to them from the dead, they would repent." 31 But he said to him, "If they do not hear Moses and the prophets, neither will they be convinced if one should rise from the dead."'*

Redaction and tradition

Note that v. 19 is attached to v. 18 without a transition. Verse 19 presupposes the discourse to the disciples (v. 1, 'and he also said to the disciples'). The address to the disciples is next marked in 17.1. The Lukan sense of the passage is to illustrate how one can make friends with the unrighteous mammon (cf. v. 9). 'This is not a real parable but a story with two types invented for purposes of teaching, like 189.9ff.* In vv. 27–31 a continuation has been attached to the main piece, vv. 19–25' (Wellhausen).

[19a] The theme is still mammon.
[19b–25] The story tells of compensation for earthly fortunes in the next world. In this respect it has countless parallels in ancient popular literature and wisdom. The figure of Abraham makes it probable that the story originates in Judaism. Its point is to comfort the poor and/or warn the rich.

[26] This verse is a Lukan transition to the second part of the narrative.

[27–31] This part is a continuation of the conversation between the rich man and Abraham which began in v. 24. As the torment of the rich man cannot be relieved for the reason given in v. 26, Lazarus is at least to warn the five brothers of the dead rich man. But Abraham refuses this. Moses and the prophets, who are known to the five brothers, have already taught them the will of God. Therefore the resurrection of a dead man like Lazarus is unnecessary. At the same time Luke's formulation here looks back on the resurrection of Jesus, in which many Jews did not believe. Now it becomes clear wherein Luke sees the will of God which the five brothers and their dead brother have not done. It consists in caring for the poor, not being greedy and giving alms.

Historical

[19–25] The passage no more goes back to Jesus than the parable of the rich farmer (12.16–20). For the reason see there.

Luke 17.1–10: Discipleship

1 *And he said to his disciples*, 'Offences are sure to come; but woe to him by whom they come! 2 It would be better for him if a millstone were hung round his neck and he were thrown <u>in the sea</u>, than that he should cause one of these little ones to fall. 3 Take heed to yourselves.

If your brother sins, rebuke him, and if he *repents, forgive him*. 4 And if he sins against you seven times in the day, and turns to you seven times, and says, *"I repent,"* you should forgive him.'

5 *And the apostles said to the Lord, 'Increase our faith.'* 6 *And the Lord said,* 'If you had faith like a grain of mustard seed, you could say to this *sycamore tree*, "Be rooted up, and plant yourself <u>in the sea</u>," and it would obey you.

7 But who among you, who has a servant ploughing or herding (cattle), will say to him when he has come in from the field, "Come at once and recline at table"? 8 On the contrary, will he not say to him, "Prepare supper for me, gird yourself and serve me, until I have eaten and drunk, and afterwards you eat and drink"? 9 Will he thank the servant for doing what was commanded? 10 *So you also, when you have done all that was commanded you, say, "We are useless servants; we have done what was our duty."*'

Redaction and tradition

[1–3a] Verse 1a is a redactional introduction (cf. 9.14; 12.22; 17.22). The rest reproduces Q material (cf. Matt. 18.6–7). Verse 3a, the first admonition, belongs to this.

[3b–4] These verses derive from Q (cf. Matt. 18.15, 21–22). But Luke has put other emphases on the tradition. Redactionally he sets sin and conversion over against each other. Repentance is an expression of remorse and a will for improvement. Then follows forgiveness.

[5–6] It is hard to say why Luke puts this piece from Q (cf. on Matt. 17.20; cf. further Thomas 48 and 106) here. At any rate it is striking that both v. 2 and v. 6 mention the sea in which the seducer is to be cast (v. 1) or the sycamore tree planted (v. 6). As 18.8 makes clear, in talking of faith Luke is probably thinking of faith which is maintained in the face of the delay of the return of Jesus. The faith of the apostles is later given special power for strengthening the brethren (22.31f.).

[7–9] The reason why this passage, which in terms of tradition is to be described as a similitude, is put here is the overarching perspective of discipleship rightly understood in relation to God, but also in relation to the weak members of the community. As a parallel see the tractate from the Mishnah, Aboth I 3, which at the latest comes from the second century: 'Do not be like servants who serve their lord on condition that they receive reward; be rather like servants who serve the Lord on condition that they receive no reward.'

[10] As the closing sentence, this verse draws the conclusion from what has been said since 16.1 and especially in vv. 1–9: the disciples have a duty to do the will of God.

Historical

[1–6] These verses are certainly unhistorical. They reflect conditions in the Christian communities and in no way go back to Jesus. The only exception may be the saying about faith in v. 6. But this goes back to Jesus only in a modified form (see on Matt. 17.20).

[7–9] The similitude probably goes back to Jesus. Its world of ideas is that of a small farmer. Its content, that one has no claim to reward, is characteristic of Jesus. It is unclear to whom it was said. The widespread view that the similitude is aimed at the self-righteousness of the Pharisees, according to whom one gets a claim to reward by serving God, is not compelling. Cf. the parallel (probably Pharisaic) given under 'Redaction and Tradition'.

Luke 17.11–19: The healing of ten lepers

11 *And it happened, when he was travelling to Jerusalem, that he passed through the midst of Samaria and Galilee.* 12 *And as he entered a village,* ten lepers ran towards him, who stood at a distance from him. 13 And they lifted up their voices and said, 'Jesus, Master, have mercy on us.' 14 When he saw (them), he said to them, '*Go,* show yourselves to the priests.' *And it happened that as they were going away,* they were cleansed. 15 One of them, when he saw that

he had been healed, *turned back, praising God with a loud voice.* 16 And he fell on his face *at his feet*, to thank him. Now he was a Samaritan. 17 And Jesus answered and said, 'Were not ten cleansed? Where are the nine? 18 Was no one found *to return and give praise to God* except this foreigner?' 19 *And he said to him, 'Rise and go, your faith has saved you.'*

Redaction and tradition

The present narrative occurs only in Luke, but is doubtless a variant to the healing of a leper from Mark 1.40–45 (= Luke 5.12–16). Its climax comes at the end, where the gratitude of the healed Samaritan is described (vv. 15–16) and Jesus comments on the event (vv. 17–19). The narrative serves as introduction to the discourse vv. 20–37 which follows and makes it clear 'that the rule of God is present in the history of Jesus as a symbolic reality. Until the parousia of the Son of man, it is important to keep faith (18.8b)' (Schneider).

[11] This verse is an introduction. Jesus is on his journey to Jerusalem.

[12–18] This is a unitary composition which is based on the miracle story Mark 1.40–45. It has come into being in order to legitimate the mission to Samaria (cf. Acts 1.8). As the rigorous saying of Jesus in Matt. 10.5b–6 shows, this was disputed. But in Acts 8.4–25 Luke himself reports the successful mission to Samaria under the leadership of the Hellenist Philip. Therefore the story of the healing of ten lepers must have been important to him. He inserts it into his Gospel and shows by means of a person hated by the Jews how, unlike the nine Jews who are lepers, this is the one who is grateful to his benefactor.

[19] This verse is a schematic conclusion (cf. 7.50; 8.48, etc.).

Historical

Against the authenticity of the narrative is the fact that it is based on Mark 1.40–45. Furthermore, there is a series of inconsistencies. Thus it is impossible that a Samaritan should present himself to a Jewish priest (v. 14) and that he should go to Jerusalem so quickly that he still meets Jesus at the same place: 'Such realistic questions should not be asked of our story' (Wellhausen). In other words, the original significance of sending the lepers to the priests was for them to establish the healing, whereas here, in order to make the point, the healing must take place on the way, to provide a parallel to II Kings 5.10–19. The further question whether there may not be a historical nucleus in the fact that Jesus once healed a Samaritan must probably be answered in the negative, since Jesus worked exclusively within the Jewish sphere.

Luke 17.20–37: The coming of the kingdom of God and the days of the Son of man (prospect for the future)

20 *Now when he was asked by the Pharisees when the kingdom of God was coming, he answered them and said,* 'The kingdom of God is not coming with observation, 21 nor will they say, "Look here or there!" *For look, the kingdom of God is in your midst.*'

22 *And he said to the disciples,* '*The days are coming when you will desire to see one of the <u>days of the Son of man</u>, and you will not see (it).* 23 And they will say to you, *"Look there, look here!"* Do not go and run after (them). 24 For as the lightning when it flashes shines from one end of heaven to the other, so will the Son of man be in his day. 25 *But first he must suffer many things and be rejected by this generation.* 26 And as it happened in the days of Noah, so will it also be in the <u>days of the Son of man</u>. 27 <u>They ate, drank</u>, married and were given in marriage until the day when Noah went into the ark, and the flood came and destroyed them all. 28 *Likewise as it happened in the days of Lot, <u>they ate, drank</u>, bought, sold, planted, built.* 29 *But on the day when Lot went out from Sodom he made fire and brimstone rain from heaven and destroyed them all.* 30 *So will it be on the day when the Son of man is revealed.* 31 On that day let him who is on the roof, with his goods in the house, not come down to take them away; and likewise let him who is in the field not turn back. 32 *Remember Lot's wife.* 33 Whoever seeks to preserve his life will lose it, and whoever loses (it) will preserve it. 34 I tell you, in that night there will be two in one bed; one will be taken and the other left. 35 There will be two women grinding *at the same place*, one will be taken and the other left.' 36 [. . .] 37 *And they answered and said to him,* '*Where, Lord?*' *But he said to them,* 'Where the body is, there the vultures will gather over it.'

Preliminary text-critical note: v. 36 ('Two in the field, one will be taken and the other left') is secondary and comes from Matt. 24.40.

Redaction and tradition

In this section Luke is working to a greater degree with written tradition. Thus we can see a little apocalypse which consists of vv. 23–24, 26–27, 34–35. It derives from Q (cf. the Matthaean references cited at the individual passages), whereas the larger discourse on the end time in 21.6–36 follows Mark 13.

[20–21] Pharisees ask Jesus when the kingdom of God is coming. In his answer he indirectly suggests that in their view the kingdom will be preceded with preliminary signs, so that its approach can be recognized (cf. vv, 23–24). However, it is impossible in principle to calculate the time at which the kingdom of God will arrive (v. 21a). The reason for this impossibility is given in v. 21b: 'The kingdom of God is in your midst', to be specific, it is present in Jesus' activity, indeed it is preached by Jesus himself.

[22] For the introduction formula cf. 16.1; 17.1. Luke has formed the plural expression 'days of the Son of Man' (vv. 22, 26) on the basis of the singular

expression that he found in Q and in parallel to vv. 26, 28: days of Noah, of Lot. The time of tribulation is not to be interpreted by the community as the sign of a near parousia, but is to be understood as an occasion for prayer (cf. 18.1ab).

[23–24] These verses (= Q; cf. Matt. 24.26–27) are the basis of vv. 20–21 at the level of the tradition.

[25] Luke had already omitted the prediction of the resurrection in the second announcement of the passion (9.44). Here once again he introduces the notion of suffering to dampen down the acute expectation of the parousia.

[26–27] These verses derive from Q (cf. on Matt. 24.37–41). In Matthew the emphasis is that no one knows when the parousia will take place (Matt. 24.39 is lacking in Luke); the Lukan text emphasizes people's unpreparedness.

[28–30] These sentences are constructed in parallel to those that have gone before and depict the same thing. As they occur only in Luke, they probably go back to him in their entirety.

[31–33] For v. 31 cf. Matt. 24.17–18 (= Q). For Lot's wife in v. 32 cf. Gen. 19.26; for v. 33 cf. Mark 8.35.

[34–35] Cf. on Matt. 24.40–41 (= Q). Cf. further Thomas 61.1.

[37] This verse is a proverb which for the purposes of clarification Luke introduces with the question 'Where, Lord?' The logion comes from Q (cf. Matt. 24.28) and probably referred to those left behind at the parousia, who are compared with a corpse. Instead of this, Luke speaks of the (dead) body without abandoning the image altogether. He in fact thinks that the place of the parousia will be unmistakable and that at it those people who are not accepted will be left behind (dead) (cf. v. 35).

Historical

[23–24] Jesus certainly never spoke these words in this form. But they do reflect his expectation of an imminent end. For the reasons, cf. the remarks on Matt. 24.26–27.

[34–35] These verses are authentic in their original form (cf. on Matt. 24.40–41).

Luke 18.1–8: The parable of the godless judge

1 *And he told them a parable, to the effect that one should always pray and not lose heart,* 2 *and said,*

'A judge was in a city who neither feared God nor regarded man. 3 Now there was a widow in that city and she came to him and said, "Vindicate me against my adversary," 4 and for a long time he would not. But then he said to himself, "Though I do not fear even God and regard no man, 5 because this widow bothers me, I will vindicate her, lest in the end she comes once again and strikes me in the face." '

6 And the Lord said, 'Hear what the judge of unrighteousness says. 7 And will not God <u>vindicate</u> his elect, who cry to him day and night, and will he delay long over them? 8 I tell you, he will <u>vindicate</u> them speedily. *But when the Son of man comes, will he find faith on earth?'*

Redaction and tradition

[1] This verse comes from Luke and gives his interpretation of the next parable in advance.

[2–5] These verses contain the tradition of a vivid narrative which Luke has introduced here intact.

[6–8a] These verses give an interpretation of vv. 2–5 from the tradition, provided with a new introduction. The narrative of the godless judge makes it clear how the (risen) Lord Jesus himself says that God will vindicate the Christians at the last judgment in the imminent future.

[8b] This verse is an addition by Luke, who with it reverses the direction of the question as previously in 13.24; 17.21b, and asks the readers whether they will still have faith at the delayed return of Jesus at the end of the ages.

Historical

[2–5] These verses, the original stratum of the parable, certainly go back to Jesus. That is supported by (a) the criterion of growth, for here with vv. 2–5, calculated backwards, we are at the third stage, and (b) the offensive character of what is narrated. Normally a judge should pronounce judgment on a legal basis. But here he is godless and pronounces judgment only because he is forced to. In contrast to v. 1, the parable says nothing at all about prayer, but about everyday reality and what means must sometimes be used to change it. As in the parable of the unjust steward (16.1b–7), a radical situation calls for unconventional behaviour, so too here the victim must act importunately to be vindicated.

[6–8a] The words of Jesus are inauthentic, as in the time after 'Easter' they interpret a parable of Jesus that has not been understood in the light of an urgent expectation of an imminent end.

Luke 18.9–14: The parable of the Pharisee and the toll collector

9 *He also told this parable to some who trusted in themselves that they were righteous and despised others:*

10 'Two men went up into the temple to pray, one a Pharisee and the other a toll collector. 11 The Pharisee stood and prayed thus within himself, "God, I thank you that I am not like other men, extortioners, unjust, adulterers, or even like this toll collector. 12 I fast twice a

week, I give tithes of all that I get." 13 But the tax collector stood far off and did not even dare to lift up his eyes *to heaven*, but beat his breast, saying, "God, be merciful to me a sinner!" 14 I tell you, this man went down to his house justified rather than the other. *For everyone who exalts himself will be humbled, but he who humbles himself will be exalted.'*

Redaction and tradition

[9] This verse mentions those to whom the parable is addressed: disciples who pray like the Pharisee (cf. 14.11). The disciples are rather to pray like the toll collector.

[10–14a] These verses are a narrative with the point in v. 14b, which is given extra emphasis by an introductory 'I tell you' in v. 14a.

[14b] This verse is a free logion in the tradition (cf. 14.11; Matt. 23.12) which Luke has added here. In any case it is secondary in this context, as the toll collector has not humbled himself at all. The saying speaks in general terms and in principle about the right attitude of the disciples, and corresponds to the Lukan addition to the previous pericope which called for faith (v. 8b).

Historical

[10–14a] Jesus did not speak this parable. But it remains beyond dispute that: (a) Jesus had contact with toll collectors; (b) he had contact with Pharisees; (c) the prayers in v. 11 (without 'even like this toll collector') and v. 13 (= opening words of Ps. 51) are Jewish prayers; (d) any Pharisee could have prayed the prayer from v. 13. The point of the present narrative is that the Pharisees not only did not pray this prayer but could never have spoken it. And it is at this point that my criticism of the authenticity of the narrative begins. It is based on a fundamental hostility to the Pharisees which Jesus did not share.

The long tradition of anti-Judaism in New Testament scholarship can be demonstrated from the exegesis of this pericope. I would like to illustrate that by two examples:

'It was *Jesus'* special task to fight against the pure Jewish Pharisaism, albeit in a spirit which makes this battle fruitful for ages and religious communities. In Luke 18.9ff. he honoured the toll collector not as a toll collector but as a man who was ready to repent, just as Luke 10.30ff. honoured the Samaritan not as a Samaritan but as a man of compassionate love and broke with prejudices of race, religion, status and good reputation' (Jülicher).

'According to v. 9 the parable of the Pharisee and the toll collector is told to some who put their trust in themselves (instead of in God), because they are righteous and look with contempt upon others, i.e. Pharisees. *The content of the parable comes over to the hearer as correct.* The Pharisees are thus not only accused of having too good an opinion of themselves; also for them, self-confidence based on their pious way of life takes the place of trust in God. The parable must have been quite surprising and incomprehensible to the first hearers' (J. Jeremias).

Luke 18.15–17: The children and the kingdom of God

15 And they brought even small children to him that he might touch them. But when the disciples saw that, they threatened them (= the people). 16 But Jesus *called them* (= the children) *to him* and said, 'Let the children come to me, and do not hinder them; for to such belongs the kingdom of God. 17 Amen, I say to you, whoever does not receive the kingdom of God like a child will not enter it.'

Redaction and tradition

At this point, after the great insertion 9.51–18.14, Luke takes up again the thread of the Gospel of Mark which he dropped. Here he is using Mark 10.13–16.

[15–16] Luke replaces Jesus' annoyance as a reaction to the action of the disciples (contrary to Mark) with 'he called them to him'; here clumsily the children are addressed and not the disciples, as in Mark. Luke omits the closing verse Mark 10.16 ('and he embraced them and blessed them, laying hands on them').

[17] This verse corresponds word for word with Mark 10.15.

Historical

Cf. on Mark 10.13–16.

Luke 18.18–30: The rich ruler

18 And a *ruler* asked him and said, 'Good Teacher, what must I do to inherit <u>eternal life</u>?' 19 And Jesus said to him, 'Why do you call me good? No one is good but God alone. 20 You know the commandments, "Do not commit adultery, do not kill, do not steal, do not bear false witness, honour your father and your mother."' 21 And he said, 'All this I have done from my youth up.' 22 When Jesus heard it, he said to him, 'One thing you still lack. Sell all you have and *distribute* it to the poor, and you will have treasure in heaven; and come, follow me.' 23 When he heard this he became sad. *For he was very rich.* 24 When Jesus saw him (so sorrowful), he said, 'How hard it is for those who have possessions to enter the kingdom of God! 25 For it is easier for a camel to go through the eye of a needle than for a rich man to enter the kingdom of God.' 26 Those who heard it said, 'Who then can be saved?' 27 But he said, 'What is impossible with men is possible with God.'

28 Then Peter said, 'Look, we have left *our possessions* and have followed you.' 29 And he said to them, 'Amen, I say to you, there is no one who has left house or *wife* or brothers or

parents or children *for the sake of the kingdom of God,* 30 who will not receive it back manifold more in this time, and in the coming world <u>eternal life</u>.'

Redaction and tradition

Luke is using Mark 10.17–31.

[18] Luke depicts the rich questioner as a ruler and in so doing is probably thinking of the ruler of a synagogue (cf. 8.41). He thus embeds the story in Jesus' conflict with representatives of the Jewish religion who are also responsible for his death (cf. the 'rulers' in 23.13, 35; 24.24; Acts 3.17).

[19] This verse corresponds almost word for word with Mark 10.18.

[20] Luke groups the commandments according to the order in Ex. 20, while Mark follows Deut. 5.

[22] Luke, like Matthew, omits the sentence '(Jesus) looked on him and loved him' (Mark 10.21). In 5.13–14, too, he passes over Jesus' outburst of feeling narrated in 1.43; similarly in 18.14, Jesus' indignation from Mark 10.14 (cf. similarly Matt. 19.14).

[23] The rich man's departure is not narrated, since Jesus is still addressing him in v. 24.

[24] In Mark 10.23, the audience is the disciples.

[27] The look is not mentioned as in v. 22.

[29] Cf. on 14.26.

[30] The Lukan text ends with the abbreviated version of Mark 10.30. Mark 10.31 was previously used in Luke 13.30 and therefore is dropped here.

Historical

Cf. on Mark 10.17–31.

Luke 18.31–34: The third announcement of the passion and resurrection

31 He took the twelve to him and said to them, 'Look, we are going to Jerusalem, and *everything that is written by the prophets of* the Son of man *will be accomplished.* 32 He will be handed over to the Gentiles, and he will be mocked and maltreated and spit upon, 33 and they will scourge him and kill him; and on the third day he will rise.' 34 *But they understood none of this, and the meaning of the saying was hidden from them, and they did not understand what was said.*

Redaction and tradition

Luke uses Mark 10.32–34; because of the long insertion 9.51–18.14 there is a great gap between this third announcement and the first and second announcements of the passion and resurrection (9.22,44). Luke has bridged it a little with the announcement of the passion in 17.25.

[31] Luke omits Mark's ponderous introduction (10.32a) and adds the prediction of the prophets which is to be fulfilled in the future handing over of Jesus to the Gentiles (see v. 32 and also 20.20b in contrast to Mark).

[32–33] Here Luke passes over all the information from Mark 10.33 relating to the Jewish authorities. It is important for him that Jesus is handed over to the Gentiles, for thus the divine plan of salvation is fulfilled (cf. v. 31).

[34] This verse may prepare for the Emmaus scene (24.13–35), in which initially the two disciples understand nothing. At the same time the verse may be an indirect reworking and abbreviation of Mark 10.35–45).

Historical

Cf. on Mark 10.32–34.

Luke 18.35–43: The healing of a blind man near Jericho

35 *Now it happened, as he drew near to Jericho, that a* blind man was sitting by the roadside begging. *36 And when he heard the multitude going by, he asked what this was. 37 And they told* him that Jesus the *Nazorean* was passing by. 38 And he cried, 'Jesus, <u>Son of David, have mercy on me!</u>' 39 And those who were in front urged him to be silent, but he cried out all the more, '<u>Son of David, have mercy on me!</u>' 40 And Jesus stopped and *commanded* him to be brought to him. And when he came nearer, he asked him, 41 'What do you want me to do for you?' He said, '*Lord,* let me see.' 42 And Jesus said to him, '*Become seeing!* Your faith has saved you.' 43 And immediately he became seeing and followed him *and glorified God. And all the people that saw it gave praised God.*

Redaction and tradition

Luke is using Mark 10.46–52.

[35] In Mark, which Luke has in front of him, the blind man, whose name 'Bartimaeus' Luke omits, meets Jesus only *after* Jesus has left Jericho, but in Luke the encounter takes place *before* he enters the city. That happens because Luke still wants to include the narrative of Zacchaeus (19.1–10) and the Q parable of the pounds (19.11–27) in the Markan material.

[37] For Luke, 'Nazorean' is synonymous with 'coming from Nazareth' (similarly Matt. 2.23; cf. Acts 2.22; 3.6, etc.). But 'Nazorean' certainly had another meaning (which so far has not been clarified), before Luke and Matthew connected it with Nazareth.

[40] This verse abbreviates the vividly told scene Mark 10.49–50, as the blind man rushes to Jesus.

[43b] This contains a typically Lukan conclusion (cf. 5.25; 7.16; 9.43).

Historical

Cf. on Mark 10.46–52.

Luke 19.1–10: Zacchaeus

1 And he entered and went through Jericho. 2 *And look, there was a man named* Zacchaeus; he was a chief tax collector, *and rich*, 3 and he desired to see Jesus, who he was, and could not on account of the crowd, because he was small of stature. 4 And he ran ahead and climbed a sycamore tree to see him; for he was to pass that way. 5 And when he came to the place, Jesus looked up and said to him, 'Zacchaeus, come down quickly; for today I must stay at your house.' 6 So he came down quickly and received him *with joy*. 7 When they saw it they all murmured and said, 'He has gone to be the guest of a sinner.' 8 *And Zacchaeus went and said to the Lord, 'Look, the half of my possessions, Lord, I give to the poor; and if I have defrauded any one of anything, I restore it fourfold.'* 9 And Jesus said *to him*, 'Today salvation has come to this house, since he also is a son of Abraham. 10 *For the Son of man has come to seek and to save the lost.'*

Redaction and tradition

The position of the Zacchaeus story – towards the end of the travel account – shows its importance for Luke. It can be read as a summary of Lukan soteriology or also as a Lukan example of the conversion of a well-to-do person which is experienced in practice, and which serves as a model for the community. Verses 8 and 10 attest in Lukan diction why Zacchaeus and his house have experienced salvation. These verses help us to find Luke's meaning.

[2–7 (,9)] These verses contain the main part of the tradition taken over by Luke. The name Zacchaeus is either a short form for Zechariah or means 'the pure, righteous one' (cf. Ezra 2.9; Neh. 7.14).

The tradition is to be termed a personal legend of the conversion of the chief toll collector Zacchaeus. His experience 'is connected with individual characteristics of the man, with his short stature and with his relative piety despite his offensive profession' (M. Dibelius). That the tradition is late clearly emerges from the fact that

Zacchaeus no longer follows Jesus, as Levi still did according to Mark 2.13–17. A parallel is a legend like that of the centurion of Capernaum (Acts 10).

The core of the tradition is the recollection which is also reflected in v. 7 that Jesus occasionally had dealings with toll collectors (cf. Mark 2.13 par: toll collectors and sinners; Luke 7.34/Matt. 11.19, as an element of an oral rumour: Jesus is a friend of toll collectors and sinners). The present story has preserved the name of one of these toll collectors.

[8] This verse is certainly Lukan. The key to its interpretation as an invitation to rich Christians in the Lukan community comes in the redactional preaching of John the Baptist in 3.10–14. This says in v. 11, 'Let him who has two undergarments give (one) to him who has none.' Cf. also Acts 4.35. In v. 8b, for the fourfold replacement in the case of theft (of sheep), see Ex. 21.37b. Here 'four' is above all a rhetorical doubling of 'two'.

[9] This is the original conclusion of the personal legend (cf. on vv. 2–7).

[10] This verse is a Lukan construction with which 'Jesus' looks back on 15.1–32. At the same time the saying is a substitute for the saying Mark 10.45, which Luke has passed over.

Historical

The historical yield of the narrative in its present form is nil. But Jesus' positive encounter with the toll collector Zacchaeus underlies it as a fixed historical nucleus.

Luke 19.11–27: The parable of the pounds

11 *While they were listening to him, he continued and told a parable; for he was near to Jerusalem and they thought that the kingdom of God would appear immediately.*

12 *Now he said, 'A nobleman went into a far country to receive a kingdom and then return.* 13 He called ten of his servants and gave them ten pounds and said to them, "Trade with these till I return." 14 *But his citizens hated him and sent an embassy after him, saying, "<u>We do not want this king to reign over us.</u>"* 15 *And it happened, when he returned, having received the king-dom,* that he had the servants to whom he had given the money called to him, to discover what they had gained by trading.

16 The first *came up to* him, and said, "Lord, your pound has made ten pounds more." 17 And he said to him, "Well done, capable servant! Because you have been faithful in a very little, you shall have power over ten cities."

18 And the second came and said, "Lord, your pound has made five pounds." 19 And he said to him, "You too are to be (ruler) over five *cities*."

20 And the other came and said, "Lord, look, here is your pound, which I kept in a napkin. 21 For I was afraid of you, because <u>you are a severe man; you take up what you have not laid down, and reap what you have not sown.</u>" 22 He said to him, "I will condemn you out of your own mouth, you wicked servant! You knew that <u>I was a severe man, taking up</u>

what I did not lay down and reaping what I did not sow. 23 Why then did you not put my
money into the bank? Then at my coming I should have collected it with interest."

24 And he said to those standing by, "Take the pound from him, and give it to him who
has ten pounds." 25 And they said to him, "Lord, but he already has ten pounds."

26 "I tell you (he continued), whoever has, to him will be given; but from him who has not,
even what he has will be taken away. 27 But as for my enemies, who did not want me to be
king over them, bring them here and slay them before my eyes.'"

Redaction and tradition

This section stands at the conclusion of the Lukan travel account. The text of Matt.
25.14–30 is genetically connected with the present section. But the agreements in wording
are very few apart from the direct speech in the dialogues. At any rate it is certain that the
saying of 'Jesus' in Luke 19.26/Matt. 25.29 stood at the end of the parable as an interpretation. It no longer fits the meaning of the parable, since the person delivering it is not concerned with having but with behaviour. At the same time this makes it certain that v. 27 (cf.
Matt. 25.30) is not part of the original parable.

[11] The audience is the same as in the previous scene. As in Acts 1.6, 'Jesus'
teaches that there is no connection between the journey to Jerusalem and the end.
Accordingly, at the level of redaction the parable which now follows is to be understood under the aspect of the delay of the end.

[12] With the nobleman who goes to a distant land to gain a kingdom and return
Luke is of course thinking of Jesus, who has been made Lord by his journey to God
(Acts 2.36) and who will return for judgment in the distant future.

[14–15a] These verses link up with v. 12. The passage depicts how the citizens
rebel against their future king.

[15b–26] The parable of the pounds has been inserted here. Its action takes place
on the return of the nobleman, namely when he has attained his royal dignity and
now makes a reckoning with his servants. (For a further analysis of the tradition cf.
the introduction to the redaction and the remarks on Matt. 25.14–30.)

[27] This verse picks up vv. 14–15a. At the latest here it becomes evident who
were meant by the hostile citizens in v. 14: the Jews as the enemies of Jesus.

'Jesus has departed from the world to get the kingdom for himself in heaven and then return
to earth or rather to the chosen people as God's Christ. But the Jews do not want to have the
one who has gone to heaven as king, and he will take vengeance on them at his parousia. Here
as in 18.1–8 and 11.49ff. the parousia is understood as the day of vengeance on the Jews who
are hostile to Christ' (Wellhausen).

Luke again put his own view about the doom of the unbelieving Jews on the lips of
Jesus.

Historical

[13, 15b–26] Cf. on Matt. 25.14–30.

Luke 19.28–48: The entry into Jerusalem and the cleansing of the temple

28 *And when he had said this, he went on ahead and went up to Jerusalem.* 29 *And it happened,* when he came near to Bethphage and Bethany, to the *mountain that is called* the Mount of Olives, he sent two of his disciples 30 and said, 'Go into the village opposite. And when you enter, you will find a colt tied, on which no one has ever yet sat; untie it and bring it here. 31 And if any one asks you, "Why are you untying it?," then say, "The Lord needs it."' 32 And those whom he had sent went away and found (it) as he had told them. 33 And as they were untying the colt, *its lords* said to them, 'Why are you untying the colt?' 34 And they said, '*The Lord* needs it.' 35 And they brought it to Jesus and threw their garments on the colt and *set* Jesus *upon it.* 36 Now as he *was going there*, they spread their garments on the way. 37 *And as he was now drawing near at the descent of the Mount of Olives, the whole crowd of the disciples began to praise God with joy, with a loud voice, for all the mighty works that they had seen*, 38 and said, 'Blessed is the one who comes, the king, in the name of the Lord! *Peace in heaven and glory in the highest!*'

39 *And some of the Pharisees in the crowd said to him, 'Teacher, rebuke your disciples!'* 40 *And he answered and said, 'I tell you, if these were silent, the stones would cry out.'* 41 *And when he came near, he saw the city and wept over it,* 42 *and said, 'Would that even at this time you knew what makes for peace! But now it is hidden from your eyes.* 43 *For the days will come upon you, when your enemies will cast up a wall against you and besiege you and oppress you on all sides,* 44 *and will raze you to the ground along with all your children within you, and will not leave one stone upon another in you, because you did not know the time of your visitation.'*

45 And he entered the temple and began to drive out the traders, 46 and said to them, 'My house shall be a house of prayer; but you have made it a robbers' den.' 47 *And he taught daily in the temple.* But the chief priests and scribes sought to destroy him, *and the principal men of the people.* 48 And they did not find anything they could do; for all the people *clung to him and listened to him.*

Redaction and tradition

The basis of the following definition of the redaction is the assumption that apart from vv. 39–44 this section is based on Mark's report (11.1–20). At the same time it should be pointed out that Luke omits the episode of the cursing of the fig tree (Mark 11.12–14.20) and effectively inserts in its place Jesus' prophecy on the destruction of Jerusalem, the content of which is equivalent to the pericope about the fig tree. The deletion of the scene with the fig tree better expresses the goal of Jesus in Jerusalem: without any deviation, Jesus 'occupies' the temple.

[28] Luke connects the journey to Jerusalem closely with the parable of the pounds which he has reported previously.

[29–36] Luke follows Mark 11.1–8 closely.

[37] The public scene in Mark is limited to the disciples; only they rejoice, while the people look on.

[38] Luke removes the name of David from the cry of joy in his original (Mark 11.10), in order to make clear, like 19.11, that the kingdom of God will not dawn in the immediate future, nor will it be a political entity. Instead of this he alludes to the song of the angels from the infancy narrative (2.14), which finds its fulfilment here.

[39–40] These verses prepare for Jesus' following prediction of the destruction of Jerusalem which follow and are already themselves an indirect prediction.

[41–44] These verses anticipate the text of Mark 13. Luke draws on all the registers of his descriptive skill in making Jesus weep in a lyrical effusion while the crowd of disciples rejoices at him. At any rate, the deep pain over the fall of the city 'differs from the cry of vengeance in Luke 18.7f.; 19.27' (Wellhausen).

[45–48] Luke abbreviates the Markan account (11.15–19). The teaching in the temple is not just the event of a particular day but happens 'daily' (v. 47; cf. Mark 14.49). From now on Jesus 'occupies' the temple preaching and goes to the Mount of Olives each night. Now it also becomes clear that there will be no more time for an anointing in Bethany (cf. Mark 14.1–9). For that reason, too, Luke has moved his variant of this anointing story forward (7.36–50).

Historical

Cf. the remarks on Mark 11.1–20.

Luke 20.1–8: The question of authority

1 *And it happened one day, as he was teaching the people in the temple and preaching the gospel, that* the chief priests and scribes *with* the elders *came up to him* 2 and said to him, 'Tell us by what <u>authority</u> you do these things? Or who has given you this <u>authority</u>?' 3 He answered them, 'I also will ask you a question; tell me, 4 the baptism of John – was it from heaven or from men?' 5 And they discussed it among themselves and said, 'If we say, "From heaven," he will say, "Why did you not believe him?" 6 But if we say, "From men, " *all the people will stone us*; for they are convinced that John was a prophet.' 7 And they answered that they did not know whence it was. 8 And Jesus said to them, 'Nor will I tell you by what <u>authority</u> I do these things.'

Redaction and tradition

Luke is using Mark 11.27–33.

[1a] This verse picks up Jesus' teaching in the temple from 19.47 and emphasizes those to whom the teaching is addressed, the people. Note the full significance of the preaching of Jesus for salvation (= 'preach the gospel') like 7.22 and 9.6. Although the mode of expression is the same, John the Baptist's preaching (3.18) is somewhat different.

[2] Jesus' teaching in the temple, not the cleansing of the temple as in Mark, is the occasion for the question about authority. Therefore Luke deletes 'that you do this' (Mark 11.28 end).

[3] From the start Jesus stands above his opponents and does not engage them, as he knows the result of the disputation. Therefore Luke omits Mark 11.29b.

[4–8] These verses follow the Markan original without any changes worth mentioning. The fear of stoning (v. 6b) is a motif which heightens the drama of the scene.

Historical

Cf. on Mark 11.27–33.

Luke 20.9–19: The wicked tenants

9 And he began to tell *the people* this parable: 'A man planted a vineyard and leased it to tenants, and went abroad *for a long time.* 10 *And when the time came,* he sent a servant to the tenants, that they should give him his share of the fruit of the vineyard. But the tenants beat him and sent him away empty-handed. 11 And he sent another servant; but they also beat him and treated shamefully, and sent him away empty-handed. 12 And he sent yet a third; but they also wounded him and cast him out. 13 Then the lord of the vineyard said, "What shall I do? I will send my beloved son; perhaps they will respect him." 14 But when the tenants saw him, they discussed among themselves and said, "This is the heir; let us kill him, that the inheritance may be ours." 15 And they cast him out of the vineyard and killed him. What *now* will the owner of the vineyard do to them? 16 He will come and destroy those tenants, and give the vineyard to others.'

When they heard this, they said, 'God forbid!'

17 *But he looked at them* and said, 'What then is this that is written, "The stone that the builders rejected has become the cornerstone?" 18 *Everyone who falls on this stone will be broken to pieces; but when it falls on any one it will crush him.'*

19 *And the scribes and chief priests sought to lay hands on him in that same hour,* but they feared the people; for they perceived that he had told this parable against them.

Redaction and tradition

Luke uses the section Mark 12.1–12 and develops its allegorical interpretation further.

[9] This verse has the parable addressed to the people. The omission of Mark 12.1b corresponds to the tendency towards simplification.

[11–12] Luke passes over the sending of many other servants after the sending of the third (Mark 12.5b) for reasons of narrative technique. In contrast to Mark 12.4–5, in Luke there is no mention of any killing of the servants.

[15] The tenants first kill the son. Luke thus makes it clear who the parable is about, Jesus. In contrast to Mark 12.8, the son is first cast out of the vineyard and then killed outside it (cf. similarly Matt. 21.39). Thus Luke takes account of the historical evidence that Jesus was crucified outside Jerusalem (= vineyard) before the gates of the city.

[16] The defensive statement of the people heightens the drama.

[17–18] Luke abbreviates the second part of the scriptural proof in Mark 12.10f. (Mark 12.11), but supplements it in v. 18 with the following text: 'Everyone who falls on this stone will be broken to pieces; but when it falls on any one it will crush him' (cf. Matt. 21.44). This threat is unambiguously aimed at the Jews.

Cf. Acts 4.10f. (Peter on the occasion of the healing of a sick man, addressing the authorities, elders and scribes in Jerusalem): 10 'So be it known to you all, and to all the people of Israel, that by the name of Jesus Christ of Nazareth, whom you crucified, whom God raised from the dead, this man is standing before you well. 11 This is the stone which was rejected by you builders, which has become the cornerstone.'

[19] This verse heightens the opposition between the Jewish authorities and Jesus; for the expression 'lay hands on' cf. 22.53.

Yield: In this text Luke intensifies the anti-Jewish tendency of Mark's original and clarifies it with a view to Jesus.

Historical

Cf. on Mark 12.1–12.

Luke 20.20–26: The question of tax for the emperor

20 *And they watched him, and sent spies, who pretended to be sincere, in order to* <u>catch</u> *him* <u>in his word</u>, *so that they could deliver him up to the authority and jurisdiction of the governor.* 21 *And they asked him and said, 'Teacher, we know that you speak and teach honestly and show no partiality, but in truth teach the way of God.* 22 *Is it lawful for us to pay tribute to Caesar, or not?'*

23 But he perceived their *deceit*, and said to them, 24 'Show me a denarius! Whose likeness and inscription has it?' They said, 'Caesar's.' 25 He said to them, 'Then give to Caesar what is Caesar's, and to God what is God's.'

26 *And they could not* catch *him* in his word *before the people* and marvelled at *his answer and kept silent.*

Redaction and tradition

Luke is using Mark 12.13–17.

[20] Luke substantially changes the beginning of the Markan account. In so doing he deletes the Markan information that these were Pharisees and Herodians. He does not know the latter at all, and he paraphrases the former as in 18.9.

[21–25] These verses follow Mark 12.14–17 closely. The position taken by Jesus in v. 25 is later reversed by his opponents to slander him (23.2).

[26] This verse takes up v. 21. The plan to catch Jesus in his word has failed. Therefore later people act violently towards him.

Historical

Cf. on Mark 12.13–17.

Luke 20.27–40: The question of the resurrection

27 There came also some of the Sadducees, who dispute that there is a <u>resurrection</u>, and asked him and 28 said, 'Teacher, Moses has written for us, "If a man's brother dies, who has a wife and this man is childless, his brother must take her to wife and father descendants for his brother." 29 Now there were seven brothers. The first took a wife and died childless. 30 And the second, 31 and the third took her; likewise all seven left no children and died. 32 Lastly the woman also died. 33 Now the woman in the <u>resurrection</u> – whose wife among them will she be? For all seven had her as wife.'

34 And Jesus said to them, *'The sons of this world marry and are given in marriage;* 35 *but those who are accounted worthy to attain to that world* and to the <u>resurrection</u> from the dead, they will neither marry nor be given in marriage. 36 *For they cannot die from then on, for they are equal to the angels and are sons of God, because they are sons of the* <u>resurrection</u>. 37 But that the dead are raised, *even* Moses *pointed to that,* in the passage about the bush, where he calls the Lord the God of Abraham and God of Isaac and God of Jacob. 38 Now God is not (a God) of the dead, but of the living; *for all live to him.'*

39 *Then some of the scribes answered and said, 'Teacher, you have spoken well.'* 40 *For they no longer dared to ask him any question.*

Redaction and tradition

Luke is using Mark 12.18–27.

[27–33] These verses largely correspond to Mark 12.18–23.

[34–36] Luke inserts a commentary here. For this world and its sons (cf. 16.8b; 17.27) a particular order applies: that of fathering or giving birth and being fathered or being born (cf. Gen. 1.28). In the world in which there is no more death, one does not need marriage, which is necessary for procreation.

[38] Luke omits the general comment by Mark (12.27b) on the error of the Sadducees because he had made the matter clear in vv. 34–36. For the end of v. 38 cf. Acts 17.28. Is that an offer to people who were inclined towards Stoic doctrines?

[39–40] Luke has introduced the passage here from Mark 12.32, 34, from the Markan pericope about the great commandment which follows immediately in the Markan outline, but which has partly been put ahead of it by Luke (10.25–28).

Historical

Cf. on Mark 12.18–27.

Luke 20.41–21.4: The question about the son of David. A warning against scribes. The widow's mite

41 And he said to them, 'How can they say that the Christ is David's son? 42 For David himself says in the Book of Psalms, "The Lord said to my Lord, Sit at my right hand, 43 until I make your enemies a stool for your feet." 44 David thus calls him a lord; how then is he his son?'

45 And in the hearing of *all* the people he said to his disciples, 46 'Beware of the scribes, who like to go about in long robes, and love greetings in the market place and the seats of honour in the synagogues and places of honour at feasts. 47 Who devour widows' houses and for a pretence make long prayers. They will receive the sharper condemnation.'

21.1 And he looked up and saw the rich putting their *sacrificial gifts* into the chest for offerings. 2 And he also saw a poor widow, how she put in two lepta. 3 And he said, 'Truly I tell you, this poor widow has put in more than all of them. 4 For they all put something of their abundance (into the chest for offerings) for the *sacrificial gifts*, but she out of her poverty put in all the living that she had.'

Redaction and tradition

Luke had the three pericopes available in Mark (12.35–44) and he has changed their wording only slightly. Luke had brought forward the pericope which precedes them in Mark, Mark 12.28–34 ('The question of the great commandment)' (cf. 10.25–28), because the passage fits better in the context of his great parables and would have destroyed the flow of the account of the time in Jerusalem.

[41–44] In his language Luke largely follows what he has in front of him in Mark (12.35–37), but he certainly has a different purpose from Mark and his tradition. In 3.23–38 Luke explicitly attests the Davidic sonship of Jesus and the angel's announcement to Mary (1.32–33) and speaks of David as the father of Jesus. But according to Luke the correct answer to the question of how Jesus, the Christ, is David's son becomes possible only after the resurrection of Jesus. The same Psalm 110.1 which Jesus quotes in the present pericope is cited in Acts 2.34b–35 by Peter to show that God has made the crucified Jesus Christ and Lord (2.36). Thus Luke is indicating that God has made Jesus the son of David Lord and Christ through the resurrection. That is why no answer is possible to the question of the Davidic sonship of the Messiah before the resurrection. To be consistent, Luke omits the positive reaction of the people (Mark 12.37b).

[45–47] Luke largely follows what he has in front of him in Mark (12.38–40). But the audience sometimes differs from that in Mark. He has Jesus' remarks addressed to the people and the disciples. For v. 46 cf. 11.43 (= Q; cf. Matt. 23.7).

[21.1–4] Luke's formulation follows Mark 12.41–44 closely. Here he tightens up the pericope and reinforces its connection with the previous passage (v. 45–47) by not having Jesus change location, as happens in Mark 12.41.

Historical

Cf. on Mark 12.35–44.

Luke 21.5–36: Jesus' discourse about the end time

5 And as some were speaking of the temple, how it was adorned with fine stones and offerings, he said, 6 'As for these things which you see, *days will come* when of all this there shall not be left here one stone upon another that will not be shattered in pieces.' 7 And they asked him, 'Teacher, when will this happen, and what will be the sign when this *is about to happen?'*

8 And he said, 'Take heed that you are not led astray; for many will come in my name, saying, "I am he!" and, *"The time is at hand!" Do not go after them.* 9 And when you hear of wars and tumults, do not be terrified. For this must *first* take place, but the end will not be so *soon.'*

10 *Then he said to them,* 'One people will rise against another and one kingdom against another, 11 and there will be great earthquakes, and in various places famines *and pestilences; and there will also be terrors and great signs from heaven.*

12 *But before all this they will lay hands on you and persecute you,* and will deliver you up to the synagogues and prisons, and you will be brought before kings and governors for my name's sake. 13 That will happen to *you* as a testimony. 14 *So take it to heart* that you are not

anxious beforehand *how you are to defend yourselves.* 15 For I will give you *a mouth and wisdom, which none of your adversaries will be able to withstand or contradict.* 16 And *you* will be betrayed by parents, brothers, kinsmen and friends, and *some of you* they will kill. 17 And you will be hated by all for my name's sake. 18 *And not a hair of your head will perish.* 19 *By your steadfastness you will gain your souls.*

20 Now when you see *Jerusalem besieged by an army*, then know that its desolation has come near. 21 Then let those who are in Judaea flee to the hills, *and let those who are in it (Jerusalem) depart, and let not those who are out in the country enter it.* 22 *For these are days of vengeance, to fulfil all that is written.* 23 But woe to the pregnant and those who are breast-feeding in those days! For great distress shall be upon the earth and *wrath (happen) to this people*; 24 *and they will fall by the edge of the sword and be led captive to all peoples; and Jerusalem will be trodden down by the Gentiles, until the times of the Gentiles are fulfilled.*

25 And there will be signs in sun and moon and stars, and on earth *distress of peoples in perplexity at the roaring and waves of the sea*, 26 *and the people will perish for fear and the expec- tation of the things which are to come upon the whole earth;* for the powers of the heavens will be shaken. 27 And then they will see the Son of man coming in a cloud with power and great glory. 28 *Now when these (things) begin to take place, look up and raise your heads, because your redemption is drawing near.'*

29 *And he told them a parable:* 'Look at the fig tree, and all the trees. 30 As soon as they come out in leaf and you see it, you know that the summer is already near. 31 So also, when you see these things happening, know that the *kingdom of God* is near. 32 Amen, I say to you, this generation will not pass away till all happens. 33 Heaven and earth will pass away, but my words will not pass away.

34 *But take heed to yourselves lest your hearts be weighed down with dissipation and drunken- ness and daily cares and this day does not come upon you suddenly* 35 *like a snare, for it will come upon all inhabitants on the whole earth.* 36 *But watch at all times, praying that you may become strong to escape all these things that will take place, and to stand before the Son of man.'*

Redaction and tradition

The present passage is the second discourse of Jesus on future events. The first is in 17.20– 27 and is based on Q; the second, here, is based on Mark 13.1–37.

There are sometimes marked deviations from Mark 13.1–37, but on the whole the indivi- dual sections are in the same order and the sections before and after the discourse correspond with those in Mark (21.4 has a parallel in Mark 12.41–44; 22.1f. has a parallel in Mark 14.1f.). Therefore it is probable that the differences from Mark 13 in the Lukan text derive from the redaction of the author himself.

[5–7] The scene and the situation are shaped redactionally: Jesus remains in the temple and speaks to the people (cf. 21.38), but in what follows at the same time addresses his readers and characterizes the events which precede the parousia as fulfilled predictions of Jesus. The former corresponds to the redactional scheme: by day Jesus is in the temple and by night on the Mount of Olives (21.37f.).

[8b] Here the motif of imminent expectation is inserted.

[12] With 'but before all this' Luke (contrary to the Markan original) puts the attacks on Christians, which are described differently (lay hands on, persecutions) before the signs of vv. 10–11. The hearings before kings and governors suggest Acts 24–26, where Paul is exposed to such situations.

[13] Luke has left out the statement about the preaching of the Gospel addressed to all peoples (Mark 13.10). It is made up for in Acts 1.8.

[14–15] It is not the holy Spirit which speaks in the place of the disciples (thus Mark 13.11), but Jesus himself gives his followers 'a mouth and wisdom' to defend themselves. For wisdom cf. Acts 6.10.

[16] By the second-person-plural address, this verse is assimilated to the context.
[18] Cf. 12.7.

[19] Luke explains that the believers' souls will be preserved when they die. This corresponds to his notion of the fate of souls (16.19–31; 23.43) which enter paradise immediately after death.

[20–24] These verses clearly refer to the destruction of Jerusalem. Luke looks back on it and presents it as a historical event, not an event of the end-time.

[25–28] 'Mark 13.24–27 hardly glimmers through, and has been completely Christianized' (Wellhausen). Luke deletes Mark 13.24, a note which had linked in time the destruction of Jerusalem and the end of the world. He probably thinks that the prediction of the parousia will be fulfilled all the more certainly since part of the prophecies of Jesus have already been fulfilled (vv. 6, 12–13, 16–17, 20–24).

[29–33] For dogmatic reasons Luke passes over the saying of Jesus (Mark 13.32) about the day and the hour of the parousia which only the Father knows (cf. Acts 1.7). According to him the Son knows the day and hour, but the Christians are not to know it. In v. 32, Luke reads 'all happens' instead of 'all this happens' (Mark 13.30). Because of the deletion of 'this', the statement in Luke does not refer to the time-table of events but to the totality of the divine counsel. In that case 'this generation' does not refer to the Jews but to all human beings.

[34–36] This 'Pauline' section evaluates redactionally what is to come. Pauline echoes are I Thess. 5.3, 6; Rom. 13.13, where independent reference to pre-Pauline tradition is possible. Note in addition that in the Lord's Supper Luke (22.19–20) makes use of a tradition from the Pauline mission sphere, as Paul does in I Cor. 11.23–26. For the metaphor of the heart in v. 34 cf. already v. 14.

Historical

Cf. on Mark 13.1–37.

Luke 21.37–38: Jesus' teaching activity in the temple

37 And by day he taught in the temple; but at night he went out and lodged at the place called the Mount of Olives. 38 And early in the morning all the people came to him in the temple to hear him.

Redaction

This passage is a summary report which concludes the preceding discourse of Jesus on the end time. In typically Lukan fashion it relates Jesus' teaching activity in the temple (cf. previously 2.41–52; 19.47; 20.1). Jesus's stay in the temple is of fundamental importance for Luke. It is there that he speaks his first words at the age of twelve (2.49): 'There he gives his concluding teaching, which is dominated by two themes, questions about the law and teaching about the last things; there Luke makes Jesus give the critical account of the future significance of the city of Jerusalem (Luke 21.20ff.)' (Conzelmann).

Luke 22–23: The passion narrative

Luke 22.1–6: Conspiracy and contract

1 Now the feast of Unleavened Bread was *near, the so-called Passover*. 2 And the chief priests and scribes were seeking how they could do away with him; *for they feared the people.*

3 *And Satan entered into* Judas, called Iscariot, who was *of the number* of the twelve. 4 And he went away and spoke with the chief priests *and with the main people how* he might deliver him up to them. 5 And they were glad, and *arranged* to give him money. 6 *And he agreed*, and sought an opportunity to hand him over *to them behind the backs of the people.*

Redaction and tradition

Luke is using Mark 14.1–11.

[1–2] Luke omits the wish of Jesus' opponents for the execution of Jesus not to take place at the feast (Mark 14.2). At the same time, through v. 1 he gives the impression that Jesus has already been in Jerusalem for a long time (cf. 22.53 as a commentary). Elsewhere too in the passion story he passes over the Markan scheme of days. Luke omits the narrative of the 'anointing at Bethany' which follows (Mark 14.3–9). For the possible reasons see on Luke 7.36–50.

[3] This verse refers back to 4.13, which spoke of Satan departing from Jesus until an appointed time. But now Satan is back again, and the time of salvation which has been described in 4.18–21.38 has come to an end. A new phase of the temptation begins with the reappearance of Satan (cf. 22.28, 40, 46).

[4–5] These verses agree in essentials with Mark 14.10b–11a.

[6] This verse emphasizes for the second time (after v. 2) that the people are on Jesus' side and therefore must not be aware of any betrayal. Therefore in this pericope, over and above Mark Jesus emphasizes the contrast between Jewish authorities on the one hand and Jesus and the people on the other.

Historical

Cf. on Mark 14.1–11.

Luke 22.7–23: Preparation of the Passover meal. The supper. Prediction of the delivering up

7 Then came the day of Unleavened Bread, on which the Passover lamb had to be slaughtered. 8 *And he sent Peter and John and said, 'Go and prepare the Passover lamb for us, that we may eat (it).'* 9 And they said to him, 'Where will you have us prepare (it)?' 10 And he said to them, 'Look, when you enter the city, a man will meet you carrying a jar of water; follow him into the house which he enters, 11 and say to the householder, "The Teacher says to you, Where is the guest room, where I can eat the Passover with my disciples?" 12 And he will show you a large upper room furnished (with cushions); there make (it) ready.' 13 And they went and found it, as he had told them; and they prepared the Passover lamb.

14 And when *the hour* came, he reclined (at table) *and the apostles with him*. 15 And he said to them, 'I have earnestly desired to eat this Passover lamb with you before I suffer. 16 For I tell you I shall not eat it again until it is fulfilled in the kingdom of God.' 17 And he took the cup, gave thanks and said, 'Take this, and divide (it) among yourselves; 18 for I tell you that from now on I shall not drink of the fruit of the vine until the kingdom of God comes.' 19 And he took the bread, gave thanks and broke (it) and gave it to them, saying, 'This is my body which is given for you. Do this in remembrance of me.' 20 And likewise the cup after the meal, saying, 'This cup is the new covenant in my blood which is shed for you.

21 But look, the hand of him who delivers me up is with me on the table. 22 For the Son of man indeed goes as it has been determined; but woe to that man by whom he is betrayed!' 23 *And they began to question one another who it was among them who would do this.*

Preliminary text-critical comment: vv. 19–20b, i.e. the words 'which is given to you' up to 'which is shed for you', are lacking in one important witness (Codex D). But this is a secondary deletion, 'since the text was related closely to Mark/Matthew (v. 19b) and v. 17 was related to the eucharistic cup and a repetition of the action over the cup was thought irrelevant' (Schneider). Moreover the text printed above is the more difficult reading.

Redaction and tradition

Luke uses Mark 14.12–25 and at the same time weaves in a tradition of his own about the supper (vv. 14–20). He turns round the order of the prediction of the delivering up and the supper to make a smoother transition to the farewell discourses (22.34–38).

[7–13] Luke is using Mark 14.12–16. Whereas in Mark (14.12) the disciples approach Jesus with the question where they are to prepare the Passover meal, in Luke (v. 8) it is the other way round. He also mentions both disciples by name. These are Peter and John, who will play an important role in the first chapters of Acts (cf. Acts 3–4; 8.14). For vv. 9–10 cf. Mark 14.12b–13; for vv. 11–13 cf. Mark 14.14–16.

[14] Luke initially passes over the dramatic scene of Mark 14.18–21, which contains the prediction of the betrayal and the designation of the betrayer, and introduces it in vv. 21–23, in order to make a transition to Jesus' farewell discourse (22.24–38). Indicating the traitor at table at the supper, i.e. before the distribution, might perhaps have been detrimental to the gift.

[15–18] These verses do not derive from a special tradition but are a Lukan version of Mark 14.25. Luke shapes this report of a Passover meal with a twofold anticipation of the death of Jesus (vv. 16, 18).

[19–20] Luke combines Mark 14.22–24 and a eucharistic text which also appears in I Cor. 11.23–25. Luke knows it from the worship tradition of his community.

[21–23] For the transposition cf. on v. 14. Verse 23 is narrative framework.

Historical

Cf. on Mark 14.22–25.

Luke 22.24–38: Conversations with the disciples

24 *A dispute also arose among them, who of them was to be regarded as the greatest.* 25 *And he said to them, 'The kings* rule over their peoples and those in authority have themselves called *benefactors.* 26 But not so with you. Rather let the greatest among you become as the youngest, and the leader as a <u>servant</u>. 27 *For who is the greater, the one who reclines at table, or the one who serves? Is it not the one who reclines at table? But I am among you as a <u>servant</u>.*

28 *You are those who have persevered with me in my temptations.* 29 *And I assign to you the kingdom, as my Father assigned it to me,* 30 *that you may eat and drink at my table in my kingdom,* and sit on thrones judging the twelve tribes of Israel.

31 Simon, Simon, look, Satan has desired to sift you like wheat. 32 But I have prayed for you, that your faith may not fail. *And when you have turned again, strengthen your brothers.'* 33 *And he said to him, 'Lord, I am ready to go with you even to prison and to death.'* 34 But he said, 'I tell you, Peter, the cock will not crow this day, until you have three times denied that you know me.'

35 And he said to them, 'When I sent you out without purse, without bag and without shoes, did you lack anything?' And they said, 'Nothing.' 36 And he said to them, '*But now*, let him who has a purse take it, and likewise a bag, and let him who does not have one, sell his cloak and buy a sword. 37 For I tell you that this scripture must be fulfilled in me, "He was reckoned with the transgressors." For what is (written) about me finds a fulfilment.'

38 *And they said, 'Lord, look, here are two swords.' And he said to them, 'It is enough.'*

Redaction and tradition

This scene does not stand in its original place in Luke and was probably deliberately transposed by him here as a kind of table talk in the framework of which Jesus gives instructions about the parting (cf. John 14–17).

[24] This verse takes up v. 23 and leads to Jesus' farewell discourse in Luke's Gospel.

[25–26] Cf. Mark 10.42–43. For 'benefactor' cf. Acts 10.38 (of Jesus).

[27] This verse is an individual saying attached by the key word 'serve', which seems to have a genetic connection with John 13.12–14.

[28–30] The connection between this passage and vv. 24–27 is grounded in the general meal situation and expands the admonitions of vv. 24–27 with the promises. Verse 28 refers to the disciples being with Jesus. From this there follows as a reward in v. 29 the assigning of the kingdom to the disciples. Verse 30a is a redactional assimilation to the situation of the meal given by the context. Verse 30b contains the core of the section vv. 28–30 from the tradition, and like the tradition Matt. 19.28 predicts for the twelve an honourable task as judges in the future kingdom of God.

[31–34] Verses 31–32a may come from the tradition, since vv. 32b–33 seem really displaced, as v. 32a ended with the prospect of the great role of Peter, whereas v. 32b has only the sorry obverse as its content. With the conditional clause 'when you have turned again' in v. 32b, Luke links the passage by way of anticipation with the story of the denial in Luke 22.56–62.

The piece of tradition in vv. 31–32a shows that some ingredients of the passion story derive from a separate tradition. Furthermore it presupposes that in the testing (the sifting) of the disciples all but Peter have fallen away; only his faithfulness has not wavered. This piece of tradition does not know the story of the denial. The picture of the sifting of the wheat presupposes that not all the disciples have fallen away, but that a remnant has survived the process of sifting. And Jesus' statement 'that your faith may not fail' excludes apostasy on the part of Peter.

[35–38] These verses look back to the previous sendings of the disciples in 9.1–6 and 10.1–12. Verse 35 is addressed to the twelve, whose sending out was depicted in 9.1–6, but 'purse, bag, shoes' refer to the sending out of the seventy-two (10.4). Since Luke is formulating the passage in retrospect and 'Jesus' is *doing away with* the instructions given them, 'twelve' and 'seventy-two' bring the disciples together into one body. For the disciples of Luke's time there is martyrdom. But the context suggests a symbolic interpretation of the sword in vv. 36f., namely in terms of the daily Christian battle against tribulation, especially in persecution, i.e. against Satan, whom they have to resist. Up to now in the Gospel there have been no references to inner struggles or sacrifice on the part of the disciples (but cf. immediately below, 22.40, 46). Verse 37 is about the fulfilment of Isa. 53.12. Verse 38, which probably derives from the evangelist, prepares for the disciple's sword stroke at the arrest of Jesus, which Luke relates (v. 50) following Mark (14.47).

Historical

[30b] Cf. on Matt. 19.28.

[31–32a] This passage is historically worthless. The tradition stands in contradiction to the historically reliable tradition of the denial (see on Mark 14.66–72). Possibly it is meant to correct an existing report of the denial of Jesus by Peter.

Luke 22.39–46: Jesus in Gethsemane

39 *And he went out, as was (his) custom, to the Mount of Olives. And the disciples also followed him.* 40 And when he came to the place, he said to them, '*Pray that you do not enter into temptation.*' 41 *And he withdrew from them about a stone's throw, and knelt down* and prayed and said, 42 'Father, *if you are willing,* remove this cup from me; nevertheless not my will, but yours be done.' 43 *And an angel appeared to him from heaven and strengthened him.* 44 *And he struggled with death and prayed more vigorously. And his sweat became like drops of blood which fell to the earth.* 45 And he arose *from prayer* and came to his disciples and found them sleeping   *for* sorrow. 46 And he said to them, 'Why are you sleeping? *Rise* and pray that you do not enter into *temptation.*'

Redaction and tradition

Luke is using Mark 14.32–42 and abbreviates very markedly what he has in front of him: 'The emphasis on the three favourite disciples, the repetition of the prayer and the sayings Mark 14.34 and 14.38b all fall away. The saying Mark 14.38a is duplicated (Luke 22.40 and 46), the saying in Mark 14.41b is shifted to later (22.48)' (Wernle).

[39] Instead of 'Gethsemane' Luke writes 'Mount of Olives' (cf. Mark 14.26). He designates Jesus' going there as a custom, in order to give Judas the possibility of finding him there. As a disciple he knew Jesus' custom.

[40] The second part of the verse forms one frame of the pericope. It contains the admonition to the disciples to pray, not to fall into temptation (cf. 11.4c). This admonition includes the fact that the trial of Jesus which is to follow will be a temptation for the disciples.

[41] For the kneeling down cf. Acts 7.60; 9.40; 20.36.

[42] Right at the beginning, in contrast to Mark 14.36, the prayer contains a subjection to the will of the Father. Cf. also the third petition of the Our Father, 'Your will be done' (Matt. 6.10b), which is lacking in 11.2.

[43–44] These verses give the impression of being an elaboration added later and moreover do not appear in important witnesses. But the appearance of the angel is God's answer to Jesus' prayer, which is strengthened by it. Angels also act in other parts of the Gospel of Luke (cf. 1.11–13, 26–30), so that the verses fit Luke. Moreover the feelings of Jesus are also a Lukan theme elsewhere (cf. 19.41).

[45–46] Luke tones down the rebuke to the disciples, whereas in Mark 14.37 Jesus still criticized Peter sharply. The disciples' sleep is caused by their sorrow. They themselves are admonished to pray, which as in v. 20 is described as prayer to be kept from temptation. Thus v. 46 forms the other frame of the pericope, which describes Jesus' prayer as the model for the prayer of the disciples.

Historical

Cf. on Mark 14.32–42.

Luke 22.47–53: The arrest of Jesus

47 While he was still speaking, *look,* there (came) a crowd of people and one of the twelve, *the one with the name* Judas, was leading them and drew near to Jesus, to kiss him. 48 *But Jesus said to him, 'Judas, would you deliver up the Son of man with a kiss?'* 49 *And when his companions saw what would follow, they said, 'Lord, shall we strike with the sword?'* 50 And one of them struck the slave of the high priest and cut off his *right* ear. 51 *Then Jesus answered and said, 'Stop! No more!' And he touched his ear and healed him.* 52 And Jesus said *to the chief priests and officers of the temple and the elders who had come out against him,* 'You have come out as against a robber with swords and clubs. 53 I was daily with you in the temple, and you did not lay hands on me. *But this is your hour and the power of darkness.'*

Redaction and tradition

Luke is using Mark 14.43–52.

[47–48] Contrary to Mark 14.45, it is not actually said that the kiss is given. Jesus does not let himself be kissed, but offers himself voluntarily for arrest (cf. v. 54a).

[49–51] In Mark, which Luke has in front of him (14.47), the sword stroke is seen as a kind of attempt at liberation, but in Luke as defence. Luke uses it to emphasize Jesus' healing power and his love for the enemy. For without delay Jesus heals the ear of the high priest's servant which has been cut off (v. 51b). The question by the disciples, which occurs only in Luke (49b), seems artificial by comparison with the impulsive action of the one who according to Mark 14.47 uses the sword. That can be explained only by the use of Mark.

[52–53] Luke has inferred the group of persons from Mark 14.43 but makes them appear far cruder. In Mark it is said that the crowd have got swords and staves from the chief priests, scribes and elders, while in Luke the chief priests, officers of the temple and elders have come to him as henchmen and Jesus addresses them as such. Only because Jesus declares that the 'hour' of the opponents and the power of darkness has come (v. 53b) can the arrest take place (v. 54a).

Luke omits the flight of the disciples (Mark 14.50) and the flight of the naked young man (Mark 14.51f.). Like Matthew, he probably found the latter incomprehensible and did not want to relate the former, because he needed the disciples in Jerusalem for his later description.

Historical

Cf. on Mark 14.43–52.

Luke 22.54–62: Peter's denial

54 Then they seized him and led him away and took him into the high priest's house. And Peter followed at a distance. 55 Then they kindled a fire in the middle of the courtyard and sat down together, and Peter sat among them. 56 Then a maid saw him sitting by the fire and looked closely at him and said, '*This man* also was with him.' 57 But he denied it and said, 'Woman, I do not know him.' 58 And *after a little while someone else* saw him and said, 'You also are one of them.' But Peter said, '*Man, I am not.*' 59 And after *an interval of about an hour* yet another confirmed it and said, 'Truly, this man also was with him; for he is a Galilean.' 60 But Peter *said,* 'Man, I do not know what you are saying.' And immediately, while he was still speaking, the cock crowed. 61 *And the Lord turned and looked at Peter.* And Peter thought of *the word of the Lord,* how he had said to him, 'Before the cock crows *today*, you will deny me three times.' 62 And he went out and wept bitterly.

Redaction and tradition

Luke is using Mark 14.53f., 66–72.

[54–55] Cf. 14.53–54. Luke takes apart Mark's sandwich and narrates Peter's denial in one passage without the interruption of a nocturnal trial (against Mark).

[56] This verse continues the narrative of the denial of Jesus by Peter, whereas in Mark the scene before the Supreme Council follows (Mark 14.55–65). Luke puts this next.

[57] Peter denies Jesus even *before* the beginning of the interrogation of Jesus.

[58–60] In the second denial a man (Mark: a serving girl) addresses Peter, where-upon Peter distances himself from Jesus and the group of disciples (v. 58). The accusation against Peter is intensified by the use of the verb 'confirm' (v. 59). Instead of the curse and oath in Mark (14.71), in v. 60 there is a simple statement, 'I do not know what you are saying.' That is a clear sparing of Peter. His act of denial is not intensified, in contrast to the accusation (see v. 59). But Jesus' prediction from v. 34 is fulfilled in it.

[61] Luke has invented Jesus' touching look at Peter, which first arouses his bad conscience. This corresponds to Luke's psychologizing throughout, which some-times allows the reader to look into the heart of his characters (cf. on 22.43–44). The 'word of the Lord' introduces a perspective of the whole church according to which the words of the Lord are to be remembered together (cf. Acts 20.35).

[62] Cf. Mark 14.72.

Historical

Cf. on Mark 14.54, 66–72.

Luke 22.63–71: Jesus before the Supreme Council

63 Now the *men* who were holding Jesus prisoner mocked him and beat him, 64 and they blindfolded him and asked, 'Prophesy! Who is it that struck you?' 65 *And they reviled him with many other insults.*

66 *And when day came*, the elders of the people assembled, the chief priests and scribes, and led him away to their council 67 and said, 'If you are the Christ, *tell us.*' But he said to them, 'If I tell you, you will not believe; 68 and if I ask you, you will not answer. 69 But from now on the Son of man *will* sit at the right hand of the Power *of God.*' 70 And they all said, 'Are you then the Son of God?' And he said to them, 'You say that I am.' 71 And they said, 'What further testimony do we need? We have heard it ourselves from his mouth.'

Redaction and tradition

Luke is using Mark 14.53, 55–64; 15.1.

[63–64] The passage corresponds to Mark 14.65. Verse 63 links up with v. 54.

[65] Luke adds a summary note about the mocking by the Jewish guards (and will later pass over the narrative provided by Mark 15.26a that Jesus is mocked by Roman soldiers).

[66] In contrast to Mark, the hearing before the Supreme Council takes place by day and not in the night (thus Mark 14.55–65). Luke passes over the interrogation of witnesses (Mark 14.55–61a), because the messiahship of Jesus was always a fact that was publicly known (cf. 22.53).

[67–68] These verses contain a dialogue shaped by Luke (cf. v. 70) with the motif of misunderstanding.

[69] Cf. Mark 14.62. Luke omits the coming on the clouds of heaven and adds to the veiled mention of the 'Power' the genitive 'of God' (cf. 12.8f.). Furthermore Luke does not say that the Jewish leaders will see the coming of the Son of man (thus Mark 14.62), but that Jesus will be exalted to the right hand of God.

[70] Note the dialogue form (cf. on vv. 67–68): 'The divine sonship is inferred from the eligibility to "sit at the right hand". The Son of God will receive "the throne of his father David" and "rule over the house of David for ever" (1.32–33)' (Schneider).

[71] No declaration of Jesus' guilt is yet made (thus Mark 14.64), as this is only a preliminary hearing which is to make possible the accusation before Pilate.

Historical

Cf. on Mark 14.53, 55–64; 15.1.

Luke 23.1–5: Jesus before Pilate

1 *And the whole company of them arose,* and brought him before Pilate, 2 *and began to accuse him, and said, 'We have found this man stirring up our people, and forbidding us to give tribute to Caesar, and saying that he himself is Christ, a king.'* 3 And Pilate asked him and said, 'Are you the King of the Jews?' He answered him and said, 'You say so.' 4 *Pilate said to the chief priests and the multitudes, 'I find no crime in this man.'* 5 *But they were even more importunate, saying, 'He stirs up the people and teaches throughout Judaea, from Galilee to this place.'*

Redaction and tradition

[1] Cf. Mark 15.1b.

[2] This verse has been added to the text of Mark and refers back to 20.20–26 ('The question of tax for the emperor'). In constructing the link between 23.2 and 20.20–26 Luke makes it clear that the accusation of the Jewish authorities is based on a *lie*. For Jesus had explicitly affirmed the payment of taxes. Therefore the only Jewish proceedings against Jesus are based on an evil slander, but Pilate has not fallen for this (cf. v. 4).

[3] Cf. Mark 15.2.

[4] This verse contains the first assertion of the innocence of the person of Jesus by a Roman official; it will be repeated twice more, 23.14–15 and 23.22. Here Luke himself is speaking as an apologist who wants to show to the Roman state that Christianity is not dangerous. Cf. further 3.10–14; Acts 10 (a Roman centurion, Cornelius, as one of the first Gentiles to be converted).

[5] This verse is a redactional summary. The link word 'Galilee' already leads to the next section.

Historical

Apart from v. 3, the section is a complete fiction constructed by Luke. For v. 3 cf. on Mark 15.3.

Luke 23.6–16: Jesus before Herod Antipas

6 *Now when Pilate heard this, he asked whether the man was a Galilean.* 7 *And when he learned that he belonged to the jurisdiction of Herod (Antipas), he sent him to Herod, who was also in Jerusalem at that time.* 8 *And when Herod saw Jesus, he was very glad, for he had long desired to see him, because he had heard about him, and was hoping to see some sign done by him.* 9 *And he put many questions to him. But he made no answer.*

10 *And the chief priests and the scribes stood by and vehemently accused him.* 11 *And Herod with his soldiers treated him with contempt and scorn, put a white garment on him and sent him back to Pilate.* 12 *On that day Herod and Pilate became friends; for previously they had been at enmity with each other.*

13 *Pilate then called together the chief priests and the rulers and the people,* 14 *and said to them, 'You brought me this man as one who was perverting the people; and look, I have examined him before you and have not found any guilt in him;* 15 *nor Herod, for he has sent him back to us. And look, he has done nothing that deserves death.* 16 *Therefore I want to beat him and release him.'*

Redaction and tradition

The composition of this scene is completely redactional and goes back to an early Christian exegesis of Ps. 2.1f. Luke has read the friendship between Herod and Pilate out of this psalm. Cf. especially Acts 4.27, where Ps. 2 is understood as a scriptural proof for the joint proceedings of the two against the Anointed. No questions should be raised about the significance of the figure of Herod in Luke for the history of Jesus, but rather about its redactional role. In that case, light is being shed from here on 13.31–33. As Luke understands it, Jesus' statement in v. 33b, 'It cannot be that a prophet perishes outside Jerusalem', in connection with Herod's intention to kill him, means that only after the time free from Satan, which extends from 4.13 to 22.3, can the adversary, whose instruments include Herod as well as e.g. Judas, have power over him. Alongside this, in its relationship to the saving event the person of Herod seems to be depicted in a kind of climax: according to 3.19 Herod seizes the herald and witness to Christ, in 9.9 he is interested in Jesus himself, and in 13.31–33 even wants to kill him, until the prediction of Ps. 2.1f is fulfilled in the present section.

[6–7] These verses serve as brackets along with the context (cf. v. 5).
[8] Cf. 9.9.

[9] Herod's curiosity is not further satisfied. He is not given an answer, whereas the Roman authorities in the figure of Pilate had got information (cf. 23.3).

[10] Cf. 23.2.

[11] This possibly serves as a replacement for the mocking of the king of the Jews by Roman soldiers which is narrated in Mark 15.16–20a; Luke passes that over.

[12] This is a Lukan echo of Mark 3.6.

[13–16] This passage contains Pilate's second declaration of Jesus' innocence (v. 14c; cf. v. 4). It leads to the Barabbas pericope (vv. 18–25), for in it Pilate undertakes the first attempt to let Jesus go free (vv. 20, 22).

Historical

The yield is nil.

Luke 23.18–25: The condemnation of Jesus

[17] 18 They all cried out together, 'Away with this man, release to us Barabbas!' 19 <u>He had been thrown into prison for a rebellion</u> which had taken place in the *city*, and for murder. 20 And Pilate addressed them once more, *because he wanted to release Jesus*. 21 But they cried out, 'Crucify, crucify him.' 22 And he said to them the third time, 'Why, what evil has this man done? I have found nothing in him which deserves death; *therefore I will have him beaten and release him.'* 23 *But they set on him with loud cries* and demanded that he should be crucified. *And their shouting prevailed.* 24 And Pilate gave sentence that their demand should be granted, 25 and released the man who <u>had been thrown into prison for rebellion and murder</u>; but he handed over Jesus *to their will.*

Preliminary text-critical note: v. 17 ('And he had to release someone to them at the feast') is certainly secondary and comes from Mark 15.6 or Matt. 27.15.

Redaction and tradition

Luke is using Mark 15.11–15.

[18] Luke omits the Markan report about the custom of the release of a prisoner at the feast (Mark 15.6). This makes the cry of the Jews for the release of Barabbas incomprehensible.

[19] This verse adds the information from Mark 15.7.

[20] Cf. on v. 22.

[21] Luke has the Jews repeat the call for crucifixion in order to emphasize their wickedness.

[22] With its declaration of Pilate's intent ('therefore I will have him beaten and release him') this verse picks up v. 16 and v. 20b.

[23] This verse lends emphasis to the desire for crucifixion over and above Mark 15.14b.

[24–25] The demand of the Jews prevails. And not only this, the criminal Barabbas is released instead of the innocent Jesus. According to Luke he, the murderer and political agitator (v. 19), belongs closely with the Jews, who are the real troublemakers in the Roman empire: Acts 13.50; 14.19; 17.5–8; 18.12–17; 21.27–28.

Historical

Cf. on Mark 15.6–15.

Luke 23.26–32: Jesus' way to Golgotha

26 And when they were leading him away, they seize a man, Simon of Cyrene, who was coming from the country, and *laid* the cross *upon him, to carry it behind Jesus.*

27 And there followed him a great crowd of people and women, who bewailed and lamented him. 28 But Jesus turned to them and said, 'You daughters of Jerusalem, do not weep for me, but weep for yourselves and for your children. 29 For look, the time will come when they say, "Blessed are the barren, and the wombs that never gave birth, and the breasts that never gave suck!" 30 Then they will begin to say to the mountains, "Fall on us," and to the hills, "Cover us." 31 For if they do this when the wood is green, what will happen when it is dry?'

32 And two other criminals were also brought to be executed with him.

Redaction and tradition

The attribution of guilt to the Jews reaches a climax in the fact that according to Luke it was Jews who executed Jesus – not Romans. Luke omits the scourging scene (Mark 15.16–20), so that Jesus is handed over immediately after being led away. Accordingly the text is to be read a follows: Pilate handed Jesus over to the will of the Jews (v. 25). They led him away (v. 26) . . . They crucified him (v. 33). From this it follows that those who call for Jesus' death also judge him.

That the Third Evangelist was really of this opinion also follows from 24.20. Here the disciples on the Emmaus road explain to the Risen Jesus, who encounters them unrecognized in the figure of a traveller, that the chief priests and authorities handed Jesus over to be executed and crucified him. The lack of any mention of the people here can hardly lead to the assumption that according to Luke the responsibility for the death of Jesus is to be limited to the Jewish elite. For guilt is being assigned to the people in Luke 23.4, 13–16 and this group is explicitly also 'burdened' with guilt in Acts 3.15 (cf. v. 12).

[26] Luke thoroughly alters what he has in front of him in Mark (14.21) so that

Simon carries the cross behind Jesus and thus becomes a model of discipleship, cf. 9.23, 'let him . . . take up his cross daily and follow me'. Luke has deleted the note that Simon of Cyrene was the father of Alexander and Rufus (Mark 15.21) because these names were unknown to him and his readership (cf. e.g. the deletion of the disciple who fled from Mark 14.51 in 22.47–53).

[27–31] These verses are a Christian prophecy which 'was put into the mouth of Jesus on the way to the cross' (Bultmann) here by Luke. It reinforces the anti-Judaism of the Lukan passion story further. The lamentation should not be for Jesus but for the inhabitants of Jerusalem, who will receive a harsh punishment. The lamenting women represent the Jewish people, which is a witness to the crucifixion (vv. 35, 48). Verse 29, as a paraphrase of Isa. 54.1, is a kind of counterpart to 11.27. If there it was said of the mother of Jesus, 'Blessed is the womb which bore you and the breasts which you sucked,' so here the opposite is said of the women of Jerusalem. Verse 30 takes up Hos. 10.8. Verse 31 gives the reason for the punishment coming upon Jerusalem with a proverb (cf. Prov. 11.31).

[32] This verse forms a transition to the next scene and prepares for the narrative about the conversation between Jesus and the two criminals on the cross. That is why in contrast with Mark (15.27) Luke makes early mention of the two robbers here. Thus also the notion of 22.37 that Jesus was reckoned among the lawless is expressed.

Historical

[27–41] Jesus never spoke these words, as they are rooted in anti-Jewish polemic. They come from a community situation in which the guilt for the death of Jesus has been foisted on the Jews.

Luke 23.33–49: The crucifixion and death of Jesus

33 And when they came to the place which is called The Place of the Skull, there they crucified him and the criminals with him, one on the right and one on the left. 34 And Jesus said, *'Father, forgive them; for they do not know what they are doing.'* And they divided his garments and cast lots for them. 35 And the people stood by and looked on. But the rulers mocked and said, 'He helped others; let him help himself, if he is the Christ, the Chosen One of God!' 36 The soldiers also mocked him, came up and offered him vinegar, 37 and said, 'If you are the King of the Jews, help yourself!' 38 There was also an inscription over him, 'This (is) the King of the Jews.'

39 *And one of the criminals hanging (beside him) reviled him and said, 'Are you not the Christ? Help yourself and us!' 40 But the other rebuked him and said, 'And do you not fear God, since you have received the same verdict? 41 And it is just for us, for we are receiving the due reward of our deeds; but this man has done nothing wrong.' 42 And he said, 'Jesus, remember me when you come*

into your kingdom.' 43 *And he said to him, 'Amen, I say to you, today you will be with me in Paradise.'*

44 And it was already about the sixth hour, and a darkness came over the whole land until the ninth hour, 45 and the sun lost its light, and the curtain of the temple was torn in two. 46 And Jesus cried, *'Father, I commend my spirit into your hands.'* And when he had said that, he departed.

47 Now when the centurion saw what had happened, he praised God and said, 'This man was *really righteous!'* 48 *And when all the multitudes who had come there and were looking on, saw the events that took place there, they beat their breasts and returned* (home). 49 But *all his acquaintances* stood afar off, also the women who had followed him from Galilee, and saw all this.

Redaction and tradition

Luke is using Mark 15.20b–41.

[33] Cf. Mark 15.22.

[34] The first part of the verse, the prayer for Jesus' enemies, is missing in important manuscripts. It has either been inserted there later or here deliberately stands in parallel with the dying cry of Stephen, Acts 7.60: 'Lord, do not impute this sin to them.'

[35] Perhaps the Christian community is prefigured in the people who look on.

]36] Luke has made the twofold offer of a drink in Mark 15.23, 36 into one.

[37–38] For v. 37 cf. Mark 15.30; for v. 38 cf. Mark 15.26. Luke has skilfully brought the two Markan verses together.

[39–43] The passage is a Lukan compendium dealing with christology (Jesus as a just man), forgiveness (prayer for forgiveness, consciousness of guilt) and eschatology (entering paradise immediately after death). There is a dispute over the text of v. 42. However, I think that it is certainly original.

[44–45] Luke skilfully combines the great darkness (Mark 15.33) with the tearing of the curtain of the temple (15.38).

[46] This conciliatory saying from a psalm (= Ps. 30.6) replaces the psalm saying about forsakenness by God in Mark 15.36 (= Ps. 22.2).

[47] The centurion does not confess that Jesus is son of God (Mark 15.39) but that as a righteous man he is innocent.

[48] The multitudes smite their breasts as a sign of repentance (cf. 18.13) and return home. 'The events' are important as a designation of the days of Jesus' activity in Jerusalem. It is unclear whether with the repentance of the multitudes Luke is indicating that the Jews responsible for the death of Jesus still have a chance of repenting, or whether the repentance is only a narrative element, for example in the sense that when confronted with the death of such a righteous man one must smite one's breast. (I incline to the latter possibility.)

[49] Cf. Mark 15.40. But Luke adds 'all his acquaintances', since he had deleted the flight of the disciples from Mark 14.50. He omits the names of the women, as in 23.55.

Historical

Cf. Mark 15.33–41. The redactional parts have no historical value.

Luke 23.50–56: The burial of Jesus

50 And look, there was a man *named* Joseph, a member of the council, *who was a good, pious man,* 51 *and he had not approved of their council and their action.* He was from Arimathea, *a city of the Jews,* and was awaiting the kingdom of God. 52 He went to Pilate and asked him for the body of Jesus, 53 and he took it down, wrapped it in a linen cloth, and laid it in a rock tomb, *in which no one had yet laid.* 54 And it was the day of preparation, and the sabbath was dawning. 55 *And the women who had come with him from Galilee followed, and saw the tomb, and how his body was laid in it.* 56 *They returned and prepared fragrant oils and ointments. And on the sabbath they rested according to the law.*

Redaction and tradition

[50–51] Luke depicts the figure of Joseph even more positively than Mark (15.43).

[52] Mark 15.44f. does not appear either in Luke or in Matthew. Either they did not yet read it in their copy of Mark or they left it out as superfluous information.

[53] The burial of Jesus is similarly depicted more positively than in Mark (15.46). The tomb is even new.

[54] Luke introduces a note of time here based on Mark 15.42.

[55–56] These verses improve on Mark (16.1) and make the women buy the spices in time. Resting on the sabbath corresponds to the faithfulness which Luke's main characters show to the Jewish law; cf. 2.41–52; Acts 3–4; 16.3; 21.26.

Historical

Cf. on Mark 15.42–47.

Luke 24.1–12: The proclamation of the Risen One in the empty tomb

1 But on the first day of the week very early they came to the tomb and brought with them the fragrant oils which they had prepared. 2 And they found the stone rolled away from the tomb, 3 and went in *but did not find the body of the Lord Jesus.* 4 *And while they were perplexed*

about that, look, two men came to them with shining garments. 5 And as they were frightened *and bowed their faces to the ground,* they (the men) said to them, '*Why do you seek the living among the dead?*' 6 He is not here, but he has been raised. *Remember how he told you, while he was still in Galilee,* 7 *the Son of man must be delivered into the hands of sinful men and crucified and on the third day rise.*' 8 *And they thought of his words.* 9 *And they returned from the tomb and proclaimed all this to the eleven disciples and to all the rest.* 10 Now it was Mary Magdalene and Joanna and Mary the mother of James and the other women with them; *they told this to the apostles.* 11 *And these words seemed to them like idle gossip, and they did not believe them.* 12 But Peter *rose* and ran to the tomb and stooped and saw only the linen cloths and went away and *wondered* at *what had happened.*

Preliminary text-critical note: v. 12 is lacking in some manuscripts. However, it is probably part of the original text, especially as it clearly has characteristics of Lukan language.

Redaction and tradition

[1–11] The Lukan significance of the pericope and its basis in tradition can best be discovered from a comparison with Mark, on which it is based. Small details apart, the texts differ at the following points:

1. The women saw the tomb of Jesus (Luke 23.55) and prepared spices and oil for anointing the evening before. They rested during the ensuing sabbath in accordance with the commandment (Luke 23.56). In Mark the women saw only (from afar) where the body of Jesus had been laid (15.47). They bought spices to anoint the body *after* the sabbath (Mark 16.1). Luke 24.1 does not explicitly mention the intention to anoint the body, but probably the women brought the fragrant oils early in the morning.

2. The names of the women are mentioned by Luke only towards the end of the pericope (v. 10), by Mark right at the beginning (v. 1).

Here Luke smoothes out the style, since in the Markan account some women who had already been mentioned immediately beforehand (Mark 15.47) reappear in Mark 16.1. By speaking of women in 23.55 (and 23.49) only generally and mentioning them by name in 24.10 he avoids the harsh transition which takes place in Mark 16.1.

The names of two women correspond in Luke and Mark: Mary Magdalene and Mary the mother of James. Salome (Mark 16.1) does not appear in Luke, but Joanna does; she had already been mentioned in Luke 8.3 as the wife of Chuza. (She probably comes from there and is redactional here.) In addition Luke mentions the other women who had accompanied Jesus – here, too, he is probably thinking of Luke 8.2–3.

3. In Luke the women do not worry about who will roll away the stone for them (Mark 16.3 differs), but, as in the Markan account, they find the stone rolled away from the tomb and enter it (Mark 16.4/Luke 24.2f.).

4. The next remark, 'but they did not find the body of Jesus', has no parallel in Mark at this point. There it is the young man, having given his message of the resurrection, who first points to the empty tomb. This shift of accent, along with the observation that Luke 24.3 explicitly mentions the *body* of Jesus (see above, Luke 23.55), indicates a stronger emphasis on the empty tomb and the bodily resurrection.

5. In Luke two men meet the women (in Mark a young man [16.5]), in shining garments (Luke 24.4); they recall the 'two men in white garments' in the scene of the ascension in Acts 1.10 (cf. 9.30,32). The scenes with the angels in 24.4–6 and Acts 1.10–12 correspond in mode of expression and order. They derive from Luke.

6. The message of the young man in Mark ran, 'You seek Jesus of Nazareth, the crucified one. He has been raised, he is not here; see the place where they laid him' (16.6). In Luke 24.5b–6a this becomes, 'Why do you seek the living among the dead?' He is not here, but he has been raised.

This last sentence is not contained in important manuscripts. For the question of the originality of this reading cf. on v. 12. Cf. on v. 5b the question expressing a similar reproach in Luke, 2.49; Acts 1.11.

7. Verses 6b–8 differ considerably from Mark 16.7. In Mark (and similarly Matt. 28.7) the women are charged to tell Jesus' disciples and Peter that they are to *go to Galilee*, where they will see Jesus, as they have been told. By contrast, in Luke (in Lukan language, cf. 'into the hands of *sinful* men' [v. 7]), the two men refer the women back to the message of Jesus which they *had been given* earlier *in Galilee*, that the Son of Man *had to* suffer and rise again on the third day (9.22; cf. 9.44; 18.32f.). (Accordingly Mark 14.28f. is *not* picked up by Luke.) It should be noted that only 9.22,44 was spoken in Galilee and that the women were not explicitly thought to be present at these instructions. For that 'must' cf. on Luke 24.26.

8. In Mark the women are silent despite the charge to them; in Luke they are convinced and pass on to the eleven disciples and all the rest the message of the resurrection without having to be told to do so (v. 9), but meet with unbelief (v. 11).

[12] From where has Luke (or his tradition) got the report of a visit of Peter to the tomb? The following answer suggests itself: Luke (or his tradition) knows the account of an appearance of Jesus to Peter (cf. Luke 24.34) and similarly the tradition of a visit of the women to the tomb. Both are combined in Luke v. 12, and added where they belong, namely at the end of the women's visit to the tomb. The 'logic' of this combination runs as follows: if the tomb was empty and if Jesus appeared to Cephas, then Peter must have inspected it beforehand in order to be persuaded of the reality of the appearance. Either Luke himself or, more probably, the report which he used must have been the author of this combination (for the parallel John 20.3–10 cf. there.) But it any case it has become clear that the tradition appearing in

v. 12 is a development of the account of the tomb in Mark 16.1–8 using the tradition of a first appearance to Peter. So the tradition behind Luke 24.12 is a secondary construction and therefore without historical value for the question of the 'resurrection events'.

Historical

Cf. on Mark 16.1–8.

Luke 24.13–35: Jesus encounters the two disciples on the Emmaus road

13 *And look*, on the same day two of them were going to a village about two hours' journey from Jerusalem; its name is Emmaus. 14 And they were talking with each other about all these things that had happened. 15 *And it happened*, while they were talking and discussing together, that Jesus himself approached and went with them. 16 But their eyes were kept from recognizing him.

17 And he said to them, 'What were the things that you were discussing on the way?' And they stood still, looking sad. 18 And one of them, named Cleopas, answered and said to him, 'Are you the only one visiting Jerusalem who does not know what happened there in these days?' 19 *And he said to them, 'What, then?' And they said to him, 'Concerning Jesus of Nazareth, who was a prophet mighty in deed and word before God and all the people; 20 how our chief priests and rulers delivered him up to be condemned to death and crucified him. 21 But we had hoped that he was the one to redeem Israel. And besides all this, it is now the third day since this happened. 22 Moreover, some women of our company terrified us. They were at the tomb early in the morning 23 but did not find his body; and they came back saying that they had even seen a vision of angels, who claimed that he was alive. 24 And some of us went to the tomb, and found it just as the women said; but him they did not see.' 25 And he said to them, 'O foolish men, and slow of heart to believe all that the prophets have spoken! 26 Was it not necessary that the Christ should suffer these things and enter into his glory?' 27 And beginning with Moses and all the prophets, he interpreted to them what had been said about him in all the scriptures.*

28 And they were approaching the village to which they were going. And he seemed to want to go farther. 29 But they constrained him and said, 'Stay with us, for it is toward evening and the day is now declining.' And he went in to stay with them. 30 *And it happened*, when he was at table with them, he took the bread, gave thanks, broke (it), and gave it to them. 31 Then their eyes were opened and they recognized him. *And he vanished out of their sight.*

32 *And they said to each other, 'Did not our hearts burn within us while he was talking to us on the road and opened the scriptures to us?' 33 And they rose that same hour, returned to Jerusalem and found the eleven gathered together and those who were with them. 34 They said, 'The Lord was truly raised, and appeared to Simon!' 35 And they told them what had happened on the road, and how he became known to them in the breaking of the bread.*

Redaction and tradition

The present narrative about the disciples on the Emmaus road, shaped with special love, is constructed as follows:

vv. 13–16: Exposition: two disciples meet Jesus on the way from Jerusalem to Emmaus
vv. 17–27: Conversation on the way
vv. 28–31: Meal scene
vv. 32–35: Return from Emmaus to Jerusalem.

[13] 'And look' is a Lukan introduction (see most recently 23.50); 'of them' links the narrative with what has gone before; 'on the same day': according to Luke all the resurrection appearances take place on one and the same day.

[14] This refers back to 'all these things' of v. 9, the report by the women. The disciples did not believe them (v. 11). But Peter nevertheless inspected the tomb (v. 12).

[15] The two disciples, too, cannot leave alone what has happened and what the women have related. They converse and discuss it (cf. Luke 22.23; Acts 6.9). The sequel picks this up: Jesus joins them and travels on with them.

[16] Their eyes were kept from recognizing him (not right at the beginning of the encounter).

That is the end of the introduction. The 'resolution' will consist in their eyes being opened (v. 31). But before that can happen the two, and thus the readers, are to undergo a recognition process. This begins with the conversation on the way in vv. 17–27.

[17–19] Jesus begins – in genuine Lukan fashion (cf. Acts 8.30; 9.4,10, etc.) – with a question which opens the dialogue, about what the two disciples have been talking about on the way. Their sorrow is emphatically noted by means of the pause in the external scene (they remain at a standstill), which heightens the tension. In the two-fold exchange of a question from Jesus (v. 17) and a more allusive counter-question from a disciple (Cleopas, v. 18), expressing a reproach, a further question from Jesus and a first brief piece of information (v. 19), it finally becomes clear that they are talking about Jesus himself, who is termed a 'prophet, mighty in deed and word before God and all the people'. Verse 19 is completely shaped by Luke. Only he uses the Greek word for 'before' which appears here (Luke 1.6; 20.26; Acts 7.10; 8.32 [= Isa. 53.7]). The people call Jesus 'prophet' in 7.16; 9.8,19 and indirectly in 7.39. For the phrase 'mighty in deed and word' see Acts 7.22. But it has to be asked why the two disciples give Jesus a christological title (' prophet') here which otherwise is not central in Luke. The answer is that Luke attributes to the disciples, who are caught up in incomprehension, a doctrine of Christ which is later to be corrected (v. 26). So v. 19 produces a tension (like v. 18 before it) which looks for resolution.

[20] This verse describes the death of Jesus in a Lukan way: the Jews crucified Jesus (cf. Acts 7.51–53 and the exoneration of Pilate in the Lukan passion narrative).

[21] This points back to the original but disappointed hope of the disciples that Jesus would redeem Israel (cf. Luke 1.68; 2.38; Acts 1.6). The hope has evidently been superseded by the creation of a church of the Gentiles (see the end of Acts). With the note of time 'third day' Luke refers back to the chronology of the Easter stories and in vv. 22–24 paraphrases what has been reported so far.

[22] This links up with the story of the visit of the women to the tomb which has been told previously.

[23] This repeats their vision of the angel and the message to them that Jesus is alive (a link to v. 5: 'Why do you seek the living among the dead?').

[24] This refers back to v. 12, where the word 'some' generalizes the visit of an individual, Peter.

[25] This introduces the development of the previous faith of the disciples – first of all through a reproach from Jesus (which is similar to the reproach to the women in Luke 24.5–8): 'And he said to them, "O foolish men, and slow of heart to believe all that the prophets have spoken!" '

[26] This characterizes the suffering of Christ as necessary and in accordance with the scriptures (v. 27; cf. v. 25). It is wholly in accord with the Lukan notion of salvation history (cf. also 24.6b, 44), the course of which is thought of as being necessary in all its elements. Here Luke puts particular emphasis on the paradoxical discovery that the Christ destined for glory had to suffer.

[27] This expresses the general Lukan conviction that Christ is mentioned in the books of Moses and in the Prophets (cf. Acts 8.35); but he does not produce a single passage to attest this.

[28] The destination has almost been reached. Jesus' intention to go farther increases the tension. Now, where everything is moving towards the climax, the recognition of Jesus by the two disciples, Jesus cannot just go farther and disappear.

[29] Accordingly, the two disciples urgently ask Jesus to stay (cf. Rev. 3.20).

[30] Jesus breaks bread at the common meal, blesses it and gives it to them. The many verbal allusions to the eucharistic words in Luke 22.19 from v. 30 on indicate that here Luke is thinking in terms of the eucharist.

[31] Their eyes are opened and they recognize him. Thus their 'blindness' of v. 16 is removed. What Luke wants to convey is that communion with Jesus is experienced in the eucharist. Once that is clear, all has been said: Jesus can vanish (v. 31b). This explicit statement that the one who appears vanishes is typically Lukan: Luke 1.38; 2.15; 9,33; Acts 10.7; 12.10.

[32] In retrospect the disciples recognize that their hearts were already burning within them when Jesus opened the scriptures to them on the way.

[33] Now the two disciples can return to Jerusalem, to the eleven and the rest (just as the women did in v. 9).

[34] Before the two disciples can communicate to the eleven the knowledge that they have just gained, these say to them, 'The Lord was truly raised and has

appeared to Simon.' This spoils their story. Here, as in other passages (Acts 8.14ff.; 11.1,22), Luke makes room for a Jerusalem perspective. He corrects his tradition at this point and establishes the first appearance to Peter (= Cephas in Aramaic), as it already occurs in the tradition in I Cor. 15.5 (Christ appeared to Cephas, then to the twelve). Now in a historical literal understanding, the second half of the sentence in v. 34 is strange, since after all Simon is one of the twelve. How could the eleven 'neutrally' make such a statement? Therefore we must ask what Luke means to say to his readers with this verse. The answer is that the experience which the two disciples and all the members of the Lukan community have at the supper, namely that Jesus is present there, is confirmed by the primitive Christian confession that Jesus is risen and has appeared to Simon. In other words, all other Easter experiences are based on the primitive Christian credo. In Acts Luke will then also depict Peter as a leader of the primitive community (cf. Peter's speeches in Acts 2.14–40; 3.12–26) and the Jerusalem church as the primitive community to which Luke's community is a successor.

[35] This sums up Luke's understanding once again: the two disciples relate what has happened to them on the way (viz. that the scriptures have been opened to them) and that they recognized Jesus in the breaking of the bread.

A reconstruction of the tradition which Luke used faces great difficulties, although it is certain that Luke worked with existing material. As a test one could take out all the references to the context of the story to see whether the result provides the basic features of a tradition. What is left is a story which with reference to Gen. 18.1–15 (cf. Judg. 6.12–24; Tobit 5 could be paraphrased like this:

'Here Christ appears unknown, as a wanderer – the role that the deity loved from of old, in simple human form, for example clad as a traveller to wander among human beings – and reveals his mysterious divine being at particular points; but as soon as he is recognized, he disappears. This outline of the story is very similar to the earliest narratives about the appearance of the deity; in style the story could be put in Genesis' (Gunkel).

At the same time it should be added that there were also similar sagas in the Graeco–Roman sphere (cf. Philemon and Baucis in Ovid).

If we presuppose such a legend as the earliest stratum, we could distinguish from it the eucharistic tradition in vv. 28–31, which may have been added at a second stage. However, this was possibly already bound up with the earliest tradition.

Historical

[34] The appearance to Simon is to be termed historical as a visionary event.

Individual elements of the pericope are beyond doubt old: thus possibly behind the name Cleopas (v. 18) lies Jesus' cousin, whose son Symeon succeeded James (Eusebius, *Church History* III, 11; IV, 22, 4). In that case, in this story we would have a recollection of an appearance of Jesus to one of his relatives, which might go back to the earliest period. It is also remarkable that in John 19.25 one of the women at the cross is called 'Mary (the wife) of Cleopas'.

The place Emmaus might also derive from historical knowledge, but it can no longer be located.

Luke 24.36–53: Jesus' appearance to the (eleven) disciples

36 As they were saying this, he himself, Jesus, stood *in their midst* and said to them, 'Peace (be) with you!' 37 *But they were terrified and frightened*, and supposed that *they saw a spirit.* 38 And he said to them, 'Why are you troubled, and why do such thoughts enter *your hearts?* 39 See my hands and my feet, that it is I myself. Handle me, and see; for a spirit has not flesh and bones as you see that I have.' 40 *And when he had said that, he showed them his hands and feet.* 41 And while they still disbelieved for joy, and wondered, he said to them, 'Have you anything here to eat?' 42 And they gave him a piece of baked fish. 43 And he took it and ate before them.

44 *And he said to them, 'These are my words which I have spoken to you, while I was still with you: everything written about me in the law of Moses, in the prophets and in the psalms must be fulfilled.'* 45 *Then he opened their minds to understand the scriptures,* 46 *and said to them, 'Thus it is written, that the Christ will suffer and on the third day rise from the dead,* 47 *and that repentance and forgiveness of sins will be preached in his name to all peoples, beginning in Jerusalem.* 48 *You are witnesses of these things.* 49 *And look, I will send the promise of my Father down upon you. But you are to stay in the city until you are clothed with power from on high.'*

50 *Then he led them out as far as Bethany, and raised his hands and blessed them.* 51 *And it happened that as he was blessing them, he parted from them and went up into heaven.* 52 *And they worshipped him and returned to Jerusalem with great joy,* 53 *and were continually in the temple blessing God.*

Redaction and tradition

The section is composed of three parts: vv. 36–43 are a recognition scene (= narrative), vv. 44–49 are instruction of the disciples (= discourse of Jesus) and vv. 50–53 are a farewell (= narrative).

[36] 'As they were saying this' is a Lukan link between what follows and the previous scene.

[37–38] For the scene cf. Acts 12.8f.

[39] Jesus' invitation to the disciples to see his hands and his feet in order to recognize his identity gives a first demonstration (whether the disciples did look at them is not said, but is presupposed); the invitation to touch him and see is the *second* demonstration of the resurrection of Jesus. The risen Jesus is no spirit (to be concrete, no demon of the dead) but consists of flesh and blood. With such realism one can hardly avoid seeing this as a thrust against docetism. Evidently in this verse

Luke is combatting challenges to the bodily reality of Jesus as Ignatius, To the Smyrnaeans 3.2, does at the beginning of the second century:

> For I know and believe that he (viz. Jesus) was in the flesh even after the resurrection. And when he came to those with Peter he said to them, 'Take, handle me and see that I am not a phantom without a body.' And they immediately touched him and believed, being mingled both with his flesh and spirit.

[40] This verse is a variation on and intensification of v. 39. It probably comes in its entirety from Luke.

[41] The disciples have been half-convinced by Jesus. The third demonstration which now follows is meant to remove any doubt. Jesus asks whether the disciples have anything to eat (v. 41b).

[42] They give him a piece of baked fish.

[43] He eats it before their eyes and thus proves that he is neither a spirit nor an angel. Angels do not eat (cf. Tobit 12.19); human beings do. The narrator takes the probative force of this last demonstration so much for granted that he does not even have to emphasize that the disciples are convinced. Later Acts 1.4; 10.41 says that Jesus ate with his disciples. By stressing the physical reality of the risen Jesus, Luke evidently wants to strengthen the certainty of his readers, as he announced in the preface (Luke 1.3–4). For this reason he has woven into vv. 36–43 the tradition of an appearance story in which the risen Jesus appears to his anxious disciples in bodily form. The central statement is the real bodily form of Jesus after the resurrection. The presupposition is a discussion within a community about the nature of the corporeality of the risen Christ of the kind that we find in the Johannine communities (cf. John 20; I John) and in its beginnings even earlier in the Pauline community of Corinth (I Cor. 15). Accordingly this is a secondary formation – probably from the second generation, which no longer had any connection with the primary witnesses to the 'resurrection' of Jesus. It is a composition formed from reflection which documents for the disciples in three progressive stages the bodily nature of the Risen One.

[44–49] These verses are a redactional composition. In v. 44 Jesus refers in retrospect to what he has said to the disciples. The main content is explained further by the second part of the verse. Just as Jesus already argued from the scriptures during his lifetime, so he does after his resurrection. In v. 45 Jesus discloses to the disciples the meaning of the scriptures as he did earlier in the Emmaus story (cf. esp. v. 27). The content of this disclosure is then made specific in the following verse in the form of a proof from scripture. Verse 46 corresponds to 9.22, Jesus' prediction that he would suffer and rise again on the third day. Verse 47 directs attention towards the future and the task of the disciples. Part of the proof from scripture is that in Jesus' name 'repentance and forgiveness of sins' should be preached 'among all peoples, beginning in Jerusalem' (cf. Acts 2.32f., 38; 3.15f.,19; 5.28–32; 10.39, 43).

Verse 48 is no longer part of the proof from scripture. Here Jesus addresses the disciples in direct speech as witnesses to 'these things', i.e. as eye-witnesses to the passion and resurrection (cf. Acts 1.22). Verse 49 corresponds to Acts 1.4. The prophecies about receiving the Spirit are fulfilled in narrative form in Acts 2.

[50–53] These verses derive from Luke. Verse 50: the section has a parallel in Acts 1.9–11, where the ascension takes place from the Mount of Olives (v. 12); here by contrast it is from Bethany. However, that need not lead us to suppose that the two scenes are rival traditions. Luke knows from Mark 11.1 that the 'Mount of Olives' and 'Bethany' are geographically close together or are identical as place names. So here the use of Bethany instead of Mount of Olives can be a variation. Thus the scene is redactional. For the blessing cf. the word-for-word parallels in Lev. 9.22 (see also Sir. 50.22). For the disappearance of Jesus in v. 51 cf. the comments on v. 31. 'Great joy' in v. 52 takes up the same motif from v. 41. In v. 53, the presence of the community in the temple is in accord with Lukan theology. The twelve-year-old Jesus remains in the temple (Luke 2.46), as does the early community (Acts 2.46; 3.1; 5.42). In terms of form, v. 53 is a short summary which has parallels in Luke-Acts (1.65f., 80; 2.20, 40, 52; Acts 1.14). We must in any case attribute the last sentence to the evangelist, because here the intention of the author is most to be expected.

Historical

The historical yield is nil, both in respect of the real historical event and in connection with the visions which were the catalyst for the rise of Christianity. For vv. 44–53 are redactional, and vv. 36–43 derive from the formation of the second Christian generation: they are conditioned by discussions within the community on the bodily nature of the 'Risen One'.

IV

The Gospel of John

FRANK SCHLERITT

Introduction

1. The Gospel of John and the historical Jesus

Anyone who is in search of the historical Jesus will not find him in the Gospel of John. For the Fourth Gospel has already left far behind what Jesus really said and did. This verdict is a consensus among New Testament scholars. Certainly John contains some historically reliable information about Jesus: for example that he comes from Nazareth (1.45), that he had disciples and brothers (2.12; 7.3), that he taught publicly and that he was finally crucified in Jerusalem. But apart from such general information, which is also known from the Synoptics, a critical analysis of the Gospel of John leaves hardly anything for the historical Jesus. Whereas at least some interconnected features of the message and activities of Jesus can be reconstructed from the Synoptic Gospels, in John it is almost exclusively the theologically interpreted Jesus, i.e. Christ, who appears.

Despite this sobering finding, which anticipates a primary result of the following survey of the Fourth Gospel, it would be illegitimate within the framework of the present work to appeal *a priori* to the consensus of scholars and to fail to take account of John. For on the one hand there is also a consensus that the majority of what Mark, Matthew and Luke report about Jesus is unhistorical. And on the other, knowledge about authentic sayings and actions of Jesus can be achieved only if at the same time it can be demonstrated with some probability which words and actions are certainly unhistorical: the negative and positive parts of the analysis are inseparably linked.

2. A preliminary text-critical note

The section 7.53–8.11 does not appear in the earliest textual witnesses to the Gospel of John. It represents a late addition and therefore is left completely out of account in the following considerations and also in the analysis of John (for the exegesis of this section cf. Chapter VI).

3. The structure of the Gospel of John

For a first rough survey, it is convenient to divide the Gospel of John into five parts, leaving details aside: the prologue (1.1–18), the report of the public activity of Jesus (1.19–12.50), the farewell discourses of Jesus in the circle of the disciples (chs. 13–17), the passion story (chs. 18–19), and the Easter narratives (chs. 20–21).

4. The relationship between the Gospel of John and the Synoptics

'Anyone who has understood John will never open the Synoptics again except out of anti-quarian interest, which John would have regarded as the inspiration of the devil' (H. Windisch).

The relationship between the Synoptic Gospels and John is like that of three variations on one and the same theme to a new piece. Whereas for example the narrative in the Synoptics comes to a climax in Jesus' first and last visit to Jerusalem, the Gospel of John reports several stays of Jesus in Jerusalem. Where the Jesus of the Synoptic Gospels tells brief, impressive parables, the Jesus of the Gospel of John delivers long discourses, often without a point. According to Mark, Matthew and Luke Jesus proclaims above all the dawn of the rule of God, and against that background speaks about commandments relating to the sabbath, cleanness and food, and about divorce, taxation, riches, poverty, prayer, etc. By contrast, according to the Gospel of John Jesus speaks almost exclusively about one theme, namely himself. Furthermore, the Fourth Gospel reports neither the temptation of Jesus by the devil, nor the expulsions of demons, nor the institution of the Lord's Supper; on the other hand it does know of some miraculous actions by Jesus which are not known to the Synoptics, and depicts the washing of the disciples' feet by Jesus on the eve of the passion, etc.

However, there are also a number of narratives which, more or less diverging from each other, appear both in the Synoptics and in the Fourth Gospel, e.g. the cleansing of the temple, the feeding of the five thousand and Jesus walking on the sea, the anointing in Bethany, Jesus' entry into Jerusalem, and above all the passion story. An attempt is often made to explain these common features – for example in the case of the passion story – by assuming that Mark and the Fourth Evangelist were independently drawing on an earlier report of the passion, and that none of the Synoptic Gospels was known in the Fourth Evangelist's community. However, that is very improbable for the following reasons. *First*: the sequence of individual narratives which correspond to each other agrees with Mark; cf. e.g. the appearance of John the Baptist (Mark 1.2ff.//John 1.19ff.), the miracle of the feeding and the walking on the sea (Mark 6.32ff.//John 6.1ff.), Peter's confession (Mark 8.27ff.//John 6.67ff.), the announcement of the delivering up by Judas (Mark 14.17ff.//John 13.21ff.), the prophecy of Peter's denial (Mark 14.29ff.//John 13.36ff.), the passion and resurrection (Mark 14.43ff.//John 18.1ff.). *Secondly*: there are not only striking agreements in wording and content between John and Mark (sometimes against Matthew and Luke) but also passages which evidently presuppose Mark's redactional activity, mainly in the passion story (cf. e.g. 18.12–27). *Thirdly*: the Gospel of John shows several agreements in word and content, over and above those with Mark, with what in all probability are in part redactional passages of Matthew and Luke (cf. e.g. John 6.1–3 with Matt. 15.29–32; John 20.1–23 with Luke 24.1–12, 36–43). *Fourthly*: it is extremely improbable that the genre of Gospel was created twice in different places independently of each other.

While these points would of themselves be open to other patterns of explanation, taken together they are clear indications that the Gospels of Mark, Matthew and Luke were known in the community of the Fourth Evangelist. Now, however, a problem arises: within the narratives of John in which the Synoptic Gospels are manifestly presupposed, many deviations cannot be derived from motives of the Fourth Evangelist. Moreover some of the passages which go beyond the Synoptics show tensions and fractures for which one would have to make the Fourth Evangelist himself responsible if one were to assume a direct literary dependence of John on the Synoptics. (For a concrete illustration of these general remarks see the introductory comments on John 18–19.)

The following hypothesis does justice to all these phenomena. Certainly the Synoptic Gospels were known in the community of the Fourth Evangelist. But in many respects they did not correspond (or no longer corresponded) to the special interests and theological views of this community. Therefore – already *before* the Fourth Evangelist began on the composition of his work – they were subjected to a new interpretation by a group of scholars commonly called the 'Johannine school' to which (later) the Fourth Evangelist also belonged. (The three letters of John came from this school after the Gospel of John.) In the process of the interpretation of the Synoptic Gospels some narratives were rejected; others, however, were developed, in the course of time changed and finally taken over by the Fourth Evangelist in a form which recalls the original Markan, Matthaean or Lukan text, sometimes more and sometimes less. Here it was inevitable that the Markan, Matthaean and Lukan texts, above all those with the same or similar content, gradually became fused together, so that the corpus of tradition which the evangelist finally found before him represented a peculiar synthesis of all three earlier Gospels (cf. e.g. 12.1–8, where the Markan/Matthaean story of the anointing has been mixed with the Lukan story, which is of quite a different kind; and 6.1–15, where the five Synoptic stories of the feeding have been fused into one).

The evangelist has used this corpus of tradition which is dependent on the redactional final form of the Synoptic Gospels. For the sake of simplicity in what follows it will be referred to as Z (= an abbreviation of the German word *Zwischentradition*, namely the tradition which chronologically stands *zwischen*, 'between', the Synoptics and John).

Whether, however, the Fourth Evangelist himself used the Synoptic Gospels, i.e. whether in composing his work he looked at these Gospels, which had already been set aside by the Johannine community, is a secondary question on which a decision is no longer possible. But if the hypothesis offered above is correct, this seems somewhat improbable. Therefore in what follows no direct use of any of the Synoptic Gospels by the Fourth Evangelist will be presupposed.

The above hypothesis about the relationship between John and the Synoptics is based on a monograph by Hans Windisch which appeared in 1926 (*Johannes und die Synoptiker. Wollte der vierte Evangelist die älteren Evangelien ergänzen oder ersetzen?*, UNT 12) but is not identical with it: Windisch came to the conclusion that the Fourth Evangelist knew all the Synoptic Gospels and that he composed his work with the intention of replacing them. Taking this thesis further, I go on the assumption – to make the point once again – that the process of a reinterpretation of the Synoptic Gospels which itself suppressed them had begun in the Johannine school *before* the composition of the Gospel of John. However, the Fourth Evangelist was the first person who then wanted to make the Synoptic Gospels quite superfluous and suppress them, at least in his community. He did not succeed in this, at any rate not in the long run. He would surely not have been pleased to know that towards the end of the second century the church put the work which he had composed (in a revised form, at that) with the Synoptic Gospels in the canon of the New Testament that was in the process of formation, and thenceforward attempted to harmonize it with these works and read it as a supplement to them.

5. The history of the origin of the Gospel of John

Whereas the so-called two-source theory has largely established itself as an explanation of the origin of Matthew and Luke, the question of the literary origin of John is still highly controversial. The model which has proved to be plausible and usable in the course of the following analysis occupies a middle position among the various hypotheses which have been developed in the course of the last century. To present it very briefly: the final form of the Gospel of John does not come from a single author. The one who deserves the designation 'evangelist' is rather responsible only for the main body of the Fourth Gospel in its canonical form. He knew a corpus of tradition (= Z) dependent on the Synoptic Gospels, and by using further non-Synoptic traditions created with great poetic freedom a counter-scheme to the 'Synoptic' picture of Jesus. After his death his work was revised by others in several stages.

6. The later revisions

The starting point for the assumption of later revisions is the observation that ch. 21 forms a secondary appendix (20.30f. is the explicit conclusion to a book; for further explanation of this cf. the introduction to ch. 21). For in that case, the question arises whether later expansions have also been made *within* the corpus of the Gospel. That is manifestly the case. However, why this verdict is passed on particular parts of the text can be demonstrated only during the analysis of the individual sections.

Various terms are used by scholars for those who expanded the work of the evangelist ('church redaction', 'post-Gospel redaction', 'deutero-Johannine redaction'). To avoid confusion over the term 'redaction', which can also be applied to the redactional activity of the evangelist, in what follows I shall speak simply of the 'later revisers'. That there are in fact several of these, following one another chronologically, and not just a single reviser – in other words, that the revision did not take place all at once – emerges from the fact that not all the passages which were added later follow the same theological line and that sometimes the additions are not a unity in themselves. The gradual growth of the Gospel of John can be traced particularly well in chs. 15–17. The individual sections of these chapters clearly show that they have been added successively (see there).

So we must also once again separate different strata within the parts of the text which were later added. However, because of the narrow textual basis it is impossible to assign every added verse or passage to one of these strata. But at least some strata of revision stand out from others. One of these strata seems to be present in 11.5; 13.1b, 12b–17, 20, 34f.; 14.14f., 24 and 15.1–17; the (group of) reviser(s) responsible for it was particularly interested in the theme of love. Another (group of) reviser(s) apparently had a marked interest in the figure of Judas, who delivered Jesus up (cf. 6.64b–65; 12.4b, 6; 13.2–3, 10b–11, 18f.; 17.12b; 18.5c).

And yet another was above all interested in the disciple whom Jesus loved (13.23–26a; 19.26–27, 35; 20.3–10; 21; cf. also the remarks on the later revision of 1.35–51). Further attempts at bringing strata together must remain very hypothetical.

The thesis of a later revision of the work composed by the evangelist is not new, as has already been indicated. It has been carried through with seductive clarity and impressive consistency by the Kiel New Testament scholar Jürgen Becker (*Das Evangelium nach Johannes*, 2 vols, ÖTK 4/1–2, ³1991). With a few small exceptions, the later additions marked off in the present chapter correspond to the passages attributed by Becker to the 'church redaction'.

7. The Gospel of John as a pseudepigraphical writing

In the supplementary chapter 21, the author of John is named as an eye-witness. (Here it is not completely clear to what verse his authorship is to extend [to 20.31; 21.23 or even to 21.24?].) The author is said to be 'the disciple whom Jesus loved' (21.24). Now the Gospel of John cannot have been composed by an immediate disciple of Jesus (cf. point 8), quite apart from the fact that it does not have one but several authors (cf. point 6). Rather, it was only subsequently put under the authority of the beloved disciple – and thus under the authority of an alleged eye-witness. In this respect the Gospel of John is a particularly refined species of early Christian pseudepigraphy. It has been authorized not by attribution to an apostle mentioned by name (such as the deutero-Paulines, I and II Peter, James and Jude) but by being presented as the work of a special disciple who was loved by Jesus. He is said to have been witness above all to the last hours of Jesus' life on earth; he was the first to believe in the resurrection of Jesus, and was put on at least the same level as Peter by the Risen One himself.

It is quite another question whether the authors of ch. 21 – and there is much to suggest that these are also responsible for the passages about the beloved disciple *within* the Gospel (cf. already point 6) – thought of the disciple whom Jesus loved as a particular historical figure. That is very probable, because 21.20–24 evidently reflect the death of the 'beloved disciple' (see there). It is a plausible assumption that behind him lies the founder of the Johannine community or the head of the Johannine school. The revisers declared this man a disciple of Jesus and projected him back into the life of Jesus.

8. The question of authorship

The interpretation that the author of the Fourth Gospel is John, son of Zebedee, Jesus' disciple, can be found for the first time in Irenaeus of Lyons (c. AD 180) and is probably already presupposed in the heading 'Gospel according to John' attested in Papyrus 66 (c.AD 200). This interpretation, which is of course completely untouched by considerations about a growth of the Gospel in several stages, is incorrect. (a) We can rule out the possibility that the Gospel of John goes back to an eye-witness of the activity of Jesus; otherwise, for example, it would be impossible to explain why the term 'kingdom of God', which certainly stood at the centre of Jesus' message, plays virtually no role in the Fourth Gospel. (b) It probably emerges from Mark 10.35–40 that John the son of Zebedee suffered a martyr's death at a very early stage, at any rate before the composition of Mark; but the Gospel of John presupposes the composition of Mark. (c) The use of sources (or Z) is hardly to be expected of an eye-witness. (d) Nowhere within John 1–21 is it hinted that the beloved disciple whom the later revisers present as the author is identical with the son of Zebedee.

In contrast, if the hypotheses mentioned under point 6 are right, the question of *the* author does not arise at all in the form it took in the early church. If we reduce it to the question of the identity of the *evangelist*, i.e. the author of the basic core of John, we have to say that the evangelist retreats completely behind his work. We do not know his name – any more than we know the names of the subsequent revisers of his work.

9. Time and place of the composition of the Gospel of John

The question of the time of composition of the Fourth Gospel is extraordinarily difficult, and becomes additionally complicated if one reckons on later revisions of the work created by the evangelist. It will therefore be answered only in a very rough and brief way. On the one hand the Gospel of John is later than the Synoptic Gospels and presupposes their dissemination. On the other hand, the first letter of John (I John) already refers to the Gospel. And the composition of I John seems already to be presupposed in the letter of Polycarp of Smyrna to the Philippians (probably around AD 135, cf. Phil. 7.1 with I John 4.2f.). If in addition we note that John is already attested at an early stage (Papyrus 52) in Egypt (which can hardly be considered the place where it was written), the evangelist's work was probably composed in the first decade of the second century. The Gospel must then have assumed its final form in the first quarter of the second century.

The question of the place of composition cannot be decided with certainty. According to the testimonies of the church fathers it is Ephesus. However, if we go exclusively by perspectives immanent in the work (Semitizing Greek, polemic against the Baptist community, mission to the Samaritans), Syria is more probable.

10. Terminology

(a) 'Fourth Evangelist': the first three evangelists are traditionally called Matthew, Mark and Luke. This custom makes sense in so far as the Gospels of Mark, Matthew and Luke each come from a single author. In contrast, the Gospel of John is the end-product of a lengthy history of literary development (see point 6). Therefore it is not advisable in connection with this Gospel to work with a name corresponding to Mark, Matthew and Luke (e.g. John). That explains why in what follows the term used will always be 'the (fourth) evangelist', when the author of the basic core is being referred to.

(b) 'Johannine': this term cannot always be avoided. It does not refer to the Fourth Evangelist as such but rather to his environment or to the Gospel of John as a whole (cf. e.g. 'the Johannine community/school'; 'Johannine terminology'). So it is not equivalent to 'Markan', 'Matthaean', etc.

(c) 'Later revisers': of course it cannot be decided whether an individual reviser was responsible e.g. for the texts about Judas which were added later, or rather a group of revisers. Hereafter, in the case of smaller additions I shall speak mainly of the later *revisers*, and in longer passages predominantly of the *author* in question. However, no conclusions are to be drawn from this.

(d) 'Z': this abbreviation (which is not usual in scholarly literature) is explained under point 4.

11. How to read the following translations

(a) In keeping with the procedure in the chapters on Mark, Matthew and Luke, the parts of the text which probably derive from the work of the evangelist as redactor or author are indicated with *italics* and the traditions used by him with normal type.

(b) What have been demonstrated in the individual analyses as additions to the completed work of the evangelist have been printed in **bold**. Of course, these additions in turn rest on earlier traditions; but in order not to spoil the clarity, no attempt will be made within the supplements to distinguish typographically the parts which derive from later redaction and those which derive from tradition. So verdicts on this can be inferred only from the relative analyses. Special rules apply to the extensive sections 10.1–18; 15–17 and 21, which have been added at a later stage, and these will be explained at the beginning of each of these passages.

(c) Underlinings serve various purposes, each of which is indicated in the analysis of the relevant individual sections. They serve not only to make the text more transparent (thus e.g. in 8.30–59 and in 15.1–17) but also, for example in some passages dependent on Z, to indicate verbatim agreements with the Synoptics (thus e.g. in chs. 18–20) or to distinguish different strata in the later revision from one another (thus only in 13.1–20).

The Prologue

John 1.1–18: The pre-existence, mediation at creation and incarnation of the Logos

1 In the beginning was the Logos,
and the Logos was with God,
and a God was the Logos.
2 *This was in the beginning with God.*
3 All things came into being through him
and without him nothing came into being.
That which came into being, 4 in it he was life,
and the life was the light of men.
5 And the light shines in the darkness,
yet the darkness has not grasped it.
6 *A man appeared, sent by God, his name (was) John. 7 This man came for witness, to bear witness to the light, that all might come to believe through him. 8 He was not the light, but to bear witness to the light. 9 It was the true light that enlightens every man who comes into the world. 10 He (the*

Logos) was in the world, and the world came into being through him, yet the world did not know him.

11 He came into his own
yet his own did not receive him.
12 But all who received him,
to them he gave power
to become children of God,
to those who believe in his name,
13 **who were begotten neither from blood nor from the will of the flesh nor from the will of man, but from God.**
14 And the Logos became flesh
and dwelt among us.
And we saw his glory,
a glory like (that of the) only-begotten with the Father,
full of grace and truth.
15 *John bears witness to him and cries, 'This was he of whom I said: The one who comes after me has become before me, for he was earlier than me.'*
16 For from his fullness
we have all received,
grace upon grace.
17 *For* the law was given through Moses,
grace and truth have come into being through Jesus Christ.
18 *No one has ever seen God. The only-begotten God, who is in the bosom of the Father, he has declared (him).*

Later revision

Verse 13 is probably an addition by the revisers (for the reason see below under v. 12d), which is meant to allude to Christian baptism (cf. the analogous terminology in 3.3, 5). The revisers make it clear that baptism is as necessary for salvation as faith (v. 12d).

Redaction

At the beginning of Mark and the Logia source Q Jesus immediately comes into view as a grown man. Matthew and Luke were dissatisfied with this and therefore prefaced their accounts of the activity of Jesus with stories about his birth and infancy, and with genealogies of Jesus (cf. Matt. 1–2; Luke 1–2; 3.23–38). The Fourth Evangelist has drawn this line even wider, to infinity: his story of Jesus, the 'Logos' (i.e. the 'Word'), goes back to the creation of the world. For the 'in the beginning' with which the prologue begins alludes to 'In the beginning God created heaven and earth', the first sentence of the Bible.

As is generally recognized, the evangelist has composed the opening text of his work on the basis of a community hymn. In order to get to the underlying hymn it is therefore necessary first of all to remove the expansions which derive from the evangelist himself.

[2] This verse is a really superfluous repetition of v. 1. The evangelist has added it in order to stress once again the nearness of the Logos Christ to God.

[6–8] Suddenly John the Baptist bursts into eternity (J. Wellhausen). This section shows the evangelist's interest in toning down the significance of the Baptist's person and work (cf. 1.19–34; 3.22–30; 4.1; 5.33–36; 10.41).

[9–10] After the insertion in vv. 6–8 these verses link back into the original and for this purpose take up some notions from vv. 3–5.

[12d] The closer definition 'to those who believe in his name' is lame and contains a formulation which is typical of the evangelist (cf. 2.23; 3.18; 20.31). The evangelist makes it clear that 'receive' in v. 12a means 'believe'. Now v. 13 does not fit well syntactically with v. 12d, and is distinguished by language untypical of the evangelist. Therefore it seems likely that we should see this verse as the first expansion which the later revisers have made in the work of the evangelist (see above).

[14d] This apposition shows itself by its explanatory character to be an addition by the evangelist. In contrast to the hymn, he does not speak of 'God' but of the 'Father'.

[15] This verse interrupts the connection of the confession of the group which in vv. 14 and 16 speaks in the first person plural; it takes the same line as vv. 6–8 (cf. 1.30).

[17] This is an originally independent saying (see under 'Tradition'), which the evangelist has added here because of the key words 'grace' and 'truth' (vv. 14*, 16). Several observations show that it did not initially belong to the hymn being used: (a) the confession of the first-person group from v. 14* and 16 is not continued; (b) the opposition between Mosaic law on the one hand, and the grace and truth which are given only in Christ on the other, does not play any role in what goes before; (c) the mention of Moses as a human person is unparalleled in primitive Christian hymns to Christ; (d) the name 'Jesus Christ' stands in tension with the title 'Logos' in the rest of the hymn.

[18] This verse shows itself to be redactional by the parallel formulations in 5.37b and 6.46 and by the reference back to v. 14d.

Yield: the hymn on which the prologue is based comprised vv. 1, 3–5, 11–12c, 14*, 16.

Despite the prominent position of the hymn at the beginning of the Gospel, it does not contain the quintessence of the theology of the Fourth Evangelist. For example, the evangelist does not once return to the incarnation of the Logos; for he himself does not present a theology of incarnation, but a theology of the one who has been sent. The same negative findings apply to the theme of the mediation of the Logos at creation and the title Logos generally. Only the unity of Jesus with God which is expressed in the hymn (cf. 10.30; 14.7–11) and the pre-existence of Jesus (cf. e.g. 8.58) are also significant in what follows.

Tradition

The hymn vv. 1, 3–5, 11–12c, 14*, 16 is not without its internal tensions. For if vv. 5, 11 already speak of the activity of the Logos on earth and his repudiation by human beings, the incarnation comes too late in v. 14, all the more so since the goal of salvation already seems to have been reached in v. 12a–c. Furthermore, after the proclamatory 'he' style, from v. 14 the hymn adopts a confessional 'we' style. These observations suggest that a Logos hymn which originally comprised only vv. 1–12c* (in the translation underlined once) was expanded at a pre-redactional stage by vv. 14*, 16 (underlined twice) (J. Becker).

The original form of the hymn (vv. 1, 3–5, 11–12c) is a pre-Christian wisdom hymn which is rooted in Jewish-Hellenistic wisdom speculation (cf. Prov. 8.22ff.; Sir. 24; Wisdom 7–11; SyrBar 3.14–38; EthEnoch 42.1ff.; see also the Nag Hammadi writing 'The Trimorphic Protennoia' [NHC XIII,1]). It can be divided into two strophes. The first strophe (vv. 1, 3–4) tells of the unique personal communion of wisdom or the Logos with God which has existed from eternity (v. 1). The Logos played an active part in creation (v. 3; cf. Job 28.27; Prov. 3.19; 8.30; Wisdom 7.12; 8.6; 9.9) and continuously grants life to all that is created (v. 4). The second strophe (vv. 5, 11–12c) reports the general repudiation of the Logos by 'his own', i.e. by human beings as a part of the world which he created (vv. 5, 11). The Logos makes only the few who receive him children of God (v. 12a–c; cf. Wisdom 2.13).

Only through the expansion by v. 14* and v. 16, i.e. through the secondary addition of a third strophe, has the hymn been Christianized (cf. a similar hymn in Col. 1.15–20). The poet saw Christ in the Logos and praised his incarnation in the confessional first-person-plural style (cf. Rom. 8.3; Phil. 2.7; I Tim. 3.16b). The Logos has come to human beings in the concrete form of Jesus and has brought to them the divine fullness of salvation (cf. Col. 1.19) by which from now on they can live.

The isolated saying v. 17, which the evangelist has added to the hymn, is governed by the Pauline opposition of law and grace (cf. Gal. 2.16, 21; 5.4) and thus polemically contrasts the old and new orders of salvation.

Historical

The Logos hymn contributes nothing to the question of the historical Jesus.

John 1.19–12.50: The public activity of Jesus

John 1.19–34: The witness of John the Baptist

19 *And this is the witness of* John, when *the Jews* sent to him priests and Levites from Jerusalem to ask him, 'Who are you?' 20 *And he confessed and did not deny, and* he confessed, 'I am not the Christ.' 21 And they asked him, 'What then? Are you Elijah?' And he says, 'I am not.' 'Are you the prophet?' And he answered, 'No.' 22 *Then they said to him, 'Who are you? – so that we can give an answer to those who sent us. What do you say about yourself?'* 23 He said, 'I am the voice of one crying in the wilderness, "Make level the way of the Lord," as the prophet Isaiah *has said.'* 24 *And they had been sent from the Pharisees.* 25 And they asked him and said to him, 'Why then do you baptize, if you are not the Christ, nor Elijah, nor the prophet?' 26a John answered them and said, b 'I baptize with water. c In your midst stands one whom you do not know, 27 who comes after me, the thong of whose sandal I am not worthy to untie.' 28 *This happened in Bethany, beyond the Jordan, where John was baptizing.*

29a *The next day he sees that* Jesus is coming *to him, and says,* b **'Look, the Lamb of God, which takes away the sin of the world!** 30 *This is he of whom I said, "After me comes a man who was before me, for he was earlier than me."* 31 Even I did not know him; but so that he may be revealed to Israel, that is why I have come, baptizing with water.' 32 *And John bore witness and said, 'I have* seen the Spirit descend as a dove from heaven, *and it remained* on him. 33a *Even I did not know him, but the one who sent me to baptize with water, he said to me,* b *"He on whom you see the Spirit descend and remain, this is he* who baptizes with Holy Spirit." 34 *And I have seen (this) and bear witness:* This is the Son *of God.'*

Later revision

In all probability v. 29b is an addition by the later revisers formulated on the basis of 1.36. It introduces into the text a theology of atoning sacrifice which is not put forward by the evangelist, and moreover does not fit v. 30.

Redaction and tradition

Like the Synoptics, the Fourth Evangelist introduces the report of the activity of Jesus with a description of John the Baptist (he was already mentioned in the prologue, cf. 1.6–8, 15). The section consists of two parts. In vv. 19–28 the testimony of John the Baptist to himself stands in the centre, and in vv. 29–34 his testimony to Jesus. Some verbatim and almost verbatim agreements with Mark 1.1–11 (underlined once) and with Matt. 3.1–17/Luke 3.1–22 (underlined twice) are striking.

[19] With the term 'witness' the evangelist refers back to the word with which he has already described the function of the Baptist in 1.7f., 15. 'Witness' and 'bear witness' are also regularly used in connection with the Baptist in what follows, cf. 1.32, 34; 3.26; 5.33, 36. Priests and Levites appear in the Gospel of John only at

this point. By contrast, the vague reference to 'the Jews' is typical of the Fourth Evangelist.

[20] The redundant introduction to the discourse is evidently meant to put special emphasis on the negative confession of the Baptist. However, 'he did not deny' is excessive as compared with the question in v. 19, and the twofold 'he confessed' seems disruptive.

[21] The attempts of the delegation to identify John fail.

[22–24] These verses interrupt the connection between vv. 20f. and v. 25. The question from v. 19 ('Who are you?') is repeated in v. 22. Verse 23 is the beginning of the series of remarkable parallel formulations with Synoptic accounts of John the Baptist; cf. Mark 1.3 parr. (= Isa. 40.3 LXX) and Mark 1.2a ('as is written in Isaiah the prophet'; similarly Matt. 3.3a; Luke 3.4a). Verse 24 proves confusing by the sudden mention of the Pharisees, for it is not clear what relation these have to the Jews or to the priests and Levites from v. 19. However, we should note that the evangelist is particularly interested in the Pharisees as the enemies of Jesus (cf. e.g. 4.1; 7.32, 47; 8.13; 9.16, 40f.; 11.47, 57; 12.42; 18.3).

[25] The delegates seem to have missed the fact that John has just described himself as the voice of one crying in the wilderness (v. 23). Instead of this they take up the Baptist's threefold negation from vv. 20f. Thus their question ignores vv. 22–24; it would fit very much better after vv. 20f.

[26] Verse 26b (= Matt. 3.11a; cf. Mark 1.8a; Luke 3.16) is not an answer to the question of the reason for the baptizing (v. 25). A reason is mentioned only in v. 31 ('that is why'). Verse 31 would in turn fit admirably after v. 26c ('know').

[27] 'Who comes after me' agrees word for word with Matt. 3.11b; 'the thong of whose sandal . . .' etc. essentially corresponds to the formulation in Mark 1.7b (cf. Luke 3.16).

[28] The preceding episode is given a location only subsequently (cf. similarly 6.59; 8.20).

[29a] This verse makes a new beginning with the note of time (= 1.35; 6.22; 12.12); it is related to vv. 26–27 as Mark 1.9 ('and it happened in these days that Jesus . . . came') is related to Mark 1.7. The evangelist is silent about the baptism of Jesus; instead of this he makes John testify again. However, we do not learn whom he is addressing.

[30] This verse corresponds almost word for word with 1.15b.

[31] As has been said, this verse would fit well after v. 26c and with it give a suitable answer to the question of the delegation in v. 25.

[32] Although the Baptist was speaking in v. 31, here a further introduction to his discourse appears – a clear indication of a redactional seam. What the Baptist says displays a notable parallelism with Mark 1.10b; Matt. 3.16b; Luke 3.21b–22. However, what Mark and Matthew report in their own words ('Jesus saw . . .') appears here in the mouth of the Baptist ('I have seen . . .').

[33a] This verse in part runs parallel with v. 31: 'Even I did not know him, but' recurs word for word; 'baptize with water' takes up 'baptizing with water'.

[33b–34] The Baptist makes clear after the event that what he saw according to v. 32 had been announced by God beforehand. The statement 'This is he who baptizes with Holy Spirit', which in Mark 1.8 (cf. Matt. 3.11; Luke 3.16) is an element of the proclamation of John the Baptist, is here regarded as a statement of God which is merely handed on by John the Baptist. Conversely the statement of God in Matt. 3.17 ('This is my beloved son', cf. Mark 1.11b; Luke 3.22c) has here become the confession of the Baptist ('This is the Son of God').

Yield: it is striking that v. 25 attaches as well to v. 21 as v. 31 does to v. 26. If we note this and in addition remove all the parts of the text which evidently presuppose the Synoptic accounts of the Baptist, a surprisingly integral narrative about a questioning of the Baptist emerges. It was probably worded as follows (deviations from the present text in square brackets):

19* When [they] sent to John priests and Levites from Jerusalem to ask him, 'Who are you?', 20* he confessed, 'I am not the Christ.' 21 And they asked him, 'What then? Are you Elijah?' And he says, 'I am not.' 'Are you the prophet?' And he answered, 'No.' 25 And they asked him and said to him, 'Why then do you baptize, if you are not the Christ, nor Elijah, nor the prophet?' 26a John answered them and said, c 'In your midst stands one whom you do not know. 31 Even I did not know him; but so that he may be revealed to Israel, that is why I have come, baptizing with water.'

This narrative emphasizes the inferiority of the Baptist: he baptizes only that Jesus may be manifest to Israel. Here, remarkably, an identification of the Baptist with Elijah (or with 'the prophet') is expressly repudiated (by contrast cf. Mark 9.11–13; Matt. 11.14; 17.10–13; Luke 1.17). The evangelist has enriched this story with individual elements from Z and some of his own additions and torn it apart by v. 28 and the note of time in v. 29. He is concerned to emphasize the inferiority of John the Baptist even more strongly: he reduces his significance to that of a mere witness and is silent about the baptism of Jesus.

Historical

The story adopted is unhistorical. The Baptist did not regard himself as a forerunner or a witness to Jesus. For this question and the historical value of the elements coming from Z cf. on Mark 1.2–11.

John 1.35–51: The first disciples

35 *The next day John was again standing there and two of his disciples; 36 and looking at Jesus as he went around, he says, 'Look, the Lamb of God!' 37 And the two disciples heard him speak and followed Jesus. 38 And Jesus turned round and saw them following and says to them, 'What do you seek?' And they said to him, 'Rabbi,' which translated means Teacher, 'where are you staying?' 39 He says to them, 'Come, and you will see.' Then they came and saw where he was staying, and they stayed with him that day. Now it was about the tenth hour.*

40 *Andrew, Simon Peter's brother, was one of the two who had heard John speak and had followed him. 41 He first finds his own brother Simon and says to him, 'We have found the Messiah', which translated is Christ. 42a He brought him to Jesus. b Jesus looked at him and said, 'You are Simon the son of John, you will be called Cephas', which is translated Peter (= stone).*

43 **The next day he wanted to go away to Galilee and finds Philip. And Jesus says to him, 'Follow me.'**

44 *Now Philip [the other of the two disciples?] was from Bethsaida, the city of Andrew and Peter. 45 Philip finds Nathanael, and says to him, 'We have found him of whom Moses wrote in the law and also the prophets, Jesus the son of Joseph, from Nazareth.' 46a And Nathanael said to him, 'Can anything good come out of Nazareth?' b Philip says to him, 'Come and see!' 47 Jesus saw Nathanael coming to him and says of him, 'Look, truly an Israelite in whom is no guile!' 48 Nathanael says to him, 'Whence do you know me?' Jesus answered and said to him, 'Before Philip called you, when you were under the fig tree, I saw you.' 49 Nathanael answered him, 'Rabbi, you are the Son of God, you are the King of Israel!' 50 Jesus answered and said to him, 'Because I said to you that I saw you under the fig tree, do you believe? You will see greater things than these.' 51And he says to him, 'Amen, amen, I say to you* (pl.), You will see the heaven opened and the angels of God ascending and descending upon the Son of man.'

Later revision

The section displays some strange features. (a) Verses 37–39 report about two disciples of the Baptist who follow Jesus. The name of the first is given later in v. 40; it is Andrew, the brother of Peter. The other remains anonymous. This is strange, seeing that this is one of Jesus' first two disciples. (b) The little word 'first' in v. 41 is left hanging in the air. (c) Verse 43 mentions Jesus' intention to go to Galilee, but we hear nothing about his doing so. Rather, according to 2.2 Jesus is in Cana in Galilee, without any previous mention of his journey there. (d) Verses 36f., 41f. and 45ff. seem to want to emphasize that one can get to Jesus only through an intermediary – a principle which is expressed in a very similar way in 12.20–22. Verse 43 does away with this principle; instead, it contains a 'Synoptic' type call of a disciple (cf. Mark 2.14 parr.; 10.21 parr.; Luke 9.59; see also 21.19). (e) It is striking that there is no mention of a direct reaction on the part of Philip to Jesus' call to discipleship. Rather, although Jesus is in the process of departing (v. 43), he immediately seems to go away again, and then finds Nathanael elsewhere (v. 45). (f) Verse 45 is enigmatic in yet another respect. First, the question arises why Philip speaks in the plural, for according to v. 43 he alone has met Jesus. Secondly, his remark contradicts what has in fact happened according to v. 43: he has not found Jesus, but Jesus has found him.

All these difficulties are resolved if we assume that v. 43 is an addition by the later revisers and that the beginning of v. 44 originally did not run, 'Now Philip was from Bethsaida . . .', but, say, 'Now Philip, *the other of the two disciples,* was from Bethsaida' (cf. the square brackets in the translation). The structure of the section would then prove to be substantially clearer and more coherent: first one of the two disciples who has gone over to Jesus, Andrew, finds his brother Peter; then the second disciple, Philip, finds Nathanael. It is in keeping with this that the evangelist also makes Andrew and Philip appear as a pair elsewhere (cf. 6.5–8; 12.20–22).

But what would have caused the revisers to make this aggravating intervention? An answer can be given only by looking ahead to the appendix, ch. 21. There the Gospel is put under the authority of the disciple whom Jesus loved; he is said to be the witness to all that is written in the Gospel and at the same time the author of the book (21.24; cf. the introduction, point 7). This conception now confronted the revisers with the problem that the beloved disciple must have been present as a witness from the beginning. But the Gospel did not mention him. So he had to be introduced in some way. This is what v. 43 achieves: the bright idea of the revisers was to make one of the two disciples from vv. 37–39 an anonymous figure by the insertion of this verse and thus make room for the beloved disciple. Now he comes to Jesus even before Peter.

Of course, no one who reads this section for the first time will think that the beloved disciple is concealed behind one of the first two disciples. But it must have been almost necessary for the authors of 21.24 to offer at least this preliminary indication of this disciple's existence.

Redaction and tradition

The starting point of the analysis of 1.35–42, 44–51 is the recognition that this passage was composed by the evangelist himself. Three observations above all support this assumption. *First,* the section can be understood only as part of a wider context; it creates the presuppositions for the appearance of Jesus in the company of the disciples in what follows. *Secondly,* here all the christological titles and several important basic christological statements which are significant for what follows are listed: Jesus is the Lamb of God (v. 36) and the Messiah, i.e. the Christ (v. 41); the scriptures bear witness to him (v. 45); he has a supernatural omniscience (vv. 42, 47); he is the Son of God, the King of Israel (v. 49), and the Son of man (v. 51). *Thirdly,* the passage is very carefully structured and (with the exception of v. 51) shows no narrative breaks. It is divided into three scenes (vv. 35–39, 40–42, 44–51); here the second and third scenes each grow out of the first.

However, the assumption of a redactional composition of the section does not rule out the possibility that here and there the evangelist has referred back to individual pieces of traditional material. To work these out is the task of the following survey of the text.

[35–36] The scene is constructed in parallel to 1.29a, 30, the beginning of the previous sub-section, and refers back to it by 'the next day' and 'again'. 'The Lamb of God' is certainly a title from the tradition, for it is not used again elsewhere in the

Gospel of John. However, its origin in the history of the tradition and its original meaning are obscure. The evangelist probably intends it as a foreshadowing of the death of Jesus: Jesus is handed over to be crucified at the very hour when people are slaughtering the Passover lambs in the temple (19.14). In this way he proves to be the true Passover lamb (cf. 19.33, 36), i.e. the one who surpasses the Jewish cult.

[37] The report that the first disciples of Jesus were former adherents of the Baptist is sometimes regarded as a historically reliable tradition; it is said that this report is too offensive to have been invented. But we should note that the evangelist – even more strongly than the Synoptists – pursues the interest of emphasizing the inferiority of John to Jesus (cf. 1.6–8; 1.19–34; 3.22–30; 5.33f.). It is in keeping with this purpose that the Baptist has to yield his disciples to Jesus (cf. 3.30: 'he must increase, but I must decrease').

[38–39] These verses confirm that John's disciples go over to Jesus and in their terse narrative style at the same time emphasize the exemplary character of the event. It is hardly by chance that 'What do you seek?' are the first words that Jesus says according to the Fourth Evangelist: the reader should take account of this question at the beginning; it is probably because of it that the evangelist does not indicate any answer from the disciples. The translation of the word 'rabbi' makes the Greek-speaking readers at the beginning of the Gospel familiar with an expression which is often used in what follows (cf. 1.49; 3.2, 26; 4.31; 6.25; 9.2; 11.8); cf. similarly the translations in vv. 41 and 42.

[40–42] These verses contain three elements from the tradition: (a) the news that the brothers Andrew and Peter were among the first disciples of Jesus (cf. Mark 1.16f.); (b) the tradition that Simon was given the (Aramaic) name Cepha(s) (Greek Petros) by Jesus (cf. Mark 3.16; see also Matt. 16.17f.); (c) the information that Peter's father bore the name John (cf. 21.15–17). From these bits of tradition the evangelist has shaped a scene which has its climax in the demonstration of Jesus' divinatory capacities: Jesus knows Peter's name without ever having seen him before.

This 'knowledge of the heart', which in practice amounts to omniscience, is reserved for God in the Old Testament (cf. e.g. I Sam. 16.7; I Kings 8.39; Ps. 38.10; 44.22; 139.1–4; Jer. 17.10). Thus in depicting Jesus as omniscient (cf. 1.47; 2.24f.; 13.1a; 18.4, etc.) the evangelist is emphasizing Jesus' divinity. In this way at the same time he makes it clear from the start that Jesus cannot be surprised by anything or anyone. The one who knows everything is the sovereign lord of his own fate. However, the motif of the omniscience of Jesus also appears in the Synoptics (cf. Mark 2.8; 8.16f.; 12.15, etc.).

That Peter comes to Jesus through his brother as an intermediary – as does Nathanael next, through Philip – is probably a construction of the evangelist. He is concerned to show that full access to Jesus is possible also through the mediation of others (cf. 12.20ff.)

[44] This verse (in the form reconstructed above) has a parallel structure to v. 40. The name of the disciple Philip derives from tradition (cf. Mark 3.18), as does the information that Andrew, Peter and Philip come from Bethsaida, which cannot be derived from redactional motives.

[45] This verse runs parallel to v. 41. For the content of Philip's remark cf. 5.39, 46. The names of Jesus' father (cf. e.g. Matt. 1.16ff.; Luke 1.27) and his place of origin (cf. Mark 1.9), and probably also the report of a disciple (?) named Nathanael come from the tradition.

[46a] This is probably based on an objection made by Jews against Christians (cf. 7.41f., 52; see also 7.27). The context in which the evangelist has embedded it shows it to have no basis.

[46b] This fulfils the same function as v. 42a. The wording recalls v. 39.

[47] This verse corresponds in form to v. 42b. Again Jesus can see through the newcomer immediately.

[48] This verse makes it clear that Jesus' knowledge demonstrated in v. 47 is in fact supernatural, and at the same time again confirms it: although Jesus was not there, he knows where Philip met Nathanael.

[49] Nathanael's initial doubt (v. 46), which in v. 48a is already toned down to a surprised astonishment, turns into an effusive confession in the face of the renewed evidence of divine omniscience.

[50] Jesus' question (cf. 3.10; 14.9a; 20.29) refers back word for word to v. 48b. The promise (for the formulation cf. 5.20b; 11.40; 14.12) is fulfilled in the miracles and discourses of Jesus which are dealt with in chs. 2ff.

[51] The new and superfluous introduction to the discourse and the sudden address to all the disciples are indications that the evangelist is quoting a traditional saying in this verse. This seems to be a saying about the Son of man from Jewish apocalyptic, formulated on the basis of Gen. 28.12, which originally was meant literally. In contrast, the evangelist – who will not report a literal fulfilment of this promise – has probably understood it in a metaphorical sense: in seeing the 'greater things' announced in v. 50, the disciples are to become witnesses to Jesus' ongoing communion with God.

Historical

For Andrew, Peter and Philip as disciples cf. the remarks on Mark 1.16f. and Mark 3.16–19; for the giving of the name Cephas to Simon cf. on Matt. 16.17–19; for Jesus' father cf. on Mark 6.1b–6; Matt. 1.18–25; for Jesus' place of origin cf. on Matt. 9.1.

No certainty can be achieved about the historical value of the following elements of tradition in the passage because either there are no parallel traditions or there are rival traditions: (a) According to Mark 1.29 the home of Simon Peter and Andrew was Capernaum. However, that does not rule out the possibility that they and Philip originally came from Bethsaida (v. 44). (b) According to Matt. 16.17, Peter's father was not called John (v. 42) but Jonah. (c) Only the Gospel of John reports a disciple called Nathanael. It is no longer possible to say whether he was in fact a disciple of Jesus or only a personality from the evangelist's community stylized as a disciple of Jesus. The reviser's report about his origin from Cana in Galilee (21.2) has probably been inferred from 1.43 and 2.1.

The saying about the Son of man in v. 51* does not go back to Jesus, for Jesus probably did not speak about the Son of man at all.

John 2.1–12: The miracle with wine at the wedding in Cana

1 And *on the third day* there was a wedding at Cana in Galilee, and the mother of Jesus was there. 2 And Jesus and his disciples were also invited to the wedding. 3 And when the wine ran out, the mother of Jesus says *to him, 'They have no wine.'* 4 *And Jesus says to her, 'What is (between) me and you, woman? My hour has not yet come.'* 5 *His mother says* to the servants, 'What he tells you, do!' 6 Now six stone jars were standing there *according to the Jews' (custom of) purification*, and each held two or three measures. 7 Jesus says to them, 'Fill the jars with water.' And they filled them up to the brim. 8 And he says to them, 'Now draw, and take it to the steward of the feast.' And they brought it to him. 9 And when the steward of the feast tasted the water that had become wine – *he did not know where it came from; though the servants who had drawn the water knew* – *the steward of the feast* called the bridegroom 10 and says to him, 'Every man serves first the good wine, and when they are drunk, the poorer; but you have kept the good wine until now.'

11 *This Jesus did as the beginning of the signs in Cana in Galilee, and he revealed his glory; and his disciples came to believe in him.* 12 *After this* he went down to Capernaum, he and his mother and his brothers and his disciples, *and they stayed there not many days.*

Redaction and tradition

Tensions within the story indicate that the evangelist has based it on a piece of tradition.

[1–2] These verses sketch out the situation presupposed in what follows. Only the note 'on the third day' which refers back to 1.35 is redactional.

[3–5] The observation that the wine ran out (v. 3a) creates the occasion for the miracle. However, before the description of how Jesus supplies the need, the narrative first runs into a dead end as a result of Jesus' objection (v. 4). For if Jesus rejects his mother's indirect request for a miracle (v. 3b), remarking that his hour has not yet come, no miracle should really take place next. Rather, first it needs to be reported that the provisional refusal by the miracle worker was overcome by a word from the person making the request (cf. Mark 7.27f. and perhaps Matt. 8.7f.); or a plausible reason should have been given why the hour which according to v. 4c has not yet come is suddenly there in v. 7. Neither is the case, and a way out of the narrative dead end is possible only because Jesus' mother ignores her son's objection (v. 5). So it is probable that Jesus' dialogue with his mother was inserted only by the evangelist. This assumption is supported by the fact that in 7.1–10 there is a very similar inconsistency on the part of Jesus: Jesus rejects his brothers' request to go to Jerusalem (7.6, 8: 'My time has/is not yet come/fulfilled') and then goes there. In both cases the evangelist wants to make it clear that Jesus does not make himself dependent on human wishes. By contrast, in 2.4c a reference to the hour of Jesus' *death* is improbable despite the parallel formulation in 7.30; 8.20 ('his hour had not yet come').

[6] If the jars are standing there for purposes of purification, they can hardly be empty. But this is assumed in v. 7. So 'according to the Jews' custom of purification' is an addition by the evangelist.

[7–8] These verses report the miracle, keeping quiet about the real miraculous event.

[9–10] These verses form a conclusion in keeping with the style. Here the tasting of the wine by the steward and the humorous 'wine rule' serve as public confirmation of the miracle. The evangelist's only contribution is the intrinsically superfluous parenthesis in v. 9 and the repetition of the subject, the 'steward of the feast', who is already mentioned in the subordinate clause.

[11] This is the redactional conclusion to the story. As the 'beginning' of the signs, the miracle of the wine refers not only to the second sign performed in Cana (4.54) but also to all the other signs which are narrated and merely mentioned (2.23).

[12] This verse appears to have no function in the present context, since a journey of Jesus to Jerusalem is reported in the next verse, with no mention of what happened in Capernaum. One possible explanation of this is that v. 12 represents the original link between the miracle stories 2.1–10* (scene Cana) and 4.46b–53* (original scene Capernaum), which were joined together at a pre-redactional level. In that case only 'after this' (cf. 3.22; 5.1, 14; 6.1; 7.1; 11.7, 11; 19.28, 38) and the phrase 'and they stayed there not many days', which evidently takes account of v. 13 (cf. also 10.40; 11.54) are to be marked out as redactional additions.

But questions remain open here, since neither the family nor the disciples of Jesus play any role in 4.46b–53*. Thus it is also conceivable that the whole of v. 12 derives from the evangelist. In that case v. 12 would be reflecting the Synoptic account, according to which Jesus was active in Capernaum at the beginning of his public activity (cf. Mark 1.21–39; Matt. 4.13).

Yield: the traditional gift miracle narrative probably has its home in the Christian mission. It seeks to arouse faith in the miracle-worker Jesus.

The motif of the transformation of water into wine is not attested unequivocally in ancient texts. Rather, only a sudden presence of wine is presupposed. Cf. the two following examples: 'When one struck the rock with the thyrsos, immediately a cool spring arose, and on striking the narthex on the ground, the god's sweet wine flowed out' (Euripides, *The Maenads*, 704–7). '. . . The priests bring three vessels to the count and set them down empty (viz. in a building) . . . The next day . . . they find the vessels filled with wine' (Pausanias, *Description of Greece*, VI 26, 1–2). However, in the Old Testament there are narratives about the transformation of water into some other matter; cf. Ex. 7.19–22 (Moses turns water into blood); Ex. 15.23–25 and II Kings 2.19–22 (each time undrinkable water is transformed into drinkable water). Moreover, it should be noted that according to many Old Testament texts the time of salvation will be marked not least by an inexhaustible supply of wine (cf. e.g. Amos 9.13f.; Hos. 2.24; Zech. 8.12; see also Mark 14.25).

Historical

The narrative is unhistorical.

John 2.13–22: The cleansing of the temple and the demand for a sign

13 *And the Passover of the Jews was near, and Jesus went up* <u>to Jerusalem</u>. 14 <u>And</u> he *found* <u>in the temple the sellers</u> of oxen and sheep and pigeons, <u>and the</u> money-changers sitting. 15 And he made a scourge from cords and <u>drove them all out</u> of <u>the temple</u>, also the sheep and oxen; and he poured out the money <u>of the money-changers</u> and over<u>turned their tables</u>, 16 and to <u>the pigeon sellers</u> he said, 'Take these things away from here; you shall not make my Father's <u>house</u> a <u>house</u> of trade.'

17 **His disciples remembered that it is written, 'Zeal for your house will eat me up.'**

18 The *Jews* then answered and said to him, 'What kind of *sign* have you to show us, <u>that you do this</u>?' 19 *Jesus answered and said to them, 'Destroy this temple, and in three days I will raise it up.'*

20 *The Jews then said, 'It has taken forty-six years to build this temple, and will you raise it up in three days?'* 21 *But he spoke of the temple of his body.* 22 *Now when he was raised from (the) dead, his disciples remembered that he had said this. And they believed* **the scripture and** *the word which Jesus had spoken.*

Later revision

In all probability, v. 17 is an addition formulated on the basis of v. 22a (E. Hirsch). It interrupts the connection between v. 16 and v. 18 and speaks of an immediate recollection of the disciples, whereas it is explicitly mentioned in v. 22 that the disciples recalled Jesus' saying in v. 19 only after Easter. With the quotation of Ps. 69.10, the revisers are referring back to one of the psalms of the Suffering Servant which in early Christianity was often used to interpret the death of Jesus (cf. the adoption of Ps. 69 in Mark 15.36; Matt. 27.34, 48; Luke 23.36; John 19.29; Rom. 15.3). Earlier, in 1.29b they had put into the mouth of John the Baptist an interpretation of the death of Jesus which was alien to the context.

If v. 17 is an addition, then the words 'the scripture and' in v. 22b, which have no basis in v. 22a, cannot be original. They refer back to v. 17 through vv. 18–21.

Redaction and tradition

A new major section begins in 2.13. It contains the account of Jesus' first stay in Jerusalem and ends in 3.21. The present section consists of two parts which are closely connected: vv. 14–16 report the cleansing of the temple, and vv. 18–22 a demand by the Jews for a sign, which is provoked by this action. Here the basis of vv. 14–16, 18 is Z (cf. Mark 11.15–17; Matt. 21.12–13). Verbatim and almost verbatim agreements with Mark are underlined once; possibly additional agreements with Matthew are underlined twice.

[13] This is a redactional transition (cf. 5.1; 7.2; 11.55; in each case note the general reference to the feasts of 'the Jews'). Certainly, according to the Synoptic Gospels, too, the cleansing of the temple takes place in connection with a Passover feast; but this is the last in the life of Jesus, not the first of two in his activity (6.4 is probably an addition). The Fourth Evangelist has put the cleansing of the temple at the beginning of the public activity of Jesus in Jerusalem in order to provide an effective prelude to the harsh controversies between Jesus and the Jews by which his work is largely characterized (cf. on 5.18). In so far as he makes this action lead into a conversation which refers cryptically to Jesus' death and resurrection (vv. 18–22), at the same time he builds a bridge to ch. 18–20 and thus gives his Gospel a slant which is also characteristic of the Synoptics.

[14–16] This passage has been composed on the basis of Z (cf. Mark 11.15f.; Matt. 21.12). Only the motif of finding comes from the evangelist (cf. 1.41, 45; 5.14; 9.35, etc.). The other deviations from the Synoptics which heighten the drama of the event probably derive from Z: the weaving of the scourge, the scattering of the money and the ejection of the animals. Jesus' first command (v. 16a) is more effective than the pale note in Mark 11.16. Mark 11.17 parr. echoes in the second command (v. 16b); cf. the similar contrasts 'house of prayer'/ 'my house'/ 'cave of robbers' and 'my Father's house'/ 'house of trade', and the similarity of the accusation 'you make or have made' to the command 'you shall not make' (however, the two sayings Isa. 56.7 and Jer. 7.11 used in Mark 11.17 parr. are no longer recognizable). 'House of trade' is certainly weaker than 'cave of robbers' (Mark 11.17 parr.), but fits better the bustling activity of the traders and money-changers whom Jesus drives out.

[18] In the Synoptics too, Jesus is confronted with a question about his legitimation in connection with the cleansing of the temple (Mark 11.27f. parr.). But as the conversation in vv. 19f. takes a completely different course from that in Mark 11.29–33 parr., we have to assume that the evangelist himself is speaking from v. 19 on.

[19] This verse is similar to Mark 14.58; Matt. 26.61. However, in view of the fact that according to the Synoptics the saying about the temple is false testimony, it seems questionable whether the evangelist has taken it over from Z. It is more probable that he got to know it as an individual logion and independently connected it with the narrative about the cleansing of the temple. In so doing – consciously or unconsciously – he may have restored it to its original place. For the question of the precise wording of the saying taken up cf. on v. 21.

[20] The Jews think that Jesus' answer to the demand for a sign is meant literally. But here, as v. 21 shows, they are on the wrong track.

The motif of misunderstanding, typical of the Fourth Evangelist, appears here for the first time (cf. 3.4; 4.11, 15, 33; 6.34, 42; 7.35; 8.22, 52, 57; 11.12). It serves him primarily as a means of illustrating human unbelief and blindness to the revelation, or the way in which human beings are rooted in the earthly. No wonder, then, that the misunderstandings almost always occur in the mouths of the unbelieving Jews. Only twice is Jesus misunderstood by the disciples (4.33; 11.12). But in contrast to the Jews, they are immediately given an explanation of what is really meant (4.34; 11.14). The motif of the incomprehension of the disciples (cf. e.g. 14.5) is to be distinguished from the motif of misunderstanding.

[21] The question of the Jews in v. 20 is left hanging. In contrast to the readers, they are given no information about the true meaning (= the interpretation developed by the evangelist) of v. 19: Jesus did not mean the temple in Jerusalem, but the temple of his body. So really the answer to the demand for a sign ran, 'Kill me, and in three days I will rise.' (Cf. similarly Matt. 12.38–40.). It follows from this that in v. 19 the evangelist might deliberately have chosen the term 'raise up' (instead of 'rebuild'). For in Greek, too, the term 'raise up' has two meanings ('erect' and 'resurrect').

It also becomes clear from v. 21 that it is no longer possible to decide with certainty the precise wording of the saying underlying v. 19. For not only the term 'raise up' but also the invitation 'Destroy this temple' which occurs instead of Jesus' statement about himself in Mark 14.58a ('I will destroy this . . . temple) are evidently already conditioned by the interpretation of the temple in terms of Jesus' body, which the *Jews* will put on the cross and which after three days will be *raised up*.

[22*] The content of this verse corresponds to 12.16. The real meaning of the saying in v. 19 (namely that formulated in v. 21) was disclosed to the disciples only after

the resurrection of Jesus, to which it referred in a cryptic way. This view fits the theological conception of the evangelist, according to which the Paraclete is sent to the disciples after the return of Jesus to the Father. He teaches and reminds them of all that Jesus has said (cf. 14.16f., 26).

Yield: whereas vv. 13–16, 18 derive from Z, vv. 19–22 have been composed by the evangelist himself, using a saying from the tradition.

Historical

For the question of the historicity of the cleansing of the temple see the remarks on Mark 11.15–19.

Verse 19 is a variant on the saying which has also been handed down in Mark 14.58 and probably goes back to an authentic saying of Jesus to the effect that *God* will destroy the earthly temple and instead of this erect a heavenly one (cf. on Mark 11.15–19).

John 2.23–25: Signs of Jesus in Jerusalem

23 Now when he was in Jerusalem, at the Passover, at the feast, many came to believe in his name when they saw his signs which he did. 24 But Jesus did not trust himself to them, as he knew all men 25 and because he needed no one to bear witness about man; for he himself knew what was in man.

Redaction and historical

The section links the preceding account of the cleansing of the temple with the description of the conversation with Nicodemus which follows (3.1–21). There are similar transitions e.g. in 4.43, 45; 10.40–42 and 11.55–57. They serve to give the reader the impression of an ongoing narrative context. However, the evangelist also succeeds in inserting his theological reflections into these compositional bridges.

[23a] This verse links to 2.13: with Jerusalem and the feast of the Passover, what follows presupposes the same time and place as the cleansing of the temple.

[23b] That Jesus' signs lead or can lead to faith in him (= 'in his name', cf. 1.12; 3.18) is also indicated directly or indirectly in 2.11; 4.48, 53; 7.31; 10.41f.; 11.45, 47f.; 12.11, 37 and 20.30f.

[24a] Although many believe in him, Jesus distances himself from them.

[24b–25] These verses give the reason why: in a threefold variation on one and the same notion (vv. 24b, 25a, b) it is emphasized that Jesus has the capacity to see into people (cf. on 1.42). However, this reason raises more questions than it gives answers: what is it that Jesus sees in people's hearts and that leads him to distance himself from them? Initially the evangelist leaves this question open. The answer will be given only later in the course of the account, when the evangelist presents his specific understanding of Jesus' 'signs' (cf. above all the remarks on 6.26).

Yield: the section is a transition created by the evangelist and has no historical value.

John 3.1–21: The conversation between Jesus and Nicodemus

1 *Now there was a man of the Pharisees, Nicodemus by name, a councillor of the Jews.* 2 *This man came to him by night and said to him, 'Rabbi, we know that as a teacher you have come from God. For no one can do these signs that you do, unless God is with him.'*

3 *Jesus answered and said to him, 'Amen, Amen, I say to you,* unless one is born anew, he cannot see the kingdom of God.'

4 *Nicodemus says to him, 'How can a man be born when he is old? Can he enter a second time into his mother's womb and be born?'*

5 *Jesus answered, 'Amen, Amen, I say to you,* unless one is born of water and Spirit, he cannot enter the kingdom of God. 6 That which is born of the flesh is flesh, and that which is born of the Spirit is spirit. 7 *Do not marvel that I said to you, "You (pl.) must be born anew."* 8 The wind (= *the Spirit*) blows where it wills and you hear the sound of it, but you do not know whence it comes or whither it goes; *so is every one who is born of the Spirit.'*

9 *Nicodemus answered and said to him, 'How can this happen?'*

10 *Jesus answered and said to him, 'Are you a teacher of Israel, and do not know that?* 11 *Amen, amen, I say to you, what we know we speak and to what we have seen we bear witness, and you (pl.) do not accept our witness.* 12 *If I have told you earthly things and you do not believe, how will you believe if I tell you heavenly things?* 13 *And* no one has ascended into heaven but he who descended from heaven, the Son of man. 14 *And as Moses lifted up the serpent in the wilderness, so must the Son of man be lifted up,* 15 *that whoever believes may have eternal life in him.* 16 *For* God so loved the world that he gave his only-begotten Son, that anyone who believes in him should not perish but have eternal life. 17 For God did not send the Son into the world to judge the world, but that the world might be saved through him. 18 *Whoever believes in him is not judged; but whoever does not believe has been judged already, because he has not come to believe in the name of the only-begotten Son of God.*

19 *And this is the judgment:*
The light has come into the world,
but men loved the darkness more than the light,
because their works were evil.

20 For every one who does evil hates the light
and does not come to the light,
lest his works should be exposed.

21 But he who does the truth comes to the light,
that his works may become manifest,
that they have been wrought in God.'

Redaction and tradition

In this section, Jesus himself develops his message at length for the first time, in the framework of a conversation with the Pharisee Nicodemus. However, the situation of a conversation is vividly depicted only at the beginning. From v. 11 the dialogue begins to turn into a monologue of Jesus, and from v. 13 on Jesus suddenly speaks about himself in the third person. So a division of the section by the external course of the conversation, i.e. by statement and counter-statement, does not seem very helpful. A division by points of content is more appropriate. This is intended by 'Jesus' himself: the saying in v. 12 divides the section into two halves: remarks about 'earthly things' and 'heavenly things'.

[1–2a] These verses give details of the situation: after Jesus had been addressed by 'the' Jews in 2.18–20, now a specific person encounters him in the form of Nicodemus, the Pharisee and councillor (= member of the Supreme Council). However, he again appears as a representative of a group, namely official Judaism (cf. the plural 'we' in v. 2), and is also regarded as such by Jesus (cf. the plural 'you' in vv. 7,11f., and the designation 'teacher of Israel' in v. 10).

[2b] The beginning of the conversation shows that Nicodemus was impressed by the signs of Jesus (2.23). He has already formed a final judgment on Jesus: the signs show him to be a teacher accredited by God and with special gifts. Therefore it is not surprising that Nicodemus does not present any concern: for someone who already knows everything does not need to ask any questions at all.

[3] The term 'kingdom of God', which occurs in John only here and in the variant v. 5, and the parallel formulations in Matt. 18.3; Mark 10.15; Thomas 22 and Justin, *Apology* I 61.4, suggests that a saying from the tradition underlies Jesus' reply (cf. on v. 5). However, the fact that at first sight this reply seems to show no reference to v. 2b results only to a small degree from the evangelist's being bound by the tradition in his formulation. Rather, the apparent lack of a reference is deliberate: it indicates that the response is an abrupt rebuff to Nicodemus. For with his respectful compliment Nicodemus has not gone into what is ultimately decisive, the question of salvation (= seeing the kingdom of God). Jesus indirectly makes it clear that 'knowledge' (v. 2b) gained in the framework of traditional ideas is not enough for this question. Rather, fundamental renewal is needed to be able to see the kingdom of God. It is so radical that it can appropriately be spoken of only as a 'rebirth'.

[4] Jesus has spoken metaphorically of rebirth. However, Nicodemus understands Jesus' metaphorical form of expression in a literal sense (for the motif of misunderstanding cf. on 2.20).

[5] The misunderstanding leads Jesus to express himself in concrete terms. He does this by repeating what he has said before in a different way, i.e. by means of a variant of v. 3 which similarly comes from the tradition (cf. likewise 8.51b/8.52b).

Verses 3 and 5 were originally focussed on the necessity of baptism for salvation. This is supported by (a) the mention of the water in v. 5, (b) the comparable talk of the 'bath of rebirth' in Titus 3.5, and (c) the widespread early Christian notion that the individual receives the spirit at baptism.

[6] This verse makes it clear that the person who is not born of the spirit belongs on the side of the 'flesh', i.e. transitoriness and death, and the one who is born of the spirit (= the believer) belongs on the side of the spirit, i.e. God (cf. 4.24). Not so much the saying itself as the opposition of flesh and spirit expressed in it might come from the tradition (cf. e.g. Gen. 6.3; Isa. 31.3; Gal. 5.16–26; Rom. 8.5ff.).

[7] This verse refers back to v. 3 and presupposes the situation of the conversation.

[8] The way in which the spirit is under no control and cannot be calculated is expressed by the form of a comparison. Like the wind, it can be experienced only in its effects. (Note that the word for 'wind' used here also means 'spirit'.)

That again a saying from the tradition provides the basis emerges first from the fact that the interpretation 'so is every one' which is given, picking up vv. 5f., does not follow in a completely organic way. Secondly, the image is often used in antiquity to express not only the effectiveness of the invisible things but also the incomprehensible nature of the divine working. Cf. e.g. Xenophon (c.430–355 BC), *Recollections of Socrates* IV 3.14: 'One does not see the winds themselves, but what they do is visible to us and we feel them coming'; cf. also Koh.11.5.

[9] With his question about the manner of being born of the Spirit, Nicodemus disappears from the scene (he does not appear again until 7.50). What follows will show that it is now Jesus who 'misunderstands' this question – though deliberately. He will answer it in vv. 13ff., not in the sense meant by Nicodemus (what must one do to be born of the Spirit?), but on a deeper level (from what does the possibility of rebirth result?).

[10] Jesus' rebuke (cf. 9.30) is conditioned by the situation of the conversation.

[11] This verse expresses a notion which will recur later in different variations: Jesus' speaking and actions are in harmony with God (cf. e.g. 5.19; 8.26, 38, 40). It is striking that Jesus abruptly begins to address Nicodemus no longer in the second person singular but in the second person plural (cf. v. 12). That indicates that the evangelist now wants to see the conversation between Jesus and the Pharisee expanded into a controversy with the Jews generally. (One can also imagine the statement in the mouths of the Johannine Christians against the Jews.). The motif of a refusal to accept the testimony – or Jesus himself – corresponds to 5.39ff.

[12] This verse has a twofold function: first, it serves to emphasize the incomprehension of Nicodemus or the Jews represented by him; and secondly, it marks off what has been said previously from what follows: after the previous talk of 'earthly

things', namely how it is possible for human beings to gain possession of salvation, now follows an account of 'heavenly things', namely what corresponds to this possibility on the part of God or Jesus.

[13] The evangelist now goes over to making Jesus speak of himself in the third person. The result is that now a post-Easter perspective shows through which has no meaningful relationship to the point in time presupposed. For Jesus' ascent into heaven, which here is supposed already to have taken place (perfect), is still to come (cf. 6.62; 20.17). Probably the evangelist has woven in a saying from the tradition spun out of Prov. 30.4 ('Who has ascended to heaven and descended again? Who has held the wind in his hands? . . . What is his name? And what is the name of his son? Do you know that?').

[14–15] These verses point forward to the passion of Jesus. They explain the need and the purpose of lifting Jesus up by means of an exegesis of Num. 21.6–9. The evangelist sees in Moses' lifting up of the (bronze) serpent, which banishes death, a 'prefigurement' of the lifting up of Jesus. The seamless continuation of v. 14 in v. 15, which clearly derives from the evangelist (cf. 5.24; 6.40ab, 47; 11.25f.; 20.31), and the presupposed ambiguity of 'lift up' (12.32f.) suggest that this typological interpretation of Num. 21.6–9 was his own idea.

[16–17] Several observations indicate that these verses are a saying from the tradition.

(a) The statement that God has loved or loves the world (v. 16a) is unique in the Gospel of John. (b) The evangelist does not use elsewhere the formulation that God 'gave'/'has given' the Son, but he does speak of the *sending* of the Son ('give' occurs only with reference to the Paraclete, cf. 14.16). (c) Verses 16–17 are interpreted by the evangelist in v. 18.

As the saying shows a similarity to Rom. 4.25; 5.8; 8.32; Gal. 1.4; 2.20, it probably comes from a sphere of the tradition with a Pauline stamp.

[18] This verse is the interpretation of the tradition adopted by the evangelist in vv. 16f. Here the negative part of the statement is not the simple reversal of the positive (= '*is* judged') but is given a special tone as a result of the use of the perfect ('*has been* judged already'; cf. 5.24: '*has* passed'): the judgment takes place in the present, in the encounter of human beings with Jesus or his word, and not at the end of days.

[19–21] These verses round off Jesus' remarks with a piece of tradition introduced by the definition formula in v. 19a (cf. 1.19).

Several reasons suggest that the evangelist has taken over a tradition, though it does not in any way belong with that in vv. 16f. (a) The introductory formula v. 19a ('and this is the judgment') is not continued organically by vv. 19b–21. (b) Verses 19b–21 form a self-contained piece with three tripartite parallelisms. (c) The words 'light', 'darkness', 'works', 'do evil', 'do the truth', etc. go beyond what Jesus has said previously. (d) The passage displays a theological tendency which is different from that of the evangelist (J. Becker). According to the evangelist, in principle all human beings – except the Jews (cf. 8.30–59) – have the opportunity to attain salvation through faith in Jesus. By contrast, vv. 19b–21 divide human-kind into two groups, which have already qualified themselves for salvation or doom before the coming of Jesus. The coming of Jesus merely serves the purpose of *disclosing* the twofold determination of human beings.

The only explanation of why the evangelist appropriates this tradition is that, as 6.28f. shows, he tacitly identifies the 'doing of works' with faith in Jesus.

Yield: the evangelist has composed the passage himself, using disparate traditions.

Historical

[3, 5] The assumption that Jesus made participation in the kingdom of God dependent on a (Christian) baptism with the spirit would be an anachronism.

[8a] In view of the parallel formulations in ancient literature, it is not possible to attribute this saying to Jesus.

[13, 16–17, 19b–21] These verses presuppose a post-Easter perspective; their formulation in the third person even suggests that they were not originally sayings of Jesus at all, but Christian confessional statements.

John 3.22–30: The Baptist's last witness to Jesus

22 *After this Jesus and his disciples went into the land of Judaea, and there he dwelt with them and baptized.* 23 *And* John *also* was baptizing at Aenon near Salim, because there was much water there; and people came and were baptized. 24 *For John had not yet been thrown into prison.*

25 Now a dispute arose on the part of John's disciples with *a Jew* over *purification.* 26 And they came to John, and said to him, 'Rabbi, *he who was with you beyond the Jordan, to whom you bore witness,* look, he is baptizing, and all are coming to him.'

27 John answered and said, '*A man can receive nothing unless it has been given him from heaven.* 28 *You yourselves bear witness to me that I said, "I am not the Christ, but I have been sent before him."* 29 He who has the bride is the bridegroom; but the friend of the bridegroom, who stands and hears him, rejoices greatly at the bridegroom's voice. This joy of mine is now full. 30 He must increase, but I must decrease.'

Redaction and tradition

In this section the evangelist yet again turns to a clarification of the right relationship between Jesus and the Baptist (cf. 1.19–34). Several observations suggest that the passage is based on a story in the tradition. (a) In view of the fact that according to v. 23 the Baptist is pursuing his activity unhindered, the allusion to his imprisonment, which has not yet taken place (v. 24), is markedly superfluous. (b) The Jew from v. 25 has no significance for the development of the action. (c) It is not clear why a dispute about 'purification' (v. 25) leads to a complaint that Jesus has a great following (v. 26). (d) It is implausible that the disciples of John are complaining about Jesus' success, although they know that their Master has borne witness to Jesus (v. 26).

[22] This verse introduces the section. It presupposes the previous stay in Jerusalem (cf. 2.23) and is to be attributed to the evangelist. The information that Jesus baptized is taken from v. 26.

[23] The detail about place, which is precise by comparison with v. 22, and the commentary in v. 24, show that this verse is the beginning of the original narrative.

[24] The reference to the imprisonment of the Baptist, which has yet to take place, comes from the evangelist. His purpose here may be to lessen the conflict between the tradition that Jesus made his first public appearance only after the imprisonment of the Baptist (cf. Mark 1.14f.; Luke 3.19f., 23; Matt. 11.2–6) and the parallel activity which is reported here, by 'predating'.

[25] This verse is puzzling. Its manifest intention is to create an occasion for the disciples of John to complain to their master about the growing influence of Jesus (v. 26), but it cannot perform this function. For a dispute which they carry on with some Jew about 'purification' is not an appropriate occasion for this. (It is not said that this Jew had been baptized by Jesus.) Could the evangelist have replaced another party in the dispute – the disciples of Jesus or even Jesus himself – with the 'Jew'? In that case the story would make good sense: after a dispute with Jesus or his disciples about the meaning or the legitimacy of the baptism practised by Jesus (v. 25), the disciples turn to their master for advice (v. 26).

This hypothesis of a deliberate correction is more defensible than the common assumption of a *mistake* by an early *copyist* (who confused 'Jesus' with 'Jew'). A conflict about Christian baptism which had already broken out during the earthly activity of Jesus did not fit the evangelist's concept; therefore by a slight correction he reduced this dispute to mere jealousy on the part of the disciples of John.

If this is correct, we may also suppose that the evangelist further replaced 'baptism', which was originally mentioned quite unmistakably, by the term 'purification', which blurs the basic character of the dispute.

[26] The introduction to the discourse and the clause beginning with 'look' are part of the tradition. By contrast, the first relative clause is probably a reference by the evangelist back to 1.19–34 ('beyond the Jordan' = 1.28). Perhaps he replaced what was originally a different mark of identification. Be that as it may, the second relative clause is clearly redactional; it undermines the sense of the complaint made by the disciples and corresponds to the previous account by the evangelist (cf. e.g. 1.6–8, 15; 1.27, 30, etc.).

[27] The similarity of the formulation to 19.11 shows the verse to be a product of the evangelist.

[28] This verse presupposes the second relative clause from v. 26 and explicitly refers back to 1.20.

[29] The simile (v. 29a, b) and the following application (v. 29c) form the beginning of the Baptist's original answer. John as naturally and readily withdraws in favour of Jesus as a friend withdraws in favour a bridegroom and even rejoices for him.

[30] This verse says that both Jesus' success and the declining influence of John the Baptist are willed by God ('must'). The words 'increase' and 'decrease', which do not occur elsewhere in John, suggest that this closing statement too belongs to the tradition.

Yield: the purpose of the narrative in the tradition was on the one hand to have Jesus confirmed by John, and on the other explicitly to limit the significance of the Baptist to his mere function as a forerunner. The narrative evidently arose from the same situation of rivalry that is also visible in the background to 1.19ff. With an eye to the Baptist community it emphasizes that the one to whom the community appeals cannot legitimate its special existence. In complete agreement with the aim of this statement, the evangelist has taken over the story, and by his additions emphasized even more strongly the role of the Baptist as forerunner.

Historical

The Baptist who bears witness to Jesus is a fiction of the Christian interpretation of history (Bultmann). He did not understand himself as a forerunner of Jesus, but was made one only by the Christians (cf. on 1.19–34).

That Jesus himself baptized is sometimes regarded as one of the few pieces of historical information in the Gospel of John by which the Synoptic picture of Jesus can be corrected (J. Becker). In fact this would be a plausible explanation of the rise of baptism in the Christian community. But it is also conceivable that the assertion that Jesus himself baptized was a counter-reaction to a charge by the rival Baptist community that with the baptism that Christians practised they were dependent on John. It is similarly possible that after Jesus had become the centre of the cult, the view arose that he himself had baptized.

John 3.31–36: A subsequent commentary on the first stay of Jesus in Judaea

31 He who comes from above is over all; he who is of the earth is of the earth, and speaks of the earth. He who comes from heaven is over all. 32 He bears witness to what he has seen and heard, and no one accepts his witness. 33 Whoever accepts his

witness has sealed this, that God is truthful. 34 For he whom God has sent speaks the words of God, for it is not by measure that he gives the Spirit. 35 The Father loves the Son, and has given all things into his hand. 36 Whoever believes in the Son has eternal life. But whoever is disobedient to the Son shall not see life, but the wrath of God rests upon him.

Analysis

Verses 31–36 are not marked off from what has gone before; so they seem still to belong to the discourse of the Baptist in 3.27–30. After the Baptist has modestly withdrawn in v. 30, however, it is quite surprising that he lets himself be carried away and continues his discourse. Moreover it is strange that his remarks seem like a paraphrase of the previous statements of *Jesus* and that he suddenly speaks about truths which are otherwise reserved for Jesus to speak. It follows from this that vv. 31–36 are manifestly no longer part of the Baptist's discourse, nor are they meant to be. Rather, they give the impression that Jesus is the speaker or that the evangelist himself is beginning to preach suddenly. But it would be both improbable and without analogy for the evangelist to have neglected to mark off a discourse of Jesus or his own commentary from the discourse of the Baptist in vv. 27–30 (there are no quotation marks in Greek). All this indicates that the present section is an addition (J. Becker). The detailed analysis will show whether this conjecture is correct.

[31] The contrast 'from above'/'of the earth' recalls 3.6 ('of the spirit'/'of the flesh'). For 'from above' ('anew') cf. moreover 3.3, 7; for 'he who comes from heaven' cf. 3.13. 'Over' is unique in this form in the Gospel of John. The word 'earth' does not have any dualistic connotations elsewhere in the Gospel.

[32] Taken as a whole this verse is very similar to 3.11. Verse 32b ('no one accepts his witness') contradicts 3.26 ('all are coming to him').

[33] In its present form this statement is unique in John. 'Seal' (= 'authenticate') appears elsewhere only in the addition in 6.27. (For the statement that God is truthful cf. 7.28; 8.26.)

[34] Verse 34a takes the same line as v. 32 (cf. 8.47). Verse 34b evidently presupposes 3.8. 'Measure' is a *hapax legomenon*.

[35] The statement that the Father loves the Son occurs once in the work of the evangelist (5.20) and five times in the later additions (10.17; 15.9; 17.23, 24, 26); the formulation that God 'has given all things into his (Jesus') hands' recurs in the addition 13.3.

[36] Verse 36a corresponds to the evangelist's main soteriological confession (cf. 5.24; 6.40ab, 47; 11.25f.); by contrast, the negative version differs in both language and theology from comparable formulations by the evangelist: 'be disobedient' and 'wrath of God' are unique in the Gospel of John; 'shall not see life' stands in tension to the realized eschatology advanced by the evangelist (cf. 3.18). All in all, the verse has the same slant as 12.48.

Yield: on the one hand the content of vv. 31–36 comes very close to the context, above all 3.1ff.; on the other hand the language and theology of these verses diverge from it. Together with the observation that the passage has no speaker, this finding confirms that the section is an addition. Those adding it probably did not regard vv. 31–36 as part of the Baptist's discourse. Rather, at the end of the account of Jesus' first stay in Jerusalem and Judaea (2.13–3.30) they made a kind of stocktaking of what they had read so far, as they understood it (cf. the analogous procedure in 12.44–50). The explanation of the absence of any demarcation of the passage from what has gone before may be that when they were added, vv. 31–36 were externally marked off from the original text.

Historical

The historical value of this secondary literary product is nil.

John 4.1–42: Jesus in Samaria

1 *Now when Jesus knew that the Pharisees had heard 'Jesus is making and baptizing more disciples than John'* 2 – **although Jesus himself did not baptize, but his disciples** – 3 *he left Judaea and departed again to Galilee.* 4 *But he had to pass through Samaria.*

5 Now he came to a city of Samaria called Sychar, near the piece of land that Jacob gave to his son Joseph. 6 And Jacob's well was there. Now Jesus, wearied from his journey, sat down beside the well. It was about the sixth hour.

7a A woman from Samaria comes to draw water. b Jesus says to her, 'Give me a drink.' 8 *For his disciples had gone off into the city to buy food.* 9 The Samaritan woman says to him, 'How is it that you, a Jew, ask a drink of me, a Samaritan woman?' **For Jews have no dealings with Samaritans.** 10 *Jesus answered and said to her, 'If you knew the gift of God, and who it is that is saying to you, "Give me a drink," you would have asked him and he would have given you living water.'* 11 *The woman says to him, 'Lord, you have nothing to draw with, and the well is deep. Where do you get that living water?* 12 *Are you greater than our father Jacob, who gave us the well, and drank from it himself, and his sons, and his cattle?'* 13 *Jesus answered and said to her, 'Every one who drinks of this water will thirst again.* 14 *But whoever drinks of the water that I shall give him will never thirst; but the water that I shall give him will become in him a spring of water welling up to eternal life.'* 15 *The woman says to him, 'Lord, give me this water, that I may not thirst, nor come here to draw (again).'*

16 He says to her, 'Go, call your husband, and come here.' 17 The woman answered and said to him, 'I have no husband.' Jesus says to her, 'You are right in saying, "I have no husband." 18 For you have had five husbands, and he whom you now have is not your husband. This you have said truly.' 19 *The woman says to him, 'Lord, I see that you are a prophet.* 20 *Our fathers worshipped (God) on this mountain, and you say, "In Jerusalem is the place where one must worship (God)."'* 21 *Jesus says to her, 'Believe me, woman, an hour is coming when you will worship the Father neither on this mountain nor in Jerusalem.* 22 **You**

worship what you do not know; we worship what we know, for salvation is from the Jews. 23 *But an hour is coming, and now is, when the true worshippers will worship the Father in spirit and truth, for the Father also seeks such to worship him. 24 God is spirit, and those who worship him must worship him in spirit and truth.' 25 The woman says to him, 'I know that the Messiah is coming, who is called Christ; when he comes, he will proclaim to us all things.' 26 Jesus says to her, 'I who speak to you am he.' 27 Just then his disciples came and marvelled that he was talking with a woman. But no one said, 'What do you seek?' or, 'Why are you talking with her?'*

28 Now the woman left her water jar behind and went away into the city and said to the people, 29 'Come, see a man who told me all that I ever did. *Is this perhaps the Christ?'* 30 They went out of the city and came to him.

31 *Meanwhile his disciples urged him saying, 'Rabbi, eat.' 32 But he said to them, 'I have food to eat which you do not know.' 33 Then the disciples said to one another, 'Has any one brought him (something) to eat?' 34 Jesus says to them, 'My nourishment is to do the will of him who sent me, and to accomplish his work. 35a Do you not say,* "There are still four months, then comes the harvest"? b *Look, I tell you, lift up your eyes, and look at the fields: they are white for harvest. Already* 36 *he who reaps receives wages, and gathers fruit for eternal life, so that sower and reaper may rejoice together.*

37 *For here the saying holds true,* "One sows and another reaps." 38 *I sent you to reap that for which you did not labour; others have laboured, and you have entered into their labour.'*

39 *Now many Samaritans from that city came to believe in him because of the word of the woman, who testified, 'He told me all that I ever did.'* 40 *Now when the Samaritans came to him,* they asked him to stay with them; and he stayed there two days. 41 *And (yet) many more came to believe in him because of his word.* 42 *And they said to the woman, 'It is no longer because of your speech that we believe, for we have heard for ourselves, and we know that this is indeed the Saviour of the world.'*

Later revision

[2] This verse brings an unexpected correction to v. 1 and moreover contradicts 3.22, 26. Therefore it can hardly derive from the evangelist.

[9b] This verse is a typical later commentary. It provides help in understanding for readers who are not familiar with the conflict between Jews and Samaritans which the evangelist takes for granted (cf. vv. 20f., 23f.).

[22] In view of 5.45–47; 8.41–47, the statement that 'salvation is from the Jews' (v. 22b) cannot possibly derive from the evangelist (Bultmann). Verse 22a is in an irresolvable contradiction with 5.37 and 8.19, according to which God is the very one whom the Jews do *not* know. It follows from this that v. 22 has evidently been inserted by a glossator who wanted to safeguard the priority of the Jews in salvation history and thus introduced into the text a devaluation of the Samaritans which is alien to the evangelist. Incidentally, without v. 22 there is a smooth transition from v. 21 to v. 23: 'neither . . . nor . . . but'.

Redaction and tradition

By telling this story in connection with the saying of the Baptist in 3.30 which immediately precedes it, the evangelist gives a vivid example of the 'increase' of Jesus. The narrative itself displays some tensions and breaks which suggest that the evangelist has composed it on the basis of a piece of tradition. Just three particularly striking instances may be mentioned here: (a) the woman's request in v. 15 is followed by the strikingly abrupt invitation that she should call her husband (v. 16); (b) in v. 29 the woman refers exclusively to vv. 17b–18; she does not mention Jesus' remarks about the living water and the abolition of the opposition between Jews and Samaritans; (c) it is twice reported that the Samaritans come to Jesus (vv. 30, 40).

[1, 3] These verses form the redactional transition: that Jesus has greater success than John refers back to 3.22–30; similarly 'Judaea' takes up the place of abode mentioned in 3.22 ('land of Judaea'); in what follows the Pharisees play no further role, but their jealousy serves simply to motivate the journey to Galilee; that Jesus knows the level of knowledge of the Pharisees without having encountered one of them corresponds to the motif of omniscience which the evangelist often weaves in (cf. on 1.42).

[4] This verse presupposes the journey from Judaea to Galilee mentioned in v. 3 ('pass through'), and similarly derives from the evangelist (cf. also the repetition of the place name 'Samaria' in v. 5, which is superfluous in the present context).

[5–6] These verses form the beginning of the story in the tradition (for the local tradition presupposed in the precise indication of the scene cf. Gen. 33.19; 48.22; Josh 24.32). With the placing of Jesus by the well the first precondition of the following conversation is fulfilled. The indication of time (twelve noon) is meant to put special emphasis on Jesus' thirst in the noonday heat.

[7a] This concludes the introduction to the story in the tradition.

[7b] The action begins with Jesus' request.

[8] This verse fulfils a twofold purpose: (a) the absence of the disciples explains why Jesus has to ask the *woman* for something to drink; (b) the mention of the food which the disciples want to buy prepares for the conversation about the 'food' of Jesus in vv. 31–34. As vv. 31–34 derive from the evangelist, we have to regard this verse, like the report of the return of the disciples (v. 27), as redactional.

[9a] The point of the story is already contained in the woman's amazement at Jesus' twofold breach of a taboo. For Jesus' answer could only be: because for me the line which is traditionally drawn between us by religion and gender is less important than a sip of water. However, the story could no more have ended with such an answer than with the woman's question.

[10] In a flash, the vivid scene ends. Jesus ignores the woman's concrete objection from v. 9a and instead begins to theologize on the term 'water'. This is all the more artificial as Jesus indirectly concedes the justification for her objection ('*If* you knew . . .'). Therefore it is natural to assume that v. 10 is not the original continuation of v. 9a but the beginning of a (first) block of conversation which was inserted by the evangelist into the story from the tradition. This assumption is supported by the fact

that the following section, which is based on the metaphorical use of the term 'water', clearly has a redactional stamp.

[11–12] These verses contain the motif of misunderstanding which is typical of the evangelist (cf. on 2.20). The woman assumes that Jesus is speaking of the water from the well by which he is sitting (cf. v. 15). The beginning of v. 12 corresponds word for word with 8.53.

[13–14] Jesus begins to clear up the misunderstanding, but without abandoning the metaphorical mode of expression in favour of a direct designation of things. However, what is meant is unmistakably clear to the reader who remembers 3.15f. For if eternal life is promised there to the believer and here to the one who drinks of the 'water' which Jesus gives, then this 'water' cannot be other than Jesus' word or the exclusive content of this word, that is, Jesus himself (cf. also 5.24).

[15] Whereas Jesus' metaphorical mode of expression discloses itself automatically to the reader, the woman misunderstands these words too. Just as previously she had regarded the 'water' of which Jesus spoke as normal water from the well (vv. 11f.), now she regards it as a kind of miraculous drink which she hopes will provide a more comfortable life in the future. Her request for water, wrongly understood, corresponds to the people's request for bread, wrongly understood in a similar way, in 6.34 ('Lord, give us always this bread!').

[16–18] The completely unmotivated transition from v. 15 to v. 16 indicates that the evangelist is now again returning to what he had before him. Here vv. 16–18 can be understood as originally the direct continuation and at the same time as an ironic resolution of the point already contained in v. 9a (J. Becker). For if Jesus invites the woman who is amazed at his unusual behaviour to call her husband, although he already knows in advance that she has no husband (or at any rate no legitimate husband), then the statement 'This you have said truly' becomes the implicit answer to her question ('If you have no husband, why then are you surprised that I ask *you* for something to drink?').

If this is correct, we can even say that v. 18 adds to the two social restrictions already overcome by Jesus (those relating to religion and gender) yet a third, which is now similarly overcome. The fact that the woman is living in a common-law marriage does not deter Jesus from turning to her. Looked at in this way, the story contains a remarkable echo of Jesus' dealings with the shady and socially outcast (cf. on Matt. 11.18f.).

In the original story, v. 18 was followed by vv. 28f. That emerges from the fact that the content of the intervening conversation plays no role in vv. 28f. So with vv. 19–26 the evangelist is inserting a second block of conversation into the tradition before him.

[19] This verse is a bridge built by the evangelist between v. 18 and vv. 20ff.: the confession that Jesus is a prophet (cf. 6.14; 7.40; 9.17) is both a meaningful conclu-

sion to the clairvoyance of Jesus attested in v. 18 and an appropriate point of contact for the cultic and religious opposition between Jews and Samaritans which becomes a theme in what follows: if Jesus is a prophet, he has to be able to say something about this.

[20] The woman presents the theme of Jesus' following remarks: how does the Samaritan cultic place, Mount Gerizim, relate to Jerusalem, the cultic place of the Jews?

[21, 23–24] Jesus goes beyond this alternative by referring to the hour in which any cult with a local tie will lose its significance: it is not God's will to be worshipped either 'on this mountain' or 'in Jerusalem' but 'in spirit and truth' – and that is possible everywhere. In order to express the eschatological character of this hour, as in 5.25, it is described as both present and coming. 'Even if it is present, its "coming" is never over' (Bultmann).

[25–26] The woman's appeal to her knowledge (cf. 3.2; 7.27) and the following self-revelation of Jesus correspond to 11.24f. (Martha: 'I know that he will rise again . . .'; Jesus: 'I am the resurrection . . .'); for the self-revelation cf. 9.37 ('it is he who speaks to you'). Verse 25 shows that the woman is still locked in misunderstanding (cf. vv. 11f., 15). This now consists in the fact that she does not grasp the characteristic of the hour as present. Instead of this she hopes for further enlightenment on the future Messiah. In indicating to her that he himself is this Messiah, Jesus confirms not only that the hour is present but additionally makes it clear that he is the Messiah of the Samaritans also.

[27] The disciples had been removed from the scene since v. 8. By bringing them back now, the evangelist prepares for the dialogue in vv. 31–38.

[28–29] In the present context the woman makes use of the interruption in v. 27 to return to the city and inform the inhabitants about the remarkable encounter. In the original narrative her sudden departure – the fact that she leaves her jar behind indicates her haste – followed immediately after v. 18 (cf. on vv. 16–18). Only the question 'Is this perhaps the Christ?' presupposes vv. 25f. and derives from the evangelist.

[30] This verse reports the reaction of the inhabitants of the city. They take up the woman's invitation from v. 29. The clumsy resumption of the verse in vv. 39f. again indicates that the following interlude has been inserted by the evangelist.

[31] With the note 'meanwhile' the evangelist makes the following conversation run parallel to the events depicted in vv. 28–30. The invitation to eat, made by the disciples who have been present again since v. 27, has been prepared for by v. 8.

[32–33] The game of vv. 10–15 is repeated: just as according to v. 11 and v. 15 the woman regarded the 'water' of which Jesus spoke as ordinary water, so now the disciples think that by 'food' Jesus means a form of natural nourishment.

[34] However, Jesus has not spoken of nourishment at all but of his task to do God's will (cf. 5.30c; 6.38) and to acccomplish his work (cf. 5.36).

[35–36] Verse 35a is possibly a proverb taken up by the evangelist which is comparable with the phrase 'Tomorrow is another day'. With the term 'harvest', v. 35b uses a word which is common as an image for mission (cf. Matt. 9.37f.; Luke 10.2). Contrary to the assumption (put into the mouths of the disciples) that it is still some time until harvest, Jesus makes it clear that the harvest is already ripe (v. 35b); indeed the harvesting is already under way (v. 36).

[37–38] These verses are formulated from a post-Easter perspective (cf. 20.21) and introduce a new notion: the disciples are to continue what 'others' have already begun. These others are probably meant to be the Hellenists from Acts 8. Thus vv. 37f. reflect knowledge that the mission carried on by the Johannine community in Samaria could pick up the work of the Hellenists.

[39] This verse ignores the coming of the Samaritans mentioned in v. 30 and derives from the evangelist.

[40] Verse 40a provides the link back to v. 30; v. 40b is probably the original conclusion of the narrative.

[41–42] These verses come from the evangelist (v. 41 presupposes v. 39; v. 42 presupposes v. 41). In what has gone before, knowledge of who Jesus is has grown step by step (v. 12, 'greater than Jacob'; v. 19, 'a prophet'; v. 29, 'the Christ'). In the confession by the Samaritans ('Saviour of the world'; cf. I John 4.14) this intensification reaches its climax.

Yield: the evangelist found a story which comprised vv. 5–7, 9a, 16–18, 28–29a, 30, 40b and has inserted three major blocks of conversation into it: vv. 10–15, 19–26 and 31–40a. The original story is a mission legend. It legitimates the Christian mission in Samaria.

Historical

The interest mentioned above, which led to its formation, and its implausible features, tell against the historicity of the narrative from the tradition. Cf. also on Matt. 15.21–28.

John 4.43–45: Jesus travels on to Galilee

43 *Now after two days he went away from there to Galilee.* 44 **For Jesus himself testified, 'A prophet has no honour in his own ancestral city.'** 45 *Now when he came to Galilee, the Galileans received him, as they had seen all that he had done in Jerusalem at the feast; for they too had gone to the feast.*

Later revision

Verse 44 reports a saying which also occurs in the Synoptics in a similar form (cf. Mark 6.4; Matt. 13.57; Luke 4.24). However, what the saying is supposed to mean at this point is a complete riddle, since it contradicts v. 45. It is sometimes assumed that the evangelist wants to indicate that despite the friendly reception which according to v. 45 he finds in Galilee, Jesus distanced himself from the Galileans (cf. 2.23–25). But in that case v. 44 would have had to follow v. 45 and might not be introduced with 'for' but would have to be introduced with 'but'. Thus this must be an addition which was later (for whatever reason) written in the margin.

Redaction

After 2.23–25, the section 4.43, 45 forms the second redactional summary within the Gospel of John. It introduces the report of Jesus' second, short stay in Galilee (4.46–54).

[43] 'After two days' corresponds to the duration of Jesus' stay in Samaria (4.40); similarly, 'from there' refers back to Samaria, the scene of 4.1–42. The destination which had already been mentioned in 4.3 is recalled.

[45] This verse reports the arrival. 'All that he had done in Jerusalem' refers back to the cleansing of the temple (2.13–22) and the signs done in Jerusalem (2.23–25).

Historical

[44] Cf. on Mark 6.4.

John 4.46–54: The healing of the son of the royal official

46a *Now he came again to Cana in Galilee, where he had made the water wine.* b And there was a royal (official) whose son was ill in <u>Capernaum</u>. 47 When he <u>heard</u> that <u>Jesus</u> had come *from Judaea to Galilee*, he went <u>to him</u> and <u>begged</u> him to come down and heal <u>his</u> son; for he <u>was on the point</u> of death. 48 *Then Jesus said to him, 'Unless you see signs and wonders, you will not believe.'* 49 *The royal (official) says to him, 'Lord, come down before my child dies.'* 50 <u>Jesus says</u> to him, 'Go; your son lives.' The man believed the word that Jesus spoke to him and went his way. 51 And as he was going down, his servants met him and said, 'Your <u>child</u> lives.' 52 Now he asked them the hour when things had got better (with him). Then they said to him, '*Yesterday* at the seventh hour the fever left him.' 53a Now the father knew that (it was) <u>in that hour</u> when Jesus had said to him, 'Your son lives'. b And he himself came to believe, and all his household.

54 *Now Jesus did this as a second sign when he had come from Judaea to Galilee.*

Redaction and tradition

Tensions within the story and the fact that there is a similar narrative in Matt. 8.5–13/Luke 7.1–10 (= Q) show that the evangelist has composed this passage on the basis of a piece of tradition. In what follows we need to investigate the extent of the story in the tradition and its relationship to the two parallel Synoptic pericopes (the most important verbatim and almost verbatim agreements with Matthew are underlined once, agreements with Luke twice).

[46a] This is a redactional introduction; the evangelist is explicitly referring back to 2.1–11.

[46b] This represents the beginning of the story in the tradition. As in Luke 7.1 and Matt. 8.5 the petitioner lives in Capernaum. (For the question of a pre-redactional connection between this narrative and the story of the miracle with the wine cf. on 2.12.)

[47] Cf. Luke 7.2–3: the servant of a centurion 'was on the point of passing away'; when the centurion 'heard of Jesus, he sent elders of the Jews to him begging him to come and cure his servant'. Only 'from Judaea to Galilee' presupposes the narrative framework which the evangelist himself has created.

[48–49] These verses have been inserted by the evangelist. That becomes clear from the fact that the royal official has not required any miracle at all as a legitimation of Jesus: 'on the contrary, his request proves his faith, and so his answer (v. 49) can only be a repetition of his request. So we cannot see how this overcomes Jesus' refusal' (Bultmann).

[50] Originally, this verse followed directly after v. 47. Cf. Matt. 8.13a ('And Jesus said to the centurion, "Go! As you have believed, be it done to you"').

[51–52] There is no equivalent in Matthew or Luke to the report that the petitioner is told by his servants about the healing of his son while he is on the way home. This information authenticates the miracle: the servants are witnesses beyond suspicion, because they do not know the reason for the healing. Merely the 'yesterday' in v. 52 derives from the evangelist, for it presupposes that the official sought Jesus in Cana.

[53a] This similarly serves to confirm the miracle: the healing took place at the precise time when Jesus spoke the word that effected the miracle. The verbatim agreement with Matt. 8.13b ('And his servant was healed in that hour') is all the more striking since the motif of the hour probably derives from Matthew's redactional activity.

[53b] This is the conclusion to the miracle story in the tradition. This note (alongside vv. 51–52) indicates that the story represents a later stage in the history of the tradition than Q.

[54] Verse 54a corresponds with 2.11; v. 54b takes up v. 47a.

Yield: the story in the tradition comprised vv. 46b, 47*, 50–53*. It shows remarkable similarities with the Matthaean and Lukan versions of the narrative, and also clear divergences. The simplest explanation for this state of affairs is as follows: the story taken up by the evangelist comes from Z, and is thus dependent on both the Matthaean and Lukan versions of the story in their redactional final forms (A.Dauer). A fusion of the two Synoptic stories took place in Z, leading to a concentration on the miracle proper (Matt. 8.7–12; Luke 7.4–9 were omitted).

Historical

Cf. on Matt. 8.5–13 and Luke 7.1–10.

John 5.1–18: The healing of a sick man on the sabbath

1 *After this there was a feast of the Jews, and Jesus went up to Jerusalem.* 2 Now there is in Jerusalem by the Sheep Gate a pool which in Hebrew is called Bethzatha, with five porticoes. 3a In these sat a multitude of invalids, blind, lame, paralysed. 5 Now a man was there who had been ill for thirty-eight years. 6 When Jesus saw him lying there *and knew that he had already been (sick) for a long time*, he says to him, 'Do you want to recover?' 7 The sick man answered him, 'Lord, I have no one to put me into the pool when the water is stirred up; while I am going, another steps down before me.' 8 Jesus says to him, 'Rise, take up your pallet, and walk.' 9 And at once the man recovered, and he took up his pallet and walked.

Now it was the sabbath on that day. 10 The Jews now said to the man who was healed, 'It is the sabbath, and it is not lawful for you to carry your pallet.' 11 But he answered them, 'The man who restored me to health said to me, "Take up your pallet, and walk."' 12 They asked him, 'Who is the man who said to you, "Take (it) and walk"?' 13 Now the man who had been cured *did not know who it was, for Jesus had withdrawn, because the people were in the place.* 14 *After this Jesus found him in the temple, and said to him,* 'See, you have recovered, sin no more, that nothing worse befall you.' 15 *The man went away and* reported to the Jews that it was Jesus who had restored him to health. 16 Therefore the Jews persecuted Jesus, because he had done this on the sabbath. 17 *But Jesus answered them, 'My Father is working until now, and I am working.'* 18 *Therefore the Jews sought all the more to kill him, because he not only broke the sabbath but also called God his own Father, making himself equal with God.*

Preliminary text-critical note: vv. 3b–4 run: 'who waited for the movement of the water. For at an appointed time an angel of the Lord came down and moved the water. Whoever then was the first to descend after the water had moved recovered from whatever illness he suffered from.' They do not appear in the earliest manuscripts.

Redaction and tradition

5.1 is the prelude to a new major section. This contains the account of Jesus' second stay in Jerusalem and comprises not only the whole of ch. 5 but also the section 7.15–24, which originally attached directly to 5.47 but was put in the wrong place by the editors (for the reason cf. on 7.14, 25–36). 5.2–18 is divided into two parts: the miracle story (vv. 2–9a) and the narrative about the conflict over the sabbath sparked off by the miracle (vv. 9b–18).

[1] This verse is the introduction by the evangelist. The festival, which is not defined further, has no significance for what follows and merely serves to bring Jesus back to Jerusalem (cf. on 2.13).

[2–9a] These verses form a self-contained miracle story which was not originally meant to have a continuation. No redactional intervention can be established. The only exception is the motif that by virtue of his clairvoyance (cf. on 1.42) Jesus knows how long the man has been ill.

[9b] The dating of the healing on a sabbath is lame (cf. the parallel in 9.14) and indicates that the following conflict over the sabbath was added to vv. 2–9a only at a secondary stage (cf. Luke 13.15f.).

[10] The conflict breaks out between the man who has been healed and the Jews (cf. Jer. 17.21f.).

[11–12] The man who has been healed denies being responsible for the breach of the sabbath. Thereupon the Jews want to know the name of the man who is really responsible.

[13–14] However, before the man who has been healed can give the name of the culprit (v. 15), the narrative takes a detour. Whereas up to v. 12 it seemed to be heading purposefully for a climax, now it goes off course and even gives the impression of a degree of carelessness.

(a) On the one hand, the note that Jesus had withdrawn comes too late; on the other it is superfluous, since in any case vv. 10–12 would not have suggested that Jesus was still at the scene of the event. (b) Moreover, the question arises how the ignorance of Jesus' name by the man who has been healed can be explained from Jesus' absence. (c) The reason for Jesus' absence is also surprising, since in the context 'the people' play no role. (d) Furthermore, Jesus' warning to the man who has been healed is strange. Previously there had been no mention of his sinfulness nor is there mention of it afterwards. (e) Finally, it is completely impossible to understand how it is that the man learns Jesus' name as a result of the admonition addressed to him to sin no more.

These inconsistencies suggest that vv. 13f. have been inserted by the evangelist. This is also indicated by the motif which recurs in 9.35, that Jesus later 'finds' the man who has been healed (for the motif of 'finding' cf. also 1.41, 45; 2.14, etc.). (However, the observation that in v. 12 'the man' is Jesus, but in v. 15 the man who has been healed, necessitates a more precise demarcation of the evangelist's elaboration: it must begin with 'did not know' in v. 13 and end with 'went away and' in v. 15.) By making the insertion the evangelist probably intended to show that Jesus secretly commands the situation. For in causing the new encounter with the man who has been healed, Jesus to some degree himself betrays his name. In other words,

Jesus has not become involved in the conflict with the Jews, but has brought it on himself (cf. on 11.4).

The surprising admonition in v. 14 is thus only a means (albeit an inadequate one) to an end. Therefore the fact that in 9.3 the evangelist shows an opposed understanding of the connection between sin and sickness cannot be the basis of assigning v. 14 to the tradition – all the less so since what is said in 9.3 does not formulate any general principle. Rather, it is limited to the man who was born blind. Moreover his affliction is again, and indeed explicitly, only a means to an end.

[15] In the pre-existing story, the disclosure of the name of Jesus by 'the man who had been cured' (not by 'the man') followed immediately after v. 12. Because of the insertion of vv. 13f., however, the evangelist had to add 'went away and'. 'Reported' may also derive from him and may perhaps replace a simple 'said'.

[16] In the tradition, the hostile reaction of the Jews formed the climax of the conflict but not the conclusion of the story. However, the original continuation, in which Jesus shows the breach of the sabbath in its true light, has been moved a great deal further away by the redactional insertion of a long interlude. In 7.21–24 (if we remove the redactional additions), it runs as follows:

21 Jesus answered and said to them, 'I did one (single) work . . . 22 Therefore (I ask you), Moses gave you circumcision . . . and (accordingly) you circumcise a man upon the sabbath. 23 (Now) if a man receives circumcision on the sabbath, so that the law of Moses may not be broken, are you angry with me because on the sabbath I restored a man's whole body to health? 24 Do not judge by appearances, but judge with right judgment.'

That this is in fact the original conclusion to 5.2–16* is a well-founded assumption because here after prolix remarks on other themes (5.17–47; 7.15–20) Jesus suddenly returns to the starting point of the dispute (see on 7.21–24).

[17] This verse prepares for the extensive monologue which the evangelist has inserted between 5.2–16* and the original conclusion in 7.21–24. Verse 17 goes far beyond the original reply of Jesus, which ultimately still moves within the framework of the 'law'. Jesus' authority to break the sabbath is grounded in the unity with God which he claims (cf. especially 10.30, 38; 14.6–11).

[18] Occasioned by v. 17, the charge of blasphemy logically follows the charge of sabbath-breaking. This leads to an aggravation of the persecution of Jesus mentioned in v. 16. From now on the intention of the Jews to kill Jesus, provoked by his tremendous claim, runs through the account like a scarlet thread (7.19f.; 7.1, 25; 8.37, 40, 59; 10.31; 11.53; cf. 7.30, 32, 44; 10.39; 11.57) until it finally comes to a climax before Pilate: 'We have a law, and by that law he must die, for he has made himself the Son of God' (19.7; cf. 19.6, 15).

Yield: the core of the tradition is formed by the miracle story in 5.2–9a*. In form it is similar to Synoptic healing stories; the verbatim agreement between 5.8 and Mark 2.9b (cf. Mark 2.11) is particularly striking.

In the form expanded by 5.9b–12,15f.*; 7.21–24*, the narrative is comparable to Mark 3.1–6 (there similarly a self-contained miracle story has been associated with the problem of the sabbath at a secondary stage). It serves to disarm the charge brought from the Jewish side that Jesus' liberal attitude to the sabbath is an offence against the law: if circumcision, which involves only one part of the body, can be carried out on the sabbath, the healing of all of a man cannot be unlawful. The observation that the passage 7.21–24* is not completely related organically to 5.9b–12, 15f.*, since it justifies the healing and not the carrying of the pallet, could be an indication that in vv. 22f. it is based on an originally independent saying which has been adapted to the context only at a secondary stage. However, its wording can no longer be reconstructed.

Finally, the evangelist has put new accents on the sabbath conflict by transforming it into a controversy over the equality with God which Jesus claims.

Historical

The nucleus of the tradition (vv. 2–9a*) is unhistorical. The same is true of its secondary expansion, since this presupposes the miracle story. However, comparable statements of the historical Jesus on the sabbath commandment are echoed in the saying 7.21–24* (cf. on Mark 2.27).

John 5.19–30: The judgment discourse

19a *Then Jesus answered and said to them,*
b '*Amen, amen, I say to you,*
c the Son can do nothing of his own accord,
but only what he sees the Father doing;
d for whatever he does,
the Son also does likewise.
20a For the Father loves the Son
and shows him all that he himself is doing, b *and greater works than these will he show him, that you may marvel.*
21 For as the Father raises the dead and makes (them) alive,
so also the Son makes alive whom he will.
22 For neither does the Father judge any one,
but he has given all judgment to the Son,
23a that all may honour the Son,
as they honour the Father. b *Whoever does not honour the Son does not honour the Father who has sent him.*

24 *Amen, amen, I say to you, whoever hears my word and believes him who sent me has eternal life and does not come into judgment, but has passed from death to life.* 25 *Amen, amen, I say to you,* the hour is coming, *and now is,* when the dead will hear the voice of the Son of God, and those who hear will live. 26 *For as the Father has life in himself, so he has granted the Son also to have life in himself.* 27 *And he has given him authority to execute judgment, because he is the Son of man.* 28 **Do not marvel at this; for the hour is coming when all who are in the tombs will hear his voice** 29 **and those who have done good will come forth to the resurrection of life, but those who have done evil, to the resurrection of judgment.** 30a *I can do nothing of my own accord.* b *As I hear, I judge; and my judgment is just.* c *For I do not seek my own will but the will of him who sent me.'*

Later revision

[28–29] In vv. 24–27 the evangelist emphasizes strongly that anyone who believes in Jesus already partakes in eternal life. Verses 28–29 show two important differences from this emphasis on the presence of salvation: (a) that the hour 'now is' (v. 25) is not said; rather it is regarded exclusively as being in the future; (b) whereas according to v. 24 the believers have already passed from death to life, according to v. 29 the 'resurrection of life' is still to come. In other words, the popular eschatology which had been radically removed by the evangelist is here re-established (Bultmann). All this indicates that vv. 28–29 represent an addition by the later revisers formulated on the basis of v. 25 (cf. Dan. 12.2). Further observations support this view. First, the statement that the fate of human beings is decided by their works is inconceivable for the evangelist, just as the phrases 'do good' and 'do evil' are untypical of him (3.20 is based on tradition). Moreover, in 11.24–26 the evangelist explicitly rejects the notion expressed in vv. 28f. Finally, the invitation not to marvel (v. 28 beginning) is not in accord with v. 20b ('that you may marvel').

Redaction

The section forms the first part of Jesus' response to the intention of the Jews in 5.18 and is to be read against the background of the charge of blasphemy raised there in connection with 5.17. Jesus disarms this accusation by emphasizing that he is acting in full accord with the Father. However, his remarks soon expand and lead into a comprehensive account of the unity of his activity as judge with the activity of God. The discourse is continued in 5.31.

[19a, b] Those addressed in Jesus' discourse are the Jews from 5.9b–18 who are hostile because of the breach of the sabbath and the 'blasphemy'.

[19c–23] The elevated style, the evidently far-reaching strophic division and the change from the third person to the first in v. 24 suggest that the passage is based on a tradition (J. Becker). Verses 20b and 23b can be identified as redactional additions: v. 20b is formulated in prose and contains a reference back to the miracle in 5.2–9a ('greater works than these', cf. 1.50; 14.12); with the address to the hearers ('that you may marvel') it presupposes the situation of the conversation. Verse 23b (cf. Luke

10.16b) stands out from what goes before by the change of subject and the sending formula which is typical of the evangelist. Evidently each time the evangelist made his additions at the end of a strophe.

In v. 20b the plural 'than these' is striking: probably the evangelist has in view not only the miracle in 5.2ff. but also 2.1ff. and 4.46ff. By contrast, 'greater works' (cf. 1.50; 14.12) refers less to the miracles narrated in chs. 6; 9 and 11 (with the exception of the raising of Lazarus these are hardly 'greater' than the previous ones) than to the activity of the Son mentioned in vv. 21f. which gives life and overcomes death.

Whereas the piece of tradition deals with the heavenly Son to whom the Father has transferred the office of judge on his exaltation (v. 22), by the addition of v. 23b and generally by the fact that the earthly Jesus speaks these words, the transfer of office and the sending now coincide.

[24] This verse is a key formulation by the evangelist. As in 6.47; 11.25f. he sums up his new interpretation of the traditional eschatology. The decision on salvation and doom is not made at the end of days but in the present. Thus the traditional future eschatology becomes a realized eschatology. As is shown by the negative version of v. 24 in 3.18, the realized eschatology, too, has a twofold outcome: 'Whoever does not believe has been judged already.'

[25] The nearness of this verse to the world of ideas in e.g. I Thess. 4.15–17 (cf. on Mark 9.1) suggests that it is based on 'a traditional apocalyptic promise of primitive Christian prophecy' (J. Becker). Whereas that dealt with the *future* resurrection of the dead, the evangelist reinterprets it in the sense of v. 24 by adding 'and now is' (cf. 4.23).

[26] This verse is constructed in parallel to v. 21.

[27] This verse echoes v. 22.

[30] Verse 30a gives the section a framework by the word-for-word adoption of v. 19c; v. 30b recurs similarly in 8.16 ('But if I judge, my judgment is true') and moreover runs parallel to 8.26 ('what I have heard from him [= God] I speak') and 8.28 ('as the Father has taught me, so I speak'); v. 30c has verbatim equivalents in 4.34 and 6.38.

Yield: the section has been composed by the evangelist himself, using two pieces of tradition (vv. 19c–23a*; v. 25*).

Tradition

[19c–23a*] These verses form a hymn of praise in two strophes, which in the descriptive present announce the dignity of the exalted Son in unity with the Father. Here it should be noted that the hymn expresses a view which has developed far beyond primitive Christian apocalyptic. For there is mention neither of a judgment at the last day nor of a general resurrection of the dead. Rather, the judgment is given in the present, and not all people are made alive, but only those to whom the Son wills to give life (cf. v. 21).

[25*] For this verse see above.

Historical

Verses 19c–23a* and v. 25* are products of theological reflection after Easter; they do not go back to Jesus. Probably these words were not even meant to be sayings of Jesus (or of the Exalted One) originally. Rather, they may originally have been confessional statements by the community.

John 5.31–47; 7.15–24: The witness to Jesus

31 *'If I bear witness to myself, my witness is not true. 32 There is another who bears witness to me, and I know that the witness which he bears to me is true.*

33 *You have sent to John, and he has borne witness to the truth. 34 But I do not receive witness from man; but I say this that you may be saved. 35 He was a burning and shining lamp, but you were willing to rejoice (only) for an hour in his light.*

36 *But I have a witness greater than that of John; for the works which the Father has given me to accomplish, these very works which I do, bear witness that the Father has sent me. 37 And the Father who sent me has himself borne witness to me. You have neither heard his voice nor seen his form. 38 And you do not have his word abiding in you, for you do not believe him whom he has sent.*

39 *You search the scriptures, because you think that in them you have eternal life; and it is they that bear witness to me. 40 Yet you are not willing to come to me that you may have life.*

41 *I do not receive glory from men; 42 but I know that you do not have the love of God in you. 43 I have come in my Father's name, and you do not receive me. If another comes in his own name, him you will receive. 44 How can you believe, who receive glory from one another and do not seek the glory that (comes) from the only God?*

45 *Do not think that I shall accuse you before my Father! There is one who accuses you, Moses, on whom you have set your hope. 46 For if you believed Moses, you would believe me, for he wrote of me. 47 But if you do not believe his scriptures, how will you believe my words?'*

7.15 *Then the Jews marvelled and said, 'How does this man know the scriptures, when he has never received instruction?'*

7.16 *Then Jesus answered them and said, 'My teaching is not mine, but his who sent me. 7.17 If anyone will do his will, he will know of the teaching whether it is from God or whether I am speaking of my own accord. 7.18 Whoever speaks of his own accord seeks his own glory; but whoever seeks the glory of him who sent him is truthful, and in him there is no unrighteousness. 7.19 Did not Moses give you the law? Yet none of you does the law. Why do you seek to kill me?'*

7.20 *The people answered, 'You have a demon! Who is seeking to kill you?'*

7.21 Jesus answered and said to them, 'I did one (single) work, *and you all marvel. 7.22 Therefore (I ask you), Moses gave you circumcision – not that it is from Moses, but from the fathers* – and (accordingly) you circumcise a man upon the sabbath. 7.23 (Now) if a man receives circumcision on the sabbath, so that the law of Moses may not be broken, are you angry with me because on the sabbath I restored a man's whole body to health? 7.24 Do not judge by appearances, but judge with right judgment.'

Redaction and tradition

With the shift of 7.15–24 to the end of ch. 5, account is taken of a result of the analysis of ch. 7. In the evangelist's work the section probably stood at this point (for the reasons see on 7.14, 25–36).

The present passage contains the end of the discourse of Jesus begun in 5.19 and thus at the same time the conclusion of the account of his second stay in Jerusalem. The following division of 5.31–47; 7.15–24 is possible: 5.31–32 mention the theme of the discourse ('witness'). This is then developed in three directions: 5.33–35 are about the witness of the Baptist, 5.36–38 about the witness of the works of Jesus and God, 5.39–47 about the witness of the scriptures. (Here 5.41–44 form an excursus on the failure of the Jews to accept Jesus, centred on the term 'glory'.) 7.15–24 stand apart in so far as here once again the Jews are speaking. However, we cannot see too deep a division between 5.47 and 7.15, since both sections are held closely together by the key words 'scriptures' (5.47; 7.15; a synonymous word in 5.39), 'glory' (5.41, 44; 7.18) and 'Moses' (5.45–47; 7.19, 22). On the whole, 5.31–47 and 7.15–24 are marked to a much greater degree by the opposition of the Jews than 5.19–30; this passage seems almost to have been conceived after the pattern of a defence speech in a court. It answers the question of the legitimation of Jesus which arises in connection with his tremendous claim in 5.19–30 and which is tacitly presupposed.

[31] Jesus formulates the same legal principle that is held against him in 8.13 by the Pharisees. (This may reflect a charge which was in fact made from the Jewish side against the witness to Christ by the Johannine community.)

[32] The vague reference to the 'other' witness suggests John the Baptist to the reader. For he has previously been the only one of whom it has often been said that he is bearing witness to Jesus (1.7f., 15, 32, 34; 3.26).

[33] By the explicit reference back to 1.19–28, v. 33 first seems to confirm the supposition provoked by v. 32.

[34a] But this brings a surprising turn: if Jesus does not accept witness from any-one, John cannot be the 'other' witness. Rather, John's witness is devalued (cf. on 1.6–8). This is all the more remarkable, as at this particular point it is important to offer witnesses to Jesus. Thus the Baptist sinks to insignificance.

[34b–35] The evangelist has made his Jesus digress into a criticism of the Baptist in v. 34a. Since, however, the opponents presupposed in ch. 5 are not followers of John but the murderous Jews of 5.18, it is necessary to return here to the legal dispute which is really to be carried on. For this purpose, in the simile the evangelist once again takes account of the positive role of the Baptist. On that basis it is then possible to rebuke the Jews: they have forfeited the opportunity which the Baptist gave them despite the defectiveness of his witness.

[36–38] Throughout, these verses bear the stamp of the evangelist: v. 36a is the natural conclusion from vv. 32 and 34a; v. 36b corresponds to 10.25b (for the 'which the Father has given me to accomplish' that goes beyond 10.25b cf. 4.34; cf. also 10.37f.); v. 37a has a parallel in 8.18; v. 37b refers back to 1.18a; v. 38a is similar to 8.37b; for the charge of unbelief to the Jews in v. 38b cf. 8.45f.

As in 8.18, the evangelist is concerned to offer *two* witnesses to Jesus (cf. 8.17). There these are Jesus himself and the Father, here the Father and the works which he has given Jesus to do.

[39–40] These verses are constructed in parallel to vv. 33, 35b ('you have sent'/ 'you search'; 'and he has'/ 'and it is they'; 'but you were willing'/'yet you are not willing'). The Jews' questioning of the Baptist was as fruitless as their study of the scriptures is vain. For the scriptures themselves cannot give eternal life, as the Jews think (cf. e.g. PsSol. 14.2: 'The pious of the Lord will have eternal life in it [= the law]); they merely bear witness to the one who alone can give eternal life (cf. 3.15f.; 4.14, 36; 5.24, 26; 6.33, 40ab, 47; 11.25f., etc.).

[41] This verse corresponds to v. 34a; this similarity makes it clear that the term 'glory' (cf. 5.44; 7.18) is here evidently interchangeable with the term 'witness', which stood at the centre of vv. 31–39 ('witness' four times, 'bear witness' seven times).

[42] This verse echoes v. 38a, where 'word of God' stands in place of 'love of God'.

[43] There is evidently an allusion to 1.11 in v. 43a. Verse 43b hardly has a concrete historical figure in view; rather, the opposition between 'in my Father's name' and 'in his own name' is merely meant to illustrate the absurd reaction of the Jews.

[44] This is along the same lines as 12.43. For not being able to believe cf. 12.39 (cf. also 8.43).

[45–47] These verses pick up vv. 39f. Jesus' remarks about Moses represent one of the climaxes of the evangelist's anti-Jewish polemic. For in contemporary Judaism Moses was regarded as being not only the mediator of the Torah but also an intercessor with God (cf. e.g. Ascension of Moses 12.6: 'He [= God] also appointed me [= Moses] for them and their sins: I was to implore and pray for them'). This function is reversed in 5.45: Moses is not the intercessor for whom the Jews have hoped but the accuser whom they must fear. Verses 46 (cf. 1.45) and 47 repeat vv. 39b–40 in other words.

[7.15] The question of the Jews who want to disqualify Jesus with a reference to his lack of scribal learning is meant to show that the Jews continue to close their minds to Jesus' claim despite his remarks in 5.19–47. The evangelist often puts similar and equally aggressive and incomprehending objections into the mouths of the Jews or the people (cf. 7.20, 35f.; 8.22, 48, 52; 10.20; 12.34).

[7.16] This verse corresponds to 8.28b.

[7.17] For 'do the will of God' cf. 4.34; 6.38; 9.31; for the opposition between 'from God' and 'of my own accord' cf. 5.30; 7.28; 8.28, 42, 54; 14.10b.

[7.18] For v. 18a cf. 8.50a ('But I do not seek my glory'); for v. 18b cf. 5.44.

[7.19] Verse 19a (cf. 1.17) and v. 19b on the one hand refer back to 5.45–47 and on the other prepare for 7.21–24. With v. 19c the evangelist recalls the starting point of the discourse in 5.18.

[7.20] The sudden appearance of the people, which have not been mentioned previously except in 5.13, is to be explained from the fact that the 'Jews' do not come into question here as speakers. They are indeed the ones who according to 5.18 want to kill Jesus. The charge of demonic possession (v. 20a) is also made against Jesus in 8.48, 52 and 10.20.

[7.21–24] The position of this passage within the context is not without problems.

First, it is remarkable that Jesus leaves 7.20 unanswered and abruptly returns to the discussion of the sabbath healing (5.2–18). Secondly, it is striking that in 7.23 Jesus grants that the same Jews whom he has just accused of violating the law of Moses (7.19) do *not* want to abolish the law of Moses. And finally, not only is 7.24 as the conclusion of the major section 5.1ff; 7.15ff. remarkably abrupt, but the question also arises how Jesus can still trust the Jews to make a just judgment in view of the sharp accusations in 5.35, 38, 40–47; 7.19.

These tensions suggest that the basis of the passage is the original end of the narrative 5.2–16* which the evangelist has taken up (cf. on 5.1–18). 7.21c ('marvel' picks up the same word from 7.15 and fits as badly with 'persecute' [5.16] as with 'be angry' [7.23]), the corrective parenthesis in 7.22b and possibly the 'you' in 7.22a (cf. 7.19a) can be removed as redactional additions.

 Yield: with the exception of 7.21–24* the section is a construction by the evangelist.

Historical

For 7.21–24* cf. on 5.1–18.

John 6.1–21: Feeding and walking on the sea

1 *After this* Jesus went away to the other side of the Sea of Galilee of Tiberias. 2a And many people followed him, b *for they saw the signs that he did to the sick.* 3 But Jesus went up the mountain and sat down there with his disciples. 4 **Now the Passover, the feast of the Jews, was near**.

5a Now when Jesus had lifted up his eyes and seen that many people were coming to him, b he says to *Philip*, 'Where are we to buy loaves, so that these (can) eat?' 6 *But he said this to test him, for he himself knew what he would do.*

7 *Philip* answered him, 'Loaves for two hundred denarii are not sufficient, that everyone may take (even a) little.'

8 One of his disciples, *Andrew, Simon Peter's brother*, says to him, 9 'There is a lad here who has five barley loaves and two fishes. But what are these among so many?' 10a Jesus said, 'Make the people settle down.'

b Now there was much grass in the place. c So the men settled down, d about five thousand in number. 11 Then Jesus took the loaves, spoke the thanksgiving, and distributed (them) to those who had settled down, in the same way also the fishes, as much as they wanted. 12 And when they were full, he says to his disciples, 'Gather up the fragments left over, so that nothing is lost.' 13 Then they gathered them up and filled twelve baskets with fragments from the five barley loaves which were left by those who had eaten. 14 *Now when the people saw the sign which he had done, they said, 'This is truly the prophet who comes into the world!'* 15 Now when Jesus perceived that they wanted to come and take him by force to make him king, he withdrew again to the mountain himself alone.

16 And when evening came, his disciples went down to the sea and 17a got into a boat and were going to the other side of the sea to Capernaum. b And it had already become dark, and Jesus had not yet come to them. 18 And the sea became turbulent because a strong wind was blowing. 19 Now when they had travelled about twenty-five or thirty stadia, they saw Jesus walking on the sea and drawing near to the boat, and they were afraid. 20 But he says to them, 'It is I; do not be afraid.' 21 Now they wanted to take him into the boat, and immediately the boat was at the land to which they were going.

Later revision

The later revisers of the Gospel speak in 21.1 of the 'Sea of Tiberias'; the only further mention of the town of Tiberias in 6.23 similarly derives from them. Therefore we may assume that they are also responsible for the overloaded naming of the sea in v. 1. They have assimilated the designation 'Sea of Galilee' to their terminology by the addition 'of Tiberias'.

[4] The mention of the imminent feast of the Passover, used elsewhere as a motivation for Jesus' journeys to Jerusalem (2.13; 11.55; cf. 7.2), appears somewhat out of place here. The verse gains meaning only from the eucharistic section 6.51c–58 which has been subsequently inserted: evidently it seeks to indicate that Jesus replaces the Jewish Passover by the Lord's Supper (J. Becker).

Redaction and tradition

The transition from ch. 5 (both with and without 7.15–24) to 6.1 is harsh. Jesus can hardly go from Jerusalem, the scene of what has gone before, to the other side of the Sea of Galilee. Therefore many exegetes conjecture that chs 5 and 6 were subsequently exchanged. However, a sufficient explanation of the abrupt transition is that here the evangelist's formulation is governed by tradition. For again the section is based on Z. In the Z version of vv. 1–15 not only have the three Synoptic stories of the feeding of the five thousand (Mark 6.32–44; Matt. 14.13–21; Luke 9.10b–17) been fused together but so have the Markan and Matthaean narratives of the feeding of the four thousand (Mark 8.1–10; Matt. 15.32–39), including the Matthaean redactional introduction Matt. 15.29–31 (cf. Mark 7.31–37). The Z basis for vv. 16–21 rests on Mark 6.45–52 and Matt. 14.22–33. In the text above the most important verbatim and almost verbatim agreements with Mark have been indicated with single underlinings and possibly additional agreements with Matthew and Luke with double underlinings.

As the following survey shows, in composing the whole section 6.1–71 the evangelist is evidently dependent on Z (Mark 6.32–53; 8.10–33 and Matt. 14.13–33; 15.29–16.20):

Feeding miracle	Mark 6.32–44 par.	John 6.1–15;
Walking on the sea	Mark 6.45–52 par.	John 6.16–20;
Crossing	Mark 6.53; 8.10 par.	John 6.21;
Demand for a sign	Mark 8.11–13 par.	John 6.30f.;
Confession of Peter	Mark 8.27–33 par.	John 6.67–71.

[1*] 'After this' is a transitional formula typical of the evangelist (cf. 2.12; 3.22; 5.1, 14; 7.1, etc.). As in Mark 6.32 parr., the multiplication of bread and fish is preceded by a change of place near the sea (for the 'Sea of Galilee' cf. Matt. 15.29). The explicit indication of 'the other side' of the sea as a destination interlocks the narratives of the feeding and the walking on the sea better: in vv. 19–21 Jesus will cross the sea on foot in the opposite direction.

[2a] This verse corresponds to Luke 9.11a (cf. Matt. 14.13) and thus presupposes the revision of Mark 6.32–44 by the parallels. For Mark 6.33 does not say that the crowd follows Jesus, but that it goes ahead of him.

[2b] In this form (cf. 2.23) this is an addition by the evangelist (but cf. Matt. 15.30f. and Luke 9.11b). In the context, the 'signs that he did to the sick' refer back to 4.46–54 and 5.1–9a.

[3] Cf. the striking verbatim agreements with Matt. 15.29.

[5a] Cf. Mark 6.34a = Matt. 14.14a ('And when he got out he saw many people').

[5b] This verse presupposes Mark 6.37b and is probably additionally influenced by Mark 8.4b (cf. Matt. 15.33). In contrast to Mark 6.35f. parr., Jesus himself (and not the disciples) takes the initiative in providing food for the multitude. The mention of Philip derives from the evangelist (cf. 1.44–46; 12.21f.; 14.8f.).

[6] The evangelist clears Jesus of the suspicion that he does not know what to do in the emergency. That is necessary because Z has placed a question on the lips of Jesus in v. 5b which is put by the disciples in Mark 6.37b.

[7] The detail 'two hundred denarii' agrees with Mark 6.37b. In Mark, loaves to the value of two hundred denarii are enough to satisfy all. If now this sum is not enough to allow each to have just a bit of bread, the need (and thus also the following miracle) becomes all the greater.

[8] Here Andrew alone speaks instead of all the disciples (cf. Mark 6.38b parr.); for him cf. 1.40–42 and 12.22, where he similarly appears together with Philip (see on v. 5b).

[9] The numbers agree with those from Mark 6.38b parr. The introduction of the 'lad' of whom the Synoptics tell us nothing is probably due to a recollection of II Kings 4.42–44, the narrative of the feeding of the hundred men by Elisha. There Elisha is supported by a 'servant' (cf. II Kings 4.43) who in the preceding story is twice called a 'lad' (cf. II Kings 4.38, 41 LXX). It must also be a result of the influence of the Elisha story that here 'barley loaves' (instead of 'loaves') are mentioned (cf. II Kings 4.42 LXX). The concluding question ('But what are these among so many?') corresponds to the expectations of the hearers: five thousand men cannot be filled with five loaves and two fishes. Thus the magnitude of the miracle which follows is heightened.

[10] As in Luke 9.14 Jesus has the *disciples* see to it that the people settle down (v. 10a), whereas in Mark 6.39 par. and Mark 8.6 par. he addresses the invitation to sit down directly to the crowd. However, in contrast to Luke 9.15 the execution of the order by the disciples is not reported; rather, in v. 10c the narrative continues on the basis of Mark 6.40. For the 'much grass' in v. 10b cf. the 'green grass' in Mark 6.39 (see also Matt. 14.19). For the number of those fed (v. 10d) cf. the agreement with Mark 6.44 parr. ('five thousand men'); as in Luke 9.14 and Matt. 14.21 ('around five thousand') and in Mark 8.9 ('about four thousand') the number is relativized.

[11] In the Synoptics Jesus gives the food to the disciples and these set it before the multitude (Mark 6.41 par.; cf. Mark 8.6f. par.). Here Jesus himself distributes the bread and the fishes. That Jesus 'spoke the thanksgiving' corresponds verbatim with Mark 8.6 par.; 'also the fishes' is as lame as the corresponding formulation in Mark 6.43. The addition 'as much as they wanted' emphasizes the sudden abundance of food.

[12] The picking up of the 'remains' is motivated by a command of Jesus (by contrast cf. Mark 6.43 parr.; Mark 8.8 par.).

[13] The formulation 'twelve baskets with fragments' appears in this form only in Matt. 14.20 and Luke 9.17; Mark speaks of 'twelve basketsful'.

[14] This verse comes from the evangelist: for 'doing signs' cf. above on v. 2b; for the confession of the people that Jesus is truly the prophet, cf. 7.40; for the addition 'who comes into the world' which goes beyond 7.40 cf. 11.27.

[15] This verse has been added to the story in Z; here 'to the mountain' has been borrowed from Mark 6.46 par. and 'himself alone' from Mark 6.47b. Jesus withdraws from the attempt to make him king. This illustrates that he is no claimant to a political messiahship. 'Again' refers back to v. 3. However, it was not said before that Jesus descends from the mountain. This inconsistency results from the fact that Z has also used Matt. 15.29 in v. 3.

[16–17a] Cf. the agreements with Mark 6.47, 45 par. Whereas in Mark and Matthew Jesus urges the disciples to get into the boat, here they do so on their own initiative.

[17b] This does not appear in the Synoptics in this form, but cf. Mark 6.47b ('and he [was] alone on the land'). It emphasizes that the disciples are all by themselves.

[18] Cf. Mark 6.48 par. ('for the wind was against them').

[19] For the note about distance (three or four miles) cf. Matt. 14.24 ('the boat was already many stadia distant from the land') and Mark 6.47 ('in the middle of the sea'). The rare word for 'travel' used here is the same as that used in another form in Mark 6.48 for 'row'. 'They saw Jesus walking on the sea' corresponds almost word for word with Mark 6.49 par. 'They were afraid' replaces 'they were terrified' (Mark 6.50 par.).

[20] This verse occurs word for word in Mark 6.50 (cf. Matt. 14.27).

[21] The original conclusion of the story (cf. Mark 6.51f. par.) has been reshaped by Z. It reports neither Jesus getting into the boat nor a sudden calm. Instead of this Z links a second miracle to the walking on the sea: the boat flies to the shore like an arrow.

Yield: Z does not presuppose any Jesus traditions other than the five Synoptic feeding stories and the two Synoptic stories of walking on the sea. As far as can be seen, the evangelist has largely taken over Z unaltered.

Historical

Cf. on Mark 6.35–44 and on Mark 6.45–56.

John 6.22–59: The bread of life

22a *On the next day the people who stood on the other side of the sea saw* b **that there had been no other boat there, except one, and that Jesus had not entered the boat with his disciples, but that the disciples had gone away alone.** 23a **Other boats came from Tiberias near the place** b **where they had eaten the bread after the Lord had spoken the prayer of thanksgiving.** 24a **Now when the people saw** b *that Jesus was not there, nor his disciples,* c **they themselves got into the boats** d *and they went to Capernaum, and sought Jesus.* 25 *And when they found him* **on the other side of the sea,** *they said to him, 'Rabbi, when did you come here?'*

26 *Jesus answered them and said, 'Amen, amen, I say to you, you seek me, not because you saw signs, but because you ate of the loaves and were filled.* 27 **Do not labour for the food which perishes, but for the food which endures to eternal life, which the Son of man will give to you; for he has been authenticated by the Father, God.'**

28 *Then they said to him, 'What should we do, to work the works of God?'*

29 *Jesus answered and said to them, 'This is the work of God, that you believe in him whom he has sent.'*

30 *Then they said to him, 'Now what sign do you do, that we may see, and believe you? What do you work?* 31 *Our fathers ate the manna in the wilderness; as it is written, "He gave them bread from heaven to eat."'*

32 *Jesus then said to them, 'Amen, amen, I say to you, it was not Moses who gave you the bread from heaven, but my Father gives you the true bread from heaven. 33 For the bread of God is that which comes down from heaven, and gives life to the world.'*

34 *They said to him, 'Lord, give us this bread always.'*

35 *Jesus said to them,* 'I am the bread of life. Whoever comes to me shall not hunger, and whoever believes in me shall never thirst. 36 *But I have said to you, you have seen me, yet do not believe. 37 All that the Father gives me will come to me; and him who comes to me I will not cast out. 38 For I have come down from heaven, not to do my own will, but the will of him who sent me.* 39 **And this is the will of him who sent me, that I should lose nothing of all that he has given me, but raise it up at the last day.** 40 *For this is the will of my Father, that whoever sees the Son and believes in him should have eternal life;* **and I will raise him up at the last day.'**

41 *The Jews then murmured at him, because he said, 'I am the bread which came down from heaven,' 42 and said, 'Is not this Jesus, the son of Joseph, whose father and mother we know? How does he now say, "I have come down from heaven"?'*

43 *Jesus answered and said to them, 'Do not murmur among yourselves!* 44 No one can come to me unless the Father *who has sent me* draws him; **and I will raise him up at the last day.** 45 *It is written in the prophets, "And they shall all be taught by God." Whoever has heard and learned from the Father comes to me. 46 Not that any one has seen the Father except him who is from God; (only) he has seen the Father.*

47 *Amen, amen, I say to you, whoever believes has eternal life. 48 I am the bread of life. 49 Our fathers ate the manna in the wilderness, and they died. 50a This is the bread which comes down from heaven, b that one may eat of it and not die. 51a I am the living bread which came down from heaven. b If anyone eats of this bread, he will live for ever.*

51c **And the bread which I will give is my flesh for the life of the world.'** 52 **Then the Jews disputed among themselves, saying, 'How can this man give us his flesh to eat?'** 53 **Then Jesus said to them, 'Amen, amen, I say to you, unless you eat the flesh of the Son of man and drink his blood, you have no life in you.** 54 **He who consumes my flesh and drinks my blood has eternal life, and I will raise him up at the last day.** 55 **For my flesh is food indeed, and my blood is drink indeed.** 56 **He who consumes my flesh and drinks my blood abides in me, and I in him.** 57 **As the living Father has sent me, and I live through the Father, so he who consumes me will live through me.** 58a **This is the bread which came down from heaven, b not as the fathers ate and have died. c Whoever consumes this bread will live for ever.'**

59 *This he said in the synagogue as he was teaching at Capernaum.*

Later revision

The following analysis of 6.22–59 derives from an insight into the special character of vv. 51c–58. This passage emphasizes the necessity of the eucharist for salvation. This fact alone is puzzling because elsewhere the evangelist is evidently indifferent to cultic sacramental piety, if not critical of it; thus e.g. in connection with the account of the last supper of Jesus (ch. 13) he offers no report on the institution of the eucharist. In addition, vv. 51c–58 represent an alien body in the context of ch. 6.

(a) In v. 51a Jesus is identical with the 'bread which came down from heaven' (cf. similarly vv. 35, 41, 48); according to v. 51c the bread is his flesh. Here there is as little preparation for this identification in vv. 31–51b as for the mention of the blood (vv. 53–55) which now additionally comes into play.

(b) According to v. 32 it is the *Father* who *gives* (present) the bread; according to v. 51c it is *Jesus* who *will give* (future) the bread.

(c) 'Bread' and 'eat' evidently have a symbolic meaning in vv. 32–51b: Jesus is the 'bread' of which one is to 'eat' by faith (v. 51b). By contrast, in vv. 51c–58 'bread' (or 'flesh'), 'eat', 'blood' and 'drink' are meant in a real sense: here consumption of the flesh and blood of Jesus is called for. The use of the word 'consume' (= 'chew') instead of 'eat' reinforces the literal understanding.

(d) In 6.33, 35, 40, 47–51b life is promised to the one who believes; according to 6.51c–58 the gift of life is bound up with the sacramental consumption of the flesh and blood of Jesus, and there is no mention of faith at all.

(e) The offence taken by the disciples in v. 60 is sparked off, as v. 62 shows, by Jesus' claim to have come down from heaven; in other words, v. 60 is directly linked with v. 51ab; the eucharistic statements in vv. 51c–58 are passed over.

(f) Whereas the flesh in vv. 51c–58 is regarded as a saving gift, according to v. 63 it is of no use.

Verses 51c–58 thus stand out not only through a variety of differences from what has gone before, but also by a lack of anchorage in the context. The most probable explanation for this state of affairs is that vv. 51c–58 are an addition by the later revisers of the Gospel (Bultmann). Here their view corresponds to the view of the eucharist attested by Ignatius of Antioch as a 'medicine of immortality' or an 'antidote against dying' (Ignatius, Eph.20.2).

However, by no means all the problems of 6.22ff. are removed by the extraction of vv. 51c–58. In what follows those elements of the text will be identified which similarly have to be attributed to the revisers (cf. the bold type in the translation).

The account in vv. 22–25 of the renewed meeting between Jesus and the people is extraordinarily complicated and confusing: first of all it is impossible to understand how the next day the people can see something which had already happened the evening before (v. 22). Then it is striking that the people twice note the absence of the disciples (vv. 22 and 24ab). Furthermore, the phrase 'after the Lord had spoken the prayer of thanksgiving' (v. 23c) can be dispensed with in the description of the situation. Moreover it is surprising that the crowd which according to v. 22 knows that there was only one boat asks Jesus *when* – and not rather *how* – he has got to Capernaum (v. 25). Finally the note 'on the other side of the sea' in v. 25 seems superfluous in view of the mention of Capernaum in v. 24.

These difficulties resolve themselves if we see that the phrase 'The people . . . saw' is taken up again from v. 22a in v. 24a. Then it is natural to assume that vv. 22b–24a have been inserted later. If this assumption is correct, we will also have to attribute v. 24c (which presupposes v. 23a) and probably also 'on the other side of the sea' in v. 25 to the revisers. The interest pursued with these expansions is clear: v. 22b emphasizes the reality of the walking on the sea for the reader. Verse 23a serves the same purpose: the people cannot come to Jesus before 'other boats' have arrived from Tiberias; i.e. in fact previously there was only one boat there. Verse 23b gives the feeding of the 5000 a eucharistic tone after the event ('speak the prayer of thanksgiving' is attested in Justin, *Apology* 66.1 as a stereotyped expression for the celebration of the eucharist) and thus points forward to vv. 51c–58.

Verse 27 disrupts the context; it has been inserted by the revisers as a preparation for the eucharistic section; cf. the resumption of the terms 'food' (v. 55), 'eternal life' (v. 54) and 'Son of man' (v. 53), and the parallel between 'will give' (future) and 'I will give' (v. 51c).

[39, 40c and 44c] In vv. 40 and 44 the phrase 'and I will raise him up at the last day' is so clearly lame (change of subject) that it almost begs to be seen as a subsequent elaboration, all the more so as the notion of an eschatological raising of the dead contradicts the realized eschatology of the evangelist (cf. on 5.24). This casts suspicion on the corresponding phrase in v. 39. Here, however, it is firmly bound up with the preceding sentence. Thus the whole of v. 39 must be an addition – a conclusion which is confirmed by the observation that in the present text the will of God mentioned in v. 38 is defined twice (vv. 39, 40).

[51c–58] The reasons for assuming this passage to be secondary have already been given above. Here it should additionally be pointed out that in v. 58 the revisers have evidently made an effort to interlock their addition with what has gone before by picking up terms and phrases from vv. 49–51b (cf. v. 58a with vv. 50a and 51a; v. 58b with v. 49 and v. 50b; v. 58c with v. 51b).

Redaction

The text freed from the additions of the revisers can now be considered by itself.

[22a, 24bd, 25*] These verses are a redactional transition: the people must now meet Jesus again so that the following conversation can develop. That in v. 26 Jesus does not respond to the question expressing the people's curiosity is hardly an indication that v. 25 has a basis in the tradition. Rather, the evangelist's Jesus often passes over superficial statements and questions from his conversation partners in order to get straight to the point (cf. e.g. 3.2f., 8.25; 12.34–36).

[26] This verse refers back to v. 24d and to vv. 11f., 14. The evangelist's distinctive understanding of the signs of Jesus is illustrated particularly clearly by the distinction between 'eating bread' and 'seeing signs'. In a way, for him the signs have two sides: on the one hand they are indications of the divine mystery of the person of Jesus; but on the other they can also be perceived as mere miracles. With regard to v. 26 that means that the people have seen only the external miracle (cf. v. 14), but have not grasped the deeper significance of the feeding (cf. v. 36). Verses 30–35 say what this consists in.

[28–29] These verses lead on to the demand for a sign in v. 30 (cf. the parallel between 'What should we do, to work the works . . .?' and 'What do you do . . .? What do you work?'). Here v. 29, in which all the following statements are already summed up, is formulated in a similar way to 5.24.

[30–35] Some regard this passage as the beginning of a discourse on the bread of life used by the evangelist; this is then assumed to be continued in vv. 41–51b or even in vv. 48–58. Not only the combination of 'see' and 'believe' in v. 30 (cf. v. 36; 20.29), which is hardly fortuitous, but above all the observation that the expression of the misunderstanding in v. 34 stands in the same relationship to vv. 32–33 as 4.15 ('Lord, give me this water') to 4.13f. tell against this assumption. The evangelist himself has thus composed the section. Against the background of the story of the manna in Ex. 16 and starting from a psalm quotation which has already been assimilated to v. 35 (Ps. 77.24 LXX: 'He [= God] gave them bread of heaven'; cf. Neh. 9.15; Wisdom 16.20), he discloses the real significance of the miraculous feeding: Jesus is the bread of life. Similarly, the evangelist later sees expressed in the healing of the blind man and the raising of Lazarus the truth that Jesus is the light of the world (cf. 9.5) or the resurrection and the life (cf. 11.25f.). Only the 'I am' saying in v. 35 is a saying from the tradition, for the motif of thirst no longer plays a role in what follows.

[36–38, 40ab] These verses expound v. 35 and thus additionally confirm that this saying derives from the tradition. The passage comes completely from the evangelist: v. 36 refers back to v. 26 (for 'see' and 'believe' cf. also v. 30); v. 37 interprets the 'come to me' (= 'believe') from v. 35; v. 38 has parallels in 4.34 and 5.30c. Verse 40ab (cf. v. 47) corresponds to 3.15f.; 5.24 and 11.25f.

[41–42] The 'murmuring' of the Jews is an allusion to the murmuring of the Israelites in connection with the miracle of the manna (cf. Ex. 16.2, 7, 8f., 12 LXX). The statement quoted in v. 41b has not occurred previously in this form, but arises from the combination of vv. 35 and 38. The objection of the 'Jews' in v. 42 corresponds to that of the 'Jerusalemites' in 7.27a: in both cases knowledge of Jesus' earthly origin allegedly contradicts his divine claim.

[43] This verse presupposes v. 41.

[44ab, 45] After v. 37, the theme of these verses is once again the 'come to me' from v. 35. Here v. 44ab is a saying from the tradition. That becomes clear from the fact that the evangelist reverses the original meaning of this saying by his interpretation in v. 45 (cf. Isa. 54.13): according to v. 44ab God *a priori* bars access to Jesus for certain people; according to v. 45 all who hear from the Father can believe.

[46] This verse corresponds to 1.18.

[47] This is probably the most pregnant expression of the message of the evangelist. With a reference back to v. 40, it introduces the conclusion of the discourse.

[48–51b] These verses round off the section (v. 48 = v. 35b; for v. 49 cf. v. 31; for v. 50 cf. the similarly present formulation in v. 33; v. 51a = v. 41b). Here the truth expressed without an image in vv. 40 and 47 is expressed metaphorically once again by the adoption of the bread metaphor from vv. 31–35.

[59] This verse refers back to v. 24. As in 1.28 and 8.20 the note about place stands at the end.

Yield: vv. 22–51b*, 59 are a composition by the evangelist. Only the revelation saying in v. 35 and the saying v. 44ab can be identified as independent traditions.

Tradition

[35] In form the 'I am' saying resembles the sayings 8.12 and 14.6, both similarly sayings from the tradition, and in content 7.37b–38a. It promises the believer the overcoming of earthly mortality, in a terminology which is common above all in Jewish wisdom literature but also in eschatological texts. Cf. e.g. Sirach 24.21 ('Whoever eats of me [= wisdom] always hungers for me, and whoever drinks of me always thirsts for me') and Isa. 49.10 ('they will neither hunger nor thirst . . .'); see also Matt. 5.6; Rev. 7.16.

[44ab] This is a saying of Jesus which gives an answer to the problem that the Christian message is not accepted by everyone.

Historical

[35] This saying is inauthentic; Jesus did not understand himself as a bringer of salvation.

[44ab] This does not come from Jesus. Rather, as an answer to the problem of unbelief (of the Jews) the saying proves to be a product of the (Johannine) community.

The addition by the revisers in vv. 51c–58 presupposes the eucharistic cult after Easter and for that reason alone cannot have preserved any authentic sayings of Jesus.

John 6.60–71: The falling away of many disciples and Peter's confession

60 *Now many of his disciples heard it and said, 'This is a hard speech. Who can listen to it?'* 61a *But because Jesus knew in himself that his disciples were murmuring about it,* b *he said to them, 'Does this cause offence to you?* 62 *What then if you see the Son of man ascending where he was before?* 63a *It is the spirit that gives life, the flesh is of no avail.* b *The words that I have spoken to you are spirit and life.* 64a *But there are some of you who do not believe.'*

b **For Jesus knew from the beginning who those were who did not believe, and who would deliver him up.** 65 **And he said, 'This is why I have told you that no one can come to me unless it is granted him by the Father.'**

66 *From this time many of his disciples went back and no longer went around with him.*

67 *Then* Jesus said *to the twelve, 'Do* you *also wish to go away?'* 68 Simon Peter answered *him, 'Lord, to whom shall we go? You have words of eternal life,* 69 *and we have come to believe and have come to know,* You are the *Holy One* of God.' 70 Jesus answered them, 'Did I not choose you twelve? And one of you is a devil.' 71 He meant Judas the (son) of Simon Iscariot, for he, one of the twelve, was to deliver him up.

Later revision

As emerges from the following observations, vv. 64b–65 have probably been inserted by the revisers (J. Becker): (a) v. 64b is a doublet of v. 71 and robs it of its point. (b) 'And he said' in v. 65 stands in isolation. (c) Verse 65 quotes 6.44ab but completely leaves out of account the reinterpretation of this saying made in 6.45. (d) The theological tendency expressed in vv. 64b–65 also proves in other sections to be a mark of later revision: unbelief is understood as divine predestination (cf. 10.1–18, 26–29; 17).

Verses 64b–65 are the first addition by a group of revisers who evidently had a particular interest in the figure of Judas (cf. 12.4b, 6; 13.2–3, 10b–11, 18–19; 17.12b; 18.5c). Probably this group saw Judas, who delivered Jesus up, as the embodiment of a heretical group which was excluded from the Johannine community.

Redaction and tradition

Over and above v. 59, v. 60 refers to the sayings of Jesus in 6.32–51ab* ('this speech'). So the section is closely connected with the previous one. Now, however, the disciples of Jesus appear; they have not had a role since 6.22a.

[60] The offence felt by many disciples corresponds to that felt by the Jews in vv. 41f.; it is sparked off by the claim made by Jesus to have come down from heaven (vv. 47–51b).

[61a] On the basis of his omniscience (cf. on 1.42) Jesus knows what the disciples are discussing among themselves. 'Murmuring' refers back to the same word in vv. 41 and 43. This makes the behaviour of the disciples explicitly parallel to that of the Jews.

[61b–62] The 'ascending' corresponds to the 'descending' (= 'coming down') which had been mentioned in 6.33, 41f., 50f. If the revelation of the heavenly origin of Jesus is already offensive to the disciples, then they must be even more shaken by his return to heavenly glory. For this return takes place through his death on the cross.

[63] The antithesis between spirit and flesh which appears abruptly indicates that the evangelist is quoting a saying from the tradition in v. 63a (cf. e.g. Gal. 5.16f.; 6.8; Rom. 2.28f.; 8.1–17; see also on 3.6). In the redactional context this means that knowledge of Jesus' 'fleshly' origin (cf. v. 42) may not affect his claim (cf. 7.28f.), nor is it relevant for the question of salvation. Rather, spirit and life disclose themselves exclusively in Jesus' revelation of himself (v. 63b; cf. 5.24; 11.25f.).

[64a] By virtue of his clairvoyant capacities (cf. v. 61a), Jesus can see into the disciples.

[66] The Synoptics do not report a split in the circle of disciples and a falling away of many. Possibly here the evangelist is projecting back into the life of Jesus a corresponding event from the history of his community. At all events, we can easily

imagine that a number of Jewish Christians turned their backs on the community when its members were excluded from the synagogue association (cf. 9.22; 12.42; see also 16.2).

[67–69] These verses have been formulated on the basis of the Z account of Peter's confession (cf. above the introductory remarks to the analysis of 6.1–21). Here the closeness to Matt. 16.15f. is greatest (see the agreements in double under-lining; but cf. also Mark 8.29; Luke 9.20). In this scene the 'twelve' appear for the first time in the Gospel of John. As the evangelist has little interest in the fact that there are twelve disciples (as well as vv. 70f. cf. elsewhere only 20.24), the mention of them will be explicable from the use of Z. Otherwise the evangelist has strongly assimilated the scene to the context which he has created. Thus the talk about 'going away' presupposes v. 66, and the phrase 'you have words of eternal life' refers back to v. 63b.

[70–71] The word 'choose', which is not used elsewhere by the Fourth Evangelist, the emphasis that there are twelve disciples, the announcement of the delivering up which is premature by comparison with 13.21c, and the fact that according to 13.27a Satan enters into Judas only at the Last Supper suggest that these verses, too, have been formulated on the basis of Z. Accordingly in Z the designation of *Peter* as Satan (cf. Mark 8.33; Matt. 16.23) has passed over to Judas.

Yield: the section has been composed by the evangelist using Peter's confession from the tradition and the individual saying v. 63a.

Historical

Verse 63a does not go back to Jesus since the opposition between flesh and spirit was not a subject of his preaching.

For Peter's confession cf. on Mark 8.27–30.

John 7.1–13: Jesus' secret journey to Jerusalem for the Feast of Tabernacles

1 *And after this Jesus went about in Galilee; for he would not go about in Judaea, because the Jews sought to kill him. 2 Now the feast of the Jews, the (Feast of) Tabernacles, was near. 3 Then his brothers said to him, 'Depart hence, and go into Judaea, that your disciples (there) may also see the works you are doing. 4a For no one does anything in secret if he seeks to be known openly. b If you do these things, reveal yourself to the world.' 5 For not even his brothers believed in him. 6 Then Jesus says to them, 'My time has not yet come, but your time is always here. 7 The world cannot hate you, but it hates me because I testify of it that its works are evil. 8 Go up to the feast yourselves! I am not going up to this feast, for my time is not yet fulfilled.'*

9 *And after he had said this, he remained in Galilee. 10 But after his brothers had gone up to the feast, he also went up, not publicly but as in secret. 11 Now the Jews sought him at the feast, and*

said, 'Where is he?' 12 And there was much muttering about him among the multitudes. Some said,
'He is a good man,' but others said, 'No, he is leading the people astray.' 13 However, no one spoke
openly of him for fear of the Jews.

Redaction and Tradition

The Feast of Tabernacles constitutes a major section which extends from 7.1f. to 10.21; it
ends with the mention of the Feast of the Dedication of the Temple in 10.22. The present
passage, 7.1–13, forms the prelude: Jesus goes up to Jerusalem in secret. A section then
begins in 7.14 which deals with extended discussions between Jesus and the Jews. Here the
constant presence of Jesus in the temple is evidently presupposed from 7.14,25 to 8.59.
7.14–8.59 accordingly comprise a regular 'temple controversy'. This is in turn divided up
temporally with rough strokes: 7.14, 25–36 presuppose the middle of the feast, 7.37–8.59 the
last day of the feast as a background. For lack of any further indication of time, the healing of
the blind man (9.1–41; 10.19–21) also seems to take place on the same day. But from 9.1 on
the evangelist might finally have lost sight of the Feast of Tabernacles.

[1] This is a redactional transition: at first Jesus remains in Galilee, where he has
been since 6.1. That the Jews are attempting to kill Jesus has been known since 5.18
(cf. 7.19,20; see later 8.37, 40, 59; 10.31; 11.53, etc.).

[2] This verse corresponds to 2.13; 11.55.

[3] The brothers take offence that since 6.1 Jesus has demonstrated his power,
which has just been shown (in the walking on the sea and) in the feeding of the 5,000,
exclusively in the secluded Galilee. They think that such works will have the desired
success only if they are done in Judaea and if the disciples (there, cf. 2.23; 3.26; 4.1)
see them. (Incidentally, in connection with the last miracle performed by Jesus in
Jerusalem [5.1ff.] no disciples were mentioned as eye-witnesses.) Therefore they ask
him to transfer his activity wholly to Judaea and thus call for precisely what Jesus
according to v. 1 does not want to do.

[4] With the terms 'in secret'/ 'openly', the saying in v. 4a cited by the brothers
as the reason for their request introduces a pair of opposites which will be significant
in what follows (cf. 7.10, 13, 26; 8.59). Its basis is probably a general wisdom
sentence (cf. Mark 4.22 par.; Matt. 10.26/Luke 12.2). By contrast, v. 4b betrays its
redactional character by its reference back to v. 3 (cf. also 14.22).

[5] This is an incidental remark which describes as unbelief the request by the
brothers which is wholly orientated on outward effect. The characterization of the
brothers as 'unbelievers' is not an invention of the evangelist: Mark 3.21, 31–35 also
reflects the tradition that the relationship between Jesus and his family was a
strained one.

[6] Verse 6a corresponds to 2.4; 7.8, 30; 8.20: the point in time determined by God
to reveal himself to the world (v. 4b) has not yet come. By contrast, the time of the
brothers who represent unbelief is not determined (and *therefore* is 'always here').

[7] The 'world', the scene recommended by the brothers for public demonstrations of power (v. 4), is in reality the subject of the hatred directed against Jesus. Jesus' remarks contain a sharper condemnation of the brothers than appears at first sight: if the world cannot hate them, this is because (as they have proved by their 'worldly' request in vv. 3f.) they are themselves of the world (thus also the train of thought in the later insertion 15.19a). But if they are of the world, they themselves belong with those who hate Jesus and whose works he unmasks as evil.

[8] This verse rounds off Jesus' answer, picking up v. 6a.

[9] This verse forms the expected conclusion of the discussion with the brothers: by remaining in Galilee, Jesus acts in accordance with what he has said in vv. 6–8.

[10] It is all the more surprising that he then follows his brothers after all. We can hardly assume that the point of time which according to vv. 6, 8 is still outstanding has now come. For the time of Jesus is fulfilled only with 13.1ff., and moreover Jesus had not said that he was not yet going to the feast, but rather that he was not going at all (v. 8).The evangelist must have deliberately shaped this contradiction between Jesus' announcement and what he actually does – not to show that Jesus is clever enough to avoid the burdensome company of the unbelieving brothers by a lie, but to make it clear that Jesus acts in a sovereign way and does not allow himself to be constrained by human wishes (cf. similarly 2.4). This is emphasized by the fact that Jesus does not travel to Jerusalem publicly (as the brothers wanted), but incognito.

[11] This verse directs attention to those who are assembled in Jerusalem to share in the feast. That they seek Jesus and do not find him is hardly to be understood (as in 11.56) as meaning that Jesus has not yet come. Rather, his presence is already presupposed. So the verse serves as an illustration and reinforcement of Jesus' incognito (v. 10).

[12] The description of various views about Jesus also occurs in 7.40–43; 9.16; 11.36f.; 12.29; the motif of leading astray additionally corresponds to 7.47.

[13] Strictly speaking, this verse means that the Jews do not dare to speak publicly about Jesus for fear of themselves ('for fear of the Jews' = 19.38; 20.19; cf. 9.22). This makes particularly clear the broad gulf between the Johannine community and the Jews. The further this community distances itself from the Jews, the more closely they come together for it.

Yield: the scene is a composition shaped by the evangelist using individual elements from the tradition.

Historical

In so far as the saying Mark 4.22 shimmers through v. 4a, it is an irony of history that this saying appears in the Fourth Gospel in the mouths of the brothers of Jesus, who are described as unbelieving.

Thus the only historical reminiscence within an otherwise wholly fictitious scene is the unbelief of the brothers of Jesus mentioned in the redactional remark in v. 5. The brothers in fact repudiated Jesus during his lifetime and regarded him as crazy (cf. on Mark 3.21).

John 7.14, 25–36: In the middle of the feast: discussions about where Jesus has come from and where he is going

14 *Now when the feast was already half over, Jesus went up into the temple and taught.* 25 *Then some of the people of Jerusalem said, 'Is not this the man whom they seek to kill? 26 And look, he is speaking openly, and they are saying nothing to him! Can it be that the authorities have really come to know that this is the Christ? 27 Yet we know where this man comes from; but when the Christ comes, no one knows where he is from.' 28 Then Jesus cried as he taught and spoke in the temple, 'Indeed you know me, and you know where I am from. Yet I have not come of my own accord; but he who sent me is truthful, (and) him you do not know. 29 I know him, for I am from him, and he has sent me.' 30 Then they sought to seize him; but no one laid hands on him, for his hour had not yet come.*

31 *Yet many of the people came to believe in him and said, 'When the Christ appears, will he perhaps do no more signs than this man has done?' 32 The Pharisees heard the people muttering this about him, and the chief priests and Pharisees sent servants to seize him. 33 Jesus then said, 'Yet a little while I am with you, and (then) I go to him who sent me. 34 You will seek me and you will not find me; and where I am you cannot come.' 35 Then the Jews said among themselves, 'Where will this man go that we shall not find him? Surely he will not go to the Dispersion (Diaspora) among the Greeks and teach the Greeks? 36 What is this word that he said, "You will seek me and will not find me; and where I am you cannot come"?'*

Later 'revision'

The section 7.15–24 has already been translated and analysed after ch. 5. The most important reasons for the thesis that in the canonical text 7.15–24 is in the wrong place and originally followed 5.47 are: (a) While the connection between 7.15 and 7.14 is smooth, 7.15–24 *as a whole* interrupt the connection between 7.14 and 7.25. (b) 7.19–24 continue the dispute sparked off by the healing of the sick man on the sabbath, especially the dispute over the significance of Moses and the scriptures (5.45b–47), and do so as if this were an event which had been described shortly beforehand and was still topical. Such a reference extending back across ch. 6 seems improbable. (c) The question of the people, 'Who is seeking to kill you?' (7.20b), stands in contradiction to 7.25 ('Is not this the man whom they seek to kill?'); by contrast, the intention of the Jews to kill Jesus is mentioned in 5.18.

Since on the one hand there is no reason for a deliberate postponement of the section to this point, and on the other 7.15 follows well after 7.14, it seems likely that 7.15–24 stood on a leaf which had fallen out of the evangelist's manuscript. The revisers sought an indication of its original location and because of the occurrence of the word 'teach' in 7.14 and the word 'teaching' in 7.16 found it between 7.14 and 7.25.

Redaction and tradition

The section 7.14, 25–36 consists of two scenes (vv. 14, 25–30 and vv. 31–36) which are held together by the note of time in v. 14 (middle of the feast). They show a parallel structure: indication of situation (v. 14/v. 31a); statement by the hearers (vv. 25–27/v. 31b); Jesus' answer (vv. 28f./vv. 33f.); concluding reaction from the hearers (vv. 30/35f.). Here the question where Jesus comes from stands at the centre of the first scene and the question where he is going at the centre of the second. Verse 32 prepares for the following section 7.37–52. For the embedding of 7.14, 25–36 in the wider context cf. the introduction to 7.1–13.

[14] The note about the advanced stage of the feast marks off the section from what has gone before: only in the middle of the feast does Jesus lift his incognito (v. 10), now to teach publicly in the temple (cf. 6.59; 7.28, 35; 8.20; 18.20).

[25–26] The people of Jerusalem wonder at the contradiction that Jesus can teach publicly (v. 14), although he is to be killed (cf. 5.16, 18; 7.19; 7.1). (The opposition 'openly'/ 'in secret' was already significant in vv. 4 and 10, cf. v. 13.) The only explanation that they have for it is that the authorities have undergone a radical change of mind (for the formulation cf. 9.27). However, if this supposition does not seem erroneous from the start, it is finally proved to be false by v. 32 and 7.48 (but cf. 12.42). But if a sudden change of mind on the part of the authorities is to be ruled out as a reason for the unmolested appearance of Jesus, then the talk of the people becomes an indirect testimony (for the reader) to the powerful sovereignty of Jesus who himself determines the beginning and end of his activity.

[27] Whereas v. 26 left it open whether the people of Jerusalem themselves recognized the Christ in Jesus, it now becomes clear that this is not the case. Their knowledge of Jesus' origin cannot be reconciled with their notions of the Christ. Rather, in their view the origin of the Christ will be unknown. (This argument probably reproduces an objection made against Christians from the Jewish side; cf. Justin, *Dialogue* 8.4; but see 7.41b–42.) Verses 28f. serve to refute this objection and show that the statement by the people of Jerusalem that no one knows the origin of the Christ (v. 27b) is an unconscious testimony against themselves.

[28–29] 'As he taught in the temple' takes up the same note of the situation from v. 14. Jesus answers the talk of the town in vv. 25–27, although he has not been addressed (cf. 4.34; 6.43; 6.61; 7.16, 33). The drift of the statement is worth noting. Jesus begins with a concession to the people of Jerusalem: he does not question that they know of his origin, namely from Galilee (cf. 7.41). However, he then declares this knowledge to be information wholly on a superficial level which does not at all grasp the real mystery of his person (cf. 8.14, 19); the only important thing is that he has been sent by God. (That God in addition is 'truthful' is an incidental notion which as in 8.26 obscures the real argument.) And finally Jesus turns the tables: *God* is the one whom they do not know (cf. 8.19). So all their speculations about where

Jesus comes from and how by contrast things must be with the Christ (v. 27) are merely empty chatter.

[30] This verse rounds off the first scene: the people of Jerusalem respond to Jesus' verbal attack with physical force. The first part of the verse corresponds almost word for word with 7.44 (cf. 10.39), the second corresponds to 8.20b (cf. 2.4; 7.6,8). The Jews *cannot* seize Jesus because his hour has not yet come.

[31] The remark that 'many of the people' came to believe (v. 31a; cf. 2.23; 4.39; 8.30; 10.42; 11.45; 12.11, 42) follows very abruptly after the aggressive reaction of the inhabitants of Jerusalem (v. 30), as does the recourse to the signs through which (as in 2.23; 10.42; 11.45; 12.11) faith is brought about (v. 31b). The verse merely serves to give an occasion for v. 32.

[32] The focus shifts to the Jewish authorities who, having had their attention drawn to Jesus by the gossip of the people, send servants to arrest him – a plan which, as v. 30 has emphasized shortly beforehand, cannot possibly succeed (yet). (A little later 7.45 reports the failure of their efforts.)

[33] The link to v. 32 is remarkable. In the face of the preparations by the Jewish authorities to kill him, Jesus seems to be nothing but a passive object. But then Jesus makes it clear that *he* is the one who determines how long he continues to dwell on earth, and *he* determines when it is time to return to the Father. 'Basically it is not at all *their* work if they do away with him, but *his* action' (Bultmann). For v. 33a ('yet a little while'), which refers to the remaining time of the earthly activity of Jesus, cf. 12.35; 13.33 (explicit reference back to 7.33) and 14.19. In what follows reference is often made back to Jesus' 'going away' (v. 33b; cf. 8.14, 21f.; 13.33, 36; 14.4f., 28).

[34] Once Jesus has returned to God, it will be too late for the Jews; then they will finally have forfeited their opportunity to 'find' Jesus (cf. 8.21).

[35] The Jews misunderstand Jesus' testimony about his departure to God as an indication of a journey to the Greeks (for the motif of misunderstanding cf. on 2.20). However, in so doing, at the same time they express a truth without knowing it: as soon as Jesus can no longer be found by the Jews he will in fact have gone to the Greeks (mission to the Gentiles).

[36] The word-for-word repetition of v. 34 as a question reinforces the impression of ignorance on the part of the Jews, who are imprisoned in their misunderstanding and closed to the testimony of Jesus.

Yield: vv. 14, 25–36 are a double scene shaped by the evangelist.

Historical

The section is not based on any preformed traditions. Accordingly the historical yield is nil.

John 7.37–52: Controversies on the last day of the feast

37a *On the last, the great day of the feast, Jesus stood there and cried,* b 'If anyone is thirsty, let him come to me; and let him drink 38a who believes in me. b *As the scripture has said,* "Rivers of living water shall flow from within him."'

39a **Now this he said about the Spirit, which those who came to faith in him were to receive. b For (the) Spirit was not yet there, because Jesus had not yet been glorified.**

40 *Now (some) of the people heard these words and said, 'This is truly the prophet.'* 41a *Others said, 'This is the Christ.'* b *But (others) said, 'Does the Christ come from Galilee?* 42 *Has not the scripture said that the Christ comes from the seed of David, and from Bethlehem, the town where David was?'* 43 *So a division arose among the people over him.* 44 *And some of them wanted to seize him, but no one laid hands on him.*

45 *Then the servants came to the chief priests and Pharisees, and these said to them, 'Why did you not bring him?'*

46 *The servants answered, 'Never has a man spoken like this!'*

47 *Then the Pharisees answered them, 'Have you too been led astray?* 48 *Have any of the authorities come to believe in him, or of the Pharisees?* 49 *But this crowd, which does not know the law – they are accursed.'*

50 *Nicodemus, who had gone to him before (and) who was one of them, says to them,* 51 *'Does our law judge a man without first giving him a hearing and coming to know what he does?'*

52 *They answered and said to him, 'Are you from Galilee too? Search, and see that no prophet arises from Galilee!'*

Later revision

Verse 39 identifies the 'rivers of living water' (v. 38) with the spirit which is present only after the glorification of Jesus (cf. 20.22). This is probably an addition. (a) Verse 39 interrupts the connection between vv. 37f. and v. 40. (b) All in all, 7.37–52 serve to illustrate the increasing conflict between Jesus and the Jews; v. 39 introduces a delaying element which seems out of place in the dramatic scene. (c) In a sense v. 38b already represents an interpretation, albeit put in the mouth of Jesus himself: the invitation in vv. 37b–38a is the fulfilment of a word of scripture. That this 'interpretation' is in turn subjected to an interpretation is at least remarkable. (d) Only v. 39 shows itself to be interested in the *content* of the saying vv. 37b–38a; from v. 40 this no longer plays a role, but only the *claim* of Jesus which is articulated in it (cf. similarly 8.12, 13–19). (e) If the spirit is really meant by the water but the spirit is not yet there, the invitation to 'drink' makes no sense in the situation which is presupposed. (f) The invitation to come and drink actively (vv. 37f.) is slightly out of keeping with the passive 'receive' (v. 39). (g) As in the additions 15.26; 16.7, Jesus is presupposed as the giver of the spirit, whereas according to the evangelist the Father sends the spirit (14.16f., 26).

Redaction and tradition

The section comprises three closely related scenes. Verses 37–38 introduce the account of the last day of the feast with a saying of Jesus. Verses 40–44 depict the split reaction of the people to this call, and vv. 45–52 in conclusion direct attention to the Pharisees and chief priests. For the position of 7.37–52 in the wider context cf. the introduction to 7.1–13.

[37a] The note of time 'on the last, the great day of the feast' (cf. 19.31) marks the section off from what has gone before. It is not said explicitly that the temple is again presupposed to be the scene, but that is a matter of course. For it would make no sense if on the last day of the festival, which was evidently particularly important, Jesus were to be in a less conspicuous place than in the middle of the feast.

[37b–38] These verses contain the only saying spoken by Jesus in this section. Here vv. 37b–38a seem to be a saying of Jesus from the tradition. It is an invitation to seek salvation only in Jesus. (E.g. Prov. 9.5; Sirach 24.19; 51.23f.; Matt. 11.28 are comparable.) Verse 38b, by contrast, represents an addition by the evangelist to this individual saying. With the quotation formula and the scriptural quotation (which cannot be demonstrated) he makes Jesus himself justify from scripture the claim which has been previously formulated.

[40–42] Jesus' words on the one hand evoke faith, but on the other doubt and repudiation (cf. 7.12; 11.36f.; 9.16; 12.29). The first of the two *positive* reactions (v. 40b) corresponds word for word with 6.14; the second (v. 41a) repeats a confession which occurs previously in this form only in the mouth of Philip (cf. 1.41; but see also 4.25). The *doubt* (vv. 41b–42) is sparked off by the question of the geographical origin (cf. 7.27) and bodily descent of Jesus (cf. similarly 6.42). It has already been said in the analysis of 7.27 that the reference to the origin of Jesus from Galilee is probably an objection which was in fact made to the messiahship of Jesus at the time of the evangelist.

[43] Cf. 9.16 and 10.19.

[44] This verse corresponds to 7.30a (cf. 10.39). The reason for the intrinsically unimaginable event (10.39, 'he *escaped* from their hands' differs) is to be supplied from 7.30b: 'for his hour had not yet come'. That in contrast to 7.30 there are only 'some' who want to seize Jesus takes into account the positive reaction of part of the people mentioned in vv. 40–41a.

[45] This verse takes up the thread of 7.32 and thus links the section with 7.14, 25–36. The servants sent by the Pharisees and chief priests return with their mission unfulfilled.

[46] The reason that the servants give for their failure emphasizes the power of Jesus: even Jesus' opponents come under the spell of the superhuman authority of his words. 7.30,44 show that the thought is in fact more of a spell than merely being impressed by Jesus' words: although people want to seize Jesus, they do not. The

servants will be able to fulfil their task of arresting Jesus only when the time pre-destined by God, 'Jesus' hour', has come (cf. 18.12). But even then – despite being supported by a Roman cohort (cf. 18.3) – they will fall back before Jesus and finally seize him only because he voluntarily offers himself to them (cf. 18.8, 11b).

[47] The suspicion expressed in the form of a question that the servants could have been 'led astray' by Jesus like many of the people, whose whispering the Pharisees have heard (cf. 7.31f.), corresponds to the opinion which according to 7.12 part of the crowd had formed about Jesus.

[48] The second question asked by the Pharisees is rhetorical – as opposed to the first, which is meant seriously (v. 47). Those who have not yet grasped it finally learn here that the supposition cherished by the inhabitants of Jerusalem, that the authorities could have recognized the Christ in Jesus (7.26b), has no basis. On the contrary, the Pharisees and high priests will soon pass a death sentence on Jesus (cf. 11.47, 53). Later the cry 'Crucify him!' will first ring out from the very mouths of the chief priests (cf. 19.6).

[49] The Pharisees think that belief in Jesus is incompatible with the law; they claim to be its best interpreters. So anyone who does not adopt the same attitude of repudiation of Jesus as they do does not know the law and is therefore accursed. But the reader knows that in reality they are the ones who do not know the law (cf. 5.46f.). So the curse falls back on them (cf. on v. 52).

[50] There is only one exception in this gathering of the enemies of Jesus: Nicodemus, to whose appearance in ch. 3 there is an explicit reference. (In what follows he causes what amounts to another 'division', cf. v. 43.)

[51] Nicodemus has to remind the self-assured Pharisees of a general principle (cf. Deut. 1.16f.; 17.4) in that very law which they allegedly know so well (v. 49) – an almost humorous moment in a scene which, however, already falls under the shadow of coming disaster: in 11.53 the high priests and Pharisees will in fact condemn Jesus to death without giving him a hearing.

[52] The Pharisees stifle Nicodemus' objection and for their part refer him to scripture (for their objection cf. vv. 41b–42: again Jesus' origin speaks against him). But in so doing they again (cf. on v. 49) only confirm what Jesus has accused the Jews as a whole of in 5.39ff. ('search' occurs only in 5.39 and 7.52), and therefore in both instances it is the case that their accuser is Moses, in whom they have hoped (5.45).

Yield: the section 7.37f., 40–52 is a free composition by the evangelist, using a saying from the tradition in vv. 37b–38a.

Historical

Verses 37b–38a do not go back to Jesus, as he did not require any faith in himself.

John 8.12–20: Controversy over the legitimation of Jesus

12a *Then again Jesus spoke to them and said,* b 'I am the light of the world; he who follows me will not walk in darkness, but will have the light of life.' 13 *The Pharisees then said to him, 'You are bearing witness to yourself; your witness is not true.'* 14 *Jesus answered and said to them, 'Even if I do bear witness to myself, my witness is true, for I know where I have come from and where I am going to, but you do not know where I come from or where I am going to.* 15 *You judge according to the flesh, I judge no one.* 16 *But if I judge, my judgment is true, for I am not alone, but I and the Father who has sent me (belong together).* 17 *In your law it is written, "The witness of two men is true";* 18 *I bear witness to myself, and the Father who sent me bears witness to me.'* 19 *Then they said to him, 'Where is your Father?' Jesus answered, 'You know neither me nor my Father. If you knew me, you would know my Father also.'* 20a *These words he spoke at the treasury, as he taught in the temple.* b *And no one seized him, because his hour had not yet come.*

Redaction and tradition

For the place of the section in the context cf. the introductory remarks on 7.1–13.

[12a] The link with the previous section is quite careless: Jesus is speaking to the Pharisees (cf. v. 13) from 7.45–52 as if he is suddenly present in their gathering; but in fact v. 20 presupposes that the Pharisees have meanwhile gone to him in the temple.

[12b] The evangelist has taken this self-contained revelation saying from the tradition. This emerges from the fact that its content has no significance for the legal dispute which follows. Rather, the saying could be replaced by another without any problem.

[13–14] In 5.31 Jesus himself had used the principle cited by the Pharisees (v. 13). Here he rejects it (v. 14). However, the contradiction is only formal, since indirectly God is also claimed as a witness in v. 14 (cf. the direct reference to the Father in 5.36f.). For the ignorance of the Jews over Jesus' origin cf. 7.27; 9.29f.

[15] There are plenty of examples in the Fourth Gospel of the Jews 'judging according to the flesh' (cf. 5.18; 7.15, 20; 6.15, 41f.; 7.31, 42), most recently in v. 13. (Incidentally, the statement that Jesus does not judge was probably the reason for the insertion of the pericope about the adulteress, John 7.53–8.11, in immediate proximity to this section; cf. the introduction, point 2.)

[16] This verse says the same thing as 5.30, partly with other words.

[17] For the term 'your law' by which Jesus dissociates himself from it cf. 7.19; 10.34. The principle quoted is a free rendering of Deut. 17.6 or Deut. 19.15.

[18] This verse corresponds to 5.36b–37a.

[19] For Jesus' charge that the Jews do not know God cf. 5.37b; 7.28 and 8.55. For the notion that God is known in Jesus cf. 14.9.

[20] The subsequent location of the scene (v. 20a) corresponds to 1.28 and 6.59. Verse 20b corresponds word for word with 7.30.

Yield: with the exception of v. 12b, the section is a creation of the evangelist.

Historical

The 'I am' saying in v. 12b with the universal claim which it expresses is unthinkable in the mouth of the historical Jesus.

John 8.21–29: Jesus' witness about his departure

21 *Then he said to them again, 'I am going away, and you will seek me, and you will die in your sin(s). Where I am going, you cannot come.' 22 Then said the Jews, 'Will he kill himself, since he says, "Where I am going, you cannot come"?' 23 And he said to them, 'You are from below, I am from above; you are of this world, I am not of this world. 24 Now I have said to you, "You will die in your sins". For if you do not believe that I am, you will die in your sins.' 25a Then they said to him, 'Who are you?' b Jesus said to them, 'Why do I speak to you at all? 26 I have much to say about you and to judge; but he who sent me is truthful, and I speak to the world what I have heard from him.' 27 They did not know that he was speaking to them of the Father. 28a Then Jesus said to them, 'When you have lifted up the Son of man, then you will know that I am (he), b and that I do nothing of my own accord, but as the Father has taught me – so I speak. 29 And he who sent me is with me. He has not left me alone, for I always do what is pleasing to him.'*

Redaction and tradition

The controversy on the last day of the Feast of Tabernacles (cf. 7.37) continues (for the embedding of the section in the wider context cf. the introductory remarks on 7.1–13). The scene also remains the same: like the one which precedes it (8.12–20) and the one which follows it (8.30–58), this controversy takes place in the temple (8.20 does not presuppose that Jesus leaves the temple; that happens only in 8.59). That Jesus is now no longer specifically talking with the Pharisees (8.13) but generally with the Jews (v. 22) does not mean much. For at other points too it proves that the two terms are virtually interchangeable for the evangelist (cf. 9.13–17, 18)

[21] As in 8.12a, 'again' marks the beginning of a new section. The saying of Jesus which points forward to his return to the Father, i.e. to his death, largely corresponds with the prophecy of disaster in 7.33f. However, the 'you will not find me' there is here replaced by the Old Testament phrase 'you will die in your sins' (cf. Deut. 24.16; Ezek. 3.19; 18.24; Prov. 24.9). This expresses more strongly the threatening aspect of the announcement of judgment.

[22] The misunderstanding of the Jews stands in the same relationship to v. 21 as 7.35 to 7.33f. In 7.35 the Jews put the stupid question whether in what he says about

his departure Jesus means a journey to the Diaspora; here they wonder whether he is announcing suicide. This misunderstanding is not only foolish but also markedly malicious, as the quotation of v. 21b in v. 22b shows. For according to the Jewish view of the time suicides went to hell. And of course the Jews could not follow the supposed suicide Jesus there, nor did they want to. For the motif of misunderstanding in general cf. on 2.20.

[23] In two terse antitheses Jesus points to the unbridgeable abyss which gapes between him and the Jews. This is one of the most pointed anti-Jewish formulations in the Gospel of John. For the opposition 'of this world'/'not of this world' cf. Jesus' answer to Pilate in 18.36.

[24] Verse 24a refers explicitly back to v. 21. The absolute 'I am' which is indicated in v. 24b as the content of faith (cf. v. 28a) is probably meant to sum up the overall content of the evangelist's christology: that the Father himself is present in the Son sent by God (cf. 1.18; 10.30; 14.9). But possibly at the same time there is an allusion to the absolute 'I am' which is often used in Isa. 40–55 to emphasize the uniqueness of God (cf. e.g. Isa. 43.10f.; 41.4; 48.12, etc.).

[25] The question in v. 25a serves, like 8.19a, as an illustration that despite Jesus' continuing activity of revelation and his invitation to believe, the Jews continue to be incomprehending; indeed, as Jesus will emphasize in 8.43, 47, they have to remain incomprehending. This is matched by the accusing yet resigned answer of Jesus in v. 25b.

[26] As in 7.28, the central idea (for this see the parallel formulations 3.11; 5.19; 8.28, 38, 40) is obscured by the statement about the truthfulness of God.

[27] This verse replaces a reply of the Jews to Jesus' statement in v. 26. The Jews do not understand that by the designation 'he who sent me' Jesus means God. Thus they confirm what Jesus has said about them in 8.19b.

[28a] Jesus begins to answer the question in v. 25a by alluding to his lifting up on the cross, through which his lifting up to God takes place (cf. 3.14). Only after the return of Jesus to the Father – and given the context that can only mean: once it is too late and the last chance has been missed – the truth about Jesus and thus at the same time the knowledge of their own lostness will dawn on the Jews. 'For then those who refuse faith now will not see him as the revealer but as the judge' (Bultmann). 'That I am (he)' here takes up the same formula, without a predicate, from v. 24 and at the same time is to be supplemented by v. 28a, 'that I am he (namely the Son of man)'.

[28b] The formulation 'not of my own accord but' is typical of the evangelist (cf. 5.30a; 7.28; 8.42); similarly the statement that Jesus speaks as the Father has taught him (cf. the parallels mentioned on v. 26).

[29] Verse 29a corresponds to 8.16b. The formulation that Jesus does 'what is pleasing to God' (v. 29b), which is unique in the Gospel of John in this form, takes the same line as the statement that Jesus 'does the will of God' (4.34; 5.30; 6.38)

Yield: the section is a creation of the evangelist.

The historical yield is nil.

John 8.30–59: The conclusion and climax of the dispute in the temple

30 *As he spoke this, many came to believe in him.* 31 *Jesus then said to the Jews who had believed him,* 'If you abide in my word, you are truly my disciples, 32 and you will know the truth, and the truth will make you <u>free</u>.'

33 *They answered him, 'We are the <u>seed of Abraham</u>, and have never been subject to anyone. How is it that you say, "You will become <u>free</u>"?'*

34 *Jesus answered them,* 'Amen, amen, I say to you, everyone who commits sin is a slave of sin. 35 *The slave does not abide in the house for ever; the son abides for ever.* 36 *Now if the son will make you free, you will be really free.* 37 *I know that you are the <u>seed of Abraham</u>; yet you seek to kill me, for my word finds no place in you.* 38 *I speak of what I have seen from the Father; so too do you: you do what you have heard from the <u>Father</u>.'*

39a *They answered and said to him,* 'Our <u>father</u> is <u>Abraham</u>.'

39b *Jesus says to them,* 'If you were <u>Abraham's</u> children, you would do the works of Abraham. 40 *But now you seek to kill me, a man who has told you the truth which he has heard from God. Abraham did not do this.* 41a *You do the works of your <u>father</u>.'*

41b *They said to him,* 'We were not born of fornication; we have one <u>Father, God</u>.'

42 *Jesus said to them,* 'If <u>God</u> were your Father, you would love me, for I proceeded and came forth from God; for I came not of my own accord, but he sent me. 43 *Why do you not understand my speech? Because you cannot hear my word.* 44a *You are of the father, (who is) the devil, and you want to do your father's desires.* b *He was a murderer from the beginning, and did not stand in the truth, because there is no truth in him.* c *When he speaks lies, he speaks from his own, for he is a liar and a father of lies.* 45 *But I – because I speak the truth, you do not believe me.* 46a *Which of you convicts me of sin?* b *If I speak the truth, why do you not believe me?* 47 *He who is of God hears the words of God; you do not hear because you are not of God.'*

48 *The Jews answered and said to him,* 'Are we not right in saying that you are a Samaritan and have a <u>demon</u>?'

49 *Jesus answered,* 'I have no <u>demon</u>; but I honour my Father, and you dishonour me. 50 *But I do not seek my glory; there is one who seeks (it) and (who) judges.* 51 *Amen, amen, I say to you,* <u>if anyone keeps my word, he will never see death</u>.'

52 *Then the Jews said to him,* 'Now we know that you have a demon. Abraham has died, and the prophets; and you say, "<u>If anyone keeps my word, he will never taste death</u>." 53 *Are you greater than our father Abraham, who died? And the prophets died! Whom do you make <u>yourself</u>?'*

54 *Jesus answered,* 'If I glorified <u>myself</u>, my glory would be nothing; it is my Father who glorifies me, of whom you say, "He is our Father," 55 *and you have not known him, but I know him. Were I to say, "I do not know him," I should be a liar like you; but I do know him and keep his word.* 56 *Abraham, your father, rejoiced that he was to <u>see</u> my day, and he <u>saw</u> it and was glad.'*

57 *Then the Jews said to him,* 'You are not yet fifty years old, and have you <u>seen</u> <u>Abraham</u>?'

58 *Jesus said to them,* 'Amen, amen, I say to you, before <u>Abraham</u> was, I am.'

59 *Then they took up stones to throw at him; but Jesus hid himself, and went out of the temple.*

Redaction and tradition

This passage forms the conclusion and climax to the temple controversy between Jesus and the Jews which extends from 7.14, 25 to 8.59 (see the introductory remarks on 7.1–13). As part of this controversy it is framed by the transition in v. 30 and the concluding note in v. 59 and thus is marked off more strongly from what follows than from what goes before. In the harsh confrontation between the Jews, who understand themselves as children of Abraham or of God but are immediately unmasked as children of the devil, and the pre-existent Son of God who overcomes death, the conflict which has been simmering since 2.13–22 and has been virulent since 5.16, 18 comes to a head; it will be surpassed in vehemence only when in chs. 18–19 the Jews bring about the execution of Jesus.

In shaping the dialogue in vv. 31–58 the evangelist follows a principle which largely makes a satisfactory division into sub-sections impossible. As the underlining in the translation shows, each time the Jews pick up word for word the previous statement made by Jesus and either take offence at it or reject it. Thereupon Jesus rejects the question or statement produced by the Jews as a rejoinder (similarly taking up word by word what has gone before) and thus causes them the next offence, etc. Thus discourse and counter-discourse (with the exception of vv. 42–47 and v. 48) are each time interlinked in the style of connections by key words. As the parts of the dialogue run on into each other in the way described, it is impossible to make a division anywhere. Only between vv. 42–47 and 48 can one see a break because the 'keyword connection' is missing. This produces two blocks of dialogue: vv. 31–47 focus on the theme that the Jews are children of Abraham, God and the devil; the theme of vv. 48–58 is that Jesus overcomes death as the real child of God who is pre-existent.

[30] This verse marks a break within the temple controversy. The evangelist inserts the note that many come to believe in Jesus often and in different contexts (cf. 2.23; 4.39; 7.31; 10.42; 11.45; 12.11, 42). But here it comes abruptly in view of the total incomprehension of the Jews in vv. 22, 25, 27. The evangelist requires the believing Jews only for a moment in order to make a link for vv. 31f. But it is not long before Jesus will declare that the faith mentioned here is worthless (cf. vv. 37ff., esp. vv. 45f.). In other words, subsequently this faith is unmasked as pseudo-faith or merely momentary assent (cf. 2.23–25).

[31a] This verse is the redactional introduction to vv. 31b–32, referring back to v. 30 which immediately precedes it.

[31b–32] This saying consisting of condition, consequence and two promises which build on each other is probably a saying of Jesus taken by the evangelist from the tradition.

The following observations support this: (a) the saying is self-contained and can be understood without its present context; (b) the theme of 'freedom' does not play a role in the Gospel of John or in the other Johannine writings (the only other instances of 'become/ be/make free' are those in vv. 33 and 36 which are dependent on v. 32; the word 'freedom' does not occur at all); (c) the theme of discipleship is not taken up again in the further course of the conversation. – The saying is an admonition and a promise to new members of the congregation and is part of initial community instruction (J. Becker).

In the framework of the evangelist's composition, the saying reaches its climax in the key word 'make free' of the second promise, which immediately sparks off the discussion about being children of Abraham.

[33] The Jews rightly understand that vv. 31b–32 describe them as slaves. In countering Jesus' remarks about freedom by reference to the fact that they are children of Abraham, they give Jesus occasion explicitly to deny both that they are free (v. 34–36) and that they are (true) children of Abraham (vv. 37–38).

[34] In the context this does not so much represent a general statement by Jesus about the connection between sin and lack of freedom but is *a priori* aimed at the Jewish conversation partners: *these* are the slaves of sin; the *sin* is the repudiation of Jesus. By contrast, the definition from the tradition which is probably used here (cf. Rom. 6.16f., 20) points to a connection in principle.

[35] This verse formulates a subsidiary notion which in a small parable excludes the 'slave' (= the Jews) from eternal saving communion with God.

[36] That here the subject of making free is 'the Son', whereas according to v. 32 it was the truth, matches Jesus' identification of himself with the truth in 14.6.

[37] Only now does Jesus take up the objection of the Jews that as descendants of Abraham they are free (v. 33). Evidently he recognizes their physical descent from Abraham. 'You seek to kill me' takes up word for word 5.18; 7.19f., 25; 7.1, 14. For 'my word finds no place in you' cf. 5.38a.

[38] Jesus outwardly puts his behaviour in parallel with that of the Jews; just as he does what he has seen from the Father (cf. 3.11; 5.19; 8.26, 40) so the Jews do what they have heard from the Father. That in both cases Jesus initially speaks of 'the Father' (and not of 'my Father' as opposed to 'your Father') is striking, for in the present confrontation a positive verdict on the Jews seems *a priori* improbable. It is therefore natural to suppose in the context that in the two cases Jesus does not mean one and the same Father. The further course of the conversation shows that this is a particularly clever idea of the evangelist: he makes Jesus reveal step by step the terrible truth about the origin of the Jews (v. 39b: Abraham is not the father of the Jews; v. 41a: the Jews have another father than Jesus has; v. 42: God is not their father; v. 44: their father is the devil).

[39a] The Jews rightly sense a concealed attack behind Jesus' saying in v. 38. Therefore once again (cf. v. 33b) they insist that Abraham is their father.

[39b] Jesus rejects the self-confident objection of the Jews in v. 39a by including it in an non-factual conditional clause (cf. similarly the adoption of v. 41b in v. 42): if it were as the Jews assert, their origin from Abraham would be reflected in their behaviour.

[40] But their murderous intent (cf. on v. 37) refutes their claim to be children of

Abraham. (For the motif that Jesus speaks what he has heard from the Father cf. above on v. 38.)

[41a] Rather, they do the works of *their* father – and now it becomes clear that he is *different* from the Father of Jesus.

[41b] The Jews again (cf. v. 39a) rightly understand these words as an attack. The evangelist now makes them bring out their strongest weapons and claim to be children of God in addition to emphasizing their descent from Abraham, because against this background the real origin of the Jews stands out all the more strongly.

[42] Jesus takes up the Jews' claim to be children of God and directly contradicts it ('If God *were* your father . . .'; cf. similarly v. 39b: 'If you *were* Abraham's children . . .'). If the Jews were children of God they would love the one sent by God. For the two 'for' sayings cf. 7.28b.

[43] Jesus' question about the reason for the repudiation of his message by his present opponents is at the same time the evangelist's question about the rejection of the Christian message by the Jews of his time. The answer is given immediately: not because they do not *want to* hear the word of Jesus but because they *cannot* hear it. (Finally from here on it becomes clear that Jesus' saying in vv. 31b–32, in so far as it was addressed to the Jews, was not meant seriously.) Verse 44 says inexorably what causes this inability.

[44] Finally Jesus resolves the more or less enigmatic remarks about the father of the Jews (vv. 38b, 41a): their father is the devil (v. 44a). It goes without saying that as his children the Jews share his properties (vv. 44b, c): the Jews are just realizing his 'murderous' nature towards Jesus (vv. 37, 40).

[45] The train of thought is worth noting: the reason for the unbelief of the Jews is that Jesus is telling the truth.

[46] The first of the two questions (v. 46a) is rhetorical: Jesus the Son of God is sinless and therefore cannot be convicted of any sin. The second (v. 46b) really goes back behind the answer which has already been given in v. 45.

[47] Jesus answers v. 46 himself: if only the one who is from God hears the words of God, then this cannot apply to the Jews, who are children of the devil (v. 44).

[48] The Jews can explain this frontal attack by Jesus only as a symptom of demonic possession (cf. 7.20; 10.20) and thus return the charge that they are children of the devil. As the suspicion that Jesus is a Samaritan (i.e. a member of the mixed people despised by the Jews and regarded as apostate), this is probably a reflection of contemporary Jewish polemic against Johannine Christianity, in which the mission to Samaria evidently played a special role (cf. 4.33–42).

[49–50] Jesus rejects the suspicion of demonic possession. Here the opposition 'I honour'/'you dishonour' recalls Jesus' saying in 5.23: 'Whoever does not honour the Son does not honour the Father who has sent him.' 'Seek glory' is a formulation sometimes used by the evangelist (cf. 5.44; 7.18 [twice]).

[51] As in vv. 31b–32, the evangelist suddenly introduces a word of promise from the tradition in order to open up a new theme.

[52] This revelation saying has an immediate result: the suspicion that Jesus is possessed by a demon, which in v. 48 has been expressed in the form of a question (albeit rhetorical), becomes a certainty for the Jews (cf. 10.20). For the saying (which they repeat almost word for word) provokes the question of the dignity of Jesus by comparison with that of Abraham and the prophets.

[53] This verse sums up this question (cf. the equivalent in 4.12). The concluding question, which takes offence that Jesus is 'making himself' something, corresponds to an accusation from the Jewish side which occurs repeatedly in the Gospel of John: cf. 5.18 and 10.33 (God); 19.7 (Son of God); 19.12 (king).

[54] Jesus takes up the key word 'yourself' and answers in the usual way: it is not to himself but to God that he owes his glory. The attached relative clause confirms once again that as children of the devil the Jews are wrong to appeal to God as father.

[55] It was already said in 7.28; 8.19 that the Jews do not 'know' God; the statement that by contrast Jesus 'knows' God occurred in 7.29. 'Liar' refers back to v. 44.

[56] The fact that despite vv. 39b, 41, 44 Jesus now designates Abraham father of the Jews either contains a sarcastic undertone ('Abraham, who is allegedly your father'), or as in v. 37 concedes only physical descent; alternatively, 'of whom you say' (as in v. 54) must be understood. The verse presupposes that in his lifetime Abraham was granted a view of the future.

According to Gen. 17.17 Abraham 'laughed' when the birth of a child was promised to him at the age of one hundred and Sarah at the age of ninety. Possibly the 'rejoicing' of Abraham mentioned here is a palliative interpretation of that scornful laughter, at the same time tailored to Jesus.

The one to whom the Jews appeal against Jesus (vv. 33, 37) in truth bears witness against them and for Jesus (cf. 5.45).

[57] The Jews cannot understand these words. As in other cases (cf. on 2.20), they are victims of a misunderstanding: how can Jesus have seen Abraham, who has already been dead for many hundreds of years?

[58] Jesus' majestic answer mocks this calculation. The verse is the crown of the whole section: Jesus speaks of his pre-existence, his eternal being with God (cf. 1.1f.). As the one who already 'is' in the beginning (cf. Ex. 3.14), of course Jesus also 'is' before Abraham.

[59a] However, in the eyes of the Jews this claim is the height of blasphemy (cf. Lev. 24.16). Now a further discussion seems to them to be neither necessary nor possible. 'At the end they have no more words but only stones in their hands' (J. Becker). Thus they vividly confirm once again what Jesus has said previously about their murderous intent (cf. vv. 37, 40, 44b).

[59b] As in 7.30,44; 8.20b; 10.39 Jesus escapes the attempt of the Jews to do violence to him. By portraying Jesus as 'hiding himself' (cf. similarly 12.36), the evangelist produces an inclusion with 7.10, where Jesus goes up 'as in hiding' (= 'as in secret') to the Feast of Tabernacles. With the departure of Jesus from the temple, the conversation in the temple which began in 7.14, 25 comes to an end.

Yield: the section represents a free composition by the evangelist using individual elements from the tradition. The evangelist's intention is to diabolize the Jews in the truest sense of the word, and against this dark background make the dignity of Jesus, the pre-existent Son of God who overcomes death, shine out all the more brightly.

Historical

[31b–32] These verses presuppose a post-Easter situation; moreover the terminology (absolute 'my word', 'know the truth', 'make free') does not accord with words that the historical Jesus used.

[34b] This verse reflects a connection which, as far as we can see, was not a subject of Jesus' preaching (but rather that of Paul).

[51, 52b] The saying underlying v. 51 or 52b presupposes an advanced stage of theological reflection: it has already left behind both Jesus' expectation of an imminent coming of the kingdom of God and also the early Christian expectation of the imminent return of Jesus (cf. I Thess. 4.15–17; Mark 9.1), and thus has taken the step to a realized eschatology. It does not go back to Jesus.

The conclusion is that none of the statements supposed to have been made by Jesus or the Jews in 8.30–59 was spoken during Jesus' lifetime.

John 9.1–41; 10.19–21: The man born blind

1 And as he passed by, he saw a man blind from his birth. *2 And his disciples asked him, 'Rabbi, who has sinned, this man or his parents, that he has been born blind?' 3 Jesus answered, 'Neither this man has sinned, nor his parents, but (he was born blind) so that the works of God might be made manifest in him. 4 We must work the works of him who sent me* while it is day; night comes, when no one can work. *5 As long as I am in the world, I am the light of the world.' 6 After he had said this,* he spat on the ground and made a paste of the spittle and anointed the man's eyes with the paste, 7 and said to him, 'Go, wash in the pool of Siloam,' *which translated means Sent.* Then he went and washed and came (back) seeing.

8 Now the neighbours and those who had seen him before, that he was a beggar, said, 'Is not this the man who used to sit there and beg?' 9 Some said, 'It is he'; others said, 'No, but he is like him.' He said, 'I am (he).' 10 Then they said to him, 'How were your eyes opened?' 11 He answered, 'The man called Jesus made paste and smeared my eyes and said to me, "Go to Siloam and wash." And when I had gone and washed, I received my sight.' *12 And they said to him, 'Where is he?' He said, 'I do not know.'*

13 *They take him to the Pharisees, the man who had formerly been blind.* 14 Now it was a sabbath day when Jesus made the paste and opened his eyes. 15 Now *again* the Pharisees *also* asked him how he had received his sight. *And he said to them, 'He put a paste on my eyes, and I washed, and I see.'* 16a *Some of* the Pharisees said, 'This man is *not from God*, for he does not keep the sabbath.' 16b *But others said, 'How can a* sinful *man do such signs?' And there was a division among them.* 17 *So they again say to the blind man, 'What do you say about him, since he has opened your eyes?' He said, 'He is a prophet.'*

18 *Now the Jews did not believe concerning him that he had been blind and had received his sight, until they called his parents – of the man who had received his sight –* 19 *and asked them, 'Is this your son, who you say was born blind? How then does he now see?'* 20 *His parents answered and said, 'We know that this is our son, and that he was born blind;* 21 *but how he now sees we do not know, nor do we know who opened his eyes. Ask him! He is of age, he will speak for himself.'* 22 *His parents said this because they feared the Jews, for the Jews had already agreed that if any one should confess him to be Christ, he was to be excluded from the synagogue.* 23 *Therefore his parents said, 'He is of age, ask him.'*

24 *So for the second time they called the man who had been blind, and said to him, 'Give God the glory! We know that this man is a sinner.'* 25 *Then he answered, 'Whether he is a sinner, I do not know; one thing I do know: I was blind, now I see.'* 26 *Then they said to him 'What did he do to you? How did he open your eyes?'* 27a *He answered them, 'I have told you already, and you have not listened. Why do you want to hear it again?* b *Do you too want to become his disciples?'* 28 *And they reviled him, saying, 'You are his disciple, but we are disciples of Moses.* 29 *We know that God has spoken to Moses, but as for this man, we do not know where he comes from.'* 30 The man answered and said to them, *'Why, this is a marvel, that you do not know where he comes from, and yet he opened my eyes.* 31 We know that God does not listen to sinners, but if any one is god-fearing *and does his (= God's) will* God listens to him. 32 *Never since the world began has it been heard that anyone opened the eyes of a man born blind.* 33 *If this man were not from God he could have done nothing.'* 34 They answered and said to him, 'You were born in utter sin, and do you teach us?' And they cast him out.

35 Jesus heard that they had cast him out *and found him* and said, 'Do you believe in the Son of man?' 36 *He answered and said, 'And who is he, Lord, that I may believe in him?'* 37 *Jesus said to him, 'You have seen him, and it is he who speaks to you.'* 38 He said, 'Lord, I believe'; and he fell down before him.

39 *And Jesus said, 'For judgment I came into this world, that those who do not see may see, and that those who see may become blind.'* 40 *Some of the Pharisees who were with him heard this, and they said to him, 'Are we also blind?'* 41 *Jesus said to them, 'If you were blind, you would have no sin; but now you say, "We see" – your sin remains.'*

10.19 *There again arose a division among the Jews because of these words.* 10.20 *And many of them said, 'He has a demon, and he is mad; why do you listen to him?'* 10.21 *Others said, 'These are not the sayings of one who is possessed by a demon. Can a demon open the eyes of the blind?'*

Later revision

The later revisers have disrupted the evangelist's narrative context of 9.1–41; 10.19–21 by inserting 10.1–18. For justification of this thesis cf. the remarks on 10.1–18.

Redaction and tradition

The division of the section is extraordinarily clear. It is highlighted by the paragraphs in the translation and by the sub-headings within the following analysis.

THE HEALING OF THE MAN BORN BLIND (vv. 1–7)

The Synoptic Gospels also report healings of the blind (cf. Mark 8.22–26; 10.46–52 par.; Matt. 9.27–31). This situation indicates that a story from the tradition underlies vv. 1–7.

[1] The brief description of the situation forms the beginning of the story from the tradition.

[2–3] Here the disciples function merely to provide a keyword: they do not occur again in what follows. Jesus corrects the 'either – or' which they formulate with a 'neither – nor'. The equivalent in 11.4 proves his answer (v. 3b) to be redactional. The widespread assumption that the original continuation of v. 3a has been replaced by v. 3b suffers from the fact that v. 3b seems to be the only possible continuation of v. 3a. Accordingly v. 3a must also be attributed to the evangelist. If this is correct, the question formulated in v. 2 with a view to Jesus' answer similarly comes from him. By the insertion of vv. 2–3 he *a priori* removes the basis for the charge of the Pharisees in v. 34, which is probably part of the tradition. (For the 'contradiction' between v. 3a and 5.14 see there.)

[4–5] These verses point forward to the passion of Jesus and like vv. 2f. can be identified as redactional additions (cf. 11.9f.). However, the basis of v. 4 is probably an individual saying from the tradition.

This is indicated by tensions which on the one hand this verse itself demonstrates and which on the other it causes in the context: (a) the first person plural ('we must work') and the first person singular ('who sent me') do not go together well; (b) 'we must work' is not only abrupt but also competes with v. 3, which speaks of the works of God; (c) whereas according to v. 5 Jesus is the 'light of the world', according to v. 4 he himself seems to belong with those who are dependent on day and night. – The saying from the tradition is a wisdom saying which is an admonition to make good use of the present in the face of individual death or the end of the world.

Evidently the evangelist has adopted v. 4* as an independent general saying and turned it into a saying of Jesus by the addition 'the works of him who sent me' (for the 'works of God' cf. 5.36; 6.28, 29; 10.37; 14.10; 'who sent me' is a formula which the Jesus of the evangelist often uses to describe God). By retaining the 'we' he brings Jesus and the disciples together.

By contrast, v. 5, which emphasizes the symbolic significance of the miracle that follows (cf. vv. 39–41), is the evangelist's own creation. The verse refers back to 8.12

(cf. 1.4–9; 3.19–21; 12.35f.) but – in contrast to 8.12 – can hardly be understood as an independent saying of Jesus.

[6a] The transitional formula 'after he had said this' (cf. 7.9; 11.28, 43; 18.1, 38; 20.14, 20, 22) produces a link to the old story.

[6b–7] These verses continue v. 1. They report the performance of the miracle and round off the story with a depiction of its success. The interpretation of the name of the pool probably comes from the evangelist as an indirect reference to the miracle-worker, Jesus, 'sent' by God.

THE CONFLICT (vv. 8–41)

Verse 7 concludes the healing story in keeping with the style. Verses 8ff. then take it further. Suddenly neighbours appear; we learn that earlier the blind man had begged and that the healing took place on a sabbath. None of this was mentioned before; thus a narrative seam can be seen in v. 8. However, it would be wrong to assume that vv. 8–41 in their entirety are a genuine creation of the evangelist attached to vv. 1–7. The following points especially tell against this: *first*, in v. 16b there is a report of a split among the Pharisees which has no further significance for the continuation of the conflict. *Secondly*, the section as a whole is not free from tension: on the one hand the Pharisees are offended that the miracle has taken place on a sabbath (cf. vv. 15–16a); on the other they doubt the reality of the miracle (cf. above all vv. 18f.). This second observation allows us to conclude that at a first stage in the development of the story the actual fact of the miracle was still presupposed. In other words, vv. 1, 6f.* were probably already expanded into a conflict over the sabbath at a pre-redactional stage. By contrast, the language and theology of those parts concerned with the identification of the blind man and with the disputing of the miracle are strongly stamped by the hand of the evangelist. They must derive from him.

The healed man is questioned by the neighbours

[8–9] The doubt expressed by the neighbours and other acquaintances about the identity of the man who has been healed corresponds to the disputing of the miracle by the Jews in vv. 18f. and prepares for it. First of all the motif of disagreement among the people with the citation of different views (v. 9) is to be attributed to the evangelist (cf. v. 16b and in addition 7.12, 40–43; 11.36f.; see also 12.29). However, without v. 9, vv. 8–12 lose their point. So this episode must come from the evangelist in its entirety. This judgment is confirmed by the fact that vv. 8–12 are untouched by the problem of a healing on the sabbath (this problem comes into view only in v. 14). The information that the blind man had previously begged, irrelevant to the further course of the story, might have occurred to the evangelist almost automatically as a result of the social conditions of his time (cf. Mark 10.46: 'a blind beggar').

[10–11] These verses correspond to vv. 15–16a. Probably in the tradition v. 11

was the answer to v. 15a* instead of v. 15b (for the reasons see on v. 15b); because he had anticipated this answer in the section vv. 8–12 which he himself had composed, the evangelist felt that in v. 15a only an abbreviated version of the same saying was necessary.

[12] By mentioning the absence of Jesus ('Where is he?' = 7.11) the evangelist explains why in what follows the Pharisees cannot call Jesus himself to account (cf. similarly 5.13); on the other hand, in this way he prepares for the return of Jesus in v. 35.

The first questioning of the blind man by the Pharisees

[13] This verse is a redactional transition from vv. 8–12 to vv. 14–17.

[14] As in 5.9b the event is subsequently dated to a sabbath. This dating is probably the beginning of the expansion of vv. 1, 6f.*, which the evangelist already found before him.

[15a] This prepares for the conflict. Here the Pharisees presuppose that the miracle has actually been performed ('how he had received his sight'). Only the words 'again' and 'also' derive from the evangelist: they make the interrogation of the healed man by the Pharisees parallel to the questioning by the neighbours which the evangelist himself has inserted.

[15b] The vague 'he' in the reply by the man who has been healed is insufficient in the narrative context. Before passing judgment on 'this man' in v. 16a, the Pharisees should first have ascertained who this 'he' was. Therefore we may assume that the original answer of the healed man to the question in v. 15a appears in v. 11. This is also matched by the resumption of 'the man' from v. 11 in v. 16a. Thus v. 15b is a redactional substitute for v. 11 which originally stood in its place.

[16a] This depicts the outbreak of the conflict. It is sparked off by the fact that both the preparation of the paste and its application to the eyes of the blind man are activities which are prohibited on the sabbath. The fact that only 'some' of the Pharisees make the accusation takes account of v. 16b, which has been inserted by the evangelist; probably 'the Pharisees' as such were mentioned in the tradition. The accusation 'This man is not *from God*' recalls 6.46; 7.29 (cf. 7.40) and in this form must derive from the evangelist. However, such an accusation is indispensable for the sabbath conflict. Therefore we may conjecture that the original accusation ran, say, 'This man is a sinner', or something similar. In that case the evangelist has used this saying in the sceptical question of the Pharisees in v. 16b.

[16b] As has already been mentioned in the introduction to vv. 8–41, this is an addition by the evangelist. For the motif of 'division' cf. 7.43; 10.19; for 'doing signs' cf. 2.11, 23; 3.2; 4.54; 6.2, 14, 30; 7.31; 10.41; 11.47; 12.18, 37; 20.30.

[17] According to v. 16a* the Pharisees have formed a final judgment on Jesus. In view of this, the fact that the Pharisees investigate what the healed man thinks about

Jesus can be explained only by the qualification that the evangelist has made in v. 16b. The confession by the healed man that Jesus is a prophet, like the identical confession of the Samaritan woman in 4.19, is only a provisional step: in v. 38 the healed man will fall down before Jesus as the Son of man.

The questioning of the parents of the healed man by the Pharisees

[18–23] These verses derive from the evangelist in their entirety. For the charge which is now made that the miracle is a deception is in tension with the charge that the miracle has taken place on the sabbath (see above). Further observations suggest that the section is redactional: abruptly, Jews (who in 8.21–59 appear as the opponents of Jesus) take the place of the Pharisees (v. 18), without it being possible to recognize whether the narrator sees them as another group than the Pharisees; the evangelist had already brought the parents of the blind man into play in v. 2; v. 21 is similar to 18.21; the motif of fear of the Jews (v. 22a) also appears in 7.13; 12.42; 19.38 and 20.19; the recourse to exclusion from the synagogue corresponds to 12.42.

With vv. 22f. the evangelist projects back into the life of Jesus a particularly prominent event in the history of his community: its exclusion from the Jewish synagogue association. Thus in connection with v. 34, vv. 22f. become an aetiology of the exclusion from the synagogue. Contrary to the change of subject brought about by the evangelist in v. 18, in what follows I shall describe the opponents of the man who has been healed as Pharisees (and not as Jews).

The second questioning of the healed man by the Pharisees

[24–25] 'For the second time' (v. 24a) refers back to the first questioning of the healed man by the Pharisees (vv. 13–17). However, the healed man has not been called to that, but taken (by contrast the parents have been called, cf. v. 18). 'Give God the glory!' (= 'Tell the truth') shows that the exchange of words still takes place within the framework of a dispute over whether the miracle in fact happened: the man who has been healed is to concede that he was not blind at all. For, the Pharisees think, as a sinner (cf. 8.46) Jesus cannot possibly be able to perform miracles (v. 24b). The evangelist deliberately does not make the Pharisees base their charge that Jesus is a sinner on the breach of the sabbath. For if he did, the narrative would fall back on the situation in v. 16, where the Pharisees still assumed the reality of the healing. In structure, the answer of the healed man corresponds to the statement by his parents in v. 20f.: 'we know'/'I do not know' – 'we do not know'/'I know'. In contrast to v. 31 the healed man here leaves open the question of whether Jesus is a sinner.

[26–27a] Verse 26, too does not go back to the sabbath conflict – say in the sense that by the invitation to give another report the Pharisees want to cause the healed man to say again (cf. v. 15b) that Jesus has broken the sabbath rest. Certainly the question 'How did he open your eyes?' makes it clear that the Pharisees again assume that the healing has actually taken place. But this is better understood as a climax: because the man who has been healed persists in his statement (v. 25), the Pharisees must put their suspicion of deception in a different way: they want to make the man concede that Jesus has not healed his blindness by divine miraculous power but otherwise, possibly with the help of a – diabolical? (cf. 10.20f.) – trick. For the reference by the healed man to what has already been said (v. 27a) cf. 18.8.

[27b–29a] The irony contained in the question of the healed man corresponds to that of 7.26. The Pharisees' appeal to being disciples of Moses recalls the Jews' appeal to being children of Abraham or God in 8.33, 39, 41b. Since 5.45–47 it has become clear that Moses is really their accuser.

[29b–30] In referring to the unknown origin of Jesus, the Pharisees want to dispute his legitimation. However, without knowing it they are merely confirming what Jesus has said about them in 8.14 and what is also presupposed in his apparently contradictory statement in 7.28.

[31] This is probably the original response of the man who has been healed to v. 16a. This is also suggested by the fact that in a formulation of his own the evangelist would hardly describe Jesus as 'god-fearing' (moreover this word appears in the New Testament only at this point). By contrast, 'do the will of God' is a phrase typical of the evangelist (cf. 4.34; 5.30; 6.38). But it can easily be detached from the sentence.

[32–33] Verse 33 shows itself to be redactional by 'not from God' (see on v. 16a) and the phrase that Jesus 'can do something' (cf. 3.2; 5.19; 11.37). But in that case we will also have to attribute v. 32 to the evangelist, since this verse is not suitable as a conclusion to the discourse of the man who has been healed; moreover it contains a different argument from v. 31.

[34] The reaction of the Pharisees was also the conclusion of the conflict in the tradition (but hardly the end of the story). In the present con-text, created by the evangelist, the Jews fall back beyond what Jesus has already repudiated in v. 2. In the evangelist's composition the expulsion of the blind man, probably originally thought of only as an expulsion from the building (cf. Mark 1.43), tacitly takes on the significance of an expulsion from the synagogue (cf. v. 22).

The further encounter between Jesus and the healed man

[35–38] In its present form this section is stamped through and through by the hand of the evangelist. Thus the motif of finding is typical of him (cf. on 5.14) and the self-revelation of Jesus corresponds to that to the Samaritan woman in 4.26 ('I who speak to you am he'). However, it is hard to imagine that the narrative adopted by the evangelist can have ended with v. 34. So it seems possible that the evangelist has used its original conclusion, which perhaps embraced only vv. 35*, 38 in this section. This is all the more probable, as in vv. 39–41 another conclusion follows, and in 10.19–21 yet a third.

Concluding controversy

[39–41] These verses, which interpret 'seeing' and 'being blind' in a metaphorical sense, derive from the evangelist in their entirety. For v. 39a cf. 5.22, 27, 30; 8.16; for v. 41 cf. 8.21, 24, 34; 19.11. It is worth noting that in the form which the evangelist has given to the passage 9.1–41 the charge of sin is first kept away from the blind man and his parents (cf. vv. 2f.) and then from Jesus (cf. vv. 16, 24, 31–33), finally to cling to the Pharisees.

Division among the Jews

[10.19–21] The motif of the 'division' among the hearers caused by Jesus also appears in 7.43 and 9.16, where it is similarly connected with the reporting of different opinions (cf. also 7.12; 11.36f.; 12.29). For the charge that Jesus is possessed by a demon cf. 7.20 and 8.48, 52 (see also Mark 3.21).

Yield: the present form of John 9 (+ 10.19–21) is the product of a process of growth in three stages: vv. 1, 6f.* form a self-contained healing story which is in accordance with the normal pattern. The location of the miracle in Jerusalem (pool of Siloam) suggests that it came into being in the Jewish-Christian-Palestinian sphere. The fact that the features in common with Mark 8.22–26 are limited to a blind man being healed and spittle playing a role in both cases tells against a direct dependence of the story on Z. Rather, it is probably a parallel construction.

In its form as elaborated into a conflict over the sabbath the story is similar to the narrative 5.2–12*, 15f.*; 7.21–24* (see on 5.1–18). In both cases the miracle is subsequently dated to a sabbath (5.9b/9.14); each time a brief description of the miracle by the person healed and the imparting of the name of the miracle worker takes place (5.11, 15/9.11); and both times a hostile reaction from the Jewish side is depicted (5.16/9.16).

The essential differences are as follows: *first*, in 5.2–16*; 7.21–24* Jesus himself puts the Jews or the Pharisees in the wrong, whereas in 9.1–38* it is the man who has been healed. (This explains why in 9.1–38* the healed man must subsequently be given *confirmation* by Jesus.) *Secondly*, 5.2–16*; 7.21–24* form a conflict story which in fact centres on the sabbath – it explains why Jesus' liberal atittude to the sabbath is not an offence against the law – whereas 9.1–38* seek to show that despite his offence against the sabbath Jesus is not a sinner, but rather his miraculous power proves that he has been legitimated by God.

The evangelist has taken up the miracle story which has already been shaped into a conflict over the sabbath and developed it into a much wider controversy (and into an aetiology of the exclusion from the synagogue) in connection with the controversy which has been going on since 7.14. Moreover he has provided the miracle with two mutually supplementary symbolic interpretations (cf. v. 5 and vv. 39–41) without putting its reality in question. He has followed the same procedure in chs. 6 and 11: Jesus, who multiplies quite real bread and fish and feeds 5000 people (6.11–13), is himself the bread of life (6.35, 48, 51a); he restores to life a man who is physically dead (11.43f.) and is himself the resurrection and the life (11.25f.).

Historical

The nucleus of the tradition, vv. 1, 6f.*, must be said to be unhistorical simply because according to the account by the Synoptics, which is in all probability accurate, Jesus did no 'miracles' in Jerusalem. Thus the sole possible historical reminiscence is the use of spittle as a means of healing the eyes by Jesus (see on Mark 8.22–26).

Verse 4* cannot be attributed to Jesus.

There is an echo of historically accurate details in the redactional passage 10.19–21: during Jesus' lifetime Jesus was in fact said (by his family) to be crazy (cf. on Mark 3.21).

John 10.1–18: The discourse about the shepherd, subsequently inserted

1a '*Amen, amen, I say to you,* b he who does not enter the sheepfold by the door but climbs in by another way, that man is a thief and robber. 2 But he who enters by the door is a shepherd of the sheep. 3 To him the doorkeeper opens, and the sheep hear his voice, and he calls his own sheep by name and leads them out. 4 When he has brought out all his own (sheep), he goes before them, and the sheep follow him, for they know his voice. 5 A stranger they will not follow, but they will flee from him, for they do not know the voice of strangers.'

6 *This riddle Jesus spoke to them, but they did not understand what he was saying to them.*

7a *Then Jesus again said, 'Amen, amen, I say to you,* b **I am the door of the sheep. 8** *All who came before me are thieves and robbers, but the sheep did not listen to them.* **9 I am the door; if any one enters by me he will be saved, and will go in and go out and find pasture.** 10 *The thief comes only to steal and kill and destroy. I have come that they may have life, and may have abundance.*

11a *I am the good shepherd.* b *The good shepherd lays down his life for the sheep.* 12 *The hired servant, who is not a shepherd, to whom the sheep do not belong, sees the wolf coming and leaves the sheep and flees – and the wolf snatches them and scatters them – 13 for he is a hired servant and does not care for the sheep.*

14a *I am the good shepherd,* b *and know my own and my own know me,* 15a *as the Father knows me and I know the Father,* b *and I lay down my life for the sheep.* 16 **And I have other sheep, that are not of this fold; them also I must lead, and they will listen to my voice, and there will be one flock, one shepherd.** 17 *For this reason the Father loves me, because I lay down my life, that I may take it again.* 18 *No one takes it from me, but I lay it down of my own accord. I have power to lay it down, and I have power to take it again. This commandment I have received from my Father.'*

The shepherd discourse as an addition

Three observations above all support the assumption that this section was only subsequently inserted into the evangelist's work (W. Langbrandtner). *First*, the transition from 9.41 to 10.1 is as abrupt as that between 14.31 and the addition 15.1–17, whereas 10.19–21 follows 9.41 without any problems. *Secondly*, the section is not at all well linked with its immediate context. *Thirdly*, 10.1–18 shows differences by comparison with the evangelist which in part are in line with other passages that have probably been added later. Only the most important of these need be mentioned here. (a) The evangelist never says that Jesus speaks in 'riddles' which need interpretation (v. 6); rather, the word occurs elsewhere only in the addition 16.16–33 (cf. 16.25, 29). (b) The evangelist does not apply the image of the flock to the community, just as the ecclesiological interest of the section in general is alien to him. By contrast, the revisers are particularly fond of ecclesiological questions (cf. e.g. 15.1–17), and the comparison of the community with a flock of sheep is known to them (cf. 21.15–17). (c) Whereas the evangelist interprets the death of Jesus as a glorification and return to God (cf. on 13.1a), vv. 11b, 15b interpret it as a representative saving death for his own (cf. similarly the additions 1.29b; 6.51c). (d) According to the evangelist, salvation and disaster are decided by whether or not a person believes in Jesus (cf. 3.16–18; 5.24; 6.40ab, 47; 11.25f.). By contrast the view prevails in 10.1–18 that Jesus' task consists in gathering together from the world those predestined to salvation by God (vv. 3f., 14; cf. similarly ch. 17).

If 10.1–18 is an addition, the translation of this section should really have been printed completely in bold in accordance with the rule elsewhere. However, this procedure has not been followed above (as in chs. 15–17 and 21) in order to make clear typographically the presumed history of the text (as far as this is possible here). Accordingly the italics within the translation and the term 'redaction' refer not to the redactional activity of the evangelist but to that of the (group of) reviser(s) (termed 'author' in what follows) responsible for inserting this passage.

Secondary additions

After being inserted into its present context, the shepherd discourse itself has evidently been yet further expanded (cf. similarly e.g. ch. 17). These expansions, which are tertiary to the work of the evangelist – and are printed in bold in the translation – must first be marked off:

[7b and 9] We can regard it as a possibility that an author should compare Jesus first with a door and then with a shepherd. But in vv. 7–10 'the image jumps about from verse to verse' (Bultmann) and the notion that all those who came before Jesus – as the *door*, not as the *shepherd* – were thieves and robbers (vv. 7f.) is hardly to be attributed to one and the same author. Moreover, the two images fit very badly together since according to v. 2 the shepherd with whom Jesus identifies himself in v. 11a enters through the door which according to v. 7b and 9 Jesus similarly claims himself to be. Thus vv. 7b and 9 are so isolated in the context that they can only be regarded as additions to an already completed text. The person responsible for these two additions has selected a subsidiary aspect from vv. 1b–5 – the door (cf. vv. 1f.) – and interpreted it in terms of Jesus as the only way to salvation (cf. 14.6).

[16] This verse interrupts the connection between vv. 15 and 17, and with the abrupt mention of the sheep outside whose existence had not been indicated previously in any way, completely destroys the cohesion of the image. The verse introduces the new notion that the church is composed not only of Jewish Christians but also of Gentile Christians. However, such a distinction is alien to the context, since in it the shepherd's 'own sheep' represent the totality of all Christians (J. Becker). As that differentiation is also expressed in the additions 11.51f. and 17.20f., we may conjecture that all three additions derive from one and the same hand or group.

Redaction and tradition

Verse 6 divides the section into two parts: the 'riddle' (vv. 1b–5) and its exegesis (vv. 7a, 8, 10–15, 17–18). Here vv. 1b–5 certainly represent the earliest element of vv. 1–18*. For on the one hand the interpretation of course presupposes what is being interpreted, and on the other it presents several images and statements which have no equivalent in vv. 1b–5.

[1a] Here as in 12.24 the 'Amen, amen' formula serves to introduce the addition.

[1b–5] This passage, which can be described as a parable with allegorical features, vividly depicts an everyday happening from a rural milieu and evidently understands this as an image of Jesus' relationship to his own. As the shepherd summons his own sheep from the various flocks lodged in the fold, so Jesus does not gather all human beings, but only his own (namely those predestined by God to salvation) from the world (vv. 2–4). (Note that according to v. 3a *the* sheep – that means all of them – *hear* the voice of the shepherd, but in vv. 3b–4 the shepherd leads out only his *own* sheep, who *know* his voice.) The two framework verses (vv. 1b, 5) indicate that Jesus is the only legitimate Lord of the community. Alongside him there can be only destroyers. However, with thieves and strangers the author of the addition may have been thinking particularly of the Pharisees from 9.40 and this may have led him to insert his addition at this point.

The image of the shepherd and his sheep is widespread in the Old Testament. There it is primarily applied to the relationship between the leader and his people or God and Israel (cf. above all Ezek. 34; also Isa. 63.11; Jer. 3.15; 23.1–4; Ps. 37.18; 119.176).

[6] 'They' is to be referred to the Pharisees from 9.40. This sparse incidental remark, which is far too 'harmless' in view of Jesus' vigorous attack in 9.41, anchors

the addition (with difficulty) in the context, and at the same time separates the image in vv. 1b–5 from the exegesis in vv. 7–18*.

[7a] The new introduction to the discourse marks the beginning of the interpretation of the image in vv. 1b–5.

It is possible that this image was already in circulation with a more or less pre-formed interpretation (and with an incidental remark corresponding to v. 6 which originally related to the disciples?) before its insertion into the Gospel of John (cf. the tradition Mark 4.3–8, 10a, 13–20 adopted by Mark). However, this interpretation can no longer be reconstructed. Above all, the elements connected with the good shepherd's surrender of his life are certainly open to the suspicion of not being original because this theme has no support in vv. 1b–5. But what remains (vv. 8, 10, 11a, 14b, 15a) not only fails to fit in with vv. 1b–5 quite organically, but moreover seems fragmentary. So we do better to assume that the author of the addition has integrated an interpretation which possibly came down with the tradition completely into his own. The similarity in language and content of vv. 11b, 15b, 17–18 to parts of the addition 15.1–17 (see on vv. 17–18), which indicates literary influence, tells against the assumption that he found vv. 6–18* (without vv. 7b, 9, 16) already complete.

[8] This verse is still relatively closely orientated on vv. 1b–5. It interprets the thieves and robbers of v. 1b allegorically in terms of all who have come earlier than Jesus. In this way the dignity of Jesus as the one and only legitimate Lord of the community is emphasized.

[10] Verse 10a forms the dark background to v. 10b, which now describes the saving function of Jesus the shepherd as well. The two half-verses are bound up with v. 8 by the key word 'come'.

[11a] This verse for the first time explicitly makes the identification of Jesus with the shepherd – an identification which is doubtless intended in vv. 1b–5 and already presupposed in vv. 8 and 10. However, a *good* shepherd has not been mentioned in vv. 1b–5, for there the contrast was not between a good and a bad shepherd but between the shepherd and the thieves.

[11b] The announcement that the good shepherd gives his life for the sheep (= Jesus for his own) goes beyond vv. 1b–5. In the imagery the shepherd's readiness for death is an excessive exaggeration which in the substantive half already looks back to the death of Jesus.

[12–13] These verses draw a contrast with the shepherd's readiness for sacrifice and no more have a basis in vv. 1b–5 than does v. 11b. For neither the hired servant nor the wolf plays a role there. So it is no wonder that the overall picture becomes increasingly blurred: whereas in v. 10 the sheep are threatened by the thief, according to v. 12 the danger comes from the wolf; and whereas in v. 5 the sheep flee from a stranger, now it is the hired servant who takes flight before the wolf.

[14–15] Verse 14a corresponds to v. 11a. Verses 14b–15a refer back to the remarks about knowing the voice of the shepherd and calling the sheep by name in v. 3. The view that the relationship between Father and Son corresponds to the relationship between Jesus and the community is typical of the revisers of the Gospel (cf. 6.56f.; 15.9f.; 17.22f. and 17.21). Verse 15b repeats v. 11b in the first person.

[17–18] These verses abandon the metaphorical form of expression which was predominant in what has gone before; here the explanation about Jesus giving his life develops the corresponding formulations in vv. 11b and 15b. All in all, the relationship in the content and terminology of these verses to the addition 15.1–17 is striking. Cf. 15.9: 'As the Father has loved me . . .'; 15.13: 'Greater love has no man than this, that a man lay down his life for his friends'; 15.10: 'as I have kept my Father's commandments' (see also 14.31). As what is said here about Jesus' active 'surrendering his life' and 'taking it up again' is fulfilled in the passion and resurrection stories in chs. 18ff., we can see vv. 17–18 as a ligature to establish the addition in the context of the Gospel as a whole (cf. v. 6).

Historical

Certainly vv. 1b–5 are characterized by motifs which also play a role in authentic parables (cf. Matt. 18.12f./ Luke 15.4–6), but because of the orientation of the 'riddle', which is ecclesiological from the start, we can rule out the possibility that this goes back to Jesus.

John 10.22–39: Jesus' defence against the charge of blasphemy

22 *It was then the Feast of the Dedication of the Temple at Jerusalem; it was winter.* 23 *And Jesus was walking in the temple, in the hall of Solomon.* 24 *Then the Jews surrounded him and said to him, 'How long will you keep us in suspense? If you are the Christ, tell us plainly.'* 25a *Jesus answered them, 'I have told you, yet you do not believe.* b *The works that I do in my Father's name, they bear witness to me.* 26 **But you do not believe, because you are not of my sheep.** 27 **My sheep hear my voice, and I know them, and they follow me,** 28 **and I give them eternal life, and they shall never perish, and no one will snatch them out of my hand.** 29 **My Father, who has given (them) to me, is greater than all, and no one can snatch them out of the Father's hand.** 30 *I and the Father are one.'*

31 *The Jews took up stones again to stone him.* 32 *Jesus answered them, 'I have shown you many good works from the Father. For which of these works do you want to stone me?'*

33 *The Jews answered him, 'It is not for a good work that we stone you but for blasphemy, and because you, being a man, make yourself God.'* 34 *Jesus answered them, 'Is it not written in your law, "I said, you are gods"?* 35 *If he (= God) called them gods to whom the word of God came, and the scripture cannot be broken,* 36 *do you say to him whom the Father has sanctified and sent into the world, "You are blaspheming," because I said, "I am the Son of God"?* 37 *If I am not doing the works of my Father, then do not believe me.* 38 *But if I do (them),*

even if you do not believe me, (at least) believe the works, that you may know and understand that the Father is in me and I am in the Father.'

39 *Again they sought to seize him, but he escaped from their hands.*

Later revision

Verses 26–29 are not only marked by the same imagery as the addition 10.1–18 but also contain several clear allusions to this section (for v. 27 cf. 10.3, 14; for v. 28 cf. vv. 10, 12). The surmise thus suggested – that this is a secondary insertion – is reinforced by the observation that the passage disrupts the structure and train of thought of the section. For whereas vv. 24–25, 30–39 are devoted to a stringent repudiation of the charge of blasphemy made against Jesus, vv. 26–29 emphasize the community's certainty of salvation in a way alien to the context (vv. 27–29). Verse 26a ('But you do not believe') attests the concern of the revisers to anchor the insertion in the context, taking up the relevant statement from v. 25 ('yet you do not believe').

Redaction and tradition

Like 5.31–47 + 7.15–24 and 8.12–20, the section takes the form of a legal dispute in which the legitimation of Jesus as the one sent by God is a matter of debate (and is decided in favour of Jesus).

[22–23] The depiction of the situation mainly pursues the aim of marking off the controversy which follows from the previous section (9.1–41; 10.19–21). But possibly the note of time is also meant to indicate that the Passover of Jesus' death is approaching.

[24–25a] The opening of the controversy bears a remarkable similarity to a scene within the Lukan depiction of the interrogation of Jesus before the Supreme Council: '"If you are the Christ, tell us!" But he said to them, "If I tell you, you will not believe" '(Luke 22.67). That could be coincidence, especially as v. 25a is strongly reminiscent of 6.36, which is certainly redactional. But it is striking that the key word 'blasphemy' from the Markan pendant to the Lukan scene mentioned appears in v. 33. It follows from this that here the evangelist has evidently been inspired by Z (Luke 22.67; Mark 14.64). 'Plainly' (= 'openly', v. 24) is one of his favourite words (cf. 7.4, 13, 26; 11.14, 54; 18.20).

[25b] This represents a short version of 5.36b. For the power of testimony in the works of Jesus cf. also v. 38.

[30] This is a key christological saying of the evangelist. He himself uses such a pointed formulation elsewhere only in 1.18 and 14.9 (but cf. also 5.17 etc.). However, the evangelist does not put forward the view that Jesus is *identical* with God: Jesus and God are *one*, but not *one person* (cf. also 14.28: 'The Father is greater than I').

[31] This verse explicitly ('again') refers to 8.59a.

[32] Jesus counters the intention of the Jews to kill him with a question the irony of which could hardly be surpassed (cf. 7.19). For the formulation 'show works' cf. 5.20b.

[33] Cf. Lev. 24.16: 'Whoever blasphemes the name of the Lord shall die the death; the whole community shall stone him . . .' For the charge by the Jews that Jesus is making himself God cf. 5.18 (see also on 8.53).

[34–36] While the Jews are still standing around with stones in their hands, Jesus goes on arguing calmly (cf. similarly 5.19ff. in relation to 5.18). By a proof from scripture (cf. Ps. 82.6) he refutes them through the very scriptures on which they think that they can rely in their verdict in v. 33.

In this respect vv. 34–36 make complete sense within the context: the Jews are struck by their own weapons. However, it cannot be disputed that the proof from scripture falls below the theological level of the evangelist elsewhere. For it cannot give a reason for the unique dignity of Jesus as the one sent by God. Here, rather, Jesus appears only as a special exception among all those who are addressed by God (J. Becker). The evangelist therefore cannot have developed this argument himself but formulated it on the basis of an apologetic proof from scripture in the tradition. This is also supported by the fact that according to v. 30 Jesus did not say, 'I am the Son of God,' but 'I and the Father are one.' Probably the additions by the evangelist are limited to the phrase 'in your law' (cf. 7.19; 8.17), which distances and disparages, and the formula about sending.

[37–38] In terms of thought and wording these verses have a parallel in 14.10f.

[39] 7.30, 44 and 8.20 also report unsuccessful attempts by his opponents to seize Jesus.

Yield: the controversy is a literary fiction which the evangelist has composed himself under the influence of Z, taking up a traditional proof from scripture.

Historical

Since Jesus did not understand himself as Son of God but was regarded as such by his adherents only as a consequence of the resurrection visions, vv. 34–36* cannot go back to him.

John 10.40–42: Jesus at the place where John first baptized

40 *And he went away again to the other side of the Jordan, to the place where John had first baptized, and there he remained.* 41 *And many came to him and said, 'John did no sign, but everything that John said about this man was true.'* 42 *And many came to believe in him there.*

Redaction and historical

With this transition (cf. 2.23–25; 4.43–45), after the vigorous controversies by which the previous chapters were stamped, the evangelist grants his readers a short pause. By doing so, at the same time he manages to give full emphasis to Jesus' greatest miracle, which follows.

[40] This verse refers back to 1.28. Here the 'first' corresponds to the evangelist's account, according to which John had shifted the place of his activity in baptizing from Bethany to Aenon near Salim (cf. 3.23). Possibly the evangelist does not mention 'Bethany' specifically in order to avoid a confusion of this place with the Bethany of the same name near Jerusalem, the scene of the following miracle.

[41] The evangelist uses the transition to have his own image of John the Baptist confirmed from the mouths of the people. In this way, for one last time, he emphasizes that the Baptist, being merely a witness, is inferior to Jesus (cf. 1.6–8, 15, 19–34; 3.22–30; 4,1; 5.33–36).

[42] This verse corresponds to 2.23; 4.39; 7.31; 8.30; 11.45; 12.42.

Yield: as a redactional summary the section has no historical value.

John 11.1–44: The raising of Lazarus

1 Now a certain man was sick, Lazarus of Bethany, from the village of Mary and Martha, her sister. **2 And it was Mary who had anointed the Lord with ointment and wiped his feet with her hair; her brother Lazarus was sick.** 3 Then the sisters sent to him, saying, 'Lord, look, the one whom you love is sick.' 4 But when Jesus had heard (it), he said, '*This sickness is not to death, but for the glory of God, that the Son of God may be glorified by means of it.*' **5 And Jesus loved Martha and her sister and Lazarus.** 6 *Now when he heard that he was sick, he remained two days longer in the place where he was.*

7 *Only after this does he say to the disciples, 'Let us go into Judaea again.'* 8 *The disciples say to him, 'Rabbi, the Jews are now seeking to stone you, and are you going there again?'* 9 *Jesus answered, 'Are there not twelve hours in the day?* If anyone walks in the day, he does not stumble *because he sees the light of this world.* 10 But if anyone walks in the night, he stumbles, *because the light is not in him.'* 11 *He said this, and after that he says to them, 'Our friend Lazarus has fallen asleep, but I am going to rouse him.'* 12 *Then the disciples said to him, 'Lord, if he has fallen asleep, he will recover.'* 13 *Now Jesus had spoken of his death, but they thought that he spoke of taking rest in sleep.* 14 *Thereupon Jesus told them plainly, 'Lazarus is dead.* 15a *And for your sake I am glad that I was not there – so that you may come to believe.* 15b *But let us go to him.'* 16 *Then Thomas, who was called Twin, said to his fellow disciples, 'Let us also go, that we may die with him.'*

17 Now when Jesus had come, he found that he (= Lazarus) had already been in the tomb four days. 18 *And Bethany was near Jerusalem, about fifteen stadia away.* 19 *And many of the Jews had come to Martha and Mary to console them over their brother.* 20 *Now when Martha heard that Jesus was coming, she went to meet him; but Mary sat in the house.* 21 *Then Martha*

said to Jesus, 'Lord, if you had been here, my brother would not have died. 22 And even now I know that whatever you ask from God, God will give you.' 23 Jesus says to her, 'Your brother will rise again.' 24 Martha says to him, 'I know that he will rise again in the resurrection at the last day.' 25 Jesus says to her, 'I am the resurrection and the life; he who believes in me, even if he dies, shall live, 26 and whoever lives and believes in me shall never die. Do you believe this?' 27 She says to him, 'Yes, Lord; I have come to believe that you are the Christ, the Son of God, who comes into the world.'

28 And when she had said this, she went away and called her sister Mary secretly, and said, 'The Teacher is here and is calling for you.' 29 And when she heard it, she rose quickly and went to him. 30 Now Jesus had not yet come to the village, but was still in the place where Martha had met him. 31 Now when the Jews who were with her in the house, consoling her, saw Mary rise quickly and go out, they followed her, supposing that she was going to the tomb to weep there. 32a Now Mary, when she came where Jesus was, (and) when she had seen him, threw herself at his feet and said, b 'Lord, if you had been here, *my brother* would not have died.' 33 Now Jesus, when he saw her weeping, and the *Jews* who had come with her weeping, was moved with indignation in the spirit *and troubled* 34 and said, 'Where have you laid him?' They say to him, 'Lord, come and see.' *35 Jesus began to weep. 36 Then the Jews said, 'See how he loved him.' 37 But some of them said, 'Could not this man who opened the eyes of the blind man have caused this man also not to die?'*

38 Now Jesus, *again being moved with indignation in himself,* comes to the tomb; but it was a cave, and a stone lay in front of it. 39a Jesus says, 'Take away the stone.' 39b *Martha, the sister of the dead man, said to him, 'Lord, he is already stinking, for he has been (dead) four days.' 40 Jesus says to her, 'Did I not tell you, "If you will believe, you will see the glory of God"?'* 41a Then they took away the stone. b *And Jesus lifted up his eyes and said, 'Father, I thank you that you have heard me. 42 I knew that you always hear me, but I have said (this) because of the people standing by, that they may believe that you have sent me.' 43 And after he had said this,* he called with a loud voice, 'Lazarus, come out.' 44 The dead man came out, his feet and hands bound with bandages, and his face wrapped with a cloth. Jesus says to them, 'Unbind him, and let him go.'

Later revision

In all probability v. 2 is a gloss: the verse 'reminds' the reader of an event (12.3) which has not yet been narrated.

Verse 5 too seems to be a later addition, probably by the author of 15.1–17 (see there). It tones down v. 6, which is felt to be offensive, and makes it clear that the fact that Jesus did not set off immediately but deliberately took the death of the sick man into account was not because of a lack of affection for Lazarus or the sisters who were seeking help.

Redaction and tradition

The last miracle of Jesus that the Fourth Evangelist reports is not only the greatest but also has the most serious consequences. It becomes the occasion for the final decision to put Jesus to death (cf. 11.45–54). Thus it represents a decisive turning point in the composition of the Gospel.

Even after taking away vv. 2 and 5, the story still displays numerous inconsistencies in form and content. It can be concluded from this that the evangelist has based it on an earlier narrative. Just one striking tension might be mentioned here in advance: the 'I am' saying in vv. 25f really makes the raising of Lazarus superfluous: 'The saying . . . robs the whole episode of all significance' (Wellhausen). Further discrepancies and fractures will be discussed in the course of the following analysis.

The report of the sickness of Lazarus (vv. 1–6)

[1, 3] The action begins without any link to what has gone before. The introduction of the protagonists of the narrative, the description of the distress and the informing of the miracle worker by a third party form the exposition of the basic story. It is striking that in this Lazarus is merely regarded as someone who lives in the village and not as the brother of the sisters Mary and Martha. That has aggravating consequences for the reconstruction of the tradition. Evidently Martha and Mary were made Lazarus' sisters only by the evangelist.

[4] The parallel in 9.3b shows that the definition of the purpose of the sickness (v. 4b) is redactional: just as the works of God were revealed in the man born blind, so the glory of God is to be made visible in the raising of Lazarus. By means of the addition 'that the Son of God may be glorified by means of it', the evangelist at the same time points to the approaching events of the passion: the raising of Lazarus will be the occasion for the Sanhedrin's decision to put Jesus to death (cf. 11.45ff.) and thus lead to his final glorification (cf. 12.23, 27f.; 13.1a; for the mutual glorification of God and Jesus cf. also 13.31f.). In other words, in performing the miracle, Jesus himself initiates his passion.

[6] For a second time (cf. v. 4a), v. 6a reports that Jesus hears of Lazarus' sickness. It thus shows itself to be redactional and at the same time suggests that v. 4a derives from the tradition. The motif of the deliberate delay to the departure (v. 6b) has been inserted by the evangelist to emphasize the sovereignty of Jesus the miracle-worker. Whereas in the story of the tradition it was presupposed that Jesus came too late unintentionally (v. 17), according to the evangelist Jesus even waits for the death of Lazarus.

Jesus' conversation with his disciples (vv. 7–16)

[7] 'Only after this' in v. 7a is understandable only against the background of the redactional v. 6. Verse 7b presupposes earlier stays in Judaea (cf. 2.13; 5.1; 7.14) and the withdrawal to the other side of the Jordan (cf. 10.40–42). Now it is striking that v. 7b ('Let us go into Judaea again') is taken up again in v. 15b ('But let us go to

him'). If we further note that the disciples no longer play a role from v. 17 on, we may assume that v. 15b (without 'but') was the original continuation of v. 4a and that the whole passage in between has been inserted by the evangelist. This conjecture is confirmed by the following observations on vv. 8–15a.

[8] This verse refers back to the attempts of the Jews to stone Jesus in 8.59 and 10.31–33.

[9–10] As in 9.4f., before performing the miracle Jesus speaks of the time limit put on his activity, in a quite similar terminology (cf. 'day', 'night', 'world', 'light'). Evidently the evangelist has taken up a general wisdom saying and has expanded it by the introductory rhetorical question and the two 'because' clauses.

[11a] The ponderous introduction to v. 11b can be explained by the insertion of the rule of life used in vv. 9–10.

[11b–12] These verses contain two motifs which are typical of the evangelist: the omniscience of Jesus (cf. on 1.42) and misunderstanding (cf. on 2.20).

[13] As in 2.21 the misunderstanding is explained afterwards for the reader.

[14] For the plain speaking of Jesus cf. 10.24; 18.20; for his supernatural knowledge cf. 1.42.

[15a] That Jesus rejoices over the death of Lazarus presupposes that he has deliberately postponed his departure (v. 6). For the statement that miracles (can) arouse faith cf. 2.11; 20.31.

[15b] This is the original continuation of v. 4a (see on v. 7). Only the 'but' derives from the evangelist.

[16] Thomas' invitation to his fellow-disciples can be understood as an expression either of hopelessness or of an unconditional readiness for discipleship. Since in 20.24–29 the evangelist stylizes Thomas (cf. Mark 3.18 parr.) as a representative of doubt, the first alternative is more likely. At all events, the statement about 'dying with' points forward to the approaching events of the passion and has no place in the original miracle story.

Jesus and Martha (vv. 17–27)

[17] This verse fits seamlessly on to v. 15b and is part of the narrative from the tradition. The purpose of its specific mention of four days which have passed since the death of Lazarus may be to emphasize the reality of his death and thus heighten the magnitude of the miracle. For according to Jewish understanding the soul remained for three days near a dead person; on the fourth day hope of a resuscitation was in vain. The proposal that the verse presupposes that Jesus already knows the precise place of burial, and therefore contradicts v. 34, is hardly compelling.

[18] The information about the short distance between Bethany and Jerusalem again gives the story an orientation to the passion of Jesus. This is explained by the

evangelist's conception that the raising of Lazarus will bring Jesus to the cross in Jerusalem (cf. vv. 4b, 8, 16).

[19] Within the miracle story 'the Jews' are merely bystanders (cf. vv. 31, 33, 36f.). However, they fulfil an important function for the further course of the Gospel. For immediately after the raising of Lazarus, some of them will give the Pharisees a report on the miracle (11.46) and thus provide the decisive impetus for the final resolution of the Sanhedrin to condemn Jesus to death (cf. 11.53). It is striking that here, in contrast to v. 1, Martha is mentioned first. Her new priority reflects the evangelist's new version of the story; for we shall see that the main female role in the story was assigned to Martha only by the evangelist.

[20] This verse creates the dramatic preconditions for what follows: by the note that Mary remains in the house, the narrator saves her for later. However, that Martha goes to meet Jesus stands in remarkable tension with the arrival of Jesus, which according to v. 17 has already taken place. Together with v. 30, which yet again emphasizes that Jesus has not yet come into the village, this is a first indication that the conversation between Jesus and Martha is to be attributed completely to the evangelist. This indication is reinforced by the analysis of the following verses.

[21] Martha's statement is identical with that of her sister Mary in v. 32b.

[22] For the formulation cf. 14.13a.

[23–26] The motif of misunderstanding (cf. on v. 12) and the correction of the traditional future eschatology (cf. 5.24f.; 6.40ab, 47) prove the passage to be redactional. Incidentally, v. 25 shows that the realized eschatology advocated by the evangelist does not exclude a salvation which goes beyond the death of the individual: Jesus saves the believer over and above death (cf. 12.32).

[27] For Martha's confession cf. 20.31: '. . . that you may believe that Jesus is the Christ, the Son of God . . .'; for the addition 'who comes into the world' cf. 6.14 (see also 1.9).

Jesus, Mary and the Jews (vv. 28–37)

[28–31] These verses are a transition by the evangelist. They presuppose the division of the scene in v. 20, the conversation between Jesus and Martha in vv. 21–27 and the introduction of the Jews in v. 19.

[32a] After the long insertion vv. 18–31 this verse has probably been formulated on the basis of the narrative in the tradition. We cannot rule out the possibility that the tradition merely reported a meeting between Mary and Jesus, but in view of vv. 1 and 3 that is improbable. So it is reasonable to assume that originally the sisters appeared together in vv. 32–33. The evangelist has to limit himself to naming Mary because in his new version of the story Martha has already met Jesus. The note 'when she came where Jesus was' can be dispensed with if v. 17 is connected directly

to v. 32a; it has probably been inserted by the evangelist with a view to the somewhat confusing coming and going in vv. 28–31.

[32b] This corresponds to Martha's statement in v. 21. As according to the narrative in the tradition Mary and Martha were not Lazarus' sisters (cf. on vv. 1, 3), 'my brother' has to be removed as a redactional addition.

[33–34] Given the agreements in 12.27 and 13.21, first of all 'and troubled' has to be regarded as an insertion by the evangelist. On the basis of vv. 19 and 31, the mention of the weeping Jews also arouses the suspicion of being redactional. But it is conceivable that only the word 'Jews' derives from the evangelist; in this case the tradition would have spoken of an undefined crowd of companions. However, if the hypothesis that the sisters originally appeared together is correct, the presence of these companions does not seem at all necessary for what follows.

[35–37] These verses undoubtedly come from the evangelist in their entirety. The weeping of Jesus (v. 35) can hardly be reconciled with the fact that he had just been angry at the weeping of those present (v. 33). Verse 36 presupposes v. 35; v. 37 refers back to 9.1–7. Moreover the quotation of various opinions is a stylistic means often used by the evangelist (cf. 7.12, 40–43; 9.16; see also 12.29).

The raising of Lazarus (vv. 38–44)

[38–39a] With the phrase 'again being moved with indignation in himself', the evangelist takes up v. 33 and continues the original narrative thread that was broken by vv. 35–37.

[39b–40] The brief exchange of words between Jesus and Martha, who apparently emerges from nowhere, has been inserted by the evangelist. Here the mention of the odour of the corpse (v. 39b), which goes beyond v. 17, is a particularly drastic means of emphasizing that Lazarus really has died. To the reader who is thus confronted with the horror of decay, the following miracle must appear all the more glorious. The saying of which Jesus reminds Mary in v. 40 was not spoken in this form in the course of the dialogue vv. 21–27. Rather it seems to be a mixed quotation made up of vv. 4b and 25f.

[41–44] The execution of Jesus' command (v. 41a), the calling forth of the dead man (v. 43b), his emergence from the tomb (v. 44a), and Jesus' last word, which illustrates the return of the raised man to everyday life (v. 44b), form the end of the original story. By contrast, the prayer of Jesus (vv. 41b–42) which interrupts the connection between vv. 41a and 43b has been inserted by the evangelist. This is indicated by the unity between Father and Son which it presupposes (cf. e.g.10.30), the talk of belief in the one whom God has sent (cf. 5.36b; 6.29, etc.) and the similarity between v. 42 and Jesus' commentary on the heavenly voice in 12.30.

Yield: the uncertainties with which the analysis is burdened, especially in vv. 32 and 33, show that the underlying miracle story can be reconstructed only hypothetically. But after removing the parts printed in italics in the translation the text may approximately correspond to the wording of the original story. To show this better, it is reprinted below in one piece, with changes from the existing text indicated by square brackets:

1 Now a certain man was sick, Lazarus of Bethany, from the village of Mary and Martha, her sister. 3 Then the sisters sent to him, saying, 'Lord, look, the one whom you love is sick.' 4a And when Jesus had heard it, he said, 15b '. . . let us go to him.' 17 Now when Jesus had come, he found that Lazarus had already been in the tomb four days. 32 Now Mary [and Martha] . . . when [they] had seen Jesus, threw [themselves] at his feet and said, 'Lord, if you had been here, he would not have died.' 33 Now Jesus, when he saw [them] weeping, and those . . . who had come with [them] weeping, was moved with indignation in the spirit . . . 34 and said, 'Where have you laid him?' They say to him, 'Lord, come and see.' 38 Now Jesus . . . comes to the tomb; but it was a cave, and a stone lay in front of it. 39a Jesus says, 'Take away the stone.' . . . 41 Then they took away the stone. And Jesus . . . 43 . . . called with a loud voice, 'Lazarus, come out.' 44 The dead man came out, his feet and hands bound with bandages, and his face wrapped with a cloth. Jesus says to them, 'Unbind him, and let him go.'

This self-contained story is related to other New Testament narratives of raisings of the dead both in its extent and also in its motifs (cf. Mark 5.22–24, 35–43; Luke 7.11–17; Acts 9.36–42; 20.7–12): the name of the sick man is mentioned (v. 1; cf. Acts 9.36); people from the sick man's neighbourhood ask the miracle-worker for help (v. 3; cf. Mark 5.22f.; Luke 7.12f.); news of the sickness is given by a delegation (v. 3; cf. Acts 9.38); the miracle-worker arrives at the place of the event too late (v. 17; cf. Mark 5.35); the lament of those present arouses the indignation of the miracle-worker (v. 33; cf. Mark 5.38f.); the dead man is restored to life by a word of the miracle-worker (v. 43; cf. Mark 5.41; Luke 7.14; Acts 9.40); a concluding order of the miracle-worker illustrates the return of the raised man to life (v. 44b; cf. Mark 5.43).

The narrative has its origins in the Christian mission: the raising of Lazarus is a 'gaudy poster' (J. Becker) which campaigns for Jesus. There is no demonstrable influence by Luke 10.38–42 (Mary and Martha) or by Luke 16.19–31, where the possibility of the raising of a Lazarus is considered but then dropped.

Historical

Several reasons tell against the historicity of the underlying narrative. *First,* the dead cannot be made to live again; *secondly,* it would be impossible to explain why the story – assuming its historicity – did not find its way into the Synoptic Gospels; *thirdly,* there are parallels in the history of religion (cf. e.g. I Kings 17.17–24, Elijah raises the son of the widow at Zarephath; II Kings 4.18–37, Elisha raises the dead son of a Shunammite woman). That Lazarus was only apparently dead is an untenable supposition which does not take the story at its word and mistakes its intention of showing Jesus as the conqueror of death.

The proverb in vv. 9–10* is too pale to permit its attribution to Jesus.

John 11.45–54: The decision of the Supreme Council to put Jesus to death

45 *Now many of the Jews, who had come to Mary and had seen what he did, came to believe in him. 46 But some of them went away to the Pharisees and told them what Jesus had done.*

47 Then the <u>chief priests and the</u> *Pharisees* <u>gathered</u> a council, and <u>said</u>, '*What are we doing? For this man does many signs. 48 If we let him go on like this, everyone will believe in him, and the Romans will come and take away from us both the place and the people.' 49 But one of them,* **Caiaphas, who was high priest of that year,** *said to them, 'You know nothing, 50 nor do you consider that it is expedient for you that one (single) man should die for the people, and that the whole people should not perish.'*

51 **But he did not say this of his own accord, but because he was high priest of that year he said prophetically that Jesus should die for the people, 52 and not for the people only, but to gather together the scattered children of God.**

53 From that day on they <u>were resolved</u> <u>to kill him.</u>

54 *Now Jesus no longer went about openly among the Jews, but went from there to the region near the wilderness, to a town called Ephraim; and there he stayed with the disciples.*

Later revision

The thesis that the specific detail 'Caiaphas who was high priest of that year' in v. 49 was introduced only by the revisers (E.Hirsch) is supported by the following considerations: the phrase 'one of them', the precise translation of which would be 'any one of them', clashes stylistically both with the mention of a concrete person and with that of a sole holder of office (cf. the other New Testament instances: Mark 14.47 = Luke 22.50; similarly Luke 7.18 and Acts 23.23, which speak of 'any two'; note in addition that some manuscripts omit 'any' in v. 49 to tone down the break in style). This thesis is later confirmed by the analysis of 18.12–27, 28 which indicates that all the references to Caiaphas in the Gospel of John derive from subsequent revision. (The evangelist erroneously regarded *Annas* as the high priest in office at the time of Jesus; cf. on 18.12–27.) It is no longer certain whether it is presupposed, wrongly, that the high priest always held office only for a year. For the phrase 'high priest of that year' (similarly v. 51 and 18.13) can also mean 'high priest in that year'.

[51–52] These verses similarly come from the revisers. They make the anonymous speaker of vv. 49f., whom they identify with Caiaphas, an involuntary prophet, and interpret the saying 'die for the people' in terms of the saving death of Jesus, which benefits the Jews and some select non-Jews. Here there are three differences from the theology of the evangelist (J. Becker): *first*, the notion of a vicarious saving death of Jesus is alien to him; *secondly*, the statement that Jesus is dying for the Jewish people is hardly compatible with what the evangelist says, for example in 8.41–47 to the Jews as the children of the devil (cf. on 4.22). And *thirdly*, according to him salvation is not merely for two predestined groups but for all human beings who believe in Jesus by their own free decision (cf. 3.16; 5.24; 6.40ab, 47). By contrast, all the views expressed in these deviations can also be demonstrated in other passages the secondary character of which is probable (for the saving death of Jesus cf. 1.29b; for the community made up of Jews and Gentiles cf. 10.16; and for the notion of predestination cf. 10.1ff. and 17.1ff.).

Redaction and tradition

From 11.45–54 on, the evangelist has composed most sections on the basis of Z: 12.1–11; 12.12–19; 13.21b–30; 13.31–38; 18.1–20.23 (see also 12.23, 27f. and 14.31; chapters 15–17 are additions). In 11.45–54 Z is based on Mark 14.1–2 (word-for-word agreements = single underlining) and Matt. 26.3–5 (double underlining); cf. Luke 22.1–2.

[45–46] These verses are to be attributed to the evangelist. For the Jews, some of whom become believers and some of whom denounce Jesus, are the same people that he has introduced in 11.19, 31, 33–37 as witnesses to the preceding miracle. Jesus' plan to make the raising of Lazarus the occasion for his passion is realized with their help (on this cf. the introductory remarks on 11.1–44 and the remarks on 11.4, 18f.).

[47a] Cf. Mark 14.1b parr. In Mark (and Luke) the 'scribes' are mentioned instead of the Pharisees, and in Matthew 'the elders of the people'. Their replacement by 'the Pharisees' probably derives from the evangelist, since elsewhere too he draws a gloomy picture of the Pharisees as the main opponents of Jesus (cf. 7.32, 45–52; 8.13; 9.40f.; 12.19, 42; 18.3).

[47b] Its dependence on vv. 45–46 and the connection between 'doing signs' and 'believe' (v. 48a) show this remark to be redactional (cf. on 2.23b).

[48] The fear put into the mouths of the members of the Sanhedrin that they could lose their rule over 'the place' (= the temple) and the people is a vivid illustration of the irony practised by the evangelist. For despite the execution of Jesus brought about by the chief priests and Pharisees, the very thing that they wanted to avoid took place: the Christian community spread, and Jerusalem, including the temple, was destroyed by the Romans (in AD 70). The evangelist seems to have been stimulated to make this remark by Z (Mark 14.2; Matt. 26.5: the Jewish authorities fear a revolt among the people).

[49*–50] This censure, made by some member of the Supreme Council, formulates a shrewd and purely political consideration. There are parallels in antiquity both to the underlying idea (cf. e.g. II Sam. 20.20–22; Jonah 1.12–15) and to the wording; cf. e.g. Dio Cassius (c. AD 155–235), who reports the following exclamation of the Roman emperor Otho (AD 69): 'It is surely far better and far more just that one should perish for all than many for one' (LXIII 13). The evangelist has probably woven in the cynical remark here to emphasize the moral depravity of the Jewish leaders.

[53] Cf. Mark 14.1b parr. In the redactional context the decision to kill Jesus shows that the members of the Supreme Council immediately adopt their colleague's consideration.

[54] This is the redactional conclusion to the scene (cf. 10.40). For avoiding the public cf. 7.10; 'from there' means Bethany, the scene of 11.1–44.

Yield: Z does not presuppose any traditions other than Mark 14.1–2 parr.

Historical

The historical value of the scene is nil, since its very core, Mark 14.1–2, is a redactional construction by Mark (see there).

John 11.55–57: The approaching feast of the Passover

55 *Now the Passover of the Jews was near. And many went up from the country to Jerusalem before the Passover, to hallow themselves.* 56 *Now they were seeking Jesus and saying to one another as they stood in the temple, 'What do you think? That he will not come to the feast?'* 57 *Now the chief priests and the Pharisees had given orders that if any one knew where he was, he should report it, so that they might seize him.*

Redaction and historical

This section predominantly fulfils a dramatic function. It opens the account of the last days of Jesus. The depiction of the expectant mood among the host of pilgrims and the report on the measures taken by the Jewish authorities against Jesus have the purpose of heightening tension for the reader.

[55] This verse corresponds to 2.13. The feast of the Passover is the second and last within the evangelist's account (the note 6.4 probably comes from the revisers). The evangelist introduces the festival pilgrims to prepare for 12.12f. For 'hallowing' cf. Num. 9.6–13; II Chron. 30.15–19.

[56] The motif of the search for Jesus corresponds to 6.24 and 7.11.

[57] Cf. 7.32. The mention of the chief priests and Pharisees refers back to 11.47ff.; similarly, the note that these have already made preparations to arrest Jesus corresponds to the decision to kill him reported in 11.53.

Yield: the section is a redactional transition with no historical value.

John 12.1–11: The anointing of Jesus in Bethany

1a Now six days before the Passover, Jesus came to <u>Bethany,</u> b *where Lazarus was, whom Jesus had raised from the dead.* 2a There they made him a supper, b *and Martha served.* c *And Lazarus was one of those who* <u>reclined</u> *with him* <u>at table.</u> 3a Now *Mary* took a pound of <u>costly ointment of pure nard,</u> <u>anointed the feet</u> of Jesus, and <u>wiped his feet with her hair.</u> b And <u>the house</u> was filled with the fragrance of the ointment.

4a But *Judas* says, b **the Iscariot, one of his disciples, who was to deliver him up,** 5 'Why <u>was this ointment</u> not <u>sold for three hundred denarii and</u> (the proceeds) <u>given to poor people?</u>' **6 Now he said this, not because he cared for the poor but because he was a thief and, having the money box, used to take what was put into it.**

7 Then <u>Jesus said,</u> '<u>Leave her</u>! (It has not been sold) so that she may keep it for the day of my <u>burial.</u> 8 <u>For you always have the poor with you, but you do not always have me.</u>'

9 *Now a great crowd of the Jews learned that he was there. And they came not only on account of Jesus but also to see Lazarus, whom he had raised from the dead.* 10 *And the chief priests also resolved to put Lazarus to death,* 11 *because many of the Jews were going away and believing in Jesus because of him.*

Later revision

The analysis of other sections shows that within the various groups of revisers of the Gospel there is one which has a special interest in the figure of Judas, who delivers Jesus up (cf. on 6.64b–65). Hence it is natural to see this one also at work in vv. 4b and 6 (J. Becker), especially as: (a) the 'one of his disciples . . .' is lame; (b) in vv. 7–8 the omniscient Jesus seems to suspect nothing of Judas' purpose; and (c) there is no redactional motive for v. 6. Through the additions the revisers make it clear that even Judas' concern for the poor is a pretence. For had the oil been sold, he would have misappropriated the money.

Redaction and tradition

The section has been formulated on the basis of Z. Here in Z there are elements both of the anointing of Jesus in Bethany in Mark 14.3–9; Matt. 26.6–13 and also of the story of the anointing of Jesus by a woman who was a sinner in Luke 7.36–50 (verbatim and almost verbatim agreements with Mark/Matthew are underlined once and agreements with Luke twice). Accordingly 12.1–11 represents a peculiar synthesis of the final form of several Synoptic texts and can be regarded as a prime example of how the Synoptic Gospels were treated in Z (cf. a similarly clear fusing of Synoptic accounts in 6.1–21; 18.28–19.16a; 19.38–42).

In Mark (14.3–9) and Matthew (26.6–13) the story of the anointing *follows* considerably after the account of Jesus' entry into Jerusalem (Mark 11.1–10; Matt. 21.1–9); in the Fourth Gospel it immediately precedes this. Probably the evangelist himself is responsible for this predating, for 'a story taking place in Bethany can well be put before the entry into Jerusalem, as the way led through Bethany' (H. Windisch).

[1a] The location of the anointing agrees with Mark 14.3; Matt. 26.6. However, the dating diverges from the Synoptics (two days before the Passover). As the following sections do not demonstrate any developed scheme of days, we have to attribute the note of time to Z.

[1b] By the reference back to 11.43f., v. 1b proves to be redactional.

[2a] Here the evangelist has probably omitted a note about the precise place of the anointing which still appeared in Z (Mark 14.3/Matt. 26.6, 'the house of Simon the Leper'; Luke 7.36, 40, the house of a Pharisee named Simon). For he cannot have liked either the notion that Jesus is the guest of a leper or that he reclines at table with a Pharisee (cf. v. 57). However, the 'house' still resonates in v. 3b.

[2b] The mention of Martha points back to 11.1–44 and accordingly derives from the evangelist.

Since for him that Simon who was probably mentioned in Z was out of the question (cf. on v. 2a), the evangelist made Lazarus, Mary and Martha the hosts. That was natural, since the tradition had provided him with Bethany as a scene both for the Lazarus narrative (cf. 11.1) and for the story of the anointing. In formulating v. 2b he was possibly also influenced by another Z narrative (Luke 10.38–42) which (by chance) also told of two sisters named Mary and Martha (cf. Luke 10.40: 'Martha made much effort to serve him').

[2c] This comes from the evangelist. That Lazarus, who will play no further role in this story, is also present at the meal once again emphasizes vividly the reality of his resurrection (11.43–44). However, the phrase 'when he (= Jesus) was reclining at table' appears in Matt. 26.7 (cf. Mark 14.3; Luke 7.36, 37). Evidently the evangelist has transferred to Lazarus a remark from Z that Jesus was reclining at table.

[3a] Only the identification of the 'woman' who was probably anonymous in Z (Mark 14.3; Matt. 26.7; cf. Luke 7.37) with Mary from 11.1–44 derives from the evangelist. Otherwise Z has mixed Mark 14.3 and Luke 7.38, 44, 46 into a tangle which is almost impossible to unravel. Instead of an 'alabaster flask' (Mark, Luke), Z speaks of a 'pound' (cf. 19.39b = Z) and thus intensifies the amount and value of the oil. By contrast with Luke 7.38, drying Jesus' feet with the woman's hair makes no sense, as the feet have not been covered with the woman's tears.

[3b] This is an elaboration of the scene. As the mention of the house (Mark 14.3; Matt. 26.6; Luke 7.36) still shows, it derives from Z (cf. on v. 2a).

[4a] The specific name 'Judas' probably comes from the evangelist (cf. on 6.5b). In Z, as in the Synoptics (Mark 14.4a: 'some'; Matt. 26.8: 'the disciples'), several people must have made the objection which follows (cf. the plural in v. 8).

[5] This verse corresponds almost word for word with Mark 14.5 (cf. Matt. 26.9). However, either Z or the evangelist turns the statement into a question.

[7] Cf. Mark 14.6, 8; Matt. 26.12. As in Mark and Matthew, despite the different formulation the meaning is that the anointing for Jesus' burial has taken place in

advance, i.e. at that moment. For according to both Z and the evangelist the woman (Mary) is not present at the real burial (19.38–42).

[8] The statement appears word for word in Mark 14.7; Matt. 26.11. As in Matthew, the Markan 'and as often as you will you can do good to them' is omitted.

[9–11] As the further reference to 11.1–44 shows, this passage has been constructed by the evangelist. Because many people believe in Jesus on the basis of the miracle of the resurrection, Lazarus is a thorn in the flesh of the chief priests. The contrast could not be greater: the chief priests immediately want to kill the one who has just been snatched from decay (an intention the execution of which is not, however, subsequently reported in the Gospel of John). The remark about their murderous intent (v. 10) is formulated on the basis of 11.53.

Yield: all the deviations of Z from the Synoptics and of the evangelist from Z are secondary elaborations and changes to the scene.

Historical

Cf. on Mark 14.3–9.

John 12.12–19: The ceremonial reception of Jesus

12 *The next day*, the great <u>crowd</u> which had come to the feast, when they heard that Jesus was coming <u>to Jerusalem</u>, 13a they took palm branches and went out to meet him, crying, b '<u>Hosanna, blessed (be) he who comes in the name (of the) Lord</u>, the <u>King</u> of Israel!' 14 And Jesus <u>found</u> a young ass and <u>sat upon it</u>; as it is written, 15 'Fear not, <u>daughter of Zion</u>; <u>look, your king is coming</u>, sitting on the <u>foal</u> of an <u>ass</u>'.

16 *His disciples did not understand this at first. But when Jesus was glorified, then they remembered that this had been written of him and that they had done this to him.*

17 *The crowd that was with him when he called Lazarus out of the tomb and raised him from (the) dead now bore witness. 18 Therefore the crowd went to meet him because they heard that he had done this sign. 19 The Pharisees now said to one another, 'You see that you can do nothing. Look, the world is running after him.'*

Redaction and tradition

The section is based on Z (Mark 11.1–10; Matt. 21.1–9; Luke 19.28–38); verbatim and almost verbatim agreements with Mark are underlined once, and possibly additional agreements with Matthew/Luke are underlined twice. It is particularly striking that by comparison with the Synoptics (cf. Mark 11.11 parr.) there is no report of the real entry into Jerusalem. 'If we did not know otherwise, we would not understand this narrative at all' (J. Wellhausen).

[12] Cf. Matt. 21.8a ('crowd') and Mark 11.1 parr. For the note of time cf. 1.29, 35; 6.22.

[13a] Cf. Mark 11.8b; Matt 21.8b. In contrast to the Synoptic reports, the ovations are not offered by the crowd accompanying Jesus but by the festival pilgrims who come out of Jerusalem especially for this purpose. Palm branches (Mark: bunches of foliage; Matthew: branches of trees) were used to greet victorious rulers (cf. I Macc. 13.51; II Macc. 10.7; Rev. 7.9). Similarly, the particular Greek term which has been translated by 'meet' is a stereotyped expression for the reception of kings and other highly-placed figures outside the town.

[13b] Cf. Mark 11.9b parr. As in Luke 19.38a, Jesus is designated king in the cry of Hosanna (cf. Ps. 117.26a LXX), namely as 'king of Israel' (cf. the quotation of Zech 9.9. in v. 15).

[14] In Z, the episode of the miraculous discovery or obtaining of the ass which is narrated at length in the Synoptics (cf. Mark 11.1b–7 parr.) is condensed into the brief sentence that Jesus found an ass 'and sat upon it' (Mark 11.7). Probably Z mentions this only because of the fulfilment of Zech 9.9 (v. 15). (Z also shows a marked interest in proof from scripture in 19.23–24b, 28–30, 36f.)

[15] The (free) quotation of Zech 9.9 also occurs in Matthew (21.5), but there in the framework of the episode of the finding of the ass.

[16] Cf. on 2.21; 'that this had been written of him' refers to v. 15; 'that they had done this to him' to v. 13.

[17–18] These verses prove to be redactional by their reference back to 11.1–44 (cf. vv. 9–11). The crowd mentioned in v. 17 are the Jews from 11.33, 42, 45 (not the people from 12.9); the crowd from v. 18 are the festival pilgrims from v. 12. The lame explanation that the festival pilgrims went to meet Jesus because of the reports on the miracle with Lazarus does not harmonize with v. 12, according to which they come out simply because of the news of Jesus' coming.

[19] This exaggeration, which is put in the mouths of the Pharisees, prepares for 12.20–36.

Yield: Z is not based on any traditions other than the Synoptic accounts of the entry. Z tightens up the Synoptic reports and emphasizes the royal status of Jesus more strongly than the Synoptists.

Historical

Cf. on Mark 11.1–10.

John 12.20–36: The last public discourse of Jesus

20 *And there were some Greeks among those who went up to worship at the feast.* 21 *These now came to Philip, (who was) from Bethsaida in Galilee, and asked him, saying, 'Sir, we wish to see Jesus.'* 22 *Philip goes and tells Andrew; Andrew and Philip go and tell Jesus.*

23 And Jesus answered them, 'The hour has come that the Son of man should be glorified.

24 Amen, amen, I say to you, unless a grain of wheal falls into the earth and dies, it remains by itself alone; but if it dies, it bears much fruit. 25 He who loves his life loses it, and he who hates his life in this world will keep it for eternal life. 26 If anyone serves me, let him follow me; and where I am, there shall my servant be also. If anyone serves me, the Father will honour him.

27 Now is my soul troubled. And what shall I say? "Father, save me from this hour?" But, for this purpose I have come to this hour. 28a Father, glorify your name.'

28b Then a voice came from heaven, 'I have glorified (it), and I will glorify (it) again.'

29 Now the people who were standing by and had heard (it) said that it had thundered. Others said, 'An angel has spoken to him.'

30 Jesus answered and said, 'This voice has not come for my sake, but for yours. 31 Now is judgment on this world: now the ruler of this world will be cast out, 32 and I, when I am lifted up from the earth, will draw all to me.'

33 Now he said this to show by what death he was to die.

34 Then the people answered him, 'We have heard from the law that the Christ remains for ever. How can you say, "The Son of man must be lifted up"? Who is this Son of man?'

35 Then Jesus said to them, 'The light is among you yet a little while. Walk while you have the light, lest the darkness overtake you; he who walks in the darkness does not know where he goes. 36a As long as you have the light, believe in the light, that you may become sons of light.'

36b Jesus said this and went away and hid himself from them.

Later revision

Verses 24–26 are probably to be attributed to the revisers (W.Langbrandtner). This verdict is obvious first with regard to vv. 25 and 26: in contrast to the context they do not have a christological but a paraenetic orientation, and thus anticipate a theme which arises appropriately only in vv. 35f. In the light of vv. 25f. the assumption of a secondary addition can then be extended to v. 24, for this simile gains its christological meaning only from the preceding context (Jesus' death is the presupposition for rich mission fruit); together with vv. 25f. it destroys the connection between vv. 23 and 27. The existence of parallels in Paul or in the Synoptics to v. 24 (cf. I Cor. 15.36–37), v. 25 (cf. Mark 8.35 parr.; Matt. 10.39/ Luke 17.33) and v. 26 (cf. Mark 8.34 parr.) shows that here the revisers are formulating on the basis of tradition. Only the introductory formula 'Amen, amen, I say to you' (v. 24a) and perhaps also the lame v. 26b might have been added in the course of the insertion.

Redaction and tradition

In this section the evangelist turns to three interconnected questions: first to the access of the non-Jewish world to Jesus; secondly to the meaning of the death of Jesus; and thirdly to the saving outcome of Jesus' return to heavenly glory.

To understand vv. 23, 27–28a it is important to note that the Synoptic Gethsemane scene Mark 14.32–42 parr. stands in the background. If we compare vv. 23, 27–28a with the corresponding Markan parallels it emerges how freely and radically the Fourth Evangelist has reinterpreted this scene: for v. 23 cf. Mark 14.41: 'The hour has come, look, the Son of man is delivered up into the hands of sinners.' For v. 27a cf. Mark 14.34: 'My soul is troubled to death . . .'; for vv. 27b–28a cf. Mark 14.35–36: 35 '. . . and he prayed that if it were possible the hour should pass by him. 36 And he said, "Abba, Father . . . take this cup from me! But not what I will, but what you will." '

[20–22] The link to 12.19 is worth noting: as confirmation of the flocking of the 'world' to Jesus complained of by the Pharisees, some Greeks (cf. elsewhere only 7.35) express the wish to see Jesus. It seems all the more remarkable that this scene has no continuation: the wish of the Greeks is not fulfilled. But the lack of a conclusion to the scene is evidently intended by the evangelist. In this way he expresses in a symbolic concentration that access to Jesus is mediated to the non-Jewish part of humankind by the disciples. Nor is it likely to be a coincidence that the Greeks seek contact with Jesus specifically through Philip and Andrew. For first, these two disciples are the only ones in the Gospel of John to have Greek names; secondly, according to the evangelist they are the first to have followed Jesus – through the mediation of John the Baptist (cf. 1.37 with 1.40 and 1.44 [in the reconstructed form]); and thirdly, they have already functioned once as middlemen: Andrew took his brother Peter to Jesus (cf. 1.40f.) and Philip took Nathanael (1.45f.). With the information about Philip's origin (v. 21) the evangelist is explicitly referring back to this part of his account (cf. 1.44).

[23, 27–28a] There was a reference forward in 7.30 and 8.20 (cf. 7.6) to the 'hour' of Jesus, the hour of his death, which had not yet come. This hour – it is not to be understood in the strictly temporal sense but comprises the totality of the events connected with the death of Jesus (cf. 13.1a) – is now dawning. According to the theological conception of the evangelist, through his death Jesus returns to God in heavenly glory (cf. 3.14f.; 6.62; 7.33; 8.14; 13.1a; 14.12, 28). Therefore the evangelist can speak of the hour of death as the hour of the glorification of Jesus. As such it is at the same time the hour of the glorification of God, as v. 28a shows (cf. 13.31f.). Thus any element of offensiveness in the death of Jesus is radically removed.

This is matched by the way in which the evangelist has used the Gethsemane scene from Z in this passage. (a) Whereas according to Mark 14.35–36a Jesus prays that the hour may pass by him, according to the Fourth Evangelist he declares such a prayer to be excluded (v. 27b). (b) Whereas in Mark 14.36b Jesus first has to force himself to comply with the will of God (which is different from his own will), here he utters the exalted saying, 'But for this purpose I have come to this hour' (v. 27c); there is no longer any trace of a struggle in prayer. (c) The hour of being delivered 'into the hands of sinners' has become the hour of glorification. (There is a further allusion to the Gethsemane scene in 18.11b; for Jesus' being 'troubled' cf. 11.33; 13.21.)

[28b] This fulfils a theological function in the truest sense of the word: the unprecedented statement that the hour of the death of Jesus is the hour of his glorification – and thus at the same time the glorification of God (cf. on v. 28a) – is confirmed by God himself; moreover, 'I *have* glorified it' looks back to the previous activity of Jesus in which God has already been glorified (cf. 11.4; see also 9.4). Furthermore the mention of the voice of God serves a purpose in the composition: it forms a hinge between vv. 23, 27, 28a and vv. 29–33.

[29] This verse serves only to provide a link to the discourse of Jesus which follows (for the quotation of various views cf. 7.12; 7.40–43; 9.16; see also 11.36f.).

[30] Cf. 11.42. Jesus himself needs neither a prayer to God nor confirmation from a heavenly voice, for he is one with God (cf. 10.30).

[31a] 'Now' refers back to v. 27. The hour of the glorification of Jesus means judgment for the world.

[31b, 32] Each of these verses develops an aspect of the basic statement in v. 31a. The judgment which is taking place in Jesus' return to the Father is identical with a fundamental change in rule: the devil (cf. 8.44) is stripped of his power (v. 31b) and Jesus, exalted to God, from now on draws all (each at the individual's hour of death) to him (v. 32; cf. 11.25f.).

[33] Through his death, Jesus is lifted up from earth to God in heaven. This event is miraculously reflected in the particular manner of his death, for in a vivid sense the crucifixion is itself a lifting up from the earth. The evangelist does not think that Jesus' lifting up is in a paradoxical way identical with his crucifixion, but wants to indicate that Jesus knew in advance the particular form of his execution.

[34] The content of the questions asked by the people is not of interest in what follows. As in 7.20, 35f.; 8.22, 48, 52; 10.20, the interjection is merely meant to illustrate the incomprehension of the people.

[35–36a] The concluding invitation to believe refers back to much that has already been hinted at: Jesus, the 'light' (cf. 1.4f., 7–9; 8.12; 9.5; 11.9f.) is among human beings 'yet a little while' (cf. 7.33). For v. 35c cf. 9.9 and 1.5b. Verse 35d recalls 11.10.

[36b] Jesus' hiding of himself (cf. 8.59) concludes not only the scene but also his whole public activity, and bridges over the time up to the eve of the Passover feast in 13.1a.

Yield: vv. 20–23, 27–36 are a composition of the evangelist; however, Mark 14.32–42 glimmers through vv. 23, 27–28a in a shadowy way. The secondary addition vv. 24–26 is based on individual sayings from the tradition.

Historical

For the splinters of tradition which come from the Gethsemane story cf. on Mark 14.32–42; for v. 25 cf. the remarks on Mark 8.35; for v. 26 cf. on Mark 8.34.

John 12.37–43: Conclusion of the account of the public activity of Jesus

37 Although he had done such great signs before them, they did not believe in him, 38 that the word of Isaiah, the prophet, might be fulfilled, which he said: 'Lord, who has believed our message? And the arm of the Lord, to whom has it been revealed?' *39 Therefore they could not believe, because Isaiah again said,* 40 'He has blinded their eyes and hardened their heart, lest they should see with (their) eyes and perceive with their heart, and turn for me to heal them.' *41 Isaiah said this because he saw his glory, and he spoke of him. 42 Nevertheless many even of the authorities came to believe in him, but because of the Pharisees they did not confess it, so as not to be put out of the synagogue. 43 For they loved the glory of men more than the glory of God.*

Redaction and tradition

This résumé forms the conclusion to the first main part of the Gospel of John, which reports the public activity of Jesus. The following chapters will be about the discourses of Jesus in the circle of the disciples.

[37] This verse marks a deep break: Jesus has hidden himself (12.36b); now the evangelist takes stock. But despite the caesura there is still a connection with what has gone before: Jesus' last call for faith addressed to the people (12.36a) has fallen on deaf ears. The mention of the general unbelief has been well prepared for by the preceding chapters (cf. esp. chs. 5–10).

[38] This verse interprets the unbelief as a fulfilment of the prophetic saying Isa. 53.1 LXX. Here the parallel drawn between 'doing signs' (v. 37) and 'message' shows that for the evangelist 'signs' are not simply identical with 'miracles' (cf. 6.26; 20.30).

[39–40] Taken by itself and in its original context, the saying quoted in v. 38 is a disappointed complaint. But if, as the evangelist thinks, the general unbelief repre-sents the *fulfilment* of this complaint, then it follows that the unbelief has already been foreseen in scripture – in other words, from the beginning it has been con-tained in the plan of God. So the Jews *could* not believe at all (v. 39; cf. 8.43b). To express this even more clearly, the evangelist attaches a taut and remarkably free reformulation of Isa. 6.10 LXX. Blinding and hardening are presupposed as a fact in the LXX version of the saying ('The heart of this people is hardened . . .'). The evangelist mentions God as the source of the hardening and in this way shows that God *a priori* wanted to block access to salvation for the Jews.

[41] This verse confirms (not quite correctly) that v. 40 was spoken by the prophet. That Isaiah saw the glory of Jesus recalls the saying in 8.56 according to which Abraham saw Jesus' day.

[42a] This contains information that we can note only with amazement after the previous account by the evangelist and vv. 37–40: many of the authorities have come to believe.

[42b–43] These verses suggest the reason for this surprising statement. By it the evangelist wants to demonstrate something that is very important to him: those people did not dare to confess their faith openly for fear of being excluded from the synagogue (v. 42b; cf. 9.22). But that showed that their faith was inauthentic (v. 43). This is a clear appeal by the evangelist to his community, which has been excluded from the synagogue association and therefore made uncertain. For this congregation, dismay at exclusion from the Jewish community is not a valid excuse for a faith which is not confessed publicly (and is therefore incomplete). Those who let themselves be governed by this fear attach more importance to human approval and the security of social ties than to the 'glory' promised to believers by Jesus and given by God; indeed, they demonstrate a typical characteristic of unbelief (5.44; cf. 5.41; 8.50). But this admonition is at the same time a promise: the fact that only faith in Jesus opens up the way to salvation for the community (14.6) is in no way affected by their being cast out of their original religious home.

Yield: the passage is a composition by the evangelist.

Historical

Verse 42 is an anachronism, which reflects a traumatic experience from the immediate past of the Fourth Evangelist's community.

John 12.44–50: A discourse of Jesus inserted subsequently

44 And Jesus cried and said, 'He who believes in me, believes not in me but in him who has sent me. 45 And he who sees me, sees him who has sent me. 46 I have come as light into the world, that whoever believes in me may not abide in darkness. 47 And if anyone hears my sayings and does not observe them, I do not judge him; for I did not come to judge the world but to save the world. 48 He who rejects me and does not receive my sayings has a judge; the word that I have spoken, it will judge him on the last day. 49 For I have not spoken of my own accord; but the Father who sent me has himself given me commandment what to say and what to speak. 50 And I know that his commandment is eternal life. What I now speak: as the Father has told me, so I speak.'

Analysis

There is no connection between this passage and 12.37–43. Nothing indicated that after the résumé by the evangelist Jesus would speak once again. It is not said where, when and to whom he speaks. He seems to be speaking either directly to the readers or into thin air.

[44–45] The two verses are formed in parallel. Verse 44b has a negative equivalent in 5.23 (cf. also 5.24; 13.20); v. 45 has considerable similarity with 14.9 (cf. 7.16).

[46] This verse recalls above all 3.19–21 and 8.12, but also 1.4–10; 9.5 and 12.35f.

[47] The expression 'observe (the sayings of Jesus)' in v. 47a does not occur elsewhere in the Gospel of John (instead it is always 'keep'); v. 47b refers back to 3.16.

[48a] The word 'reject' is unique in the Gospel of John (but cf. Luke 10.16); 'has a judge' (literally, 'has [one] who judges him') recalls 8.50 ('there is [one] who . . . judges') and first suggests God as judge.

[48b] But then v. 48b contains two surprising statements: first that the *word* spoken by Jesus has the function of judging, and secondly that it will exercise this function on the *last day*.

The first notion looks like an attempt to draw a balance between sayings in which Jesus speaks of himself as a judge (5.22, 27, 30; 8.16) and those according to which Jesus has not come to judge but to save the world (cf. the saying 3.16b quoted in v. 47b). With 'on the last day' the second notion refers back to the same phrase in 6.39, 40c, 44c, 54 – verses which according to the analysis above have been added later. Just as there the notion of the resurrection 'on the last day' clashes with the notion that the believer is already in possession of eternal life, so here the notion of a judgment 'on the last day' is in conflict with the view put forward by the evangelist that the one who does not believe has already been judged (cf. 3.18).

[49–50] These verses are similar to 3.11; 5.19; 8.26, 28, 38, 40.

Yield: verses 44–50 apparently seek to give a brief summary of the public teaching of Jesus by a selective adoption of individual notions from chs. 1–12. Here v. 48b does not correspond to the theology of the evangelist, but stands in the horizon of thought of the later revision of ch. 6 and the addition in 5.28f. However, in contrast to 5.28f.; 6.39 and the phrase 'and I will raise him up at the last day' in 6.40c, 44c, v. 48b is firmly rooted in its context. Therefore it is a well-founded assumption that not only v. 48b or the words 'on the last day' but vv. 44–50 as a whole derive from the revisers (J. Becker). They took this seam in the Gospel as an occasion to formulate a tightly condensed summary of chs. 1–12 (cf. the analogous proceeding in 3.31–36).

Historical

This secondary literary product does not contain authentic sayings of Jesus.

John 13–14: Jesus' farewell to the disciples

John 13.1–20: The foot-washing

1a *Now before the Feast of the Passover,* **when** *Jesus knew that his hour had come to depart out of this world to the Father,* b **as he had loved his own (who were) in the world, he showed** them his love to the end; 2 and at a supper – the devil had already put it into the heart of Judas Iscariot, the (son) of Simon, that he would deliver him up; 3 when he knew that the Father had given all things into his hands and that he had come from God and was going (back) to him – 4 he arose from the supper, took off his upper garment, picked up a linen cloth and girded himself with it. 5 Then he poured water into a basin and began to wash the disciples' feet and to dry them with the linen cloth with which he was girded.

6 *Now he comes to Simon Peter. He says to him, 'Lord, do you want to wash my feet?'* 7 *Jesus answered and said to him, 'What I am doing you do not yet know now, but afterwards you will understand it.'* 8 *Peter says to him, 'You shall never ever wash my feet.' Jesus answered him, 'If I do not wash you, you have no part with me.'* 9 *Simon Peter says to him, 'Lord, not my feet only, but also my hands and my head!'* 10a *Jesus says to him, 'He who has bathed does not need to wash* [except for the feet], *but he is completely clean.* b And you are clean, but not all.' 11 For he knew the one who delivered him up; that was why he said, 'You are not all clean.'

12a Now when he had washed their feet and put on his upper garment and resumed his place, b he said to them, 'Do you know what I have done to you? 13 You call me "Teacher" and "Lord", and you say so rightly, for so I am. 14 Now if I have washed your feet as Lord and Teacher, you must also wash one another's feet. 15 For I have given you an example, that you also should do as I have done to you.

16 Amen, amen, I say to you, the slave is not greater than his lord, nor one who is sent (= apostle) greater than the one who has sent him. 17 If you know these things, blessed are you if you do them.

18 I am not speaking of you all; I know whom I have chosen. But that the scripture may be fulfilled, "He who consumes my bread has lifted his heel against me." 19 I tell you this now already, before it takes place, that when it does take place you may believe that I am (he).

20 Amen, amen, I say to you, he who receives one whom I shall send receives me; and he who receives me, receives him who sent me.'

Preliminary text-critical comment: In v. 10a the majority of manuscripts add 'except for the feet' to 'does not need to wash'. This qualification does not fit in with the verse. For if it is still necessary to wash the feet after a bath, then the one who has bathed is not *completely* clean (R. Bultmann). So we can assume that these words are a gloss. However, the long text is so well attested that we cannot rule out the possibility that in terms of textual criticism 'except for the feet' is original. But even if that were so, it would not change the secondary character of the words, in that they would then have to be attributed to the (first) later revisers, who will be mentioned next; they certainly do not derive from the evangelist.

First and second later revision

The narrative of the foot-washing has obviously gone through an extremely complicated history before it assumed its present, final form. In what follows, first all elements and passages added at a secondary stage will be identified. However, once this has been done it will prove that the phenomenon of later revision is even more complicated in the case of 13.1–20 than in other passages which have been expanded at a secondary stage.

There is no monster sentence elsewhere in the Gospel of John comparable with vv. 1–4. Several observations are important for extracting the original text from this bombastic and overloaded construction. (a) The evangelist hardly ever speaks of the love of Jesus for his own (v. 1b); the only exception is 14.21, a verse from the tradition. On the other hand this love is a dominant theme of the addition 15.1–17. (b) According to v. 2 the devil has already prompted Judas to deliver Jesus up. That is in conflict with 13.27, according to which Satan goes into Judas only after Jesus has given him a piece of bread. (c) In content, v. 3 is a doublet of v. 1a.

Here is a plausible explanation for this situation: first of all the revisers added v. 1b (a preparation for vv. 12b–15). In order to tie this addition closely to v. 1a, they replaced the original predicate 'knew' with the participle 'knowing' (which has been broken up in the translation by the 'when' clause). Accordingly v. 1a originally had the following wording: 'Now before the Feast of the Passover Jesus knew that his hour had come to depart out of this world to the Father.' Then v. 2 (from 'the devil' to the end of the verse) is probably an addition: by placing Judas under Satanic influence even before the meal began, the revisers responsible are trying to remove the embarrassing fact that the one who delivered Jesus up participated in the meal. In so doing they make it clear that Judas was truly not to be counted as one of 'his own' (v. 1b). Because of this addition it was again necessary to create a counter-balance to the devil who has now come into play. That was achieved by v. 3, formulated on the basis of v. 1a (for the formulation cf. also the additions 3.35; 16.28). The parenthesis has now assumed grotesque proportions, and every reader has forgotten the situational note 'at a supper' from v. 2; accordingly, the revisers finally inserted 'from the supper' in v. 4 as a reminder.

[10b–11] In v. 10a, only Peter is addressed; in v. 10b Jesus is abruptly addressing all the disciples. The revisers used the keyword 'clean' from v. 10a in order to weave in another note about Judas after the expansions in vv. 2–3. That vv. 10b–11 are an addition emerges also from the fact that otherwise it would be incomprehensible why Jesus can be troubled when announcing the delivering up in 13.21b (the same goes for vv. 18f.).

[12b–15] In the framework of the dialogue between Jesus and Peter (vv. 6–10a) the foot-washing is interpreted as a *symbol*. This interpretation clearly derives from the evangelist (see under 'Redaction and tradition'). By contrast, vv. 12b–15 give the foot-washing a completely different interpretation. Here it is an *example* which calls for imitation. 'The two interpretations stand over against each other as monoliths with no reference to each other, and in substance are mutually exclusive' (J. Becker).

[16–20] This passage similarly derives from the revisers, since first, vv. 16f., 20 are closer to the second interpretation of the foot-washing than to the first, and secondly, the note about Judas in vv. 18f. is in line with the expansions in vv. 2–3 and vv. 10b–11; thirdly, none of the statements in vv. 16–20 can be attached to v. 12a (including the introduction to the discourse in v. 12b).

Now it is clear that these extensive expansions of the text composed by the evangelist are not a unity in themselves and are sometimes even in tension with one another. In particular it is striking that by the remark about Judas (vv. 18f.) v. 20 is torn away from vv. 16f., with which it is connected by the key word 'send', so that it is now in complete isolation. Moreover v. 18 does not fit well with the beatitude in v. 17. It follows from these tensions *within* the secondary expansions that in the case of 13.1–20 we have to reckon not just with one but with two successive revisions (J. Becker; cf. also the introduction, point 6). The *first* reviser or circle of revisers (vv. 1b, 12b–17, 20) is responsible for the interpretation of the foot-washing as an example to be imitated (for this stratum of the revision cf. the introductory comments on 15.1–17). The *second* (circle of) reviser(s), whose additions are underlined in the translation, finally devoted itself to the problem of Judas (cf. on 6.64b–65). Here in formulating vv. 18f. he has evidently leaned on 6.70; 8.28; 14.29 (cf. Ps. 41.10).

Redaction and tradition

After removing the tertiary and secondary additions we can now look separately at the text composed by the evangelist: vv. 1a, 2*, 4*, 5–10a, 12a.

[1a] This is a redactional introduction: 'before the Feast of the Passover' refers back to 11.55 and 12.1; the motif of the coming of the hour picks up 12.23; the interpretation of the death of Jesus as a return to the Father is characteristic of the evangelist (cf. 6.62; 7.33; 8.14; 12.32; 14.12, 28).

[2*, 4*, 5] The surprising transition from the highly theological statement in v. 1a to the foot-washing scene, which is described vividly and in detail, indicates that these verses are the beginning of a narrative taken over by the evangelist. It is about an unprecedented exchange of roles: the disciples do not wash their Lord's feet, but the Lord washes his disciples' feet.

[6a] It may be said in anticipation that the dialogue between Peter and Jesus (vv. 6b–10a) introduced with v. 6a interprets the foot-washing as a symbol of Jesus' crucifixion. This interpretation does not emerge organically from vv. 2*, 4*, 5 and therefore hardly represents the original continuation of these verses. Rather, this must be the specific interpretation of the evangelist, for it is stamped through and through by his theology.

[6b–7] Peter rejects Jesus' intention (v. 6b); this emphasizes the offensiveness of the action. When Jesus instructs his disciple that he will experience the meaning of the action only 'afterwards' (v. 7), this 'afterwards' without doubt refers to the time after Easter (cf. 2.22; 12.16).

[8] Despite the reference in v. 7 Peter now protests energetically against Jesus' humiliation of himself (v. 8a). By contrast, Jesus' retort (v. 8b) emphasizes the need for his self-humiliation: if Peter does not allow this service to be performed, he can have no fellowship with Jesus. It is clear that the evangelist is not concerned to speak up for some act of foot-washing initiated by Jesus. Rather, his aim is to 'answer the burning christological question of the time whether or not the crucifixion – symbolically depicted by the foot-washing – is in harmony with the messiahship of Jesus' (G. Richter). Therefore in v. 8b he states in symbolic concentration that

anyone who wants to belong to Jesus must accept the scandal that Jesus' return to God takes place through the cross. Thus to put it in a pointed way, the evangelist does not want to emphasize the saving significance of the *death* of Jesus on the cross, but rather to show that the saving significance of *Jesus* is not limited by his death on the cross. 'Jesus' death is a necessary transition to life, the last testing in the mission of the Son' (U.B.Müller).

[9–10a] Peter has now evidently understood that he must have his feet washed in order to be able to have communion with Jesus. Therefore after his initial protest he goes to the other extreme and asks for a cleansing of his whole body (v. 9). The answer which he is thereupon given (v. 10a*), which sounds like a proverb, is hard to interpret. Probably it serves to avoid the misunderstanding that v. 8b is an insistence on the need for a cultic-sacramental rite. By contrast, again in symbolic concentration, it is made clear that the salvation that the believer receives when he overcomes the last offence given by the cross of Jesus (v. 8b) is complete; it does not need to be supplemented by anything else.

[12a] This again takes up the threads of the story, vv. 2*, 4*, 5, adopted by the evangelist which were dropped in v. 6. As vv. 12b–20 are later additions, immediately after v. 12a the evangelist continued with the prophecy of Jesus about the delivering up by Judas. Accordingly, the present and the following narrative formed a unit in the work of the evangelist.

It is often assumed that v. 12a belongs with the later expansions vv. 12b–20 and that in the work of the evangelist v. 10a was continued by 13.21a. But the evangelist must also have reported that after vv. 6–10a Jesus again dressed and reclined at table. Otherwise we would have the somewhat comic conclusion that from 13.21 onwards Jesus is acting in a half-naked state.

Now, however, the following problem arises: if vv. 6–10a come from the evangelist and vv. 12b–20 are later additions, what was the original continuation of the story in vv. 2*, 4*, 5, 12a adopted by the evangelist? The obvious hypothesis for answering this question is complicated, but attractive: the original continuation corresponds to the one which was added by the revisers in vv. 12b–15 (J. Becker). They reintroduced into the text the original interpretation broken off by the evangelist and replaced by vv. 6–10a.

It is difficult to find a place for vv. 16f., 20. Certainly it is clear that these verses are secondary to vv. 12b–15, for first the story has a meaningful conclusion with v. 15, and secondly there are Synoptic variants to v. 16 (which is reinforced by v. 17) and v. 20 (for v. 16 cf. Matt. 10.24 par; for v. 20 cf. Matt. 10.40 par.; Mark 9.37). But it is no longer possible to decide whether vv. 16f., 20 were already added to the narrative at the level of tradition and then adopted by the revisers, or whether they were added only in the course of the revision itself. However, this question is unimportant for an identification of the core of the tradition.

Accordingly, the *original* form of the foot-washing narrative had the following wording:

2* And at a supper 4* he arose, took off his upper garment, picked up a linen cloth and girded himself with it. 5 Then he poured water into a basin and began to wash the disciples' feet and to dry them with the linen cloth with which he was girded. 12 Now when he had washed their feet and put on his upper garment and resumed his place, he said to them, 'Do you know what I have done to you? 13 You call me "Teacher" and "Lord", and you say so rightly, for so I am. 14 Now if I have washed your feet as Lord and Teacher, you must also wash one another's feet. 15 For I have given you an example, that you also should do as I have done to you.'

This narrative is a community rule with a scenic introduction. It calls upon the members of the community to imitate the example of Jesus and to serve one another (cf. Mark 10.42–45; Luke 22.27). The foot-washing is certainly a vivid metaphor for this mutual service, but in principle it can be replaced by any other act of humility. Moreover it should be noted that the narrative shows no reference to the passion of Jesus. It was put in this context only by the evangelist.

Yield: the evangelist has used a narrative about a foot-washing which comprised vv. 2*, 4*, 5, 12–15 (,16f., 20?) and framed it with v. 1a. He omitted the original conclusion of the narrative (from v. 12b) and instead provided it with an interpretation of his own (vv. 6–10a). The original conclusion was then restored to the narrative by those who subjected the evangelist's text to a first revision (v. 1b is also to be attributed to them). A later reviser (or group of revisers) finally added the long parenthesis in vv. 2–3, the words 'from the supper' (in v. 4), and vv. 10b–11, 18f.

In conclusion, to illustrate the matter more clearly, here is a list of which verses the narrative presumably comprised at the individual stages in the eventful history of its composition.

Original form	2*, 4*, 5, 12–15
Expanded form?	2*, 4*, 5, 12–15 (,16f., 20?)
Evangelist	1a, 2*, 4*, 5, 6–10a, 12a
Revision 1	1a, 1b, 2*, 4*, 5, 6–10a, 12a, 12b–15, 16f., 20
Revision 2	1–20

Historical

The narrative of the foot-washing in vv. 2*, 4*, 5, 12–15 serves as paraenesis for the disciples. This ecclesiological interest shows it to be unhistorical.

For v. 16 cf. the observations on Matt. 10.24 and Luke 6.40a. The saying is not authentic.

For v. 20 cf. the remarks on Matt. 10.40/Luke 10.16 (= Q) and Mark 9.37. The saying does not go back to Jesus.

John 13.(12a) 21–30: The prophecy of the delivering up by Judas

[12a Now when he had washed their feet and put on his upper garment and resumed his place . . .]

21a **When Jesus had said this,** b *he was troubled in the spirit, and testified and said,* c 'Amen, *amen,* I say to you, one of you will deliver me up.' 22 The disciples looked at one another, uncertain of whom he spoke.

23 **One of his disciples, whom Jesus loved, was reclining in the bosom of Jesus. Simon Peter now beckons to him to enquire who it is of whom he was speaking. 25 So he reclines on Jesus' breast and says to him, 'Lord, who is it?' 26a Jesus answers, 'It is he to whom I shall give the morsel when I have dipped it.'**

26b *Now he* dips *the* [a] *morsel, takes and gives it to* Judas Iscariot, *the (son) of Simon.* 27a *And after the morsel,* Satan entered into *him.* b *Then Jesus says to him, 'What you want to do, do quickly.' 28 But no one of those who were reclining at the table knew why he said this to him. 29 For some supposed that, because Judas had the money box, Jesus was telling him, 'Buy what we need for the feast,' or that he should give something to the poor. 30 Now after he had received the morsel, he immediately went out. And it was night.*

Later revision

[21a] In the course of the insertion of 13.12b–20 the revisers were compelled to create a smooth transition to v. 21b. To this end they made use of the transitional formula 'When he had said this', which is also often used by the evangelist.

[23–26a] In v. 28 it is emphasized that *none* of those reclining at the table could make sense of Jesus' command in v. 27b. (This corresponds to the motif of misunderstanding or incomprehension which is typical of the evangelist, cf. on 2.20.) This statement is in sheer contradiction to vv. 23–26a, which say that the beloved disciple has explicitly been informed by Jesus of the identity of the one who will deliver him up (v. 26a). Thus at least the beloved disciple can be in no doubt about the meaning of the command in v. 27b.

Now the beloved disciple plays an important role in ch. 21, which was added later by the revisers; indeed his real significance (as the – alleged – author of the whole Gospel) is disclosed to the reader only in ch. 21. So it is natural to suppose that the authors of ch. 21 are also responsible for the insertion of the scene with the beloved disciple at this point. This assumption is confirmed by the fact that all the other beloved disciple passages within chs. 1–20 (19.26f., 35; 20.3–10; see also on 1.35–51) cause tensions in the context and thus prove to be additions. By making clear that the beloved disciple is the only one to be informed in advance of the identity of the one who is to deliver Jesus up, they emphasize the advantage in knowledge he has over his fellow disciples and at the same time bring him into a unique proximity with Jesus. This proximity is further heightened by v. 23. For by reclining in the bosom of Jesus, the beloved disciple is as close to Jesus as Jesus himself is to his Father (cf. 1.18: 'who is in the bosom of the Father'). For the conception of the beloved disciple cf. already the introduction, point 7.

If vv. 23–26a are an addition, there is no preparation for the mention of 'the' morsel in v. 26b. However, this can easily be explained if we assume that under pressure from v. 26a, the definite article was inserted only by the revisers. According to the evangelist, thus Jesus probably spoke of 'a morsel' in v. 26a.

Redaction and tradition

This section, which is closely connected with the previous one (13.1a, 2*, 4*, 5–10a, 12a; see on 13.12a) has been composed on the basis of Z; cf. Mark 14.18–20; Matt. 26.21f. (underlinined once) and Luke 22.3 (underlined twice).

[21b] This verse is the seamless continuation of v. 12a. The verse shows itself to be redactional by the motif of Jesus' being troubled (cf. 11.33; 12.27) and the word 'testify', which the evangelist favours.

[21c] The prophecy of the delivering up by one of the disciples corresponds word for word with Mark 14.18 (= Matt. 26.21); the evangelist inserts only an additional 'amen'.

[22] The reaction of the disciples corresponds to Mark 14.19 or Matt. 26.22.

[26b] Jesus reacts to the perplexity of the disciples with a wordless gesture.

[27a] Cf. Luke 22.3: before the Passover meal 'Satan entered into Judas'.

[27b] Jesus directs Judas to implement his plan as quickly as possible. This emphasizes that Jesus himself has control over his fate.

[28–29] Judas' actual purpose is brought out all the more strongly by the naive interpretations attributed to the disciples.

[30a] This verse takes up the narrative thread of v. 27b again and ends it with the notice of Judas' departure. He is no longer present at the farewell discourse of Jesus which follows (13.31–14.31). The next time he encounters Jesus he will deliver him up (18.3), as has been announced.

[30b] The note of time which is put emphatically at the end of the scene makes it clear that now the night is beginning in which Jesus is completing his work (cf. 9.4; 12.35).

Yield: the section 13.21b–22, 26b–30 presupposes Mark 14.18–21 and Luke 22.3. The evangelist is above all concerned to emphasize the sovereignty of Jesus in the approaching passion: Jesus was not surprised by the events which led to his execution, but staged them himself.

Historical

As the basis of the report is itself a fiction (for the reason see on Mark 14.18–22), the elements which differ from the Markan account and go beyond it cannot lay any claim to historicity.

John 13.31–38: The prophecy about Peter's denial

31 Now when he (= Judas) had gone out, Jesus says, 'Now has the Son of man been glorified, and God has been glorified in him. 32 But if God has been glorified in him, God will also glorify him in himself, and he will glorify him soon. 33 Children, yet a little while I am with you; you will seek me; and as I said to the Jews, "Where I am going, you cannot come," (so) I now also say to you.

34 A new commandment I give to you, that you should love one another, as I have loved you, so that you also love one another. 35 By this all will know that you are my disciples, if you have love for one another.'

36 Simon Peter says to him, 'Lord, where are you going?' Jesus answered him, 'Where I am going, you cannot follow me now; but you will follow later.' 37 <u>Peter</u> <u>says to him</u>, '<u>Lord</u>, *why can I not follow you now?* I will lay down my life for you.' 38 <u>Jesus</u> answers, 'Will you lay down your life for me? <u>Amen</u>, *amen,* <u>I say to you: the cock will not crow until you have denied me three times.</u>'

Later revision

[34–35] The commandment to love one another stands in isolation in the context. For Peter does not take any notice of it in v. 36, but refers directly to Jesus' announcement in v. 33. It follows from this that vv. 34–35 have been inserted into this section later, probably by the author of the addition 15.1–17 (see there).

Redaction and tradition

This section is the beginning of the farewell discourse of Jesus which continues in 14.1 and in the evangelist's work extended to 14.31 (chs. 15–17 are additions). As is shown by the verbatim and almost verbatim agreements between vv. 37–38 and above all Luke 22.33–34 (double underlining), the evangelist has shaped this section using Z (agreements with Mark 14.29–31 = Matt. 26.33–34 are underlined once).

[31a] This takes up the note of Judas' departure (13.30). In this way the section is closely linked with the previous one.

[31b–32] These verses are wholly stamped by the key word 'glorify' (5 times) and express the notion characteristic of the evangelist that Jesus' glorification takes place in his passion (cf. on 12.23, 27f.). Since the death of Jesus is at the same time the completion of the divine mission, the glorification of God also takes place in it.

[33] 'Yet a little while' (cf. 7.33; 12.35; 14.19) corresponds to the 'soon' from v. 32; the rest explicitly relates to 7.34 and 8.21, where the formulation is very similar.

[36a] Cf. 7.35; 14.5.

[36b] Only when Jesus has completed the task for which he has been sent and has returned to the Father through death can Peter follow him. Only Jesus himself can lay the foundation for salvation (cf. 12.32).

[37] Peter is not content with the 'later' (cf. 13.8), but wants to follow Jesus now. He is even ready to stake his life on this. Cf. Luke 22.33 ('Lord, I am ready to go with you even to prison and to death'); cf. also Mark 14.31 = Matt. 26.35 ('even if I had to die with you . . .').

[38] Jesus' answer, which rebukes Peter's over-hasty zeal, stands in sharp contrast to this. The prophecy, which corresponds almost word for word with Luke 22.34, will be fulfilled in 18.12–27.

Yield: the section has been composed by the evangelist himself on the basis of Z.

Historical

Cf. on Mark 14.29–31.

John 14.1–31: The farewell discourse to the disciples

1 *'Let not your hearts be troubled! Believe in God, and believe in me.* 2 In my Father's house are many dwellings; *if (it were) not (so), would I then say to you that* I go away to prepare a place for you? 3 And when I have gone away and prepared a place for you, I will come again and will take you to myself, that where I am you may be also.

4 *And where I am going, you know the way.'* 5 *Thomas says to him, 'Lord, we do not know where you are going; how can we know the way?'* 6 *Jesus says to him,* 'I am the way and the truth and the life; no one comes to the Father, but by me. 7 *And if you have known me, you will know my Father also. And even now you know him and see him.'* 8 *Philip says to him, 'Lord, show us the Father, and that suffices us.'* 9 *Jesus says to him, 'Have I been with you so long, and yet you do not know me, Philip? He who has seen me has seen the Father; how can you say, "Show us the Father"?* 10a *Do you not believe that I am in the Father and the Father in me?* b *The words that I say to you I do not speak of my own accord; rather, the Father who abides in me does his works.* 11 *Believe me that I (am) in the Father and the Father in me. If not, believe for the sake of the works themselves.*

12 *Amen, amen, I say to you, he who believes in me will do the works that I do; and greater than these will he do, for I go to the Father.* 13 *And* whatever you ask in my name, I will do it, *that the Father may be glorified in the Son.* 14 **If you ask me anything in my name, I will do it.** 15 **If you love me, you will keep my commandments.** 16 *And I will ask the Father, and he will give you another Paraclete, to be with you for ever,* 17 *the Spirit of truth, whom the world cannot grasp, because it neither sees him nor knows (him). You know him because he abides with you, and will be in you.*

18 *I will not leave you behind as orphans; I am coming to you.* 19 *Yet a little while, and the world sees me no more; but you will see me, because I live and you will live.* 20 *On that day you will know that I (am) in my Father, and you in me, and I in you.* 21 He who has my commandments and keeps them, he it is who loves me; and he who loves me will be loved by my Father, and I will love him and manifest myself to him.' 22 *Judas – not Iscariot – says to him, 'Lord, how is it that you will manifest yourself to us, and not to the world?'* 23 *Jesus answered and said to him, 'If a*

man loves me, he will keep my word, and my Father will love him; and we will come to him and dwell with him. 24 **He who does not love me does not keep my words; and the word which you hear is not mine, but (that) of the Father who has sent me.** 25 *I have spoken this to you while I was with you.* 26 *But the Paraclete, the Holy Spirit, whom the Father will send in my name, he will teach you all things, and bring to your remembrance all that I have said to you.*

27 *Peace I leave with you; my peace I give to you; not as the world gives do I give (it) to you. Let not your hearts be troubled, and do not let them be afraid.* 28a *You have heard me say to you, "I am going away, and coming to you."* b *If you loved me, you would rejoice that I am going to the Father; for the Father is greater than I.* 29 *And now I have told you before it takes place, so that when it does take place, you may believe.* 30 *I will no longer talk much with you, for the ruler of the world is coming. He has nothing in me,* 31 *but (this happens) so that the world may know that I love the Father and do as the Father has commanded me.* Arise, let us go from here!'

Later revision

[14–15] Verse 14 does not say anything new by comparison with v. 13a but largely agrees word for word with it. By contrast, v. 15 with its paraenetic undertone seems displaced in the context, but has precisely the same structure as v. 14. This suggests that vv. 14–15 have been added by a later hand – probably the author of the addition 15.1–17 (see there). This assumption is supported by the fact that v. 16 takes up 'Father' from v. 13b.

[24] This verse probably derives from the same reviser. His concern was evidently, after the statement about the one who loves Jesus (v. 23), also to take a look at the one for whom the opposite is the case. For v. 24a merely represents the negative counterpart to v. 23a. By contrast, v. 23b cannot so easily be turned into the opposite; therefore the reviser helped himself by adopting for v. 24b a statement which occurs often in a similar form in the Gospel of John (most recently in v. 10b; cf. further 8.28, 42; 12.49). However, it does not fit well at this point.

Redaction and tradition

The situation presupposed in ch. 14 is still the same as that in ch. 13: the signal to set out from the place of the last supper is given only in 14.31. Jesus' discourse, which is interrupted by individual disciples only in vv. 5, 8, 22, can be divided up as follows. Verses 1–3 introduce the discourse. Here a revelation saying from the tradition is quoted which is about Jesus' going away and returning. In vv. 4–26 this saying is interpreted in two directions: vv. 4–17 develop the theme of 'going away'; vv. 18–26 interpret the theme of the renewed coming. Verses 27–31 form the conclusion of the discourse; they bring together individual sayings from the main part and lead into the passion story.

Introduction and theme of the discourse (vv. 1–3)

[1] The invitation to fearlessness in the face of the imminent departure of Jesus (v. 1a) recurs word for word in v. 27b. The admonition to faith in God and in Jesus (v. 1b) prepares for the remarks about the unity of Father and Son in vv. 7–11.

[2–3] The talk of heaven as the house of God and the many heavenly dwellings, which is unique in the New Testament, indicates that these verses are based on a revelation saying from the tradition. Only the words 'if not, would I then say to you that' have been inserted by the evangelist, probably to anchor this saying better in the discourse situation. Accordingly, the tradition was worded as follows:

2 'In my Father's house are many dwellings,
[and] I go away to prepare a place for you.
3 And when I have gone away and prepared a place for you,
I will come again and will take you to myself,
that where I am you may be also.'

This word of promise moves in the thought-world of apocalyptic: by his death Jesus returns to heaven and there makes ready the 'dwellings' for the disciples; after that he comes again to fetch them, to lead them into the heavenly dwellings, and then to be united with them for ever.

This mythological-apocalyptic saying differs from the theological conception of the evangelist which has become apparent in the previous chapters. For whereas the evangelist emphasizes time and again that the eschatological salvation is present in Jesus and in his word (cf. on 5.24), according to v. 2f. salvation dawns only with the return of Jesus at the end of days. Until then the disciples must persevere in a time void of salvation. Is the evangelist now going to give up the emphasis on the presence of salvation in favour of a notion according to which the goal of salvation is still to come? If no more followed vv. 2f., we would doubtless have to accuse him of such an inconsistency. But what is said later in the discourse will show that the evangelist is reinterpreting the faith of the community articulated in vv. 2f. step by step as he understands it, so that the traditional view is at the end 'reversed' in the truest sense of the word (cf. v. 23). Cf. also 5.25.

Jesus' departure (vv. 4–17)

[4] This verse skilfully leads on to the theme of the 'way', which hitherto has played no role.

[5] The disciples, who here are represented by Thomas (cf. 11.16; 20.24–29), do not understand Jesus' remarks (for the motif of the incomprehension of the disciples cf. on 2.20) and thus offer Jesus an occasion to explain the mystery of the 'way'.

[6] This 'I am' saying is most probably a saying from the tradition (cf. 6.35; for the

claim to exclusiveness cf. Ex. 20.2f.; Acts 4.12), for in the context only the term 'way' is significant; Jesus' identification of himself with the 'truth' and the 'life' is left unnoticed. In the redactional context, v. 6 discloses the meaning of v. 4: Jesus has not been speaking at all about his own way into the house of the Father but about the way of the disciples. For them Jesus himself, exclusively, is the way to God. The subsequent remarks will show that this way is at the same time the destination, and in what sense that is the case.

[7–11] With the notion of the unity of Jesus and his Father, the claim articulated in v. 6 is enlarged – first by way of a hint (v. 7), then indirectly (v. 9a), and finally quite directly (vv. 9b–11). None of the key christological formulations of vv. 7–11 appears here for the first time: for v. 7 cf. 8.19; for v. 9 cf. 1.18; for vv. 10a, 11a cf. 10.30; for v. 10b cf. 8.28, 42 (for v. 11b cf. 10.39). But here they appear in such a concentrated form that together with v. 6 this passage may be termed a summary of the evangelist's christology. Furthermore it is also already becoming evident here what direction the reinterpretation of the saying about the heavenly dwellings (vv. 2–3) will take. For if God can be known and seen in *Jesus*, then the one who believes in Jesus is already in a state of final and complete salvation.

[12–13] Verse 12 takes up the theme of 'works' which has been introduced through the skewed contrast in v. 10b. Jesus promises those who believe in him that they will continue his works and do even 'greater works' than he. The end of v. 12 ('for I go to the Father') and v. 13 say how that is possible: the Jesus who will have returned to the Father will hear the prayers of the community which remains behind (v. 13a comes from the tradition; cf. Mark 11.24; Luke 11.13; for v. 13b cf. 13.31f.). In concrete terms the thought behind the 'greater works' is probably that after the departure of Jesus, Christian preaching will no longer be limited in time and place (cf. 20.29).

[16–17] These verses contain a further promise to the disciples: the Father will give them 'another Paraclete', the Spirit of truth, who will remain with them for ever. In view of the fact that this Paraclete has not been mentioned previously, however, that is an unexpected and remarkable promise. Above all, the question arises how the Paraclete relates to Jesus. This question is answered in vv. 18–26.

The new coming of Jesus (vv. 18–26)

[18] This verse takes up the 'I will come again' from v. 3 and thus introduces the interpretation of the notion of the further coming. The verse is the key to understanding vv. 16–17 and thus at the same time the whole farewell discourse. Whereas the preceding remarks of Jesus gave the impression that he himself will shortly be completely removed from the disciples and that from now on the Paraclete will take his place, now it is said that 'I am coming to you.' But this can only mean that Jesus himself is coming in the Paraclete. The evangelist probably thought of this 'identity

with a difference' (J. Becker) in accordance with the relationship of Jesus to God (cf. 10.30).

[19–20] These verses deal with the question of when Jesus' new coming will take place. The expression 'yet a little while', the exclusion of the world from seeing Jesus, and the 'I live' show that it will take place at Easter. On that day the disciples will know not only the unity of Jesus with God (cf. v. 10a and v. 11a) but also their own unity with Jesus. Here the phrase 'you in me and I in you' refers back to v. 17 (the *Paraclete* will be 'in you'). Thus it is confirmed that according to the evangelist, Jesus and the Paraclete are one (cf. on v. 18).

Now if the return of Jesus and the coming of the Spirit take place at Easter, according to the Fourth Evangelist Easter, Pentecost and parousia are one and the same event – an event which takes place time and again in the community (cf. vv. 16f.). The present of the community is therefore no empty time but the present of salvation.

[21] This verse clarifies the question of the presupposition on which the disciples will be granted this experience of the new coming of Jesus. The abrupt mention of keeping the commandments and the equally abrupt motif of love make it probable that for this purpose the evangelist is referring back to a traditional statement of promise.

[22] Judas (cf. Luke 6.16; Acts 1.13), who is distinguished from that Judas who delivers Jesus up, takes up the key word 'manifest' from v. 21 in order to ask Jesus about the reason for the exclusiveness of revelation (cf. 7.4b). Behind this question there is probably an objection made by non-Christians against the Christian Easter testimony: why can it not be confirmed by independent witnesses? Cf. Acts 10.40f.

[23] Jesus does not give a direct answer, and thus does not engage in any apologetic, but repeats v. 21 in a slightly different form: it is enough if the disciples know to whom and on what presuppositions Jesus comes. With v. 23, at the same time the reinterpretation of vv. 2–3 achieves its goal: the promise that Jesus will one day take the believers into the heavenly dwellings is replaced by the promise that in a reverse movement, Father and Son will come to the believers and take up a dwelling place *in them*. This indwelling is promised to all those who love Jesus and keep his word; accordingly it does not take place in an indeterminate future but is already reality in the community of the readers.

[25–26] In vv. 16f. Jesus had already mentioned a function of the Paraclete, namely of always being with and in the disciples. This task is now made concrete: it consists in keeping alive Jesus' sayings and time and again giving them a new validity (in contrast to this see 16.12–14). Thus in the Paraclete Jesus remains present among the disciples.

The conclusion of the discourse (vv. 27–31)

[27] The promise of peace, together with the word of comfort, 'Let not your hearts be troubled' (cf. v. 1a), introduces the end of the discourse. The negative evaluation of the world corresponds to vv. 17 and 19.

[28a] This verse sums up the basic statement of the previous remarks by taking up vv. 4a and 18b word for word.

[28b] The death of Jesus is his return to heavenly glory and thus the presupposition for the fulfilment of the promises from vv. 1–26. It should therefore really be cause for joy for the disciples caught up in the sorrow of farewell.

[29] Seen purely from the outside, the approaching events of the passion will not show that the exaltation of Jesus to God is taking place in them. But because Jesus has explained the meaning of his departure to the disciples beforehand, they need not be afraid in the face of the circumstances in which his glorification takes place.

[30–31] These verses lead into the passion story in chs. 18f. The ruler of the world, i.e. the devil, now goes into action through Judas (cf. 13.27; 18.3). But he has no power over Jesus (cf. 12.31), for the following events only apparently represent the triumph of Satan over Jesus. In reality they are an element in and the conclusion of the Son's task. The evangelist has evidently based vv. 30–31 on Z, since it is obvious that the conclusion of the Gethsemane scene shines through them; cf. Mark 14.42 (= Matt. 26.46): 'Arise, let us go! See, the one who is delivering me up is near.' In the evangelist's work, 14.31 was directly continued by 18.1 (cf. the introductory remarks on chs. 15–17).

Yield: the evangelist himself has composed the farewell discourse of Jesus using individual sayings from the tradition. His bold reinterpretation of Easter, Pentecost and Parousia has no parallel in the New Testament.

Historical

The saying vv. 2f.* is not authentic, for it presupposes post-Easter faith in the parousia of Jesus.

The 'I am' saying in v. 6 is a saying of the Exalted One and therefore inauthentic.

The word of promise in v. 13a does not go back to Jesus. Jesus spoke of a direct hearing of prayer by God (cf. on Matt. 7.7–11).

[21] This verse shows itself to be inauthentic by its language, which is not characteristic of Jesus.

John 15–17: The farewell discourses added subsequently

Chapters 15–17 are not part of the evangelist's work, but were added only later (J. Wellhausen). The following observations tell in favour of this statement. *First,* 18.1 is the organic continuation of the signal to depart in 14.31c ('Arise, let us go from here!'); cf. the analogous transition from Mark 14.42 to Mark 14.43ff. *Secondly*, the transition from 14.31 to 15.1 is particularly harsh. *Thirdly*, the farewell discourse in 13.31–14.31 represents a coherent and self-contained whole: in it Jesus has said all that the disciples need to know. Moreover the impression that any further word would be a word too many is reinforced by 14.30: in view of the announcement 'I will no longer talk much with you', it seems strange that Jesus once again begins on a discourse – and the longest to appear in the Gospel of John at that. *Fourthly*, the discourses in chs. 15–17 hang in the air without any situation. In the present context the somewhat absurd notion arises that they are given at the point of departure from the place of the supper to the garden beyond the brook Kidron (18.1). *Fifthly*, chs. 15–17 show numerous deviations and shifts of accent from the theological tendency of the evangelist (cf. the remarks on the individual sections).

However, chs. 15–17 were not introduced into the work of the evangelist all at once. Rather, there are several indications that the individual sections contained in them, namely 15.1–17; 15.18–16.15; 16.16–33; and 17.1–26, were added in stages by different authors. First, these sections display differences not only from the work of the evangelist but also from one another. Secondly, the sections are each well-rounded in themselves. And finally, the repeated occurrence of particular concluding phrases (e.g. 'I have spoken this to you'; 'I have yet many things to say to you, but . . .') indicates that different authors are each time coming to an end.

Since chs 15–17 are not part of the evangelist's work, the following translations should all have been printed in bold, in keeping with the procedure used elsewhere. However, I shall dispense with this procedure in the present complex of texts so that here too it will be possible to demonstrate typographically the traditions which have presumably been used. Accordingly, the passages in chs 15–17 printed in *italics* indicate not the redactional contributions by the evangelist but those of the authors of the particular individual additions. (In what follows the term 'redaction' is also to be referred to their writing, and not to that of the evangelist.) However, there is every reason to believe that some further secondary additions were made in chs. 15–17. These additions (which are tertiary by comparison with the work of the evangelist) are in turn printed in **bold**.

John 15.1–17: The discourse about the vine

1 I am the true vine,
and my Father is the vine-dresser.
2 Every branch in me which does not <u>bear fruit</u> he removes,
and every (branch) that <u>bears fruit</u> he cleans,
that it may <u>bear</u> (yet) more <u>fruit</u>. 3 *You are already clean because of the word which I have spoken to you. 4 ABIDE in me, so I (abide) in you. As the branch cannot <u>bear fruit</u> by itself, unless it ABIDES in the vine, neither can you, unless you ABIDE in me.*
5 I am the vine,
you (are) the branches.

He who ABIDES in me and I in him,
he <u>bears</u> much <u>fruit</u>,
for without me you can do nothing. 6 *If a man does not ABIDE in me, he is cast out as the branch and withers; and they gather them and cast them into the fire, and they burn.* 7 *If you ABIDE in me, and my words ABIDE in you, (then) ask whatever you will, and it will be done for you.* 8 *In this my Father is glorified, that you <u>bear</u> much <u>fruit</u>, and prove to be my disciples.*

9 *As the Father has <u>loved</u> me, so too I have <u>loved</u> you. ABIDE in my <u>love</u>.* 10 *If you keep my commandments, you will ABIDE in my <u>love</u>, just as I have kept my Father's commandments and ABIDE in his <u>love</u>.* 11 *I have spoken this to you that my joy may be in you, and that your joy may be complete.*

12 *This is my commandment, that you <u>love</u> one another, as I have <u>loved</u> you.* 13 Greater <u>love</u> has no man than this, that a man lay down his life for his friends. 14 *You are my friends if you do what I command you.* 15 *I no longer call you slaves, for the slave does not know what his lord is doing; but I have called you friends, because all that I have heard from my Father I have made known to you.* 16a *You did not choose me, but I have chosen you* b *and appointed you that you should go and <u>bear fruit</u> and that your fruit should ABIDE,* c *so that whatever you ask the Father in my name, he may give it to you.* 17 *This I command you, that you <u>love</u> one another.*

Redaction and tradition

This first addition (cf. the introduction to chs. 15–17) is an artistically composed literary unit. It is divided into three sections (vv. 1–8: discourse on the vine; vv. 9–11: admonition to abide in love; vv. 12–17: admonition to mutual love), which thematically are closely related and are held together by the terms 'bear fruit' (7×), 'abide' (11×) and 'love' (9×) (cf. the underlinings and the CAPITALS in the translation). In view of the planned structure of the discourse, the question arises whether it already existed in essentials before being inserted into the Gospel of John or whether it was especially composed for its present context. The first possibility is supported not only by the abrupt transition from 14.31 to 15.1 but also by the observation that in contrast to the preceding discourse the passage is in no way shaped by the situation of farewell: Jesus is not speaking here as one who is taking his leave but already as the exalted Lord who is looking back on his completed work on earth and who now has the post-Easter community in view as a present entity. Nevertheless the second alternative is preferable, because the passage displays several clear references to the discourse 14.1–31 which was composed by the evangelist (cf. vv. 7, 16 with 14.13a; v. 8 with 14.13b; vv. 9f. with 14.21, 23). Thus the abrupt transition from 14.31 to 15.1 and the lack of any reference to the situation of farewell probably results from the fact that only in vv. 1–8 are the author's formulations bound by the tradition (see below).

It emerges from the content of the present addition that its author evidently had a special interest in Jesus' love for his own and the demand addressed to the disciples which is derived from this, i.e. to abide in Jesus' love and also to love one another. This makes it natural to assume that the same author is also responsible for the insertion of the verses identified above as additions, which are similarly stamped by the theme of love: 11.5; 13.1b, 12b–15, 16f., 20; 13.34f. and 14.14f., 24. Particularly in inserting the commandment to love in 13.34f., he probably had the intention of preparing for the present addition and thus fixing it in the context of the Gospel of John (cf. the partly verbatim agreements between 15.12 and 13.34 and the similarity between 15.8 and 13.35). In other words, in the light of 15.1–17 it is possible to specify some of the results of the analysis of the previous chapters: with a quite specific purpose, the author of the present passage stands out from the group which else-where has been summed up under the heading 'later revisers'. The vehemence with which he advocates this concern suggests that he inserted his additions at a time when the cohesion of the community was seriously threatened by external tribulations and/or inner disputes. (For the assumption that several strata can be distinguished within the additions of the later revisers cf. already the remarks in the introduction, point 6, and e.g. the analysis of 13.1–20.)

[1–8] The discourse about the true vine, which is strongly stamped by Old Testament-Jewish motifs (cf. e.g. Isa. 5.1–7; Jer. 2.21; 6.9; Ezek. 15.1–8; 17.1–10; 19.10–14; Hos. 10.1; Sir. 24.17f.; see also Matt. 15.13), is an admonition to abide in Christ and to bear fruit. Those who heed this admonition are promised that their prayers will be heard (v. 7); those who are closed to it are threatened with judgment (vv. 2a, 6). Several inconsistencies indicate that the author based this sub-section on an earlier simile.

(a) The statement about the cleanness of the disciples (v. 3), which recalls 13.10b, makes the cleansing activity of the vine-dresser (= God) spoken of in v. 2b superfluous. (b) Verse 4 contains the only imperative within the sub-section and anticipates the identification of the branches with the community of disciples which is made explicitly only in v. 5; moreover the frequent occurrence of the word 'abide' is suspicious, as the author also uses this term several times in vv. 9–10, which certainly come from him. (c) The broad depiction of the judgment in v. 6 gives the impression that the 'remove' of v. 2a was not drastic enough for the author. Furthermore, v. 6b introduces an undefined group of people; this runs counter to the first part of the image, which is concentrated on vine, vine-dresser and branches. (d) Verse 7 similarly breaks out of the picture: evidently 14.13 prompted the promise of the hearing of prayer and the following statement about the glorification of the Father (v. 8).

If we remove the verses which cause tension or in all probability are influenced by the previous discourse, only vv. 1–2 and v. 5 are left. It is quite possible that the image used by the author extended only this far, especially as the two parts of the image, each of which begins with an introduction of himself by Christ, seem to display an elevated style and have a coherent meaning. Nevertheless this reconstruc-tion must remain completely hypothetical. For vv. 1–2, 5 themselves are not free from tensions. For example, it is striking that the Father from vv. 1–2 no longer has a role in v. 5; and it is at least remarkable that first the disciples are required to bear fruit (vv. 1–2) and only then to abide, though according to v. 5 this is the pre-requisite for bearing fruit. So we must note that the deeper we hope to get into the heart of the image, the more it falls apart in our hands.

[9–11] These verses have the function of leading from vv. 1–8 to vv. 12–17: on the one hand they refer back to the discourse on the vine in that they make specific the communion with Jesus that is emphasized there by the term 'love', which has not occurred previously (cf. especially the imperative in v. 9b with that in v. 4a). On the other hand, with the mention of the commandments they prepare for the following section. Probably in formulating this transitional section the author relied on 14.21, 23, for there too the (indirect) admonition to keep the commandments is linked with the motif of the love of Jesus for the disciples and the love of the disciples for Jesus.

[12–17] This admonition shows itself to be a sub-unit in the composition by the correspondence between vv. 12a and 17 (inclusion). It builds on the intermediate passage vv. 9–11 by focussing the commandments from v. 10, the content of which is not defined, on the one commandment, the invitation to mutual love. Here the christological foundation with which the author provides this commandment (v. 12b; cf. v. 9b) is developed in three directions: Jesus' love showed itself in the vicarious offering of his life (v. 13; cf. 10.11, 15, 17f.; I John 3.16), in the transmission of the knowledge of revelation received from God (v. 15; cf. 17.8, 14), and in choosing the disciples (v. 16a; cf. 13.18). With the term 'bear fruit' (cf. vv. 2, 4, 5, 8), and with the promise that prayer will be heard (cf. v. 7), verses 16b and 16c refer back to the first part of the discourse. Only in the case of v. 13 is a basis in the tradition probable, for this verse is an aphorism which corresponds with the Hellenistic ideal of friendship. It has numerous parallels in ancient literature (cf. e.g. Aristotle, *Nichomachean Ethics* IX 8.9: 'Of a noble man it can also be truly said that he does everything for the sake of his friends and his fatherland and, if need be, even dies for them').

By comparison with the evangelist's theological view and terminology the section 15.1–17 displays clear shifts of accent. (a) The author proves to be interested in community paraenesis in a way which is alien to the evangelist. Here the fact cannot be overlooked that according to him heeding admonitions is even a factor that decides salvation. In contrast, the evangelist sees belief in the one sent by God as the only condition of salvation. This emphasis on the ethical imperative brings the section 15.1–17 close to I John. (b) The emphasis on right church practice is matched by a change in the idea of judgment: whereas according to the evangelist judgment comes about in the encounter with Jesus (cf. 3.18; 5.24), now it hovers over the community as a permanent threat (vv. 2, 6). (c) The evangelist does not know the use of the word 'abide' in the sense of 'abide in (or outside) Christ (or God)'. By contrast, this use of the term is as typical of the later revisers of the Gospel as it is of the author of I John (cf. 6.56; 12.46; I John 2.6, 24, 27f.; 3.6, 24, etc.). (d) The evangelist uses the word 'glorify' (cf. v. 8) exclusively with regard to the relationship between God and Jesus (cf. 8.54; 11.4; 12.16, 23, 28; 13.31f.; 14.13).

Historical

[1–8*] There can be no doubt about the inauthenticity of the discourse about the vine, even if its original form can no longer be reconstructed with certainty. For it is shaped throughout as a discourse of the Exalted One and is imaginable only as such. In other words, it does not go back to Jesus, but to a prophet or a teacher who thought that he could speak in the name of the exalted Christ.

[13] On the basis of the parallels within ancient literature (cf. the instance cited above) this saying cannot be attributed to Jesus.

John 15.18–16.15: The hatred of the world and the coming of the Paraclete

18 'If the world <u>hates</u> you, know that it has <u>hated</u> me before (it hated) you. 19a *If you were of the world, the world would love its own.* b *But because you are not of the world, but I have chosen you out of the world, therefore the world <u>hates</u> you.* 20a *Remember the word that I said to you, "The slave is not greater than his lord."* b If they persecuted me, they will also persecute you. c If they have kept my word, they will keep yours also. 21 *But all this they will do to you for my name's sake, for they do not know him who has sent me.* 22 If I had not come and spoken to them, they would not have sin. But now they have no excuse for their sin. 23 *He who <u>hates</u> me, <u>hates</u> my Father also.* 24 If I had not done among them the works which no one else did, they would not have sin. But now they have seen (them) and have nevertheless <u>hated</u> *both* me *and my Father.* 25 *But it is to fulfil the word that is written in their law, "They <u>hated</u> me without a cause."*

26 *But when the Paraclete comes, whom I will send to you from the Father, the Spirit of truth, who proceeds from the Father, he will bear witness to me.* 27 *And you also bear witness, because you have been with me from the beginning.*

16.1 *I have spoken this (to) you so that you do not fall away.*

2 They will exclude you from the synagogue; but an hour is (even) coming when whoever kills you will think he is doing God a service. 3 And they will do this because they have not known the Father, nor me. 4a But I have spoken this (to) you, so that when their hour comes, you may remember these (things) that I have told you of them.

4b *I did not say this to you from the beginning, because I was with you.* 5 *But now I am going to him who sent me, and none of you asks me, "Where are you going?",* 6 *but because I have said these things to you, sorrow has filled your hearts.* 7 *Yet I tell you the truth: it is to your advantage that I go away. For if I do not go away, the Paraclete will not come to you. But if I go away, I will send him to you.*

8 *And when he comes, he will convict the world in respect of sin, in respect of righteousness, and in respect of judgment:* 9 *in respect of sin, because they do not believe in me;* 10 *in respect of righteousness, because I go to the Father and you see me no more;* 11 *and in respect of judgment, because the ruler of this world has been judged.*

12 *I have yet many things to say to you, but you cannot bear them now.* 13 *But when he comes, the Spirit of truth, he will guide you into all the truth. For he will not speak of his own accord, but*

whatever he hears, he will speak, and he will declare to you the things that are to come. 14 *He will glorify me, for he will take of what is mine and declare it to you.* 15 **All that the Father has is mine; therefore I said that he takes of what is mine and will declare it to you.'**

Secondary additions

The second addition (cf. the introduction to chs. 15–17) has probably in turn been expanded at a secondary stage.

[16.2–4a] After the general remarks about the hostility of the 'world' in 15.18–25, two concrete reprisals on the part of the Jews are mentioned in 16.2: exclusion from the synagogue (cf. 9.22; 12.42) and killing (cf. Matt. 24.9; Luke 21.16). Two observations lead to the assumption that this passage has been added only at a secondary stage: first the concluding phrase 16.1 is repeated word for word in 16.4a ('I have spoken this to you so that you . . .'). Secondly, 16.3 looks like a mixed quotation of 15.21 and 15.24 end.

[16.15] As a result of the thrice repeated 'and he will declare (it) to you' (vv. 13, 14, 15, each time at the end) the end of the addition seems very heavy. Therefore at least v. 15, which quotes the verse immediately preceding it, might be judged to be an addition to bring clarification; the formulation 'all that the Father has is mine' suggests that it should be attributed to the author of ch. 17 (cf. 17.10).

Redaction and tradition

The theme of this section, the hatred of the world towards the community and the coming of the Paraclete, no longer has anything to do with the admonition to abide in Christ and to love one another, which stood at the centre of the previous discourse. This mere fact suggests that in 15.18–16.15* another author is speaking than was in 15.1–17. This assumption is reinforced by the fact that 15.20a refers to 13.16 in a different way from 15.15: whereas according to 15.15 Jesus will no longer call the disciples slaves, in 15.20 he derives the world's enmity towards the disciples from the fact that these are 'slaves' and as such must suffer the same fate as their Lord.

[18–25] The wording of the revelation saying underlying this section was probably as follows (J. Becker):
18 'If the world <u>hates</u> you,
know that it has <u>hated</u> me before (it hated) you.
20b If they persecuted me,
they will also persecute you.
c If they have kept my word,
they will keep yours also.
22 If I had not come and spoken to them,
they would not have sin.
But now they have no excuse for their sin.
24* If I had not done among them the works which no one else did,
they would not have sin.
But now they have seen (them) and have nevertheless <u>hated</u> me.'

The first part of this saying which consists of five 'if' sentences depicts the communion of fate between Jesus and his own in a threefold variation (vv. 18, 20b, 20c); by contrast, in the second part (vv. 22, 24*) the verdict is passed on the sinful behaviour of the world. Here v. 24* rounds off the revelation saying by taking up the motif of hatred from v. 18. The very monotonous structure of this saying makes it probable that it is a collection of what were (in part) once independent individual sayings which originally had their home in the community catechesis. This also explains v. 20c, which surprisingly reckons with an acceptance of the word.

The author of the addition has commented on this collection through vv. 19, 20a, 21, 23, 25, and an addition in v. 24. Here in part he has used motifs which also appear in Synoptic traditions about persecution (cf. esp. Matt. 10.5–26):

[19a] In form this statement certainly resembles the 'if' sentences of the revelation saying from the tradition, but it seems to be formulated with an eye to v. 19b and falls out of the framework by virtue of its use of the subjunctive. Moreover, in contrast to vv. 18, 20b, 20c, it can hardly be understood as a formerly independent individual saying. So we have to assume that the author himself composed this verse, imitating the style of his tradition. This is all the more probable since the key word 'love' refers back to 15.1–17.

[19b] The author takes up the notion of choosing from 15.16, adopting the vocabulary of 15.18, and in this way dovetails his own contribution with the previous one.

[20a] This verse builds a bridge to 13.16 and thus anchors the addition in the context of the Gospel as a whole (cf. also Matt. 10.24).

[21a] This verse is similar to Matt. 10.22a (cf. Mark 13.13; Matt. 24.9; Luke 21.17).

[21b] This verse recalls 7.28b (cf. 8.19, 55) and thus fulfils the same purpose as v. 20a.

[23–24] Both v. 23 and the expansion of v. 24 ('and my Father') introduces the reference to the Father missing in the revelation saying from the tradition.

[25] This verse interprets the hatred of the world from v. 24 as the fulfilment of the scriptural saying Ps. 34.19 LXX or Ps. 68.5 LXX (quoted freely). Here the phrase 'in their law', which corresponds to the same way of speaking by the evangelist (cf. 7.19; 8.17; 10.34), makes it unmistakably clear that by the 'world' the author understands the Jews (cf. similarly 16.2).

[26–27] The promise of the support of the Holy Spirit occurs also in Synoptic traditions about persecution (cf. Mark 13.11–13; Matt. 10.19f.; Luke 12.11f.). In contrast to the evangelist (cf. 14.16f., 26), the author does not identify the Paraclete with the Exalted One. Rather, for him the Paraclete is an independent entity who is sent by Jesus himself (and not by the Father); cf. similarly 16.7.

[16.1] This verse sums up the remarks so far and indicates their purpose. They serve to immunize the disciples against falling away.

[4b–7] For the first time since 13.31–14.31 Jesus explicitly mentions the situation of farewell. In view of the sorrow with which the disciples are stricken as a consequence of the announcements in 15.18–25, Jesus speaks of the benefit of his going away. This consists in the coming of the Paraclete (cf. 15.26–27). In v. 5 the author gets into a contradiction with the farewell discourse composed by the evangelist. In that framework the question 'Where are you going?' was certainly addressed to Jesus (cf. 13.36).

[8–11] These verses deal with the task of the Paraclete towards the world ('penal office'). This is first described summarily in v. 8 and then developed in a threefold way in vv. 9–11. The sense of the remarks, which are compressed and therefore difficult to understand, is probably as follows: the Paraclete will convict the world of its sin, because it is hostile to Jesus as the Revealer sent by God (v. 9); he will disclose the righteousness of Jesus, because he has been proved to be righteous by his exaltation to God (v. 10); and finally he will show that the violent death of Jesus is in truth the defeat of the ruler of this world (v. 11; cf. 12.31; 16.33).

[12] This verse introduces the end of the present addition.

[13–14] These verses deal with the activity of the Paraclete in the community ('teaching office'). After Jesus' departure the Paraclete will make up for what Jesus can no longer say to the disciples now because they could not bear it in the sorrowful situation of the farewell (v. 12). This again does not correspond to the evangelist's conception. For according to him the Paraclete is merely to remind the disciples of what the earthly Jesus has already revealed completely and finally (cf. 14.26).

Historical

None of the individual logia brought together in the revelation saying vv. 18–24* represents an authentic saying of Jesus. For they all derive from the situation of a community which is stamped by the experience of hostility and failure.

John 16.16–33: Sorrow and joy. Speaking in riddles and open speaking

16 *'A little while, and you see me no more, and again a little while, and you will see me.'* 17 *Then (some) of his disciples said to one another, 'What is this that he says to us, "A little while, and you do not see me, and again a little while, and you will see me"; and, "I go to the Father"?'* 18 *Now they said, 'What is this that he says, "a little while"? We do not know what he speaks.'* 19 *Jesus knew that they wanted to ask him, and said to them, 'Are you thinking among yourselves concerning this, that I said, "A little while, and you do not see me, and again a little while, and you will see me"?* 20 *Amen, amen, I say to you, you will weep and lament, but the world will rejoice; you will be sorrowful, but your sorrow will turn to joy.* 21 *A woman, when she is giving birth, has sorrow, because her hour has come; but when she has given birth to the child she no longer remembers the tribulation, for joy that a human being has come into the world.* 22 *So you too indeed have sorrow now, but I will see you again and your hearts will rejoice, and no one takes your joy from you.* 23 *And on that day you will ask me no question. Amen, amen, I say to you, if you ask anything of the*

Father, he will give it to you in my name. 24 Hitherto you have asked nothing in my name. Ask, and you will receive, that your joy may be complete.

25 I have said this to you in riddles. (The) hour is coming when I shall no longer speak to you in riddles but proclaim to you openly from my Father. 26 On that day you will ask in my name; and I do not say to you that I will pray the Father for you. 27 For the Father himself loves you, because you have loved me and have come to believe that I came forth from the Father. 28 I came forth from the Father and have come into the world; again, I am leaving the world and going to the Father.' 29 His disciples say, 'Look, now you are speaking plainly, and not uttering any riddles. 30 Now we know that you know all things, and do not need anyone to ask you. From this we believe that you have come from God.' 31 Jesus answered them, 'Do you now believe? 32a Look, an hour is coming and has already come that you will be scattered, every man to his own, and will leave me alone. Yet I am not alone, for the Father is with me. 33 I have spoken this to you so that you may have peace in me. In the world you have tribulation; but be consoled, I have conquered the world.'

Redaction and tradition

The author of this third addition (cf. the introduction to chs. 15–17) is not identical with the author of 15.18–16.15. This emerges above all from the fact that in contrast to that other he does not refer to the Paraclete. As numerous parallel formulations and allusions show, in writing 16.16–33 the author has orientated himself especially on the farewell discourse 13.31–14.31 but also on other parts of the Gospel of John (cf. the references in the following analysis). So in literary terms the section is dependent on its context and was specially composed for it.

[16] Jesus announces to his disciples the imminent separation and promises them that they will see him again soon (cf. 14.19; see also 7.33; 13.33). Here the first span of time is meant to be the time from the situation imagined for the discourse to the death of Jesus, and the second the time from Jesus' death to Easter. There can be no doubt that Easter is in fact in view and not the parousia. For first, the prayer of supplication to which Jesus invites the disciples in vv. 23–24 would be superfluous after the parousia. And secondly, it cannot be a coincidence that several phrases and terms appear in 16.16–33 which the reader will meet again in connection with the Easter narratives: cf. 'on that day' (16.23, 26 and 20.19; see already 14.20); 'joy' (16.20, 22, 24 and 20.20); 'peace' (16.33 and 20.19, 21); 'see' (16.16, 17, 19, 22 and 20.20).

[17–18] For the first time since 13.31–14.31 the disciples again play a role. However, they do not appear here as individuals (cf. 14.5, 8, 22) but as a group. They express their incomprehension about the announcement in v. 16.

According to v. 17 they also ask about the meaning of the saying 'I go to the Father'. This is strange, since Jesus did not say any such thing in v. 16. But this saying does appear in 16.10 (cf. previously 13.3, 33, 36; 14.4f., 28; 16.5). Evidently this is a redactional hook which the author of 16.16–33 has used to fix his own addition in the context of the farewell discourses.

[19] By virtue of his capacity to see into people, Jesus knows the thoughts of his disciples (for this motif, which is also often used by the evangelist, cf. on 1.42).

[20–22] These verses are governed by the key words 'sorrow' and 'joy'. Here vv. 20 and 22 correspond in content: the time of the seeing-no-longer will be a time of sorrow, and that of the seeing-again at Easter a time of joy. Verse 21 illustrates the transition from one to the other with the help of an image common in the Old Testament (cf. Isa. 66.7–10; see also Isa. 21.3; 26.17f.; 37.3).

The statement 'no one takes your joy from you' shows that by 'Easter' the author evidently does not merely understand the short space of time in which the Risen One will dwell visibly and physically among the disciples, but the post-Easter period generally. Thus v. 16 can also be referred to the situation of the post-Easter community. And we can probably go a stage further and say that this transparency applies not only to the promise of the Easter joy but also to the announcement of the sorrow: 'What the disciples experienced for the first time and fundamentally at Easter . . . is repeated in the post-Easter existence of the community whenever the forsaken and sorrowing community becomes aware of the presence of Jesus' (C.Dietzfelbinger).

[23–24] With Easter (which keeps taking place time and again) the questions of the disciples have an end (v. 23a) because they will then have direct access to God (vv. 23b–24). God himself will hear their prayers (cf. 15.7, 16). (According to the evangelist the exalted Jesus will hear the prayers of the disciples; cf. 14.13.) For 'complete joy' cf. 15.11.

[25] This verse introduces the second part of the addition, in which the theme is the opposition between riddle and open talk.

[26–27] The promise that prayer will be heard corresponds to vv. 23–24. The saying about the Father's love refers to 14.21b, 23a.

[28] For the formulation cf. 13.3b.

[29–30] The disciples think that they are now already in possession of what according to v. 25 Jesus has promised them only for the time after Easter. Here v. 30a in part refers back to 2.25.

[31–32] Because the disciples presume already to understand now, whereas complete understanding can be granted them only by the Easter experience, they are rebuked by Jesus (for the question in v. 31 cf. 1.50; 20.29; see also 13.38a). By predicting that they will leave him alone in his passion he shows them the questionable nature of the certainty of faith which they have expressed prematurely. Here there is evidently an allusion to the tradition of the flight of the disciples as this appears in Mark 14.27, 50 par. (In view of 18.8, where he makes Jesus gives 'orders' for the disciples to be allowed to depart freely, the evangelist could not have referred to this tradition in this way.) Verse 32b corresponds to 8.16b and possibly represents an indirect criticism of Mark 15.34.

[33a] With the promise of peace (cf. 14.27), this verse introduces the end of the discourse.

[33b] This verse recalls Jesus' statement about his superiority to the ruler of the world in 14.30 (cf. 12.31), but in contrast to that it is already spoken from the standpoint of the exalted Christ: despite the crucifixion of the Son of God, the world has not been able to put Jesus' union with the Father in question. That is its defeat and Jesus' victory.

Historical

The historical yield is nil.

John 17.1–26: Jesus' farewell prayer

1a *Jesus said this, and he lifted up his eyes to heaven and said,*

1b '*Father, the hour has come; glorify your Son, that the Son may glorify you,* 2 *as you have given him authority over all flesh, that he may give eternal life to all those whom you have given to him.* 3 **And this is eternal life, that they know you, the only true God, and Jesus Christ, whom you have sent.**

4 *I have glorified you on earth, having accomplished the work which you have given me to do.*

5 *And now, Father, glorify me with your glory which I had with you before the world was.*

6 *I have revealed your name to the men whom you gave me out of the world. They were yours, and you have given them to me and they have kept your word.* 7 *Now they know that everything that you have given me is from you.* 8a *For I have given them the words that you have given to me.* b *And they have received them and have come to know in truth that I have come forth from you, and have believed that you have sent me.*

9 *I am praying for them; I am not praying for the world, but for those whom you have given me, for they are yours;* 10 *and all that is mine is yours, and what is yours is mine, and I am glorified in them.* 11a *I am no longer in the world, but they are in the world, and I am coming to you.*

11b *Holy Father, keep them in your name, which you have given me, that they may be one as we are.*

12a *While I was with them I kept them in your name, which you have given me;* b **and guarded (them), and none of them perished but the son of perdition, that the scripture might be fulfilled.** 13 *But now I am coming to you, and these things I (still) speak in the world, that they may have my joy fulfilled in themselves.*

14 *I have given them your word; and the world has hated them, because they are not of the world, even as I am not of the world.*

15 *I do not ask you to take them out of the world, but to keep them from evil.* 16 **They are not of the world, as I am not of the world.**

17 *Sanctify them in the truth! Your word is truth.*

18 *As you sent me into the world, so too I have sent them into the world.* 19 *And I sanctify myself for them, that they too may be sanctified in truth.* 20 **And not only for these do I pray, but**

also for those who through their word believe in me, 21 that they may all be one, as you, Father, are in me and I in you, so that they also may be in us, so that the world believes that you have sent me.

22 *And I have given them the glory that you have given me, that they may be one even as we are one, 23 I in them and you in me, so that they may be perfected into one, so that the world may know that you have sent me and have loved them even as you have loved me.*

24 *Father, what you have given me – I will, that where I am, they also are with me, so that they see my glory which you have given me, because you loved me (even) before (the) foundation of the world.*

25a *Righteous Father, the world has not known you, but I have known you,* b *and these have come to know that you have sent me.* 26a *And I have made your name known to them, and I will make it known,* b *that the love with which you have loved me may be in them, and I in them.'*

Secondary additions

This section represents the fourth and last of the additions inserted between 14.31 and 18.1 (see the introduction to chs. 15–17). There are several indications that it has in turn been subjected to a revision (J. Becker).

[3] Jesus explains to God what eternal life (cf. v. 2) is, and designates himself as 'Jesus Christ' (cf. elsewhere in the Gospel of John only 1.17). This definition falls outside the context of the prayer.

[12b] This is a long-winded explanation of why Jesus can say that he has preserved his own (v. 12a) although Judas (= 'the son of perdition') was lost. The verse probably goes back to the same reviser(s) who already dealt with the problem of Judas in 6.64b–65; 12.4b, 6; 13.2f., 10b–11, 18f. This is all the more probable as the formula 'that the scripture might be fulfilled' seems to refer to the saying quoted in 13.18 (Ps. 41.10).

[16] This is a superfluous repetition of v. 14b, which interrupts the connection between vv. 15 and 17.

[20–21] The incorporation of the later believers stands in isolation in the context, for in v. 22 the disciples present are again in view without any transition. Moreover 'word' (v. 20) does not elsewhere in ch. 17 refer to the mission preaching of the disciples but exclusively to the word of God revealed by Jesus (see vv. 6, 14, 17). The one making the addition, who in formulating v. 21 doubtless went by vv. 22b–23, is possibly the same redactor who is responsible for the insertion of 10.16 into the addition 10.1ff. and for the addition 11.51–52.

Redaction and tradition

Even after removing the evidently secondary additions, the judgment that ch. 17 gives the impression of a 'monotonous peal of bells in which the elements of the same chord move to and fro in a random sequence' (J. Wellhausen) seems to be justified. This impression rests not least on the many overlaps in thought (cf. only vv. 1b/5; 6/26; 8/14; 11b end/22b), and the frequent occurrence of the word 'world' (17x) and the phrase 'you have given me (or him)' (12x). But once the structure of the text has been recognized (J. Becker), it proves to be a well-ordered whole. The scenic introduction (v. 1a) is followed by a main petition (vv.

1b–2) which is then developed in four individual petitions (vv. 4–5, 6–13*, 14–19*, 22–26). In all four developing sections the petition proper (vv. 5, 11b, 17, 24) is preceded by a report given by Jesus which each time begins with a verb of revealing in the aorist or the perfect ('I have': vv. 4, 6–8, 14, 22–23). In addition the last three petitions contain a concluding reason (vv. 12a–13, 18–19, 25–26), and the second and third also contain an introduction (vv. 9–11a, 15).

Like all the previous farewell discourses added at a later stage, ch. 17 too has probably been composed specifically for its present context. For first, the isolated existence of such a prayer would in any case be hard to imagine, and secondly, there are a number of references back not only to the preceding farewell discourses but also to other parts of the Gospel of John.

Scenic introduction and basic petition

[1a] The phrase 'Jesus said this' (cf. 12.36b) clearly marks off the prayer from the preceding discourses. Lifting his eyes to heaven – a typical gesture of prayer (cf. Ps. 123.1; Mark 6.41; 7.34; Luke 18.13; Acts 7.55) – is also mentioned with reference to Jesus in 11.41.

[1b–2] The motif that the hour (of the passion) has come recalls 12.23 (cf. 12.27) and 13.1 (see also 7.30; 8.20). With the following petition, which is about the reciprocal glorification of God and Jesus, the author probably wants to build a bridge back to 13.31–32, the beginning of the farewell discourses (cf. moreover 14.13: 'that the Father may be glorified in the Son'). This is also suggested by the fact that here as in 13.31–32 Jesus speaks of himself in the third person, whereas from v. 4 he will use the first person. Verse 2 makes a distinction: certainly Jesus has been given authority (cf. 5.27) over 'all flesh' – a Jewish term for 'all human beings' – but he bestows eternal life only on a group chosen by the Father. This group of those entrusted to Jesus is summed up in the formula 'those whom you have given to him' (cf. 6, 9, 24), which is characteristic of ch. 17.

In this stereotyped phrase, which significantly appears also in the two additions 6.39 and 10.29, a fundamental difference from the theology of the evangelist becomes evident. That becomes particularly clear in comparison with 3.16, which presumably prompted the formulation of v. 2. In 3.16 anyone who believes in Jesus is promised eternal life, and so the decision about salvation or doom is made in the encounter with Jesus or his word (cf. 5.24; 6.40ab, 47; 11.25f., etc.). By contrast, v. 2 says that Jesus gives eternal life to all those whom the Father has given him (cf. similarly 6.65). In other words, there is no longer an offer of salvation for all human beings, but salvation is *a priori* reserved for a particular group pre-destined by God. The evangelist had reinterpreted this view, also expressed in the saying 6.44ab which he takes up, in 6.45f. (see there).

The first development of the basic petition

[4] Jesus' first report about what he has done was evidently influenced by 4.34 and 5.36.

[5] The first individual petition concerns Jesus himself, whereas the three following ones (vv. 11b, 17, 24) represent intercessions for his own. It corresponds to the basic petition v. 1b (including the address 'Father'), but expands this with the notion that the glory of Jesus is to be the same as that which he had in pre-existence.

The second development of the basic petition

[6–8] The second report introduces the motif of the 'name' of God (v. 6; cf. 12.28), which is taken up again both in the petition (v. 11b) and in the concluding reason for it (v. 12a; cf. moreover v. 26a). Again it is emphasized that salvation is limited to those who are predestined to it by God (cf. on vv. 1b–2). For the keeping of the word of God by the disciples (v. 6b) cf. 8.51, 52 and above all 14.23f.; 15.20c. The knowledge of the disciples (v. 7) is once again emphasized in vv. 8 and 25 (here in contrast to the lack of knowledge of the world). In literary terms v. 8 is influenced by 16.27 and 11.42.

[9–11a] The introduction to the second petition once again draws a clear line between the world and those entrusted to Jesus: the world is explicitly excluded from Jesus' intercession (vv. 9–10). Verse 11a recalls the farewell situation and refers back to 13.1, 33, 36; 14.2–4, 12, 28; 16.5, 7, 28; for the statement 'they are in the world' cf. the addition 13.1b ('his own in the world').

[11b] With the formulation 'keep in your name' the petition refers back to the report in vv. 6–8. The concluding notion of unity which is repeated in v. 22b has a basis in the evangelist's work in 10.30; 10.38 and 14.20.

[12a, 13] These verses give the reason for the petition: during his presence on earth (for 'while I was with them' cf. 16.4b, 'because I was with you') Jesus was responsible for keeping the disciples in the name of God. Now that he is leaving the disciples, he must return to God the task of keeping the disciples in his word. For v. 13 see the parallels indicated at v. 11a; the concluding statement about perfect joy recalls 15.11 (cf. also 16.20–22, 24).

The third development of the basic petition

[14] 'I have given them your word' is a variation of v. 8a. Otherwise the report refers back word for word to the remarks in the second addition (15.18–16.15) about the hatred of the world (cf. above all 15.19). 'As I am not of the world' has a parallel in 8.23.

[15] In its first part, formulated in the negative, the introduction to the third

petition picks up v. 14b: despite the world's hatred the disciples are not to be taken out of the world. The positive part bears a similarity to a petition of the Our Father (cf. Matt. 6.13b: 'Deliver us from evil!').

[17] The connection between this petition and the 'word' mentioned in the report becomes clearer when one introduces into v. 17a the identification made in v. 17b (= 'Sanctify them in your word!').

[18–19] These verses form the reason for the petition. Verse 18 bears a great similarity to 20.21 is probably dependent on this verse (for the form of this statement cf. also 15.9). Verse 19 refers back to 'sanctify' in v. 17, a term which in the evangelist's work merely appears within the traditional scriptural proof 10.34–36*. The expression has its quite original meaning within ch. 17: 'separate from the sphere of the profane'.

The fourth development of the basic petition

[22–23] With the keyword 'glory' (v. 22a), the last report and the following petition (v. 24) take up the central term of the basic petition and its first development (vv. 1–2a, 4–5: 1x 'glory'; 4 x 'glorify'). This gives the prayer a kind of framework. The notion of unity (vv. 22b–23) is developed more broadly than in v. 11b, on the basis of v. 8b ('that you have sent me') and 15.9a ('as the Father has loved me'). Here it should be noted that the world is not the object of God's love, but is merely to become the witness of the loving communion existing between God, Jesus and the community; the world itself is excluded from this communion.

[24] In contrast to vv. 5, 11b and 17, the petition is formulated not as an imperative but with 'I will'. For its content cf. the addition 12.26; 14.3 (this passage has been used here); 1.14 and 15.9. In connection with the motif of the glory of Jesus God's love for Jesus before time refers back to v. 5.

Verse 24 denotes a further striking difference from the theological view of the evangelist. For according to this verse the goal of salvation is that the elect will one day see the glory of the exalted Jesus in the heavenly world (cf. similarly I John 3,2). Thus eternal life is understood as a transmortal state. The evangelist, by contrast, while not limiting salvation to earthly life (cf. 11.25f.; 12.32), puts all his emphasis on the fact that eternal life is already present in Jesus or his word: 'Whoever believes has eternal life' (6.47; cf. 5.24–26; 3.15–18; 6.40ab; 20.31).

[25–26] These verses form the reason for the last petition. At the same time, by taking up individual motifs from the other developments of the basic petition, they sum up the whole prayer and thus give it a solemn conclusion. For the closedness of the world to God noted in v. 25a cf. 8.55 (Jesus says to the Jews, 'You have not known him, but I know him') and the numerous parallels within the previous farewell discourses (14.17, 22; 15.18–25; 16.2–4a, 8f., 20, 33). Verse 25b corresponds to

v. 8b end. Verse 26a takes up v. 6 and adds a corresponding future statement (cf. similarly the voice of God in 12.28). The motif of the love of God for Jesus, coupled with the notion of unity, picks up the end of v. 23.

Historical

Jesus' farewell prayer is a literary product dependent on the other parts of the Gospel of John, above all chs. 13–16. Consequently it is of no value for the question of the historical Jesus.

John 18–19: The passion story

The content and structure of the passion story in the Gospel of John is essentially that of the Synoptic Gospels: Jesus is arrested outside the city (18.1–11; cf. Mark 14.32–52 parr.); Jesus is brought before the high priest while Peter denies him three times (18.12–27; cf. Mark 14.53–65 parr.); Jesus is handed over to Pilate (18.28–19.16a; cf. Mark 15.1–20a parr.); Jesus is crucified on Golgotha along with two other men (19.16b–30; cf. Mark 15.20b–41 parr.) and finally buried by Joseph of Arimathea (19.38–42; cf. Mark 15.42–47 parr.). In addition to this common outline there are analogies in detail. Thus for example the account of the hearing by the high priest and the depiction of Peter's denials are dovetailed both in Mark (and in Matthew) and in John; here the sequence of the events narrated by both evangelists corresponds as a mirror image – with one exception:

	Mark 14	John 18
Jesus led off to the high priest	53	13f.
Peter follows Jesus	54a	15a
First denial	–	17
Peter warms himself	54b	18
Hearing by the high priest	61b–64	19–21
Jesus is struck	65	22
First denial	66–68	–
Second denial	69–70a	25
Third denial	70b–71	26–27a
Cock crow	72a	27b

The difference is that Mark initially introduces Peter's situation (14.54a, b) and then narrates all three denials only after the description of the hearing (14.66–72a), whereas the Fourth Evangelist makes the first denial (v. 17) take place before the hearing. But this difference is minimal and does not alter the fact that there is a dovetailing of the two narrative strands in both Mark 14 and John 18.

Now the idea of interlocking the two reports in all probability derives from Mark (see on Mark 14.53–65), who in general has a predilection for this literary technique (cf. Mark

5.21–24, 25–34, 35–43; 6.7–13, 14–29, 30–34; 11.12–14, 15–19, 25; 14.1–2, 3–9, 10–11). This is an important argument for the assumption that the Fourth Evangelist's passion story presupposes Mark 14–15. If we note further that the Johannine passion story also displays numerous verbatim agreements with Matt. 26–27 and Luke 22–23 and that not all the deviations of John 18–19 from the Synoptics can be derived from redactional motives (cf. e.g. 19.23–24b), the most probable assumption seems to be that the passion narrative of the Fourth Gospel is based on Z (for Z cf. the introduction, point 4).

Here, in brief, are some further comments. (a) Since in chs 18–19 the additions by the evangelist to Z often seem like additions to an already fixed text, we may assume that he had Z in written form (at least for the passion story). (b) It is impossible to make a complete reconstruction of the Z passion story. For the question of what parts of Z the evangelist could have omitted is of course as impossible to answer as the question of what elements of the Synoptics Z may have omitted. (c) All deviations of John 18–19 from Mark 14–15; Matt. 26–27; Luke 22–23 derive either from Z or from the evangelist or from the later revisers. The additions by the revisers can be marked off quite simply; cf. on 18.5c, 6a, 9; 18.13b–14, 24, 28, 32; 19.24c, (25,) 26f.; 19.35. By contrast, a decision between Z and the evangelist is not always possible. In case of doubt, in what follows preference is given to Z. Accordingly, in the translation only passages which in all probability derive from the evangelist are printed in italics.

John 18.1–11: Jesus in the garden beyond the brook Kidron

1a *After he had said this,* b Jesus <u>went out</u> with his disciples across the brook Kidron, where there was a garden, *which he and his disciples entered.* 2 Now Judas, <u>who delivered him up,</u> also knew the place, because Jesus often met there with his disciples. 3 Now <u>Judas</u> takes the cohort and (also) servants of <u>the chief priests and the</u> *Pharisees,* and goes there <u>with</u> lanterns and torches and weapons.

4 *Now Jesus, who knew all that was to befall him, went out and says to them, 'Whom do you seek?'* 5a *They answered him, 'Jesus, the Nazoraean.'* b *He says to them, 'I am he.'* c **And Judas also, who delivered him up, was standing with them. 6 Now when he said to them, 'I am he,'** *they drew back and fell to the ground.* 7 *Now again he asked them, 'Whom do you seek?' And they said, 'Jesus, the Nazoraean.' 8 Jesus answered, 'I have told you that I am he. Now if you seek me, let these men go.'* 9 **(This was) to fulfil the word which he had spoken, 'Of those whom you have given me I have not lost one.'**

10 Now Simon Peter had a <u>sword</u>, drew it and <u>struck the high priest's slave and</u> cut off <u>his right ear</u>. The servant's name was Malchus. 11a <u>Jesus said</u> to Peter, 'Put <u>the sword into</u> its sheath! <u>The cup</u> *which* <u>the Father</u> *has given me, shall I not drink it?'*

Later revision

[5c] The mention of Judas stands in isolation in a context which was evidently created by the evangelist himself (cf. under 'Redaction and tradition'). Moreover it is superfluous; for because of v. 3 it goes without saying that Judas was among the troop which arrested Jesus.

Finally it is suspicious that Judas is once again explicitly characterized as the one 'who delivered him up' (cf. v. 2). The verse has probably been inserted by the same revisers who were also at work in 6.64b–65; 12.4b, 6; 13.2–3, 10b–11, 18f.; 17.12b (cf. on 6.64b–65). For the last time, they emphasize quite clearly to which side Judas belongs.

[6a] This verse takes up the narrative thread which was interrupted by the insertion of v. 5c. The seam is also visible in that Judas seems to be the subject of this subordinate clause, although of course Jesus is meant.

[9] This verse refers back either to 6.39 or to 17.12b. Neither of these verses comes from the evangelist. Accordingly we will also have to attribute this fulfilment saying to the revisers.

Redaction and tradition

In the evangelist's work this passage attached directly to 14.31 (for the reason cf. the introduction to chs 15–17). As is shown by the verbatim and almost verbatim agreements with Mark 14.26, 43–47 (underlined once) and with Matt. 26.47–56 and Luke 22.47–53 (underlined twice), the section is based on Z.

[1a] The evangelist attaches what follows to 14.31 in the usual way (cf. 7.9; 9.6; 11.28, 43; 20.14, 20) with the phrase 'after he had said this'.

[1b] As in Mark 14.26 parr., it is reported that Jesus and the disciples go out of the city after the last supper. Whereas according to the Synoptics the events connected with the arrest of Jesus take place at the Mount of Olives (according to Mark 14.32 and Matt. 26.36, more precisely, on a piece of land called Gethsemane), Z locates them in a garden (cf. 19.41 = Z) beyond the brook Kidron. As Jerusalem is separated from the Mount of Olives by the Kidron Valley, this note of place can be understood as a free rendering of the Synoptics.

[1c] This is lame and derives from the evangelist.

[2] This verse explains how Judas 'who delivered him up' (= Mark 14.44; Matt. 26.48) knows the place where Jesus is. The evangelist has not previously mentioned that Jesus regularly spent time in the garden.

[3] This verse is based on Mark 14.43 par. and reports the fulfilment of the prediction of Jesus in 13.21c. The mention of the Pharisees probably derives from the evangelist as in 11.47 (cf. on 1.24). By contrast, the mention of the Roman cohort, which goes beyond the Synoptics, probably derives from Z. How little the Z report is interested in the historical plausibility of the account is evident from the fact that Judas appears as the leader of the two groups – 'as if the Roman forces occupying Jerusalem along with their centurion had subordinated themselves to a Jewish civilian' (E.Haenchen).

[4] This verse forms the beginning of an interlude inserted by the evangelist (vv. 4–8*). In sovereign fashion Jesus steps up to the contingent in order to give himself up (the scene with Judas' kiss in Mark 14.44f. par. must therefore be

omitted, if it was contained in Z at all). As Jesus knows in advance of all that is to come (cf. on 1.42; see also 13.1a), he must also know whom the henchmen are seeking. The fact that he nevertheless asks them is evidently only to compel them to mention his name; thereupon he can strike them to the ground with his mighty 'I am he' (vv. 5ab, 6b). For the question 'Whom do you seek?' cf. 1.38; 20.15.

[5a] As the evangelist does not use the designation 'Nazoraean' (cf. on Luke 18.37) elsewhere, we have to assume that he has taken it here from 19.19 (= Z).

[5b] 'I am he' is the only conceivable reply to v. 5a. But possibly an allusion to 8.28 is also intended.

[6] Jesus' identification of himself has its effect. Probably the evangelist is alluding to Ps. 34.4 LXX ('Those who devised evil for me . . . shall draw back') and Ps. 26.2 LXX ('When evildoers fell upon me . . . my oppressors became weak and fell'). Incidentally, a Roman cohort consisted of 600 or 1000 men. That all these fell to the ground is as fantastic a notion as that they had previously put themselves under the command of Judas. For the magic power of Jesus' words cf. also on 7.46.

[7] This verse corresponds to vv. 4b–5a. Whereas the purpose of the question in v. 4b was for Jesus to demonstrate his power, here it serves as a point of contact for Jesus' order to let the disciples go free.

[8] The evangelist emphasizes that Jesus arranged for his companions to depart unhindered (cf. by contrast Mark 14.50).

[10] This verse is based on Mark 14.47; Matt. 26.51; Luke 22.50. In contrast to the Synoptists, Z 'knows' both the name of the one who wields the sword (= Peter) and the name of the wounded slave (= Malchus). As in Luke, the ear cut off is the right one.

[11a] This is the Z rendering of Matt. 26.52.

[11b] With this question, put into the mouth of Jesus, the evangelist corrects the petition 'Father, . . . take this cup from me' from the Gethsemane scene (cf. Mark 14.36 parr.), which he had already turned into its opposite in 12.23, 27f.

Yield: Z does not presuppose any traditions other than the Synoptic accounts of the arrest of Jesus. The evangelist emphasizes in a way which cannot be surpassed the powerful sovereignty of Jesus, his overwhelming superiority in the truest sense of the word, and his voluntary self-surrender.

Historical

Cf. on Mark 14.43–52.

John 18.12–27: The arrest of Jesus. The hearing before Annas. Peter's denials

12 Now the cohort and the centurion and servants *of the Jews* <u>seized</u> Jesus and bound him 13 <u>and</u> they <u>led</u> him first <u>to</u> *Annas*; for he was the father-in-law of Caiaphas, *who was* <u>high priest</u> *of that year*. 14 It was Caiaphas who had advised the Jews that it was expedient that one (single) man should die for the people.

15 <u>Now</u> Simon <u>Peter</u> <u>followed</u> Jesus, and another disciple. And that disciple was known to the high priest, and he <u>went</u> with Jesus <u>into the courtyard of the high priest</u>. 16 But Peter stood outside at the door. Then the other disciple, who was known to the high priest, went out and spoke to the woman who kept the door, and brought Peter in. 17 The <u>maid</u>, the woman who kept the door, <u>says</u> to <u>Peter</u>, 'Are not <u>you also</u> one <u>of</u> <u>this man's</u> disciples?' He says, '<u>I am not</u>.' 18 Now the slaves and <u>servants</u> were standing there, having made a charcoal fire because it was cold, and they were warming themselves; Peter also stood <u>with</u> them <u>and warmed himself</u>.

19 <u>The high priest</u> *now* <u>questioned Jesus</u> *about his disciples and his teaching.* 20 *Jesus answered him, 'I have spoken openly to the world; I have always taught in (the) synagogue and in the temple, where all Jews come together, and I have said nothing secretly. 21 Why do you ask me? Ask those who have heard me, what I have said to them. Look, they know what I said.'* 22a Now when he had said this, one of the <u>servants</u> standing by <u>slapped</u> Jesus' face b *and said, 'Is that how you answer the high priest?'* 23 *Jesus answered him, 'If I have spoken wrongly, bear witness to the wrong; but if I have spoken rightly, why do you strike me?'* 24 Annas then sent him bound to Caiaphas the high priest.

25a Now <u>Peter</u> was standing there and warming himself. b Then they said to him, 'Are not you also (one) of his disciples?' c He <u>denied</u> it and said, 'I am not.' 26 One of the slaves of the high priest, a kinsman of the man whose ear Peter had cut off, says, 'Did I not see you in the garden with him?' 27 Peter <u>again denied</u> it; <u>and immediately a cock crowed</u>.

Later revision

The section displays a number of peculiarities which suggest that it has been subsequently revised. In v. 13 (and v. 24) Caiaphas is explicitly designated as high priest of that year. However, in v. 19 Annas is regarded as high priest. Certainly Annas still held the title high priest after his removal from office in AD 15, but it is also remarkable that the hearing before Caiaphas, the real office-holder, is only hinted at in v. 24. For v. 28 next reports Jesus' being taken from Caiaphas to Pilate. So the question arises why it is reported at all that after questioning by Annas Jesus is brought before Caiaphas. The assumption that Z reported a hearing before Annas and that the evangelist wanted to indicate that after it Jesus was taken to Caiaphas as well is improbable: the evangelist would surely have depicted the second hearing in greater detail. That suggests the following explanation: the evangelist reported only a single hearing before the high priest, who was Annas. The revisers missed the name of the high priest who was officially in office at the time of Jesus (= Caiaphas) – either because of better historical knowledge or on the basis of Matt. 26.57 – and introduced it subsequently. That required relatively little effort. *First*, they added the words 'for he was the father-in-law of Caiaphas' in v. 13. Through this addition the following designation of office passes over to Caiaphas. At the same time, the detail about the kinship explains ('for') why Jesus was brought to Annas at all. However, this explanation is 'more than silly' (E. Hirsch). *Secondly*, they added v. 14. It points back to 11.49f. (where for stylistic reasons 'Caiaphas, who was high priest of that year' proves to be an addition) and thus anchors the additions connected with Caiaphas in the context of the Gospel as a whole. *Thirdly*, they inserted v. 24. And *fourthly*, in v. 28 they either replaced an original 'from Annas' by 'from Caiaphas' or – if the evangelist's text did not contain any name – they simply inserted 'from Caiaphas'.

Redaction and tradition

Despite considerable differences in details the section has a good deal in common with the corresponding Synoptic reports (Mark 14.53–72; Matt. 26.57–75; Luke 22.54–71). Thus Z is the basis for this section too (cf. already the explanations and the survey in the introduction to John 18–19). Verbatim and almost verbatim agreements with Mark are underlined once, possible additional agreements with Matthew/Luke twice.

[12] The arresting party is that of 18.3. As in Luke 22.54a the arrest of Jesus is reported only after the scene involving the sword in 18.10f. (cf. Luke 22.50f.), since at this point Jesus must still be free because of 18.11.

[13*] They take Jesus to Annas (for the problem of the phrase 'high priest of that year' cf. on 11.49). Evidently Z, on the basis of Mark 14.53 and Luke 22.54a, simply spoke of the 'high priest' without mentioning a name (by contrast cf. the correct detail 'Caiaphas' in Matt. 26.57). So it could happen that the Fourth Evangelist erroneously inserted 'Annas'. This error may have been caused by the fact that even after being removed from office Annas still had great influence, or at least was regarded by later generations as the one who really held power in the time of Jesus (some other New Testament passages also support this: Luke 3.2; Acts 4.6; 5.17 v. l.). The little word 'first' points forward to the transfer to Pilate reported in v. 28 (or similarly derives from the revisers and then refers to v. 24).

[15–16] These verses are based on Mark 14.54a; Matt. 26.58a; Luke 22.54b, but go beyond the Synoptics in the mention of another disciple. Z evidently saw the need to explain how it was possible for Peter to get into the courtyard of the high priest (cf. a similar explanation in 18.2). An intermediary was needed for that, a figure who was known both to Peter and to the high priest.

The anonymous disciple is often regarded as the beloved disciple, but such an identification is improbable. Since that disciple was already mentioned in 13.23–26a, he cannot be reintroduced here as '*another* disciple'. The fact that the beloved disciple in 20.2 is called 'the other disciple' (with the definite article) does not support the assumption that the beloved disciple is meant in 19.15f., but rather tells against it.

[17] Cf. Mark 14.66, 71; Matt. 26.69, 73; Luke 22.56, 58. Jesus' prophecy of the denials of Peter (13.38; cf. Mark 14.30 parr.) is beginning to be fulfilled. In the redactional context, Peter's 'I am not!' (cf. similarly Luke 22.58) is an effective contrast to Jesus' 'I am' from 18.5b.

[18] This verse corresponds in essentials to Mark 14.54b. Z elaborated the scene with some details.

[19] This verse takes up v. 13* (cf. Mark 14.60). The high priest's question about the 'disciples' and the 'teaching' is redactional ('teaching' only in 7.16, 17; but cf. 'teach', 6.59; 7.14, 28, 35; 8.20, 28; 9.34; 14.26).

[20–21] These verses derive from the evangelist; for v. 20 cf. 7.26 ('Look, he is speaking openly'); 6.59 (Jesus teaches in the synagogue); 7.14, 28; 8.20 (Jesus teaches in the temple); for v. 21 cf. 9.21. However, Mark 14.49, the rebuke addressed by Jesus to the henchmen ('I was daily with you in the temple teaching'), is echoed in v. 20.

[22a] Cf. Mark 14.65b.

[22b–23] These verses probably come from the evangelist. Jesus comments on the violent action (which according to Mark 14.65 and Matt. 26.67f. he endures in silence) with a question (cf. 8.46b) which discloses the nonsensical nature of the blow; thus Jesus shows his sovereignty in the face of death.

[25a] This takes up v. 18b word for word. (Similarly, Mark 14.66 par links up with Mark 14.54 par.) That reinforces the impression of the simultaneity of the two courses of events.

[25b–c] For the second denial cf. on v. 17. The questioners are the slaves and servants from v. 18.

[26] The third time Peter is suspected by a kinsman of Malchus (cf. 18.10 = Z) because of his presence in the garden.

[27a] Cf. Matt. 26.72. With the third denial Peter leaves the stage; he will appear again only when Jesus has risen (20.3–10*).

[27b] This corresponds word for word with Matt. 26.74b (cf. Mark 14.72a; Luke 22.60b). With the cock crow the fulfilment of the prophecy of the denial from 13.38 is complete.

Yield: the Z report, part of which has been preserved only in fragments, does not presuppose any traditions other than the corresponding Synoptic accounts.

Historical

Cf. on Mark 14.46, 53–72.

John 18.28–19.16a: Jesus before Pilate

28a Now they <u>lead</u> Jesus **from Caiaphas** into the praetorium; and it was <u>early morning</u>. b *And they themselves did not enter the praetorium, so as not to become unclean, but to be able to eat the Passover (meal).* 29 *Now Pilate came out to them and says, 'What accusation do you bring against this man?'* 30 *They answered and said to him, 'If this man were not an evildoer, we would not have delivered him up to you.'* 31 *Then Pilate said to them, 'Take him yourselves and judge him by your own law.' The Jews said to him, 'We may not kill anyone';* 32 **(this was) to fulfil the word which Jesus had spoken to show by what death he was to die.**

33 *Now* <u>Pilate</u> *again went into the praetorium and called Jesus and* said to him, '<u>Are you the King of the Jews?</u>' 34 *Jesus answered, 'Do you say this of your own accord, or have others said it to you about me?'* 35 *Pilate answered, 'Am I a Jew? Your people and* <u>the chief priests</u> *have* <u>delivered</u> *you* <u>up</u> *to me.* <u>What</u> *have you* <u>done</u>*?'* 36 *Jesus answered, 'My kingdom is not of this world. If my kingdom were of this world, my servants would have fought, that I might not be delivered up to the Jews. But now my kingdom is not from here.'* 37 *Then Pilate said to him, 'So you are a king?'* <u>Jesus answered,</u> '<u>You say it</u>: *I am a king. For this I was born, and for this I have come into the world, to bear witness to the truth. Every one who is of the truth hears my voice.'* 38a *Pilate says to him, 'What is truth?'*

38b *And after he had said this, he went out to the Jews again, and says to them, '*<u>I find no guilt in</u> him. 39 **But** you have a custom that I should <u>release one man</u> for you at the Passover. Will you have me <u>release for you the King of the Jews</u>?' 40 Then they cried out again and said, 'Not <u>this</u> man, but <u>Barabbas</u>!' <u>Now Barabbas was</u> a robber.

19.1 <u>Thereupon</u> Pilate took Jesus and had him scourged. 2 And <u>the soldiers</u> <u>wove a crown of thorns</u> and <u>put</u> it on <u>his head,</u> and arrayed him in a <u>purple</u> robe, 3 and came up to him and said, '<u>Hail, King of the Jews</u>!' And they slapped him on the face.

4 *And Pilate came out again, and says to them, 'Look, I am bringing him out to you, that you may know that* <u>I find no guilt in</u> *him.'* 5 *Now Jesus came out, wearing the* <u>crown of thorns</u> *and the purple robe. And he said to them, 'That is the man!'* 6a *Now when the chief priests and the servants saw him,* they cried out and said, '<u>Crucify, crucify</u>!' b *Pilate says to them, 'Take him yourselves and crucify him. For* <u>I find no guilt in him.</u>' 7 *The Jews answered him, 'We have a law, and by that law he must die, for he has made himself Son of God.'*

8 *Now when Pilate heard this saying, he was even more afraid* 9a *and went into the praetorium again and says to Jesus, 'Where are you from?'* b *But Jesus gave* <u>him</u> *no answer.* 10a *Pilate says to him, 'Do you* <u>not</u> *speak to me?* b *Do you not know that I have power to release you, and power to crucify you?'* 11 *Jesus answered him, 'You would have no power over me unless it had been given you from above. Therefore he who delivered me up to you has greater sin.'*

12a Therefore <u>Pilate</u> sought to <u>release</u> him. b *But the Jews cried out and said, 'If you release this man, you are not Caesar's friend. Every one who makes himself a* <u>king</u> *sets himself against* <u>Caesar</u>*.'* 13 *Now when Pilate heard these words, he brought Jesus out and* sat down <u>on</u> a <u>judgment seat</u> at a place called 'Mosaic Pavement', and in Hebrew Gabbatha. 14a *Now it was the day of preparation for the Passover (festival); it was about the sixth hour.* b *And he says to the Jews, 'That is your King!'* 15a Then they cried out, '<u>Away</u>, away! <u>Crucify him</u>!' b *Pilate says to them, 'Shall I crucify your King?'* c *The chief priests answered, 'We have no king but Caesar.'* 16a <u>Thereupon</u> he now <u>delivered</u> him <u>up</u> to them <u>to be crucified</u>.

Later revision

The detail 'from Caiaphas' in v. 28 comes from the revisers. It has either been added, or replaces an original 'from Annas' (for the reasons see on 18.12–27).

[32] This incidental remark refers back to 12.33. But whereas there the allusion was to the symbolic character of the crucifixion of Jesus as 'lifting up', the point of v. 32 lies in the fact that even the lack of capital jurisdiction on the part of the Jews was included in the divine plan. Since the only other example of a saying of Jesus being treated like a word of scripture occurs in the addition 18.9, this note is probably a secondary addition (R. Bultmann). Cf. also 21.19.

Redaction and tradition

This passage shows agreements with several elements from all three Synoptic descriptions of the hearing before Pilate. This suggests that the evangelist also based this section on the Z passion account. In the translation verbatim and almost verbatim agreements with Mark 15.1–20b are underlined once and possibly additional agreements with Matt. 27.1–31a and Luke 23.1–25 twice (cf. the individual references in the following analysis). However, the evangelist has evidently revised the account strongly, enriched it, and above all put it into a new mould. For the whole complex of the hearing before Pilate is divided up by changes of place: Pilate is sometimes in front of the praetorium and sometimes in it. Four times Pilate goes *out* (18.29, 38b; 19.4; presupposed in 19.12) and three times he comes in (again) (18.33; 19.9; presupposed in 19.1). This produces seven individual scenes.

Scene 1: Jesus is handed over to Pilate (vv. 28–31)

[28a] Cf. Luke 23.1; Mark 15.1 ('into the praetorium' as in Matt. 27.27). As v. 28b shows, apparently only the Jews are the subjects of the sentence (by contrast cf. 18.12–13a).

[28b] This creates the presupposition for the principle which the evangelist goes on to use as the basis for his composition, the division of the hearing into two settings: only because for cultic and religious reasons the Jews cannot enter the building is it plausible that Pilate constantly moves between the inner and outer part of the praetorium.

Here v. 28b shows for the first time that the chronology of the events of the passion in the Fourth Gospel differs from that in the Synoptics. For the Passover meal was taken at the beginning of the feast of the Passover, i.e. by our reckoning about 6 o'clock in the evening of the day before. Whereas according to the Synoptics Jesus celebrated this meal with his disciples (cf. Mark 14.12–25 parr.), according to the Fourth Evangelist at this point of time he was already dead (cf. 19.14a and the remarks in the section 'Historical').

[29] Pilate opens the hearing by asking what charge is made against Jesus, and thus shows himself to be an impartial judge.

[30] The reaction of the Jews then appears all the more reprehensible. As they cannot bring any firm charge against Jesus they give an answer which is both arrogant and evasive: if they have taken the trouble to bring Jesus, then he must be a criminal. For the phrase 'If this man were not an evildoer' cf. 9.33 ('If this man were not from God'); but cf. also Mark 15.14 parr.: 'Why, what evil has he done?'

[31] Pilate draws an understandable conclusion from v. 30: the Jews should settle the matter among themselves in accordance with their own law (v. 31a). But the Jews are not calling on Pilate as a judge who is to decide whether Jesus is innocent or guilty. They merely need him to carry out the death sentence on which they have long since decided (cf. 11.53).

Scene 2: The first interrogation of Jesus by Pilate (vv. 33–38a)

[33] This verse reports the first direct encounter between Pilate and Jesus. The question 'Are you the King of the Jews?' corresponds to Mark 15.2a parr. and refers to a possible political claim on the part of Jesus.

[34] The point of Jesus' counter-question is that Pilate should account to himself for why he is engaged in the charge against him.

[35] Pilate has no cause of his own to proceed against Jesus. Indeed, the fact that he has to ask the *accused* what guilt he has incurred shows that he has allowed the Jews to force him into the position of judge. (The underlinings relate to Mark 15.1, 14a.)

[36] Only now does Jesus begin to answer the question in v. 33. The way in which Jesus speaks of his kingdom first in negative terms must reassure Pilate. If Jesus' kingdom 'is not of this world' (cf. 8.23) and if moreover he has no earthly means of power (cf. Matt. 26.53), there is no occasion for the state authorities to take proceedings against him.

[37] Jesus is indeed a king ('you say it' corresponds to Mark 15.2b parr.), but he makes no political claims. Rather, he has come into the world (cf. 6.14; 11.27) to bear witness to the truth (cf. 8.40, 45; see also 5.33). For the last sentence of Jesus' answer cf. 8.47.

[38a] What Jesus says remains quite alien to Pilate; he evades the claim in Jesus' words which also applies to him. But his question also shows that he does not regard Jesus as a political rebel.

Scene 3: Jesus or Barabbas? (vv. 38b–40)

[38b] Pilate communicates the result of the interrogation to the Jews and for the first time confirms the innocence of Jesus (cf. Luke 23.4).

[39] The Jews have a last chance to avert the immeasurable guilt that they would load upon themselves through the death of the Son of God (cf. Mark 15.6, 9).

[40] But the Jews do not take advantage of this opportunity: they ask, not for the release of Jesus, but for that of a criminal (cf. Luke 23.18; Mark 15.7, 11).

Scene 4: Jesus is scourged and mocked (19.1–3)

[19.1–3] For v. 1 cf. Matt. 27.27 ('thereupon'); Mark 15.15 par. (Pilate had him flogged); for v. 2 cf. Mark 15.16f.; Matt. 27.27–29a; for v. 3 cf. Mark 15.18 par. In Mark and Matthew the mocking of Jesus follows Jesus' being handed over to be crucified (Mark 15.16–20a; Matt. 27.27–31a). Probably this scene was put forward not by Z but only by the evangelist: according to him the maltreatment and mockery of Jesus are an attempt staged by Pilate to assuage the Jews and to deter them from their murderous intent.

Scene 5: The Jews call for the crucifixion of Jesus (vv. 4–7)

[4] Cf. Luke 23.14. Pilate emphasizes the innocence of Jesus to the Jews for the second time (cf. v. 38b).

[5] Pilate presents Jesus to the Jews as the 'caricature of a king' (R. Bultmann) and thus appeals to them indirectly to let Jesus go ('crown of thorns' as in Mark 15.17).

[6a] Pilate's attempt fails: the chief priests and servants unanimously call for the execution of Jesus (cf. Mark 15.13; Luke 23.21).

[6b] With the invitation 'Take him yourselves and crucify him' which precedes the third declaration of innocence (cf. Luke 23.22), Pilate rejects 'with grim irony' (R. Bultmann) the request of the Jews: they do not have capital jurisdiction (cf. 18.31).

[7] Only now do the Jews come out with the answer that they had dodged in v. 30: Jesus has made himself Son of God (cf. on 8.53) and therefore he must die (cf. Lev. 24.16). They cannot bring forward a political charge.

Scene 6: The second interrogation of Jesus by Pilate (vv. 8–11)

[8–9a] Pilate is afraid not of the Jews but of Jesus: if he is in fact the Son of God (cf. v. 7), it would be madness to become an accomplice in his death. Therefore Pilate wants to achieve certain knowledge and asks Jesus where he is from (cf. 7.27f.; 8.14; 9.29).

[9b–10a] Cf. Mark 15.5, 4; Luke 23.9.

[10b–11] Jesus puts the balance of power in its true light: Pilate would have no power over Jesus were it not given to him by God (= 'from above'). If *therefore* the Jews ('he who delivered me up to you' = generalizing singular) have greater sin, it is clear that *their* power is not in God's hand.

Scene 7: The condemnation of Jesus (vv. 12–16a)

[12a] Cf. Luke 23.20 (see also Luke 23.16, 22a).

[12b] The Jews play their last trump card by accusing Pilate of being disloyal to the emperor. Cf. Luke 23.2.

[13] That Pilate sits down on the judgment seat corresponds to Matt. 27.19 and derives from Z. But the information over and above Matthew, that this stood on a place called 'mosaic floor' ('Gabbatha' = dais), must also derive from Z, since it is unimaginable that the evangelist invented it.

[14a] By giving the day and the hour (cf. 1.39; 7.2; 11.55a; 13.30; 18.28a) the evangelist indicates that Jesus is handed over to crucifixion at the very hour (12 noon) when preparations were begun in the temple for slaughtering the Passover lambs. Thus Jesus proves to be the true Passover lamb, the one who supersedes the Jewish cult (cf. 1.36).

[14b] This verse reports Pilate's penultimate attempt to deter the Jews from aggression against their maltreated 'king'.

[15a] This corresponds to v. 6a and emphasizes the stubborn attitude of the accusers (cf. Luke 23.18: 'Away', Mark 15.14b).

[15b] Pilate points out to the Jews the absurdity of their desire.

[15c] In order to get rid of Jesus, the chief priests do not even shrink from abandoning the people's messianic claim. They submit to the pagan Roman emperor.

[16a] Cf. Matt. 27.26; Mark 15.15. Pilate confesses himself beaten. But the fact that in the end he gives in to the demand of the Jews cannot alter in any way the impression given by what has gone before: Pilate is not so much a guilty man entangled in the event but rather a tragic figure.

Yield: (a) All the parts of the text which have no equivalent in one of the parallel Synoptic accounts can be understood as creations by the Fourth Evangelist (the only exception is v. 13b). (b) The Z account, which can be reconstructed only in fragments, does not presuppose any traditions except the Synoptic accounts of the interrogation by Pilate and the specific detail of place in 19.13b. (c) One of the main interests of the evangelist is to heighten the guilt of the Jews for the death of Jesus. *Therefore* – and not out of sympathy for the prefect or for apologetic motives towards the Roman state – he minimizes Pilate's guilt.

Historical

Cf. on Mark 15.1–20a. The detail that Pilate's judgment seat was at a place called 'mosaic floor' or Gabbatha is historically beyond suspicion.

At this point we need to go very briefly into the question of whether v. 14a (which is probably redactional) reflects reliable information about the date of Jesus' death. The problem here is as follows: the Synoptics and the Fourth Evangelist agree that Jesus died on the day of preparation for a sabbath, i.e. on a Friday. But whereas according to the Synoptics the Friday on which Jesus died was the first day of the Passover feast (= 15 Nisan), the Fourth Evangelist reports that Jesus died on the day *before* the feast of the Passover (= 14 Nisan), which incidentally is likewise called 'day of preparation'. Now the question whether the Synoptic dating is credible cannot be decided here. But this much can be said about the date given in the Fourth Gospel: according to the present analysis, the Fourth Evangelist has composed his account of the passion on the basis of an account dependent on the Synoptics, which evidently itself assumes the Synoptic chronology (cf. on 19.31). So we must reckon that the evangelist is deliberately correcting the earlier dating. However, it is highly improbable that he made this correction because he wanted to restore the historically correct date, given all the other passages in his work in which he has failed to show a comparable interest – and this is quite apart from the question of how, at the beginning of the second century, he could have received knowledge of this date. In other words, those who regard the Synoptic dating as untrustworthy cannot automatically give preference to the dating of the Fourth Evangelist. If the correct date of Jesus' death has in fact been preserved in the Gospel of John, then it must be because of the fortuitous coincidence of a historical fact with a theological conception (Jesus as the true Passover lamb).

John 19.16b–30: The crucifixion and death of Jesus

16b Now they took Jesus. 17a And *he himself* bore <u>the cross</u> b and <u>*came*</u> out <u>to</u> the <u>so-called</u> <u>place of a skull, which</u> in Hebrew is <u>called</u> <u>Gologotha,</u> 18a where <u>they crucified him</u> b <u>and</u> <u>with him two</u> others, one on either side, *and Jesus in the middle.*

19 And *Pilate* also *wrote* a title *and* <u>fixed</u> (it) to the cross. <u>And</u> there was written: '<u>Jesus</u> the Nazoraean, <u>the King of the Jews.</u>' 20 *Now many of the Jews read this title, for the place where Jesus was crucified was near the city. And it was written in Hebrew, in Latin, (and) in Greek.* 21 *Now the chief priests of the Jews said to Pilate, 'Do not write, "The King of the Jews", but, "This man said: I am King of the Jews".'* 22 *Pilate answered, 'What I have written I have written.'*

23 *Now* the soldiers, *when they had crucified Jesus,* took his garments and made four parts, one for each soldier; and also the undergarment. But the undergarment was without seam, woven from top to bottom. 24a So they said to one another, 'Let us not tear it, but cast lots for it, whose it shall be.' b (This was) to fulfil the scripture, '<u>They parted</u> my <u>garments</u> among them, and <u>over</u> my vesture they <u>cast</u> <u>a lot.</u>'

c **Now the soldiers did this. 25 But there were standing by the cross of Jesus his mother and his mother's sister, (and then) Mary the (wife) of Clopas, and Mary Magdalene. 26 Now when Jesus saw his mother, and the disciple whom he loved standing near, he says to his mother, 'Woman, that is your son!' 27 Then he says to the disciple, 'That is your mother!' And from that hour the disciple took her to his own home.**

28 After this, *when Jesus knew that all was already finished,* he says, so that the scripture might receive its final fulfilment, 'I thirst.' 29 A bowl full of vinegar stood there; they <u>stuck</u> a

<u>sponge</u> full of the <u>vinegar</u> on a hyssop (branch) and <u>held</u> it to his mouth. 30 Now when <u>Jesus</u> had taken the vinegar, *he said, 'It is finished', and* he bowed his head and gave up <u>the spirit</u>.

[25 <u>But there were standing</u> by the cross of Jesus his mother and his <u>mother</u>'s sister, (and then) <u>Mary the</u> (wife) <u>of</u> Clopas, <u>and Mary Magdalene</u>.]

Later revision

In view of the fact that four women by the cross are mentioned in v. 25, it is surprising that according to vv. 26f. Jesus overlooks three of them but does catch sight of the beloved disciple. Now the analysis of 13.21–30 has already shown that the scene with the beloved disciple in 13.23–26a was added by the revisers. Therefore it seems reasonable to assume that vv. 26f. also are a later addition. However, v. 25 stands in an impossible place before v. 28. That suggests the following conjecture: in the original text, in accordance with the Synoptic accounts (Mark 15.40f.; Matt. 27.55f.; cf. Luke 23.49) the mention of the women followed v. 30, and only the revisers brought it forward in the course of the insertion of vv. 26f. (J. Becker). This was necessary in that it would have been remarkable if Jesus had continued to speak after his death. By the clumsy addition 'Now the soldiers did this' (v. 24c), the revisers tried to fix v. 25 in its new place.

The purpose of the revisers in rearranging and expanding the scene is to make the beloved disciple as the representative of the Johannine community a witness to an important stage in the life of the earthly Jesus, namely the last. At the same time they emphasize once again (cf. 13.23) the particularly intimate relationship of trust between Jesus and the beloved disciple. It is to the beloved disciple that Jesus addresses his last words and to whom he transfers the obligation of care of his mother. (Given 2.4, the evangelist could not have formulated the latter in this way.)

Redaction and tradition

The section comprises five scenes (vv. 16b–18: the crucifixion; vv. 19–22: the controversy over the inscription on the cross; vv. 23–24b: the division of the garments; vv. 28–30: the death of Jesus; v. 25: the women as witnesses). It is based on Z (Mark 15.20b–41; Matt. 27.31b–56; Luke 23.26–49). In the translation, verbatim and almost verbatim agreements with Mark are underlined once and possibly additional agreements with Matthew/Luke are underlined twice.

[16b] This verse corresponds to Mark 15.20b; Matt. 27.31b; Luke 23.26a. The fact that the Fourth Evangelist attaches this note directly to 19.16a gives the impression that the high priests or the Jews from 19.15 lead Jesus off to be crucified. This may be done not carelessly but deliberately, even if it then emerges from v. 23 that (Roman) soldiers carry out the crucifixion.

[17a] Cf. Mark 15.21; Matt. 27.32; Luke 23.26b. The statement that Jesus himself bore the cross contradicts the description in all three Synoptic Gospels according to

which Simon of Cyrene was compelled to take the burden from Jesus. We will not go wrong in attributing this correction to the evangelist: the notion that Jesus needs the help of others is not in keeping with Jesus being the sovereign Lord of his fate who has staged the events of the passion himself (cf. 11.4; 18.4–8).

[17b] Almost all the words appear (in a similar form) in Mark 15.22 or Matt. 27.33 (cf. Luke 23.33a). As in Luke, there is no observation on the wine refused by Jesus (Mark 15.23; Matt. 27.34). Probably the evangelist has changed an original 'they came out' (cf. Matthew) into the singular, in order after v. 17a to emphasize once again that Jesus actively accepts death.

[18a] This agrees almost word for word with the corresponding phrase in Luke 23.33 (cf. Mark 15.24a; Matt. 27.35a).

[18b] Cf. Mark 15.27; Matt. 27.38; Luke 23.33b (see also Luke 23.32). As in Luke, the two other men who are executed are mentioned immediately after the crucifixion of Jesus, and not after the distribution of the garments (thus Mark, Matthew). Either Z or the evangelist has deleted their characterization as robbers (Mark/Matthew) or evildoers (Luke). The note 'and Jesus in the middle', which is really superfluous, derives from the evangelist, who wants to focus the attention entirely on Jesus.

[19] Cf. Mark 15.26; Matt. 27.27; Luke 23.38. The elaboration of the titulus on the cross with the designation 'the Nazoraean' (cf. Matt. 2.23; 26.71; Luke 18.37) derives from Z; the information that Pilate was the author of this title comes from the evangelist (see below).

[20–22] These verses have been composed in their entirety by the evangelist: in refusing to alter the inscription on the cross, Pilate takes his revenge on the Jews, who have compelled him to act against his will (cf. especially the controversy over the 'King of the Jews' in 19.12–15). The trilingual inscription composed by Pilate expresses the universal significance of Jesus, who is now returning to the Father.

If vv. 20–22 derive from the evangelist, we can conjecture that in Z (as in the Synoptics) v. 19 came only after the division of the garments (vv. 23–24b). Also in support of this is the fact that v. 23 would follow well after v. 18 (A.Dauer). The evangelist would then have made a link back from v. 23a to v. 18 by the temporal clause. All in all, in this case there would be a strong similarity between the Z and the Lukan outlines of the whole scene.

[23–24b] These verses have been spun out of Mark 15.24b; Matt. 27.35b; Luke 23.34b at a secondary stage (for 'whose it shall be' cf. 'who should get what' in Mark). A shrewd person noted that Ps. 21.19 LXX (= v. 24b), to which the Synoptics merely allude, does not say that garments are divided by casting lots but that the garments are divided and lots are cast for the *vesture*. Thus for the psalm verse to be fulfilled literally there also had to be an undergarment – one without a seam, for one that had been sewn together could equally have been divided. Cf.

similarly Matt. 21.2–9, where the First Evangelist makes Jesus ride on two asses at the same time so that (his misreading of) Zech. 9.9 can be fulfilled literally. For the evangelist such scriptural proofs are of secondary importance; they are all the more important for Z (cf. 12.14f.; 19.28, 36f.).

[28–30] If the scripture still has to be fulfilled, not everything can have been finished previously (v. 28). Moreover it seems strange that the last word of Jesus, which is surely meant to refer to all the events of the passion, if not indeed to the whole of his work accomplished on earth (cf. 4.34), in the present context seems to focus merely on the drink of vinegar. That indicates that the evangelist has added the phrase 'when he knew that all was already finished' (cf. 13.1a; 18.4) in v. 28 and 'he said "It is finished!" and' in v. 30. Accordingly Z merely reported that with Jesus' last breath the scripture received its final fulfilment (cf. Ps. 69.22b: 'in my thirst they gave me vinegar to drink'). Here Z evidently drew on Mark 15.36; Matt. 27.48; Luke 23.36. For the death of Jesus itself cf. Matt. 27.50, 'he yielded up the spirit' (see also Luke 23.46, 'I commend my spirit into your hands').

[25] Cf. Mark 15.40; Matt. 27.55 and Luke 23.49 ('but there were standing'). In the evangelist's work this verse likely followed v. 30 (see above). Probably the evangelist took over the list of women unchanged from Z, for – apart from Mary Magdalene (cf. 20.1, 11b–18), who is the only one also to appear in the lists in the Synoptics – otherwise he has little or no interest in the women mentioned (cf. 2.4; 6.42). Again, Z seems not to have known what to do with the women mentioned in the Synoptics. Therefore (with the exception of Mary Magdalene) they have been displaced by Jesus' mother and aunt and by the wife of a certain Clopas (who was probably known in the community). In contrast to the Synoptics, according to which the women observe the event 'from afar', Z or the evangelist (or only the revisers?) put them directly under the cross.

Yield: Z does not presuppose any traditions other than the Synoptic accounts of the crucifixion.

Historical

Cf. on Mark 15.20b–41.

John 19.31–37: The confirmation of the death of Jesus

31 Now since it was the day of preparation, so that the bodies should not remain on the cross on the sabbath – *for great was the day of that sabbath* – the Jews asked Pilate that their legs might be broken, and that they might be taken away. 32 Now the soldiers came and broke the legs of the first, and of the other who had been crucified with him. 33 But when they came to Jesus (and) saw that he was already dead, they did not break his legs, 34 but one of the

soldiers stabbed into his side with a lance, and at once there came out blood and water. 35 **And he who saw it has borne witness, and his witness is true, and he knows that he is telling the truth, that you also may believe.** 36 For this took place that the scripture might be fulfilled, 'Not a bone of him shall be broken.' 37 And again another (passage of) scripture says, 'They shall look on him whom they pierced.'

Later revision

Verse 35 is clearly an addition by the revisers. *First*, v. 37 sees the point of what is narrated in the lance thrust itself, whereas v. 35 is interested in the consequence of the thrust, the flow of blood and water. *Secondly*, the eye-witness brought into play in v. 35 can only be the beloved disciple, since according to the description so far he is the only male witness under the cross (cf. 19.26f.); but he was put there only by the revisers. *Thirdly*, v. 35 is manifestly formulated on the basis of the conclusion to the added chapter 21 (21.24: 'the disciple who bears witness . . . and we know that his witness is true'). And *fourthly*, v. 35 addresses the readers directly, contrary to the usual style; the evangelist does this for the first and last time at the end of his work (20.31: 'that you may believe' – a passage which also seems to have been used here). It is unclear what deeper sense the revisers attached to the flow of blood and water from the wound in Jesus' side. Possibly they saw it as a mysterious indication that the sacraments of baptism (water) and the eucharist (blood) are grounded in the death of Jesus (cf. 1.13; 6.51c–58).

Redaction

The scene has no parallel in the Synoptics. Thus the question arises whether the evangelist composed it himself, or integrated it into the account as an individual tradition, or found it already in the account of the passion which he used. The last must be the case. For first, in v. 31 an addition by the evangelist to an existing text can be marked off. And secondly, the section is stamped by the same interest in scriptural proof that the Z account of the passion also shows in 19.23–24b and 19.28–30.

[31] This verse shows a remarkable parallelism to 19.38: there Joseph 'asks Pilate' to be allowed to 'take away' the body of Jesus; here the Jews 'ask Pilate' to allow the bones of the crucified men to be broken and for them to be 'taken away'. Moreover it is striking that the phrase 'since it was the day of preparation' occurs word for word in the introduction to the Markan account of the burial (Mark 15.42–47), which is presupposed in 19.38–42. Thus Z formulated v. 31 on the basis of 19.38 and here appropriately anticipated the note of time from Mark 15.42.

The request of the Jews has to be seen against the background of the regulation in Deut. 21.22f. according to which an executed man was not to hang on a tree overnight. (However, that means any night and not just the night of the approaching sabbath.) That in what follows the soldiers carry out only the first of the two demands is explained by the fact that on the one hand the request for the bodies to be taken away is necessary for the present story, and on the other there is still a story to follow which reports that Jesus is taken down from the cross by Joseph of Arimathea – a narrative clumsiness which, however, the author *had to* accept if he wanted to find any place for the present story at all.

Only the explanation 'for great was the day of that sabbath' derives from the evangelist (cf. 7.37). With this addition he takes account of his chronology of the events of the passion, which diverges from the Synoptics and Z. For according to him, in the year of Jesus' death the day of the preparation for the sabbath (= Friday) on which Jesus died was not the first day of the feast of the Passover (thus the Synoptics) but the eve of the Passover, i.e. the day of preparation for the sabbath and the day of preparation for the Passover at the same time. So the story from the tradition must have presupposed the 'Synoptic' chronology. For the chronological question cf. further the remarks on 18.28–19.16a ('Historical').

[32–34] The breaking of the legs meant that the crucified men could no longer support themselves with their feet; the weight of the body was then borne only by the arms, and death by suffocation followed more quickly. However, if Jesus had already died, the cruel procedure was unnecessary. Simply to make sure, one of the soldiers thrusts with a lance into the area of Jesus' heart. The resultant flow of blood and water shows that death has in fact taken place. Mark 15.44–45 (Pilate was amazed 'that he was already dead') probably glimmers through v. 33 ('when they saw that he was already dead'). This episode is omitted in 19.38–42.

The evangelist probably included the present story above all because of the mention of the wound in Jesus' side in v. 34. For he will return to it in 20.24–29, using it to demonstrate the bodily resurrection of Jesus vividly.

[36–37] Verse 33 is interpreted as the fulfilment of Ex. 12.10, 46 LXX (no bone of the Passover lamb is to be broken) or of Ps. 34.21 (the Lord preserves all the bones of the righteous, 'none of them will be broken'); Zech. 12.10 is fulfilled with v. 34.

Yield: the account is spun out of Ps. 34.21 (Ex. 12.10, 46) and Zech. 12.10 and shows that the Old Testament scriptures are fulfilled even in Jesus' body. At the same time it is made clear with a subsidiary apologetic intent that Jesus was really dead. Proof of that is (a) the impartial verdict of the soldiers (v. 33), (b) the lance thrust to make sure Jesus is dead (v. 34a), and (c) the flow of water and blood from the body (v. 34b). We need not immediately assume that this proof has an anti-docetic slant. There is no intention to dispute that Jesus merely seemed to suffer; the intention is to show that it was not a seemingly dead person who rose again.

Historical

The historical yield is nil.

John 19.38–42: The burial of Jesus

38a *And after this* Joseph of Arimathea, who was a <u>disciple of Jesus</u>, *but secretly, for fear of the Jews,* asked <u>Pilate</u> that he might take away <u>the body of Jesus</u>. b And <u>Pilate</u> allowed it. c So <u>he came</u> and took away his body. 39a *And Nicodemus also came, who had at first come to him by night,* b bringing a mixture of myrrh and aloes, about a hundred pounds' weight. 40 Now *they* <u>took the body</u> of Jesus and wrapped <u>it</u> in linen cloths with the <u>spices</u>, *as is the burial custom of the Jews.* 41a Now in the place where he had been crucified there was a garden, b and in the garden a <u>new tomb</u> wherein <u>no one had ever</u> yet been laid. 42 There *now – because of the Jews' day of preparation, as the tomb was near –* they <u>buried Jesus</u>.

Redaction and tradition

This section is based on Z (cf. Mark 15.42–47; Matt. 27.57–61; Luke 23.50–56). Verbatim and almost verbatim agreements with Mark are underlined once and possibly additional agreements with Matthew and Luke are underlined twice.

[38a] Cf. Mark 15.43; Matt. 27.57–58a; Luke 23.50–52. In Z, on the basis of Matthew, the 'respected councillor' Joseph of Arimathea 'who was also awaiting the kingdom of God' (thus Mark; cf. Luke) has become a disciple of Jesus. The evangelist adds that Joseph keeps his discipleship hidden for fear of the Jews (cf. 7.13; 9.22; 12.42). That Joseph himself is a Jew plays no role (cf. 7.11–13). Mark 15.42 has been used by Z in 19.31 (see there).

[38b] Cf. Mark 15.45; Matt. 27.58.

[38c] The taking down of the body (from the cross), which is tacitly presupposed by the Synoptics, is specifically mentioned by Z. For 'he came' cf. Matt. 27.57 (Mark 15.43; Luke 23.52).

[39a] With explicit reference to the nocturnal scene 3.1–21, the evangelist gives Joseph a companion.

Mark and Luke know that *Joseph of Arimathea* was a 'councillor who was awaiting the kingdom of God' (see on v. 38a). In view of that it cannot be chance that with *Nicodemus* the Fourth Evangelist introduces someone who according to 3.1 (cf. 7.50f.) is similarly a councillor and with whom Jesus had carried on a conversation about the 'kingdom of God' (3.3, 5). Thus in Z (v. 38a*) Joseph was evidently described not only as a disciple of Jesus (as in Matthew) but also as a councillor who was waiting for the kingdom of God (as in Mark and Luke). The evangelist omitted this, but was prompted by it to introduce Nicodemus.

[39b] Such elaborations are not typical of the evangelist. In Z the verse probably continued v. 38c, and thus originally referred to Joseph. In Z the burial of Jesus becomes a truly royal interment by the procurement of a tremendous amount of myrrh and aloes: 100 (Roman) pounds is almost 33 kilograms with a value of 30,000

denarii; cf. 12.5 (= Z), 'one pound' for 300 denarii (one denarius is a day's wage; cf. Matt. 20.2–4). With v. 39b Z brought forward the note about the 'spices' (which according to Mark 16.1/Luke 24.1 women bring to the tomb) to the right place, namely the burial.

[40] Cf. Matt. 27.59; Luke 23.53a (Mark 15.46a); 'spices' as in Luke 23.56. The evangelist merely puts the predicates in the plural and adds the explanation v. 40b. Through this he 'somewhat clumsily turns the rich burial into a normal one' (J. Becker).

[41a] Z moves the tomb of Jesus into a garden (cf. 18.1) and in this way transforms the burial into an almost idyllic scene.

[41b] Cf. Matt. 27.60 ('his new tomb'); Luke 23.53 ('where no one had ever yet lain').

[42] Cf. Mark 15.46; Matt. 27.60; Luke 23.53. The passage extending from 'now' to 'near' proves to be a redactional addition because it tears apart the main clause to the limits of the possible, and because the details about the day and the nearness of the tomb are superfluous after vv. 31, 41. The conclusion of the Z report of the passion ran: 'There he buried Jesus.'

Yield: Z does not presuppose any traditions beyond the Synoptic accounts of the burial.

Historical

Cf. on Mark 15.42–47.

John 20: The Fourth Evangelist's Easter Stories

John 20.1–23: Easter Day

1a Now on the first day of the week Mary Magdalene comes to the tomb early in the morning, while it is still dark, b and sees the stone taken away from the tomb.
2 Then she runs, and comes to Simon Peter and to the other disciple, whom Jesus loved, and says to them, 'They have taken the Lord out of the tomb, and we do not know where they have laid him.' 3 Then Peter and the other disciple came out, and they went to the tomb. 4 Now they both ran together, but the other disciple outran Peter and came to the tomb first. 5 And he stoops and sees the linen cloths lying there, but he did not go in. 6 Then Simon Peter also comes, following him, and went into the tomb, and sees the linen cloths lying there, 7 and the napkin, which had been on his head, not lying with the linen cloths but rolled up in a (special) place by itself. 8 Then the other disciple, who had reached the tomb first, also went in, and he saw and believed. 9 For as yet they did not understand the scripture, that he must rise from the dead. 10 Thereupon the disciples went back home.

11a **But Mary stood outside the tomb and wept**. b And as she wept she stooped (to look) <u>into the tomb</u> 12 and sees <u>two</u> <u>angels</u> in <u>white</u> garments sitting there, one at the head and one at the feet, <u>where the body of Jesus had lain.</u> 13a And they say to her, 'Woman, <u>why</u> <u>are you weeping?</u>' b She says to them, 'They have taken away my Lord, and I do not know <u>where they have laid him.</u>'

14a *After she had said this*, she turned round b and sees <u>Jesus</u> standing there, and she did not know that it was Jesus. 15a *Jesus says to her, 'Woman, why are you weeping? Whom do you seek?'* b *Supposing him to be the gardener, she says to him, 'Sir, if you have carried him away, tell me where you have laid him, and I will get him.'* 16a Jesus says to her, 'Mary.' b She *turns round and* says to him *in Hebrew*, 'Rabboni!', *which means: Teacher.* 17a <u>Jesus says</u> to her, 'Do <u>not</u> touch me! b *For I have not yet ascended to the Father.* c But go to <u>my brothers</u> and say to them, d *"I am ascending to my Father and your Father, and to my God and your God."'* 18 Mary Magdalene goes and <u>proclaims</u> to the disciples, 'I have seen the Lord,' *and that he has told her this.*

[3* Then <u>Peter</u> and [the other disciples] came out, and 4* they <u>ran to the tomb</u>. 5* And [they stoop] and [see] <u>the linen cloths lying there</u>, 7 and the napkin, which had been on his head, not lying with the linen cloths but rolled up in a (special) <u>place</u> by itself. [<u>And they</u> <u>wondered</u>.] 9 For as yet they did not understand the scripture, <u>that he must rise</u> from the dead. 10 Thereupon the disciples <u>went back home</u>.]

19a Now when it was evening on that first day of the week and the doors had been closed where the disciples were – *for fear of the Jews* – b Jesus came and <u>stood in the midst and says</u> <u>to them</u>, '<u>Peace be with you.</u>' 20a And <u>when he had said this, he showed them his hands and</u> *his side*. b Then the disciples <u>rejoiced</u> when they saw the Lord. 21a *Then he said to them again, 'Peace be with you.* b *As the Father has sent me, so I send you.'* 22 And *when he had said this*, he blew on (them), and says to them, 'Receive Holy Spirit. 23 If you forgive the sins of any, they are forgiven; if you retain (the sins of any), they are retained.'

Later revision

The text shows a notable number of inconsistencies. Some of them are so serious that they compel us to assume that the section has been revised subsequently. *First*, the link between v. 2 and v. 1 is suspicious: for Mary Magdalene to conclude from her observation that the *stone* has been taken away from the tomb (v. 1) that *Jesus* is no longer in his original place (v. 2) can only be said to be over-hasty. *Secondly*, there is no report of Mary returning to the tomb after she has notified the two disciples (v. 2); in v. 11 she is standing at the tomb as though the events which were narrated in vv. 2–10 had not taken place. *Thirdly*, the question arises why Mary sees two angels sitting in the tomb (v. 12), whereas previously all that there was to be seen was a napkin and some linen cloths (vv. 5–7). *Fourthly*, the charge of the Risen One to Mary Magdalene (v. 17) is robbed of its point if a disciple has already come to believe in the resurrection (v. 8).

These tensions are matched by the observation that v. 11b would follow well after v. 1. Thus the conjecture arises that the episode of the race between the two disciples and their visit to the tomb was introduced between v. 1 and v. 11b only by the later revisers. By v. 2, which is formulated on the basis of v. 13b, they anchored this episode in a makeshift way in the context, and with v. 11a they returned to the situation presupposed in v. 1, taking up v. 11b ('weep').

However, not all problems are solved with this literary-critical operation. For vv. 2–11a are not free of tension in themselves. For example, the information that first Peter and thereupon the beloved disciple 'sees the linen cloths lying there' (vv. 5, 6) is redundant. The reader is then presented with a particularly great riddle in v. 9: the observation that the two disciples had not yet understood that Jesus had to rise from the dead stands in cross contradiction to v. 8, according to which the beloved disciple has already come to believe in the resurrection. In other words, the section itself gives the impression of having been revised at a secondary stage. How can that be explained?

An answer can be given only by anticipating the further analysis of the section vv. 1–18, 19–23. For we shall see that the evangelist has composed these two Easter stories on the basis of a tradition (= Z) dependent above all on Luke 24. That is significant because Luke similarly reports an inspection of the tomb. However, in his work this takes place only after the women have passed the Easter message of the angels at the tomb on to the disciples, and is carried out only by Peter (cf. Luke 24.12: 'Now Peter stood up and ran to the tomb and stooped and saw only the linen cloths and went away and wondered at what had happened'). If one combines this fact with the previous reflections on the position and the lack of integrity of vv. 2–11a, and further notes that the beloved disciple has been introduced later into the sections 1.35–51; 13.21–30; 19.16b–30; 19.31–37, directly or indirectly, the following assumption seems likely: certainly the revisers are responsible for the insertion of vv. 2–11a between vv. 1 and 11b, but they found the basic material of this passage already in the work of the evangelist, at a place corresponding to the position of Luke 24.12, i.e. after v. 18 (M. Theobald). They added the beloved disciple and at the same time shifted the section to its present place. (Cf. the verse 19.25, which has probably also been transposed subsequently.)

In conclusion, two further questions need to be asked. *First*, what was the aim of the revisers in making these serious interventions? *Secondly*, what was the wording of the text of vv. 3–10* composed by the evangelist?

The answer to the *first* question is obvious. The insertion of the beloved disciple running a race with Peter has the aim of tangibly illustrating his priority over Peter. And the transposition of the section ensures that the beloved disciple (and not Mary Magdalene) can be the first to believe in the resurrection of Jesus.

The *second* question is harder to answer, and an answer must remain highly hypothetical. Above all it is debatable whether according to the evangelist Peter went to the tomb alone or in the company of other disciples. Because of the plural in v. 9, however, the second possibility has to be regarded as the likelier. That would also fit in well with 20.18, 19, 20, 25, where there is a general mention of 'the disciples' or 'the other disciples' (cf. also Luke 24.24, where despite Luke 24.12 we read: 'And *some* of us went to the tomb and found it as the women had said . . .'). Moreover, in the course of the revising of vv. 3–10* an observation about the incomprehension of the disciples when confronted with the empty tomb, corresponding to the conclusion of Luke 24.12, must have fallen out before v. 9. However, it must be explicitly emphasized that the reconstruction of vv. 3–10* which is printed in square brackets in the translation between vv. 18 and 19 represents only one of several possible ways in which the original text could have run (divergences from the present text similarly in square brackets).

Redaction and tradition

As has already been indicated, the basis of this section is a tradition dependent above all on Luke 24 but also influenced by Mark 16 and Matt. 28 (Z). Verbatim and almost verbatim agreements with Luke are underlined twice, agreements with Mark/Matthew are underlined once.

Mary Magdalene and the two angels (vv. 1, 11b–13)

[1] There is an equivalent in Mark 16.1, 2, 4a or Luke 24.1, 2 for almost every word. The reason why Mary, in contrast to Mark 16.1; Luke 24.1, does not bring any spices to the tomb is that according to 19.40* (= Z) the body of Jesus has already been buried in a proper fashion. However, an important difference from the Synoptics is that Mary Magdalene (cf. 19.25) goes to the tomb *alone* (Mark 16.1: three women; Matt. 28.1: two; Luke 24.1, 10: more than three). The analysis of vv. 14–18 will indicate a probable explanation of this.

[11b–13] The substance of this piece derives from Z; cf., in the order of underlinings: Mark 16.5a ('into the tomb'); Luke 24.4 ('two'); Matt. 28.2 ('angel'); Matt. 28.3/Mark 16.5 ('white'); Matt. 28.6 ('where . . . had lain'); Luke 24.3 ('the body of the Lord Jesus'); Luke 24.5 ('why . . .?'); Mark 16.6 ('where they have laid him'). However, though no assured statements can be made, the possibility cannot be ruled out that the evangelist has also intervened redactionally. Thus it should be noted that the motif of weeping in 11.35 has been inserted redactionally and that the address 'woman' derives from the evangelist in 2.4 and 4.21.

The appearance of Jesus to Mary Magdalene (vv. 14–18)

The scene with the angels in vv. 11b–13 ends quite abruptly: the angels do not proclaim the resurrection of Jesus (cf. Mark 16.6; Matt. 28.6; Luke 24.6), nor do they give instructions to pass the message of the resurrection on to the disciples (cf. Mark 16.7; Matt. 28.7). Rather, in vv. 14–17 there follows a report about a meeting between Mary Magdalene and Jesus himself which competes with the appearance of the angels. Now Matthew similarly added to his version of the Markan story of the tomb a report (presumably composed by himself) about an appearance of Jesus to Mary Magdalene (and another Mary); cf. Matt. 28.9–10. Here the charge 'Go, proclaim to my brothers' (Matt. 28.10), which corresponds to John 20.17c, is particularly striking. The following explanation of this seems likely: Z has taken up the Matthaean report about the meeting of the two women with Jesus but reshaped it and developed it into a recognition scene. In connection with this, two essential changes were made in comparison with the Synoptic stories of the tomb. First, that part of the narrative which reported the proclamation of the resurrection by one or more angels was dropped, because in view of the encounter with the Risen One himself this episode seemed superfluous. Secondly, the other Mary mentioned by Matthew was removed from the story, and the recognition scene was thus wholly focussed on Jesus and Mary Magdalene. If this latter assumption is correct, then Z must also be responsible in vv. 1, 11b–13 for the reduction of the number of several women given by the Synoptics to one. However, the Z basis of vv. 14–18 can be reconstructed only fragmentarily, for the evangelist has evidently reworked it considerably.

[14a] 'After she had said this' is a transitional formula typical of the evangelist (cf. 7.9; 9.6; 11.11, 28, 43; 18.1, 38; 20.20, 22).

[14b] Cf. Matt. 28.9a ('And look, Jesus met them'). The motif of a failure to recognize Jesus was probably already an element of the Z narrative. (The same motif also appears in the story of the disciples on the Emmaus road, cf. Luke 24.16.) The evangelist has introduced only the additional motif of misunderstanding into the traditional recognition scene (v. 15b).

[15a] 'Woman, why are you weeping?' is identical with the way in which the two angels address Mary Magdalene in v. 13. The question 'Whom do you seek?' recalls 1.38; 18.4, 7 (but cf. also Luke 24.5: 'Why do you seek the living among the dead?').

[15b] For the motif of misunderstanding cf. 2.20; for the formulation cf. 11.31; 13.29.

[16] For Mary to turn round is in tension with v. 14a, where she has already turned round. The translation of the address 'Rabboni' and the explanation that this is a Hebrew word suggest that the exchange of words belongs to Z. In being addressed by Jesus, Mary recognizes him again.

[17] The 'do not touch me' (v. 17a) probably comes from the tradition, for it seems to presuppose a reaction corresponding to Matt. 28.9b ('And they came to him and embraced his feet . . .'). The charge in v. 17c similarly comes from the tradition. This is suggested not only by the analogy in Matt. 28.10 (see above) but also by the fact that the disciples are not designated 'brothers' of Jesus elsewhere in the work of the Fourth Evangelist. By contrast, both the reason for the prohibition against touching (v. 17b) and the content of the message to be delivered (v. 17d) derive from the evangelist. He means to say that once Jesus has returned to heavenly glory, his Father will also become the Father of his own. We can no longer ascertain what originally stood in place of vv. 17b and 17d.

[18] The report 'I have seen the Lord', which does not really fit Jesus' command in v. 17d, is an additional confirmation of the assumption that the original content of the charge has been replaced by the evangelist. He takes account of his reformulation of v. 17 by the lame clause 'and that he has told her this'.

The inspection of the tomb (vv. 3–10*)

[3–10*] These verses (in the form reconstructed hypothetically above) correspond to Luke 24.12. As in Luke, so in Z the mention of the linen cloths has an apologetic purpose. They exclude the possibility of a confusion of the tomb. The mention of the carefully folded napkin, which goes beyond Luke 24.12, is probably meant to rule out the suspicion of tomb robbery (cf. Matt. 27.62–66; 28.11–15, where the same suspicion is dismissed by other means). Thus the empty tomb becomes almost a fully valid testimony to Jesus' resurrection. Luke 24.7 ('that he must rise') and Luke 24.44b–46 have evidently been used in v. 9.

The appearance of Jesus to the disciples (vv. 19–23)

[19a] The note of time refers back to v. 1. That the verse attaches well to v. 10 is an additional argument that in the evangelist's work vv. 3–10* stood between v. 18 and v. 19. Only 'for fear of the Jews' proves to be redactional through the equivalents in 7.13 and 19.38 (cf. 9.22). This addition tones down one of the points of the tradition – namely that the Risen Christ can pass through closed doors. In Luke 24.36–43 the motif of fear occurs as a reaction to the appearance (Luke 24.37).

[19b–20a] Cf. the almost verbatim agreement with Luke 24.36, 40. The only significant difference consists in the fact that the Fourth Evangelist mentions Jesus' *side* instead of his feet. Here he is referring back to 19.34 and at the same time preparing for the following scene (cf. 20.25b, 27). (As 19.34 comes from Z, however, it is also possible that the mention of the side already antedates the evangelist.)

In the redactional context the question arises how the announcement of the ascent of Jesus in v. 17 relates to his renewed appearance. For it seems as if now Jesus, who in the meantime has ascended to the Father, is once again returning to earth. But this can hardly be the view of the evangelist. For him, rather, 'He has ascended, and *as such* he appears to the disciples' (R. Bultmann).

[20b] For the motif of the joy of the disciples cf. Luke 24.41.

[21] The phrase 'he said to them again' (cf. 8.12, 21) and the repetition of the greeting from v. 19b indicate that this verse has been inserted by the evangelist (cf. 4.38).

[22] The phrase 'when he had said this' is conditioned by the insertion of v. 21. Otherwise we will see this verse as an element of Z, for the archaic nature of the transfer of the spirit (cf. Gen. 2.7; Ezek. 37.5–10, 14; Wisdom 15.1) competes with the Paraclete sayings of both the evangelist and the later revisers (cf. e.g. 14.16, 26; 16.7, 13; 7.39); similarly there is no 'holy spirit' without the article elsewhere in the Gospel of John. It is remarkable that in Z – in contrast to Luke (cf. Luke 24.49; Acts 2) – Easter and Pentecost fall on the same day.

[23] The concluding word of authority similarly belongs to Z. There it has possibly been composed of Luke 24.47 and Matt. 16.19; 18.18. The expressions 'forgive sins' and 'retain sins' do not occur elsewhere in the Gospel of John.

Historical

[1, 11b–13] These verses presuppose all the Synoptic stories of the tomb. Therefore for their historical value reference can be made to the remarks on Mark 16.1–8.

[14–18*] These verses presuppose the Matthaean redactional composition Matt. 28.9f. and therefore have no historical value.

[3–10*] For the report on the inspection of the tomb by Peter cf. on Luke 24.12.

[19–23*] Cf. the observations on Luke 24.36–43, 44–49. For v. 23 see also the remarks on Matt. 16.19 and 18.18.

John 20.24–29: The appearance of the Risen One to Thomas

24 *Now Thomas, one of the twelve, called Didymus (= Twin), was not with them when Jesus came.* 25a *So the other disciples told him, 'We have seen the Lord.'* b *But he said to them, 'Unless I see in his hands the print of the nails, and place my finger in the print of the nails, and place my hand in his side, I will not believe.'* 26a *And after eight days his disciples were again in the house, and Thomas with them.* b *Jesus comes, the doors being shut, and stood in the midst and said, 'Peace be with you.'* 27 *Then he says to Thomas, 'Put your finger here and see my hands; and put out your hand and place it in my side, and do not be faithless, but believing.'* 28 *Thomas answered and said to him, 'My Lord and my God!'* 29a *Jesus says to him, 'Because you have seen me, have you come to believe?* b *Blessed are those who do not see and (yet) believe.'*

Redaction and historical

This story has no parallel in the Synoptics. It is in tension with the preceding section vv. 19–23, because there was no indication there that one of the disciples was absent when Jesus appeared.

[24] This verse explains why the appearance to Thomas still had to take place, and refers back explicitly to v. 19. Thomas has already been mentioned in 11.16 with his nickname 'Twin' and there similarly appeared as a typical representative of doubt.

[25a] 'We have seen the Lord' takes up 'when they saw the Lord' (20.20b) and is formulated in accordance with the saying of Mary Magdalene in 20.18.

[25b] The conditions laid down by Thomas refer back to 20.20a.

[26a] The note of time, 'after eight days', dates the new gathering of the disciples, like the first one (cf. v. 19), to a Sunday.

[26b] This verse corresponds almost word for word with 20.19b; the motif of the closed doors comes from 20.19a.

[27] The invitation by Jesus accords with Thomas' wish from v. 25b. Since according to the evangelist the earthly Jesus was omniscient (cf. on 1.42), the Risen One is even more so: 'No report needs to be given to him of what happened according to v. 24f.' (J. Becker). (For touching as a means of convincing oneself of the reality of Jesus' body and the identity of his person cf. Luke 24.39–43.)

[28] Thomas does not accept Jesus' offer. Instead of this he makes a quite appropriate confession to the Risen One (cf. 11.27), which sees God himself in Jesus. The exclamation 'My Lord and my God' builds a bridge back to 1.1, 18 (cf. 5.18; 10.30).

[29a] Jesus' question is formulated like 1.50; its reproachful tone corresponds to 3.10; 6.61 and 14.9a.

[29b] This beatitude, which corresponds to the train of thought in 4.48, is the last word which according to the evangelist the risen Jesus says. Debating the relationship between 'believe' and 'see' is typical of the evangelist (cf. 6.30, 36, etc.).

Yield: the narrative is a creation of the evangelist, who in it makes concrete the motif of doubt also known from other resurrection stories (cf. Luke 24.11, 21ff., 37f., 41; Matt. 28.17). The historical value of this narrative is nil. (For the motif of doubt see also the remarks on Matt. 28.17.)

John 20.30–31: The conclusion of the Gospel

30 *Now Jesus did many other signs in the presence of his disciples, which are not written in this book.* 31 *But these are written that you may believe that Jesus is the Christ, the Son of God, and that believing you may have life in his name.*

Redaction

[30] The evangelist emphasizes at the end of his book that his account is only a selection. 'This remark is not meant to excuse the author of the Gospel but rather to make the reader aware of the inexhaustible riches of the subject' (R. Bultmann). With the passive formulation 'are written', which is repeated in v. 31, the evangelist as author deliberately retreats behind his work.

However, it is a great riddle why he sums up all that he has told of Jesus under the term 'sign', since he predominantly reserves this word for the specific miracles of Jesus (cf. 2.11, 18, 23; 3.2; 4.48, 54; 6.2, 14, 30; 7.31; 9.16; 10.41; 11.47; 12.18) and it occurs exclusively in the first part of the Gospel (chs 2–12). However, it should be noted that 6.26 and 12.37f. also transcend the predominant limitation of this shimmering term to the meaning 'miracle'.

[31] In conclusion the evangelist mentions the purpose of his book, by addressing his readers directly for the first time. Here the phrase 'that believing you may have life in his name' builds a bridge back to the beginning of the work, where the children of God were said to be those 'who believe in his name' (1.12d).

John 21: The concluding chapter added later

The whole of ch. 21 has been added by the revisers who edited the Gospel of John. The following indications above all tell in favour of this judgment. (a) 20.30f. is an explicit conclusion to the book. (b) According to 21.3 the disciples are professional fishermen. This is in radical conflict with the new status and role that Jesus conferred on them in 20.21–23. (c) The appearance of Jesus in 20.26–29 cannot be followed by any other in the work of the evangelist, since from now on, 'Blessed are those who do not see and yet believe!' (20.29). (d) The appointment of Peter to the position of leadership in the church (21.15–17) does not fit with the transfer of authority to all disciples (20.21–23). (e) In 21.24 a 'we' group distinguishes itself explicitly from the (alleged) author of the book. (f) Chapter 21 differs from chs. 1–20 in language and style.

Therefore, to be consistent with the procedure used elsewhere, the translation of all the parts of ch. 21 should have been printed in bold. But, as in 10.1–18 and 15–17, this has not been done, so that here too the various underlying traditions can be indicated typographically. That means that in what follows the *italics* and the expression 'redaction' do not refer to the redactional activity of the evangelist but to that of the later revisers or editors. These will now in turn be refered to as the 'authors'.

John 21.1–14: Jesus' appearance by the Sea of Tiberias

1 *After this Jesus revealed himself again to his disciples* by the Sea of Tiberias. *And he revealed (himself) in this way.*

2 There were together Simon Peter *and Thomas, named Didymus, and Nathanael from Cana in Galilee* and the (sons) of Zebedee, *and two other of his disciples.* 3 Simon Peter says to them, 'I am going fishing.' They say to him, 'We also come with you.' They went out and got into the boat; but that night they caught nothing. 4a Now when it was already morning, Jesus stood on the shore. b Yet the disciples did not know that it was Jesus. 5 *Then Jesus says to them, 'Children, have you anything to eat?' They answered him, 'No.'* 6 *But* he said to them, 'Cast the net on the right side of the boat, and you will find.' So they cast (the net), and they were no longer able to draw, because of the quantity of fish. 7 *Then that disciple whom Jesus loved said to Peter, 'It is the Lord!' Now when Simon Peter heard that it was the Lord, he put on his upper garment, for he was naked, and threw himself into the sea.*

8 Now the *other* disciples came in the boat, for they were not far from the land, but (only) about two hundred cubits, *dragging the fishing net.* 9 Now when they got out on land, they see a charcoal fire there, with fried fish lying on it, and bread. 10 *Jesus says to them, 'Now bring of*

the fish that you have caught.' 11 So Simon Peter went up and drew the net to land, filled with one hundred and fifty three large fish. And though there were so many, the net did not break. 12a Jesus says to them, 'Come and have breakfast.' b Now none of the disciples dared ask him, 'Who are you?' c *For they knew that it was the Lord.* 13 Jesus comes and takes the bread and gives it to them, and likewise the fried fish.

14 *This was now the third time that Jesus was revealed to the disciples after he had been raised from (the) dead.*

Redaction and tradition

The section is marked by a number of inconsistencies. Only two particularly striking ones need be mentioned here: (a) Because the disciples have nothing to eat, according to v. 5f. Jesus asks them to cast the net on the right side of the boat, which promises good fortune; but according to v. 9, fried fish is already there before the miraculous catch is landed. (b) According to v. 7 Peter evidently throws himself into the sea because he wants to get to Jesus as quickly as possible; however, v. 11 presupposes that he gets to land only later than the other disciples – and that although they have with them so full a net that they are no longer able to draw it (v. 6). These and further inconsistencies probably arise from the fact that the authors of ch. 21 have interwoven two different traditions in vv. 1–14 and cemented them with redactional additions (R.Pesch): first the story of a miraculous catch of fish and secondly an Easter recognition legend. In the translation the narrative of the catch (which has probably been preserved complete), a variant of the tradition behind Luke 5.1–11, is underlined once. The parts of the text underlined twice represent the recognition legend, only fragments of which have been preserved.

[1] Together with v. 14 this verse forms the framework of the story and essentially derives from the authors of ch. 21 ('after this' and 'again' presuppose the preceding Easter stories). Only the detail of place has been taken from the tradition of the catch (cf. Luke 5.1).

[2] The sons of Zebedee, who appear in the Gospel of John only here, and Peter originally belong to the tradition of the catch (cf. Luke 5.3, 10). Thomas (cf. 20.24) and Nathanael (cf. 1.45–49), by contrast, have been set alongside them only by the authors. The same is true of the two other disciples who are not named ('of his disciples' refers back to v. 1). All in all, therefore, seven disciples are present. This number is possibly meant to symbolize the future church (cf. the seven communities in Rev. 2–3).

[3] The failure to catch any fish (cf. Luke 5.5) sets the scene for the miracle.

[4a] After the nocturnal failure, the miracle-worker comes to the shore in the morning.

[4b] The disciples do not recognize Jesus (cf. 20.14; Luke 24.16). This motif makes sense only in an Easter narrative, but not in a miracle story. Therefore v. 4b must be part of the recognition legend. However, its beginning has been broken off

by the link with the tradition of the catch. Probably it consisted merely of a note that Jesus came to the shore and in some way made contact with the disciples who were on the sea. Here the similarity of the particular expositions (Jesus is standing on the shore, the disciples are fishing) might have favoured the combination of the recognition legend with the narrative about the catch of fish.

[5] This verse serves to link the two traditions. Here the term 'anything to eat' has been chosen deliberately. For this tones down to some degree the tension with v. 9, according to which fried fish is already lying on the charcoal fire. The familiar form of address, 'children', appears in the New Testament only here and in I John 2.14, 18 and is thus an additional argument for the secondary character of this verse.

[6] This verse originally continued v. 4a (without 'but'). It briefly reports the preparation and execution of the miracle with the fish (cf. Luke 5.4–6).

[7] This verse derives from the authors of ch. 21 in its entirety. As in 20.8 they emphasize the priority of the beloved disciple over Peter: he is the first to recognize Jesus (cf. on 13.23–26a).

[8–9] These verses continue the recognition legend of v. 4b: at a gesture or call from the unknown man the disciples make their way to the shore, which is about 100 yards away, and there find a meal completely prepared. Merely the talk of the 'other disciples' (instead of 'the disciples') is conditioned by the insertion of v. 7. But the end of v. 8 ('dragging the fishing net') might also be redactional; it again serves to link the two traditions.

[10] Jesus sees to it that a couple of fish from the miraculous catch are also used in the meal which has already been prepared long since. This gives the impression that the miracle of the fish was not completely superfluous after all.

[11] The invitation, addressed to all, to bring the fish (v. 10) is accepted only by Peter – though inadequately; for instead of immediately rushing to the fire with the catch, Peter merely counts the fish and notes that the net is unbroken. This indicates that the conclusion of the tradition of the catch is to be found in v. 11: Peter gets on land, draws up the over-full net (v. 6), and confirms the miracle.

[12a] The invitation to breakfast followed immediately after v. 9 in the Easter legend.

[12b] That the disciples do not dare to ask who the mysterious host is shows that they have not yet recognized Jesus (cf. 4b).

[12c] This verse stands in tension with v. 12b: suddenly all the disciples know who the host is, so there is no reason for investigating his identity, far less a reason for having inhibitions about this question.

[13] In Luke 24.30f. the eyes of the two disciples on the Emmaus road are opened when Jesus breaks bread before them. Probably it was precisely the same in the present recognition story: the authors of ch. 21 replaced the original conclusion of the story (e.g. 'Then the disciples know that it is the Lord') by v. 12c. The reformu-

lation and shifting of the verse before v. 13 was necessary because the authors had already made the beloved disciple establish the identity of Jesus in v. 7.

[14] This verse forms the other frame of the story and derives entirely from the authors (cf. v. 1). If the appearance in vv. 2–13 is described as the third, then 20.19–23 was the first and 20.26–29 the second. The appearance to Mary Magdalene (20.14–18) is probably not counted because it was not an appearance to 'disciples'.

Historical

Neither the miracle of the fish (cf. on Luke 5.1–11) nor the Easter meal scene is historical.

John 21.15–19: The Risen One and Simon Peter

15 *Now when they had finished breakfast, Jesus says (to) Simon Peter, 'Simon, (son) of John, do you love me more than these?' He says to him, 'Yes, Lord; you know that I love you.' He says to him, 'Feed my lambs.'*

16 *He says to him again, a second time, 'Simon, (son) of John, do you love me?' He says to him, 'Yes, Lord; you know that I love you.' He says to him, 'Tend my sheep.'*

17 *He says to him the third time, 'Simon, (son) of John, do you love me?' Peter was grieved because he said to him the third time, 'Do you love me?' And he says to him, 'Lord, you know everything; you know that I love you.' Jesus says to him, 'Feed my sheep.*

18 *Amen, amen, I say to you, when you were young, you girded yourself and walked where you wanted. But when you are old, you will stretch out your hands, and another will gird you and carry you where you do not wish to go.'* 19a *He said this to show by what death he was to glorify God.* b *And after he said this he says to him, 'Follow me.'*

Redaction and tradition

The second section of the additional chapter is loosely linked with the preceding one by the note 'now when they had finished breakfast', which refers back to 21.12f. It tells 'of the brilliant retrieval of the honour of Peter, who was seriously compromised by his denial' (W. Heitmüller).

[15–17] These verses have a unitary structure. Three times Jesus asks Simon Peter, the son of John (cf. 1.42), whether he loves him, and three times Peter confirms this. Each time his answer is followed by a command of Jesus appointing him shepherd of the sheep (cf. the addition 10.1–18), i.e. leader of the church. Peter's thrice-repeated affirmation corresponds to his threefold denial in the court-yard of the high priest (18.17, 25–27) and Peter is exonerated from this heavy guilt by the thrice-repeated charge.

[18] This verse continues the third exchange of words: Jesus predicts Peter's martyrdom. In formulating this *vaticinium ex eventu* (cf. I Clem. 5.2–4) 'the author seems to have dropped out of the situation (soon after the resurrection of Jesus) which he assumes; he should have written: as long as you are still young you gird yourself' (J. Wellhausen).

[19a] The commentary formulated on the basis of 12.33 or 18.32 says that his particular kind of death is a special mark of distinction for Peter. It is evidently assumed that he too was crucified.

[19b] Jesus extends the charge to lead and protect the community by an invitation to personal discipleship which because of vv. 18–19a is also to be understood as a call to discipleship into martyrdom (cf. 13.36).

Yield: the direct and indirect references back to 1.42; 10.1–18; 13.36–38 and 18.17, 25–27 show that the scene has been created by the authors of the additional chapter. Its purpose is to derive from the Risen One the leading position in the church which Peter holds despite his denial of his Lord (cf. Matt. 16.17–19; Luke 22.32).

Historical

The scene is unhistorical.

John 21.20–25: Peter and the Beloved Disciple. The second conclusion to the book

20 *Peter turns round and sees the disciple whom Jesus loved following, who had also reclined on his breast at the supper and had said, 'Lord, who is it who is going to deliver you up?' 21 Peter now sees him and says (to) Jesus, 'Lord, what about this man?' 22 Jesus says to him, 'If it is my will that he remains until I come, what (is that) to you? Follow me yourself!' 23a Now this saying went out to the brothers, 'That disciple will not die.' b But Jesus had not said to him that he would not die, but, 'If it is my will that he remains until I come, what (is that) to you?'*

24 *This is the disciple who bears witness to this and who has written this, and we know that his witness is true.*

25 But there are (yet) many other (things) which Jesus did; were every one of them to be written down, I suppose that the world itself could not contain the books that would be written.

Secondary addition

[25] This rhetorical exaggeration, which has been formulated on the basis of 20.30f. and stands out by virtue of the unexpected 'I', 'gives the impression that an ambitious scribe wanted to add one more brilliant conclusion . . . If this writer was also one of the circle of the editors, he was not their most capable man' (R. Schnackenburg).

Redaction and tradition

This passage forms the conclusion of the supplementary chapter. After 20.3–10 and 21.7, vv. 20–23 once again consider the question of the relationship between the beloved disciple and Peter. Verse 24 contains the second conclusion to the book.

[20] After the conversation with Jesus in 21.15–19, Peter turns round and sees the beloved disciple following, to whose presence at the last supper there is an explicit reference (cf. 13.2, 23–26a).

[21] If Peter has been charged with the leadership of the church, what significance does the beloved disciple then have?

[22] Jesus rejects Peter's question. It must be no concern of his if the beloved disciple remains (alive) until Jesus comes (at the parousia). Rather, Peter has already been told all that matters to him, and so Jesus can only repeat the call to discipleship from v. 19b. That makes it clear that the beloved disciple has a close and prominent relationship to Jesus regardless of Peter's position as leader of the whole church.

[23a] The authors quote a rumour circulating in the community: it has been assumed that Jesus has promised the beloved disciple that he will survive until the parousia.

[23b] This explicitly clarifies that such an assumption was a misunderstanding: Jesus has not predicted that the beloved disciple will survive but has merely indicated that it is possible. That fits with what was reported in v. 22.

[24] This verse unveils the secret of the beloved disciple: he is the author of the book. Despite his death (implied in v. 23) he is thus also in the future the guarantor of the Johannine community. With the Gospel of John itself, the community possesses the written testimony of a true eye-witness and reliable informant. Whereas Peter must die a martyr, the beloved disciple remains alive in this book.

Yield: the section derives completely from the authors of ch. 21. Here vv. 20–23 doubtless serve to refute the saying quoted in v. 23a. Evidently the real chronological sequence of the saying of 'Jesus' in v. 22 and the 'misunderstanding' in v. 23a was precisely the opposite: first the saying 'That disciple will not die' (v. 23a) arose in the community – probably on the basis of the advanced age of the person behind the beloved disciple – and was immediately attributed to Jesus. When the disciple then died nevertheless, it had to be corrected. Only then was it said that Jesus had merely considered the possibility that this disciple would survive (vv. 22, 23b).

Historical

The historical yield is nil. For the beloved disciple as the alleged author of the Gospel of John cf. the introduction, point 7.

V

The Gospel of Thomas

The existence of the Gospel of Thomas was already known from the testimonies of the church fathers. Greek fragments of it came to light more than a century ago, in 1897. However, they were only identified as such as a result of the spectacular find near Nag Hammadi in 1945, in which a complete Gospel of Thomas in Coptic was discovered. It contains 114 logia and is attributed to the apostle Thomas (cf. Mark 3.18; John 20.24) – though historically this attribution is certainly wrong. There are numerous points of contact between the Gospel of Thomas and the Synoptic Gospels, but also considerable divergences. Moreover the Gospel of Thomas contains special material. A Gnostic-ascetic stratum is evident at quite a large number of points in the Gospel of Thomas, the message of which corresponds with that of the early Christian Gnostics: the human being or the soul has fallen into the world of matter from which it can be freed only by self-knowledge, by the know-ledge or recollection of its heavenly resting place (cf. Logion 67 with the references given there). Otherwise there is still a dispute over the wider context of the Gospel. The main focus of my investigation is to see whether authentic sayings of Jesus are contained in it. For this reason, a good deal of space is taken up with an examination of its relationship to the Synoptic Gospels. Since not only the composition of the Greek Gospel of Thomas but also its relationship to the Coptic translation is a matter of dispute, I have investigated each logion independently, without presupposing a general theory. My only presupposition is that there was a Greek Gospel of Thomas around 125 CE.

The following English translation has been made in collaboration with John Bowden. The division of the Gospel of Thomas into logia and verses follows established usage. I would like to mention here two more recent publications which give a good account of international research into the Gospel of Thomas: Risto Uro (ed.), *Thomas at the Crossroads. Essays on the Gospel of Thomas*, 1998; Stephen J.Patterson (ed.), *Foundations and Facets Forum* 10.1–2, 1994 (1998).

Prologue

These are the hidden words which the living Jesus spoke; Didymos Judas Thomas has written them down.

Analysis

Cf. the similar introduction to the Book of Thomas from Nag Hammadi (NHC II 7):
'These are the hidden sayings which the saviour spoke to Judas Thomas which I,
Mathaias, have written down; I had been walking past, and heard them speaking to
one another.' The author uses the expression 'hidden words' to denote all the
sayings which follow; here one is inclined to see Logion 1 as a continuation of the
prologue. The Greek 'Didymos' literally means 'twin'. Cf. the continuation of the
Nag Hammadi Book of Thomas mentioned above: 'The Saviour said, "Brother
Thomas, as long as you have time in the world, listen to me, and I will reveal to you
what you have attempted to fathom in your heart. And because it has been said that
you are my twin brother and my true friend, examine yourself and know who you
are and how you are and how you will come to be."'

Logion 1

And he (Thomas) said, 'Whoever finds the interpretation of these words will not taste death.'

Analysis

The speaker is Thomas: 'these words' takes up 'the hidden words' which are spoken
by 'the living Jesus'. 'Living Jesus' and 'living Father' (cf. 3.4; 50.2) mean the same
thing. Both bestow the true life and make it possible by hidden words (cf. on 37.3).
But the correct interpretation is the prerequisite of not tasting death. For not tasting
death cf. Mark 9.1, where it is meant literally. Here, however, the author is thinking
in a metaphorical sense of overcoming (spiritual) death. Cf. 18.3; 19.3; 85.2; 111.2;
John 8.51–52.

Historical

Thomas never spoke these words, all the more so because Thomas is merely a name
(see the Introduction to this chapter).

Logion 2

1 Jesus said, 'The one who seeks is not to cease to seek until he finds. 2 And when he finds, he
will be shaken. 3 And (when) he is shaken he will be moved to wonder. 4 And he will be king
over the All.'

Analysis

[1–4] 'Find' takes up 'find' in Logion 1 and develops the thoughts expressed there. This is a chain saying (cf. Rom. 5.3–4). The Greek version has yet another element of the chain at the end: 'And when he is king, he will have rest.'

Historical

The saying is inauthentic, as it describes the Gnostic way to knowledge. On 2.1 cf. 92.1; 94.1. However, the invitation to search is an element in Jesus' understanding of faith (cf. on Matt. 7.7–8).

Logion 3

1 Jesus said, 'If those who lead you (astray) say to you, "Look, the kingdom is in the sky," then the birds of the sky will precede you. 2 And if they say to you, "It is in the sea," then the fish will precede you. 3 But the kingdom is inside you, and outside you. 4 When you know yourselves, then you will become known; and you will know that you are the sons of the living Father. 5 But if you do not know yourselves, you are in poverty and you are poverty.'

Analysis

[1–4] This saying has also been handed down in Greek and has a parallel in 113.1–3. In vv. 1–3 it is a parody of those who lead (astray) (v. 1) and in vv. 1–3a is based on Luke 17.20–21, but extends the limitation of the 'inside you' with 'outside you' (v. 3b). Verses 4–5 are a Gnostic addition. 'Sons of the living Father' in v. 4 takes up 'living Jesus' from the prologue.

Historical

The logion is inauthentic.

Logion 4

1 Jesus said, 'The man who is old in days will not hesitate to ask a small child seven days old about the place of life, and he will live. 2 For many who are first will become last. 3 And they will become a single one.'

Analysis

[1] This verse contains the Gnostic theme of the child as a revealer (cf. 22.1–2). In Gnostic texts Jesus appears as a little child (Acts of John 88), or Gnostic teachers claim to have seen a little newborn child which is identical with the divine Word (Valentinus).

[2] Cf. on Mark 10.31.

[3] The motif of being a single one also appears at other points in Thomas: 11.4; 22.4–5; 23.2; 106.1.

Historical

The logion is inauthentic and is to be understood completely in terms of the Gnostic world.

Logion 5

1 Jesus said, 'Know what is before your face, and what which is <u>hidden</u> from you will reveal itself to you. 2 For there is nothing <u>hidden</u> which will not become manifest.'

Analysis

The logion has also been handed down in Greek and at the end also contains the fragmentary sentence: 'and there is nothing buried which [will] not [be raised].'

[1] This verse has parallels in other Gnostic texts and echoes Gnostic self-knowledge.

[2] Cf. on Mark 4.22 par.

Historical

The saying 5.2 is probably authentic (cf. on Mark 4.22). However, that does not in itself establish its meaning, since it can be used in various contexts.

Logion 6

1 His disciples questioned him; they said to him, 'Do you want us to fast?' And in what way should we pray? And give alms? And what food (regulations) should we observe?' 2 Jesus said, 'Do not tell lies. 3 And do not do what you hate. 4 For all things are disclosed before heaven. 5 For there is nothing hidden which will not become manifest, and nothing covered which will remain without being uncovered.'

Analysis

The saying has also been handed down in Greek. But there at the end of v. 4 we have 'before the truth' instead of 'before heaven' and the disciples ask *how* they are to carry out the four observances of the law which are mentioned.

[1] The disciples' question is about fasting, prayer, almsgiving and the food laws. The first three also appear in the regulations about piety in Matt. 6.1–18 (cf. Tobit 12.8) and are discussed once again later (Thomas 14; cf. 104). In the present verse the question about food completes the sphere of the Jewish law.

[2–3] Jesus does not answer the disciples' question directly. The meaning is either that they are to be honest in doing the four things mentioned or that 'Jesus' generally rejects the practices cited.

[4–5] These verses take up 5.2 and in the context of Logion 6 emphasize that lying and doing what one hates are to be eschewed in view of the uncovering which will certainly take place.

Historical

Apart perhaps from v. 5a, which corresponds word for word with 5.2, the logion is inauthentic, as it is completely rooted in discussions within Gnosticism.

Logion 7

1 Jesus said, 'Blessed is the lion, this which man will devour. And the lion will (become) man. 2 And abominable is the man, this one who will devour the lion. And the man will become lion.'

Analysis

The logion consists of a beatitude (v. 1) and a curse (v. 2). For the two genres cf. on Luke 6.20–26.

[1–2] Verse 1 is about the humanization of bestial forces in human beings, v. 2 about human beings lapsing into a bestial nature. Because of the parallelism, I have emended the extant text in v. 2b, 'and the lion will become man', to the text above. The logion fits well with ascetic-Gnostic circles which are interested in a taming or humanization of bestial passions. They are often concerned with taming bestial natures, of which that of the lion is the strongest.

Historical

The saying is inauthentic.

Logion 8

1 And he said, 'The man is like a wise fisherman, this one who cast his net into the sea; he drew it up (again) from the sea full of little fishes. 2 Among them the wise fisherman found a fine big fish. 3 He threw all the little fishes (back) into the sea (and) chose the large fish without hesitation. 4 Whoever has ears to hear, let him hear.'

Analysis

[1] 'Man' is a keyword link to 'man' in 7.1, 2. Instead of 'man', originally 'kingdom of the Father/God' probably stood in v. 1.

[2] The contrast is that between the many little fishes and the one big fish (cf. 96.1–2; 107).

[3] The fisherman chooses only this big fish.

[4] The awakening call appears elsewhere in Thomas in the following places: 21.11; 24.2; 63.4; 65.8; 96.3. It recalls the hidden meaning of the words of Jesus (cf. Logion 1).

Historical

[1–3] These verses are inauthentic, since they describe the knowledge of the Gnostic. In terms of content the parable has little to do with the parable of the net in Matt. 13.47–48, which is authentic. The latter is about the separation at the end of time; this is about 'catching' the single person who will become solitary.

[4] This verse is too general to be called historical.

Logion 9

1 Jesus said, 'Look, a sower went out, filled his hand and threw (the seeds). 2 Some fell on the way; the birds came, they pecked it up. 3 Others fell on the rock and did not take root in the earth and did not bring forth ears heavenwards. 4 And others fell among the thorns; they choked the seeds and the worm ate them. 5 And others fell on the good earth and it brought forth good fruit heavenwards. It bore sixty per measure and one hundred and twenty per measure.'

Analysis and Historical

Cf. on Mark 4.3–8. Reasons are given there why the Thomas version represents the oldest stage of the tradition, and is historical.

Logion 10

Jesus said, 'I have cast fire upon the world, and look, I am guarding it (the world or the fire) until it blazes.'

Analysis

The logion is similar to Luke 12.49, but can hardly have come from there (cf. by contrast the adoption and interpretation of Luke 12.49 in the Gnostic writing Pistis Sophia IV 141: it means the cleansing of the sins of the whole world by fire). The key to its understanding is 'world' (Luke: earth), a word which appears sixteen times alone in the Gospel of Thomas and in it has a predominantly negative sense (cf. Logion 56). In Logion 82 'fire' is connected with the nearness of Jesus. So the meaning seems to be that Jesus' presence will set on fire the world, understood in negative terms.

Historical

The saying is inauthentic, as Jesus never saw the world in such negative terms. It remains God's creation.

Logion 11

1 Jesus said, 'This heaven will pass away, and the (heaven) above it will pass away. 2 The dead are not alive, and the living will not die. 3 In the days (when) you consumed what is dead, you made it alive. When you are in the light, <u>what will you do</u>? 4 On the day when you were one you became two. But when you become two, <u>what will you do</u>?'

Analysis

[1] This verse picks up the previous logion about the destruction of the cosmos (cf. 111.1).

[2] This verse describes the two groups of people: the non-Gnostics, who only seem to live, and the Gnostics, who will live and never die.

[3] Cf. 7.1.

[4] The step to duality is the real fall of human beings. Through knowledge each will again attain the original unity (cf. on 4.3). Note the parallel formulation of v. 4b and v. 3b.

Historical

The logion is inauthentic. It is utterly rooted in Gnostic thought.

Logion 12

1 The disciples said to Jesus, 'We know that you will go from us. Who is it who will (then) be great over us?' 2 Jesus said to them, 'Wherever you go, you are to go to James the righteous, for whose sake heaven and earth came into being.'

Analysis

[1–2] The logion recalls the disciples' conversations about status which we know from Mark 9.33–34. To be precise, the saying regulates the succession to Jesus (cf. the Paraclete in John 14.16, 26; 15.26; 16.7 and Peter as the follower of Jesus in John 21.15–17). James is not only given the predicate 'righteous' (cf. Acts 7.52), but is also assigned a role in creation. All these sayings came into being in Jewish-Christian circles where James later became 'the pope of Ebionite fantasy' (H. J. Schoeps).

Historical

The logion is inauthentic. James repudiated his brother during the latter's lifetime (cf. Mark 3.21) and only became the leader of the Jerusalem community in the course of its development (cf. I Cor. 15.7; Acts 21.18).

Logion 13

1 Jesus said to his disciples, 'Compare me (and) tell me whom I am like.' 2 Simon Peter said to him, 'You are like a righteous messenger.' 3 Matthew said to him, 'You are like a man (who is) a wise philosopher.' 4 Thomas said to him, 'Master, my mouth (can) in no way bear my saying whom you are like.' 5 Jesus said, 'I am not your teacher, for you have drunk, you have become intoxicated at the bubbling spring which I have measured (out).' 6 And he took him, withdrew (and) told him three things. 7 And when Thomas returned to his companions, they asked him, 'What did Jesus say to you?' 8 Thomas said to them, 'If I tell you one of the words which he told me, you will pick up stones (and) throw them at me; and fire will come out of the stones and burn you up.'

Analysis

[1] This verse recalls Mark 8.27, Jesus' question about whom people think that he is. But in Logion 13 Jesus at once asks who the disciples think that he is.

[2] In contrast to Mark 8.29, here Simon Peter (cf. Logion 114) gives an inadequate answer. 'Righteous' picks up 'the righteous' in 12.2.

[3] Matthew's designation of Jesus recalls the designation of the fisherman in 8.2.

[4–8] These verses provide the basis for the spiritual authority of Thomas, as he has been singled out by Jesus through secret instruction (cf. the prologue). Jesus is no longer his teacher, but both are of equal rank; cf. the reasons in v. 5 and the commentary in Logion 108.

Historical

The scene and the logia have no historical value.

Logion 14

1 Jesus said to them, 'If you fast, you will cause sin for yourselves. 2 And if you pray, you will be condemned. 3 And if you give alms, you will do harm to your spirits. 4 And if you go into any land and walk about in the districts (and) if they receive you, eat what they set before you; and the sick among them, heal! 5 For what goes into your mouth will not defile you. But what issues from your mouth is what will defile you.'

Analysis

[1–3] These verses give a direct answer to the question of 6.1.

[4] The connection with vv. 1–3 is obscure. For v. 4 cf. Luke 10.7–8. Luke (Q) is *specifically* about missionaries who have been sent out; Thomas is about rules of conduct generally.

[5] This develops the notion of v. 4 about eating all that is set before one, and gives a reason for it. The dependence on Luke 10.7–8 in v. 4 also decides positively the dependence of v. 5 on Mark 7.15. For the invitation to heal the sick does not fit in v. 4 at all, and is best explained by the use of Luke 10.9.

Historical

[1–3] These verses are inauthentic.
[4] Cf. on Luke 10.7–9.
[5] Cf. on Mark 7.15.

Logion 15

Jesus said, 'When you see him (or: 'one') who was not born of a woman, throw yourselves down on your faces, worship him! That one is your Father.'

Analysis

The God of the Gnostics cannot be born – he is unbegotten – as birth would include finitude. Nevertheless one can fall down before him (and pray?). It is attractive to identify the God with the All (cf. Logion 77).

Historical

The logion is inauthentic and totally rooted in Gnostic thought.

Logion 16

1 Jesus said, 'Perhaps people think that it I have come to cast peace upon the world. 2 And they do not know that I have come to cast divisions upon the earth: fire, sword, war. 3 For there will be five in a house: three will be against two, and two against three, the father against the son, and the son against the father. 4 And they will stand there as solitary ones.'

Analysis

[1–2] The unseen order of the cosmos is set forth in Gnostic terms (cf. Logion 10). Otherwise there is a close parallel in Matt. 10.34/Luke 12.51.

[3] Cf. Matt. 10.35/Luke 12.52–53.

[4] This verse shows Gnostic revision. The negation of the cosmos is focussed on the Gnostic as a single one (cf. 4.3; 11.4, etc.).

Historical

[1–3] Cf. on Luke 12.51–53.
[4] This verse is inauthentic.

Logion 17

Jesus said, 'I will give you what no eye has seen and what no ear has heard and what no hand has touched and what has never occurred to the human mind.'

Analysis

The saying – starting from Isa. 64.4 – has a rich subsequent history in Jewish and Christian writings; cf. e.g. I Cor. 2.9. However, it is unique in that unlike the parallels it mentions the sense of touch. Perhaps here there is an allusion to John 20.24–29, where the offer is made to Thomas to touch Jesus.

Historical

The saying is inauthentic.

Logion 18

1 The disciples said to Jesus, 'Tell us how our end will be.' 2 Jesus said, 'Have you already discovered the beginning that you ask about the end? For where the beginning is, there (also) will the end be. 3 Blessed is he who will stand at the beginning. And he will (also) know the end and will not taste death.'

Analysis

[1–3] The beginning and the end correspond (cf. Logion 4). Brought back to the beginning, the Gnostic will not taste death. The latter is meant in a metaphorical sense. The non-Gnostic does not live at all (cf. 11.2).

Historical

The saying is inauthentic.

Logion 19

1 Jesus said, 'Blessed is he who was before he came into being. 2 If you become my disciples (and) listen to my words, these stones will serve you. 3 For you have five trees in Paradise which do not move in summer (and) in winter and their leaves never fall. 4 Whoever comes to know them will not taste death.'

Analysis

[1] This verse picks up the previous logion. In form and content the beatitude corresponds to 18.3, for the man is called blessed before his incarnation.

[2] This verse attributes the decisive significance for knowledge to the hearing of

Jesus' words and entry into discipleship, and as in 13.8 uses stones as illustrative material.

[3–4] In other Gnostic testimonies (Jeu 50) there is mention of five trees in paradise which do not shake. Knowledge of them leads to not tasting death. This picks up 18.3b word for word.

Historical

The sayings are inauthentic.

Logion 20

1 The disciples said to Jesus, 'Tell us what the kingdom of heaven is like.' 2 He said to them, 'It is like a mustard seed. 3 It is the smallest of all seeds. 4 But when it falls on cultivated earth, it produces a great plant and becomes a shelter for the birds of the sky.'

Analysis

[1–4] The same parable occurs in Q (Matt. 13.31–32/ Luke 13.18–19) and in Mark 4.30–32. For further commentary see the comments on these passages.

Historical

Cf. on Mark 4.30–32. The Thomas parallel is at least as near to the original as the Mark and Q versions.

Logion 21

1 Mariham (Mary) said to Jesus, 'Whom are your disciples like?' 2 He said, 'They are like little children who have settled in a field is which does not belong to them. 3 When the owners of the field come, they will say, "Let us have our field back." 4 They are naked before them (or: they undress before them) in order to let them have it (and thus) to give them their field.

5 Therefore I say, if the owner of a house knows that the thief is coming, he will watch before he comes (and) he will not let him break into his house, his kingdom, to carry away his things. 6 But you, be on your guard against the world! 7 Gird your loins with great power so that the robbers do not find a way to come to you! 8 For the benefit which you expect will surely be found.

9 Let there be among you a man of understanding!

10 When the fruit ripened, he came quickly with his sickle in his hand and reaped it. 11 Whoever has ears to hear, let him hear.'

Analysis

[1–4] These verses are unique among the Jesus traditions and are hard to understand. If we begin with the evident recognition that the children symbolize the Gnostics, it is manifestly being said that they are staying in a strange field, namely the evil world, and that they are asking the owners for their own field. To this end, the exchange of fields, they bare themselves, which probably refers to baptism.

[5–8] In this parable the Gnostics are the owners who are to guard against burglars (cf. Luke 12.39–40/Matt. 24.43–44). Verse 6 confirms that this is about a Gnostic understanding (for the cosmos cf. 56.1–2).

[9] This verse is a wish that among the readers there may be those who understand what has gone before.

[10–11] These verses are later additions which derive from Mark 4.29 (v. 10) and Thomas 8.4 etc. (v. 11).

Historical

The logia are inauthentic and came into being in Gnostic communities.

Logion 22

1 Jesus saw little (children) receiving milk. 2 He said to his disciples, 'These little (children) who are receiving milk are like those who <u>enter the kingdom</u>.'

3 They said to him, 'Shall we then, because we are little, <u>enter the kingdom</u>?' 4 Jesus said to them, 'When you make the two one, and when you make the inside like the outside and the outside like the inside, and the above like the below 5 and when you make the male and the female into a single one, so that the male is not male (and) the female (is not) female, 6 when you make for yourselves eyes in place of one eye, and a hand in place of a hand and a foot in place of a foot, a likeness in place of a likeness, 7 then will you <u>enter [the kingdom]</u>.'

Analysis

[1–2] 'Little (children)' is a link by key word to 21.2. The verses formed on the basis of Mark 10.15 par. serve as a way into the explanation of being a Gnostic which follows next.

[3] This verse is a transition to vv. 4–7.

[4–7] The abolition of existing oppositions is the condition for entering the kingdom (cf. 106.1).

Historical

[1–2] These verses are secondary.

[3–7] These verses are unhistorical, as they are wholly rooted in the Gnostic world.

Logion 23

1 Jesus said, 'I shall choose you, one out of a thousand, and two out of ten thousand. 2 And they shall stand as a single one.'

Analysis

[1] For election cf. Logion 49. It has an exclusive character and happens rarely.

[2] The transition from the second person plural to the third person plural is surprising. For the motif of standing as a single one cf. on 16.4 and, in the immediate context, see 22.5.

Historical

These verses are unhistorical, as they are wholly rooted in the Gnostic world.

Logion 24

1 His disciples said, 'Show us the place where you are, since it is necessary for us to seek it.' 2 He said to them, 'Whoever has ears, let him hear. 3 There is light within a man of light, and he (or: it) lights up the whole world. If he (or: it) does not shine, there is darkness.'

Analysis

[1–2] Verse 1 is the initial question about the place of Jesus which leads through the awakening formula in v. 2 to the following answer.

[3] The disciples do not need to look outside themselves, but as people of light they have light in themselves just as much as the light figure Jesus (cf. 77.1). Indeed, without this particle of light there would be darkness in the world. This statement seems to contain an indirect command to engage in mission in the world (cf. 33.1–3).

Historical

Verses 1 and 3 are inauthentic and are to be derived in their entirety from the Gnostic world. For the awakening call in v. 2, cf. on 8.4 and Mark 4.9.

Logion 25

1 Jesus said, 'Love your brother like your soul. 2 Guard him like the apple of your eye.'

Analysis

[1] Cf. the commandment to love one's neighbour in Lev. 19.18, though in the New Testament, unlike Thomas, this usually occurs together with the commandment to love God (Deut. 6.5): Mark 12.30–31 par.

[2] This verse does not occur in the New Testament. However, the mode of expression does have parallels in the Old Testament: Deut. 32.10; Ps. 17.8; Prov. 7.2.

Historical

A genetic relationship to old Jesus traditions is improbable. Both sayings are inauthentic.

Logion 26

1 Jesus said, 'You see the splinter in your brother's eye, but you do not see the log in your own eye. 2 When you pull the log out of your own eye, you will see clearly (enough) to pull the splinter from your brother's eye.'

Analysis

[1–2] The key words 'brother' and 'eye' link Logia 26 and 25. Logion 26 corresponds to Q (Matt. 7.3–5/Luke 6.41–42) and as the simpler construction may also represent the earliest stage. But it is also conceivable that Thomas has simplified an earlier saying, the centre of which was reproof of the brother, and put self-correction at the centre.

Historical

It is impossible to derive the saying from Jesus. This is a wisdom rule the context of which we do not know.

Logion 27

(Jesus said), 1 'If you do not fast in respect of the world, you will not find the kingdom. 2 If you do not observe the sabbath as sabbath, you will not see the Father.'

Analysis

The two sayings were originally independent. They have also been handed down in Greek and have a parallel structure in both the Greek and the Coptic traditions.

[1] Cf. 14.1. 'Fast in respect of the world' is not normal fasting but Gnostic abstinence from the world (cf. 56.1–2; 80.1–2; 111.3).

[2] A literal understanding, namely sabbath observance, is to be excluded. Rather, 'sabbath' here may be synonymous with 'world'. In that case v. 2 symbolizes abstinence from worldly values. For 'seeing the Father' cf. Matt. 5.8 ('see God').

Historical

The sayings are inauthentic and completely at home in the Gnostic world.

Logion 28

1 Jesus said, 'I stood in the midst of the world, and I appeared to them in the flesh. 2 I found them all intoxicated, I did not find one of them who was thirsty. 3 And my soul suffered pain over the sons of men, because they are blind in their hearts and do not see, for they have come empty into the world, (and) again they seek to leave the world empty. 4 Now they are intoxicated. (But) when they shake off their (intoxication with) wine, then they will repent.'

Analysis

[1] For appearing in the flesh cf. I Tim. 3.16. In contrast to the New Testament parallels cited, Jesus stood in the midst of the hostile world.

[2] It is no wonder that in the world all are drunk, i.e. were ignorant.

[3] This verse gives the reason for Jesus' pain: people are incapable of gaining knowledge and surrender themselves to things of no value. 'See' is a keyword link to 'see' in 27.2 and 26.1–2.

[4a] This verse once again sums up the human state.

[4b–c] After shaking off their intoxication, people are offered the possibility of knowledge.

Historical

The logion is inauthentic, as it is completely at home in the Gnostic world.

Logion 29

1 Jesus said, 'If the flesh came into being because of the spirit, it is a wonder. 2 But if the spirit (came into being) because of the body, it is a wonder of wonders. 3 But I am amazed at how this great wealth has made its home in this poverty.'

Analysis

[1–2] 'Flesh' is a link by key word to 28.1. The whole is a praise of the spirit which has taken up its abode in human bodies or in the flesh. For 'spirit' as an element of light in human beings cf. 24.3.

[3] This verse is a summary of vv. 1–2. For 'poverty' as a designation of the body cf. 3.5.

Historical

The logion is inauthentic as it belongs to the Gnostic world.

Logion 30

1 Jesus said, 'Where there are three gods, they are gods. 2 Where there are two or one – I am with him.'

Analysis

It is possible that the Coptic translation is erroneous. Probably a Greek version is closer to the original. It combines 30.1–2 with 77.2–3 and runs as follows: 30.1 'Where (three are), they are godless. 2 And where one is alone I say, I am with him' (77.2–3 follows). This version is a further development of Matt. 18.20. However, faithful to the theology of Thomas, the focus and the emphasis lies on being single (cf. 4.3; 22.5; 23.2).

Historical

The historical value is nil.

Logion 31

1 Jesus said, 'No prophet is welcome in his village. 2 No physician heals those who know him.'

Analysis

Logion 31 has a Greek equivalent

[1] This verse is dependent on Luke 4.24, for there 'welcome' is redactional.

[2] This verse develops the notions expressed in v. 1. This has perhaps been prompted by Luke 4.23.

Historical

Cf. on Mark 6.4.

Logion 32

Jesus said, 'A city built on a high mountain (and) fortified cannot fall, nor can it be hidden.'

Analysis

The saying has a precise equivalent in Greek. It seems overloaded by comparison with the parallel Matt. 5.14. Therefore Logion 32 may be of a later date in terms of tradition. Gnostics had no difficulties in seeing themselves as inhabitants of a fortified city which could not be shaken.

Historical

Cf. on Matt. 5.14.

Logion 33

1 Jesus said, 'What you hear with your ear with the other ear, preach from your housetops. 2 For no one lights a lamp (and) puts it under a bushel, nor does he put it in a hidden place, 3 but he sets it on a lampstand so that every one who enters and leaves will see its light.'

Analysis

[1] The saying is probably corrupt. Perhaps there is also a failed word–play here. At any rate the basis is Matt. 10.27/Luke 12.3.

[2–3] The simile of the lamp often occurs in the New Testament: Matt. 4.21/Matt. 5.15; Luke 8.16; 11.33. 'Hidden place' takes up 'hidden' from Logion 32.This is likely to have been conditioned by the Matthaean sequence, for there we have the same word from Thomas 32 in Matt. 5.14, whereas it does not occur in the verse (Matt. 5.15) which corresponds to Thomas 33.2.

Historical

[2–3] Cf. on Matt. 5.15.

Logion 34

Jesus said, 'If a blind man leads a blind man, they both fall into a pit.'

Analysis

The saying is a proverb which also occurs in Matt. 15.14b/Luke 6.39b (Q).

Historical

Cf. on Luke 6.39b.

Logion 35

1 Jesus said, 'It is impossible for anyone to enter the house of a strong (person) and take possession of it by force unless (first) he binds his hands. 2 Then he will ransack his house.'

Analysis

At the level of redaction the logion recalls 21.5–8, and at the level of tradition it strongly recalls both Mark 3.27 and Matt. 12.29/Luke 11.21–22 (= Q). It has a genetic connection with these passages. However, in contrast to the parallels mentioned it does not indicate the context, which there consists in the overcoming of Satan by Jesus.

Historical

Cf. on Mark 3.27.

Logion 36

Jesus said, 'Do not be anxious from morning until evening and from evening until morning about what you will wear.'

Analysis

This saying has a parallel in the Greek version. It runs:

1 Do not be anxious from morning until evening and from evening until morning, <u>either about your food or about what you will eat</u>, or about your clothing and what you will wear. 2 You are much better than the lilies which do not grow or spin. 3 As you have no garment, with what will you clothe yourselves? 4 Who will add something to your size? He himself will give you clothing.

The key to the history of the tradition is provided by that part of the Greek version which goes beyond the Coptic translation. It contains, first, a modification of the Coptic version (underlined); secondly, at the end (= vv. 3–4), a Gnostic interpretation (the symbol of the garment); and thirdly, before that, a part (= v. 2) which recalls Matt. 6.25–31/Luke 12.22–29). As the Gnostic part is certainly secondary, the same conclusion may be drawn about the other pieces. The Coptic translation is probably an abbreviation of a Greek version.

Historical

Cf. on Matt. 6.25–31.

Logion 37

1 His disciples said, 'On what day will you reveal yourself to us and on what day will we see you?' 2 Jesus said, 'When you cast off your shame and take your garments, put them under your feet like little children (and) trample on them, 3 then [will] you see the son of the Living One, and you will not be afraid.'

Analysis

[1] This verse is an introductory formula (cf. Mark 13.4) which in contrast to the Mark passage is not to be understood in temporal terms but in an essentially timeless way.

[2] The precondition of seeing Jesus (in the spirit) is the negation of sexuality. The Gnostic is then again in a state *before* the fall, where sex plays no role.

[3] This verse leads back to v. 1. For the 'son of the Living One' cf. 'living Jesus' from the prologue.

Historical

The sayings are inauthentic and completely at home in a Gnostic thought world.

Logion 38

1 Jesus said, 'You have often wished to hear these words, these which I said to you, and you have no one else to hear them from. 2 Days will come when you will seek me and will not find me.'

Analysis

[1–2] Verse 1 has an approximate parallel in Matt. 13.16–17/Luke 10.23–24 (= Q). For v. 2 cf. John 7.34. The logion tries to cope with the absence of Jesus (v. 2) and the disciples' wish to hear the words of the living Jesus (cf. Prologue; 2; 92.1). It fits the situation of the Thomas community well.

Historical

The sayings are secondary and therefore inauthentic.

Logion 39

1 Jesus said, 'The Pharisees and scribes have received the keys of knowledge; they hid them. 2 They themselves have not entered, nor have they allowed to enter those who wanted to. 3 You, however, be as wise as serpents and as innocent as doves.'

Analysis

The logion also exists in a fragmentary form in Greekwhich – as far as can be seen – corresponds with the Coptic version.

[1–2] These verses have an equivalent in Matt. 23.13/Luke 11.52 (= Q) .

[3] This verse derives from Matt. 10.16b, for that passage is redactional. But in that case it is also probable that vv. 1–2 are dependent on Matt. 23.13, all the more so as in both Thomas and Matthew this saying is directed against the Pharisees and scribes (Luke: against experts in the law).

Historical

[1–2] Cf. on Matt. 23.13.
[3] Cf. on Matt 10.16b.

Logion 40

1 Jesus said, 'A grapevine has been planted outside (the vineyard) of the Father. 2 And as it is not established, it will be pulled up by the root and destroyed.

Analysis

[1–2] These verses come close to Matt. 15.13. Verse 2a is not contained in Matt. 15.13, but can well be understood as an elaboration by Gnostics who are concerned with inner fortification. Similarly, the use of 'vine' instead of 'planting' is not a reason for dismissing a genetic relationship to the text of Matthew. A dependence of this logion on Matthew is virtually certain, for Matt. 15.13 derives from Matthaean redaction.

Historical

Cf. on Matt. 15.13.

Logion 41

1 Jesus said, 'Whoever has (something) in his hand will be given more. 2 Whoever has nothing, from him will be taken away even the little that he has.'

Analysis

[1–2] These verses have parallels in Mark 4.25 and Matt. 25.29/Luke 19.26 (= Q). Thomas diverges from them in two points: (a) in v. 1 he reads 'in his hand' (cf. 9.1; 17; 21.10; 22.6; 35.1; 98.2) and (b) in v. 2 'the little'. The saying is a common proverb. How it was read by Gnostics is shown for example by Gospel of Philip 105: 'Is it not fitting for all who have all this also to know themselves? But some, if they do not know themselves, will not enjoy what they have. The others, who have come to know themselves, will enjoy them (= their possessions).'

Historical

Cf. on Mark 4.25.

Logion 42

Jesus said, 'Become passers-by.'

Analysis

This saying is the shortest in the Gospel of Thomas. Certainly it has no parallels in early Christian writings, but a similar Arabic version has been preserved on the portal of a mosque in India. It says, 'Jesus, peace be on him, has said: The world is a bridge. Go over it but do not settle on it.' Thomas 42 recalls 21.6; 27.1; 56.1–2; 80.1–2; 110; 111.3 and corresponds to a favourite theme of the theology of the Gospel of Thomas. But in the wider sense the logion also fits Jesus' itinerant life and homelessness (Matt. 8.20/Luke 9.58 [= Q]).

Historical

The saying is probably authentic. At the same time it should be conceded that the Thomas Christians understood it in a different way from Jesus, namely in ascetic terms and not related to the world.

Logion 43

1 His disciples said to him, 'Who are you, that you should say these things to us?' 2 Jesus said to them, 'Do you not know who I am from what I say to you? 3 You have become like the Jews, for they love the tree (and) they hate its fruit, or they love the fruit and they hate the tree.'

Analysis

[1] The disciples put the question of the identity and authority of Jesus. As in Logion 38 a crisis situation in the community is presupposed.

[2–3] With an image corresponding to 45.1, in v. 3 Jesus compares the disciples with Jews who want to separate tree and fruit or fruit and tree. However, for the disciples it is a matter of knowing Jesus exclusively from his words (v. 2) as they are to be found in the Gospel of Thomas.

Historical

The scene and the logia are inauthentic. They are to be derived completely from debates within Gnosticism.

Logion 44

1 Jesus said, '<u>Whoever blasphemes against</u> the Father will be forgiven. 2 And <u>whoever blasphemes against</u> the Son will be forgiven. 3 But <u>whoever blasphemes against</u> the Holy Spirit will be forgiven neither on earth nor in heaven.'

Analysis

[1–3] These verses have a tripartite symmetrical structure. The logion has parallels in Mark 3.28–29 and Matt. 12.32/Luke 12.10 (= Q). Only v. 1, the blasphemy against the Father, is not contained in any of the parallels mentioned. It may well have been added for reasons of symmetry and because of the doctrine of the Trinity which was developing in orthodoxy. Thomas can keep the focus on the impossibility of forgiving blasphemy against the Holy Spirit because for him this is the spark of light which guarantees the redemption of the Gnostic.

Historical

Cf. on Mark 3.28–29.

Logion 45

1 Jesus said, 'Grapes are not harvested from thorn bushes, nor are figs plucked from thistles, for they do not produce fruit.' 2 A good man <u>brings forth</u> good from his treasure. 3 A bad man <u>brings forth</u> bad things from his bad treasure, which is in his heart, and says evil things. 4 For out of the abundance of the heart he <u>brings forth</u> bad things.'

Analysis

[1–4] Verses 1–3 have a close parallel in Luke 6.44b–45b and in Matt. 7.16b; 12.35; 12.34b. The sequence grapes/figs agrees with Matt. 7.16b against Luke 6.44b (figs/grapes). Verse 4 recalls Luke 6.45c. As this part of the verse derives from Lukan redaction, the same thing may be presumed for the whole Thomas logion, which is to be designated a mixed quotation.

Historical

Cf. on Luke 6.44b–45.

Historical

Cf. on Luke 6.44b–45.

Logion 46

1 Jesus said, 'Among those born of women, from Adam to John the Baptist there is no one higher than John the Baptist, that his (John's) eyes need not be lowered. 2 But I have said, Whoever among you will be small, he will know the kingdom and will become greater than John.'

Analysis

[1–2] These verses correspond to the Q logion Matt. 11.11/Luke 7.28; a Gnostic feature is introduced in v. 2 with 'know the kingdom'.

Historical

Cf. on Luke 7.28.

Logion 47

1 Jesus said, 'It is impossible for a man to mount two horses or to stretch two bows. 2 And it is impossible for a servant to serve two masters. Otherwise, he will honour the one and insult the other. 3 No one drinks old wine and immediately desires to drink new wine. 4 And new wine is not put into old wineskins, lest they burst, nor is old wine put into a new wineskin, lest it spoil it. 5 An old patch is not sewn on to a new garment, because there would be a tear.'

Analysis

Logion 47 consists of several sayings, each of which contrast antithetically two mutually exclusive things.

[1] This verse is a wisdom saying, which has been inserted here because of its similarity to the following verse.

[2] Cf. Matt. 6.24/Luke 16.13.

[3] This verse uses Luke 5.39, as the Luke passage is redactional.

[4] Cf. Luke 5.37.

[5] Cf. Luke 5.36. As v. 3 *certainly* came about from the use of Luke, the same conclusion follows for vv. 4–5. Thomas has reversed the order of Luke, which he has in front of him, as he had placed v. 3 with the key word 'wine' after vv. 1–2, and

now Luke 5.37 automatically presented itself as the next sentence with the same key word.

Historical

[1] This verse is inauthentic.
[2] Cf. on Matt. 6.24 (with a reference there to Mark 12.17).
[3] Cf. on Luke 5.39.
[4] Cf. on Luke 5.36–37 (in the reverse order).

Logion 48

Jesus said, 'If two make (or keep) peace with each other in the same house, they will say to the mountain, "Move away," and it will move away.'

Analysis

The second half of the logion is widely attested in early Christian writings (cf. on Matt. 17.20/Luke 17.6) and also appears in Thomas 106.2. 106.1 recalls the first half of the present logion (each time a conditional sentence, the two-motif). The first half, the meaning of which can be interpreted in the light of Logion 106.1, puts the traditional saying about the faith which moves mountains into a new and thus secondary context.

Historical

Cf. on Matt. 17.20.

Logion 49

1 Jesus said, 'Blessed are the solitary ones, the elect, for you will find the kingdom. 2 For you (come) from it (and) you will return thither.'

Analysis

[1] The beatitude moves from the third person plural to the second plural in the same way as the beatitude in Logion 54. For the 'solitary ones' cf. 4.2; 16.4; 75, etc. For the notion that the solitary ones are the elect cf. 23.1–2.
[2] This verse reassures believers of their origin and their return to the kingdom, as will be further elaborated in the following logion.

Historical

The logion is inauthentic and wholly rooted in Gnostic thought.

Logion 50

1 Jesus said, 'If they say to you, "Where did you come from?", say to them, "We came from the light, the place where the light came into being on its own accord. It established [itself] and appeared in their image." 2 If they say to you, "Who are you?," say, "We are his sons and we are the elect of the living Father." 3 If they ask you, "What is the sign of your Father in you?", say to them, "It is movement and rest." '

Analysis

Logion 50 contains a typically Gnostic catechism which develops the mini-catechism from 49.2.

[1] For the place of light cf. 24.3.

[2] For 'elect of the living Father' cf. 49.1: 'Elect'.

[3] Movement and rest as a designation of one and the same thing correspond to the Gnostic paradoxical discourse (cf. the treatise Bronte from Nag Hammadi [NHC VI ,2]).

Historical

The logion is inauthentic.

Logion 51

1 His disciples said to him, 'On what day will the rest of the dead take place? And on what day will the new world come?' 2 He said to them, 'What you look forward to (= the rest) has (already) come, but you do not know it.'

Analysis

[1] This verse opens a series of three questions from the disciples (cf. 52.1; 53.1). 'Rest' picks up 'rest' in 50.3. 'Rest' is generally a technical term for salvation: 60.6; 90.2.

[2] Cf. also on 113.3. The Gnostics will not cease to seek until they have found rest (cf. 2.1).

Historical

Jesus' words are inauthentic since they relate to the Gnostic rest (cf. further on 113.3).

Logion 52

1 His disciples said to him, 'Twenty-four prophets have spoken in Israel, and all of them have spoken of you (or: through you).' 2 He said to them, 'You have left (out of account) the one who lives in your presence and you have spoken (only) of the dead.'

Analysis

[1] This verse is the second in a series of three questions from the disciples (cf. 51.1; 53.1). 'Twenty-four prophets' refers to the twenty-four books of the Old Testament (thus the numbering in IV Ezra 14.45). According to the disciples they have predicted Jesus' coming or even spoken under the inspiration of Jesus.

[2] Jesus repudiates this sharply and cuts any connection between the Old Testament and himself. The prophets are dead. ('Dead' picks up 'dead' in 51.1.) The disciples have failed to take account of the living Jesus (cf. Prologue).

Historical

Jesus' sayings are inauthentic, since in reality the historical Jesus saw a connection between himself and the Old Testament prophets.

Logion 53

1 His disciples said to him, 'Is <u>circumcision</u> of benefit or not?' 2 He said to them, 'If it were of benefit, their father would beget them (= the children) already <u>circumcised</u> from their mother. 3 But the true <u>circumcision</u> in the spirit has become completely profitable.'

Analysis

[1] This verse is the third in a series of three questions from the disciples.

[2] This verse gives an argument from nature for the uselessness of circumcision: boys are begotten and born uncircumcised.

[3] Like Paul (Rom. 2.25–29; I Cor. 7.7–19; Gal. 6.5; Phil. 3.3), this verse understands circumcision in the metaphorical sense and thus provides a further argument against the benefits of circumcision. The negative attitude to circumcision in the

Gospel of Thomas corresponds to that towards fasting, almsgiving and dietary regulations (cf. 6;14; 104), and also to the Old Testament, as it was documented in the analysis of the preceding logion, Logion 52.

Historical

Jesus' reported sayings are inauthentic. They derive from controversies in the early Christian communities about the significance of Jewish commandments.

Logion 54

Jesus said, 'Blessed are the poor, for yours is the kingdom of heaven.'

Analysis

The beatitude recalls that in Logion 49, and like it moves from the third person to the second. The logion corresponds to Luke 6.20 and Matt. 5.3*, but derives from Luke 6.20, because 'yours' corresponds to Lukan redaction. This conclusion is all the more compelling as in Luke 6.20 the Coptic translation of the New Testament reads 'their' instead of 'yours' – no doubt an assimilation to Matt. 5.3.

Historical

Cf. on Luke 6.20.

Logion 55

1 Jesus said, 'Whoever does not <u>hate</u> his father and his mother cannot become a disciple to me. 2 And (whoever) does (not) <u>hate</u> his brothers and sisters (and) take up his cross like me, will not be worthy of me.'

Analysis

[1–2] Verse 1 appears once again in 101.1 The saying consists of two sentences in synonymous parallelism (a: hate; b: be a disciple of Jesus/be worthy of Jesus). The logion is a mixed quotation made up of Matt. 10.37(–38) and Luke 14.26(–27). Thomas has woven the saying about taking up the cross (cf. Mark 8.34 parr.) into the parallelism.

Historical

Cf. on Luke 14.26–27.

Logion 56

1 Jesus said, 'Whoever has come to know the world has found a corpse. 2 And whoever has found a corpse, the world is not worthy of him (or: is superior to the world).'

Analysis

[1–2] Thomas 80 corresponds to Thomas 56, the only difference being that there we have 'body' instead of 'corpse'. For Thomas this world is a sphere opposed to God. So the commandment is to abstain from it (21.1). But the Gnostic must first recognize it as an anti-world in order to be able to turn to the true life. Cf. Gospel of Philip 93: 'This world is an eater of carrion. All things that one eats in it also die again. The truth is an eater of life. Because of this, none of those who are nourished on the [truth] will die. Jesus came from that place and brought food from there. And to those who wished he gave [life, so that] they will not die.'

Historical

The logion is inauthentic and wholly rooted in Gnostic thought.

Logion 57

1 Jesus said, 'The kingdom of the Father is like a man who had [good] seed. 2 His enemy came during the night (and) sowed weeds among the good seed. 3 The man did not allow them to pull up the weeds. He said to them, "Lest you go to pull up the weeds and pull up the wheat with them. 4 For on the day of the cutting (= the harvest) the weeds will be manifest; they will be pulled up and burned."'

Analysis

[1–4] The logion has a close parallel in Matt. 13.24–30. Here Thomas 57 clearly presupposes the Matthaean version. *First*, the course of events is told more succinctly and is to be understood as an abbreviation, for *secondly*, there is no mention of the sowing of the seed (Matt. 13.24), the process of growth (Matt. 13.30a), and especially the suggestion of the servants that they should pull up the weeds immediately (Matt. 13.27), although a remnant of that has been left, namely the owner's answer

(v. 3). In other words, this answer presupposes the conversation with the servants (Matt. 13.27–28). Thomas twists the parable to see non-Gnostics and Gnostics depicted in the weeds and in the good seed in order to emphasize the dualism between the two. Thomas has preserved the reference to the harvest (v. 4) in order to emphasize the lasting separation.

Historical

Cf. on Matt. 13.24–30.

Logion 58

Jesus said, 'Blessed is the man who toiled (or: suffered). He has found life.'

Analysis

The form of the beatitude reflects that of Logion 54. For 'the man' cf. 47.1. The theme of toiling and/or suffering is reminiscent of Paul's catalogue of his vicissitudes (cf. I Cor. 4.11–13; II Cor. 11.23–27). The finding of life is a theme which often recurs in Thomas; cf. Prologue; 18.3; 19.4; 85.2; 101.3.

Historical

The logion is a secondary construction and therefore inauthentic.

Logion 59

Jesus said, 'Look at the living one as long as you live, lest you die and (then) seek to see him and will not be able to see!'

Analysis

The key word 'living' links the present logion with the previous one ('found life'). Jesus is speaking of himself as the living one (cf. Prologue; 52.2) and emphasizing the either-or between (spiritual) life and (spiritual) death.

Historical

The saying is inauthentic and completely at home in the Gnostic world of the Gospel of Thomas.

Logion 60

1 (They saw) a Samaritan carrying a lamb on his way to Judaea. 2 He said to his disciples, 'Is that man around the lamb?' 3 They said to him, 'In order to kill it and eat it.' 4 He said to them, 'While it is alive, he will not eat it, but (only) when he has killed it (and) it has become a corpse.' 5 They said to him, 'He cannot do so otherwise.' 6 He said to them, 'You too, look for a place for yourselves for rest, so that you do not become corpses and be eaten.'

Analysis

[1–6] The meaning of this logion consisting of a dialogue between Jesus and his disciples is obscure. Nevertheless it is certain that 'alive' (v. 4) is a key word linking it to Logion 59 and Logion 58. The Gnostics are to seek a place of rest (= salvation) for themselves (v. 6), so that they are not consumed by the world, like the lamb, and become a corpse. As the living beings that they are they cannot be eaten and become corpses (v. 4).

Historical

The saying is inauthentic and completely a product of the Gnostic world.

Logion 61

1 Jesus said, 'Two will rest on a <u>bed</u>. The one will die, the other will live.' 2 Salome said, 'Who are you, man, as if you were from the One? You have obtained a place on my <u>bed</u> and eaten from my table.' 3 Jesus said to her, 'I am he who comes from the One, who is equal (or: undivided). They gave me of that which is my Father's.' 4 (Salome said,) 'I am your disciple.' 5 (Jesus said to her,) 'Therefore I say, If he is destroyed (read: equal) he will fill himself with light, but if he is divided, he will fill himself with darkness.'

Analysis

[1] This verse is a link by keyword to the theme of 'life/death' present in Thomas 58–60. The verse recalls Matt. 24.40–41/ Luke 17.34–35 (= Q), but changes the apocalyptic background presupposed in Q and refers to the death of the individual, which can take place at any time.

[2] Starting from the key word 'bed', this verse adds a question from Salome and prepares for Jesus' answer.

[3] Jesus comes from the One, who is equal. Jesus has a divine origin and is equal to God (cf. John 5.18).

[4] This verse describes Salome's reaction in the face of the self-identification of Jesus.

[5] This verse presents two possibilities: either one is – like God – equal (cf. v. 3) and is filled with light or one is separated from God. Then one is filled with darkness. On the concept of light cf. 11.3; 24.3; 50.1; 83.1–2. The theme of division is mentioned in 72.1–3.

Historical

[1] Cf. on Matt. 24.40–41.
[2–5] These verses are unhistorical and utterly at home in Gnostic thought.

Logion 62

1 'I tell my mysteries to those who [are worthy of my] mysteries. 2 Do not let your left hand know what your right hand is doing.'

Analysis

[1] This verse recalls Mark 4.11 and like that verse (cf. the parable chapter, Mark 4) forms a heading for a group of parables (Thomas 63–65).
[2] The connection between this verse and v. 1 is obscure. It has an equivalent in Matt. 6.3, where the instruction is given in the context of almsgiving.

Historical

[1] Cf. on Mark 4.11.
[2] This paradoxical sentence is a wisdom saying and, as the evidence in Matthew and Thomas clearly shows, was used in different contexts. I see no possibility of attributing it to Jesus within any degree of probability.

Logion 63

1 Jesus said, 'There was a rich man who had much money. 2 He said, "I shall use my money to sow, to reap, to plant (and) to fill my storehouse with produce, so that I lack nothing." 3 That is what he thought in his heart. And that night he died. 4 Whoever has ears, let him hear.'

Analysis

[1–3] This exemplary narrative is related to Luke 12.16–20. But the economic circumstances are slightly different. In Luke we have a farmer who wants to 'save', here a businessman who wants to put his money to work. The meaning of the two parables is the same. Sudden death can overtake even the shrewdest of rich men.

[4] Cf. 8.4; 21.11.

Historical

Cf. on Luke 12.16–20. An additional argument against the authenticity of vv. 1–3 is the slightly changed economic horizon of the Thomas parable, which is of a kind which Jesus is unlikely to have known.

[4] Cf. on 8.4.

Logion 64

1 Jesus said, 'A man had guests, and when he had prepared the supper, he sent his servants to invite the guests. 2 He went to the first one; he said to him, "My lord invites you." 3 He said, "I have (financial) claims against some merchants. They are coming to me this evening, I must go (and) give them my orders. I ask to be excused from the supper." 4 He went to another, he said to him, "My lord has invited you." 5 He said to him, "I have bought a house and am needed for a day. I shall not have any time." 6 He went to another and said to him, "My lord invites you." 7 He said to him, "My friend is getting married, and I am to prepare the banquet. I shall not be able to come. I ask to be excused from the supper." 8 He went to another, he said to him, "My lord invites you." 9 He said to him, "I have bought a village, I am going to collect the rent. I shall not be able to come. I ask to be excused." 10 The servant went (back); he said to his lord, "Those whom you invited to the supper have asked to be excused." 11 The lord said to his servant, "Go out into the streets. Bring back those whom you find, that they may join in the supper. 12 Businessmen and merchants [will] not enter the places of my Father."'

Analysis

[1–11] By comparison with the related parable Luke 14.15–24 (Matt. 22.1–14), Thomas offers an allegory-free version which may stand closest to the original parable. (For the secondary features in the present parable see on Luke 14.15–24.) This is the case despite the fact that as in Thomas 63 an urban milieu has taken the place of the rural one. The invitation expressed in the same words (vv. 2, 4, 6, 8) is in popular narrative style.

[12] This verse generalizes and orientates itself on the fact that the four people invited had commercial interests. This is a secondary interpretation which possibly already shaped the text of vv. 1–11 and gave it a milieu which is rather that of a major city of the Roman empire.

Historical

[1–11] These verses are very close to the original parable and deserve the designation 'authentic'. For further reasons see on Luke 14.15–24.

Logion 65

1 He said, 'A generous man had a vineyard. He gave it to country labourers so that they might work it and he might collect his produce from them. 2 He sent his servant so that the labourers might give him the produce of the vineyard. 3 They seized his servant, beat him; they almost <u>killed</u> him. The servant went; he told his lord. 4 His lord said, "Perhaps he did not <u>know</u> them (or, emended: perhaps they did not <u>know</u> him)." 5 He sent another servant. But the labourers beat the other (also). 6 Then the lord sent his son. He said, "Perhaps they will respect my son." 7 Those labourers, because they <u>knew</u> that he was the heir to the vineyard, seized him and <u>killed</u> him. 8 Whoever has ears, let him hear.'

Analysis

[1–7] The owner ('man') from 64.1 provides the link to this parable (v. 1). By comparison with Mark 12.1–9 parr. it does not contain any element which *must* be interpreted allegorically. However, one would hesitate to conclude from this that 65.1–7 is the basis of the Markan version. *First,* Logion 66, the content of which appears in Mark 12.10–11 directly attached to Mark 12.1–9, suggests dependence on the Synoptics. *Secondly,* v. 4, which is peculiar to Thomas, may contain a Gnostic interpretation. If we follow the text which has been handed down, the servant did not know the labourers and went to the wrong people. By contrast, v. 7 says that the labourers knew the son and killed him immediately. If the reading handed down is correct, the author is here playing on the word 'know'.

However, should the emended reading be correct, there will similarly be a play on the verb 'know', but at the same time we would have to note an inappropriate elaboration of the parable: after all, the logic in v. 3 presupposes that the labourers have recognized the servant, for otherwise they would have hardly struck him or almost killed him.

In both cases Thomas has modified the train of thought. The parable which he has handed down is not close to the original version and is in no way original.

Historical

Cf. on Mark 12.1–9.

Logion 66

Jesus said, 'Show me the stone which the builders have rejected. It is the cornerstone.'

Analysis

This piece also appears in Mark 12.10–11 par. and fits in well there, because the verses give the reason for the rejection of Israel. But as they do not fit with Thomas here, it follows that they have been taken over, together with Mark 12.1–9, from the Synoptics.

Historical

Cf. on Mark 12.10–11.

Logion 67

Jesus said, 'Whoever knows the All (but) is <u>deficient</u> in himself is <u>deficient</u> in everything.'

Analysis

The 'All' is a technical term which relates to the universe, embracing the earth and the cosmos (cf. 2.4; 77.1). 'Know' takes up the same expression from 65.4,7. According to Thomas, knowledge of the All and self-knowledge condition each other. The reason lies in the consubstantiality of the All with the Gnostic self. Thus according to Logion 77 Jesus is the light and at the same time the All. Whoever knows himself is Christ and himself becomes a person of light.

Historical

The saying is inauthentic and utterly at home in Gnostic thought.

Logion 68

1 Jesus said, 'You are blessed when they hate you and <u>persecute</u> you. 2 And they will find no room at the place where they have <u>persecuted</u> you.'

Analysis

[1] This verse corresponds to Matt. 5.11a/Luke 6.22a and promises consolation to those who are persecuted and hated.

[2] The meaning is unclear. Is this talk of the lack of success of the ones who are acting? But in what sense? Perhaps it helps to note that 'place' also appears in other passages of the Gospel of Thomas (4.1; 24.1; 60.6; 64.12) and each time denotes the place of salvation. In that case v. 2 says that the persecutors have forfeited salvation.

Historical

[1] Cf. on Luke 6.22.

Logion 69

1 Jesus said, 'Blessed are those who have been persecuted in their hearts. They (are the ones) who have known the Father in truth. 2 Blessed are the hungry, so that the belly of him who desires (it) will be filled.'

Analysis

Logion 69 continues the beatitude from Logion 68, but this time in the third person plural.

[1] The statement about persecution in the heart is unclear; perhaps the Coptic translator has mistranslated the text 'Blessed are the persecuted who are of a pure heart' (cf. Matt. 5.8). Thomas has here introduced the key word 'persecute' from Logion 68. The second part of v. 1 certainly comes from him since to attain the 'knowledge of the Father' is one of the goals of Thomas (cf. 50.2–3).

[2] This verse recalls Luke 6.21a, but is secondary by comparison with Luke (= Q), for Q expects the feeding with the heavenly meal in the future, Thomas in the present.

Historical

[1] Cf. on Matt. 5.8.
[2] Cf. on Luke 6.22a.

Logion 70

1 Jesus said, 'If you bring forth that which is in yourselves, what you have will save you. 2 If you do not have that in you, what you do not have in you will kill you.'

Analysis

[1–2] Cf. 24.3. Thomas's formulation is dualistic. It is a matter of life (= salvation) and death. Salvation is manifestly connected with knowledge of one's own self, one's heavenly origin, which is light. Otherwise, if the knowledge is not attained, the result is death.

Historical

The historical yield is nil, since the saying is completely at home in the Gnostic world.

Logion 71

Jesus said, 'I will [destroy this] house, and no one will be in a position to build it up [again].'

Analysis

The saying is reminiscent of John 2.19, where a similar saying is spoken by Jesus, and Mark 14.58, according to which a saying of Jesus to this effect has been wrongly put on the lips of Jesus. However, in the New Testament parallels there is always a reference to a rebuilding, whereas there is none in Thomas. Hence Logion 71 might be about the destruction of the world or matter in a metaphorical sense. There is no eschatological perspective at work here. Thomas presupposes the New Testament texts and on that basis formulates an ascetic–dualistic saying of Jesus about the temple.

Historical

Cf. on Mark 14.58; John 2.19.

Logion 72

1 [A man said] to him, 'Tell my brothers to divide my father's possessions with me.' 2 He said to him, 'O man, who has made me a divider?' 3 He turned to his disciples; he said to them, 'Am I then a divider?'

Analysis

[1–2] These verses correspond to Luke 12.13–14, but are probably independent of the Lukan text.

[3] This verse formulates Thomas's own viewpoint: Jesus is not a divider (on division cf. 61.5), but points people to the original unity (cf. 22.4–5; 106.1).

Historical

[2] This verse is an authentic saying of Jesus which gives an answer to the question asked in v. 1 (cf. on Luke 12.13–14).

[3] This verse is an addition which betrays a Gnostic perspective.

Logion 73

Jesus said, 'The harvest is great but the labourers are few. Ask the lord, therefore, to send out labourers to the harvest.'

Analysis

The logion corresponds to Matt. 9.37–38/Luke 10.2 (= Q), but does not read 'of the harvest' after 'the lord' as Matthew and Luke do. There is no evidence of dependence on the Synoptic parallels.

Historical

The saying is inauthentic. Cf. on Matt. 9.37–38.

Logion 74

He said, 'Lord, there are many around the cistern, but there is no one (or) nothing in the sickness (read: cistern).'

Analysis

This remarkable aphorism, which Thomas probably attributes to Jesus (or is Jesus the Lord who is addressed?), has an equivalent in the anti-Christian philosopher Celsus (c. 180 CE), who read it in a writing with the title 'Heavenly Dialogue'. It was in circulation among the Gnostic group of the Ophites (serpent worshippers). There it runs, 'Why are there many around the well and no one in the well?' Evidently the aphorism is meant to encourage the Gnostic to stop being a bystander and enter, in order also to be able to drink the water of knowledge.

Historical

The saying is inauthentic and completely at home in Gnosticism.

Logion 75

Jesus said, 'Many are standing at the door, but it is the solitary ones who will enter the bridal chamber.'

Analysis

'Many' takes up 'many' from Logion 74 which, like Logion 75, is addressed to single ones who are confronting the salvation of knowledge. For the bridal chamber cf. 104.3 and Gospel of Philip 60; 73; 79; 80; 82; 102; 122. The symbolism of the door remotely recalls Matt. 25.1–13.

Historical

The logion is unhistorical and completely rooted in Gnostic thought.

Logion 76

1 Jesus said, 'The kingdom of the Father is like a merchant who had a <u>consignment of merchandise</u> and who found a pearl. 2 That merchant was wise; he gave away the <u>consignment of merchandise</u> (and) bought the pearl alone for himself. 3 You too, seek his treasure, which does not cease to exist, where no moth comes to devour and no worm destroys (anything).'

Analysis

[1–2] This parable likewise occurs in Matt. 13.45–46. Thomas has revised it slightly and introduced his criticism of trading (cf. 64.12), which is evident from the repetition of 'merchandise'. For 'wise' (v. 2) cf. 8.2.

[3] This verse contains an interpretation of the parable in vv. 1–2. It is similar to Matt. 6.19f./Luke 12.33 (= Q) and calls on the reader to preserve the inner treasure which in the context of the Gospel of Thomas can mean only the self (= Jesus as light; cf. 50.1). In this Gnostic interpretation I presuppose that v. 3 is dependent on the Synoptic parallels mentioned (for 'treasure' cf. further Matt. 13.44).

Historical

[1–2] Cf. on Matt. 13.45–46.
[3] Cf. on Matt. 6.19–21.

Logion 77

1 Jesus said, 'I am the light, this which is above all. I am the All; from me the All came forth. And the All has come to me. 2 Split a piece of wood, I am there. 3 Lift up the stone, and you will find me there.'

Analysis

[1–3] Jesus identifies himself with light (cf. John 8.12; 9.5), which is tremendously important in Thomas: 11.3b; 24.3; 50.1; 61.5; 83.1–2. Jesus claims to be mediator at creation (cf. Romans 11.36; I Cor. 8.6; Col. 1.16). All this recalls the role of wisdom. The presence of Jesus as it is described in vv. 2–3 echoes Matt. 18.20; 28.20 – but in that passage, too, there is a wisdom background.

Historical

The logion is inauthentic and at home in Gnostic thought.

Logion 78

1 Jesus said, 'Why have you come out into the field? To see a reed shaken by the wind? 2 To see a man clothed in soft garments [like your] kings and your mighty ones? 3 These are they who wear soft garments, and they will not be able to know the truth.'

Analysis

[1–2] These verses have an equivalent in Matt. 11.7–8/Luke 7.24–25 (= Q), but avoid the reference to John the Baptist which is present in Q. This suggests a secondary stage of the tradition by comparison with Q.

[3] This verse addresses the readers and calls for asceticism. Only those who do not wear soft clothing will recognize the truth.

Historical

[1–2] Cf. on Luke 7.24–25.
[3] This verse is inauthentic, as it derives from redaction.

Logion 79

1 A woman from the crowd said to him, 'Blessed is the body (womb) which bore you and the breasts which nourished you.' 2 He said to her, 'Blessed are those who have heard the word of the Father (and) have kept it in truth. 3 For days will come when you say, "Blessed is the body (womb) which has not conceived and the breasts which have not given milk." '

Analysis

[1–2] The basis of these verses is Luke 11.27–28, as v. 28 derives from Lukan redaction and 'word of the Father' (v. 2) clearly derives from the redaction of Thomas. 'Word of the Father' is typical of Thomas, as he avoids the term 'God'. 'Truth' (v. 2) picks up the same word from 78.3.

[3] This addresses the readers ('you'). Thomas is using Luke 23.29–30 in order to protest against procreation (cf. Logion 114).

Historical

[1–2] Cf. on Luke 11.27–28.
[3] Cf. on Luke 23.29–30.

Logion 80

1 Jesus said, 'He who has known the world has found the body. 2 But he who has found the body, the world is not worthy of him.'

Analysis and Historical

Cf. on Logion 56.

Logion 81

1 Jesus said, 'Let him who has grown rich be king. 2 And let him who possesses power renounce (it).'

Analysis

For the logion cf. Thomas 110.

[1] 'Become rich' refers in a metaphorical sense to knowledge (cf. 3.5). The one who has knowledge should be king (cf. 2.3).

[2] This verse requires renunciation on the part of the one who has worldly power, so that he enters into the state denoted in v. 1.

Historical

The saying is inauthentic and is completely at home in Gnostic thought.

Logion 82

1 Jesus said, 'He who is near me is near the fire. 2 And he who is far from me is far from the kingdom.'

Analysis

[1–2] The significance of the fire follows from v. 2. Fire thus denotes nearness to the kingdom. Cf. further on Logion 10.

Historical

The logion is inauthentic and completely rooted in Gnostic thought.

Logion 83

1 Jesus said, 'The images are manifest to man; and the light in them is hidden by the image of the light of the Father. 2 He will manifest himself, but his image is hidden by his light.'

Analysis

[1–2] The logion defines the relationship between image, light and Father. Cf. Gospel of Philip 67: 'The truth did not come naked into the world, but came in types and images. It (= the world) will not (be able to) receive it otherwise.' See further 50.1–2.

Historical

The logion is inauthentic and springs wholly from Gnostic thought.

Logion 84

1 Jesus said, 'On the day when you see your <u>likeness</u>, you rejoice. 2 But when you see your <u>likenesses</u> which came into being before you – they do not die, nor are they manifest – how much will you bear?'

Analysis

'Likeness' is a keyword link to 'image' (83.1–2).

[1] This verse probably refers to knowledge of the like, for like is known by like (cf. I Cor. 2.6–16).

[2] This verse introduces the eternal heavenly likenesses to which the readers have not yet become assimilated. Thomas raises the question how long the readers can bear it, i.e. can be reminded of their earthly existence, without failing.

Historical

The logion is inauthentic and utterly rooted in Gnostic thought.

Logion 85

1 Jesus said, 'Adam came into being from a great power and a great wealth, but (nevertheless) he did not become <u>worthy</u> of you. 2 For had he been <u>worthy</u>, [he would] not [have tasted] death.'

Analysis

[1–2] Like Paul (Rom. 5; I Cor. 15), Thomas brings Adam into play in order to emphasize the special character of salvation. The Thomas Christians are far superior to Adam, for they do not taste death (for this expression cf. 1; 18.3; 19.4; 111.2).

Historical

The logion is inauthentic and wholly rooted in Gnostic thought.

Logion 86

1 Jesus said, '[The foxes have their holes] and the birds have their nests. 2 But the Son of man has no place to lay down his head and rest.'

Analysis

[1–2] The logion has a parallel in Matt. 8.20/Luke 9.58 (= Q). At the end of v. 2 Thomas alludes to the rest which in Gnosticism denotes salvation (cf. 51.1–2). The Son of man, who probably denotes the Gnostic, has no rest in the material world (cf. 28.3: 'sons of men' = human beings).

Historical

Cf. on Luke 9.58.

Logion 87

1 Jesus said, 'Wretched is the body that is dependent on a body. 2 Wretched is the soul that is dependent on the two of them.'

Analysis

[1] The Gnostic's own body, and also the world in which he lives, are described as bodies.

[2] The soul may not be dependent on either of the two (cf. 29.3). For the reasons for this dualism cf. on Logia 56 and 80.

Historical

The logion is inauthentic and completely at home in Gnostic thought.

Logion 88

1 Jesus said, 'The messengers will come to you together with the prophets, and they will give you what belongs to you. 2 And you too give them what is in your hands, and say to yourselves, "On what day will they come and receive what is theirs?"'

Analysis and Historical

Since the meaning is unclear, the historical question does not arise.

Logion 89

1 Jesus said, 'Why do you wash the outside of the cup? 2 Do you not know that he who made the inside is the same one who made the outside?'

Analysis

[1–2] The logion has a parallel in Matt. 23.25–26/Luke 11.39–41 (= Q). But it seems original by comparison with the Synoptic parallels, as it emphasizes one notion (and does not, like Matthew/Luke, include the inside of the person as well as the outside of the cup). Because the one who created the outside of the cup and what is inside is the same, washing the inside and the outside are made equal. Hence the following conclusion suggests itself: if the inside is not washed, the outside does not need to be washed either.

Historical

The logion is probably authentic and fits Jesus' criticism of the law (cf. Mark 2.27; 7.15).

Logion 90

1 Jesus said, 'Come to me, for my yoke is easy and my lordship is gentle. 2 And you will find rest for yourselves.'

Analysis

[1–2] The logion has a parallel in Matt. 11.28–30, but by comparison with it is different and shorter. The key word 'rest' was welcome to Thomas as a reference to Gnostic salvation (cf. 51.1–2).

Historical

Cf. on Matt. 11.28–30.

Logion 91

1 They said to him, 'Tell us who you are, so that we may believe in you.' 2 He said to them, 'You examine the face of the sky and of the earth, and have you not known the one who is before you, and do you not know how to examine this moment?'

Analysis

[1] This verse is an introductory question from the disciples inserted by Thomas (cf. 43.1; John 6.30; 8.25).

[2] This verse has a parallel in Luke 12.56, but unlike that verse contains a reference to the present Jesus who is before the disciples, i.e. both around and within them. Cf. 5.1; 24.3; 59.

Historical

[2] Cf. on Luke 12.54–56.

Logion 92

1 Jesus said, 'Seek and you will find. 2 But what you asked me about in the past I did not tell you on that day. Now I want to say it, and you do not ask me about it.'

Analysis

[1] Cf. on 2.1; 94.1.

[2] This verse calls on the reader not to give up the search, even though signs of neglect are becoming evident (v. 2b). Gnostic existence is grounded in a 'religion of searching'.

Historical

[1] Cf. on 2.1.

[2] This verse is rooted in the Gnostic world and is therefore inauthentic.

Logion 93

1 (Jesus said), 'Do not give what is holy to dogs, lest they throw it on the dunghill. 2 Do not throw pearls before swine, lest they do not . . . make it.'

Analysis and Historical

The meaning is obscure. Cf. on Matt. 7.6.

Logion 94

1 Jesus [said], 'He who seeks will find. 2 [And he who knocks,] to him it will be opened.'

Analysis and Historical

Cf. on 2.1; 92.1 and Matt. 7.7–8.

Logion 95

1 [Jesus said], 'If you have money, do not lend it at interest. 2 But give [it] to one from whom you will not get it back.'

Analysis

[1–2] The logion has a parallel in content in Matt. 5.42b/Luke 6.30. But the theme of interest recalls the antipathy of Thomas to merchants (cf. 64.12). However, this does not exclude the possibility that it was already contained in the tradition that Thomas is using.

Historical

The logion is probably authentic and could be the earliest form of the version behind Matt. 5.42b. But another possibility is that it is dependent on the redactional passage Luke 6.34.

Logion 96

1 Jesus said, 'The kingdom of the Father is like [a] woman. 2 She took a little leaven; [she] hid it in some flour (and) made it into large loaves. 3 He who has ears let him hear.'

Analysis

[1–2] These verses have a parallel in Matt. 13.33/Luke 13.20–21 (= Q). Their dependence on the Q parable emerges from the abnormal expression that the woman hid (one would have expected the verb 'knead') the leaven in the flour. Moreover in the parable in Thomas the woman and her activity are at the centre, and she is meant to be the model for the readers. Finally, at the end the size of the loaves is emphasized (cf. 8.1–3; 107.1–3).

[3] The awakening call is secondary, here and everywhere else in Thomas. Cf. on 8.4.

Historical

Cf. on Luke 13.20–21.

Logion 97

1 Jesus said, 'The kingdom of the [Father] is like a woman who was carrying a [jar] full of flour. 2 While she was going a long way, the handle of the jar broke. The flour poured out behind her [on] the road. 3 (But) she did not know it, she had not noticed any mishap. 4 When she reached her house, she set the jar down. She found it empty.'

Analysis

A further parable follows, which like the previous one is orientated on the action of a woman.

[1–4] This parable is preserved only here in the early Christian tradition. But its images do not match. Why should all the flour pour out of a jar if only a handle breaks? How is it that the woman did not observe this? So the parable must be interpreted in the light of these contradictions. In that case Thomas wants to say that knowledge (v. 3) is important at any point in time. The reader should always be on guard.

Historical

The parable is inauthentic, as it is an admonition to the individual Gnostic.

Logion 98

1 Jesus said, 'The kingdom of the Father is like a man who wanted to kill a powerful man. 2 He drew the sword in his house. He stuck it into the wall to know whether his hand was strong (enough). 3 Then he killed the powerful man.'

Analysis

The parable appears only at this point in the early Christian Jesus tradition. It has a high degree of offensiveness, since as in Luke 16.1–7; Matt. 13.44; Matt. 24.43–44/Luke 12.39 Jesus uses an immoral hero to make a statement about the kingdom of God. Cf. in addition the original version of the saying about 'men of violence' in Matt. 11.12/Luke 16.16 (= Q) as a further example of Jesus being deliberately offensive in what he says.

Historical

The parable is authentic. Because of its offensiveness it probably fell victim to moral censorship at an early stage and therefore does not appear in any other text. Cf. further on Luke 16.1–13.

Logion 99

1 The disciples said to him, 'Your brothers and your mother are standing outside.' 2 He said to them, 'Those here who do the will of my Father are my brothers and my mother. 3 They are the ones who will enter the kingdom of my Father.'

Analysis

[1–2] These verses have a parallel in Mark 3.31–35/Matt. 12.46–50/Luke 8.19–21. But as Thomas, like Luke, offers a shorter version (to note the most important point, he does not mention the sisters), it seems likely that Thomas is using a text dependent on the Synoptics.

[3] This verse is a generalization by Thomas.

Historical

Cf. on Matt. 3.31–35.

Logion 100

1 They showed Jesus a gold coin and said to him, 'Caesar's men are demanding taxes from us.' 2 He said to them, 'Give Caesar (what) is Caesar's. 3 Give God what is God's. 4 And give me what is mine.'

Analysis

[1–4] The logion has a parallel in Mark 12.13–17 parr. In contrast to the Synoptics, it is the disciples and not the opponents of Jesus who show Jesus a coin; this represents a further development. The whole logion has its climax in v. 4, which is without a parallel in the Synoptics. Evidently 'Jesus' expects of his disciples their own offering, i.e. in the framework of the Gospel of Thomas, that they should be aware of their own sparks of light and thus become one with Jesus, the personification of light (cf. 77.1–3; 108.1–3).

Historical

Cf. on Mark 12.13–17.

Logion 101

1 (Jesus said), 'Whoever does not hate his [father] and his mother as I do <u>will not be able to be a [disciple] to me</u>. 2 And whoever does [not] love [his father] and his mother as I do, <u>will not be able to be a disciple to me</u>. 3 For my mother . . . but [my] true [mother] gave me life.'

Analysis

[1–2] These verses are typically Gnostic paradoxical statements. (On this cf. Bronte [NHC VI, 2].) For v. 1 cf. Matt. 10.37/Luke 14.26.

[3] This verse has been preserved only in fragments and makes no sense.

Historical

[1] Cf. on Luke 14.26.

Logion 102

Jesus said, 'Woe to the Pharisees, for they are like a dog sleeping in the manger of oxen. For he neither eats, nor does he [let] the oxen eat.'

Analysis

Jesus attacks the Pharisees in the form of a woe, using a common Greek proverb (cf. e.g. Lucian, *Against the Uneducated Book Collector*, 30).

Historical

The saying is inauthentic. Moreover Jesus' rebukes of the Pharisees in the New Testament (cf. e.g. Matt. 23) also derive from the community.

Logion 103

Jesus said, ' Blessed is the man who knows at what point (of the house) the robbers will enter, so that he may get up, gather his [. . .] and gird his loins before they come in.'

Analysis

The beatitude picks up the woe from the previous logion. The logion is a free version of 21.5–7; Matt. 24.43–44/Luke 12.39–40 (= Q). It puts a new emphasis on the Q parallel by indicating the place (and not the time) of the attack. Perhaps Thomas could interpret this logion in a Gnostic way, starting from 'know'.

Historical

Cf. on Luke 12.39–40.

Logion 104

1 They said [to him], 'Come, let us <u>pray and fast</u> today.' 2 Jesus said, 'What then is the sin that I have committed? Or in what were they superior to me? 3 But when the bridegroom leaves the bridal chamber, then they are to <u>fast and pray</u>.'

Analysis

[1–3] These verses are a dialogue with an invitation by the disciples (v. 1) and two rhetorical questions from Jesus as an answer. Verse 2 rejects prayer and fasting (for the Gnostics) (cf. 6; 14.1–2). Verse 3 allows it for those who are completely initiated. Cf. the structure of the argumentation in Mark 2.19–20, which is similar to v. 3.

Historical

The logion is inauthentic and completely at home in Gnostic thought.

Logion 105

Jesus said, 'He who knows the father and the mother will be called "son of a prostitute".'

Analysis

Here Jesus is speaking about himself and his special relationship to his father and his mother. Cf. 61.3; 101.3. What he says about his father and his mother is meant literally and at the same time symbolically. How does this relate to the second half of the logion? Jesus, who knows his father and mother, is called 'son of a prostitute'. This statement probably refers to the tradition behind John 8.41, the content of which from the beginning was directed by non-Christian Jews against the conception and birth of Jesus, i.e. against his illegitimate birth. Cf. further on Mark 6.3.

Historical

Jesus' words in this logion are inauthentic. But they reflect historical facts.

Logion 106

1 Jesus said, 'If you make the two one, you will become sons of men. 2 And if you say, "Mountain, move away," it will move away.'

Analysis

[1–2] The logion has a parallel in Thomas 48. The step into duality is the real fall for human beings. Doing away with it is salvation (cf. 11.4; 22.4–7).

Historical

Cf. on Logion 48.

Logion 107

1 Jesus said, 'The kingdom is like a shepherd who had a hundred sheep. 2 One of them went astray – it was the largest. He left (the) ninety-nine behind; he looked for that one until he found it. 3 When he had toiled so hard, he said to the sheep, "I love you more than the ninety-nine." '

Analysis

[1–3] The parable has a parallel in Matt. 18.12–13/Luke 15.4–6 (= Q) and represents a further development of the Q parable. For the lost sheep has now become the largest (v. 2). This is a motif which corresponds to 8.1–3 and 96.1–2. Two interpretations of the parable in Gnostic terms are possible: (a) the shepherd stands for the Saviour, who in the large sheep seeks and finds the Gnostic self which has gone astray in the world. (b) The shepherd represents the Gnostic himself, who seeks and finds himself.

Historical

Cf. on Luke 15.4–6.

Logion 108

1 Jesus said, 'Whoever will drink from my mouth will become like me. 2 I myself will become he, 3 and the things that are hidden will reveal themselves to him.'

Analysis

[1] This is a commentary on 13.5.

[2] For the unity of Jesus with the disciples cf. the presentation of Thomas as a twin (prologue).

[3] Cf. the prologue.

Historical

The saying is inauthentic and completely at home in Gnostic thought.

Logion 109

1 Jesus said, 'The kingdom is like a man who has a [hidden] <u>treasure</u> in his field of which he <u>knows nothing</u>. 2 And [after] he had died, he left it to his [son. The] son <u>knew nothing</u>. He took that field and sold [it]. 3 And the one who had bought it went ploughing (and) [found] the <u>treasure</u>. He began to lend money at interest to whomever he wished.'

Analysis

[1–2] These verses are dependent on Matt. 13.44, since the parable has developed further. One owner has become two, and only the third makes a profit out of the treasure. The three persons represent the Gnostic self. The first two indeed have the treasure, but know nothing. Only the third finds it.

[3] The finder has done what Thomas 95 repudiates. He accepts interest. Thus a warning is attached not to misuse the find. Cf. the further interpretation of the parable in Logion 110.

Historical

Cf. on Matt. 13.44.

Logion 110

Jesus said, 'Whoever has found the world and has become rich, let him renounce the world.'

Analysis

Like Logia 56; 80; 111.3, the logion is about the renunciation of the world. This time Jesus is addressing those who like the man from Logion 109 have profited from the world, but should now withdraw from it as rapidly as possible.

Historical

Cf. on Logion 56.

Logion 111

1 Jesus said, 'The heavens will roll themselves up, and likewise the earth in your presence (or: before you). 2 And the one who lives from the Living One will not see death.' 3 Did not Jesus say, 'Whoever finds himself, the world is not worthy of him'?

Analysis

[1] This verse has a parallel in 11.1. Cf. further Isa. 34.4.
[2] This verse describes the Gnostic existence (cf. 18.3; 19.4; 85.2).
[3] This verse is an ascetical interpretation which picks up the preceding Logion 110 (keyword links are 'find' and 'world') and is typical of Thomas: cf. 21.6; 27.1; 56.1–2; 80.1–2.

Historical

The sayings are inauthentic and completely rooted in Gnostic thought.

Logion 112

1 Jesus said, 'Woe to the flesh that depends on the soul. 2 Woe to the soul that depends on the flesh.'

Analysis and Historical

Cf. on 87.1–2.

Logion 113

1 His disciples said to him, 'The kingdom, on what day will it come?' 2 (Jesus said,) 'It will not come by watching out for it. 3 It will not be a matter of saying "Look here" or "Look there", but the kingdom of the Father is spread out over the earth, and people do not see it.'

Analysis

[1–3] Like 3.1–3, this logion, which echoes Luke 17.20–21, is concerned with the coming of the kingdom of God. It rejects all speculation about the date of its arrival, giving the reason that the kingdom of God is already spread out over the earth, but is not seen by people. Other passages in which Thomas speaks of the presence of the kingdom of God are 46.2; 51, etc.

Historical

[1–3a] These verses are probably authentic. Jesus rejected speculations about the coming of the kingdom of God (cf. Luke 17.20).

[3b] This verse is not authentic. Jesus expected the imminent coming of the kingdom of God. Moreover v. 3b corresponds to the redactional verse Luke 17.21 and for that reason alone is unhistorical.

[3c] Since this verse is redactional, it is inauthentic (those who do not see are those who are not Gnostics).

Logion 114

1 Simon Peter said to them, 'Mariham (= Mary) should go from us. For women are not worthy of life.' 2 Jesus said, ' Look, I myself will lead her in order to make her male, so that she too becomes a living spirit resembling you males. 3 For every woman, if she makes herself male, will enter the kingdom of heaven.'

Analysis

[1–3] The logion contrasts with 22.5. For that speaks of the dissolution of sexuality, whereas this logion speaks of a transformation of the female into the male, of a kind that occurs in numerous Gnostic ascetic texts. Perhaps Logion 114 was added to the Gospel of Thomas only at a relatively late stage. In the framework of the version of the Gospel of Thomas which has been preserved, Logion 114 is principally to be read as a polemic against procreation and the world (cf. 79.3; 27.1, etc.).

Historical

The logion is inauthentic and reflects later discussions within Gnostic communities about the role of the woman and about the role of sex.

VI

Apocryphal Traditions of Jesus

MARTINA JANSSEN

Introduction

The origins of research into the agrapha lie in the second half of the seventeenth century, but a comprehensive monograph on this theme did not appear until 1889 when the Thesaurus by A. Resch, *Agrapha. Ausserkanonische Evangelienfragmente*, was published. This work is a comprehensive collection of scattered sayings of Jesus which are not attested in the New Testament Gospels (agrapha). Shortly afterwards, in 1896, came the investigation by J. H. Ropes, which as well as raising fundamental questions about the Ur-Markus hypothesis, which Resch had developed and used fruitfully in his research into the agrapha, with its criticism cut down the number of logia of Jesus collected in 1889. Ropes also made progress in distinguishing between authentic and inauthentic sayings of Jesus. The extra-canonical sayings of Jesus became popular as a result of J. Jeremias, *Unknown Sayings of Jesus*, which was first published in German 1948 and subsequently appeared in a whole series of new editions and translations. However, this work, too, reduced the number of extra-canonical traditions under investigation by taking into account the criteria of authenticity. This tendency has been reinforced in the first volume of the latest edition of the *New Testament Apocrypha* edited by W. Schneemelcher and R. McL. Wilson (German 1990, English 1991). Here O. Hofius prints only a handful of agrapha which are relevant to the question of authentic traditions.

There are numerous sources over and above the canonical Gospels which attest the sayings and actions of Jesus. Already in the New Testament writings there are some references to Jesus traditions, a number of which do not appear in the Synoptic Gospels or the Gospel of John but are attested in other writings (cf. I Cor. 2.9 with Thomas 17; Acts 20.35 with Didache 1.5). The New Testament manuscripts are another important source: they often contain additional Jesus material as well as textual variants.

However, earlier research into the agrapha for the most part drew its material from the church fathers, who in their homilies, commentaries and treatises report some sayings of Jesus or episodes which are not known from the canonical writings. In addition to the notes in Papias (c.125) and II Clement (c.150), the main sources here are the church father Clement of Alexandria (died before 215), Epiphanius of Salamis (died 403) and Jerome (c.347–419/20). The reports which they have handed on have often been seen as elements of apocryphal Gospels which are no longer in existence (Gospel of the Egyptians, Gospel of the Ebionites, Gospel of the Hebrews, Gospel of the Nazareans). Usually sayings of Jesus appear here which do not really cast any new light on Jesus but represent variants on the canonical traditions. One example is the Jewish Christian Gospel of the Nazareans, fragments of which have been preserved in the church fathers (Jerome, etc.); these are firmly based on the Gospel of Matthew, but occasionally embellish it with legendary material. The same can be said for the Gospel of the Ebionites (fragments in Epiphanius), which is similarly Jewish-Christian, but in addition takes up material from Luke and Mark and has its own theological emphases throughout (absence of the virgin birth, etc.). The Jewish Christian/Gnostic Gospel of the Hebrews displays greater independence from the canonical writings (fragments above all in Jerome and Clement of Alexandria). There are connections with the Gospel of Thomas (NHC II 2) and the Gospel of Philip (NHC II 3). Finally, mention should be made of the Gospel of the Egyptians, which has been preserved in Clement of Alexandria and the Excerpts from Theodotus. It takes the form of a conversation between Jesus and Salome and is sometimes (Theissen and Merz) counted among the so-called dialogue Gospels (see below). In terms of content this writing has a stamp of its own and has marked (Gnostic-)Encratite tendencies. There are related notions in the Dialogue of the Saviour from Nag Hammadi (NHC III 5; especially 140,12ff.; 144,15ff.), the Book of Thomas (NHC II 7) and, with qualifications, also in the Gospel of Thomas (cf. Thomas 114).

There are numerous agrapha and other traditions about Jesus in apocryphal Christian documents (acts of apostles, apocalypses and other revelatory writings) which for reasons of chronology and content did not find their way into the New Testament canon. Although most of these texts are relatively late, earlier traditions about Jesus, mostly handed down by word of mouth, may be hidden within them, which were unknown to the Synoptics and John or were deliberately suppressed by them. One example which was particularly discussed in earlier research is a widely attested eschatological saying of Jesus which elaborates on the abundance of Paradise and with slight changes has also been handed down in Irenaeus, *Against the Heresies* V, 33, 3. The Encomium on John the Baptist (fol. 14f.) is an additional occurrence of this logion, which is probably secondary. This late apocryphon is a homily wrongly attributed to John Chrysostom, in which the author quotes a conversation between the Risen One and his disciples about the status of John the Baptist; this is introduced by the traditional motif of the discovery of a book. In this conversation Jesus – motivated by a question from Thomas – is made to say, 'I will hide nothing from you about which you ask me. Because you have asked me about wine: every grape has ten thousand berries, and a berry usually produces six measures. And again the date branches of Paradise produce ten thousand bunches. Their measure is that of a man. It is the same with the fig tree: it has ten thousand branches. If three people eat from one fig tree, they will be full.' Similar promises are made about the wheat, etc.

The papyrus discoveries at the end of the nineteenth century are an extremely important source for the extra-canonical traditions about Jesus: in 1885 the Fayyum fragment, which is presumably to be connected with the apocryphal Gospel of Peter, was discovered in a papyrus collection. In 1889 C. Schmidt recognized in a couple of papyrus fragments a consecutive text, namely the Strasbourg Coptic Papyrus. Pride of place, however, is to be given to the Greek Oxyrhynchus Papyrus, which since 1897 has slowly been made accessible to the public, and which contains numerous early Jesus traditions from the second century (see below). The edition of Egerton Papyrus 2 followed in 1935; this is a document which on palaeographical grounds can be dated to the second century. Some of the papyri mentioned are thus very old and presumably contain yet older traditions – a notable fact, when we think that with few exceptions (Papyrus 52 from the second century with some lines from John 18), most manuscripts of New Testament texts cannot be dated before the fourth century. Certainly the papyri offer early and in part very valuable testimonies for the Jesus tradition, but the reservation must be added that the state of some papyri is very bad and some of the writings are very difficult to read. So the reconstruction of the texts, the definition of their form and their place in relation to known writings or their connection with 'new' Gospels (see below on the Gospel of Peter) is fraught with a whole series of problems. Sometimes it is a matter of considerable controversy. Thus, for example, Merton Papyrus 51 is sometimes interpreted as the fragment of an apocrypha Gospel, but often only as a commentary on Luke 6.7.

Non-Christian sources also hand on sayings and actions of Jesus. Thus there are sayings and actions of Jesus in the Talmud, in Islamic writings and in Manichaean and Mandaean texts. One prominent example is the inscription composed in Arabic on a portal of the mosque of Fathpur-Sikri in India, which displays similarities of content to Thomas 42: 'Jesus, peace be to him, has said: The world is a bridge. Go over it, but do not settle on it.' Most of these extra-Christian testimonies do not contribute much to the understanding of the historical Jesus, since they are stamped by a mythological picture of Jesus, as is shown for example by the Jesus psalms from the Manichaean psalm book or the polemical depiction of Jesus in the Mandaean Book of John.

In 1945 a further inestimable source for the extra-canonical Jesus traditions was discovered with the Nag Hammadi find. The Nag Hammadi library, which has a largely Gnostic stamp, is one of the greatest collections of Christian apocrypha. Apart from the Gospel of Thomas (NHC II 2), there are other texts in the Nag Hammadi writings which preserve earlier Jesus traditions. These are clearly to be distinguished from obviously late, Gnosticizing logia or discourses, a large number of which appear in the Pistis Sophia (Askew Codex) or in the Sophia Jesu Christi (NHC III 4), a form of pagan-Jewish document which has been Christianized by the insertion of Jesus and his disciples (Letter of Eugnostos [NHC III 3]). What H. Koester has called the dialogue Gospels from Nag Hammadi like the Letter of James (NHC I 2) or the Dialogue of the Saviour (NHC III 5) are particularly important for the authentic Jesus tradition. Sayings of Jesus are included in all these dialogue Gospels. Certain techniques can be ascertained from the way in which these writings use known sayings from the canonical Gospels, and unknown sayings of Jesus can also be reconstructed from further apocryphal discourses. Adopting Koester's results, and taking them further, we can say that the literary fiction of the dialogue Gospels is that Jesus expounds his own sayings in conversation with his disciples – almost as an actualization of himself. In this way his message keeps its validity and power of conviction even in changed social or religious contexts.

There is much argument among scholars over the value of the extra-canonical Jesus traditions. Thus in their reconstruction of the teaching and life of Jesus some scholars (Koester; Cameron; Mayeda) attach as much importance to them as to the canonical traditions, whereas others (Evans; Charlesworth) largely dispute their historical value. The solution to this question probably lies somewhere in the middle. A narrow, limited and closed understanding of the canon should not dominate investigation of the subject nor in principle exclude the possibility of authentic Jesus tradition outside the canon. Nor should enthusiasm about being able to discover in 'new' sources the real Jesus, who is even thought to have been censored in the New Testament writings, burden the analysis of the text with a hermeneutical interest which produces just as much of a caricature. Here both canonical and extra-canonical tradition from the first centuries should stand side by side on an equal footing, and contribute objectively towards the reconstruction of the teaching (and the life) of Jesus.

The criteria for discovering authentic and inauthentic Jesus traditions are in principle the same in the extra-canonical sources as they are in the canonical tradition. A further criterion to be mentioned is that of possible derivation from the canonical writings. The independent attestation of a logion in different sources is also an indication of authentic material; here, however, the dependence of the sources on one another should be noted. Jeremias has established normative criteria for ascertaining inauthentic sayings of Jesus, which include among others reshaping of sayings of Jesus from the Gospels, the translation of accounts in the Gospels into sayings of Jesus, the use of agrapha as aids in composition, the tendentious reshaping and invention of words of the Lord, and erroneous or deliberate transfers. If all these criteria can be excluded, a saying of Jesus could derive from an authentic tradition. Among positive criteria for authenticity Jeremias mentions affinity to the Synoptic material and a Hebraizing language.

The order of the Jesus traditions presented here is based on the sources from which they come; other possible systematizations which have been chosen by scholars go for example by content (apocalyptic, wisdom, etc. sayings), form (parable, saying, etc.) or authenticity. However, the choice of the texts offered here is not primarily guided by the criterion of authenticity; rather, it is meant to give a representative survey of the different Jesus traditions. Nevertheless, an attempt has been made to judge the possible authenticity of the Jesus traditions. This is not possible in all cases, either because of the uncertainty of the textual basis or the brevity or ambiguity of a logion. In some cases there are just as many reasons to suppose a saying comes from Jesus as there are against this supposition, so that sometimes the question of authenticity is deliberately left open.

To make the texts more readable, I have largely dispensed with indicating conjectures and reconstructions; however, this should not give the false impression that the text is certain. For precise information see the editions of the texts in question. For reasons of space I have usually mentioned J. Jeremias, *Unknown Sayings of Jesus*, London 1964, and W. Schneemelcher and R. McL. Wilson (eds), *New Testament Apocrypha*, Vol.I, Louisville, Ky and Cambridge 1991. The source texts for which a bibliography cannot be discovered in these works are cited at the appropriate place.

New Testament traditions outside the Gospels (Paul)

There are some sayings of Jesus and references to Jesus traditions in the New Testament itself outside the Gospels. One example is the certainly inauthentic 'agraphon' from Acts 20.35, which attributes to Jesus a sentence which is common in ancient literature ('It is more blessed to give than to receive'). In addition, I Corinthians 2.9 (cf. Thomas 17) and Ephesians 5.14 have been conjectured as further possible scattered sayings of the Lord in the New Testament writings.

In particular the Pauline writings are drawn into the search for sayings of Jesus which are not attested in the Gospels. However, opinions divide over how intensively Paul worked sayings of Jesus into his letters. One problem in Paul's use of sayings of the Lord is that he hardly ever uses the Jesus traditions with an explicit introduction (but see I Cor. 7.10f.), but seems to make use of them indirectly and by way of allusion (see e.g. Rom. 13.6–10). However, simply on the basis of the agreements between Pauline ethics and the preaching of the historical Jesus it has been conjectured that Paul grounds himself more in the Jesus tradition than is recognizable at first sight. Scholars like Dungan begin by assuming that Paul knew many more sayings of the Lord than is generally accepted. The question of (hidden) sayings of the Lord in the letters of Paul remains largely open and is an important point in the difficult question of the continuity between Jesus and Paul.

I Thess. 4.13ff.: A miniature apocalypse of Jesus?

13 But we do not want you to be ignorant, brothers, about those who are asleep, so that you may not be sorrowful like the others who have no hope. 14 If we believe that Jesus has died and is risen, so too God through Jesus will bring with him those who have fallen asleep. 15 For this we say to you in a word of the Lord, that we, the living, who are left behind, at the coming of the Lord will not precede those who are asleep. 16 The Lord himself [the Son of man] will descend from heaven with a command, with the archangel's call and the sound of the trumpet of God. And first those who have died in Christ will rise. 17 Then we, the living, who are left behind, will be transported together with them on clouds into the air to meet the Lord. And so we shall always be with the Lord. 18 Therefore admonish one another with these words.

The view that a saying of the Lord is hidden in this section from Paul's first letter to the Thessalonians is motivated above all by the introduction to verses I Thess. 4.15b–17 in 4.15a ('For this we say to you in a word of the Lord'). This assumption is not undisputed. According to some scholars, I Thess. 4.15a is not the introduction of a direct quotation but a reference to Jesus using prophetic modes of discourse (cf. e.g. Sir. 48.3). Moreover it is unclear whether the postulated quotation is to be found in I Thess. 4.15b or the apocalyptic passage I Thess. 4.16ff. Investigations using word statistics indicate that phrases untypical of Paul appear specifically in I Thess. 4.16f. Moreover the terminology which differs from the redactional context supports the assumption of an independent tradition in I Thess. 4.16f. Whereas Paul uses 'those who have fallen asleep' for the dead (I Thess. 4.13ff.), I Thess. 4.16f. speaks of the 'dead'. Originally the logion may have referred to the descent of the Son of man, which Paul has replaced by 'the Lord himself' in view of the understanding of the community in Thessalonica. The Pauline 'in Christ' may also be an addition, as may be I Thess. 4.17b as a whole (cf. the we-style as in I Thess. 4.15b).

Jeremias regards vv. 16–17 as an authentic Jesus tradition, which was perhaps spoken by Jesus on the occasion of the prophecy of martyrdom for his disciples (Matt. 10.16ff.). Their death will not put them at a disadvantage at the parousia of Jesus. In terms of content scholars have also cited some analogies to sayings of Jesus in I Thess. 4.16f. like Matt. 10.39; 16.25, 28; 20.1ff.; 24.31, 34; 25.6; 26.64; Luke 13.30. However, these instances offered by scholars are not really convincing; rather, in I Thess. 4.16f. we seem to have what Vielhauer has called a Jewish 'miniature apocalypse' which has been put into the mouth of Jesus – like the Synoptic apocalypse in Mark 13 par. The imagery attested in the logion recalls the ancient Near Eastern ceremonial reception of the king and works with motifs and ideas, many of which are to be found in Jewish apocalyptic. Alongside the report of the appearing of the Son of man (IV Ezra 13.13), reference can be made to the notion, also attested elsewhere, that the dead take part in the eschatological salvation (IV Ezra 7).

Paul puts this Jewish miniature apocalypse – which, however, he understands as a saying of the exalted Kyrios – into a wider overall argument (I Thess. 4.13–18) that he develops in view of the critical situation in Thessalonica. There the members of the community who have already died are becoming a problem. How can they attain the eschatological salvation at the parousia if they have died? The death of the members of the community leads to hopelessness and mourning in the community – probably because the notion of the resurrection of Christians was unknown in Thessalonica. Now Paul attempts to combine the notion of the parousia with faith in the resurrection. After an exposition (I Thess. 4.13), he makes use of the traditional credo of the death and resurrection of Christ, through which he also confirms that the dead, too, will have future communion with Christ (I Thess. 4.14): because Jesus has died and been raised, the dead too will have a share in paradise (cf. the further development of this causal relationship to the analogy in I Cor. 6.14). This statement, which is new to the Christians in Thessalonica, is explained further by a reference to a Jewish miniature apocalypse which is regarded as a saying of the Lord (I Thess. 4.16f.); it is applied in advance to those to whom Paul is writing in I Thess. 4.15 and summed up for them. The dead are not at a disadvantage at the return of Christ, because through their resurrection they will be put in the same situation as the living, and together with them experience communion with Christ and the result of being transported in order to meet the Lord in the air (I Thess. 4.17). I Thessalonians 4.18 serves as the concluding admonition.

Jesus traditions in New Testament manuscripts

In New Testament manuscripts there are often variants or additions to the normative text of the biblical canon. Mostly the changes are minimal and are to be assigned to the sphere of textual criticism. However, sometimes real additions can be found which indicate a particular tendency. Thus in Codex Vercellensis (fourth century) in Matt. 3.17 the baptism of Jesus is expanded as follows: 'And when Jesus was baptized, a great light shone from the water so that all who had gathered (there) were made very afraid.' Here typical elements from the classical description of a theophany (light as a sign of the divinity and the fear among those present that it provokes) are added. Such a notion is also attested elsewhere, as in Codex Sangermanensis, in Justin (died c.160), Ephraem the Syrian (died 373) and in the Gospel of the Ebionites.

In some cases whole pericopes inserted into the manuscripts can represent old pieces of tradition.

The Freer Logion

This follows Mark 16.14. And they excused themselves with these words: 'This aeon of law-lessness and unbelief is under Satan, who through the unclean spirits does not allow the true power of God to be comprehended. Therefore reveal your righteousness already (now),' they said to Christ. And Christ replied to them, 'The measure of the years of Satan is filled up. But other terrible things are drawing near, also (for those) for whom I, because they have sinned, was delivered to death, so that they might convert to the truth and no longer sin, in order to inherit the spiritual and imperishable glory of righteousness (preserved) in heaven.' *Mark 16.15 follows.*

The abrupt ending of the Gospel of Mark clearly provoked reactions at an early stage. Like most manuscripts, Codex W (Freer) from the fifth century puts the longer, inauthentic conclusion to Mark (16.9–20) after Mark 16.8. In addition how-ever, a conversation between Jesus and the disciples has been inserted after 16.14, part of which has also been handed down by the church father Jerome (*Against Pelagius* II 15).

Numerous allusions to New Testament writings can be made out (cf. for indi-vidual notions and phrases only Gal. 1.4; John 14.30; Eph.2.2; Mark 12.24; John 5.14; 8.11; I Peter 1.4), and these put in question whether Jesus is the author. The appearance of Jesus to the eleven is also attested in Luke 24.41ff.; in Luke it is similarly coupled with the motif of the unbelief of the disciples, though in contrast to the Freer Logion this disappears with the appearance of Jesus. On the other hand, in the Freer Logion the unbelief becomes an explicit theme and is 'defended' with a reference to the Satanic corruption of the existing aeon (for this connection cf. e.g. II Cor. 4.3f.). The reason for the unbelief is the absence of Jesus from the world. Therefore the disciples ask him to reveal his righteousness. Jesus instructs the disciples that while the rule of Satan is over (cf. similarly also Luke 10.18; John 12.31; Rev. 12.7–12), other tribulations are imminent. The whole section is stamped by Jewish apocalyptic terminology and radiates a mood of 'eschatological exaltation'.

There are countless equivalents to the form of the Freer Logion, namely conver-sation with the Risen One, in the apocryphal and above all in the Gnostic literature. The point of time between the resurrection and ascension of Jesus was suitable for inserting 'special revelations'. However, apart from these dialogues, which are often late (see below), the primary reference text in relation to the Freer Logion is Acts 1.6–8, where the risen Christ imparts to his disciples final revelations which relate to the future.

John 7.53–8.11: Jesus as omniscient judge

7.53 And each went to his own house. 8.1 But Jesus went to the Mount of Olives. 2 And in the morning he went again to the temple, and all the people came to him, and he sat down and taught them. 3 The scribes and the Pharisees brought a woman who had been caught in adultery, placed her in the midst 4 and said to him, 'Teacher, this woman has been caught in the act of adultery. 5 In the law Moses commanded us to stone such women. Now what do you say?' 6 But they said this because they wanted to test him, so that they might have some reason to accuse him. And Jesus bent down and wrote with his finger on the ground. 7 And as they continued to ask him, he stood up and said to them, 'Let him among you who is without sin be the first to throw a stone at her.' 8 And once more he bent down and wrote on the ground. 9 When they heard it, they went away, one after the other, beginning with the elders, and he was left alone, and the woman was in the midst. 10 Then Jesus stood up and said to her, 'Woman, where are they? Has no one condemned you?' 11 She said, 'No one, Lord.' And Jesus said, 'Neither do I condemn you; go, and do not sin again.'

The pericope about Jesus and the adulteress is not an original part of the Gospel of John. That is clear from the fact that the text is absent from many manuscripts, and in some manuscripts appears in another place (John 7.36; 7.52; 21.24 or Luke 21.38). Nor is the character of the pericope Johannine: the appearance of the scribes (and Pharisees) and the scribal teaching of Jesus in the temple are untypical of the Johannine account. On the other hand the pericope recalls the Synoptic narratives; there are close connections above all with the Lukan special material: the situational note that Jesus teaches by day in the temple and by night stays on the Mount of Olives is reflected in Luke 21.37. Jesus' concern for sinners and for social outcasts (Luke 5.27–32; 15.1–7, 11–32; 19.1–10; 7.36–50) and the significance of women (7.36–50; 8.1–3; 10.38–42; 23.27–31; cf. also the role of women in Acts) are specific features of the writer Luke (but cf. also Mark 2.13–17). For these reasons it has sometimes been assumed that John 7.53ff. is of Lukan origin. However, there are stylistic and linguistic objections to this (U.Becker). Moreover the comparison which is often made between Luke 7.36ff. and John 7.53ff. does not stand up to critical examination: the woman who is a sinner in Luke 7.36ff. is explicitly introduced as a penitent and a believer, and the forgiveness promised to her comes about precisely because of these characteristics (cf. also Luke 5.32). The adulteress in John 7.53ff. shows no penitence or veneration for Jesus; her feelings remain in the dark. Moreover the forgiveness of sins is not the real point of the story, but Jesus' wise judgment.

In terms of form, the pericope about the adulteress clearly has a 'Synoptic stamp' and has sometimes been counted among the controversies of Jesus (U. Becker, with the proviso of a redactional revision). In fact there are parallels here, particularly to the pericopes in which Jesus is tempted with a controversial question: the Pharisees and scribes approach Jesus in John 7.53ff. with a question (cf. e.g. Mark 10.2–12, the question of divorce; Mark 12.13–17, the question of the temple tax; Mark 12.18–27, the question about the resurrection of the dead). The question is asked solely to test Jesus and thus to set a trap for him. There is no real lack of clarity about the situation, since according to Lev. 20.10 the adultery is clearly to be punished with stoning. However, there are problems in classifying John 7.53ff. as a controversy, as its strong narrative features show. Moreover, the closing scene between Jesus and the adulteress (John 8.9–11) is problematical, as in addition to the real controversy (John 7.53–8.9a) it gives the pericope a second climax.

There remains the problem of mixed forms. Thus sometimes similarities are pointed out to Mark 2.1–12 par., where a miraculous healing is combined with a controversy (Schnackenburg). Furthermore, formal analogies are seen with POxy 840, but here not only is the text at the end of the fragment uncertain, but much is only conjecture, especially as in terms of form this text follows more the pattern of Mark 2.23–28 par. and Mark 7.1–23 par.: offensive behaviour on the part of Jesus provokes (controversial) questions! A further text which can be compared with the pericope of the adulteress on the formal level is Mark 3.1–6 par: here the opponents of Jesus want to test him to see whether he performs healings on the sabbath. As in the pericope of the adulteress, the 'object' of the testing is brought into the foreground (cf. Mark 3.3 with John 8.3, 9) and the opponents are routed with a terse remark by Jesus. On closer inspection, however, here too the differences are greater than the common features. It remains to be noted that while John 7.53ff. recalls Synoptic forms, it contains much that is 'novelistic and secondary' (Bultmann).

The impressive encounter between Jesus and the adulteress has often been regarded as an authentic saying of Jesus, as a 'lost pearl of old tradition' (Heitmüller). The standard 1963 monograph *Jesus und die Ehebrecherin* by U.Becker advances three primary reasons for putting the event in the life of Jesus. 1. The question of adultery and retribution for it was the subject of lively discussion in the time of Jesus. 2. Jesus' judgment goes against the Torah and its professional expositors. 3. Jesus acquits the adulteress on his own authority and unconditionally. A further criterion that can be added to Becker's observations is the originality of Jesus' symbolic action.

Jesus' answer to the scribes and Pharisees who are putting him to the test is a symbolic action which cannot really be explained satisfactorily. It is often suggested as a solution that Jesus' reaction is based on Jer. 17.13 ('Hope of Israel, Lord, all who forsake you shall be put to shame; those who turn away from you shall be written in the dust, for they have forsaken the Lord, the fountain of living water'). Accordingly, with his gesture Jesus wants to make clear that all human beings are sinners before God. However, whether those who figure in this pericope grasped this by no means obvious allusion and staging of the prophetic word is questionable, given the great scriptural and hermeneutical demands made by it on all concerned (including Jesus). Moreover renewed investigation of the symbolic action of Jesus and its repetition makes this solution improbable, especially as it is Jesus' saying that drives the accusers away, and not the action paralleled in the Jeremiah passage. However, it is worth reflecting that the reference to Jer. 17.13 was made at a very early stage in the reception history of the pericope, and possibly was responsible for its insertion after John 7.36 (cf. the streams of living water in John 7.37f.). Other attempts to explain Jesus' symbolic demonstration, like recourse to Roman legal procedures (noting the judgment before the one who gives it) or the interpretation of Jesus' symbolic action as pensiveness on his part, do not really work. Finally, the attempts to define the words which Jesus is said to have written on the ground (Derrett conjectures Ex. 23.1b in the first instance and Ex. 23.7 in the second) are speculative. Jesus' symbolic action remains enigmatic.

It is difficult to see an original Jesus tradition in the pericope of the adulteress. According to some exegetes (von Campenhausen), not only form-critical grounds but also the circumstances of the time and the subject-matter tell against it being a real event from the life of Jesus: the joint appearance of the scribes and Pharisees as a legal authority indicates an origin after 70. Moreover it is questionable whether the Jews in the time of Jesus had the right to carry out the death penalty themselves (cf. John 18.31) – Acts 7.58 reflects an act of lynch law, or whether this did not lie rather in the hands of Rome; nor is it really certain how adultery was in fact punished in the time of Jesus (death penalty? If so, by stoning or by strangling?). The main objection to an origin with Jesus, however, is the fact that in literary terms the pericope seems to take up the story of Susanna, which is known as an addition to the book of Daniel. Further reasons in support of this view will be given below.

Not only Jesus' gesture of writing in the dust is problematical; the text raises some further questions. How does the accused woman feel? Is she at all penitent over her action (cf. as a contrast Luke 7.36ff.)? Moreover where is the man who is said to have committed adultery with her? Has the woman already been condemned by a court, or does she still face trial? Why do the accusers capitulate after Jesus' statement, and desist from implementing the clear regulations of the Torah?

Old Testament tradition is often reflected in the stories of the New Testament; events and actions have their models and origins in the Hebrew Scriptures. Reflections or imitations of Old Testament pericopes can be found e.g. in Mark 5.22–43 (cf. II Kings 4. 8–37); Mark 6.35–44 (cf. II Kings 4.42–44); Mark 1.40–45 (cf. II Kings 5.1–15); Mark 3.1–6 (cf. I Kings 13.4–6). In general cf. also such phenomena as the interpretation of John the Baptist as Elijah redivivus. John 7.53–8.11 also takes a narrative from the Old Testament as a prototype; this sheds light on the problems indicated above.

In the Greek version of the Old Testament we find as an addition to the Book of Daniel the novella of Susanna, which is only very loosely connected by the figure of Daniel with the prophetic book which precedes it (Theodotion 64). The event is transferred to Babylon and documents the lawlessness of the elders-judges. They see the beautiful, married Susanna out walking and burn with desire for her. When the two of them independently make their way to Susanna with clear intentions they meet and forge a plan to seduce her together. She rejects their demands, because she knows that adultery is wrong and does not want to sin against God. The elders devise revenge: they order Susanna and her family to the synagogue and falsely accuse Susanna of adultery, claiming to have witnessed it. Susanna turns to God and he gives the spirit of insight to the young Daniel. Daniel questions the two elders separately about the type of tree under which they saw Susanna sin. Their answers do not match, and the elders are convicted of bearing false witness and executed. Susanna is freed.

Individual scholars have seen the points of contact between John 7.53–8.11 and the story of Susanna (Schmidtke; Schilling; Derrett; Becker), but have usually disputed a deeper affinity because of the difference in motifs: in Susanna the motif of the innocent beautiful woman who is persecuted – or the handsome man: Gen. 39.6b–20a – is connected with the notion of a wise, often youthful, judge; whereas in John 7.53–8.11 the love of Jesus who forgives sins stands in the foreground. As in Matt. 19.3–12 (Deut. 24.1; dismissal of the wife from a marriage) he relativizes the rigorous marriage laws in favour of co-humanity.

The narrative frameworks of the story of Susanna and the pericope of the adulteress are comparable; John 7.53–8.11 begins at the point in the plot where Susanna is allegedly discovered by the elders–judges and falsely accused. The common thrust is as follows: a woman accused of adultery and thus condemned to death according to the Old Testament legislation is acquitted by a judge who did not originally take part in the trial. She is thus saved from the death of stoning, whereas her accusers are put to shame. Certainly there is no explicit mention of stoning in the Susanna story, but one could reasonably infer a plan to stone Susanna from the gesture of laying hands on her by the elders–judges (LXX 34) with reference to Lev. 24.14 ('Bring out of the camp him who cursed; and let all who heard him lay their hands upon his head, and let all the community stone him').

The parallels between the two narratives extend beyond this basic pattern to details of language and content. One feature to be mentioned is the figure of the young wise judge, represented by Daniel (for omniscience cf. LXX 52, 56 and Theodotion 52, 56) and in John 7.53ff. interpreted in terms of Jesus (cf. similarly the motive of the wise young man in Luke 2.41–52).

Furthermore there are numerous linguistic echoes and resonances between John 7.53ff. and the story of Susanna: cf. e.g. John 8.2 with LXX 12f. and Theodotion 28, 47 (in the morning); John 8.2. with LXX 48 and Theodotion 28, 47 (people); John 8.4 with Theodotion 58 (the woman taken/discovered); John 8.5 with Theodotion 62 (according to the law); John 8.19 with LXX 12f.; Theodotion 5, 28 etc. (the elders); John 8.10 with Theodotion 48 and LXX 53 (condemn). Above all the motif of 'putting in the midst' (John 8.3, 9; Theodotion 48 and LXX 48) is striking (cf. especially John 8.3 and Theodotion 34, where the accusers present the woman in the midst of the people).

The story of Susanna can contribute to the solution of the difficulties in the subject-matter of John 7.53ff.: scholars dispute whether the adulteress in John 7.53ff. has already been condemned. According to Jeremias this must be the case, as it is the scribes and Pharisees who bring Susanna forward. Had the trial not yet occurred, the witnesses to the act should have presented Susanna. However, Jesus' question in 8.10 clearly tells against a prior condemnation; it indicates that the trial has not yet taken place. Now if we look at the Susanna story, as 'elders-judges' the witnesses who accuse Susanna are the representatives of the Jewish law like the scribes and Pharisees in John 7.53–8.11. They accuse the innocent Susanna and are themselves convicted. This development can also be transferred to the pericope of the adulteress. The Pharisees and scribes, as alleged *witnesses* to the adultery, present the adulteress; a trial has not yet taken place. This identification of the Pharisees with the witnesses who make the accusation is also supported by the following observations: first of all the decisive statement by Jesus in John 8.7f. indicates that the witnesses to the action must contribute to the event (cf. Deut. 17.7: 'The hand of the witnesses shall be the first to kill him'). In reaction to Jesus' judgment the accusers capitulate; they then depart in shame. Now it is remarkable that we are also told that the elders are the first to depart (John 8.9), i.e. they have been hardest hit by Jesus' judgment; it is natural to identify them with the Pharisee witnesses. In the Susanna story too, it is the elders-judges who falsely accuse Susanna and are then ignominiously convicted (cf. LXX 52: here it is emphatically the older false witness who is led away before the younger one!).

Despite the similarities and points of reference, there seems to be a decisive difference between the Susanna story and John 7.53–8.11: Susanna is innocent of the charge. But what about the woman in John 7.53–811? Here too on close examination her guilt is not clearly established; in her case too it is probable that the charge is unfounded. If we begin by assuming that the woman has been accused falsely (thus e.g. also Derrett) as in the Susanna story, there is an explanation for the absence of her lover and her lack of repentance. That the woman has sinned is known explicitly only through the mouth of her opponents (John 8.4–5; secondarily adopted in 8.3). She herself shows no consciousness of guilt. In that case the only thing that needs to explained is Jesus' concluding remark in 8.11: 'Go and henceforth sin no more!'

There are three possible solutions to this problem, which I shall discuss briefly:

(a) The redactional character of John 8.11b. If we do not excise the whole sentence as a redactional gloss which corrects the content of the story by introducing the concept of sin in the 'style of a formula of absolution from the early church' (U.Becker), it can be pointed out that 'henceforth', which in terms of content can be identified with the time of the adultery, is missing in many manuscripts and is taken as an interpretative addition in the sense of a Christian baptismal theology (cf. Gal. 5.1; cf. also Rom. 6.19ff.; II Cor. 5.16; Eph. 5.8; I Peter 2.10, 25; Titus 3.3–7; Rom. 13.12–14). Through baptism freedom from sins has been bestowed and now it must be preserved (Wilckens).

(b) The reference to John 5. A second possible solution to the problem is to refer to the healing of the sick man in John 5.1–17: after the sick man has been healed and asked about the identity of his saviour, he meets Jesus in the temple, where Jesus says to him, 'Now you are well; sin no more so that nothing worse befalls you' (John 5.14). Wellhausen aptly remarks on this: 'But v. 14 is offensive, because in this case it is highly unmotivated; someone who has lain sick for thirty-eight years and during that time has had no occasion to sin is told after the healing that he is to sin no more so that nothing worse happens to him.' This passage is in fact hard to explain; recourse to the notion of retribution (anyone who is sick has sinned) with reference to Mark 2.5 is not convincing here: in John 9.2ff. Jesus clearly rejects the connection between sin and sickness made by his disciples. So in John 5.14 the invitation to sin no more is not preceded by any sinful behaviour on the part of the person addressed; therefore this need not be the case in John 7.53–8.11 either.

(c) The redactional character of John 8.9b–11. Thirdly, one can consider the possibility of excising John 8.9b–11 completely as a later addition (Fiedler; Lührmann). A first round of conversation (Jesus and the scribes) already ends in John 8.9a with a concluding saying of Jesus. With its second round of conversation (Jesus and the woman), John 8.9b–11 destroys the focus of the pericope.

At first sight this literary-critical observation is supported by an apocryphal tradition in Didymus the Blind (fourth century), who reports the following 'controversy': 'A woman was condemned for a sin by the Jews and was brought for stoning to the place where this was usually done. When the Saviour . . . saw her and noted how she was ready for her stoning, he said to those who were in the process of covering her with stones, "Let the one who has not sinned take a stone and throw it. If anyone is convinced that he himself has not sinned, let him take up a stone and throw it at her." And no one dared to. As they knew themselves and were aware that they too were guilty in some things, they did not dare to stone her.' The conversation between Jesus and the sinful woman (John 8.9b–11) is lacking. By contrast, another source (Syriac Didascalia VIII) offers precisely this 'biographical apophthegm' (John 8.9b–11) and apparently knows nothing of Jesus' first round of conversation with the accusers (John 7.53–8.9a). There is vigorous discussion of the relationship between the two sources and on John 7.53–8.11: do they represent two independent pieces which have been fused together in John 7.53–8.11 (Ehrman), or do both sources use John 7.53–8.11 selectively and put the emphasis differently (McDonald)? This question cannot be resolved here. However, it is probable that John 7.53–8.11 is presupposed in both cases (thus Didymus the Blind picks up John 7.53–8.9a in order to illustrate his reflections on Eccl.7.21–22a; John 7.53–8.9a is hardly suitable for that in isolation, but is so in connection with John 7.24, 51; 8.15, so that Didymus already understands the pericope in its Johannine context). It can, however, be said that Didymus is reading John 7.53–8.9a in the light of the story of Susanna. Moreover, one parallel which goes beyond John 7.53ff. is that Jesus himself takes the initiative and like Daniel joins in the trial.

So the adoption of the Susanna material (7.53–8.9a) would be supplemented by the encounter of Jesus with the sinful woman, which introduces the theme of forgiveness and thus gives the Susanna version a new meaning. In support it should be noted that the most numerous and decisive linguistic parallels between John 7.53ff. and the Susanna story appear in the first round of conversation, 7.53–8.9a (moreover the person who made the addition could have taken 'the standing in the midst' in John 8.9b from John 8.3).

Thus the story of Jesus and the (alleged) adulteress (or its basic material in John 7.53–8.9a or John 7.53–8.11a) is one of the many different adoptions of the Susanna material.

The Susanna story exists in several versions. The often very different recensions of the Susanna material sometimes emphasize one element and sometimes another. They consist of individual complexes of motifs which each in turn have their own transformations (Baumgarten). Sometimes the material is considerably altered, as in John 7.53ff. Thus the figure of Daniel is absent from the Samaritan Susanna story: the wise judge is Susanna's father. But even the 'traditional' versions of the Septuagint and Theodotion differ in lay-out and motivation. In its Susanna material the Septuagint offers a religious didactic narrative which also gives encouragement to hold fast to God in the face of threats within. With different means like eroticizing (the story of the bath), psychologizing, individualizing, historicizing and a new conclusion to the narrative, the version of Theodotion, which was composed a century later, creates from this didactic narrative an 'edifying story of the beautiful Susanna once upon a time in Babylon and two criminal elders' (Engel).

The emphasis in this version of the Susanna material lies on the omniscience of Jesus, who becomes the victim of an intrigue of the Pharisees and scribes. These deliberately bring Jesus an innocent woman against whom false charges are being levelled, which leave nothing to be desired about the clarity of the judgment to be made. Here it is not Jesus' faithfulness to the Torah (does he observe the law?) or loyalty to the authorities (Rome alone has the right to the death penalty) which are put to the test, as elsewhere in the catch questions in the New Testament, but his omniscience. Does Jesus know of the innocence of the accused, or does he condemn her according to the law? With the help of the Susanna material Jesus is stylized as the wise, omniscient judge who sees through everything and by his judgment (John 8.7f.) brings out the true culprits. Here the salvation of the woman is an incidental matter; the reader does not learn much about it.

The incorporation of the pericope into the Gospel of John suggests some reasons. Jesus' omniscience is a central theological concern in the Gospel (cf. John 1.40ff.; 1.46ff.; 4.1, 17; 6.64b; 13.1 etc.). Furthermore in this Gospel Jesus appears in principle as a life-giver and judge (John 5, 7.15–24), a function which he also exercises in John 7.53ff. (especially in the understanding of the redaction in 8.9b–11). Moreover in John 7.24 and 8.15 Jesus warns against judging (but cf. also Matt. 7.1ff. par.; Luke 6.37). Finally, in the Gospel of John – as in the Lukan special material – Jesus' concern for women is strongly emphasized. Along with John 11 (Mary and

Martha), John 12.1–11 (the anointing in Bethany) and John 20.11ff. (the prominent role of Mary of Magdala), prime mention should be made of John 4, the conversation at Jacob's well between Jesus and the Samaritan woman who becomes a messenger of faith. This woman too was a 'notorious sinner' (Ritt) and adulteress (John 4.16–19).

The position of the pericope about Jesus and the adulteress fits its context each time. If it is incorporated after John 7.52 it fits without problem into the topographical and chronological framework: Jesus is in Jerusalem at the Feast of Tabernacles (John 7.1, 10). Half-way through the feast he is teaching in the temple (John 7.14), an activity which he continues on the last day (John 7.37). In John 8.12, as in John 8.2, Jesus again teaches in the temple (John 8.20). However, a closer look at the text shows that the incorporation of John 7.53–8.11 is very loose. Both John 7.37–52 and John 8.12–20 involve controversies of Jesus with his Jewish opponents, which each time are about his person (in John 7.37ff. the views of others about Jesus are cited; in John 8.12ff. Jesus bears witness himself), so that the novelistic pericope John 7.53–8.11 seems more like an alien body which disrupts the context. However, the redactor was able to find a point of contact for the incorporation of the pericope of the adulteress specifically after John 7.53. In John 7.30; 7.44 and in a sense also in John 7.51, a reason is sought to condemn Jesus. This could have been given at the level of the final text with the testing of Jesus' faithfulness to the Torah in John 7.53–8.11.

A plausible explanation can also be given for the other places chosen for the pericope in other manuscripts. The link with John 7.37 is made clear by the interpretation of Jesus' writing on the ground as a reference to Jer. 17.3; the link to Luke 21.38 through the details fo the situation in John 8.1 and the proximity in content to the Lukan special material. The summary note in John 21.24 also provides sufficient occasion for the insertion of traditions.

The pericope of Jesus and the adulteress, which is attested early by Papias (c.125) and which probably developed redactionally, was presumably a free-floating tradition (Koester, Bultmann) that has left its traces above all in Jewish Christian writings (Gospel of the Hebrews; Protevangelium of James; Didascalia). However, it found a way into the four-Gospel canon only at a late stage (second or third century). This was probably in the context of the questions about penance which concerned the church, the discussion about the deadly sins (which included adultery), and the possibility of forgiving adultery.

Luke 6.5 (Codex D): A saying on the sabbath

On the same day he saw a man doing his work on the sabbath. Then he said to him, 'Man, if you know what you are doing you are blessed. But if you do not know, you are cursed and a transgressor of the law!'

The sabbath was an important mark of identity for the Jews of the time of Jesus and for that reason the precise way in which it was to be observed (exceptions relating to its observance) was disputed. Jesus' way of treating the sabbath belonged in the broad spectrum of possibilities. His attitude to the sabbath appears ambivalent in the canonical Gospels (cf. John 5.18; 9.16; Luke 6.5; with Luke 4.16, 31; Matt. 24.20) and thus scholars too have different views on it. However, there is no room to go into them here.

Jesus and the sabbath is a theme which also has had an effect beyond the New Testament writings. Here Jesus is often one-sidely made someone who abolished the Sabbath. Thus in the infancy stories of Thomas the following is reported of the young Jesus: on one sabbath he forms twelve sparrows from clay. When a Jew sees this and complains to Jesus' father about the desecration of the sabbath, Jesus brings the sparrows to life and makes them fly away. The Jews marvel.

In contrast to this legendary story, the sabbath special material from Codex D is sometimes regarded as authentic. However, this is to be doubted for several reasons. First, there is no parallel in the Synoptic Gospels to the beatitude in a casuistic formulation (cf. here Matt. 5.3ff.; Luke 6.20ff., but cf. John 13.17). On the other hand, a community controversy seems to be reflected in the sabbath logion from Codex D: Jesus' condemnation of the sabbath-breaker is not about *what* he does (for example good works as an exception to the sabbath rest) but about *his attitude* to his work. In the knowledge that salvation no longer lies in keeping the law, but that God has opened up a new way to salvation through faith in Jesus, the sabbath rest is no longer to be seen as absolute for believers. Only if people know why they are break-ing the sabbath rest is this right and admissible. This notion seems to be directed against a libertinistic understanding of the sabbath on the part of particular Christians (Käser).

The positioning of this agraphon in the Gospel of Luke is plausible. The sabbath plays a major role in this Gospel in particular (cf. Luke's special material: 13.10–17, healing of the woman bent double; 14.1–6, healing of a man with dropsy), so that it seemed suitable to insert additional material here. The choice of the precise place is also significant. Luke 6.1–5 contains the pericope about the disciples plucking corn on the sabbath; in Luke 6.6–11 Jesus heals a withered hand. The insertion of the saying about the sabbath after Luke 6.5 produces a trio of sabbath narratives.

The Letter of James (NHC I 2)

The Letter of James (NHC I 2) is presented here as an example of the Nag Hammadi writings in connection with authentic Jesus traditions. This apocryphon is a mixture of a letter framework, a revelation dialogue between Jesus and his disciples, and an ascension of the disciples. The writing begins as a letter (1.1–1.7);

then follows the appearance of Christ to all the disciples (2.8–35). Following this, Peter and James are separated from the other disciples for a revelation dialogue with Jesus (2.35–15.6). This dialogue makes up the greater part of the writing and contains Jesus traditions which could be authentic. The Letter of James ends with an ascension of James and Peter and their return to the other disciples (15.6–16.12), and an epistolary conclusion (16.13–30).

The Letter of James is to be dated to the second century and presupposes a fluid Jesus tradition of oral and written elements, as is suggested by formulations like 2.9ff. ('The twelve disciples were all sitting together and recalling what the Saviour had said to them . . .'). As in the Dialogue of the Saviour (NHC III 5) 140.1ff., there is also a series of parable titles. Some of these can be connected with the canonical parables; others refer to parables unknown from the New Testament, but which seem to have the same value as the canonical parables. Thus it is said in the Letter of James (NHC I 2) 7.37ff.: 'As I have been glorified before this time, why do you hold me back, although I am eager to go? For after the toil, you have compelled me to remain a further eighteen days with you for the parables. It was enough for some (to hear) the instruction, and they understood "the shepherds" (Luke 15.1–6) and "the sower" (Mark 4.3–9) and "the building" and "the virgins' lamps" (Matt. 25.1–13) and the "labourers' recompense" (Matt. 20.1–16) and "the didrachm" and "the woman" (Luke 15.8–10).'

The parables of the kingdom of heaven are particularly impressive in this Nag Hammadi writing; these partly echo the canonical Gospels, but in part offer new perspectives. Scholars (Hedrick, Cameron, Koester) have defined some of them as very old tradition, which stands on the same footing as the related Synoptic material.

As well as the parables of the kingdom, the Letter of James contains numerous sayings and sentences about the kingdom of God:

2.30ff.: 'No one will ever enter the kingdom of heaven at my bidding, but (only) if you are full . . . Be full, so that you do not take away; those who take away will not be saved'; 3.31ff.: 'Blessed are those who were not sick and who have known rest before they became sick. Theirs is the kingdom of God'; 6.5ff.: 'But those who have believed in my cross – theirs is the kingdom of God'; 6.17ff.: 'For the kingdom of God belongs to those who have been killed'; 9.32ff.: 'Do you have nothing now to do but to sleep, when it is appropriate you to be wakeful from the beginning so that the kingdom of heaven receives you?'; 13.27ff.: (Peter said:) 'Sometimes you invite us into the kingdom of heaven, and then again you reject us, Lord. Sometimes you persuade us, draw us to faith and promise us life, and then again you cast us far from the kingdom of heaven.'

These sayings, most of which are composed on a redactional level, have one thing in common: the kingdom of heaven is put in danger by the disciples and they must make an active contribution in order to come into possession of the kingdom of heaven or to remain in it abidingly – a notion which also occurs in the parable of the palm shoot (7.23–36) and the parable of the grain of wheat (8.16–26). It is keeping with this that a large part of what Jesus says in the letter of James consists of admonitions and woes.

In principle it should be noted that all the parables or sayings about the kingdom of heaven in the Letter of James are elements in lengthy discourses by Jesus. Although they are often only loosely attached to their context, it is sometimes difficult to extract the original tradition because of the redactional revision.

Letter of James 13.16–25: Admonition about the kingdom of heaven

1 Do not let the kingdom of heaven wither in you!

2 Do not be proud because of the light which illuminates (you).

3 Rather be to one another as I myself was to you. For your sakes I placed myself under the curse, that you might be redeemed.

This complex of sayings on the kingdom of heaven, which is typical of the Letter of James, initially indicates two things: the kingdom of heaven does not lie in the future but is present now, but at the same time is exposed to danger – a notion which governs the Letter of James (see above). The disciples are admonished about the kingdom of heaven. Instead of being certain of the kingdom of heaven and behaving proudly, they are to serve one another, following the example which Jesus has set them.

These notions have near equivalents in the New Testament preaching of Jesus (cf. only the example of the false self-confidence of the rich man in Luke 12.16–21 or the admonitions of Jesus to his disciples as e.g. in Matt. 24). It is important to be observant about the kingdom of heaven, for no one knows when the Son of man will come (cf. only Matt. 24.40–51; 25.13, etc.).

Nevertheless there are substantial objections to the authenticity of this complex of sayings. Saying 1 is strongly reminiscent of the technique of the redactor of the Letter of James. For example there is a comparable imperative statement at the beginning of the palm shoot parable (7.23ff.). Because of the theme of enlightenment, Saying 2 shows Gnostic influences. Saying 3 seems to presuppose Pauline christology (cf. Gal. 3.13; II Cor. 5.20f.).

Letter of James 7.22–35: The palm shoot parable about the kingdom of heaven

1 Do not allow the kingdom of heaven to wither.

2 For it is like a palm shoot whose fruit had fallen down on the ground around it. It (the fruit? The palm shoot?) bore leaves, and when they grew they caused their pith to dry up.

3 So too it is with [or: Thus it (viz. the kingdom of heaven) is like] the fruit which grew from this single root. After it had been planted, fruits were brought forth by many (viz. labours).

4 It (viz. the root) was indeed good, (and) if it were possible for you now (or: It would be good for you] to produce the new plants, you would find it (viz. the root/the kingdom of heaven).

The text of this first parable about the kingdom of heaven presents some difficulties or ambiguities in terms of language and content. First of all we should consider whether the redactional invitation not to let the kingdom of heaven wither (1) is to be referred to the whole parable (2 and 3) or only to the first half (2). At the same time this already raises the second decisive question, whether the passage contains two parables or a coherent image in the sense of a double parable (cf. e.g. Matt. 7.24–27 and Luke 6.47–49). The question of the subject (fruit? palm shoot?) in the imagery of the first saying in the parable is connected with this. Both translations are possible. There are similar linguistic ambiguities in the application to the hearers (4).

If we take the invitation (1) as a motto over the following connected parabolic sayings (Kirchner), these would be meant to indicate a way towards protecting the kingdom of heaven from withering. Accordingly the first image (2) depicts the wrong way to deal with the kingdom of heaven almost as a negative background: the fruit which by chance drops off falls on the ground (which is useless, because it has not been carefully chosen; cf. Mark 4.1–9 [4–7]) and chokes the kingdom of heaven: because of the careless sowing it is deprived of all nourishment and thus dries up. The second image (3) presents the positive way of dealing with the kingdom of heaven: the fruit planted thoughtfully has a good root and for its part brings for good fruit. However, plausible though this interpretation of the section as a double parable is, a further interpretation can be set alongside it.

Thus Cameron and Hedrick interpret the complex of images as the final form of a redactional process of growth. The second saying (3) is a secondary addition to the parable of the palm shoot pointing in a positive direction, whereas the parable was originally meant to make only a negative statement: the palm shoot goes beyond its limits and thus perishes. In that case the putting forth of leaves in 2 will also relate to the palm shoot and not, as in the first solution, to the fruit. In order to clarify the meaning of the parable, Cameron refers to depictions of the palm shoot by ancient authors. Because the unpollinated fruits on the dioecious date palm fall to the ground, they become unfruitful.

What is probably a redactional note (4) interprets the double parable in respect of the hearer: if the person is in a position to bring forth fruit, i.e. to convert people (for the term cf. I Tim. 3.6), he can see his roots, i.e. know that he himself is the carefully planted fruit. Other references suggest the interpretation that as a result of 'bearing fruit' the person finds the kingdom of heaven.

Simply because of the difficulty of interpreting the text, it is almost impossible to decide whether this parable has a basis in the preaching of Jesus. The mere fact that rural images drawn from agriculture are used here is hardly sufficient argument for a clear attribution to Jesus. Moreover it is striking that the kingdom of heaven is possible only 'through many (labours)' (3). This stands in opposition to the 'ease' with which the seed grows by itself (Mark 4.26–28,29) and could be an indication that there is already a crisis for the kingdom of heaven (and thus for the community).

Letter of James 8.16–26: The parable of the grain of wheat

1 Be zealously concerned for the word.

2 For as to the word, its first part is faith, its second love, its third deeds. For from these (viz. the actions) comes life.

3 For the word is like a grain of wheat: when someone had sown it, he had confidence in it. And when it grew, he loved it, because he saw many grains in place of one. And after he had worked, he was saved, as he had prepared it for food. Again he left some over to sow.

4 Thus it also possible for you to attain the kingdom of heaven for yourselves. Unless you receive it through knowledge, you cannot find it.

The word-parable of the grain of wheat (3) is firmly anchored in its redactional context. A sentence about the word (1), 'Be zealously concerned for the word', prefaces the section almost as a motto. This saying is explained in the triadic formula which follows: its properties are faith, love and deeds, which in the apodosis are further defined as life-giving and thus emphasized (an alternative point of reference not discussed here is that the giving of life stems from all three partial aspects of the word). The following parable now explains the properties of the word with the image of the grain of wheat that someone sows. The motif of sowing the word has its equivalent in the interpretation of the parable of the sower (Mark 4.3–8) in Mark 4.13–20.

The relationship between the sower and the word is clarified in the parable of the grain of wheat in three stages which deliberately relate to the foregoing triad: the sower has confidence (= faith) in it, he loves (= love) it because it bears fruit, and he works (= deeds) on it, which gives him salvation (= life; cf. the addition to the triadic definition of the word in 2). The ongoing effect of this process, which is rich in blessing, is illustrated by the care taken over the coming sowing. The conclusion of the section (4), which has Gnostic colouring, refers the complex of images of the word to the kingdom of heaven and interprets the parable in terms of the hearer; here knowledge seems to fulfil the saving functions of the actions: the kingdom of heaven cannot be found without a concern for knowledge (of one's own). Here too emphasis is put on the (spiritual) action of human beings. With its emphasis on the active attitude of the disciples in the face of the kingdom of heaven or the sower in the face of the word, the parable fits in very well with the paraenetic tenor of the whole of the Letter of James (see the sayings about the kingdom of heaven above; cf. also 12.9ff.; 14.14ff.).

The extremely close connection between faith and work has a parallel in the New Testament letter of James, which sets a synergistic relationship between faith and work over against a radical Paulinism of its time. Thus James 2.14–26 says: 'My brothers, what does it profit if someone says that he has faith but does not have works? Can faith save him? If a brother or a sister is without clothing and without daily bread and one of you said to him, "Go in peace, be warmed and filled," but gives them nothing that they need for life – what use is that? So too faith by itself is dead, if it has no works to show . . . For as the body apart from the spirit is dead, so too faith apart from works is dead.'

The parable of the grain of wheat is certainly not to be reckoned genuine Jesus tradition. Certainly the demand for human beings to be active in the face of the kingdom of heaven and the word of God has a basis in the preaching of Jesus; there are references to this not only in the twofold commandment to love (Matt. 22.39 par.) but also in the sayings of Jesus about entering the kingdom of heaven (above all Mark 10.25), Jesus' threats of judgment, the references to a notion of recompense (e.g. Mark 9.41 par.), etc. Rather, the following are the reasons which tell against an authentic Jesus tradition: the parable is anchored so well in the preceding triadic formula that the parable seems to have been written for this context. Moreover the absolute use of 'word' is certainly not at home in the authentic Jesus tradition (cf. also Mark 4.13–20).

Letter of James 12.20–30: The kingdom of heaven parable about the ear

1 I tell you this so that you may know yourselves.

2 For the kingdom of heaven is like an ear which grew in a field. And when it was ripe it scattered its fruit and again filled the field with ears for another year.

3 But you, hasten now to reap an ear of life for yourselves, that you may be filled with the kingdom.

This parable too uses the images of Jesus from a rural-agricultural sphere. Attention can be drawn above all to Mark 4.26–28, 29 (the seed growing by itself). Further reference could be made to Mark 4.3–9 par. (parable of the Sower); Mark 4.30–32 par. (parable of the grain of mustard seed); Matt. 13.33 (parable of the leaven).

The real parable (2) is framed by a redactional introduction which is focussed on (Gnostic?) self-knowledge (1) and an application to the hearers (3). There is argument over the interpretation of the parable: is the kingdom of heaven compared with a single ear, which by multiplying brings forth an abundance of fruit (Severin), or is the kingdom of God described by the image of the contrast, i.e. the tension of how a tremendously great end can stem from the small beginning (cf. Mark 4.31 and Matt.

13.22 with Luke 13.18) (Hedrick?). Probably the interlocking of the two aspects indicates what the parable is saying: the kingdom of heaven is described in the tension between its presence (cf. e.g. Luke 17.20ff.; Mark 1.15ff.; Matt. 11.12; 12.22–30; Luke 10.18) and the consummation which is still to come (cf. e.g. Luke 13.28; Mark 14.25). The great end is already anticipated in the small beginning. This phenomenon is explained by the image of growth: the kingdom of heaven unstoppably spreads itself year by year with a snowball effect which has all the 'certainty of a natural event' (Weder), until the individual ears become a whole field of ears. In both its imagery and its intention this parable stands on a level with the Synoptic parables which have been mentioned.

The redactional conclusion interprets the parable in terms of the hearers. They are to advance the kingdom of heaven in themselves with their efforts. This direction of interpretation corresponds both to the image of the grain of wheat (8.16–26) and to the paraenetic tendency of the whole of the Letter of James.

The Strasbourg Coptic Papyrus

The Strasbourg Coptic Papyrus offers some apocryphal Jesus traditions. This text seems to present an independent Gospel, but it is hardly possible to define its form and content because the text is so damaged (the following translation is along the lines of the edition by A.Jacoby, *Ein neues Evangelienfragment*, 1900). It is almost impossible to relate it to known non-canonical Gospels. The date of origin of this apocryphon is difficult to define: the marked dependence on New Testament writings suggests that it is late. The recognizable thrust of the text makes the Strasbourg Coptic Papyrus look like a kind of 'farewell story of Jesus' which consists in a prayer of Jesus, a farewell conversation with the disciples, a transfiguration of Jesus (ascension? resurrection?) and the equipping of the apostles which takes the form of an account of a vision. The passion or crucifixion of Jesus is not described. With this outline the fragment corresponds closely to the Gospel of the Saviour (see below).

A prayer of Jesus

(Recto 5) (Jesus said): '. . . it (viz. the tree) will be known by its fruits so that it is praised for its strange fruit, for it surpasses the mass of the (trees) of the garden. Now give me your power, Father, so that . . . those who love . . . Amen. I have taken the crown of glory, namely the crown of those who live and are despised in their humility as no one is equal to them. I have become king through you, my Father. You subject this enemy to me. Amen. Through whom will the enemy be ground to pieces? Through the anointed. Amen. Through whom will the sting of death be destroyed? Through the Only-Begotten. Amen. To whom does the glory belong. It belongs to the Son. Amen. Through whom has everything come into being? Through the firstborn . . .'

This prayer of Jesus has a distinct form, in that its construction is very well planned. Each of the individual (rhetorical) questions with their christological answers is concluded with 'Amen'. This structure is not unique in the apocryphal literature but has equivalents in the dance hymn from the Acts of John (87–105), a liturgical interchange between Jesus and his disciples in the Gnostic Book of Jeu from the Bruce Codex (1 Jeu 41), and some hymnic discourses of Jesus from the Gospel of the Saviour (see below). In their stylized-artificial form, none of these prayers or liturgical dialogues derive from Jesus, but are elaborations of Mark 14.26 (cf. Augustine, *Letter* 237,4 about the dance hymn from the Acts of John mentioned above: 'The hymn of the Lord, which he communicated in secret to the holy apostles, the disciples, and of which it is written in the Gospel, "After he had spoken the hymn he went up the mountain," and which is not in the canonical [scriptures]').

As well as this widespread liturgical scheme, in the case of Strasbourg Coptic Papyrus R 5 the secondary character is already evident from the combination of the titles of Christ (anointed, only-begotten, firstborn).

In terms of content, in the prayer from Strasbourg Coptic papyrus R 5 there are allusions e.g. to Matt. 7.16 par.; Phil. 2.6–11 and above all to the Gospel of John (John 17, etc.). The theme seems to be the imminent suffering of Jesus, in the face of which he asks his Father for power; it is conceivable that the 'strange fruit' in the opening words is to be interpreted in terms of the passion of Jesus, the 'tree' (cf. similarly John 12.24ff.). However, in contrast, say, to the Gethsemane scene (Mark 14.32–42 par.), the rule of Jesus and his power over the enemy is the defining element.

A farewell conversation

(Verso 5) . . . now when he had completed the whole matter of his life, he turned to us and spoke to us: 'The hour is near when I shall be taken from you. The spirit is indeed willing but the flesh is weak. Remain now and watch with me.' But we, the apostles, we wept and we said to him, 'Do not rebuke us, Son of God. For what is our end?' And Jesus answered and said to us: 'Do not fear that I will be destroyed, but rather take heart. Do not fear the power of death. Remember all that I have said to you. Know that they have persecuted me as one has persecuted . . . Now rejoice that I have overcome the world. I have . . .'

If the prayer of Jesus from R 5 with its link to Mark 14.26 apparently indicates the location of the fragment in the passion story, this is confirmed in what follows. After the hymn Jesus turns to the disciples and confronts them with his imminent suffering. They react with sorrow (cf. John 16.20) and express anxiety about their own end, whereupon they are comforted by Jesus. The whole passage is filled with allusions to and quotations from the Synoptic Gospels, especially the Gospel of Matthew (Matt. 26.45; 26.41; 26.38; but cf. also John 15.18ff.; 16.33). In contrast to the high christology in the preceding prayer (R 5) and the adoption of John 16.33 (R 5), here Jesus seems in some parts to be depicted in completely human terms, as is shown by the transfer of Mark 14.36 or Matt. 26.41 ('The spirit is willing, the flesh is weak') from the mouth of the disciples to his own person. This 'remarkable mixture of the Johannine picture of Christ with the Synoptic picture' (Jacoby) indicates a late origin for the text.

An account of a vision of the apostles

(Recto 6) (Jesus said) 'I have revealed to you all my glory and I have shown you all your power and the mystery of your apostolate. I have given you, Mary . . . power . . . on the mountain.'

(Verso 6) Our eyes penetrated all places. We saw the glory of his divinity and the whole glory of his rule. He clothed us with the power of his apostolate . . . They were like . . . light.

The account of a vision which follows cannot be reconstructed precisely. Formally it describes an announcement by Jesus (R 6) that he will show the apostles his glory and endow them with their apostolate, the fulfilment of which the apostles go on to report in the first person plural report (V 6). Again there is an allusion to a passage of John, namely John 1.14 ('We saw his glory'). With its linking of the revelation of the glory to the mountain (R 6), the scene recalls both the transfiguration of Jesus (Mark 9.2–10) and also his ascension, whose witnesses the apostles will become in Acts 1.9–11 (cf. also Luke 24.50f.). The suffering of Jesus is followed by the manifestation of his glory, which is combined with the constitution of the apostolate of the disciples and the charge implied in it. The equipping of the apostles evokes associations with John 20.22; Luke 24.49 and the sending out in Matt. 28.

Oxyrhynchus Papyrus

This parchment from the fourth century offers numerous religious traditions as well as profane texts. In 1897 Oxyrhynchus Papyrus 1 (= Gospel of Thomas [NHC II 2]) was published, and shortly afterwards further fragments of the Gospel of Thomas were edited with Oxyrhynchus Papyrus 654 and 655, until in 1905 the great fragment 840 about a previously unknown dispute of Jesus with a Pharisee was made known (see below). Further fragments of this papyrus have been subsequently edited down to the present day, including parts of the Gospel of Peter (POxy 2949; 4009).

Oxyrhynchus Papyrus 840a: fragment of a discourse of Jesus

(Jesus said:) 'Before he acts unjustly he devises everything cunningly. But be careful that you do not suffer the same fate as they. For not only is retribution inflicted on transgressors among men among the living, but they must also endure punishment and great torment.'

These sentences are the conclusion of a discourse of Jesus which is no longer extant. What we have is an admonition (to the disciples?) against false security (cf. similarly Luke 13.5). The fragment is too short and the content and the context and audience of the discourse cannot be ascertained, so that nothing certain can be said about the historical probability of this originating with Jesus.

Oxyrhynchus Papyrus 840b: a controversy over true cleanness

And he took them (viz. the disciples) with him into the place of purification itself and walked about in the temple court. And a Pharisaic chief priest, Levi by name, fell in with them and said to the Saviour, 'Who allowed you to tread the place of purification and to look upon these holy vessels without bathing and without your disciples washing (even) their feet? Rather, you have trodden the temple court, this clean place, defiled, although no one who has not first bathed himself or changed his clothes may tread it and venture to view these holy vessels.' Immediately the Saviour stood still with his disciples and answered, 'And you? You too are here on the temple court. Are you then clean?' He said to him, 'Yes, I am clean. For I have bathed myself in the pool of David and have gone down by the one stair and come up by the other and have put on white and clean clothes, and (only) then have I come here and viewed these holy vessels.' The Saviour answered and said to him, 'Woe to you blind who do not see! You have bathed yourself in this water that has been poured out, in which dogs and pigs lie night and day, and you have washed yourself and scraped your outer skin, which prostitutes and flute-girls also anoint, bathe, scrape and adorn, in order to arouse the desires of men, but within they are full of scorpions and of badness of every kind. But I and my disciples, of whom you say that we have not immersed ourselves, have been immersed in the living, pure water which has come down from the Father in heaven. But woe to those who . . .'

What Jeremias has called a 'pearl of Gospel narrative art' takes place in the temple forecourt. As so often, the behaviour of Jesus and the disciples is offensive to the Jews and the starting point for a controversy or a discussion of Jesus with the Pharisees, Sadducees or scribes (cf. e.g. Mark 2.13–17; 2.23–28). The closest parallels to the Synoptic pericopes are to be found in Mark 7.1–23 or Matt. 15.1–20, where in the opinion of the Pharisees Jesus and his disciples are not observing the regulations about cleanness. Thereupon Jesus enlightens them about true cleanness and uncleanness: external cleanness cannot wipe away the true uncleanness in a person (for the theme of true cleanness see also the sayings about the scribes and Pharisees in Matt. 23.27f.)

There are numerous reminiscences in the canonical Gospels (cf. e.g. Mark 11.27; John 13.10; Matt. 15.14; Matt. 23; Matt. 7.6; also Rev. 22.15). In form, the fragmentary text is a dispute 'in Synoptic style' (Jeremias) but enriched throughout with novellistic features and related more to 'mixed forms' like Mark 2.1–12 and John 7.53–8.11.

It is questionable whether the controversy involving Jesus on the temple forecourt is historical. Among other reasons, this is because the concluding saying of Jesus cannot be reconstructed precisely. The conclusion of the fragment and thus the decisive words of Jesus are hard to read; but probably there is an allusion to baptism as a cleansing of sins. The negative attitude towards prostitution is striking (for the prostitutes and flute players see also the Gospel of the Nazarenes, Eusebius, *De theophania* IV 22) and is difficult to associate with Jesus' propensity towards social outcasts (cf. here especially Luke 7.36ff.). Moreover the cultic features in the fragment are not readily harmonized with the knowledge we have of this sphere in the time of Jesus, or at least are in need of explanation (Schürer against Jeremias). Furthermore the extended explanation of Jewish customs points to a remoteness in time and place from Palestine in the time of Jesus.

Oxyrhynchus Papyrus 1224: Sayings of Jesus

175 And when the scribes and Pharisees and priests saw him, they were angry that he reclined at table in the midst of sinners. But Jesus heard it and said, 'The healthy do not need the physician.

176 And pray for your enemies. For he who is not against you is for you. He who today is far off – tomorrow he will be near to you.'

Here Jesus' answer to the charges of the Pharisees, which are also contained in the canonical scriptures (Luke 7.36ff.; Mark 2.15ff.), consists of a collection of logia, some of which are attested in the New Testament writings. The statements of Jesus on page 175 echo Mark 12.16f., those on page 176, Matt. 5.44 and Luke 9.50. Only the sentence 'He who today is far off – tomorrow he will be near to you' has no parallel in the canonical scriptures. According to Jeremias, who sees this saying as an authentic saying of Jesus also because of stylistic characteristics (parallelismus membrorum; antithetical formulation), the sentence expresses the same message as the contrast parables about the kingdom of heaven (Mark 4.30–32): Jesus wants to give the disciples confidence and make plausible to them the breaking in of the kingdom of heaven, which today seems so remote. Here the emphasis is particularly on the interpersonal level, as is already suggested by the preceding logia: anyone who today is the enemy of the disciples can be one of them as early as tomorrow!

The Gospel of Peter

In addition to the passages from Oxyrhynchus Papyrus cited above there are also further fragments of this parchment. One is POxy 4009. This short piece is probably an element from a larger text, namely the Gospel of Peter (D. Lührmann, 'POx 4009: Ein neues Fragment des Petrusevangeliums?', *NT* 35, 1993, 390ff.). This apocryphal Gospel – already at an early stage known by name from the reports of the church fathers – is presumably further made up of the Fayyum fragment (PVindob G 2325) and above all of the famous passion story (Akhmim fragment [PCair 10759]; there are also parts in POxy 2949), which for reasons of space can only be given in summary form in what follows.

If we put the fragments of conversation from POxy 4009, PVindob G2325 and, with qualifications, II Clement 5.2–4 alongside the Akhmim fragment, we get a new picture of the Gospel of Peter with a Synoptic stamp: in addition to the extensive description of the passion it contains conversations between Jesus and Peter which Peter – and this is the big difference from the other Gospels – hands on in a first-person report. The result is an extensive apocryphon (to be expanded further?) which in the light of its basis in the sources can at least be dated to the second century AD.

The Fayyum Fragment: The announcement of Peter's denial of Jesus

After the meal according to custom he said, 'You will all take offence at me this night, as it is written, I will smite the shepherd and the sheep will be scattered.' When [I: reconstructed following Lührmann], Peter, had said, 'Even if all (do this), not I,' Jesus said, 'Before the cock crows twice, today you will deny me three times.'

The Fayyum fragment (P Vindob G 2325) was published as early as 1885. This short conversation between Jesus and Peter picks up Matt. 26.31–34 and Mark 14.27–30, though the canonical text is not taken up in its entirety. The fragment does not contain any reference forward to the meeting in Galilee after the resurrection of Jesus (Mark 14.28/Matt. 26.32); Peter's answer is notably briefer than in the New Testament texts. But like Mark 14.30, PVindob G 2325 does not know the twofold cock-crow and has sometimes been interpreted as a preliminary stage of the text of Mark. Because of its 'chreia-like abbreviation', Dibelius has attributed this logion to a source of sayings of Jesus; by contrast Lührmann is inclined to interpret the scene as part of the Gospel of Peter. The Fayyum fragment has often been regarded as a secondary précis of the Gospel text.

The Akhmim fragment: The passion of Jesus

The Akhmim fragment was discovered in 1886/1887 and made available to the public in 1892. It is a passion account which is often dated to the first half of the second century; in some points it differs from the material of the canonical Gospels. It includes accounts of Pilate washing his hands, the burial of Jesus, the guard on the tomb, the discovery of the tomb, the return of the disciples to Galilee and a scene with Peter, Andrew and Levi by Lake Gennesaret. The most important characteristics of its content are probably its anti-Judaism and the speaking cross, which time and again has led scholars to suppose that this apocryphal account of the passion has a docetic tendency. The general opinion is that the Akhmim fragment uses both earlier traditions (reference back to the Old Testament) and later ones (exoneration of Pilate, etc.) traditions, in which it is possible to make out both orthodox and heretical elements.

There is controversy over the relationship of this passion fragment to the reports in the canonical Gospels and thus over its age. Koester sees it as a very old and original tradition, independent of the canonical Gospels (similarly Crossan); Dibelius and Vielhauer disagree.

There is no usable information about the historical Jesus in the passion fragment, and knowledge of Palestine in the time of Jesus seems to be very limited. Features appear which are strongly legendary, like the exoneration of Pilate and a conversation between the robbers crucified alongside Jesus, which later became a favourite motif in the apocryphal Pilate tradition.

Oxyrhynchus Papyrus 4009: Conversation of the Risen One (?) with Peter

Oxyrhynchus Papyrus 4009: (Jesus said): '. . . the harvest. But be as guileless as the doves and as wise as the serpents. You will be like sheep among wolves.' I said to him, 'Will we be torn now?' He answered and said to me, 'If the wolves have torn the sheep they can do no more to it. Therefore I say to you: Do not fear those who kill you and after the killing can do no more' (reconstruction following Lührmann).

II Clement 5.2–4: The Lord said: 'You will be like sheep in the midst of wolves.' Peter answered and said to him, 'What if the wolves tear the sheep?' Jesus said to Peter, 'The sheep should not fear the wolves after they have died. And you should not fear those who kill you and are not in a position (really) to do anything to you. But fear the one who has power over your soul and your body, to cast it into the fire of hell after you have died.'

The dialogue between an (initially anonymous) first person narrator and Jesus in POxy 4009 is strongly reminiscent of the Synoptic Gospels. There are echoes of the mission discourse in Matt. 9.35–10.42, but some of the motifs are in a different order (cf. the reverse sequence of Matt. 10.16b). The disciples are promised confidence because of their anxiety about persecution; here the imagery is abandoned and the disciples are addressed directly. The power of their persecutors is destroyed with the death of the disciples. As the parallel from II Clement makes clear, however, the power of God extends beyond death: if the disciples are to have fear, then it should be of God, who can deliver the disciples over to eternal damnation (Matt. 10.28).

II Clement (composed around 150), which is probably the earliest Christian homily, offers a parallel to POxy 4009 and has also been used by Lührmann to reconstruct the Oxyrhynchus fragment. In both cases passages like Matt. 10.16/ Luke 10.3 and Matt. 10.28/Luke 12.4f. are combined in a dialogue; it is unclear whether one version presupposes the other or whether the Jesus material has been taken up by each independently. Moreover II Clem. 5.2–4 sheds light on the anonymous conversation partner of Jesus in POxy 4009, who now can be identified as Peter. Since a prominent feature of the Gospel of Peter is Peter as a narrator in the first person, it is appropriate to interpret POxy 4009 as an element of the Gospel of Peter.

It is not certain at what point in the gospel of Peter the fragment from POxy 4009 is to be put. If one uses the Synoptic chronology as a basis, then POxy 4009 would have to be put before the passion fragment as a mission discourse. Conceivably – and typical of second-century literature – the conversation between Jesus and Peter is to be put in the time after the passion (cf. the Freer Logion, the Letter of James and the later apocryphal conversations of the Risen One). This is also suggested by a look at the end of the Akhmim fragment: the text ends with the gathering and mourning of the disciples of Jesus, who go to the sea (cf. John 21.11ff.). An appearance of the Risen One could have been attached here, and a conversation between Jesus and Peter (cf. John 21.15ff.; also Luke 24.34; I Cor. 15.5) could have followed, of which POxy 4009 gives us a brief glimpse. The theme of the fragment (the disciples' fear of persecution) is also a frequent motif in the discourses of the Risen One (cf. e.g. the letter of Peter to Philip [NHC VIII 2] 134.3ff.; 138.10ff.).

Berlin Papyrus 11710

Nathanael's confession

He made a confession and said, 'Rabbi, Lord, you are the Son of God.' The rabbi (answered him) and said, 'Nathanael, walk in the sun!' Nathanael answered him and said, 'Rabbi, Lord, you are the lamb of God who bears the sin of the world.' The rabbi (answered him) and said . . .

Berlin Papyrus 11710 (H.Lietzmann, 'Ein apokryphes Evangelienfragment', *ZNW* 22, 1923, 153f.) represents a brief conversation between Jesus and his disciple Nathanael (cf. John 1.45–51). The papyrus is not to be dated before the fourth century, but the form of address to Jesus is archaic and not often attested in late apocrypha (but cf. also the Syrian *Transitus Mariae* traditions). On the verso of the fragment is a confession written in Coptic ('Jesus Christ God'). This suggests the magical use of the papyrus as an amulet text. The text on the recto picks up the first part of Nathanael's christological confession in John 1.49 but develops into a brief dialogue between Jesus and Nathanael. Nathanael's confession is followed by the retort of Jesus (in the text always rabbi) which is a *crux interpretum* (see below). To this is joined a further confession of Nathanael, which in the Gospel of John appears in the mouth of John the Baptist (1.29). Jesus' response to Nathanael's second confession is recognizable only from the insertion formula which has been preserved.

There are passages comparable to this text in the pericope of Peter's messianic confession (Mark 8.27–30) or in Thomas 13. In all cases the issue is the appropriate interpretation of the person of Jesus by his disciples.

Jesus' sentence 'Walk in the sun', which he gives as an answer to Nathanael's first confession, is not attested in the canonical writings and according to Lietzmann shows Manichaean influence (Augustine, *On the Heresies* 46, etc.): according to Manichaean notions, in the course of its return the soul which has been purified ascends to true being, into the heavenly kingdom of God, on the barque of the moon and the sun. If this notion underlies the logion of Jesus, then the saying is to be interpreted as a wish for a blessing and means that Nathanael has made an appropriate statement about the nature of Jesus. Eisler understands the logion differently: in his view it is a repudiation of Nathanael by Jesus (cf. similarly the repudiation of Peter in Mark 8.33) and means something like, 'You are crazy, you have sunstroke'. This rebuke declares the christological confession to be false.

Although the first interpretation is unimportant for the sayings of the historical Jesus because of the Manichaean colouring in the question, there could be an apocryphal Nathanael tradition in the second interpretation of the 'sun logion'. But as the drift and continuation of the conversation can no longer be ascertained, no certain judgment can be made.

Egerton Papyrus 2

What we have of the papyrus structurally resembles an apocryphal Gospel and displays a clear division: the first controversy of Jesus with his opponents, which almost leads to the stoning of Jesus, is followed by a demonstration of Jesus' power in the healing of a leper. To this is attached Jesus' second controversy with his opponents over the question of tax, whereupon Jesus shows his power in the form of the miracle at the Jordan. The relationship between miracles and conversations or discourses of John is likewise a striking characteristic of the divisions in the Gospel of John.

This fragment, which comes from the second century, consists of several parts:

the first part has a markedly Johannine stamp (cf. John 5.39, 45; 9.29; 12.31; 5.46; 10.31; 7.30; 10.39); the central pericopes show more Synoptic echoes (Mark 1.40–44 par.; Mark 12.13–17 par., etc.). The conclusion of the fragment, the so-called Jordan miracle, has no basis in the canonical writings nor is it attested in apocryphal writings, and thus represents special material in the papyrus. Unfortunately this particular passage is heavily damaged.

Because of its great age and its non-legendary character especially by comparison with other apocryphal Gospels, there is a dispute as to whether Egerton Papyrus 2 knows and presupposes the canonical Gospels or offers similar, if not even more original, material independently of them. Jeremias argues for a dependence on canonical traditions, but e.g. Mayeda does not think this necessary. Dodd occupies an intermediate position: Egerton Papyrus 2 is merely dependent on John.

Conversation between Jesus and the leaders of the people

Jesus said to the experts in the law: 'Punish every transgressor and lawless person but not me, for it is untested what he does, how he does it.' And he turned to the rulers of the people and said this word: 'Search in the scriptures, in which you think you have life. It is they that bear witness about me. Do not believe that I have come to accuse you to my Father. The one who accuses you is Moses, on whom you have set your hope.' And when they said, 'We know well that God has spoken to Moses. But as for you, we do not know where you have come from,' Jesus answered and said to them, 'Now your unbelief is accused in regard of what is testified by him. For if you had believed Moses you would believe me; for your fathers have written about me . . .'

This pericope presupposes an action or a saying of Jesus on the basis of which he has to defend himself against his opponents (cf. e.g. Mark 7.1ff.). Jesus' discourse shows verbal parallels to John 5.39, 45, 46; 9.29. The motif that Moses and the Old Testament would point to Jesus, which can be found in the New Testament (cf. e.g. Acts 10.43; I Peter 1.11), and above all in Matthew (the reflective quotations) is presented once again in the passage about the question of tax (see below). The same goes for the unbelief of the Jews in this connection. Moreover reference can be made to the pericopes which have the identity of Jesus as their theme (e.g. Matt. 16.13–20; Thomas 13; but especially John 7.37–52).

All in all, this controversy between Jesus with his opponents does not offer any new material. It is difficult to locate the scene in the life of the historical Jesus, because the beginning and thus the reason for the exchange of words has not been preserved. Moreover the dependence above all on the Gospel of John rules out the possibility of an origin with Jesus.

An attempt to arrest Jesus

They pulled him and gathered stones to crucify him. And the rulers laid hands on him to arrest him and to deliver him to the crowd. But they could not arrest him because the hour when he was to be delivered up had not yet come. But he himself, the Lord, escaped their hands and went away from them.

The attempt to kill Jesus seems to take place as a result of the blasphemy in the previous section (blasphemy of God is punished with death; cf. John 8.59; 10.30f.). The text is not completely clear. Is Jesus to be stoned or crucified? The decisive fact is that the intended killing of Jesus at this point had not yet been foreseen in the plan of salvation history. In a sovereign way Jesus evades his persecutors (John 8.59; 10,39; cf. also John 7.30; 8.20 and Luke 4.30).

The healing of a leper

And look, a leper came to him and said, 'Teacher Jesus, when I was travelling with lepers and ate with them in an inn, I myself became leprous. If you now will, I shall become clean.' Then the Lord said, 'I will, be clean.' And immediately the leprosy departed from him. And the Lord said to him, 'Go and show yourself to the priests, and bring (an offering) for the cleansing as Moses has ordained, and sin no more . . .'

The healing of the leper has a parallel in Mark 1.40–44 par. However, some modifications are to be noted which indicate that the version in Egerton Papyrus 2 is secondary to the Synoptic story (thus also Neirynck). Here first of all mention should be made of the special material: the reference by the sick person to the reason for his illness, namely infection in an inn, is hardly possibly historically, since according to Lev. 13.46 lepers had to keep apart from the healthy population (Burkitt; but cf. Mark 14.3). Moreover the information about the condition for the desired healing from the mouth of the sick person is untypical in the Synoptic miracles; usually there is only a request for healing (but cf. Luke 9.37ff., where the father asks for healing for his possessed son because he is his only son); in miraculous healings in the New Testament the reason for the healing is usually the faith of the sick person (cf. e.g. Mark 5.21ff.). Somewhat parallel to the healing of the leper in the Egerton Papyrus is the case in the Jewish Christian Gospel of the Nazareans, where as an extension of Matt. 12.9ff. par. (the healing of the man with the withered hand on the sabbath), the request of the sick man is elaborated as follows: 'I was a mason and earned (my) living with (my) hands. I beg you, Jesus, to restore my health so that I may not have to beg for my bread with ignomiy' (Jerome, *Commentary on Matthew*, on 12.13).

 Alongside this novellistic feature of giving some form of justification to the request for healing, the present healing of a leper offers no description of the course of healing or Jesus' action (but cf. Mark 1.41). Only the saying of Jesus makes the sick man well.

The question of tax

They came with the intention of testing him, to tempt him, by saying, 'Teacher Jesus, we know that you have come from God. For what you do bears testimony about all the prophets. Tell us now, is it lawful to give to the kings that which is due to the authorities? Should we give it to them or not?' But Jesus saw through their intention and angrily said to them: 'Why do you call me teacher with your mouth without hearing what I say? Aptly did Isaiah prophesy about you when he said, This people honours me with their lips but their heart is far from me. In vain they worship me because they do not follow my precepts (or: Vain is their worship. They teach precepts of men).'

This episode from the life of Jesus, too, is not without Synoptic parallels. The question of tax occurs in Mark 12.13–17 par. However, Jesus' answer ('give to Caesar what is Caesar's . . .') is not handed down in the Egerton Papyrus. For Crossan this is a reason to conjecture that Egerton Papyrus 2 is an earlier stage than Mark 12.13–17. Instead of Jesus' famous sentence from Mark 12.17 par., here we have a reference to the statement by Jesus' opponents which introduces their question, namely that Jesus' action bears testimony about all the prophets. Jesus unmasks the hypocrisy of the questioners: the prophet Isaiah has already seen and condemned the lip-service of the people (Isa. 29.13). This retort of Jesus as a consequence of a controversy with his opponents appears in the Synoptic tradition in the pericope about the question of cleanness (Mark 7.1–23 par.). Thus two New Testament pericopes seem to have been combined.

The miracle at the Jordan

. . . Because he shut (it) up in a hidden place, it became as though invisible underneath and its fullness was transitory. But when they were put to confusion by his displeasing question, Jesus went around and went to the bank of the river Jordan, stretched out his right hand, filled it with water, and scattered (it) on the bank. And then the earth absorbed the water that had been sown when it had taken the seed. And it was filled before them and brought forth much fruit for joy . . .

The miracle at the Jordan is very much special material of the Egerton papyrus and is almost impossible to interpret because the state of the text is so bad. It is probable that, like the healing of the leper, this miracle too is an immediate reaction to a controversy of Jesus with his opponents. Jesus puts them to confusion with a displeasing question (for the motif of amazement about Jesus cf. e.g. Luke 20.26: conclusion of the pericope about the question of tax!) and shows them a miracle.

Lietzmann wants to see the symbolic action of Jesus as analogous to the activity of an Indian fakir who before the eyes of his public sows water on the ground and immediately makes a plant spring up. This 'illusion of oriental magicians' would not tell in favour of the originality of the Jordan miracle, but assign the passage to Gnostic apocryphal traditions.

Jesus traditions from the church fathers

The following sayings are only a brief selection from the material of the sayings of Jesus handed down by the church fathers. Scholars have often regarded the examples cited here as authentic.

The Secret Gospel of Mark

And they came to Bethany and there was a woman there whose brother was dead. And she came and did honour to Jesus. And she said to him, 'Son of David, have mercy on me.' But the disciples rebuked her. And in anger Jesus turned round and went away with her into the garden where the tomb was, and immediately a loud voice was heard from the tomb. And Jesus went forward and rolled away the stone from the door of the tomb. And immediately he went in where the young man was. He stretched out his hand and raised him up, grasping him by the hand. But the young man looked upon him and loved him. And he began to ask him that he might remain with him. 32 And when they had gone out from the tomb, they went into the young man's house; for he was rich. And after six days Jesus commanded him (to come to him). And when evening had fallen, the young man went to him clothed only in a linen cloth upon his naked skin. And he remained with him there that night; for Jesus was teaching him the mysteries of the kingdom of God. And from there he arose and returned to the other bank of the Jordan.

(And he came to Jericho.) And there were there the sisters of the young man whom Jesus loved, and his mother and Salome. And Jesus did not bid them welcome.

Most recently, the so-called 'Secret Gospel of Mark' is an example of apocryphal information about Jesus traditions from the church fathers. In 1958 it was 'discovered' by M.Smith in a hitherto unknown letter attributed to Clement of Alexandria. In the letter of Clement there is a Jesus tradition which represents a supplement to Mark 10.34. The resurrection of a young man in Bethany and his subsequent instruction by Jesus is described. A second scene (insertion after Mark 10.46a) depicts the encounter of Jesus with the women. The quotations and echoes of New Testament writings are marked (cf. above all the Gospel of Mark: Mark 10.21; Mark 9.2; Mark 14.51; Mark 4.11; for the disciple whom Jesus loved cf. the Gospel of John). In addition to these phrases, for the theme of the pericope reference should be made above all to John 11 (raising of Lazarus); Matt. 9.18–26 par (raising of Jairus' daughter) and more remotely Luke 7.11–17 (raising of the young man in Nain).

According to Clement's report, this short fragment belongs to a secret Gospel of Mark which is a spiritual version of the canonical Mark and was in use among Gnostics. According to Smith, this Gospel of Mark, which is basically preserved only in the short fragment quoted by Clement, represents a revision of the canonical Mark which uses Markan material about Jesus the magician. Yet Koester and Crossan regard the fragment as a preliminary stage of the canonical Mark. However, it is probable that this is a revision and reshaping of the canonical Gospel of Mark using secondary (Gnostic?) material. This is suggested not only by the striking references to some New Testament texts but also by the close affinity to John 11.

Syriac Liber Graduum, Serm. III 3, XV 4

As you are found, so you will be led away (to judgment).

This logion is attested often and is also attributed to Jesus in Justin (*Dialogue with Trypho* 47.5: 'Wherein I encounter you, therein I will also judge you'). In other sources the logion is attributed to Ezekiel and is sometimes regarded as part of an apocryphal book of Ezekiel (cf. the link to Ezek. 33.20). But as the Syriac *Liber Graduum* offers the earliest version, the attribution to Jesus seems to be primary. In content the logion can be compared with passages like Luke 17.20–37 and Matt. 25.1–13: the judgment is always near and people should not ignore the seriousness of the hour and relax in false security.

Clement of Alexandria, Stromateis I 24, 158

Ask for the great and God will do the little for you.

This logion, which has been handed down by Origen and Ambrose in a long version ('Ask for the great and God will do the little; and ask for the heavenly and God will do the earthly for you') has close parallels in language and content to the Jesus tradition in the New Testament writings. Alongside Matt. 6.33; Luke 12.31, mention should be made above all of Jesus' sayings about right and wrong anxieties (Matt. 6.19–34 par.). It is necessary to keep one's eye on the truly important things, namely the kingdom of heaven. Everyday earthly cares will resolve themselves. There are similar notions e.g. in the parable of the true treasure (Matt. 6.19, 21 par) or also in the mission discourse to the disciples (Matt. 10.28ff.): there must be no anxiety about bodily life but only about eternal life (cf. similarly also Luke 10.20 on the true joy). This notion comes to a head in the overall view of discipleship as self-denial and the gaining of eternal life (Matt. 16.24–28): 'What does it benefit a man to gain the whole world but forfeit his life?' (Matt. 16.26).

Pseudo-Clementine Homilies II 51, 1 etc.

Be competent moneychangers.

This saying, which has been handed down often and with some variations, is one of the sayings of Jesus and primitive Christianity which uses a profession (workers, shepherds, fishermen, but also stewards and judges) as a point of comparison (Matt. 9.37; Matt. 10.6; Mark 1.17; Matt. 16.19a; Matt. 18.18). Clement of Alexandria, *Stromateis* I 28, 177, hands the saying down in a longer version which clarifies its meaning: 'Be competent moneychangers who reject some but keep the good.' Here Jesus is pleading as it were for a critical attitude of mind. Paul expresses himself in a similar way in his first Letter to the Thessalonians (I Thess. 5.21): 'Test all things, hold fast to what is good.' The specific context of this logion, which can be applied to almost all spheres of life, can only be guessed at. If the appeal in fact went back to the historical Jesus, the logion was probably spoken in connection with the temptation exercised by false prophecy (Matt. 7.15ff. par.).

Gospel of the Hebrews in Jerome, Commentary on Ephesians 5.3f.

And you are to be cheerful only when you look on your brother with love.

This saying of Jesus, which is often regarded as authentic, is about loving one's brother, and has its equivalents in canonical and apocryphal Jesus traditions. Thus Jesus calls for reciprocal forgiveness (Matt. 18.15, 21f.); the disciples are to be one another's servants (Matt. 20.20–28); dispute among them has a negative effect on relations with God (Matt. 5.22; Matt. 5.23f.; Mark 11.25). Disturbance of a brotherly spirit is also counted among the worst transgressions in the Gospel of the Hebrews (Jerome, *Commentary on Ezekiel* 18.7). Moreover a tradition in the Gospel of the Nazareans (Jerome, *Against Pelagius* III 2) takes up Matt. 18.21f., enlarging it and varying it.

Appendix on the Syriac Transitus Mariae tradition

This Gospel fragment (W.Wright, *Contributions to the Apocryphal Literature of the NT*, 1865, 63ff.) is an appendix to the Syriac *Transitus Mariae* tradition, a group of texts the theme of which is the death and assumption of Mary into heaven; it was very widespread in the Eastern national churches in the context of the Nestorian controversies. The passage about the 'True Fruits of the Tree' has no direct connection with its context and is generally (Wright, James, et al.) thought to be an independent piece of tradition which is possibly very old. While the manuscript itself comes from the fifth century, the Syriac of the pericope, because of the redundancies, is to be defined as translation Syriac. So the brief narrative has a lengthy textual history and probably also a phase of oral tradition behind it. The anti-Jewish polemic expressed in this pericope is a possible, very external point of contact for its incorporation into the *Transitus Mariae* traditions, since in these the Jews are sometimes depicted as malicious opponents of the apostles.

The True Fruits of the Tree

1 . . . them in accordance with their wish. And he had them asked by the apostles whether this was not the case. And he said, 'These are the shepherds of the house of Israel, who pray for the sheep that they may be hallowed and worthy before the sons of men. And they themselves are not worthy to hallow, for they praise themselves as being strong. Have I not given them many signs?' And the apostles said, 'Lord, look, they weep and pray and repent and fall on their knees. Why do you not hear them?' Our Lord said to them: 'Even if I wanted to hear them, there is deception in them, as you know.'

2 And when Jesus wanted to show the apostles for what reason he had not heard them, he took them up a mountain and made them fast. And when the apostles had come down, they asked him and said, 'Lord, we are hungry. What do we have now to eat in this wilderness?' and Jesus commanded them to go to the trees which were before them. And he said to them, 'Go to the trees which are before us, whose branches from a distance are numerous, full and beautiful, and from which you should be filled.' And when the apostles went, they found no fruit on the trees. And they returned to Jesus and said, 'Good teacher, you sent us to the trees opposite, and we went and we found no fruit on them, but only the branches which were full and splendid, but there was no fruit on them.' And Jesus said to them, 'You have not seen them because the trees are growing straight upwards. Go again, for the trees will bend and you will find fruit on them and can be filled.' And when they went, they found that the trees bended, but they found no fruit on them. And they returned to Jesus again in great distress and said to him, 'What is happening, teacher, that we are mocked? For first you told us, "You will find upright trees on which there is fruit," and we found none. Why are we being mocked?. You should teach us what has happened. For we think that what you want to teach us is wrong. For these trees are held upright and bowed by a visible power. If this is a temptation, let us know what it is.' And Jesus said, 'Go and sit under them and you will see what it is that is on them. But you will not be able to make them bend again.' And when the apostles went and sat under the trees, the trees immediately dropped stinking worms on them. And the apostles returned to Jesus and said to him, 'Teacher, do you want to lead us astray or to remove us from you (or remove yourself from us)?'

This episode from the life of Jesus belongs in the context of the controversy between Jesus and the Jewish authorities. Formally it is divided into two sections. The first part consists of a conversation between Jesus and his disciples. The topic is the cleanness of the shepherds of Israel, who are to hallow the people but are not themselves clean and cannot fulfil this task because of their arrogance. The disciples object that the shepherds of Israel constantly pray in public and thus give the impression of holiness. Jesus thereupon points out to his disciples that all this is deceit and hypocrisy. The shepherds of Israel are far removed from true piety, although Jesus has been concerned for them.

The references to the New Testament traditions are clear: as well as the criticism of the Pharisees and rulers of the Jews in principle, as it can be found e.g. in the discourse on the Pharisees in Matt. 23.1ff., the motif of hypocrisy and merely external piety is especially evident (cf. Matt. 6.1–4, 16–18; 15.1–20 par); such behaviour may impress and deceive other people, but not God (cf. Luke 16.14–15; Matt. 23.28). In addition to the charge of being sanctimonious, the Pharisees' overestimation of themselves and their arrogance become the object of Jesus' criticism. In Jesus' judgment, these shepherds of Israel cannot stand before God; this is all the more important, as Jesus wanted to hear them and save them (Matt. 15.21–18) and – contrary to some New Testament reports (Matt. 12.38–42 par., etc) – gave them signs (cf. also John 12.37ff.; further 2.23; 2.18; 4.48; 6.14,30; 11.47).

The description of the rulers of the Jews as *shepherds* of Israel and the designation of the Jews as sheep also breathes the language of the New Testament (for the Old Testament in addition to Ezek. 34 cf. above all Zech. 11.44ff.). In addition to Matt. 7.15; 9.35f. par.; 10.6; 18.12–14 par.; 26.31 etc., reference should be made above all to Johannine imagery: Jesus' sayings about the shepherd and the sheep in John 10.1–10 depict Jesus as the good shepherd, as opposed to robbers and day labourers. In connection with our pericope, Jesus is the good shepherd who can bring true holiness, in contrast with the unclean arrogant shepherds of Israel.

The incomprehension of the disciples about Jesus' verdict on the shepherds of Israel (cf. also the incomprehension about true cleanness in Matt. 15.15f.) leads to the second part of the pericope. This consists of a kind of symbolic action or staged parable which is meant to show the disciples the true nature of the shepherds of Israel by means of allegory. Jesus goes with the disciples to a mountain, the traditional place of revelation. He makes them get hungry; the disciples need food – just as the sheep of Israel strive for hallowing. When the disciples thereupon turn to Jesus, he points to many trees in the distance which look beautiful and bear abundant fruit – just like the shepherds of Israel in their fine garments and their ostentatious piety. The disciples vainly go their way and return to Jesus hungry. Jesus sends them again and points out to them the height of the trees, which means that the fruit can only be obtained if the branches bend. This seems to be a polemical reference to the arrogance of the shepherds of Israel and their condescension. Again the way of the disciples is not blessed with success: even when the shepherds of Israel have compassion on them by condescendingly fulfilling their tasks, the sheep must go away empty. The disciples again press on Jesus with growing impatience. Jesus requires the disciples a third and last time to go to the trees and sit under them. Now the true fruits of the trees become manifest: not food but stinking worms are sitting in their branches. The shepherds of Israel do not have sanctification to give to their sheep but filth. The apocryphal fragment breaks off with the continued incomprehension of the disciples.

This second part, too, displays allusions to the canonical Gospels. As well as the references already mentioned, note above all the 'parabolic sayings presumably collected at a very early stage from Jesus' polemic against the Pharisees' (Kremer), Luke 6.43–46 or Matt. 7.15–23; 12.33–35, and possibly also the imagery of bringing forth fruit in John 15.1–8. While the parabolic words about the fruits of the trees spoken by Jesus in this apocryphal report are made into a kind of play with a clear link to the New Testament, shifts can still be made out. An inner logic can be recognized in the Matthaean and Lukan tradition (cf. the earlier Sirach 27.6: 'The fruit corresponds to the species of tree; so everyone is judged by his disposition'): as the fruit, so the tree. A good tree produces good fruit, a bad tree bad fruit. The opposite is true in the pericope about the cleanness of the shepherds of Israel: here it is the good and high trees that promise rich fruit but only bring forth bad fruit.

The natural character of Jesus' parabolic discourses – they are immediately illuminating – has been staged in a complex and ambivalent way in the apocryphon. This high degree of reflection itself suggests a late date. This is also indicated by the combination of Synoptic and Johannine notions described above. Moreover the legendary character of the account (note particularly the vivid depiction of the impatience and urging of the disciples) tells against an authentic Jesus tradition. A last argument is the form of the apocryphon, especially in its second part. This is not a sign or symbolic action in the strict sense, but the performance of an allegory: Jesus and his disciples act out the narrative of the parable. This kind of bibliodrama in which Jesus as actor puts his own parable on the hermeneutical stage is alien to the New Testament writings and the preaching of Jesus (cf. possibly the Jordan miracle in Egerton Papyrus 2). A comparison with the symbolic actions or parabolic actions of Jesus like eating with toll collectors (Mark 2.13–17), the forming of the group of twelve (Mark 3.13–19), the cleansing of the temple (Mark 11.15–17) or the cursing of the fig tree (Mark 11.12–14), is not fruitful. In these symbolic actions Jesus on his own authority gives an 'eschatological sign of fulfilment' (Schürmann); however, this must not be thought of as an analogous depiction of the future, as in Old Testament prophecy, but as being identical with the future (Trautmann). However, our apocryphon hardly makes this kind of claim!

VII

A Short Life of Jesus

'The race of Jews and Christians is comparable with a swarm of bats or ants teeming out of a building, or frogs squatting together round a pool, or earthworms gathering in the corner of a dunghill, and argue with one another about which of them are the worst sinners. They assert: 'In the first place God reveals and proclaims everything to us. He lets go of the whole world and the course of the stars of heaven; he even neglects the wide world and concerns himself with us alone. To us alone he sends his messengers and does not cease to send them and to ensure that we are always together with him' (Celsus, c. 178).

If the images people use in their speech accurately reflect their surroundings, then it is certain that Jesus came from a village. For the world of his parables is a rural one. Jesus knows the sower on the field (Mark 4.3–8) and the mustard plant in the garden (Mark 4.30–32); he sees the shepherd with his flock (Mark 6.26), the birds under heaven (Matt. 6.26) and the lilies in the field (Matt. 6.28). Even the sparrow which falls to the ground (Matt. 10.29) brings Jesus, the man from the village, near to the omnipotent activity of God.

Jesus grew up in a circle of more than five brothers and sisters in the Galilean village of Nazareth. He was probably the oldest. His mother tongue was Aramaic, but this does not rule out the possibility that he understood some bits of Greek. He learned a building craft from his father. Like most of his contemporaries, he could not read or write. But the local synagogue near his home was the place of his religious education. Here and on other occasions he learned parts of the Torah by word of mouth: commandments, prophetic instructions and predictions, and exciting stories from the scriptures, for example the narratives about Elijah and Elisha, the prophets who did miracles, which excited many of the pious people of that time.

The limits of his environment at that time can be seen by a comparison with the apostle Paul, who was of the same age. Paul did not come from a village, but from a city. That again is indicated by the images that he uses. His letters show city life with the stalls of traders (II Cor. 2.17), past which the tutor (Gal. 3.24f.) goes to school holding the hands of his little charges, and the street through which the solemn triumphal procession moves (cf. II Cor. 2.14). Paul often takes his imagery from the life of soldiers (II Cor. 10.3–5), and even their trumpets provide him with a comparison. Similarly, he uses parallels from the legal sphere (Gal. 3.17), indeed even from the theatre (I Cor. 4.9) and from athletic competitions (I Cor. 9.24), for his argument. Jesus, however, probably never saw a theatre or an arena, though the city of Sepphoris, stamped with Greek culture, where for example he would have found work as a craftsman, was barely three miles from Nazareth. In contrast to Jesus, Paul was highly literate, indeed he had received both a Jewish and a Greek education. He also had a command of Aramaic, though his mother tongue was Greek. As a Roman citizen he was endowed with numerous privileges. In origin and education, Paul was a cosmopolitan and Jesus was a provincial. Had they ever met in person, they would presumably have had little to say to each other. Social barriers would have discouraged communication. Most likely Paul would simply have chuckled at such a country bumpkin from Galilee, or he might just have shrugged his shoulders. Jesus would probably not have reacted to Paul any differently. In any case he would hardly have understood Paul's stilted theological arguments, for the pedantic, strict exegesis of commandments, prophets and scriptures with all their fiddly distinctions would not have been to his taste.

But despite all the differences, the two would have had things in common. Jesus and Paul were committed Jews, proud of their God, who had created heaven and earth and chosen Israel. Both lived in the certainty that their God had destined Jerusalem to be the centre of the earth. Here the 'Saviour' would come at the end of days; and here, as ordained by God, sacrifices were offered for the sins of the Jews. Until then the great festivals like Passover, Pentecost and Tabernacles, also ordained by God, held the cycle of the years together. Jesus and Paul shared this basic framework of religious convictions with most other Jews. In addition it may be observed that both Jesus and Paul had the special gift of driving out demons, and that both thought that they were in contact with the devil.

Biographically, there are special features in the life of every individual, ranging from natural disposition to strokes of fortune. In the case of Paul this was probably an illness which tormented him to the end of his life and which evidently made him particularly susceptible to ecstatic experiences. He speaks about this in hints as the thorn in the flesh, the angel of Satan which – of course at God's bidding – keeps pummelling him (II Cor. 12.7). Jesus was burdened with an even harder blot on his reputation, one which also overshadowed his mother Mary. Jesus, her oldest child, had been fathered in dubious circumstances. If in the earliest source he is contemptuously called 'son of Mary' (Mark 6.3), Matthew's birth story (1.18–25) recognizes the lack of a father and immediately introduces the Holy Spirit as a begetter. At the same time Mary is defended against the charge of immoral behaviour, for the ancestors of the Messiah, too, had been entangled in immoral behaviour. But none of this had deterred God from his plan to raise up Jesus, the son of Mary, the Messiah and Son of God, from the family of these notorious women.

However, theological interpretation against a gilded background is one thing. The often brutal history in the dust of this earth is another, and Jesus came to feel this to an increasing extent. From the very first, people in his home town of Nazareth bombarded him with comments that he was a bastard without a proper father. Hence the taunt 'son of Mary'. The later adoption by Joseph – long before Jesus' public appearance – did not alter the fact that Jesus must have been stigmatized by this shadow in his background. Sooner or later he learned what it means to be regarded as the son of a prostitute. Perhaps one of the roots of his later leaning towards people who were despised, to prostitutes, toll collectors and sinners, lay here. And possibly this explains his broken relationship to his own biological family. For after the evidently early death of his adoptive father, in normal circumstances, as the oldest he would have had to look after the family, especially his mother. But here the sources tell another story. For Jesus the fourth commandment, which prescribed honouring father and mother, no longer applied. He chose the way of radical separation.

Now insults and inclinations are not in themselves enough to bring a movement to life. There must be other reasons, and stimuli from other people. That happened for Jesus in the figure of John the Baptist.

John the Baptist stood in a long line of Jewish prophets of doom who called for repentance in the face of the imminent day of God. At the same time, he combined his preaching of judgment with the announcement of a forgiveness of sins in which all those who had themselves baptized by him were to share. This guaranteed that they could escape the wrath to come. His preaching went round like lightning and led numerous Jews to come to him beside the Jordan. Among them was the Galilean Jesus of Nazareth, who had come south. He too was seized with a nagging unrest, which found at least temporary relief in the circle around John the Baptist. By joining him, Jesus had found a new family which was very different from his biological family. Now he belonged to a group of ascetics who wanted to be obedient only to God and were grateful to God for having given them one final opportunity for repentance.

The members of the priestly aristocracy in Jerusalem must have been provoked by this eccentric by the Jordan and his followers. Had not the supervision, administration and execution of the sacrifices which brought about atonement been entrusted to them alone by God in person? But as long as the temple was not in immediate danger, they left the exotic-looking Baptist sect by the Jordan alone. Moreover at that time, too, there were inspired prophets in abundance who were claiming now this, now that. But John was in fact dangerous. If people began to spell out his indirect criticism of the temple, things would heat up for the authorities, as his preaching had political implications. The ruler of the area in which Jesus lived, Herod Antipas, began to realize that, and subsequently had John executed in summary fashion as a messianic pretender.

We do not know how long Jesus spent in the company of John the Baptist.

However, it is certain that he detached himself from John well before John's execution. The rivalry between the disciples of Jesus and the disciples of John shows that Jesus must have already gone his own way before the Baptist's death. That is not to be understood as a break with the tradition, but as a development or focussing of John's preaching by Jesus. For Jesus this new beginning was connected with *three things: first*, in the long term he did not like John's fundamentally ascetic attitude. In keeping with this, *secondly*, he had a tremendous experience of the kingdom of God which was prefigured in meals with him to which anyone could come. And *thirdly*, he found his capacity to heal an overwhelming experience which he also associated with the coming of the kingdom of God.

We can no longer be completely clear about the connection between these three points, in either substance or chronology, but it is nevertheless important to note that none of the three characteristics is attested for John himself. So we have to speak of a turning point which inaugurated a new stage in Jesus' activity. However, essential features of the preaching of John the Baptist remained elements of Jesus' religious conviction: first an imminent final judgment and secondly an inexorable seriousness in expounding and following the will of God. Finally, like John, Jesus remained unmarried. The two of them had this in common with the apostle Paul. This point is all the more worth noting since it was the duty of every male Jew to father descendants.

Jesus' newly-discovered capacity for healing soon became known in Galilee. His exorcisms, in which he healed the psychologically sick, are the best-attested miracles in the New Testament. At that time sicknesses affecting the nerves and the mind were attributed to demonic possession. Satan was regarded as the chief of these evil spirits. Jesus lent reality to the battle against him. In anticipation of the kingdom of God he had seen Satan fall like lightning from heaven and thus had become stronger than Satan himself. He could therefore heal men, women and children by snatching them from the rule of the devil with the promise of the forgiveness of sins. For him, sickness and sin were joined by an unbreakable link. In this, too, Paul resembled him. Paul could explain the numerous cases of sickness in the community in Corinth only by the sinful misuse of the eucharist (I Cor. 11.29–30).

According to Jesus, however, the kingdom of God did not only consist of healings and liberation from sicknesses and evil of every kind. Its other aspect was the rule of God and the rule of Jesus together with the Twelve. Underlying the latter was the reckless hope that at the imminent end of time, when God brought in his kingdom, those ten tribes which seven hundred years previously had been crushed by the Assyrians would also be restored. At the time of Jesus only the two tribes of Judah and Benjamin remained. According to Jesus, at the end of history, each of his twelve disciples would judge one of these tribes. The status of acting as judges alongside God and his elect as representatives of Jesus could hardly be surpassed. And indeed the apostle Paul also had a similar hope. He called on the members of the community in Corinth not to go to law against one another, since they themselves, each individual, would judge angels (I Cor. 6.3). Here we see directly into the heart of the early Christians and the community gathered by Jesus. The roots of their faith were not reason or reflection, but the prospect of sharing in God's rule. And this rule did not extend only to human beings. Rather, it embraced the whole cosmos, which had to be brought back to the rightful order willed by God. Of course all this was conceived from a Jewish perspective, since it was exclusively about the Jewish people, and with the new Jerusalem in the centre; other peoples were in essence no more than neighbours. Jesus fulfilled an ardent hope that God would soon keep his promise. And in the course of his activity – after his departure from John the Baptist – he became convinced that he himself had to play the most significant role in this final drama. Here too the parallel with Paul is striking and illuminating, since Paul, too, a few years later, thought that he was the incorporation of the Gentiles into the future kingdom of God was up to him (cf. Rom. 11.13–36).

In its decisive phase, Jesus' life was shaped by the unshakable faith that he had to interpret God's law authoritatively in God's name. Broadly speaking, his interpretation was to be perceived as an accentuation of the will of God. Thus he forbade divorce with an appeal to God's good creation, by which in marriage man and woman irrevocably have become one flesh (Mark 10.8). He focussed the commandment to love on the demand to love one's enemy (Luke 6.27). He forbade judging (Matt. 7.1) and swearing (Matt. 5.34). Now and then he reduced the law in a sweeping manner and by so doing in fact made the food laws irrelevant (Mark 7.15); he focussed the sabbath on human well-being (Mark 2.27). But anything that – in modern terms – looked like autonomy was grounded in theonomy. Jesus could ordain this free and at the same time radical interpretation of the law only because he had received the authority to do so from God, whom he addressed lovingly, as Paul did later, as Abba (a term denoting deep intimacy and affection). At this point Jesus and his heavenly Father were almost one, and that must have been most offensive to his Jewish hearers.

He drove out demons and expounded the law, but at the same time he was also a poet and wisdom teacher. Jesus told exciting stories about cheats, and drew morals for himself and his own disciples from their realistic estimation of particular situations. Morally speaking, his life itself resembled that of an immoral hero, all the more so since because of his itinerant mode of living he had no income, but accepted the support of sympathizers, or simply trusted in God. Embedded in his stories are shrewd maxims, of a kind that one would have expected more from philosophers. In other parables he showed vividly how God will bring in his kingdom: gently and yet at the same time irrevocably. Yet others give a striking account of the way in which God seeks the lost. Jesus provided the commentary for this in his own life: he was often the guest of tax collectors and prostitutes. Sometimes his parables also took on a threatening tone: there will be judgment in the end, and God will destroy his enemies. At the same time God will then make good the fate of the poor, the hungry and those who weep, as the beatitudes of the Sermon on the Mount impressively indicate.

It has been asked how the almost timeless wisdom rules in Jesus relate to those passages which bear witness to an unbroken expectation of an imminent end. Some scholars cut the knot and declare that one element is authentic and the other inauthentic. That at least produces a Jesus whom we find easier to understand today. But that kind of thinking is probably too modern. What we cannot reconcile may be far from incongruous for someone living in the first century. Jesus' contemporary Paul is a striking example of the juxtaposition of timeless wisdom and the impetuous expectation of an imminent end. Paul was convinced that he himself would live to experience the coming of his Lord Jesus on the clouds of heaven and as almost obsessively wanted to carry on his mission throughout the Roman empire before the return of Jesus. But at the same time we find in his writings almost timeless remarks about human wisdom being foolishness before God (I Cor. 1–2), and he himself has left to posterity the magnificent hymn to a kind of love which knows no expectation of an imminent end. In I Cor. 13 he says that love is greater than hope (for the end) and greater also than faith (in Christ who first made possible the expectation of an imminent end). It follows from this that in the case of Paul, as with Jesus, expectation of an imminent end, wisdom teaching and ethics stand side by side, contrary to all modern logic. Probably for Jesus the expectation of an imminent end had the upper hand, as will emerge from a consideration of the last days of his life.

Jesus had experienced great success in Galilee. The crowds had responded to his call. Now that same call drew him to Jerusalem. There he wanted to call on the people and its leaders to repent. He marched to Jerusalem, accompanied by a host of disciples, men and women. In a symbolic action he expressed his hope for the new temple in the temple forecourt by overturning some tables of money changers and traders. The Jewish aristocracy could not forgive him that. What happened next bore no similarity to the occasional clashes between Pharisees and Jesus in Galilee. Whereas there Jesus had received no more than insults, here in Jerusalem things were in real earnest. Jesus was slandered as political king of the Jews, and Pilate made short shrift of him. Evidently Jesus had not prepared his disciples well for this. Otherwise they would not all have fled. Finally on the cross, Jesus became the victim in a criminal setting. He suffered here for something which he had neither attempted nor desired. Things had turned out differently from what he had told his disciples and the Jewish people. But probably he had not seen it like that. Here once again a look at the apostle Paul helps; when Paul observed that Jesus had failed to return, he did not give up his faith because people were dying, but held on to it all the more strongly. He came to the conclusion that whether he lived or died he belonged to the 'Lord'. That is how Jesus must have thought and felt on the cross, surrendering himself to his Father. No faith can ever be refuted by reality, let alone by arguments.

And, to be brief, the story of Jesus after his death is also part of his life, since it is only because of this history that we still know anything about him. The disciples who passionately appealed to Jesus began by making Jesus the Jew a problem case of the first order. For soon after his death they claimed that Jesus had been raised from the dead and would come again on the clouds of heaven as Son of God, as Saviour, as Christ, as the Son of man. Even more important, followers of Jesus drove out demons in his name and performed miracles similar to his. Indeed, some even functioned as the mouthpiece of the risen Jesus and, as his representatives, filled with the Holy Spirit, dealt with problems in their communities. The conversion of Paul, the persecutor of Christ , who after being commissioned by the heavenly Christ gave the decisive impulse to the mission to the Gentiles and organized it in grand style, became the prime example of this phenomenon.

What now followed was an unparalleled confusion, out of which emerged a church of Jesus Christ consisting almost exclusively of Gentiles, who without delay branded Jesus' fellow-countrymen as deicides. The flood of bizarre interpretations which began with the 'resurrection' of Jesus was unstoppable. Everywhere the dams of reason, which had hitherto held religious fantasies of omnipotence partly in check, broke. At many points in the Old Testament – according to the Christians – God had already spoken of Christ and announced his coming. Indeed Christ had stood at God's side at the beginning of world history. If the way in which the authoritative exorcist, the expounder of the law, the prophet, the poet and the wisdom teacher Jesus fell victim to a political intrigue in Jerusalem was already a tragedy, the way in which Jesus has been interpreted and misused for the interests of particular people throughout church history to the present day is an even greater one.

Nevertheless the question remains: what does Jesus mean for the present once his ecclesiastical trimmings are recognized as a masquerade? I have come to the conclusion that Jesus is a sympathetic, original figure, a man of humour and wit at whom I sometimes chuckle. There can be no reasonable doubt about the earnestness of his own career on the periphery of the Jewish society of his day. Jesus is the paradigm of someone who will not be deterred from following a path to the end, once he has chosen it. But in his interpretation of the law, which at the same time both accentuated the Torah and tore it off its hinges, he sometimes becomes too serious for me. I can no longer take seriously his enthusiasm which tramples reason under foot, since the kingdom of God which he announced has failed to materialize. Finally, in his confident dialogue with God, Jesus seems to me to be almost ridiculous, for here he makes the mistake of so many religious people: he sees himself at the centre of the world.

Therefore as a whole person Jesus remains a problem, and we cannot expect a problem to provide us with an answer to the questions which haunt us. So with this book I am putting him on file: 'A good world needs knowledge, goodness and courage; it does not need any painful longing for the past, any fettering of the free intelligence by words which have been spoken a long time ago by ignorant men. It needs hope for the future, not constant looking back to a dead past which we are convinced will be far surpassed by the future which our intelligence can create' (Bertrand Russell).

Index of All the Authentic Sayings and Actions of Jesus

This index lists all the passages on the basis of the analysis given above which contain authentic sayings and actions of Jesus. Those printed in *italics* have a very high degree of probability; those printed normally have a relatively high degree of probability. If a saying or an action of Jesus has multiple attestation, on each occasion only the earliest form is mentioned. Thus all the texts in Matthew and Luke which transcribe authentic passages from Mark are omitted. In the case of Q, each time I give the reference for what is presumably the earliest form and the Matthaean or Lukan text in brackets. If a variant of the same saying of Jesus occurs in Mark and/or Thomas which is independent of this, it is mentioned in connection with it. I deal in a similar way with the authentic sayings of Jesus from the Gospel of Thomas. The other historically reliable elements of the texts which have been investigated can be found in the relevant sections under 'historical'.

An asterisk* after a chapter or verse reference denotes the basic material in the relevant chapter, section or verse.

Matthew

Matt. 5. 13–14 (Luke 14.34–35; Mark 9.50)

Matt. 5.**15** (Luke 11.33; Mark 4.21)

Matt. 5.21–22a

Matt. 5.27–28

Matt. 5.34

Matt. 5.39b–42a (Luke 6.29–30)

Matt. 5.44a (Luke 6.27)

Matt. 6.9–loa, 11–13 (Luke 11.2–4)

Matt. 6.24

Matt. 6.25–33 (Luke 12.22–34)

Matt. 7.1 (Luke 6.37a)

Matt. 7.7–11 (Luke 11.9–13; Thomas 92.1; 94.1–2)

Matt. 11.11 (Luke 7.28)

Matt. 11.12* (Luke 16.16*)

Matt. 11.18b,19b (Luke 7.33b,34b)

Matt. 13.44–48

Matt. 17.20b (Luke 17.6)

Matt. 19.12

Matt. 19.28*

Matt. 20.1–15

Matt. 21.31c

Luke

Luke 2.7a

Luke 6.20b–21 (Matt. 5.3, 6)

Luke 6.43–45 (Matt. 7.17–18)

Luke *7.22–23* (Matt. 11.5–6)

Luke 7.36–50*

Luke 9.57b–58, 59b–60a (Matt. 8.19–22)

Luke 9.62

Luke 10.18

Luke 10.23b–24 (Matt. 13.16–17)

Luke 10.30–35

Luke 11.5–8

Luke 11.20 (Matt. 11.28)

Luke 11.24–26 (Matt. 12.43–45)

Luke 12.39 (Matt. 24.43)

Luke 12.54b–56

Luke 12.58–59

Luke 13.6–9

Luke 13.20–21 (Matt. 13.33; Thomas 96.1–2)

Luke 14.26 (Matt. 10.37)

Luke 14.28–32

Luke *15.4–6* (Matt. 18.12–13)

Luke 15.8–9

Luke 15.11–32

Luke 16.1b–7

Luke 17.7–9

Luke 17.34–35 (Matt. 24.40–41)

Luke 18.2–5

Luke 22.30b

John

None

Thomas

Thomas 9.1–5 (Mark 4.3–8)

Thomas 20.1–4 (Matt. 13.31–32/Luke 13.18–19; Mark 4.30–32)

Thomas 42

Thomas 64.1–11 (Matt. 22.1–10/Luke 14.15–24)

Thomas 72.1–2 (Luke 12.13b–14)

Thomas 89.1–2

Thomas 95.1–2 (Matt. 5.42b)

Thomas 98.1–3

Thomas 113.1–3a (Luke 17.20b–21a)

Apocryphal Jesus Traditions

Letter of James (NHC I.2) 12.20–30 (2)